McGraw-Hill Education

6 SAT Practice Tests

Fourth Edition

Christopher Black

Mark Anestis

and the Tutors of College Hill Coaching™

New York Chicago San Francisco Athens London Madrid
Mexico City Milan New Delhi Singapore Sydney Toronto

7 8 9   LHS   22 21 20 19

ISBN   978-1-259-64336-1
MHID   1-259-64336-0

e-ISBN   978-1-259-64337-8
e-MHID   1-259-64337-9

SAT is a registered trademark of the College Entrance Examination Board, which was not involved in the production of, and does not endorse, this product.

McGraw-Hill Education books are available at special quantity discounts to use as premiums and sales promotions or for use in corporate training programs. To contact a representative, please visit the Contact Us pages at www.mhprofessional.com.

College Hill Coaching® is a registered trademark under the control of Christopher F. Black.

Visit the College Hill Coaching website at www.collegehillcoaching.com.

ACKNOWLEDGMENTS

We would like to acknowledge the help of those who have contributed to this project: Elizabeth, Sarah, and Anna Black for their patience and support; Stephanie Anestis for her invaluable efforts in reading and editing the text and for her incredible love and support; and Robert, Janice, Michael, and Matthew Anestis, who also gave their insight on the work in progress. We appreciate the hard work of those at McGraw-Hill Education who made this project work and the thoughtful help of our agent, Grace Freedson. Finally, we would like to thank all the students of College Hill Coaching who have contributed to the growth of these materials over the years.

CONTENTS

ABOUT THE AUTHORS

Christopher Black, M.A. is the founder and director of College Hill Coaching. He has been a consultant to the nation's leading educational publishers and software developers and is coauthor of *McGraw-Hill's SAT*.

Mark Anestis is the founder and director of The Learning Edge and coauthor of *McGraw-Hill's SAT*.

SECTION I

ATTACKING THE NEW SAT: TWELVE FAQs

1

1 WHAT'S NEW IN THE REDESIGNED SAT?

Beginning in spring 2016, the redesigned SAT features ten major changes.

1. More time per question

The redesigned SAT gives you more time per question, making it less likely that you will underperform due to time restrictions.

Section	Old SAT Time Per Question	New SAT Time Per Question
Writing and Language	43 seconds (49 questions, 35 mins)	48 seconds (44 questions, 35 mins)
Mathematics	78 seconds (54 questions, 70 mins)	84 seconds (57 questions, 80 mins)
Reading	63 seconds (67 questions, 70 mins)	75 seconds (52 questions, 65 mins)

Bottom Line: The new SAT should give you a bit more time to breathe.

2. "Rights-only" scoring

The redesigned SAT no longer penalizes you a quarter point for getting a multiple-choice question wrong. Now your raw score on each section is simply the total number of correct answers on that section. The College Board claims that this will encourage you to make educated guesses, and discourage you from "thinking strategically" about whether to guess on a question, since that is not central to the reasoning skills the SAT is designed to assess.

Bottom Line: *On the new SAT, answer every question.* On the toughest questions, just pick an answer and move on rather than leaving it unanswered. You can't hurt your score, and you may help it.

3. Four choices instead of five

All multiple-choice questions now have four choices instead of five. This makes guessing on tough questions even more beneficial, since the chances of getting the question right by luck alone have now increased from 20% to 25%.

Bottom Line: All the more reason to guess rather than leaving a question unanswered.

4. Academic vocabulary in context

The SAT no longer includes "sentence completion questions" or any other specifically vocabulary-focused questions. Rather, it tests your knowledge of vocabulary by challenging you to read and analyze college-level prose in the liberal arts and sciences, and to answer questions about how vocabulary is used to clarify ideas, establish tone, and indicate point of view.

Bottom Line: Prepare to be tested on words in the context of the reading passages you encounter on test day.

5. Return to the 400-to-1600 point scale

The redesigned SAT scores return to the 400-to-1600 point scale, based on the sum of the Reading and Writing test score (from 200 to 800) and the Mathematics test score (from 200 to 800). The Essay component is no longer mandatory.

Bottom Line: Now you can compare your SAT scores with your parents' SAT scores!

6. Essay optional, and a new essay task

On the new SAT, you have the option of taking the Essay component, in which you are given 50 minutes to read and analyze an argumentative essay that examines an idea, debate, or trend in the arts, sciences, culture, or politics. You are then expected to "produce a clear and cogent written analysis in which [you] explain how the author . . . builds an argument to persuade an audience through the use of evidence, reasoning, [and] stylistic and persuasive elements."

Many competitive colleges will require you to submit the SAT Essay score with the rest of your SAT scores. If you are considering applying to any of these schools, you should choose the Essay option when you register to take the SAT. Check the college websites for their policies on the SAT Essay.

Bottom Line: Get yourself ready for the new SAT Essay by doing the six sample essays in this book.

7. More advanced math questions

The redesigned SAT Math test includes questions on topics from trigonometry and second-year algebra, such as complex numbers, trigonometric identities, and analysis of polynomials.

Bottom Line: As you do the practice tests in this book, identify which of the advanced topics give you the most trouble and use the detailed answer explanations to help you master those concepts!

8. Calculator and no-calculator math questions

The redesigned SAT Math test is composed of two sections: a calculator section and a no-calculator section. The no-calculator section is designed to assess your arithmetic and algebraic fluency, which are essential to mathematical problem solving.

Bottom Line: As with the advanced math concepts, practice makes perfect here! After each test, review the detailed answer explanation for each question you miss so you are ready for it the next time it comes your way!

9. **Graphical analysis required in some reading and writing questions**

Some of the passages in the redesigned SAT Reading and Writing tests include information in the form of graphs, diagrams, or tables that you may be expected to interpret and synthesize with the content of the passages.

Bottom Line: SAT Reading isn't just about textual analysis anymore, it also includes a bit of graphical analysis.

10. **Lots more data**

In addition to the basic Math and Reading/Writing scores, the new SAT will also supply you (and colleges) with up to *sixteen* (yes, you heard right) other "Test Scores," "Cross-Test Scores," and "Subscores."

Bottom Line: Don't worry about all these extra scores. They're just the College Board's way of showing you that it's really good at statistics. The only scores that really count are the Math score and the Reading and Writing score.

---

2 WHAT ARE THE PRIMARY SKILLS ASSESSED BY THE REDESIGNED SAT?

SAT Reading

- Interpreting, analyzing, and drawing inferences from college-level texts across the liberal arts and sciences such as arguments, narratives, and personal or expository essays
- Interpreting and drawing inferences from data in the form of graphs, tables, and diagrams that accompany reading passages

SAT Writing and Language

- Analyzing sentences and paragraphs in terms of their grammatical correctness and semantic coherence
- Analyzing essays in terms of their overall development, tone, and effectiveness

SAT Math

- Solving algebraic problems involving equations, inequalities, systems, formulas, and functions
- Solving data-analysis problems involving concepts such as ratios, proportions, percentages, units, and numerical relationships
- Solving problems in advanced mathematics involving concepts such as quadratics, polynomials, angles, polygons, areas, volumes, exponentials, complex numbers, and trigonometry

SAT Essay (Optional)

- Writing an effective essay that analyzes and critiques a given argumentative passage

---

3 WHAT IS THE FORMAT OF THE REDESIGNED SAT?

The redesigned SAT is a 3-hour test (3 hours 50 minutes with Essay) consisting of four mandatory sections and an optional Essay.

Total Time: 3 hours (3 hours 50 minutes including Essay)

1. Reading Test	52 questions	65 minutes
2. Writing and Language Test	44 questions	35 minutes
3. Mathematics Test (No calculator)	20 questions	25 minutes
4. Mathematics Test (Calculator)	38 questions	55 minutes
5. Essay (optional)	1 question	50 minutes

4 | WHAT KINDS OF SCORES ARE REPORTED BY THE SAT?

The new SAT returns to the classic 1600-point, "Math + Verbal" format (although now the sections are called "Math" and "Reading and Writing"), but these scores are enhanced with what the College Board calls "Insight Scores," which include three or four "Test Scores," two "Cross-Test Scores," and seven to ten "Subscores."

SAT Insight Scores

	Composite Score (400–1600)			Optional
Sections (200–800)	**Math**	**Reading and Writing**		
Test Scores (10–40)	**Math**	**Writing and Language**	**Reading**	**Essay** (6–24)
Cross-Test Scores (10–40)	**Analysis in History/Social Studies**			
	Analysis in Science			
Subscores (1–15)	**Heart of Algebra**	**Relevant Words in Context**		**Reading** (2–8)
	Problem Solving and Data Analysis	**Command of Evidence**		**Analysis** (2–8)
	Passport to	**Expression of Ideas**		**Writing** (2–8)
	Advanced Math	**Standard English Conventions**		

5 | WHAT WILL COLLEGES DO WITH MY SAT SCORES?

Your SAT scores show colleges how ready you are to do college-level work. Students with high SAT scores are more likely to succeed with the challenging college-level math, writing, and reading assignments. Recent studies have also shown that SAT scores correlate strongly with postcollege success, particularly in professions like medicine, law, the humanities, the sciences, and engineering. Students with high SAT scores are more likely to graduate from college and to have successful careers after college.

But let's face it: one reason colleges want you to send them SAT scores is that high scores make them look good. The higher the average SAT score of their applicants, the better their rankings and prestige. This is why most colleges cherry-pick your top subscores if you submit multiple SAT results. (It's also why some colleges have adopted "SAT-optional" policies: only the high-scoring students are likely to submit them, and so the college's average scores automatically increase, thereby improving its national rankings.) In addition to your SAT scores,

most good colleges are interested in your grades, your curriculum, your recommendations, your leadership skills, your extracurricular activities, and your essay. But standardized test scores are becoming more important as colleges become more selective. Without exception, high SAT scores will provide you with an admission advantage, even if the college does not require them. Some large or specialized schools will weigh test scores heavily. If you have any questions about how heavily a certain college weighs your SAT scores, call the admissions office and ask.

The majority of colleges "superscore" your SAT, which means that they cherry-pick your top SAT Reading and Writing score and your top SAT Math score from all of the SATs you submit. So, for instance, if you submit your March SAT scores of 520R/W 610M (1130 composite) and your June SAT scores of 550R/W 580M (1130 composite), the college will consider your SAT score to be 550R/W 610M (1160 composite). Nice of them, huh?

6 | WHAT CONTROL DO I HAVE OVER MY SAT SCORES?

No college will see any of your SAT or Subject Test scores until you choose to release them to that particular school. So you never have to worry about a college seeing a score you don't want to release. Most colleges also allow you to use Score Choice to select which particular SAT and SAT Subject Test scores are submitted to the colleges among all that you've taken. Some colleges, however, may request that you not use Score Choice, and instead submit all scores of all SATs you've taken. Typically, colleges do this for two reasons: (1) to give

you the maximum possible SAT "superscore," and (2) to identify students who are inappropriately test-obsessed (for instance, those who have taken the SAT five or more times).

So don't worry about taking the SAT two or three times, if you need to. In fact, most colleges encourage students to take multiple tests, since one data point isn't as trustworthy as multiple data points. But don't go overboard. If you take it more than four times, a college might think you're test-obsessed.

7 SHOULD I TAKE THE ACT AS WELL?

The ACT is a college admissions test—administered independently of the SAT by a completely different company—that you may submit to colleges in lieu of your SAT and perhaps even your Subject Tests. It is roughly the same length as the SAT and tests roughly the same topics: grammar, math, reading, and science, as well as an optional rhetorical essay. Many students take the ACT in addition to the SAT and Subject Tests in order to have as many possible options as possible when submitting their applications.

Some students prefer the ACT to the SAT, and some do not. You owe it to yourself to check it out and consider it as an option. You can find out more about the ACT at ACT.org.

8 WHAT IS THE BEST WAY TO PREPARE FOR THE REDESIGNED SAT?

"Start where you are. Use what you have. Do what you can."
–Arthur Ashe

Step 1: Make a testing schedule

First, decide when you will take your first SAT. Sit down with your guidance counselor early in your junior year and work out a full testing schedule for the year, taking into account the SAT, SAT Subject Tests, AP tests, and possibly the ACT. Once you have decided on your schedule, commit yourself to beginning your SAT preparation at least 3 months prior to your first SAT. Commit to setting aside 30–40 minutes per night for review work and practice, and to taking at least two or three full-scale practice tests on the weekends.

Step 2: Take a diagnostic SAT or two

When you're ready to begin your SAT preparation (ideally 3 months before your SAT), you'll first need to assess your readiness. Use the first test in this book as a diagnostic SAT. It requires 3 hours (or 3 hours and 50 minutes if you include the essay). Take it on a Saturday morning, if possible, at roughly the time you will start the real SAT (around 8:00 a.m.), and make sure that you have a quiet place, a stopwatch, a calculator, and a few #2 pencils. This will give you a solid idea of what the experience of taking the new SAT is like.

Step 3: Learn from your mistakes

The detailed answer keys after each practice test will give you plenty of feedback about the topics that you may need to review in order to prepare for your SAT. After completing each test, review each question that you have missed to help you learn from these mistakes heading forward.

Step 4: Take practice tests regularly and diagnose your performance

This book contains six full-scale practice SATs. Use them. Take one every week or two.

Step 5: Use online tutorials

You can find a lot of SAT advice and review material online, some of it good, most of it mediocre, some of it horrible. For the redesigned SAT, the College Board has partnered with Khan Academy to offer online video tutorials on many of the key topics for the SAT.

The best review, of course, comes from actually tackling the test yourself and getting direct feedback on your performance and specific advice on how to improve. Nevertheless, it can still be helpful to watch someone else working through tough problems and explaining strategies in a lecture format. Many of the Khan Academy lessons also include linked discussions where you can ask questions about the lectures.

Step 6: Read as often as you can from the College Hill Coaching Power Reading List

Engaging big ideas and honing your analytical reading skills are keys to success in college and on the SAT. Make a point of working your way though these books and checking these periodicals regularly.

Online/Periodical

The New York Times (Op-Ed, Science Times, Front Page)
BBC News (Views, Analysis, Background)
The Atlantic (Feature Articles)
Slate (Voices, Innovation)
Scientific American (Feature Articles)
The Economist (Debate, Science & Technology)
TED Talks (Innovation, Culture, Politics, Inspiration)
The New Yorker (Talk of the Town, Feature Articles)
ProPublica (Feature Articles)
Edge (Essays)
Radiolab (Weekly Podcast)

Books

To Kill a Mockingbird, Harper Lee
Macbeth, William Shakespeare

Frankenstein, Mary Shelley
The Color Purple, Alice Walker
Pride and Prejudice, Jane Austen
Jane Eyre, Charlotte Bronte
Heart of Darkness, Joseph Conrad
Narrative of the Life of Frederick Douglass, Frederick
      Douglass
The Great Gatsby, F. Scott Fitzgerald
Walden, Henry David Thoreau
The American Language, H. L. Mencken
Notes of a Native Son, James Baldwin
The Stranger, Albert Camus
Night, Elie Wiesel
Animal Farm, George Orwell
Things Fall Apart, Chinua Achebe
The Language Instinct, Steven Pinker
The Mismeasure of Man, Stephen J. Gould
The Republic, Plato

A People's History of the United States, Howard Zinn
Guns, Germs, and Steel, Jared Diamond
A Short History of Nearly Everything, Bill Bryson

Step 7: Take strong math courses

Challenge yourself with strong math courses that introduce you to the ideas, skills, and methods of advanced mathematics, such as trigonometry, analysis of polynomials, statistical reasoning, plane geometry, and even complex numbers. These advanced topics have become a greater focus for both the SAT and ACT.

Step 8: Take strong writing courses

Take courses from teachers who emphasize strong writing skills, particularly by giving challenging writing assignments and providing timely and detailed feedback. Reading and writing skills are at the core of both the SAT and the ACT, so working with strong reading and writing teachers is invaluable.

9 HOW CAN I GET THE MOST OUT OF MY STUDY SESSIONS?

1. **Create a schedule, a study log, and place to study.** Stick to a firm schedule of 30–40 minutes a day for SAT preparation. Write it down in your daily planner and commit to it like you would to a daily class. Also, keep a log of notes for each study session, including key strategies, important formulas, vocabulary words, and advice for your next test. Then make an effective study space: a well-lit desk with a straight-back chair, plenty of pencils, a timer for practice tests, flashcards, your study log, and even a stash of brain-healthy snacks.

2. **Eliminate distractions.** Turn off all alerts on your phone and laptop, and tell everyone in the house that this is your study time. Make sure everyone is in on the plan. Even kick the dog out of the room. (But do it nicely!)

3. **Stick to focused 30- to 40-minute sessions.** Set a very clear agenda for each study session, such as "Review all the explanations to the math questions I have missed in tests 1 and 2 so far." Then find your study spot, shut out all distractions, and set to work. Try not to go beyond 40 minutes for each session: stay focused and engaged, and keep it brisk.

4. **Do 30-second checks.** Once you've completed your session, take out your study log. Give yourself 30 seconds to write down the most important idea(s) that helped you through that study session. Reread your notes just before you begin your next session.

5. **Learn it like you have to teach it.** Now step away from your log and imagine you have to run into a class of eighth graders and teach them what you just learned. How would you communicate these ideas

clearly? What examples would you use to illustrate them? What tough questions might the students ask, and how would you answer them? How can you explain the concepts and strategies in different ways? How can you help the students to manage potential difficulties they might have in a testing environment?

6. **Sleep on it.** A good night's sleep is essential to a good study program. You need at least eight hours of sleep per night. To make your sleep as effective as possible, try to fall asleep while thinking about a challenging problem or strategy you're trying to perfect. As you sleep, your brain will continue to work on the problem by a process called consolidation. When you awake, you'll have a better grasp on the problem or skill whether you realize it or not.

7. **Make creative mnemonics.** Whenever you're challenged by a tough vocabulary word, grammar rule, or mathematical concept, try to visualize the new idea or word as a crazy, colorful picture or story. The memory tricks are called mnemonics, and the best ones use patterns, rhymes, or vivid and bizarre visual images. For instance, if you struggle to remember what a "polemic" is, just turn the word into a picture based on its sound, for instance a "pole" with a "mike" (microphone) on the end of it. Then incorporate the meaning into the picture. Since a polemic is a "strong verbal attack, usually regarding a political or philosophical issue," picture someone having a vehement political argument with someone else and hitting him over the head with the "pole-mike." The crazier the picture, the better. Also, feel free to scribble notes

as you study, complete with helpful drawings. Write silly songs, create acronyms—be creative.

8. **Consider different angles.** Remember that many math problems can be solved in different ways: algebraically, geometrically, with tables, through guess-and-check, by testing the choices, etc. Try to find elegant, simple solutions. If you struggled with a problem, even if you got it right, come back to it later and try to find the more elegant solution. Also, consider experimenting with pretest rituals until you find one that helps you the most.

9. **Maintain constructive inner dialogue.** Constantly ask yourself, What do I need to do to get better? Do I need to focus more on my relaxation exercises? Should I try to improve my reading speed? Should I ask different questions as I read? Should I refresh myself on my trigonometry? Having a clear set of positive goals that you reinforce with inner dialogue helps you to succeed. Banish the negative self-talk. Don't sabotage your work by saying, "This is impossible," or "I stink at this."

10. **Make a plan to work through the struggles.** Before you take each practice test, have a clear agenda. Remind yourself of the key ideas and strategies for the week. But remember that there will always be challenges. Just meet them head-on and don't let them get you down.

10 WHEN AND HOW OFTEN SHOULD I TAKE THE SATs AND SUBJECT TESTS?

Most competitive colleges require either SAT or ACT scores from all of their applicants, although some schools are "test-optional," allowing you to choose whether or not to submit your standardized test scores with your application. Many competitive colleges also require two or three Subject Test scores. The Subject Tests are hour-long tests in specific subjects like mathematics, physics, chemistry, foreign languages, U.S. history, world history, and literature.

If you want to be able to apply to any competitive college in the country, plan to take the SAT at least twice, as well two to four SAT Subject Tests, by the end of spring semester of junior year, and retake any of those tests, if necessary, in the fall of your senior year. This way, you will have a full testing profile by the end of your junior year, and you'll have a much clearer picture of where you stand before you start your college applications. Also, if you plan well, you will have some choices about which scores to submit.

Even if your favorite colleges don't require standardized tests, you may be able to submit them anyway to boost your application. The Subject Tests, specifically, can provide a strong counterbalance to any weaknesses in your grades. For instance, a strong chemistry Subject Test score can offset a poor grade in chemistry class.

Take your Subject Test when the subject material is fresh in your mind. For most students, this is in June, just as you are preparing to take your final exams. However, if you are taking AP exams in May, you might prefer to take the SAT Subject Tests in May, also. Learn which SAT Subject Tests your colleges require, and try to complete them by June of your junior year. You can take up to three SAT Subject Tests on any test date.

11 WHAT SHOULD I DO THE WEEK BEFORE MY SAT?

1. **Get plenty of sleep.** Don't underestimate the power of a good night's sleep. During sleep, not only do you restore balance and energy to your body, but you also consolidate what you've learned that day, and even become more efficient at tasks you've been practicing.

2. **Eat healthy.** Don't skip meals because you're studying. Eat regular, well-balanced meals.

3. **Exercise.** Stick to your regular exercise program the weeks before the SAT. A strong body helps make a strong mind.

4. **Visualize success.** In the days before your SAT, envision yourself in the test room, relaxed and confident, working through even the toughest parts of the test without stress or panic.

5. **Don't cram, but stay sharp.** In the days before the SAT, resist the urge to cram. Your best results will come if you focus on getting plenty of sleep and staying positive and relaxed. If you're feeling anxious, take out your flashcards for a few minutes at a time, or review your old tests just to remind yourself of basic strategies, but don't cram.

6. **Keep perspective.** Remember that you can take the SAT multiple times, and that colleges will almost certainly "superscore" the results, so don't get down about any single set of test results. Also, keep in mind that colleges don't base their acceptance decisions on SAT scores alone.

7. **Lay everything out.** The night before your SAT, lay out your admission ticket, your photo ID, your #2 pencils, your calculator (with fresh batteries), your snack, and directions to the test site (if necessary). Having these all ready will let you sleep better.

12 WHAT SHOULD I DO ON TEST DAY?

1. **Wake up early and get some cardiovascular exercise.** A good 20-minute cardiovascular workout will get your blood flowing, wake up your brain, and release stress. However, if you do not regularly exercise, we wouldn't suggest you do so for the first time on test day! Be smart about it!

2. **Eat a good breakfast.** Don't skip breakfast. Your brain needs energy for a three- to four-hour workout!

3. **Bring a snack.** You'll have a couple of short breaks, during which you can have a quick snack. Bring a granola bar or some other quick burst of energy. You'll need it!

4. **Take slow, deep breaths—often.** Most test takers feel some anxiety before and during the test. Don't worry—it's a normal physiological response to keep you on your toes. If this anxiety begins to overwhelm you, just take three long, deep breaths and remind yourself that you are prepared, and you will perform better if you are relaxed rather than tense. It works wonders.

5. **Dress in layers.** Since you won't know whether your test room will be hot or cold, dress in layers so you'll be ready for anything.

6. **Don't worry about what anyone else is doing.** If you've been practicing as this book recommends, you will have a good sense of your own pacing and game plan. Trust your preparation, and resist any temptation to take your cues from what anyone around you is doing.

7. **Don't panic when things get tough.** Don't psych yourself out every time you get to a hard question or even a hard section. That might be an experimental section! Just stay positive and keep going.

SECTION II

PRACTICE SAT 1

ANSWER SHEET

SECTION 1

1	Ⓐ Ⓑ Ⓒ Ⓓ	13	Ⓐ Ⓑ Ⓒ Ⓓ	25	Ⓐ Ⓑ Ⓒ Ⓓ	37	Ⓐ Ⓑ Ⓒ Ⓓ	49	Ⓐ Ⓑ Ⓒ Ⓓ
2	Ⓐ Ⓑ Ⓒ Ⓓ	14	Ⓐ Ⓑ Ⓒ Ⓓ	26	Ⓐ Ⓑ Ⓒ Ⓓ	38	Ⓐ Ⓑ Ⓒ Ⓓ	50	Ⓐ Ⓑ Ⓒ Ⓓ
3	Ⓐ Ⓑ Ⓒ Ⓓ	15	Ⓐ Ⓑ Ⓒ Ⓓ	27	Ⓐ Ⓑ Ⓒ Ⓓ	39	Ⓐ Ⓑ Ⓒ Ⓓ	51	Ⓐ Ⓑ Ⓒ Ⓓ
4	Ⓐ Ⓑ Ⓒ Ⓓ	16	Ⓐ Ⓑ Ⓒ Ⓓ	28	Ⓐ Ⓑ Ⓒ Ⓓ	40	Ⓐ Ⓑ Ⓒ Ⓓ	52	Ⓐ Ⓑ Ⓒ Ⓓ
5	Ⓐ Ⓑ Ⓒ Ⓓ	17	Ⓐ Ⓑ Ⓒ Ⓓ	29	Ⓐ Ⓑ Ⓒ Ⓓ	41	Ⓐ Ⓑ Ⓒ Ⓓ		
6	Ⓐ Ⓑ Ⓒ Ⓓ	18	Ⓐ Ⓑ Ⓒ Ⓓ	30	Ⓐ Ⓑ Ⓒ Ⓓ	42	Ⓐ Ⓑ Ⓒ Ⓓ		
7	Ⓐ Ⓑ Ⓒ Ⓓ	19	Ⓐ Ⓑ Ⓒ Ⓓ	31	Ⓐ Ⓑ Ⓒ Ⓓ	43	Ⓐ Ⓑ Ⓒ Ⓓ		
8	Ⓐ Ⓑ Ⓒ Ⓓ	20	Ⓐ Ⓑ Ⓒ Ⓓ	32	Ⓐ Ⓑ Ⓒ Ⓓ	44	Ⓐ Ⓑ Ⓒ Ⓓ		
9	Ⓐ Ⓑ Ⓒ Ⓓ	21	Ⓐ Ⓑ Ⓒ Ⓓ	33	Ⓐ Ⓑ Ⓒ Ⓓ	45	Ⓐ Ⓑ Ⓒ Ⓓ		
10	Ⓐ Ⓑ Ⓒ Ⓓ	22	Ⓐ Ⓑ Ⓒ Ⓓ	34	Ⓐ Ⓑ Ⓒ Ⓓ	46	Ⓐ Ⓑ Ⓒ Ⓓ		
11	Ⓐ Ⓑ Ⓒ Ⓓ	23	Ⓐ Ⓑ Ⓒ Ⓓ	35	Ⓐ Ⓑ Ⓒ Ⓓ	47	Ⓐ Ⓑ Ⓒ Ⓓ		
12	Ⓐ Ⓑ Ⓒ Ⓓ	24	Ⓐ Ⓑ Ⓒ Ⓓ	36	Ⓐ Ⓑ Ⓒ Ⓓ	48	Ⓐ Ⓑ Ⓒ Ⓓ		

SECTION 2

1	Ⓐ Ⓑ Ⓒ Ⓓ	11	Ⓐ Ⓑ Ⓒ Ⓓ	21	Ⓐ Ⓑ Ⓒ Ⓓ	31	Ⓐ Ⓑ Ⓒ Ⓓ	41	Ⓐ Ⓑ Ⓒ Ⓓ
2	Ⓐ Ⓑ Ⓒ Ⓓ	12	Ⓐ Ⓑ Ⓒ Ⓓ	22	Ⓐ Ⓑ Ⓒ Ⓓ	32	Ⓐ Ⓑ Ⓒ Ⓓ	42	Ⓐ Ⓑ Ⓒ Ⓓ
3	Ⓐ Ⓑ Ⓒ Ⓓ	13	Ⓐ Ⓑ Ⓒ Ⓓ	23	Ⓐ Ⓑ Ⓒ Ⓓ	33	Ⓐ Ⓑ Ⓒ Ⓓ	43	Ⓐ Ⓑ Ⓒ Ⓓ
4	Ⓐ Ⓑ Ⓒ Ⓓ	14	Ⓐ Ⓑ Ⓒ Ⓓ	24	Ⓐ Ⓑ Ⓒ Ⓓ	34	Ⓐ Ⓑ Ⓒ Ⓓ	44	Ⓐ Ⓑ Ⓒ Ⓓ
5	Ⓐ Ⓑ Ⓒ Ⓓ	15	Ⓐ Ⓑ Ⓒ Ⓓ	25	Ⓐ Ⓑ Ⓒ Ⓓ	35	Ⓐ Ⓑ Ⓒ Ⓓ		
6	Ⓐ Ⓑ Ⓒ Ⓓ	16	Ⓐ Ⓑ Ⓒ Ⓓ	26	Ⓐ Ⓑ Ⓒ Ⓓ	36	Ⓐ Ⓑ Ⓒ Ⓓ		
7	Ⓐ Ⓑ Ⓒ Ⓓ	17	Ⓐ Ⓑ Ⓒ Ⓓ	27	Ⓐ Ⓑ Ⓒ Ⓓ	37	Ⓐ Ⓑ Ⓒ Ⓓ		
8	Ⓐ Ⓑ Ⓒ Ⓓ	18	Ⓐ Ⓑ Ⓒ Ⓓ	28	Ⓐ Ⓑ Ⓒ Ⓓ	38	Ⓐ Ⓑ Ⓒ Ⓓ		
9	Ⓐ Ⓑ Ⓒ Ⓓ	19	Ⓐ Ⓑ Ⓒ Ⓓ	29	Ⓐ Ⓑ Ⓒ Ⓓ	39	Ⓐ Ⓑ Ⓒ Ⓓ		
10	Ⓐ Ⓑ Ⓒ Ⓓ	20	Ⓐ Ⓑ Ⓒ Ⓓ	30	Ⓐ Ⓑ Ⓒ Ⓓ	40	Ⓐ Ⓑ Ⓒ Ⓓ		

SECTION 3

1 Ⓐ Ⓑ Ⓒ Ⓓ
2 Ⓐ Ⓑ Ⓒ Ⓓ
3 Ⓐ Ⓑ Ⓒ Ⓓ
4 Ⓐ Ⓑ Ⓒ Ⓓ
5 Ⓐ Ⓑ Ⓒ Ⓓ
6 Ⓐ Ⓑ Ⓒ Ⓓ
7 Ⓐ Ⓑ Ⓒ Ⓓ
8 Ⓐ Ⓑ Ⓒ Ⓓ
9 Ⓐ Ⓑ Ⓒ Ⓓ
10 Ⓐ Ⓑ Ⓒ Ⓓ
11 Ⓐ Ⓑ Ⓒ Ⓓ
12 Ⓐ Ⓑ Ⓒ Ⓓ
13 Ⓐ Ⓑ Ⓒ Ⓓ
14 Ⓐ Ⓑ Ⓒ Ⓓ
15 Ⓐ Ⓑ Ⓒ Ⓓ

Student-Produced Responses

ONLY ANSWERS ENTERED IN THE CIRCLES IN EACH GRID WILL BE SCORED. YOU WILL NOT RECEIVE CREDIT FOR ANYTHING WRITTEN IN THE BOXES ABOVE THE CIRCLES.

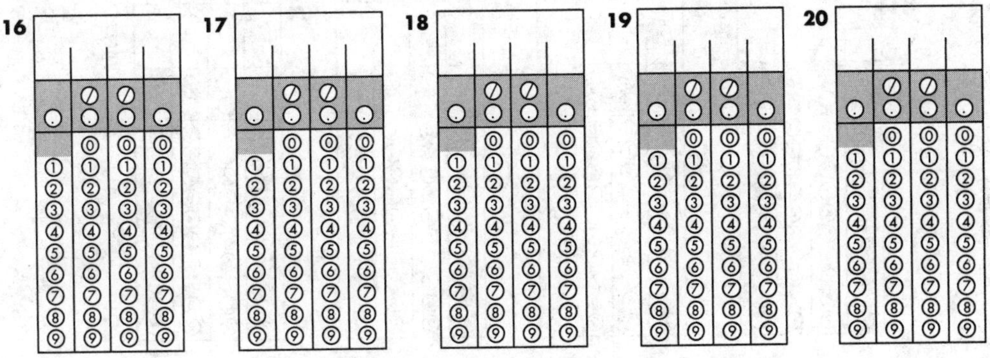

SECTION 4

1 (A) (B) (C) (D)
2 (A) (B) (C) (D)
3 (A) (B) (C) (D)
4 (A) (B) (C) (D)
5 (A) (B) (C) (D)
6 (A) (B) (C) (D)
7 (A) (B) (C) (D)
8 (A) (B) (C) (D)
9 (A) (B) (C) (D)
10 (A) (B) (C) (D)

11 (A) (B) (C) (D)
12 (A) (B) (C) (D)
13 (A) (B) (C) (D)
14 (A) (B) (C) (D)
15 (A) (B) (C) (D)
16 (A) (B) (C) (D)
17 (A) (B) (C) (D)
18 (A) (B) (C) (D)
19 (A) (B) (C) (D)
20 (A) (B) (C) (D)

21 (A) (B) (C) (D)
22 (A) (B) (C) (D)
23 (A) (B) (C) (D)
24 (A) (B) (C) (D)
25 (A) (B) (C) (D)
26 (A) (B) (C) (D)
27 (A) (B) (C) (D)
28 (A) (B) (C) (D)
29 (A) (B) (C) (D)
30 (A) (B) (C) (D)

Student-Produced Responses

ONLY ANSWERS ENTERED IN THE CIRCLES IN EACH GRID WILL BE SCORED. YOU WILL NOT RECEIVE CREDIT FOR ANYTHING WRITTEN IN THE BOXES ABOVE THE CIRCLES.

31   32   33   34

35   36   37   38

SECTION 5: ESSAY

You may wish to remove these sample answer document pages to respond to the practice SAT Essay Test.

Begin your essay here.

_____

_____

_____

_____

_____

_____

_____

_____

_____

_____

_____

_____

_____

_____

_____

_____

_____

_____

_____

_____

_____

_____

_____

_____

_____

_____

_____

_____

_____

If you need more space, please continue on the next page.

Cut Here

ESSAY

Cut Here

ESSAY

_____

_____

_____

_____

_____

_____

_____

_____

_____

_____

_____

_____

_____

_____

_____

_____

_____

_____

_____

_____

_____

_____

_____

_____

_____

If you need more space, please continue on the next page.

ESSAY

_____
_____
_____
_____
_____
_____
_____
_____
_____
_____
_____
_____
_____
_____
_____
_____
_____
_____
_____
_____
_____
_____
_____
_____
_____
_____
_____

STOP here with the Essay.

Cut Here

1   1

Reading Test
65 MINUTES, 52 QUESTIONS

Turn to Section 1 of your answer sheet to answer the questions in this section.

DIRECTIONS

Each passage or pair of passages below is followed by a number of questions. After reading each passage or pair, choose the best answer to each question based on what is stated or implied in the passage or passages and in any accompanying graphics (such as a table or graph).

Questions 1–10 are based on the following passages and supplementary material.

This passage is adapted from Holli Riebeek, "Is Current Warming Natural?" originally published in *The Earth Observatory Newspaper* (earthobservatory.nasa.gov) in 2010.

Before the Industrial Revolution, Earth's climate frequently changed due to natural causes
Line unrelated to human activity. For instance, tiny wobbles in Earth's orbit or variations in the sun's
5 intensity sometimes produced variations in sunlight intensity at different parts of the Earth's surface. Also, occasional volcanic eruptions spewed particles high into the atmosphere that reflected sunlight, brightening the planet and cooling the
10 climate. In the deep past, more frequent volcanic activity over millions of years also increased greenhouse gases, contributing to episodes of global warming.

Such natural causes are still in play today,
15 but their influence is too small or too slow to explain the rapid warming we have witnessed in recent decades. We know this because scientists closely monitor natural and human activities that influence climate with a fleet of satellites and

20 surface instruments. NASA satellites record a host of vital signs including the levels of atmospheric aerosols (tiny wind-borne particles created by such things as factory emissions, wildfires, desert sandstorms, or volcano eruptions),
25 concentrations of atmospheric gases (including greenhouse gases), the intensity of energy emitted from the sun or radiated from the Earth's surface, fluctuations in ocean surface temperatures, changes in the global sea level and the
30 extent of polar ice sheets and glaciers, changes in plant extent and growth, levels of rainfall, and even varieties of cloud structure. On the ground, many agencies and nations support networks of weather and climate-monitoring stations that
35 maintain temperature, rainfall, and snow depth records. In the ocean, buoys measure surface water and deep ocean temperatures and salinity. Taken together, these measurements provide an ever-improving record of both natural events and
40 human activity for the past 150 years.

Scientists integrate these measurements into sophisticated computerized climate models in an attempt to re-create temperatures recorded over the past 150 years. Those simulations that con-
45 sider only natural solar variability and volcanic aerosols fit the observations of global temperatures very well from 1750 until 1950. After that

CONTINUE ➡

point, the trend in global surface warming cannot be explained without including the contribution
50 of the anthropogenic greenhouse gases, that is, those produced via non-natural human activities like burning fossil fuels.

Granted, natural changes to Earth's climate have also occurred in recent times. For
55 example, two major volcanic eruptions, in 1982 and in 1991, pumped sulfur dioxide gas high into the atmosphere, creating tiny particles that lingered for more than a year. These reflected sunlight and shaded Earth's surface,
60 and temperatures across the globe dipped for about three years. However, although volcanoes are active around the world, the amount of carbon dioxide they release is extremely small compared to that released by human
65 activities. On average, volcanoes emit between 130 and 230 million tons of carbon dioxide per year, whereas the burning of fossil fuels releases about 26 billion tons of carbon dioxide every year. In other words, human influence on

70 the climate is 100–200 times the effect of all the world's volcanoes.

Changes in the brightness of the sun also can influence the climate from decade to decade, but an increase in solar intensity falls short as an
75 explanation for the warming we've seen in the last 65 years. This is because the warming pattern produced by an increase in solar radiation is different from that produced by an increase in greenhouse gases. When the sun becomes more
80 intense, it warms both the lower atmosphere (the troposphere) and the upper atmosphere (the stratosphere). However, greenhouse gases warm the troposphere and *cool* the stratosphere. The data from the last 65 years show the latter effect,
85 not the former.

Those who dismiss environmental scientists as global warming "alarmists" would do well to look more closely at the data. While it is true that "Earth's climate has always been changing,"
90 there is little doubt now that humans have fundamentally changed the equation.

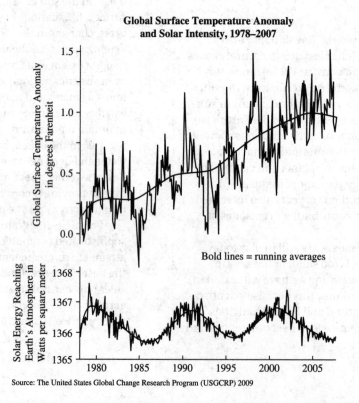

**Global Surface Temperature Anomaly
and Solar Intensity, 1978–2007**

Bold lines = running averages

Source: The United States Global Change Research Program (USGCRP) 2009

CONTINUE ▶

1

1

1

Which choice best summarizes the main point of the passage?

A) Many natural phenomena, like solar and volcanic activity, continue to drive global climate change.

B) The recent improvements in climatological data gathering will soon yield a deeper understanding of the greenhouse effect.

C) Recent trends in global temperatures cannot be explained without including data associated with human activities.

D) The Industrial Revolution provided new technologies that have allowed scientists unprecedented insight into climate change.

2

In the fourth paragraph (lines 53–71), the author anticipates which of the following objections to the main thesis of the passage?

A) Current climatic computer models are inaccurate and hence unreliable.

B) The science of climatology is still in its infancy.

C) Non-anthropogenic drivers of climate change overwhelm anthropogenic ones.

D) Natural causes have been driving climate change for much longer than humans have.

3

The passage as a whole characterizes modern-day volcanic activity as

A) a significant source of greenhouse gases.

B) a relatively minor contributor to global climate change.

C) the primary cause of stratospheric cooling.

D) a complicating factor in the gathering of global climatic data.

4

Which choice provides the best evidence for the answer to the previous question?

A) Lines 7–10 ("Also . . . climate")

B) Lines 20–32 ("NASA . . . structure")

C) Lines 44–47 ("Those . . . 1950")

D) Lines 69–71 ("In . . . volcanoes")

5

As used in line 21, "host" most nearly means

A) presenter.

B) multitude.

C) carrier.

D) subset.

6

As used in line 42, "sophisticated" most nearly means

A) highly complex.

B) refined and worldly.

C) widely appealing.

D) reliably functional.

7

Which statement is most strongly supported by the data in the graphs, taken as whole?

A) Global temperature changes correlate strongly with fluctuations in the sun's intensity.

B) Both global temperatures and solar energy have been steadily increasing since 1978.

C) Changes in solar energy cannot fully account for the recent increase in global surface temperatures.

D) Volcanic activity must be factored into climate models to better account for the steady increase in recent global temperatures.

CONTINUE ►

8

According to the graph, when the running average of global surface temperatures reached a peak in 2004,

A) solar energy was near its short-term maximum and beginning to decline.

B) solar energy was near its long-term average and declining.

C) solar energy was near its short-term minimum and beginning to increase.

D) solar energy was near its long-term average and increasing.

9

In the context of the passage, the quotation in line 89 is best regarded as

A) a widely held delusion.

B) a little-known fact.

C) an inadequate explanation.

D) a surprising discovery.

10

Which choice best supports the author's claim that recent atmospheric measurements confirm that natural causes do not explain recent global temperature trends?

A) Lines 20–32 ("NASA . . . structure")

B) Lines 41–44 ("Scientists . . . years")

C) Lines 54–58 ("For example . . . year")

D) Lines 83–85 ("The data . . . former")

1   1

Questions 11–21 are based on the following passages.

Passage 1 is from President James Monroe, *Message to Congress*, given on December 2, 1823, announcing what has come to be known as the Monroe Doctrine. Passage 2 is from President Theodore Roosevelt, *Message to Congress*, given on December 6, 1904, announcing what came to be known as the Roosevelt Corollary to the Monroe Doctrine.

Passage 1

Line
American continents, by the free and independent condition which they have assumed and maintain, are henceforth not to be considered as subjects for future colonization by any European
5 powers.

In the wars of the European powers in matters relating to themselves we have never taken any part, nor does it comport with our policy to do so. It is only when our rights are invaded
10 or seriously menaced that we resent injuries or make preparation for our defense. With the movements in this hemisphere we are of necessity more immediately connected, and by causes which must be obvious to all enlightened and
15 impartial observers. The political system of the allied powers is essentially different in this respect from that of America. This difference proceeds from that which exists in their respective Governments, and to the defense of our own,
20 which has been achieved by the loss of so much blood and treasure, and matured by the wisdom of their most enlightened citizens, and under which we have enjoyed unexampled felicity, this whole nation is devoted. We owe it, therefore,
25 to candor and to the amicable relations existing between the United States and those powers to declare that we should consider any attempt on their part to extend their system to any portion of this hemisphere as dangerous to our peace and
30 safety.

With the existing colonies or dependencies of any European power we have not interfered and shall not interfere. But with the Governments who have declared their independence and
35 maintain it, and whose independence we have, on great consideration and on just principles, acknowledged, we could not view any interposition for the purpose of oppressing them, or controlling in any other manner their destiny, by
40 any European power in any other light than as the manifestation of an unfriendly disposition toward the United States. In the war between those new Governments and Spain we declared our neutrality at the time of their recognition,
45 and to this we have adhered, and shall continue to adhere, provided no change shall occur which, in the judgment of the competent authorities of this Government, shall make a corresponding change on the part of the United States indis-
50 pensable to their security. It is still the true policy of the United States to leave the parties to themselves, in hope that other powers will pursue the same course.

Passage 2

It is not merely unwise, it is contemptible, for
55 a nation, as for an individual, to use high-sounding language to proclaim its purposes, or to take positions which are ridiculous if unsupported by potential force, and then to refuse to provide this force. If there is no intention of providing and
60 keeping the force necessary to back up a strong attitude, then it is far better not to assume such an attitude.

The steady aim of this Nation, as of all enlightened nations, should be to strive to bring
65 ever nearer the day when there shall prevail throughout the world the peace of justice. All that this country desires is to see the neighboring countries stable, orderly, and prosperous. Any country whose people conduct themselves well
70 can count upon our hearty friendship. If a nation shows that it knows how to act with reasonable efficiency and decency in social and political matters, if it keeps order and pays its obligations, it need fear no interference from the United
75 States. Chronic wrongdoing, or an impotence which results in a general loosening of the ties of

CONTINUE ▶

civilized society, may in America, as elsewhere, ultimately require intervention by some civilized nation, and in the Western Hemisphere the
80 adherence of the United States to the Monroe Doctrine may force the United States, however reluctantly, in flagrant cases of such wrongdoing or impotence, to the exercise of an international police power.
85   We would interfere with them only in the last resort, and then only if it became evident that

their inability or unwillingness to do justice at home and abroad had violated the rights of the United States or had invited foreign aggression
90 to the detriment of the entire body of American nations. It is a mere truism to say that every nation, whether in America or anywhere else, which desires to maintain its freedom, its independence, must ultimately realize that the right
95 of such independence can not be separated from the responsibility of making good use of it.

1   **1**

11

On which policy do the authors of both passages most strongly agree?

A) The United States must remain neutral in disagreements between European powers and their colonies.

B) The political systems of all European countries must remain essentially different from those in the American continents.

C) The European colonies on the American continents must be allowed to resolve conflicts on their own.

D) European nations must not attempt to control any part of the American continents.

12

Which choice provides the best evidence for the answer to the previous question?

A) Lines 1–5 ("American . . . powers") and lines 85–91 ("We . . . nations")

B) Lines 15–17 ("The political . . . America) and lines 63–66 ("The steady . . . justice")

C) Lines 31–33 ("With . . . interfere") and lines 68–70 ("Any country . . . friendship)

D) Lines 50–53 ("It . . . course") and lines 70–75 ("If . . . United States")

13

The first paragraph of Passage 1 functions primarily to

A) provide historical background.

B) announce a conciliatory initiative.

C) declare an authoritative position.

D) reject a philosophical premise.

14

The author of Passage 1 suggests that the circumstances by which the United States is "more immediately connected" (line 13) to the rest of the American continent are

A) historically unique.

B) long established.

C) self-evident.

D) reluctantly acknowledged.

15

As used in line 23, "unexampled" most nearly means

A) without precedent.

B) lacking illustration.

C) without basis.

D) lacking reliability.

16

As used in lines 37–38, "interposition" most nearly means

A) interruption.

B) interpolation.

C) intermingling.

D) intervention.

CONTINUE ➡

1　　　　　　　　　　　　　　　　　　　　　　**1**

17

The author of Passage 1 mentions the war between Spain and its former colonies in order to make the point that the United States

A) has exhibited notable restraint in a troubling situation.

B) is preparing for a vigorous defense of the American continents.

C) recognizes Spain's particular penchant for aggression.

D) is willing to act as a mediator in international disputes.

18

Both authors acknowledge that American military force may be required to

A) achieve independence from foreign oppressors.

B) rehabilitate American colonies that are becoming dissolute or corrupt.

C) support American allies in foreign wars.

D) prevent European expansionism on the American continents.

19

Which choice provides the best evidence for the answer to the previous question?

A) Lines 6–9 ("In . . . do so") and lines 50–53 (It is . . . force")

B) Lines 17–24 ("This . . . devoted") and lines 63–66 ("The steady . . . justice")

C) Lines 24–30 ("We . . . safety") and lines 85–91 (We . . . nations")

D) Lines 50–53 ("It . . . course") and lines 91–96 ("It is . . . of it")

20

The author of Passage 2 would most likely respond to the statement in lines 9–11 ("It . . . defense") by adding that

A) hostilities between nations on the American continent can be a legitimate threat to the United States.

B) European nations have a history of reneging on their agreements with foreign colonies.

C) military intervention is antithetical to the United States' policy of promoting peace in the Americas.

D) the United States respects the sovereignty of all independent nations.

21

Which choice best exemplifies the kind of "wrong-doing" mentioned in line 75?

A) Spain's founding of a new colony in Africa

B) A Central American nation instigating rebellion in a neighboring country

C) Portugal's establishment of an embassy in a former colony in South America

D) Great Britain's sending naval vessels to the North American coast

CONTINUE ▶

Questions 22–32 are based on the following passage.

This passage is adapted from Matthew Edward, "Historical Frameworks." ©2014 by Matthew Edward.

Professional historians often struggle to understand those distant historical events that
Line are "lost in the mist of time." Even those events that were depicted vividly in primary sources
5 must often be reconsidered as new information is uncovered or old information is reinterpreted.

For example, Richard III of England has long been regarded as one of the most vicious and heartless monarchs in history. Yet now
10 the Richard III Society has uncovered facts suggesting that this image was distorted by Shakespeare's famous representation, which in turn was based solely on the Tudor version of Richard's reign. Since the Tudors were eager to
15 vilify Richard and legitimize Henry VII's usurpation of the throne from the Plantagenets, their representations can hardly be regarded as historically objective.

America has its own distortions to contend
20 with. For instance, for a long time most American schoolchildren were taught that Andrew Jackson represented everything good in American democracy. Then, during the Civil Rights Era, evidence came to light regarding the land-lust and
25 latent racism behind his Indian Removal Act.

To discern reality through the mist of time, historians must turn to careful analytical methods. These methods can be organized into three predominant approaches, each with its
30 advantages and disadvantages: the "classic narrative" approach, the "quantitative-positivistic" approach, and the "cultural criticism" approach.

The classic narrative approach stresses the historian's skills in writing and discernment.
35 By this method, historians evaluate the validity of evidence by considering diverse sources. For example, when evidence in a personal journal conflicts with that in a newspaper, and both conflict with the information in a government report,

40 the historians must weigh all evidence, using the intuitive skills they have honed from years of training, before arriving at a conclusion. All of this analysis serves not merely accuracy but also narrative cogency. The objective is to construct a
45 story that provides an explanatory framework as well as a compelling tale.

The second approach, the quantitative-positivistic approach, applies methods from fields like statistics and information analysis to the
50 study of history. Historians who gravitate toward this approach adopt a paradigm very much like the scientific method, by which they construct clear historical theories and apply quantitative methods such as Bayesian logic and multivariate
55 regression in order to assess those hypotheses. Here, the key elements are the clearly defined variable and the testable hypothesis. For example, Brazil in the 19th century saw pronounced economic growth as well as increased foreign
60 investment in railroads. Whereas historians in the past might have assumed a causal relationship between the two, quantitative-positivistic historians now have the means to scrutinize this connection. Using multivariate regression, they
65 can compare one statistic gauging economic growth, such as real wages or per capita gross domestic product, to multiple other variables like trade deficits or foreign investment levels, to determine any correlations among those data.

70 The third approach, the cultural criticism approach, takes a skeptical view of hierarchies, hegemonies, and institutions and the way such power structures can misrepresent historical accounts. An essential postulate of this approach
75 is that history is written by the powerful, the victorious, and the literate. Since the vast majority of people in history were none of these things, historians must read between the lines of historical documents, which may distort, or merely
80 hint at, the lives of the less privileged classes. These documents include written laws, merchant ledgers, personal journals, government decrees, and court decisions. One notable example is the documentation of the "tribute system"

CONTINUE ➤

85 established by Christopher Columbus on the isle of Hispaniola in the early 16th century, by which natives were required to bring him gold and cotton or risk having their hands amputated or being sold into slavery. By analyzing the documents of 90 the empowered, historians can begin to assemble the lives of the downtrodden.

Each of these approaches represents a set of skills for dealing with the fundamental problems of history: distortion and deficiency. None 95 is a perfect method for determining truth, but all seek to peer more clearly through the mist of time.

CONTINUE

1　　　　　　　　　　　　　　　　　**1**

22

The passage as a whole is best regarded as

A) an argument for adopting a particular historical method over the alternatives.

B) a discussion of several obstacles to impartial historical analysis.

C) an introduction to various methodological systems for examining history.

D) an illustration of some of the technical debates among modern academic historians.

23

Compared to each of the other approaches discussed in the passage, the quantitative-positivistic approach is more

A) objective.

B) embellished.

C) skeptical.

D) popular.

24

The second paragraph mentions Shakespeare primarily as an example of

A) a famous figure whose identity and background are in dispute.

B) an exemplary author of riveting historical plays.

C) an early pioneer of the classic narrative approach.

D) an abettor to an act of historical misrepresentation.

25

The passage implies that reliable historical analysis is most significantly hindered by

A) a lack of appropriate analytical methods.

B) biased and incomplete documentation.

C) technical disputes among historians who use different methodologies.

D) political and philosophical differences among academic historians.

26

Which choice provides the best evidence for the answer to the previous question?

A) Lines 19–20 ("America . . . with")

B) Lines 28–32 ("These . . . approach")

C) Lines 74–76 ("An essential . . . literate")

D) Lines 92–94 ("Each . . . deficiency")

27

The passage suggests that historians using the classic narrative approach are most concerned with producing

A) persuasive prose.

B) even-handed portrayals.

C) imaginative stories.

D) verifiable data.

28

Which choice provides the best evidence for the answer to the previous question?

A) Lines 33–34 ("The . . . discernment")

B) Lines 35–36 ("By . . . sources")

C) Lines 36–42 ("For . . . conclusion")

D) Lines 42–46 ("All of . . . tale")

29

According to the passage, the "documentation" mentioned in line 84 is notable because it

A) confirms the validity of a well-established belief.

B) contradicts the evidence provided by other sources.

C) contributes reliable data for quantitative analysis.

D) provides insight into an often unacknowledged aspect of history.

30

In line 55, "regression" refers to an act of

A) political subjugation.

B) scientific conjecture.

C) mathematical calculation.

D) social deterioration.

31

The passage discusses the economy of Brazil in the 19th century primarily to make the point that

A) some countries can see dramatic economic growth over a matter of decades.

B) some historical theories should not be taken for granted.

C) some political leaders are inclined to suppress historical facts.

D) some historians find it difficult to frame historical phenomena in mathematical terms.

32

As used in line 90, "assemble" most nearly means

A) represent as a coherent whole.

B) forge from rudimentary materials.

C) gather for a cultural event.

D) categorize as a social group.

CONTINUE

1

Questions 33–42 are based on the following passage.

This passage is adapted from Henry Fielding, *Tom Jones*, originally published in 1749. In this story, Mrs. Deborah Wilkins is Mr. Allworthy's longtime servant.

Mr. Allworthy had been absent a full quarter of a year in London, on some very particular business. He came to his house very late in the evening, and after a short supper with his sister, retired much fatigued to his chamber. Here, having spent some minutes on his knees—a custom which he never broke through on any account—he was preparing to step into bed, when, upon opening the clothes, to his great surprise he beheld an infant, wrapt up in some coarse linen, in a sweet and profound sleep, between his sheets. He stood some time lost in astonishment at this sight; but, as good nature had always the ascendant in his mind, he soon began to be touched with sentiments of compassion for the little wretch before him. He then rang his bell, and ordered an elderly woman-servant to rise immediately, and come to him, and in the meantime was eager in contemplating the beauty of innocence, appearing in those lively colours with which infancy and sleep always display it.

Mrs. Deborah Wilkins had given her master sufficient time to dress himself; for out of respect to him, and regard to decency, she had spent many minutes in adjusting her hair at the looking-glass, notwithstanding all the hurry in which she had been summoned by the servant, and though her master, for aught she knew, lay expiring in an apoplexy, or in some other fit.

When she entered into the room, and was acquainted by her master with the finding of the little infant, her consternation was rather greater than his had been; nor could she refrain from crying out, with great horror of accent as well as look, "My good sir! what's to be done?" Mr. Allworthy answered, she must take care of the child that

evening, and in the morning he would give orders to provide it a nurse. "Yes, sir," says she, "and I hope your worship will send out your warrant to take up the hussy its mother, for she must be one of the neighbourhood; and I should be glad to see her committed to Bridewell,[1] and whipt at the cart's tail. For my own part, it goes against me to touch these misbegotten wretches, whom I don't look upon as my fellow-creatures. Faugh! how it stinks! It doth not smell like a Christian. If I might be so bold to give my advice, I would have it put in a basket, and sent out and laid at the church-warden's door. It is a good night, only a little rainy and windy; and if it was well wrapt up, and put in a warm basket, it is two to one but it lives till it is found in the morning. But if it should not, we have discharged our duty in taking proper care of it; and it is, perhaps, better for such creatures to die in a state of innocence, than to grow up and imitate their mothers; for nothing better can be expected of them."

There were some strokes in this speech which perhaps would have offended Mr. Allworthy, had he strictly attended to it; but he had now got one of his fingers into the infant's hand, which, by its gentle pressure, seeming to implore his assistance, had certainly out-pleaded the eloquence of Mrs. Deborah, had it been ten times greater than it was. He now gave Mrs. Deborah positive orders to take the child to her own bed, and to call up a maid-servant to provide it pap, and other things, against it waked.

Such was the discernment of Mrs. Wilkins, and such the respect she bore her master, under whom she enjoyed a most excellent place, that her scruples gave way to his peremptory commands; and she took the child under her arms, without any apparent disgust at the illegality of its birth; and declaring it was a sweet little infant, walked off with it to her own chamber.

---

[1]a prison and hospital

CONTINUE →

33

Which choice best summarizes the passage?

A) A man and his sister have divergent reactions to receiving an abandoned infant and different opinions about what to do with it.

B) A servant comes to resent her master because of his indifferent treatment of an abandoned infant.

C) A master orders his servant to take care of an abandoned infant, and the servant resents the task but acquiesces.

D) A master criticizes his servant for the lack of respect she shows for an abandoned infant and the infant's absent mother.

34

As used in line 11, "coarse" most nearly means

A) brusque.

B) essential.

C) rough.

D) vulgar.

35

The second paragraph suggests that Mrs. Deborah reacts to Mr. Allworthy's bell-ringing with

A) nonchalance.

B) earnestness.

C) deference.

D) contempt.

36

As used in line 40, "take up" most nearly means

A) take into custody.

B) give shelter to.

C) become friends with.

D) undertake as a project.

37

Mrs. Deborah's emotional reaction to the infant is best described as evolving from

A) shock to indignation to resignation.

B) fear to disappointment to compassion.

C) surprise to righteousness to indifference.

D) outrage to tenderness to sullenness.

38

Which choice best describes Mrs. Deborah Wilkins's general attitude toward Mr. Allworthy as characterized in the passage?

A) She regards herself as a pragmatic counterbalance to his unreasonable vanity.

B) She feels she can speak candidly with him yet she respects his authority.

C) She feigns to tolerate him but in fact considers him wretched.

D) She is openly scornful of his easygoing temperament.

39

Which choice provides the best evidence for the answer to the previous question?

A) Lines 22–29 ("Mrs. Deborah Wilkins . . . fit")

B) Lines 30–35 ("When . . . done?'")

C) Lines 46–49 ("If . . . door")

D) Lines 69–76 ("Such . . . chamber")

40

Mr. Allsworthy is not offended by Mrs. Deborah's speech primarily because

A) he has learned to ignore her tirades.

B) he cannot manage the estate without her.

C) he values her blunt opinions.

D) he is distracted by the infant.

1 1

41

The narrator indicates that Mrs. Deborah eventually takes the infant in her arms primarily because she

A) regards it with pity and compassion.

B) wants to remain in Mr. Allworth's good graces.

C) fears the wrath of Mr. Allworth if she disobeys.

D) realizes that neglecting it would be immoral.

42

As used in line 65, "positive" most nearly means

A) optimistic.

B) heartening.

C) unequivocal.

D) practical.

CONTINUE

1   1

Questions 43–52 are based on the following passage.

This passage is adapted from Edward Ditkoff, MD, "Setting Your Biological Clock by Oocyte Cryopreservation." ©2014 by Edward Ditkoff and CNY Fertility.

Today, couples are marrying much later than they did in previous generations and are starting families later still. With careers, homes, and lives comfortably in place, however, these couples are facing a new problem of modern family planning. Forty may be the new thirty, but not when it comes to having babies!

All female infants are born with approximately one million eggs in reserve. By puberty, this number diminishes by about one half, and continues to decline by approximately 750 every month thereafter. The quality of these eggs begins to decline as well when a woman hits her 20s, and after she reaches the age of about 35 her eggs begin to degenerate. For women over 40 who have never given birth, fertility rates are significantly lower than those for younger women, or for older women who have already given birth.

One cause of age-related infertility is the increased likelihood of "mitosis errors," in which the genetic material in a fertilized egg or embryonic cell fails to distribute itself evenly to daughter cells. (Mitosis is the process by which cells divide to form new cells.) This disorder is called aneuploidy, which yields embryonic cells that lack the necessary complement of 23 chromosome pairs, usually with one chromosome too few or too many. This discrepancy is significant. Missing even one of the hundreds of threadlike structures on a single chromosome can have a major effect on a developing embryo.

The vast majority of aneuploid embryos are nonviable and will not implant in the wall of the uterus. Therefore, older women often require more prolonged and more complicated fertility treatments. Even if implantation does occur, early miscarriage (pregnancy loss) is common, which not only causes emotional and physical trauma, but also delays potential childbearing. And even when aneuploid embryos are viable and do survive to term, babies can develop syndromes like Down, Turner, Klinefelter, or Cri-du-chat. Other viable aneuploid embryos that are carried to term sadly die soon after delivery, as in Edwards' syndrome. Fortunately, these complications in older first-time mothers are not universal, and this problem has not yet risen to crisis proportions. In fact, many older mothers conceive, carry to term, and deliver perfectly healthy children. Nonetheless, the medical community believes the situation certainly deserves serious consideration as more and more couples delay starting families.

Today's mature would-be mothers have a new option. The techniques of oocyte cryopreservation, or egg freezing, have improved dramatically over the past decade. In fact, egg freezing has not been considered experimental by the American Society of Reproductive Medicine since 2012. The process involves stimulating the ovaries to ripen multiple eggs, then retrieving these eggs while they are healthy and freezing them to preserve their quality. Then, when the prospective mother is ready to conceive (or to donate to a surrogate), the eggs can be thawed, fertilized, and transferred to the uterus as embryos.

Experimental evidence suggests that previously frozen oocytes work nearly as well as fresh ones with regard to fertilization and pregnancy rates. Perhaps even more importantly, frozen eggs do not seem to be as susceptible to degradation and the many associated developmental deficits that could result. This process may sound frighteningly futuristic, but it is showing a great deal of potential.

For women who are leading busier lives, obtaining advanced education, pursuing successful careers, and starting families later in life, frozen eggs can effectively slow down their biological clocks. A woman of 35 or 40 can now have a child with her own egg that was collected when she was 25, when she was in her reproductive prime. Prudent family planning in partnership with modern medicine can give today's older potential parents a better chance to have a successful pregnancy and a healthy baby.

CONTINUE ▶

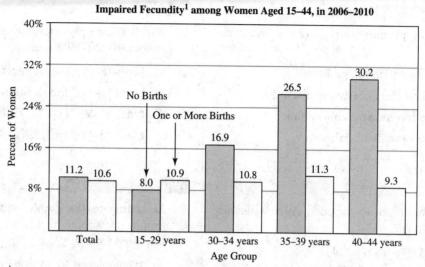

Impaired Fecundity[1] among Women Aged 15–44, in 2006–2010

[1]impaired fecundity: significant difficulty (unrelated to surgery) with getting pregnant or carrying a baby to term

Source: Centers for Disease Control and Prevention, National Center for Health Statistics, National Survey of Family Growth, 2006–2010. Analysis conducted by the National Center for Health Statistics

CONTINUE

1   **1**

43

In context, the primary purpose of the first paragraph is to

A) propose a solution to a problem.

B) describe a sociological phenomenon.

C) identify a common misconception.

D) advance a new medical theory.

44

The data in the graph best supports which statement from the passage?

A) Lines 1–3 ("Today . . . still")

B) Lines 9–12 ("By . . . thereafter")

C) Lines 12–15 ("The . . . degenerate")

D) Lines 15–18 ("For . . . birth")

45

As used in line 25, "yields" most nearly means

A) generates.

B) surrenders.

C) gives way to.

D) displaces.

46

The passage indicates that the most common result of aneuploidy is

A) oocyte degeneration.

B) miscarriage.

C) developmental syndromes.

D) failure to implant.

47

Which choice provides the best evidence for the answer to the previous question?

A) Lines 12–15 ("The . . . degenerate")

B) Lines 32–34 ("The . . . uterus")

C) Lines 36–39 ("Even . . . childbearing")

D) Lines 39–42 ("And . . . Cri-du-chat")

48

According to the graph, which of the following groups of women is LEAST likely to encounter impaired fecundity?

A) Women aged 30–34 who have never given birth

B) Women aged 30–34 who have given birth at least once

C) Women aged 40–44 who have never given birth

D) Women aged 40–44 who have given birth at least once

49

As used in lines 75 and 85, "potential" most nearly means, respectively,

A) power and latent.

B) promise and prospective.

C) prospect and undeveloped.

D) possibility and inherent.

50

The passage suggests that the promise of oocyte cryopreservation lies primarily in its ability to

A) reduce the need to utilize surrogates.

B) ensure the even distribution of genetic material during mitosis.

C) arrest the egg's degeneration process.

D) reverse the effects of aneuploidy and its associated syndromes.

CONTINUE ▶

1   **1**

51

Which choice provides the best evidence for the answer to the previous question?

A) Lines 19–23 ("One . . . cells")

B) Lines 29–31 ("Missing . . . embryo")

C) Lines 63–66 ("Then . . . embryos")

D) Lines 70–73 ("Perhaps . . . result")

52

Which of the following is a potential drawback to oocyte cryopreservation as it is described in the passage?

A) It requires advance planning.

B) It is very expensive.

C) It has not been thoroughly tested.

D) It is less effective with younger women.

STOP

**If you finish before time is called, you may check your work on this section only.
Do not turn to any other section of the test.**

2   2

Writing and Language Test
35 MINUTES, 44 QUESTIONS

Turn to Section 2 of your answer sheet to answer the questions in this section.

DIRECTIONS

Each passage below is accompanied by a number of questions. For some questions, you will consider how the passage might be revised to improve the expression of ideas. For other questions, you will consider how the passage might be edited to correct errors in sentence structure, usage, or punctuation. A passage or a question may be accompanied by one or more graphics (such as a table or graph) that you will consider as you make revising and editing decisions.

Some questions will direct you to an underlined portion of a passage. Other questions will direct you to a location in a passage or ask you to think about the passage as a whole.

After reading each passage, choose the answer to each question that most effectively improves the quality of writing in the passage or that makes the passage conform to the conventions of standard written English. Many questions include a "NO CHANGE" option. Choose that option if you think the best choice is to leave the relevant portion of the passage as it is.

Questions 1–11 are based on the following passage and supplementary material.

Cold, Flu, or Allergy?

– 1 –

You've got the sniffles, a cough, and **1**
you're throat is sore. Is it a cold, flu, or allergies?
Understanding the differences among these illnesses
will help you choose the best treatment. Dr. Teresa
Hauguel, an expert on respiratory diseases, **2** advises
that learning is important about the causes, symptoms,
and treatments of these common upper-respiratory ail-
ments. With the right knowledge, we can avoid taking
medications that at best are ineffective, and at worst
can exacerbate conditions or even create new ones.

1

A) NO CHANGE
B) your throat is sore
C) a sore throat
D) soreness in you're throat

2

A) NO CHANGE
B) advises everyone to be learning
C) advises that everyone learn
D) advises the importance of everyone learning

CONTINUE ▶

2   2

Cold, flu, and allergies all affect the respiratory

3 system, they cause breathing problems. However,

each condition has distinctive **4** symptoms that

set it apart.

3

A) NO CHANGE

B) system and cause breathing problems

C) system in causing breathing problems

D) system; to cause breathing problems

4

A) NO CHANGE

B) symptoms setting them apart

C) symptoms

D) symptoms that set them apart

Symptoms	Cold	Flu	Airborne Allergy
Fever	Rare	Usual, high (100°–102° F or sometimes higher in young children), lasts 3–4 days	Never
Headache	Uncommon	Common	Uncommon
General aches and pains	Slight	Usual, often severe	Never
Fatigue or weakness	Occasional	Usual, can last up to 3 weeks	Occasional
Extreme exhaustion	Never	Usual, at onset of illness	Never
Congested or runny nose	Common	Occasional	Common
Sneezing	Usual	Occasional	Usual
Sore throat	Common	Occasional	Occasional
Cough	Common	Common, can be severe	Occasional
Chest discomfort	Mild to moderate	Common	Rare, except with allergic asthma

Adapted from Vicki Contie and Carol Torgan and the National Institutes of Health (newsinhealth.nih.gov)

CONTINUE

– 2 –

According to Dr. Hauguel, colds and flu are caused by different viruses, while allergies are most commonly caused by airborne pathogens like pollen or dander. All three illnesses usually involve **5** congestion and sneezing, but the flu is commonly distinguished by high, prolonged fever as well as headache and often severe pain.

5

At this point, the writer wants to add specific information from the table. Which choice adds the most relevant and accurate information?

A) NO CHANGE

B) fever and sneezing, but the flu is commonly distinguished by sore throat and congestion.

C) fatigue and headache, but the flu is commonly distinguished by cough, sore throat, and mild fever.

D) congestion and headache, but the flu is commonly distinguished by high, prolonged fever and sore throat.

CONTINUE

2   2

– 3 –

6 Contrary to a cold or flu infection, a respiratory allergy is an immune response to a particular particle in the air, called an allergen. When an allergy sufferer **7** imbibes an allergen, the nose and airways **8** overreact. Delicate respiratory tissues become inflamed, and the nose may feel stuffed or drippy. Itchy and watery eyes are also common allergy symptoms **9** that are not usually seen with the cold or flu. Another sign that the problem is allergy and not illness is the duration of the symptoms. Cold and flu symptoms almost never last longer than two weeks. Allergy symptoms, on the other hand, can last as long as the allergic person is exposed to the allergen. For some sufferers, this could be as long as 6 weeks during the pollen season.

6

A) NO CHANGE
B) Differently from
C) In opposition to
D) Unlike

7

A) NO CHANGE
B) inhales
C) ingests
D) imparts

8

Which choice most logically and effectively combines the two sentences?

A) overreact: delicate
B) overreact where delicate
C) overreact because delicate
D) overreact, delicate

9

The writer is considering deleting this underlined portion to make the sentence more concise. Should the author make this change?

A) Yes, because the distinctive qualities of allergies have already been listed.
B) Yes, because these symptoms are actually common with the cold and flu.
C) No, because the sentence should stress that these symptoms are unique to allergies.
D) No, because this phrase provides important treatment advice for allergy sufferers.

CONTINUE ▶

2   **2**

– 4 –

It's important to select your medication carefully according to your condition. Specialized prescription treatments are available for flu and allergy sufferers, but over-the-counter medications can be effective for mild cases. Dr. Hauguel also suggests selecting medicines with only the active ingredients **10** convenient to your condition. One popular medication contains a pain reliever, a fever reducer, an antihistamine, and a decongestant. Such a product would overmedicate an allergy attack that typically requires only an antihistamine for relief.

– 5 –

"Read medicine labels carefully—the warnings, side effects, and dosages," Dr. Hauguel says, "and if you have questions, talk to your doctor or pharmacist, especially if you have children who are sick."

Question 11 asks about the previous passage as a whole.

10

A) NO CHANGE
B) logical
C) valuable
D) suitable

Think about the previous passage as a whole as you answer question 11.

11

To make the passage most logical, paragraph 5 should be placed

A) where it is now.
B) after paragraph 1.
C) after paragraph 2.
D) after paragraph 3.

CONTINUE

2   2

Questions 12–22 are based on the following passage.

To Catch a Cyber-Thief

In Alfred Hitchcock's classic film *To Catch a Thief*, **12** the idea of which has been reworked in many books, films, and television shows ever since, a retired jewel thief is tasked with using his skills to catch a copycat burglar. But old-time cat burglars have nothing on today's super thieves who ply their trade on the Internet and in the computer networks of corporations and governments. **13** Today, we need a new generation of detectives who can think like these cyber thieves.

14 Nevertheless, colleges and universities have begun offering both bachelor's and master's degrees in cyber security. According to *US News and World Report*, in the past few years the demand for cyber security services **15** have grown twice as fast as that for the general information technology (IT) services. As unscrupulous hackers imagine more

---

12

A) NO CHANGE

B) an idea that has been reworked

C) an idea that had been reworked

D) the idea of which being reworked

13

At this point, the writer is considering adding the following sentence.

> In Hitchcock's film, the retired thief is initially the key suspect, even though he is innocent.

Should the writer make this addition here?

A) Yes, because it provides a relevant detail about Hitchcock's film.

B) Yes, because it explains why modern detectives might want to employ ex-thieves.

C) No, because disrupts the transition to a discussion about modern crime.

D) No, because it emphasizes property theft rather than security breaches.

14

A) NO CHANGE

B) In addition

C) Next

D) Accordingly

15

A) NO CHANGE

B) has grown

C) had grown

D) will grow

CONTINUE ▶

2   **2**

ways to break into computer systems, we need a
workforce to imagine more ways [16] for stopping the
intrusions.

    FBI Director James Comey [17] encapsulated
the situation in a speech to the Senate Committee
on Homeland Security and Governmental Affairs on
November 14, 2013. He said that FBI experts "anticipate
that in the future, resources devoted to cyber-based-
threats will equal or even eclipse the resources devoted
to non-cyber-based terrorist threats." [18] Other
agencies, like the NRA and CIA, often have different
priorities with regard to national security. By accessing
personal, corporate, financial, medical, and military
[19] networks, far more than just expensive pieces of
jewelry can be stolen by hackers.

[16]

A) NO CHANGE
B) in which to stop
C) in stopping
D) to stop

[17]

A) NO CHANGE
B) enveloped
C) concocted
D) supplemented

[18]

Which choice best maintains the logical cohesiveness of the paragraph?

A) NO CHANGE
B) Nevertheless, our law enforcement agencies
    must also engage networks of potentially
    violent criminals.
C) These resources must be used to thwart
    cyber criminals attempting to exploit our
    dependency on the Internet.
D) In recent decades, the FBI has been vigilant
    against threats to our major cities and power
    sources.

[19]

A) NO CHANGE
B) networks, hackers can steal far more than just
    expensive pieces of jewelry.
C) networks, hackers would be stealing far more
    than just expensive pieces of jewelry.
D) networks, far more than just expensive pieces
    of jewelry would be stolen by hackers.

2   2

Cyber security serves a growing need, and the field is so new and dynamic [20] but it provides many opportunities for entrepreneurs. Governments, corporations, and individuals must protect their computers, networks, programs, and data so that they cannot be accessed, stolen, or destroyed by unauthorized users. The idea is simple, but the reality is not. Without physical doors and locks to protect, [21] access cannot be monitored in any conventional way by using armed guards. How can anyone guard the Cloud? This new kind of security requires a great deal of technical expertise and diligence. It also requires the ability to be [22] as clever, if not more so, than a criminal.

[20]

A) NO CHANGE

B) and

C) that

D) because

[21]

A) NO CHANGE

B) access would not be monitored in any conventional way by using armed guards

C) armed guards would not be used to monitor conventional access in any way

D) armed guards cannot be used to monitor access in any conventional way

[22]

A) NO CHANGE

B) as clever, if not more, than a criminal does

C) as clever as a criminal, if not more so

D) as clever, if not more clever than a criminal

CONTINUE

2 　 **2**

Questions 23–33 are based on the following passage.

"Satchmo"

Louis Armstrong (1901–1971) was perhaps the most famous jazz musician of all time. His music was 23 energetic and it was groundbreaking, and his trumpet playing technique stood out from 24 other musicians of his day. He mastered what came to be the hallmark of jazz—the art of improvisation—advising his music students to "never play a thing the same way twice." New Orleans at the turn of the 20th century 25 provided fertile ground in which to nurture young Armstrong's special talents. Music was in the streets, where performers played for attention and perhaps a bit of coin. As a boy, Armstrong had a job selling coal from a cart and played a tin horn to 26 accommodate customers. He also spent a lot of time in "honkey tonks," cheap bars or dance halls where live music was played by some of the most innovative musicians of the day. 27 Sadly, these establishments would largely disappear from American cities within a few decades. He idolized musicians like Bunk Johnson and Joe Oliver, who became his mentors.

23

A) NO CHANGE
B) energetic, pioneering, and groundbreaking
C) energetic and it broke ground
D) energetic and groundbreaking

24

A) NO CHANGE
B) the playing of other musicians
C) that of other musicians
D) the music of other musicians

25

A) NO CHANGE
B) nurtured young Armstrong's special talents with it's fertile ground.
C) provided fertile ground nurturing young Armstrong's special talents.
D) was providing fertile ground on which to nurture young Armstrong's special talents.

26

A) NO CHANGE
B) afford
C) assist
D) attract

27

Which choice provides the most relevant and effective transition between the previous sentence and the sentence that follows?

A) NO CHANGE
B) Armstrong knew that these establishments attracted criminal elements as well.
C) Armstrong came to these establishments not only to listen, but also to learn.
D) The energy in these establishments inspired many of the great novelists of the era.

CONTINUE ▶

2   **2**

From New Orleans, Armstrong moved to **28** Chicago, to join Joe Oliver and his King Oliver Creole Jazz Band. His next big move was to New York, where the "Harlem Renaissance" was in full swing. Here, Armstrong met and collaborated with artists of all types—painters, poets, writers, actors, and musicians **29** —and embraced an artistic culture even richer than that in New Orleans. Soon afterward, he moved back to Chicago and formed his own group, The Hot Five. Now Armstrong **30** was back in a city he knew well and had the opportunity to let his genius soar. He sought new ways to expand his style and technique. He added "scat"—rhythmic but nonsensical syllables—to his songs. He also supported aspiring young musicians in his ensembles, giving them improvisational solos to showcase their skills.

28

A) NO CHANGE
B) Chicago to join
C) Chicago; joining
D) Chicago; to join

29

At this point, the writer wants to indicate a specific effect that Armstrong's experience in New York had on his work. Which choice does this most effectively?

A) NO CHANGE
B) —many of whom became legendary artists in their own right.
C) —and so his performances became more theatrical and comedic.
D) —and later would recall this period as one of the most influential in his career.

30

Which choice most effectively sets up the information that follows?

A) NO CHANGE
B) was his own artistic director
C) had a new shot at success
D) could find new musical mentors

2   **2**

Louis Armstrong, or "Satchmo" **31** as millions called him, did more for jazz music **32** than any musician has ever done. Near the end of his career, he recorded the now-iconic "What a Wonderful World," a fitting final tribute **33** for his musical legacy.

31

A) NO CHANGE
B) that he was called by millions
C) which was what millions called him
D) being what millions called him

32

A) NO CHANGE
B) than any musician
C) than what any other musician
D) than any other musician

33

A) NO CHANGE
B) about
C) to
D) of

CONTINUE

2   **2**

Questions 34–44 are based on the following passage.

Certainty and Economic Growth

In modern political science, two competing theories about economic development have emerged. The first theory **34** <u>contends</u> that broad cultural **35** <u>factors: such</u> as social values and gender traditions, determine a nation's path to economic development. The second contends that governmental institutions play the primary role in driving this development. Scholars who subscribe to this latter theory are called "institutionalists."

Institutionalists define institutions as social constructions that regulate social activities, particularly those pertaining to exchanges of goods and services. **36** <u>The "rules of the game" are established by these institutions</u> for a society's economic activities.

Institutionalists believe that an economy grows **37** <u>on decreasing uncertainty</u>. If two parties are not secure in the belief that a mutual transaction will turn out as they believe it should, **38** <u>they are unlikely to make that transaction in the first place</u>. Therefore, in order to maximize economic growth, institutions must reduce the inherent uncertainty that curtails transactions.

34

A) NO CHANGE
B) believes
C) sustains
D) endorses

35

A) NO CHANGE
B) factors—such
C) factors, such
D) factors; such

36

A) NO CHANGE
B) These institutions will establish the "rules of the game"
C) These institutions establish the "rules of the game"
D) The "rules of the game" would be established by these institutions

37

A) NO CHANGE
B) as uncertainty decreases
C) when decreasing of uncertainty occurs
D) when they decrease uncertainty

38

Which choice provides information that best supports the main claim of the paragraph?

A) NO CHANGE
B) they may try to renegotiate the terms of their agreement.
C) they may seek professional advice on the matter.
D) it is probably because they did not do sufficient research.

CONTINUE ▶

2   **2**

One important way that a country can minimize uncertainty, according to institutionalists, is by [39] obtaining laws that ensure robust private property rights. [40] With institutionalizing such rights and establishing punishments for violating them, a nation enables individuals and companies to have confidence that their rights will be maintained as they participate in investments, purchases, and other kinds of exchanges.

[1] Consider two countries. [2] In the first, laws guarantee the terms of economic transactions, such as the purchase of a house. [3] In this country, a purchaser will have confidence putting down money for the house and securing a mortgage with a bank, because the future is relatively clear. [4] Even though the purchaser understands that such transactions bear inherent risks, he or she can nevertheless plan in relative security. [41]

In the second country, private property rights are [42] unconvincing, so a potential purchaser cannot be sure that a seller will be held accountable for possible cheating. Additionally, without structured and regulated institutions like banks [43] to boot, a purchaser would likely have to pursue unreliable loans at usurious rates. Furthermore, the lack of stable economic institutions would make runaway inflation more likely, making it much harder for buyer and seller to agree on a price.

39

A) NO CHANGE
B) adopting
C) achieving
D) completing

40

A) NO CHANGE
B) Because of
C) From
D) By

41

The author is adding the following sentence to this paragraph.

> In addition, well-regulated institutions like banks ensure a dependable third party to these transactions.

Where should this sentence be placed?

A) Immediately after sentence 1
B) Immediately after sentence 2
C) Immediately after sentence 3
D) Immediately after sentence 4

42

A) NO CHANGE
B) tenuous
C) exhausted
D) timid

43

A) NO CHANGE
B) in addition
C) on top of that
D) DELETE the underlined portion

CONTINUE ▶

2   2

Uncertainty hinders economic activity and thereby impedes growth. Without the stability, enforcement, and predictability that [44] is afforded by a reliable system of institutions, a nation cannot prosper.

[44]

A) NO CHANGE
B) are afforded by
C) affords
D) afford

STOP

If you finish before time is called, you may check your work on this section only. Do not turn to any other section of the test.

3 | | **3**

Math Test—No Calculator

25 MINUTES, 20 QUESTIONS

Turn to Section 3 of your answer sheet to answer the questions in this section.

DIRECTIONS

For questions 1–15, solve each problem, choose the best answer from the choices provided, and fill in the corresponding circle on your answer sheet. **For questions 16–20**, solve the problem and enter your answer in the grid on the answer sheet. Please refer to the directions before question 16 on how to enter your answers in the grid. You may use any available space in your test booklet for scratch work.

NOTES

1. The use of a calculator **is not permitted**.

2. All variables and expressions used represent real numbers unless otherwise indicated.

3. Figures provided in this test are drawn to scale unless otherwise indicated.

4. All figures lie in a plane unless otherwise indicated.

5. Unless otherwise indicated, the domain of a given function f is the set of all real numbers x for which $f(x)$ is a real number.

REFERENCE

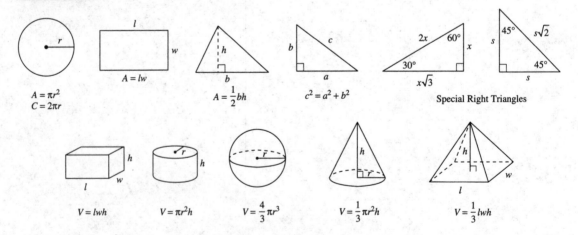

The number of degrees of arc in a circle is 360.
The number of radians of arc in a circle is 2π.
The sum of the measures in degrees of the angles of a triangle is 180.

CONTINUE ▶

3 **3**

1

If $\frac{3}{4}a + \frac{2}{3}b = 7$, what is the value of $9a + 8b$?

A) 64

B) 72

C) 84

D) 96

2

Raj can exchange 15 Euros for 11 British Pounds. At this exchange rate, approximately how many British Pounds should he receive in exchange for 100 Euros?

A) 21

B) 73

C) 137

D) 340

3

If $ax + b = x$, where $a > 1$ and $b > 1$, which choice expresses the value of x in terms of a and b?

A) $\frac{1-a}{b}$

B) $\frac{a-1}{b}$

C) $\frac{b}{a-1}$

D) $\frac{b}{1-a}$

4

Jeff received a gift card worth $50 and plans to use it to download music and movies. Each song download costs $1.25 and each movie costs $3. If Jeff downloads 4 songs and 1 movie each month, which of the following indicates the number of dollars, d, left on Jeff's gift card after m months?

A) $d = 53 - 5m$

B) $d = 50 - 2m$

C) $d = 50 - 8m$

D) $d = 45 - 3m$

5

$$2x + y = 3x + 4$$
$$x + 5y = 2$$

Based on the system of equations above, what is the value of $x + y$?

A) −3

B) −2

C) −1

D) 1

6

$$4(2x + 3)^2 + 2x$$

Which of the following is equivalent to the expression above?

A) $4x^2 + 14x + 9$

B) $8x^2 + 12x + 9$

C) $16x^2 + 48x + 36$

D) $16x^2 + 50x + 36$

7

$$y = ax^3 + 2x^2 + 5x + d$$

The graph of the function above in the xy-plane has an x-intercept at $x = 3$ and a y-intercept at $y = 2$. What is the value of a?

A) $-\frac{35}{27}$

B) $-\frac{31}{27}$

C) $\frac{31}{27}$

D) $\frac{35}{27}$

CONTINUE

3   **3**

8

$$\frac{1}{6}+\frac{1}{x}=\frac{1}{4}$$

Mrs. Perry can paint a fence in 6 hours, but if her son Jason helps her, they can finish it in 4 hours. If the equation above models this situation, what does the term $\frac{1}{x}$ represent?

A) The number of hours it takes Mrs. Perry and Jason to paint the fence working together

B) The number of hours it would take Jason to paint the fence alone

C) The part of the job Jason completes in one hour

D) The part of the job Mrs. Perry completes in one hour

9

Luis budgeted no more than $500 to purchase a suit and shirts for his new job. He found the suit for $264 and shirts for $24 each. Which of the following could be used to find the number of shirts, x, Luis could purchase while staying within his budget?

A) $500 \le 264 - 24x$

B) $500 \ge 264x + 24$

C) $500 \ge 264 + 24x$

D) $500 \le 264x - 24$

10

$$f(x) = ax^2 + b$$

In the function above, a and b are constants, $f(0) = 2$, and $f(1) = 5$. What is the value of $f(-3)$?

A) -43

B) -25

C) 29

D) 47

11

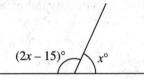

In the figure above, what is the measure of the larger angle?

A) $65°$

B) $80°$

C) $115°$

D) $125°$

12

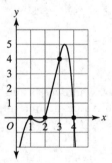

The function $y = g(x)$ is graphed in the xy-plane above. Which of the following equations could describe $g(x)$?

A) $g(x)=(x+1)(x+2)(x-4)^2$

B) $g(x)=-(x-1)^2(x-2)(x-4)$

C) $g(x)=(x-1)^2(x-2)(x-4)$

D) $g(x)=-(x+1)^2(x+2)(x+4)$

---

3   **3**

13

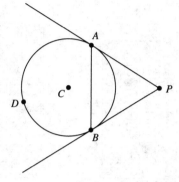

In the figure above, two tangent segments, AP and BP, are drawn to the circle with center C, and the measure of arc ADB is 240°. Which of the following must be true?

A) $\triangle ABP$ is a right triangle

B) $AB > AP$

C) $\triangle ABP$ is an equilateral triangle

D) $BP < AP$

14

$$y = 3x - 4$$
$$2x + y = 1$$

When graphed in the xy-plane, the lines described by the equations above each include a diameter of a circle. If the circle includes the point $(-2, -5)$, which of the following is the equation of the circle?

A) $(3x-4)^2 + \left(\dfrac{1}{2} - \dfrac{1}{2}y\right)^2 = 29$

B) $(x+2)^2 + (y+5)^2 = 29$

C) $(x-1)^2 + (y+1)^2 = 29$

D) $(x-1)^2 + (y+1)^2 = 25$

15

$$\frac{3-2i}{4+5i}$$

Which of the following expressions is equivalent to the expression above? $(i = \sqrt{-1})$

A) $-\dfrac{2}{9} - \dfrac{23}{9}i$

B) $\dfrac{2}{41} - \dfrac{23}{41}i$

C) $\dfrac{22}{41} + \dfrac{7}{9}i$

D) $\dfrac{22}{41} - \dfrac{23}{9}i$

CONTINUE ➡

3   3

DIRECTIONS

For questions 16–20, solve the problem and enter your answer in the grid, as described below, on the answer sheet.

1. Although not required, it is suggested that you write your answer in the boxes at the top of the columns to help you fill in the circles accurately. You will receive credit only if the circles are filled in correctly.

2. Mark no more than one circle in any column.

3. No question has a negative answer.

4. Some problems may have more than one correct answer. In such cases, grid only one answer.

5. **Mixed numbers** such as $3\frac{1}{2}$ must be gridded as 3.5 or $\frac{7}{2}$.

   (If $3\frac{1}{2}$ is entered into the grid as [3 | 1 | / | 2], it will be interpreted as $\frac{31}{2}$, not $3\frac{1}{2}$.)

6. **Decimal answers**: If you obtain a decimal answer with more digits than the grid can accommodate, it may be either rounded or truncated, but it must fill the entire grid.

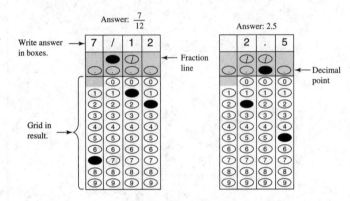

Answer: $\frac{7}{12}$

Answer: 2.5

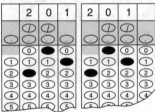

Answer: 201
Either position is correct.

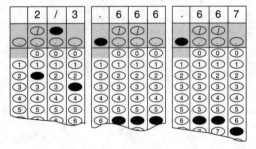

Acceptable ways to grid $\frac{2}{3}$ are:

3   3

16

A bag of apples and oranges contains twice as many apples as oranges. If there are 15 total pieces of fruit in the bag, how many apples are in the bag?

17

A shade of green paint called *Groovy Green* is made by combining yellow paint and blue paint so that the ratio, by volume, of yellow to blue paint is 12 to 5. How many <u>tablespoons</u> of blue paint are needed to make 34 cups of Groovy Green? (1 cup = 16 tablespoons)

18

Points A, B, and C do not lie on the same line. If the distance from A to B is 4 units, and the distance from B to C is 5 units, then what is the largest possible integer distance between points A and C?

19

Pei-Sze has an average score of 89 on the six tests she has taken in her Physics class. She has two more tests left to take, and wants to raise her average to at least 90. If all tests are weighted equally, what is the minimum possible average score Pei-Sze must get on the two remaining tests to raise her average for the eight tests to at least 90?

20

If $x = 2\sqrt{3}$ and $5x = \sqrt{3y}$, what is the value of y?

STOP

**If you finish before time is called, you may check your work on this section only.
Do not turn to any other section of the test.**

Math Test—Calculator

55 MINUTES, 38 QUESTIONS

Turn to Section 4 of your answer sheet to answer the questions in this section.

DIRECTIONS

For questions 1–30, solve each problem, choose the best answer from the choices provided, and fill in the corresponding circle on your answer sheet. **For questions 31–38**, solve the problem and enter your answer in the grid on the answer sheet. Please refer to the directions before question 31 on how to enter your answers in the grid. You may use any available space in your test booklet for scratch work.

NOTES

1. The use of a calculator **is permitted**.

2. All variables and expressions used represent real numbers unless otherwise indicated.

3. Figures provided in this test are drawn to scale unless otherwise indicated.

4. All figures lie in a plane unless otherwise indicated.

5. Unless otherwise indicated, the domain of a given function f is the set of all real numbers for which $f(x)$ is a real number.

REFERENCE

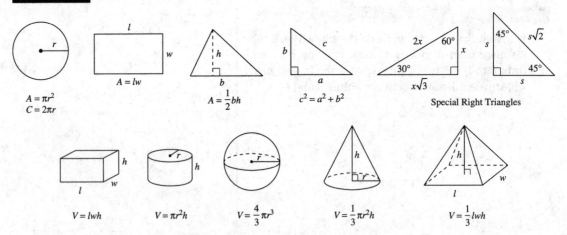

$A = \pi r^2$
$C = 2\pi r$

$A = lw$

$A = \frac{1}{2}bh$

$c^2 = a^2 + b^2$

Special Right Triangles

$V = lwh$

$V = \pi r^2 h$

$V = \frac{4}{3}\pi r^3$

$V = \frac{1}{3}\pi r^2 h$

$V = \frac{1}{3}lwh$

The number of degrees of arc in a circle is 360.
The number of radians of arc in a circle is 2π.
The sum of the measures in degrees of the angles of a triangle is 180.

CONTINUE ▶

4 **4**

1

When Shondra makes an online purchase, a 15% discount is applied to the retail price and then a 6.25% tax is added to this discounted price. Which of the following represents the amount Shondra pays, in dollars, for an item with a retail price of x dollars?

A) $x - 0.15 + 0.0625x$

B) $1.0625x - 0.15x$

C) $1.0625(0.85x)$

D) $x - 0.15(1.0625x)$

2

In Connecticut, the highest recorded temperature over the past 100 years was 109°F in 1995 and the lowest recorded temperature was −37°F in 1943. How many degrees higher than the lowest recorded temperature was the highest recorded temperature?

A) 72°F

B) 95°F

C) 124°F

D) 146°F

3

At Petro's Restaurant, the owner will sometimes push smaller tables together to form one long rectangular table. If she pushes two tables together, she can seat 10 people. If she pushes three tables together, she can seat 14. Which equation best describes the relationship between the number of people, P, who can be seated at t tables that have been pushed together?

A) $P = 4t + 2$

B) $P = 5t$

C) $P = t + 4$

D) $P = 4t - 1$

4

Mark took a test with two kinds of questions: some worth 5 points and some worth 8 points. He answered a total of 14 questions correctly and earned a total of 94 points. How many 5-point questions did Mark answer correctly?

A) 9

B) 8

C) 7

D) 6

5

A pool in the shape of a right rectangular prism holds 450 cubic feet of water. If the length and width of the pool are 10 feet and 15 feet, respectively, what is the depth of the water in the pool?

A) 3

B) 6

C) 7

D) 10

CONTINUE ➡

4   **4**

6

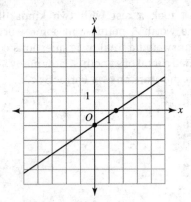

Which of the following equations best describes the graph above?

A) $y = \frac{2}{3}x + \frac{3}{2}$

B) $y = 2x - 1$

C) $2x - 3y = 0$

D) $2x - 3y = 3$

7

$$f(x) = 4x^2 - 7x + 3$$
$$g(x) = 2x^2 - 5x - 4$$

If $h(x) = f(x) - g(x)$, which of the following is equivalent to $2h(x)$?

A) $4x^2 - 4x + 14$

B) $4x^2 - 4x - 2$

C) $12x^2 - 24x - 2$

D) $4x^2 - 4x - 14$

8

$$y + 2 = x^2 - k$$

In the equation above, k is a constant less than zero. Which of the following graphs in the xy-plane could represent the solutions to this equation?

A)

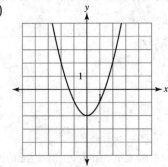

B)

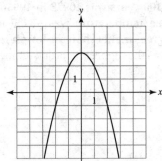

C)

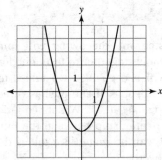

D)

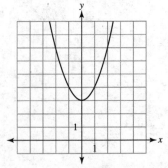

CONTINUE ➡

4   **4**

Questions 9 and 10 refer to the following information.

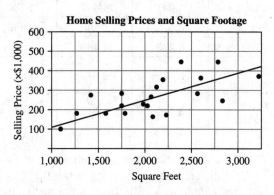

The scatterplot above shows the selling price and area, in square feet, for 20 homes in a suburban area, as well as the line of best fit for the data.

9

The Lees have budgeted between $200,000 and $300,000 for their new home. Approximately what percentage of the houses shown in the graph are priced within the range of this budget?

A) 35%

B) 40%

C) 45%

D) 55%

10

The line of best fit for these data has the equation $y = 0.12x + 3.37$, where x represents the total square footage of the house, and y represents the selling price, in thousands of dollars, for the house. Which choice best describes the meaning of the number 0.12 in this equation?

A) The selling price of the smallest house in the area is about $1,200.

B) The average selling price of a house, in thousands of dollars, is about 12% of the size of the house in square feet.

C) For every increase of 1 square foot in the size of the house, the average selling price increases by about $120.

D) For every increase of 1 square foot in the size of the house, its average selling price increases by about $0.12.

11

Approximately 3 million U.S. students graduated from high school in 2014, and of those, 70% of the women and 65% of the men enrolled in college. The U.S. school population is approximately 49% male and 51% female. Which of the following is the best estimate of the number of 2014 female high school graduates who did <u>not</u> enroll in college?

A) 459,000

B) 509,000

C) 907,000

D) 1,080,000

CONTINUE

4 **4**

12

$$x^{-2}\left(\frac{x+x+x}{x+x}\right)$$

Which of the following is equivalent to the expression above for all positive values of x?

A) $\dfrac{1}{x}$

B) $\dfrac{3x^3}{2}$

C) $\dfrac{3}{2x}$

D) $\dfrac{3}{2x^2}$

13

$$h(x, y) = \frac{Kx^2}{y}$$

If K is a constant in the definition of the function h above, and $h(m, n) = 2$, what is the value of $h(3m, 2n)$?

A) 4.5

B) 6

C) 9

D) 18

14

STATE	1990 Population	2000 Population	2010 Population
Alabama	4.041	4.447	4.780
Georgia	6.478	8.186	9.688
Louisiana	4.220	4.469	4.533
North Carolina	6.629	8.049	9.535
South Carolina	3.487	4.012	4.625

The table above shows the populations, in millions, of 5 Southern states, according to the U.S. Census for 1990, 2000, and 2010. How many of the states shown saw a population increase of 10% or more from 2000 to 2010?

A) One

B) Two

C) Three

D) Four

15

The legs of a right triangle have measures 15 and 36. What is the sine of the smallest angle in this triangle?

A) $\dfrac{15}{36}$

B) $\dfrac{15}{39}$

C) $\dfrac{36}{15}$

D) $\dfrac{36}{39}$

CONTINUE ▶

4   4

16

$$-\frac{2}{x} < -\frac{1}{3}$$

Which of the following describes all solutions of the inequality above?

A) $x > -6$

B) $x < -6$

C) $x > 6$ or $x < -6$

D) $0 < x < 6$

17

The current price of a share of stock A is one-fifth the price of a share of stock B. If the price of stock A were to increase at a constant rate of $5 per month and the price of stock B were to decrease at a constant rate of $3 per month, then in 6 months the two stock prices would be equal. What is the current price of a share of stock A?

A) $12

B) $18

C) $42

D) $60

18

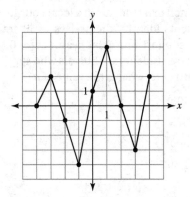

The function $y = f(x)$ is graphed on the xy-plane above. On the interval $-4 \le x \le 4$, for how many distinct values of x does $f(x) = \frac{1}{2}$?

A) Zero

B) Three

C) Four

D) Five

19

Mr. Johnson collected data on salaries of 20 randomly selected employees in his company. He found that their median salary was $37,500, but their average salary was $49,500. Which of the following would best explain the discrepancy between the median and the average values?

A) More than 20 employees were included when calculating the median.

B) One or more very high salaries pulled the average up.

C) One or more very low salaries pulled the median down.

D) Fewer salaries were included in calculating the median than the average.

CONTINUE

4 **4**

20

In a poll of n students at a local college, 45% of these students identify themselves as liberals. Of these, 60% support universal health care. If 405 students of these students are liberals who support universal health care, what is the value of n?

A) 109

B) 675

C) 900

D) 1,500

21

Light travels through a vacuum at a speed of approximately 186,000 miles per second. Approximately how many miles will a ray of light travel through a vacuum in one day?

A) 6.7×10^8 miles

B) 1.6×10^{10} miles

C) 3.2×10^{10} miles

D) 4.6×10^{13} miles

22

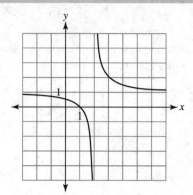

$$f(x) = \frac{x-1}{x-2}$$

The function $y = f(x)$ is graphed on the xy-plane above. If the equation $y = x - 1$ is drawn on the same set of axes, which of the following is a point of intersection of the two graphs?

A) (0, 1)

B) (0, 0.5)

C) (1.5, −1)

D) (3, 2)

23

$$f(x) = x^2 - 6x - 475$$
$$g(x) = 3 - 4x$$

Given the definitions of the functions above, if $f(2a) = 3g(a)$, which of the following could be the value of a?

A) −9

B) 11

C) 12

D) 121

CONTINUE ▶

4 **4**

24

$$y = x^2 + k$$
$$2x + y = 5$$

When the equations above are graphed in the *xy*-plane, they intersect in exactly one point. What is the value of k?

A) 6

B) 5

C) 1

D) 2.5

25

Every box of Weitz water crackers has a label that indicates it contains 6.5 ounces of crackers. However, industry standards allow these boxes to contain anywhere between 6.45 and 6.75 ounces of crackers. If x represents the number of ounces of crackers inside a box of Weitz water crackers that meets industry standards, which of the following expresses all possible values of x?

A) $|x - 6.60| \le 0.10$

B) $|x - 6.60| \le 0.15$

C) $|x - 6.50| \le 0.05$

D) $|x - 6.50| \le 0.25$

26

$$a + b < b < a - b$$

Let a and b be numbers that satisfy the inequality above. Which of the following must be true?

   I. $a < 0$

   II. $b < a$

   III. $b < 0$

A) I only

B) I and III only

C) II and III only

D) I, II, and III

27

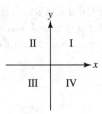

If the system of inequalities $y \le 2x + 3$ and $y > x - 4$ are graphed in the *xy*-plane above, which quadrant contains <u>no</u> solutions to the system?

A) Quadrant II

B) Quadrant III

C) Quadrant IV

D) There are solutions in all four quadrants.

28

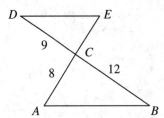

In the figure above, segment *AB* is parallel to segment *DE*, and segment *AE* is perpendicular to segment *DB*. What is the area of triangle *DCE*?

A) 27

B) 28

C) 32

D) 36

CONTINUE

4 **4**

29

If the average of a and b is x, the average of b and c is $2x$, and the average of a and c is $3x$, what is the average of a, b, and c, in terms of x?

A) $\dfrac{2x}{3}$

B) $\dfrac{5x}{3}$

C) $2x$

D) $6x$

30

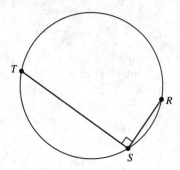

In the figure above, $SR = 10$ and $TS = 24$. If the area of the circle is $k\pi$, what is the value of k?

A) 13

B) 26

C) 169

D) 531

CONTINUE

DIRECTIONS

For questions 31–38, solve the problem and enter your answer in the grid, as described below, on the answer sheet.

1. Although not required, it is suggested that you write your answer in the boxes at the top of the columns to help you fill in the circles accurately. You will receive credit only if the circles are filled in correctly.

2. Mark no more than one circle in any column.

3. No question has a negative answer.

4. Some problems may have more than one correct answer. In such cases, grid only one answer.

5. **Mixed numbers** such as $3\frac{1}{2}$ must be gridded as 3.5 or $\frac{7}{2}$.

   (If $3\frac{1}{2}$ is entered into the grid as [3 1 / 2], it will be interpreted as $\frac{31}{2}$, not $3\frac{1}{2}$.)

6. **Decimal answers**: If you obtain a decimal answer with more digits than the grid can accommodate, it may be either rounded or truncated, but it must fill the entire grid.

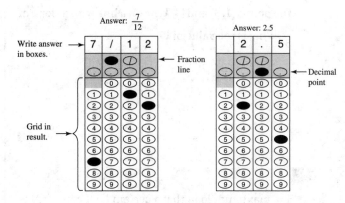

Answer: $\frac{7}{12}$ — Write answer in boxes. ← Fraction line — Grid in result.

Answer: 2.5 ← Decimal point

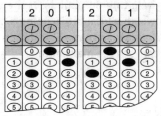

Answer: 201
Either position is correct.

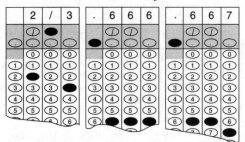

Acceptable ways to grid $\frac{2}{3}$ are:

CONTINUE →

31

The points $(1, 3)$ and $(4, k)$ lie on a line with a slope of $\frac{2}{3}$. What is the value of k?

32

The maximum load that a certain boat can carry is 4,000 pounds. The boat is to carry n identical crates, each weighing 60 pounds. If the crew and equipment weigh a total of 950 pounds, what is the maximum value for n that will still keep the weight of the load beneath the maximum?

Questions 33 and 34 refer to the following information.

Opinions on Immigration Reform				
Age Group	Support	Oppose	No Opinion	Total
21–40	68	22	10	100
41–60	55	39	6	100
61+	30	45	25	100
Total	153	106	41	300

A questionnaire about immigration reform was given to 300 people whose opinions were tabulated in the table above.

33

If one of the supporters of immigration reform is chosen at random from the table above, what is the probability that he or she is in the 21–40 age group?

34

The "indifference factor" for a group of people is defined as the number of people in the group who indicate no opinion on an issue divided by the number of people in the group who do indicate an opinion on the issue. According to the table, how much greater is the "indifference factor" on the issue of immigration reform for the 61+ age group than for the 21–40 age group?

4 **4**

35

If $(x - a)(x - b) = x^2 - 9x + 7$ for all values of x, what is the value of $a + b$?

36

Degrees Awarded by Hawthorne University in 2015			
	Bachelors	Masters	Doctorate	Total
Male	45	48	27	120
Female	55	52	23	130
Total	100	100	50	250

The table above shows the numbers of bachelor's, master's, and doctoral degrees awarded by Hawthorne University in 2015, broken down by gender. What fraction of the males who earned a degree from Hawthorne University in 2015 earned doctorates?

Questions 37 and 38 refer to the following information.

Ms. Hamid has established a trust fund for her daughter, Aisha. Aisha will be allowed to withdraw 4% annually from this fund once she reaches 21 years of age. Ms. Hamid uses the formula

$$A = 5,000r^n$$

to approximate the amount of money, in dollars, remaining in the trust fund n years after Aisha turns 21.

37

What should Ms. Hamid use for the value of r?

38

To the nearest cent, how much more money, in dollars, can Aisha withdraw from the trust fund in the second year after she turns 21 than she can in the third year? (Note: Disregard the $ sign when gridding your answer.)

STOP

If you finish before time is called, you may check your work on this section only.
Do not turn to any other section of the test.

5   5

Essay
50 MINUTES, 1 QUESTION

DIRECTIONS

The essay gives you the opportunity to show how effectively you can read and comprehend a passage and write an essay analyzing the passage. In your essay, you should demonstrate that you have read the passage carefully, present a clear and logical analysis, and use language precisely.

Your essay must be written on the lines provided in your answer booklet; except for the Planning Page of the answer booklet, you will receive no other paper on which to write. You will have enough space if you write on every line, avoid wide margins, and keep your handwriting to a reasonable size. Remember that people who are not familiar with your handwriting will read what you write. Try to write or print so that what you are writing is legible to those readers.

You have 50 minutes to read the passage and write an essay in response to the prompt provided inside this booklet.

As you read the passage below, consider how Zeba Khan uses

- evidence, such as facts or examples, to support claims
- reasoning to develop ideas and connect claims and evidence
- stylistic or persuasive elements, such as word choice or appeals to emotion, to add power to the ideas expressed

---

Adapted from Zeba Khan, "Muslim Americans Missing from the Political Fray." ©2009 by Zeba Khan. Originally published November 21, 2009, in the _Huffington Post_. Reprinted by permission of Zeba Khan.

1   I remember the day my Indian Muslim family became Latino. It was 2006 and Ted Strickland was running as the Democratic nominee for governor of Ohio. My father declared our new identity with a "Latinos Unidos por Strickland" bumper sticker on the back of our minivan. "We want him to win, right?" he reasoned.

2   My father's attempt to change our family's ethnic and religious identities into something he believed would be more acceptable to our neighbors reflects the sad reality of the role of Muslims in public life in the United States.

3   It is no secret that many Americans are wary of Muslims. A 2007 report published by the Pew Forum indicated that just 43 percent of Americans held a favorable view of Muslims. This fact was not lost on the Republicans who launched a whisper campaign the following year to frame Obama as the Muslim Manchurian Candidate.

CONTINUE

5   **5**

4   The "Tea Party" demonstration in Washington, D.C., on September 12, 2009, illustrated that using the term "Muslim" as a slur is still acceptable in many parts of the country as protesters exclaimed they were afraid "Muslims are moving in and taking over"—an echo of their leader Mark Williams' comments about candidate Obama being an "Indonesian Muslim" during the presidential campaign.

5   That Muslims aren't well liked hasn't been lost on Muslim Americans themselves. But rather than confront the stereotypes and misunderstandings that led to the negative views, most Muslim Americans seem to have gone into hiding and decided not to participate in American political life.

6   During the 2008 presidential campaign, for example, Muslim American leaders debated for months whether or not to publicly support Barack Obama's candidacy. Although Muslim Americans lean overwhelmingly towards the Democratic Party, many community leaders feared that their public support of then-candidate Obama would ultimately hurt his campaign. So, instead of mobilizing the community, many determined they could best help Obama by sitting quiet. One such leader, who ran MuslimsforKerry.com in 2004, went so far as to register a website for Muslim supporters of Obama but then ultimately decided not to develop the site, concerned that public support from Muslims would hurt the candidate.

7   If we think we're that toxic, how do we expect anyone else to think differently?

8   Muslim Americans certainly have a legitimate reason to complain about the discrimination and stereotyping we face in America, but if we want to actually do something about it, we need to reach the hearts and minds of our fellow Americans. A poll conducted by the Pew Forum last week suggests that higher levels of familiarity with Islam, and especially knowing someone who is Muslim, are associated with more positive views of the religion. In our case, familiarity breeds regard and respect.

9   Muslims also need to be politically invested in the country. A recent Gallup report showed that Muslims vote in far lesser numbers than other religious groups. This trend is particularly acute with young Muslims. Some 78 percent of Protestants under 30 are registered to vote, while only 51 percent of young Muslims are registered.

10 Finally, Muslim Americans need to field some candidates for political office, where we are painfully absent. Like the Muslim American community, both the Jewish and the Mormon American communities each comprise approximately two percent of the U.S. population. But unlike these two groups, Muslim Americans have virtually no representation in our federal legislative body. Currently in the Senate, there are 15 Jewish senators, five Mormon senators, but no Muslim senators. In the House of Representatives, Keith Ellison, the first Muslim congressman in history, was elected in 2006 and was joined by the second, Andre Carsen, in 2008. By comparison, there are currently 33 Jewish and 14 Mormon Representatives.

11 Until Muslim Americans claim their seat at the political table, we will continue to be vulnerable to slurs and misperceptions, and our many contributions and service to this country we love will go unnoticed. We will continue to be defined by extremists abroad and political fearmongerers at home because we have not fully stepped into our American identity.

CONTINUE →

12 Our lack of political involvement at the local, state, and federal levels not only hurts the community but hurts the political health of the entire country. This democracy cannot work without its citizens participating and we all suffer when one group is silent.

13 Our presence in our country's political life is the most powerful testament to the Muslim World that the United States truly is a nation founded on the idea that all are created equal. It is time to peel away any false bumper sticker identities and educate our fellow Americans on who Muslims really are while demonstrating to the Muslim World the ideals of this great country.

Write an essay in which you explain how Zeba Khan builds an argument to persuade her audience that Muslim Americans should be more politically active. In your essay, analyze how she uses one or more of the features listed in the box above (or features of your own choice) to strengthen the logic and persuasiveness of her argument. Be sure that your analysis focuses on the most relevant features of the passage.

Your essay should NOT explain whether you agree with Khan's claims, but rather explain how she builds an argument to persuade her audience.

SAT PRACTICE TEST 1 ANSWER KEY

Section 1: Reading	Section 2: Writing and Language	Section 3: Math (No Calculator)	Section 4: Math (Calculator)
1. C	1. C	1. C	1. C
2. C	2. C	2. B	2. D
3. B	3. B	3. D	3. A
4. D	4. C	4. C	4. D
5. B	5. A	5. B	5. A
6. A	6. D	6. D	6. D
7. C	7. B	7. A	7. A
8. B	8. A	8. C	8. D
9. C	9. C	9. C	9. B
10. D	10. D	10. C	10. C
11. D	11. A	11. C	11. A
12. A	12. A	12. B	12. D
13. C	13. C	13. C	13. C
14. C	14. D	14. D	14. C
15. A	15. B	15. B	15. B
16. D	16. D	16. 10	16. D
17. A	17. A	17. 160	17. A
18. D	18. C	18. 8	18. D
19. C	19. B	19. 93	19. B
20. A	20. C	20. 100	20. D
21. B	21. D		21. B
22. C	22. C		22. D
23. A	23. D		23. B
24. D	24. C		24. A
25. B	25. A		25. B
26. D	26. D		26. B
27. A	27. C		27. D
28. D	28. B		28. A
29. D	29. C		29. C
30. C	30. B		30. C
31. B	31. A		31. 5
32. A	32. D		32. 50
33. C	33. C		33. 4/9 or .444
34. C	34. A		34. 2/9 or .222
35. A	35. C		35. 9
36. A	36. C		36. 9/40 or .225
37. A	37. B		37. .96
38. B	38. A		38. 7.68
39. D	39. B		
40. D	40. D		
41. B	41. B		
42. C	42. B		
43. B	43. D		
44. C	44. B		
45. A			
46. D			
47. B			
48. D			
49. B			
50. C			
51. D			
52. A			

Total Reading Points (Section 1)

Total Writing and Language Points (Section 2)

Total Math Points (Section 3 + Section 4)

Scoring Your Test

1. Use the answer key to mark your responses on each section.

2. Total the number of correct responses for each section:

    1. Reading Test   Number correct: _____ **(Reading Raw Score)**

    2. Writing and Language Test   Number correct: _____ **(Writing and Language Raw Score)**

    3. Mathematics Test—No Calculator   Number correct: _____

    4. Mathematics Test—Calculator   Number correct: _____

3. Add the raw scores for sections 3 and 4. This is your **Math Raw Score:** _____

4. Use the table on page 73 to calculate your **Scaled Test and Section Scores (10–40).**

    Math Section Scaled Score (200–800):   _____

    Reading Test Scaled Score (10–40):   _____

    Writing and Language Test Scaled Score (10–40):   _____

5. Add the **Reading Test Scaled Score** and the **Writing and Language Test Scaled Score (sum will be 20–80)**, and multiply this sum by 10 to get your **Reading and Writing Test Section Score (200–800).**

    Sum of Reading + Writing and Language Scores: _____ × 10 =

    Reading and Writing Section Score: _____

Scaled Section and Test Scores

Raw Score	Math Section Score	Reading Test Score	Writing/ Language Test Score	Raw Score	Math Section Score	Reading Test Score	Writing/ Language Test Score
58	800			29	540	27	29
57	790			28	530	26	29
56	780			27	520	26	28
55	760			26	510	25	27
54	750			25	510	25	27
53	740			24	500	24	26
52	730	40		23	490	24	26
51	730	39		22	480	23	25
50	720	39		21	470	23	24
49	710	38		20	460	23	24
48	700	37		19	460	22	23
47	690	36		18	450	22	23
46	680	35		17	440	21	22
45	670	35		16	430	21	21
44	660	34	40	15	420	20	20
43	660	33	39	14	410	20	20
42	650	33	38	13	390	19	19
41	650	32	37	12	370	18	18
40	640	32	37	11	360	18	17
39	630	31	36	10	350	17	16
38	620	31	35	9	340	16	16
37	610	30	34	8	320	16	15
36	600	30	33	7	300	15	14
35	590	29	33	6	280	14	13
34	580	29	32	5	270	13	12
33	570	28	32	4	250	12	11
32	570	28	31	3	230	11	10
31	560	28	31	2	210	10	10
30	550	27	30	1	200	10	10

PRACTICE SAT 1 ANSWER EXPLANATIONS

Section 1: Reading

1. C — **General Meaning**

This passage focuses on the impact humans have had on the climate since the 1950s. Lines 47–52 state, *After that point (1950), the trend in global surface warming cannot be explained without including the contribution of the anthropogenic [human-created] greenhouse gases, that is, those produced via non-natural human activities like burning fossil fuels.*

2. C — **Interpretation**

The fourth paragraph begins by stating: *Granted, natural changes to Earth's climate have also occurred in recent times.* It then goes on to cite two recent volcanic eruptions that occurred in 1982 and 1991.

Immediately after mentioning the two volcanic eruptions, the passage states: ***However**, although volcanoes are active around the world, the amount of carbon dioxide they release is **extremely small** compared to that released by human activities. . . . In other words, human influence on the climate is 100–200 times the effect of all the world's volcanoes.*

<u>General tip:</u> Underline contrast words like *but* and *however* in reading passages, as they often precede crucial author opinions.

All of this information refutes the notion that *non-anthropogenic drivers of climate change overwhelm anthropogenic ones.*

3. B — **Inference**

In lines 62–71, the author classifies volcanoes as a relatively minor contributor to global climate change: *the amount of carbon dioxide they (volcanoes) release is extremely small compared to that released by human activities. On average, volcanoes emit between 130 and 230 million tons of carbon dioxide per year, whereas the burning of fossil fuels releases about 26 billion tons of carbon dioxide every year. In other words, human influence on the climate is 100–200 times the effect of all the world's volcanoes.*

4. D — **Textual Evidence**

As mentioned in the explanation to question 3, lines 62–71 contain the best evidence for the answer.

5. B — **Word in Context**

In saying that *NASA satellites record a **host** of vital signs including . . .* the author indicates that these satellites provide a *wide variety* of information, or a *multitude of vital signs.*

6. A — **Word in Context**

In lines 41–44, the passage states that *Scientists integrate these measurements into **sophisticated** computerized climate models in an attempt to re-create temperatures recorded over the past 150 years.* A computer model that attempts to incorporate vast amounts of information to make difficult predictions must be *highly complex.*

7. C — **Inference from Data**

The data show that changes in solar energy cannot fully account for the recent increase in global surface temperatures. The bottom curve is sinusoidal, that is, oscillating in a fairly steady cycle. However, the top curve (for global surface temperature) shows a steady climb, implying that the solar energy change is not telling the entire story.

8. B — **Inference from Data**

When the running average of global surface temperatures reached a peak in 2004 (top graph), the solar energy was near its long-term average and declining (bottom graph). In 2004, the general trend line on the bottom curve is near the "midline" (the long-term average value) for the curve, and heading downward.

9. C — **Interpretation**

In the final paragraph, the passage states that *those who dismiss environmental scientists as global warming "alarmists"* might argue that *"Earth's climate has always been changing"* and that there is no reason to be so concerned about human impact. However, the passage states that *there is little doubt now that humans have fundamentally changed the equation.* Thus, the author disagrees with the quotation in line 89 and considers it to be an inadequate explanation of the current environmental situation.

10. D — **Interpretation**

The fifth paragraph (lines 72–85) gives the evidence supporting the hypothesis that solar intensity cannot fully explain recent global warming. In particular, lines 83–85, *The data from the last 65 years show the latter effect, not the former,* refers directly to the fact that recent data supports the "greenhouse gas" theory and not the "solar intensity" theory.

11. D — **Cross-Textual Inference**

The first sentence of Passage 1 states, *American continents, by the free and independent condition which they have assumed and maintain, are henceforth **not to be considered as subjects for future colonization by any***

European powers. In other words, Monroe is cautioning European nations against trying to control lands in the American continents (North and South America).

In lines 85–91 of Passage 2, Roosevelt states that *We would interfere with them only in the last resort, and then only if it became evident that their inability or unwillingness to do justice at home and abroad had **violated the rights of the United States** or had invited foreign aggression to the detriment of the entire body of American nations.* In other words, Roosevelt is saying that anyone who violates the rights of the United States or any of the Americas would face consequences.

---

12. A   **Cross-Textual Evidence**

As mentioned in the explanation to question 12, lines 1–5 and lines 85–91 contain the best evidence to answer that question.

---

13. C   **Specific Detail**

In the first paragraph of Passage 1, Monroe cautions the European nations not to attempt to control nations in the Americas. The President of the United States is *declaring an authoritative position*.

---

14. C   **General Purpose**

In lines 12–15, Passage 1 states that the United States is *of necessity more immediately connected [to other countries in the Western hemisphere], and **by causes which must be obvious to all** enlightened and impartial observers.* That is, they are *self-evident*.

---

15. A   **Word in Context**

In saying that *we have enjoyed unexampled felicity*, Monroe is saying that there has never before been an example of this felicity, and therefore it is *without precedent*.

---

16. D   **Word in Context**

The phrase *any **interposition** [by any European power] for the purpose of oppressing [the Governments of the Americas who have declared their independence]*, Monroe is referring to the *intervention* in the affairs of American countries to which he objects.

---

17. A   **Interpretation**

Monroe refers to Spain's war with its former colonies as an example of the United States' policy of neutrality, even in times of war. Thus, the United States is exercising *restraint in a troubling situation*.

---

18. D   **Cross-Textual Inference**

In lines 27–30 of Monroe states that *we should consider any attempt on [the part of European nations] to extend their system to any portion of this hemisphere as dangerous*

to our peace and safety. In lines 85–91, Roosevelt declares that the United States would intervene if a foreign country *had violated the rights of the United States or had invited foreign aggression to the detriment of the entire body of American nations.* Thus, both men indicate that force may be required to *prevent European expansionism on the American continents.*

---

19. C   **Cross-Textual Evidence**

As mentioned in the explanation to question 18, lines 24–30 and lines 85–91 contain the best evidence for the answer.

---

20. A   **Cross-Textual Interpretation**

Roosevelt would agree with Monroe's statement that *It is only when our rights are invaded or seriously menaced that we resent injuries or make preparation for our defense,* but would make a special point that *our rights* include the right to protect against *flagrant cases of . . . wrongdoing or impotence* (lines 82–84) that could prevent neighboring countries from being *stable, orderly, and prosperous* (line 68). In other words, hostilities that destabilize American nations are considered a legitimate threat to the rights of the United States.

---

21. B   **Interpretation**

Lines 76–77 indicate that the "wrongdoing" is the type that *results in a general loosening of the ties of civilized society* among the American nations. The only choice that gives an example of such disruption on the American continents is B.

---

22. C   **General Purpose**

This passage introduces three methodological systems for examining history: the *classic narrative approach* (line 33), the *quantitative-positivistic approach* (lines 47–48), and the *cultural criticism approach* (lines 70–71).

---

23. A   **Interpretation**

The quantitative-positivistic approach uses statistics and information analysis to study historical evidence and evaluate historical theories. Because it uses data rather than opinion, it is a more *objective* approach.

---

24. D   **Specific Meaning**

The passage states that *Even those events that were depicted vividly in primary sources must often be reconsidered as new information is uncovered or old information is reinterpreted* (lines 3–6), then gives the example of Richard III, who *has long been regarded as one of the most vicious and heartless monarchs in history* (lines 7–9), but whose reputation has been *distorted by Shakespeare's famous representation* (lines 11–12). That is, Shakespeare aided in *an act of historical misrepresentation*.

25. B   **Inference**

In lines 92–94, the passage states that *Each of these approaches represents a set of skills for dealing with the fundamental problems of history:* **distortion and deficiency**. In other words, reliable historical analysis is most significantly hindered by *biased and incomplete documentation*.

26. D   **Textual Evidence**

As indicated in the previous explanation, the final paragraph provides the best evidence for the answer.

27. A   **Inference**

In lines 33–34, the passage states that the classic narrative approach *stresses the historian's skills in writing and discernment*. Lines 42–46 point out that *this analysis serves not merely accuracy but narrative cogency. The objective is to construct a story that provides an explanatory framework as well as a compelling tale.* In other words, those who use this approach are concerned with producing persuasive prose.

28. D   **Textual Evidence**

As mentioned in the explanation to question 27, lines 42–46 provide the best evidence for the answer.

29. D   **Specific Purpose**

The opening sentence of the *cultural criticism approach* paragraph (lines 70–74) states that *the cultural criticism approach . . .* **takes a skeptical view** *of hierarchies, hegemonies, and institutions and the way such power structures* **can misrepresent historical accounts**. The documentation referenced in lines 83–89 is notable because it provides insight into an *often unacknowledged aspect of history*, namely Columbus's exploitation of the natives.

30. C   **Specific Meaning**

This sentence is discussing *quantitative methods*, which are the *mathematical calculations* used to analyze data.

31. B   **Interpretation**

The reference to Brazil's economy begins with the phrase *for example*, indicating that it exemplifies the use of the quantitative-positivistic approach to examine *testable hypotheses*. In this case, the example shows that the assumed relationship was *not* causal and was in fact merely a correlation. This refutation demonstrates that some theories are not to be taken for granted.

32. A   **Word in Context**

In saying that *historians can begin to* **assemble** *the lives of the downtrodden*, the author means that historians are trying to *represent* those lives *as a coherent whole*.

33. C   **General Purpose**

In this passage, Mr. Allworthy finds an infant in his room and sends for his servant to help take care of the baby overnight until he can assign a nurse to it in the morning. In lines 38–58 we hear the servant's tirade against the baby and the mother who abandoned it. But the final paragraph (lines 69–76) states *that her scruples gave way to his peremptory commands; and she took the child under her arms, without any apparent disgust.* Despite her disdain for the child, she does what her master tells her to do.

34. C   **Word in Context**

The word *coarse* is being used to describe the texture of the sheets, so *rough* is the best fit.

35. A   **Word in Context**

Nonchalance is the state of being coolly unconcerned and indifferent, which perfectly describes Mrs. Deborah when she receives an urgent call from Mr. Allworthy. She responds without haste or concern, *[spending] many minutes in adjusting her hair at the looking-glass, notwithstanding all the hurry in which she had been summoned by the servant, and though her master, for aught she knew, lay expiring in an apoplexy or some other fit.*

36. A   **Inference**

Mrs. Deborah wants her master to send out a *warrant to take up the hussy its mother.* A warrant is a document issued by a legal or government official authorizing the police or some other body to make an arrest. Mrs. Deborah wants the mother to be arrested or *taken into custody.*

37. A   **Tone/Attitude**

When Mrs. Deborah first walks in the room to see the infant, *she [cannot] refrain from crying out, with great horror of accent,* so she is clearly shocked. She then goes on a tirade about the *hussy mother* (line 40) and the baby that *stinks* (line 46), revealing her indignation. Finally, she becomes resigned, accepting what Mr. Allworthy wants her to do despite her indignation.

38. B   **Inference**

Mrs. Wilkins' vicious verbal attack against the abandoned infant and his mother clearly demonstrate that she feels secure enough in her position to speak openly, or *candidly*, to Mr. Allworthy. On the other hand, she changes her attitude in an instant when she realizes that he does not share her opinions. As the narrator explains, she is a woman of *discernment* who respects Mr. Allworthy's authority and power over her and *the most excellent place* she *enjoyed* in his household, and she does not want to risk his bad opinion.

39. D — **Textual Evidence**

As mentioned in the explanation to question 38, the evidence for this answer can best be found in the last paragraph (lines 69–76). Notice that she leaves the room *without any* **apparent** *disgust* at the baby. Again, the narrator makes her hypocrisy evident to the reader if not to Mr. Allworthy.

40. D — **Interpretation**

Lines 59–64 indicate that Mrs. Deborah's speech *perhaps would have offended Mr. Allworthy, had he strictly attended to it; but he had now got one of his fingers into the infant's hand, which, by its gentle pressure, seeming to implore his assistance, had certainly out-pleaded the eloquence of Mrs. Deborah.* That is, Mr. Allworthy is not paying attention to what Mrs. Deborah is saying because he is distracted by the baby who is grabbing one of his fingers.

41. B — **Interpretation**

The final paragraph indicates that because of the great respect Mrs. Deborah has for her master's authority, and because she has *enjoyed a most excellent place* as his servant, she does what he asks and ignores her own negative feelings. She wants to remain in his good graces.

42. C — **Word in Context**

The sentence *He now gave Mrs. Deborah positive orders...* indicates that Mr. Allworthy gave her *definitive, unambiguous,* or *unequivocal* directions.

43. B — **General Purpose**

The paragraph sets the stage for a discussion about the *sociological phenomenon* that more couples are starting families later in life: *couples are marrying much later than they did in previous generations and are starting families later still.*

44. C — **Inference from Data**

The graph indicates that as women get older, the percent of women who experience impaired fecundity increases for women who have not previously given birth. This supports the statement in lines 12–15 that *The quality of these eggs begins to decline as well when a woman hits her 20s, and after she reaches the age of about 35 her eggs begin to degenerate.*

45. A — **Word in Context**

The statement that aneuploidy *yields embryonic cells that lack the necessary complement of 23 chromosome pairs* indicates that this disorder *generates* genetically malformed cells.

46. D — **Inference**

In lines 32–34, the passage states that *the vast majority of aneuploid embryos are nonviable and* **will not implant** *in the wall of the uterus.*

47. B — **Textual Evidence**

As mentioned in the explanation to question 46, the best evidence for the answer is in lines 32–34.

48. D — **Inference from Data**

Just look at each choice and pick the one with the **lowest** *impaired fecundity* rate:
Choice A: Women ages 30–34 with NO BIRTHS: 17%
Choice B: Women ages 30–34 with 1+ BIRTHS: 11%
Choice C: Women ages 40–44 with NO BIRTHS: 30%
Choice D: Women ages 40–44 with 1+ BIRTHS: 9%
Choice D is the winner!

49. B — **Word in Context**

In line 75, the statement that oocyte cryopreservation *is showing a great deal of* **potential** means that it is showing *promise* of being successful and a real treatment. In line 85, the statement that this process can *give today's older* **potential** *parents a better chance to have a successful pregnancy* means that it gives *prospective* parents more hope.

50. C — **Inference**

In lines 67–73, the passage states that *experimental evidence suggests that previously frozen oocytes . . . do not seem to be as susceptible to degradation and the many associated developmental deficits that could result.* In other words, the promise of oocyte cryopreservation lies in its ability to *arrest the egg's degeneration process.*

51. D — **Textual Evidence**

As mentioned in the explanation to question 50, the best evidence can be found in lines 70–73.

52. A — **Specific Meaning**

The final sentence of the passage states that *prudent family planning* is required to take advantage of oocyte cryopreservation. In other words, a woman must plan ahead carefully and harvest the eggs many years before she intends to use them.

Section 2: Writing and Language

1. C   Standard English Conventions/Parallelism

Words or phrases in a list should have the same grammatical form. This is the *Law of Parallelism.* In this case, all three items are common nouns that represent symptoms.

2. C   Clear Expression of Ideas/Idiom

The original phrasing does not coordinate well with the prepositional phrase that follows. Advises is most often followed by a *that-clause* in which the *subjunctive* form of the verb is used to indicate a suggestion or indirect command.

3. B   Standard English Conventions/Punctuation/ Comma Splices

The original phrasing contains a comma splice. A comma splice variation of a run-on sentence occurs when two independent clauses are connected with only a comma. Many good corrections to this problem are possible. Choice B creates two parallel predicates.

4. C   Clear Expression of Ideas/Redundancy

The original phrasing is redundant: *distinctive* means "set apart."

5. A   Clear Expression of Ideas/Support/Data Analysis

Choice A is the only one that correctly matches conditions with symptoms in accordance with the table.

6. D   Clear Expression of Ideas/Diction

Although all four choices correctly signal a contrast, only *Unlike* offers a logical one. Infection and allergy are not in a contest (*in opposition*), nor are they *contrary* (opposite or contradictory). *Differently from* does not match the structure of the rest of the sentence.

7. B   Clear Expression of Ideas/Diction

Choices A, B, and C all have variations of "taking in" as a meaning, but only *inhales* also logically relates to the upper respiratory effects that follow. Choice D, *impart,* means "bestow or disclose," which is unrelated to the context.

8. A   Punctuation/Coordination

The two sentences are related in that the second provides an explanation for the statement in the first, The colon in choice A provides a logical way of linking the two clauses, since it implies that the second clause explains the first. Choice B misuses the pronoun *where,* choice C incorrectly signals a cause-and-effect relationship rather than an explanatory relationship, and choice D contains a comma splice.

9. C   Clear Expression of Ideas/Development

Paragraph 3 is about allergies and how they differ from infections. The underlined portion of the sentence supports this purpose.

10. D   Clear Expression of Ideas/Diction/Idiom

The point of this paragraph is that medicines should contain only active ingredients that are *suitable to* treating specific symptoms. Though *logical* might not seem totally incorrect, it would be idiomatically incorrect to follow it with the preposition *to.*

11. A   Clear Expression of Ideas/Organization

Paragraph 5, where it is now, aptly concludes the passage with general advice to the reader about treating all sorts of illnesses.

12. A   Coordination/Verb Tense

Choice A may seem awkward but is semantically and grammatically sound. Choices B and C illogically equate the film *To Catch a Thief* with an *idea,* and choice D is missing a required verb.

13. C   Development

Although you might want to know more about the film, the passage is about modern-day cyber thieves, and the sentence disrupts the transition from introduction to thesis.

14. D   Clear Expression of Ideas/Diction

The transition here should signal a cause-and-effect relationship between the thesis and the first body paragraph, which indicates a logical consequence of the situation described in the first paragraph. Choice A indicates a contrast, and choices B and C merely signal sequence.

15. B   Number Agreement/Verb Tense

Notice that the subject of this clause is *demand,* not *services;* therefore, the plural verb *have grown* disagrees in number with the subject. Since the verb indicates a *present consequence* of a situation that extends into the past, the "present perfect" (or "present consequential") form is required, as in choice B. Choice C is incorrect because it indicates the "past perfect." Choice D is the future tense.

16. D   Idiom

The phrase *ways for stopping* is not idiomatic. The infinitive form *to stop* is needed to indicate function or purpose. Choice B is incorrect because the preposition *in* is illogical.

17. A   **Clear Expression of Ideas/Diction**

Choice A is the correct answer because the sentence requires a word that means *summarize* or *express the essential features of succinctly.*

18. C   **Cohesiveness**

Choice C is the only one that does not detract from the main topic of the passage, cybersecurity.

19. B   **Misplaced Modifiers/Verb Tense**

In the original sentence, the participle *accessing* dangles, because its subject is not the subject of the main clause. Choices A and D illogically imply *pieces of jewelry* are accessing networks. Choices B and C both indicate, correctly, that *hackers* are doing the *accessing,* but the verb mood in choice C is incorrect.

20. C   **Idiom**

This sentence uses the idiomatic phrase *so [adjective phrase] that [clause],* which is only completed correctly with choice C.

21. D   **Misplaced Modifiers/Verb Tense**

The original phrasing and the phrasing in choice B are incorrect because they cause the prepositional phrase that starts the sentence to dangle. The subject of the main clause must represent the noun modified by the phrase *without physical doors and locks.* Choices C and D both contain the proper subject, but only choice D correctly indicates the *inability* of armed guards to implement cybersecurity.

22. C   **Idiom/Comparisons**

A sentence must remain grammatically intact even when interrupting modifiers are removed. Notice that choices A and B violate this rule, since the phrase *as clever than* is unidiomatic. Choice D is incorrect, because the comparative idiom *as clever as* is not completed.

23. D   **Parallelism**

Words or phrases in a list should follow the same grammatical form. In this case, choice A and choice C do not do so. While choice B presents a list in parallel structure, it contains an error of redundancy by adding *pioneering.*

24. C   **Logical Comparisons**

The original comparison is illogical: Armstrong's *trumpet playing technique* is compared to *other musicians.* The only choice that indicates a logical comparison is C, which compares Armstrong's *technique* to *that of other musicians.*

25. A   **Clarity of Expression**

The original phrasing is best. Choice B is incorrect because *it's* is the contraction of *it is,* which is illogical. Choice C is awkward, and choice D is in the wrong tense.

26. D   **Cohesiveness/Diction**

The previous sentences states that *performers played for attention and perhaps a bit of coin.* Similarly, Armstrong played his horn to *attract* customers.

27. C   **Cohesiveness/Organization**

The sentence that follows this one mentions musicians that Armstrong idolized; therefore, this sentence should introduce this idea. Choice C is the only one that indicates that Armstrong *came to these establishments . . . to learn* from his idols.

28. B   **Punctuation**

The phrase requires no punctuation.

29. C   **Development**

Choice C is the only choice to present any *specific effect* that Armstrong's New York experience had on his work.

30. B   **Development**

Choice B aptly moves from the Armstrong's career from the creation of a new group to his seeking new ways to expand style and technique.

31. A   **Standard English Conventions**

The sentence is correct as written.

32. D   **Logical Comparisons**

The original phrase forms an illogical comparison. Armstrong cannot do more than he, himself, did; therefore, the logical phrasing is that he did more *than any* <u>*other*</u> musician.

33. C   **Clear Expression of Ideas/Idiom**

Choice C correctly completes the idiomatic phrase *tribute to.*

34. A   **Clarity of Expression/Diction**

A theory cannot logically *believe* or *endorse* anything. The nature of a theory is to make a *contention.*

35. C   **Punctuation**

The correct available choice creates a parenthetical phrase that must be set off by commas. This means that there must be a comma before and after the phrase.

36. **C** — Verb Tense, Mood, and Voice

This phrase must indicate a clear idea as well as coordinate logically with the prepositional phrase that follows. The original phrase is in the passive voice, which is stylistically weak, and it separates the prepositional phrase from the noun phrase it modifies, *the "rules of the game."* Choice D commits the same error and is in the wrong mood to boot. Choice B is in the wrong tense. Only choice C is clear and effective.

37. **B** — Clarity of Expression

The underlined phrase is an adverbial phrase that modifies the verb *grows*. The context of the sentence requires that it indicate some way that an *economy* grows. The only choice that does this logically and idiomatically is choice B.

38. **A** — Clarity of Expression/Cohesiveness

The original phrasing most logically supports the main claim of the paragraph because it is the only one that expresses the idea that *uncertainty hinders economic activity.*

39. **B** — Diction

The correct choice must express what *a* country might do with *laws* in order to *ensure robust property rights*. The only reasonable choice is C, *adopting.*

40. **D** — Coordination

Choice D establishes the correct cause-and-effect relationship between the two parts of the sentence.

41. **B** — Coordination/Cohesiveness

The new sentence indicates an additional benefit provided by countries with strong economic institutions, so this sentence should follow the sentence that indicates the *first* economic benefit of such countries, which is sentence 2.

42. **B** — Clarity of Expression/Diction

This sentence conveys the relative weakness of economic institutions in the second country. The only word among the choices that indicates this relative weakness is B, *tenuous.*

43. **D** — Redundancy

Since the sentence begins with the word *Additionally*, choices A, B, and C are all redundant.

44. **B** — Subject-Verb Agreement

The subject of this clause, *the stability, enforcement, and predictability*, is plural and so requires a plural verb. Choice D provides a verb that agrees with the subject, but forms an illogical idea. Choices A and C include verbs that disagree with the subject.

Section 3: Math (No Calculator)

1. **C** — Algebra (linear equations) EASY

$$\frac{3}{4}a + \frac{2}{3}b = 7$$

Multiply by 12 (the common denominator):

$$12\left(\frac{3}{4}a + \frac{2}{3}b = 7\right)$$

Distribute:

$$\frac{36}{4}a + \frac{24}{3}b = 84$$

Simplify:

$$9a + 8b = 84$$

2. **B** — Algebra (ratios) EASY

Set up a proportion:

$$\frac{15 \text{ Euros}}{11 \text{ Pounds}} = \frac{100 \text{ Euros}}{x \text{ Pounds}}$$

Cross-multiply: $15x = 1,100$
Divide by 15: $x = 73.33$

3. **D** — Algebra (solving equations) EASY

$$ax + b = cx + d$$

Subtract cx and b from each side: $ax - cx = d - b$
Factor out x: $x(a - c) = d - b$
Divide by $(a - c)$:

$$x = \frac{d - b}{a - c}$$

4. **C** — Algebra (equation writing) EASY

In one month, Jeff spends 4($1.25) = $5 on music and $3 on a movie, for a total of $8 per month. Therefore, in m months, he spends $8m$. The amount remaining on his card after m months is, therefore, $50 minus the amount he spends in m months: $d = 50 - 8m$.

5. **B** — Algebra (systems) EASY

First equation: $2x + y = 3x + 4$
Subtract $2x$: $y = x + 4$
Substitute $y = x + 4$ into the second equation:

$$x + 5(x + 4) = 2$$

Distribute: $x + 5x + 20 = 2$
Simplify: $6x + 20 = 2$
Subtract 20: $6x = -18$
Divide by 6: $x = -3$
Substitute $x = -3$ into the equation to solve for y:

$$y = -3 + 4 = 1$$

Therefore, $x + y = -3 + 1 = -2$.

6. **D** — Advanced Mathematics (polynomials) MEDIUM

$$4(2x + 3)^2 + 2x$$

Factor: $4(2x + 3)(2x + 3) + 2x$
FOIL: $4(4x^2 + 6x + 6x + 9) + 2x$
Simplify: $4(4x^2 + 12x + 9) + 2x$
Distribute: $16x^2 + 48x + 36 + 2x$
Combine like terms: $16x^2 + 50x + 36$

7. **A**   **Advanced Mathematics (analyzing quadratics) MEDIUM**

If the graph has a y-intercept of $y = 2$, then $y = 2$ when $x = 0$:
$$2 = a(0)^3 + 2(0)^2 + 5(0) + d$$
Simplify: $2 = d$
If the graph has an x-intercept at $x = 3$, then $x = 3$ when $y = 0$:
$$0 = a(3)^3 + 2(3)^2 + 5(3) + 2$$
Simplify: $0 = 27a + 18 + 15 + 2$
Simplify: $0 = 27a + 35$
Subtract 35: $-35 = 27a$

Divide by 27: $-\dfrac{35}{27} = a$

---

8. **C**   **Algebra (expressing relationships) MEDIUM**

Equations about work are framed in terms of the part of the job each participant can complete in one unit of time. If Mrs. Perry can do the job in 6 hours, she does one sixth of it in an hour. Together, she and Jason do the job in 4 hours, so they do one fourth in an hour. The time it would take Jason alone is unknown, so if it is represented by x, $\dfrac{1}{x}$ will represent the part of the job Jason can do in one hour.

---

9. **C**   **Algebra (inequalities) MEDIUM**

If each shirt costs \$24, then Luis's total expenditure for x shirts is \$24x. If he also purchases a suit for \$264, the total expenditure is $264 + 24x$ dollars. If this must be less than or equal to 500, then $500 \geq 264 + 24x$.

---

10. **C**   **Advanced Mathematics (functions) MEDIUM-HARD**

If $f(0) = 2$: $2 = a(0)^2 + b$
Simplify: $2 = b$
If $f(1) = 5$: $5 = a(1)^2 + b$
Simplify: $5 = a + b$
Substitute $b = 2$: $5 = a + 2$
Subtract 2: $3 = a$
Therefore, the function is: $f(x) = ax^2 + b = 3x^2 + 2$
Therefore: $f(-3) = 3(-3)^2 + 2 = 27 + 2 = 29$

---

11. **C**   **Additional Topics (angles) MEDIUM**

Since the two angles form a linear pair, their sum is 180°:
$$2x - 15 + x = 180$$
Combine like terms: $3x - 15 = 180$
Add 15: $3x = 195$
Divide by 3: $x = 65$
Therefore, the larger angle has a measure of $2(65) - 15 = 130 - 15 = 115°$.

12. **B**   **Advanced Mathematics (polynomials) MEDIUM-HARD**

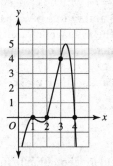

Notice that every choice is a polynomial function in factored form. Since the graph clearly has x-intercepts at $x = 1$, $x = 2$, and $x = 4$, then by the Factor Theorem the polynomial must have factors of $(x - 1)$, $(x - 2)$, and $(x - 4)$. This rules out choices A and D. Notice, also, that the graph contains the point $(3, 4)$. This point satisfies the function in B because $g(3) = -(3 - 1)^2(3 - 2)(3 - 4) = -(4)(1)(-1) = 4$. Notice that the function in choice C gives $g(3) = -4$.

---

13. **C**   **Additional Topics (angles in circles) HARD**

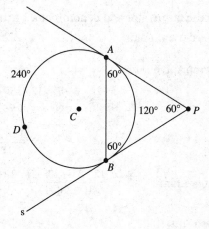

We can analyze this triangle completely by just marking up the diagram with the measurements we are given. First, let's mark arc ADB with its measure: 240°. Since a circle has 360°, the minor arc AB must have measure $360° - 240° = 120°$. Now we must recall an important theorem called the Inscribed Angle Theorem: **an angle that has its vertex on a circle intercepts an arc that is twice its measure.** Since points A and B are both on the circle, we can use this theorem. Since angle ABP intercepts an arc of 120°, it must have a measure of $120/2 = 60°$. We can say the same of angle BAP. Then, since the angles in a triangle must have a sum of 180°, the remaining angle in the triangle must have a measure of $180 - 60 - 60 = 60°$. Since all of the angles in triangle ABP are equal, it is an equilateral triangle.

14. D   **Additional Topics (circles) HARD**

First notice that each choice is an equation in the form $(x - h)^2 + (y - k)^2 = r^2$, which is the equation of a circle with radius (h, k) and radius r. We can find the radius (h, k) by finding the intersection point of the two lines (because all diameters of a circle must intersect at the center).

Substitute first linear equation $(y = 3x - 4)$ into the second:

$$2x + (3x - 4) = 1$$

Simplify: $5x - 4 = 1$

Add 4: $5x = 5$

Divide by 5: $x = 1$

Substitute $x = 1$ into first equation to find the y-coordinate of the center: $y = 3(1) - 4 = -1$

Therefore, the center of the circle is $(1, -1)$, so the equation must have the form $(x - 1)^2 + (y + 1)^2 = r^2$.

This rules out choices A and B. We can finalize the equation by noticing that it must be satisfied by the point $(-2, -5)$:

$$(-2 - 1)^2 + (-5 + 1)^2 = r^2$$

Simplify: $(-3)^2 + (-4)^2 = 9 + 16 = 25 = r^2$

Therefore, the equation is: $(x - 1)^2 + (y + 1)^2 = 25$

---

15. B   **Special Topics (complex numbers) HARD**

$$\frac{3 - 2i}{4 + 5i}$$

Multiply the numerator and denominator by the conjugate of the denominator: $\dfrac{3 - 2i}{4 + 5i} \times \dfrac{4 - 5i}{4 - 5i}$

FOIL the top and bottom:

$$\frac{3 - 2i}{4 + 5i} \times \frac{4 - 5i}{4 - 5i} = \frac{12 - 15i - 8i + 10i^2}{16 - 25i^2}$$

Combine terms: $\dfrac{12 - 23i + 10i^2}{16 - 25i^2}$

Substitute -1 for i^2: $\dfrac{12 - 23i + 10(-1)}{16 - 25(-1)} = \dfrac{12 - 23i - 10}{16 + 25}$

Combine terms: $\dfrac{2 - 23i}{41}$

Distribute division to get standard $a + bi$ form: $\dfrac{2}{41} - \dfrac{23}{41}i$

---

16. 10   **Algebra (ratios/word problems) EASY**

Let a represent the number of apples in the bag, and let r represent the number of oranges in the bag. If there are twice as many apples as oranges, then $a = 2r$. If there are 15 total pieces of fruit in the bag, then $a + r = 15$. Substitute $2r$ for a and solve:

$$r + 2r = 15$$

Combine terms: $3r = 15$

Divide by 3: $r = 5$ oranges

The bag contains twice as many apples as oranges, so it contains $2(5) = 10$ apples.

17. 160   **Algebra (ratios) EASY**

Let's leave the conversion for the last step, and first find the number of cups of blue paint required. First set up a proportion in which x represents the number of cups of blue paint required. Since this will produce 34 total cups of paint, this mixture must also contain $34 - x$ cups of yellow paint.

$$\frac{12}{5} = \frac{(34 - x) \text{ cups of yellow paint}}{x \text{ cups of blue paint}}$$

Cross-multiply: $12x = 5(34 - x)$

Distribute: $12x = 170 - 5x$

Add $5x$: $17x = 170$

Divide by 17: $x = 10$

Therefore, it requires 10 cups of blue paint, or $10(16) = 160$ tablespoons of blue paint.

---

18. 8   **Additional Topics (triangles) MEDIUM**

If the three points are not all on the same line, they are the vertices of a triangle. If the distance from A to B is 4 units, and the distance from B to C is 5 units, then the distance between A and C must be less than the sum of these two differences, so less than 9 miles. The largest integer less than but not equal to 9 is 8.

---

19. 93   **Data Analysis (central tendency) MEDIUM-HARD**

If Pei-Sze has an average of 89 for 6 tests, she has earned $6(89) = 534$ points thus far. To earn an average of 90 for all 8 tests, she needs a total of $8(90) = 720$ points. That means she needs an additional $720 - 534 = 186$ points. If she earns those 186 points on 2 tests, she will average $186 \div 2 = 93$ points per test.

---

20. 100   **Advanced Mathematics (radicals) HARD**

First equation: $x = 2\sqrt{3}$

Multiply by 5: $5x = 10\sqrt{3}$

Second equation: $5x = \sqrt{3y}$

Use the Transitive Property of Equality: $\sqrt{3y} = 10\sqrt{3}$

The square root of a product is the product of the square roots. $\sqrt{3}\sqrt{y} = 10\sqrt{3}$

Divide both sides by $\sqrt{3}$: $\sqrt{y} = 10$

Square both sides: $y = 100$

Section 4: Math (Calculator)

1. C   **Algebra (representing quantities) EASY**

If x represents the retail price of the order, then $x - 0.15x = 0.85x$ is the price after the 15% discount. If a 6.25% tax is added, the final price $0.85x + 0.0625(0.85x) = 1.0625(0.85x)$.

2. D   **Data Analysis (data spread) EASY**

This requires simply finding the difference between $-37°F$ and $109°F$: $109°F - (-37°F) = 146°F$

---

3. A   **Algebra (linear functions) EASY**

We are given that $P = 10$ when $t = 2$ and $P = 14$ when $t = 3$. The only equation among the choices that is satisfied by both of these ordered pairs is A: $P = 4t + 2$.

---

4. D   **Algebra (word problems) EASY**

If Mark answered 14 questions correctly, and if x is the number of 5-point questions he answered correctly, then $14 - x$ must be the number of 8-point questions he answered correctly. He earned $5x$ points for the 5-point questions and $8(14 - x)$ points for the 8-point questions. If he earned a total of 94 points:

$$5x + 8(14 - x) = 94$$

Distribute: $5x + 112 - 8x = 94$

Combine like terms: $112 - 3x = 94$

Subtract 112: $-3x = -18$

Divide by -3: $x = 6$

---

5. A   **Additional Topics (volume) EASY**

The pool holds 450 cubic feet of water with a length and a width of 10 feet and 15 feet. The volume of water can be expressed in the equation:

$$V = lwh$$

Substitute $V = 450$, $l = 10$, and $w = 15$: $450 = (10)(15)(h)$

Simplify: $450 = 150h$

Divide by 150: $3 = h$

---

6. D   **Algebra (linear analysis) EASY**

The graph shows clearly that the line has an x-intercept at $(1.5, 0)$ and a y-intercept at $(0, -1)$, so we want to find the linear equation that has these features. One way to tell is simply to substitute these ordered pairs into the choices, and eliminate those that don't work. Let's start by testing $(0, -1)$:

A) $-1 = \frac{2}{3}(0) + \frac{3}{2} = \frac{3}{2}$ (Nope. Eliminate.)

B) $-1 = 2(0) - 1 = -1$ (Yes. Keep.)

C) $2(0) - 3(-1) = 3 = 0$ (Nope. Eliminate.)

D) $2(0) - 3(-1) = 3 = 3$ (Yes. Keep.)

Next we can test $(1.5, 0)$ in the remaining choices:

B) $0 = 2(1.5) - 1 = 2$ (Nope. Eliminate.)

D) $2(1.5) - 3(0) = 3 - 0 = 3$ (Yes.)

---

7. A   **Advanced Mathematics (polynomials) MEDIUM**

$$2h(x) = 2f(x) - 2g(x)$$

Use definitions of $f(x)$ and $g(x)$:

$$= 2(4x^2 - 7x + 3) - 2(2x^2 - 5x - 4)$$

Distribute: $8x^2 - 14x + 6 - 4x^2 + 10x + 8$

Combine like terms: $4x^2 - 4x + 14$

---

8. D   **Advanced Mathematics (quadratic functions) MEDIUM**

This equation represents a quadratic function in x, so its graph is a parabola. Since all of the choices are parabolic graphs, we must analyze the equation further to find the correct graph.

Given equation: $y + 2 = x^2 - k$

Subtract 2: $y = x^2 - k - 2$

Express in vertex form: $y = (x - 0)^2 + (-k - 2)$

This means that this is an "open-up" parabola with a vertex at $(0, -k - 2)$, which is on the y-axis.

If k is negative: $k < 0$

Multiply by -1 (and "flip" the inequality): $-k > 0$

Subtract 2: $-k - 2 > -2$

This means that $-k - 2$ (the y-coordinate of the vertex) is greater than -2, so the vertex must be on the y-axis above the point $(0, -2)$. The graphs in choices B and D both satisfy this criterion, but since the graph in B is open down instead of up, the correct answer is D.

---

9. B   **Data Analysis (scatterplots) MEDIUM**

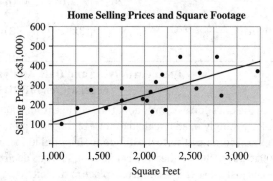

The shaded region shows the range of prices that are within the Lees' budget. Eight of the 20 data points are in this region, and these represent $8/20 = 0.40 = 40\%$ of the total.

---

10. C   **Data Analysis (scatterplot) MEDIUM-HARD**

This is a linear equation in slope-intercept form, and 0.12 represents the slope. The slope is the rate of change of the y variable with respect to the x variable. This means that the average selling price of the house increases by (0.12) thousand dollars for every additional square foot, or $120 per square foot.

---

11. A   **Data Analysis (percentages) MEDIUM**

Of 3 million graduates, approximately $(0.51)(3 \text{ million}) = 1.53$ million are female. Of those, 70% enrolled in college. Therefore, 30% are <u>not</u> enrolled: 30% of 1.53 million young women is $(0.3)(1.53 \text{ million}) = 0.459$ million or approximately 459,000.

12. D   **Advanced Mathematics (exponentials)**
MEDIUM-HARD

Original expression: $x^{-2}\left(\dfrac{x+x+x}{x+x}\right)$

Rewrite x^{-2} as $\dfrac{1}{x^2}$: $\dfrac{1}{x^2}\left(\dfrac{x+x+x}{x+x}\right)$

Simplify: $\dfrac{1}{x^2}\left(\dfrac{3x}{2x}\right)$

Simplify: $\dfrac{1}{x^2}\left(\dfrac{3}{2}\right)$

Multiply fractions: $\dfrac{3}{2x^2}$

---

13. C   **Problem Solving and Data Analysis**
(variation) MEDIUM-HARD

Definition of function: $h(x,y)=\dfrac{Kx^2}{y}$

If $h(m,n)=2$: $\dfrac{Km^2}{n}=2$

We want to evaluate $h(3m, 2n)$:

$$h(3x, 2y)=\dfrac{K(3m)^2}{2n}=\dfrac{9Km^2}{2n}=\left(\dfrac{9}{2}\right)\left(\dfrac{Km^2}{n}\right)$$

Substitute $\dfrac{Km^2}{n}=2$: $h(3x, 2y)=\left(\dfrac{9}{2}\right)(2)=9$

---

14. C   **Problem Solving and Data Analysis**
(set relations) MEDIUM

Since the question asks only about the change from 2000 to 2010, we simply need to calculate 10% of the 2000 populations and compare this to the difference in population from 2000 to 2010. (Remember that calculating 10% of a decimal is easy: just move the decimal one place to the left.

	10% of 2000 pop.	Increase from 2000 to 2010
Alabama	0.4447	0.333
Georgia	0.8186	1.502
Louisiana	0.4469	0.064
North Carolina	0.8049	1.486
South Carolina	0.4012	0.613

For three of these states—Georgia, North Carolina, and South Carolina—the increase is greater than 10%.

---

15. B   **Additional Topics (trigonometry) MEDIUM**

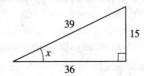

If the two legs of a right triangle have lengths 15 and 36, we can find the hypotenuse, h, with the Pythagorean Theorem: $15^2 + 36^2 = h^2$

Simplify: $225 + 1{,}296 = h^2$
Simplify: $1{,}521 = h^2$
Take the square root: $39 = h$

The question asks for the sine of the smallest angle. The smallest angle in a triangle is always across from the smallest side, so the smallest angle in this triangle must be the one marked x. The sine ratio is defined as the opposite side divided by the hypotenuse, so $\sin x = 15/39$.

---

16. D   **Algebra (inequalities) MEDIUM**

Original inequality: $-\dfrac{2}{x}<-\dfrac{1}{3}$

Multiply by -1 and "flip": $\dfrac{2}{x}>\dfrac{1}{3}$

Notice that this inequality tells us that $\dfrac{2}{x}$ is a positive number, so x must be a positive number, and $3x$ (the common denominator) must also be a positive number. This means that if we multiply both sides by $3x$, we don't need to "flip" the inequality.
Multiply by $3x$ (and don't flip): $6 > x > 0$

---

17. A   **Problem Solving and Data Analysis**
(rates) MEDIUM-HARD

Let x denote the current price of stock A, and $5x$ denote the current price of stock B. In 6 months, stock A will have gained $5 per month, so it will have gained a total of $($5)(6) = 30, so its new price will be $x + 30$. After the same six months, stock B will have lost $3 per month, so it will have lost a total of $($3)(6) = 18, giving it a new price of $5x − 18$. If the two stock prices are then the same:

$$x + 30 = 5x - 18$$
Subtract x: $30 = 4x - 18$
Add 18: $48 = 4x$
Divide by 4: $12 = x$

---

18. D   **Advanced Mathematics (functions)**
MEDIUM-HARD

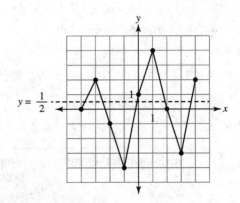

Drawing a horizontal line at $y = \frac{1}{2}$ shows that the function intersects with this line 5 times.

---

19. B — Data Analysis (central tendency) MEDIUM-HARD

The median of a set is not affected by extreme values, but the average is. Consider a simple set of numbers like 1, 2, and 3. It should be clear that the median and the average of this set are both 2. Compare this to the set 1, 2, and 300. The median of this set is still 2, but the average is now much larger: 101. If the average of a set is much larger than its median, the likely explanation is that some very large outliers are pulling the average up without changing the median.

---

20. D — Problem Solving and Data Analysis (percents) MEDIUM-HARD

If n students were polled, then the 45% of these who identify as liberals can be represented as $0.45n$. The 60% of this group that support universal health care can be expressed as $0.60(0.45n) = 0.27n$. If there are 405 students in this group, then $0.27n = 405$. Dividing by 0.27 gives $n = 1,500$.

---

21. B — Problem Solving and Data Analysis (conversions) MEDIUM-HARD

This is a fairly straightforward conversion problem. Just make sure you set up your conversion factors carefully and convert the answer to scientific notation.

$$1 \text{ day} \times \frac{24 \text{ hours}}{1 \text{ day}} \times \frac{60 \text{ minutes}}{1 \text{ hour}} \times \frac{60 \text{ seconds}}{1 \text{ minute}}$$

$$\times \frac{186,000 \text{ miles}}{1 \text{ second}} = 1.6 \times 10^{10} \text{ miles}$$

---

22. D — Advanced Mathematics (functions) MEDIUM-HARD

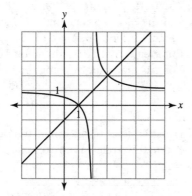

Since the graph is given, one way to solve this problem is to simply graph the line $y = x - 1$ and notice that the two graphs appear to intersect at (1, 0) and (3, 2). Then we can confirm that these are solutions by plugging these values back into the equations and confirming that they work.

If you prefer the algebraic method, you can solve the equation $x - 1 = \dfrac{x-1}{x-2}$ for x:

$$x - 1 = \frac{x-1}{x-2}$$

Multiply by $(x - 2)$: $\qquad (x-1)(x-2) = x - 1$

FOIL: $\qquad\qquad\qquad x^2 - 3x + 2 = x - 1$

Subtract x and add 1: $\qquad x^2 - 4x + 3 = 0$

Factor: $\qquad\qquad\qquad (x-1)(x-3) = 0$

Solve with the Zero Product Property: $\quad x = 1$ or $x = 3$

Plugging these values of x back into either equation gives the ordered pair solutions (1, 0) and (3, 2).

---

23. B — Advanced Mathematics (functions) HARD

Given functions: $\qquad\qquad\qquad f(x) = x^2 - 6x - 475$

$$g(x) = 3 - 4x$$

If $f(2a) = 3g(a)$: $\qquad (2a)^2 - 6(2a) - 475 = 3(3 - 4(a))$

Simplify: $\qquad\qquad 4a^2 - 12a - 475 = 9 - 12a$

Add $12a$: $\qquad\qquad\qquad 4a^2 - 475 = 9$

Add 475: $\qquad\qquad\qquad\qquad 4a^2 = 484$

Divide by 4: $\qquad\qquad\qquad\qquad a^2 = 121$

Take the square root: $\qquad\qquad\qquad a = \pm 11$

---

24. A — Advanced Mathematics (non-linear systems) MEDIUM-HARD

Although the question gives us information about the graphs of these equations, it is impossible to graph the first equation precisely, because k is unknown. Therefore, it is probably easier to treat this as an algebraic system of equations with only one solution.

Given equations: $\qquad\qquad\qquad y = x^2 + k$

$$2x + y = 5$$

Substitute $y = x^2 + k$ into the second equation:

$$2x + (x^2 + k) = 5$$

Express in standard quadratic form: $\quad x^2 + 2x + k = 5$

Subtract 5: $\qquad\qquad\qquad x^2 + 2x + (k - 5) = 0$

Recall that if a quadratic equation has only one solution, then its discriminant, $b^2 - 4ac$, must equal 0.

The discriminant is 0: $\qquad (2)^2 - 4(1)(k - 5) = 0$

Simplify: $\qquad\qquad\qquad 4 - 4k + 20 = 0$

Combine like terms: $\qquad\qquad 24 - 4k = 0$

Add $4k$: $\qquad\qquad\qquad\qquad 24 = 4k$

Divide by 4: $\qquad\qquad\qquad\qquad 6 = k$

---

25. B — Algebra (absolute values) MEDIUM-HARD

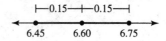

It helps a lot to draw the number line and indicate the range of "industry standard weights." Since the problem states that any weight between 6.45 and 6.75 ounces satisfies industry standards, we can represent this range with the dark line above. Notice that the midpoint of this segment is $(6.45 + 6.75)/2 = 6.60$, and that this midpoint is 0.15 away from each endpoint. This means that every value in this set is 0.15 units or less away from 6.60. Another way to put this is that "the distance from x to 6.60 is less than or equal to 0.15" or $|x - 6.60| \leq 0.15$.

26. B   **Problem Solving and Data Analysis**
                                   (numerical reasoning) HARD

Original inequality: $a + b < b < a - b$

Subtract a: $b < b - a < -b$

Subtract b: $0 < -a < -2b$

Multiply by -1 and "flip": $0 > a > 2b$

This indicates that both a and b must be negative, so we have proven that statements I and III must be true. This rules out choices A and C. To choose between B and D, we must determine whether b must be less than a. Here, we might choose simple values for a and b that satisfy the inequality. Notice that $a = -1$ and $b = -1$ work, because $0 > -1 > 2(-1)$. Since this shows that a and b can be equal, statement II is not necessarily true. Therefore, the correct answer is B, I and III only.

27. D   **Algebra (graphing systems) HARD**

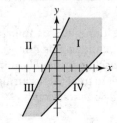

Since both linear inequalities are written in slope-intercept form, you should be able to graph each line based on its slope and y-intercept, and then shade accordingly. The first line has a slope of 2 and a y-intercept of 3, and is shaded below, to catch all of the y values that are <u>less than or equal to</u> this line. The second line has a slope of 1 and a y-intercept of -4, and is shaded above, to catch all of the y values that are <u>greater than</u> this line. This gives the shaded region shown above, which clearly contains points in all four quadrants.

28. A   **Additional Topics (Triangles) HARD**

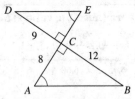

Because AB is parallel to DE, alternate interior angles A and E are congruent, as shown above. Also, since AE is perpendicular to DB, the triangles contain right angles as shown. This proves that the triangles are similar, and so corresponding sides must be proportional. We can find the length of CE by setting up a proportion:

$$\frac{CE}{AC} = \frac{DC}{CB}$$

Substitute values: $\dfrac{CE}{8} = \dfrac{9}{12}$

Cross-multiply: $12(CE) = 72$

Divide by 12: $CE = 6$

Therefore, the area of triangle DCE is $(6)(9)/2 = 27$.

29. C   **Problem Solving and Data Analysis**
                                   (averages) MEDIUM-HARD

Recall the average formula: $\text{average} = \dfrac{\text{sum}}{\text{\# of numbers}}$

And therefore: $\text{sum} = (\text{average})(\text{\# of numbers})$

Therefore, if the average of a and b is x:

$$a + b = x(2) = 2x$$

If the average of b and c is $2x$: $b + c = 2x(2) = 4x$

If the average of a and c is $3x$: $a + c = 3x(2) = 6x$

Add these three equations together:

$$2a + 2b + 2c = 2x + 4x + 6x = 12x$$

Divide by 2: $a + b + c = 6x$

The average of a, b and c is $\dfrac{a+b+c}{3}$:

$$\frac{a+b+c}{3} = \frac{6x}{3} = 2x$$

30. C   **Additional Topics (Circles) HARD**

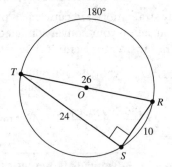

First recall the Inscribed Angle Theorem: if an angle is inscribed in a circle, it intercepts an arc that is twice the measure of the angle. Since angle RST has a measure of $90°$, it must intercept an arc of $180°$, which is a semicircle. This means that TR is a diameter. We can find the measure of this diameter by using the Pythagorean Theorem: $(TR)^2 = 10^2 + 24^2$

Simplify: $(TR)^2 = 676$

Take the square root: $TR = 26$

Since this is the diameter of the circle, the radius must be $26 \div 2 = 13$, and the circle has an area of $\pi(13)^2 = 169\pi$. Therefore $k = 169$.

31. 5   **Algebra (graphs of lines) EASY**

Slope formula: $\text{slope} = \dfrac{y_2 - y_1}{x_2 - x_1}$

Substitute known values: $\dfrac{2}{3} = \dfrac{k-3}{4-1}$

Simplify: $\dfrac{2}{3} = \dfrac{k-3}{3}$

Multiply by 3: $2 = k - 3$

Add 3: $5 = k$

32. **50**   Problem Solving and Data Analysis
                                     (inequalities) MEDIUM

If the total weight of the crew, equipment, and cargo
cannot exceed 4,000 pounds: $950 + 60n < 4,000$
Subtract 950: $60n < 3050$
Divide by 60: $n < 50.83$
Since n must be a whole number, the greatest value it can
take is 50.

---

33. **4/9 or .444**   Problem Solving and Data
                                 Analysis (probability) MEDIUM

The table shows 153 respondents in support of immigration support, 68 of which are in the 21–40 age group.
Therefore, the probability of a supporter being in the
21–40 age group is $68/153 = 4/9 = .444$.

---

34. **2/9 or .222**   Data Analysis (analysis of
                                     tabular data) MEDIUM

The "indifference factor" for the 61+ age group is $25 \div (30 + 45) = 1/3$ or .333. The "indifference factor" for the
21–40 age group is $10 \div (68 + 22) = 1/9$ or .111. The differ-
ence is $.333 - .111 = .222$ or $2/9$.

---

35. **9**   Algebra (identities) MEDIUM
                                  $(x - a)(x - b) = x^2 - 9x + 7$
FOIL: $x^2 - ax - bx + ab = x^2 - 9x + 7$
Combine like terms: $x^2 - (a + b)x + ab = x^2 - 9x + 7$
If this equation is true for all values of x, then the two
quadratics must be identical, and so their coefficients
must match perfectly. This means that $a + b = 9$ and
$ab = 7$.

---

36. **9/40 or .225**   Data Analysis (percentages)
                                                   MEDIUM

According to the table, 27 men were awarded doctorates.
The question asks what percentage *of the males*, so the
fraction is $27/120 = .225$ or $9/40$.

---

37. **.96**   Advanced Mathematics
                                 (exponential functions) MEDIUM

The formula is designed to find the amount of money
remaining in the account. If 4% is withdrawn, 96% will
remain. Ms. Hamid should use $r = 0.96$.

---

38. **7.68**   Algebra (extended analysis) HARD

According to the formula, the trust fund started with
$5,000, so Aisha can withdraw $(0.04)(\$5,000) = \$200$ the
first year. This means that the fund will have $5,000 −
$200 = $4,800 remaining, so Aisha can withdraw $(0.04)(\$4,800) = \$192$ the second year. This means that the fund
will have $4,800 − $192 = $4,608 remaining, so Aisha can
withdraw $(0.04)(\$4,608) = \$184.32$ the second year. This is
a difference of $192 − $184.32 = $7.68.

PRACTICE SAT 2

ANSWER SHEET

SECTION 1

1 Ⓐ Ⓑ Ⓒ Ⓓ	13 Ⓐ Ⓑ Ⓒ Ⓓ	25 Ⓐ Ⓑ Ⓒ Ⓓ	37 Ⓐ Ⓑ Ⓒ Ⓓ	49 Ⓐ Ⓑ Ⓒ Ⓓ
2 Ⓐ Ⓑ Ⓒ Ⓓ	14 Ⓐ Ⓑ Ⓒ Ⓓ	26 Ⓐ Ⓑ Ⓒ Ⓓ	38 Ⓐ Ⓑ Ⓒ Ⓓ	50 Ⓐ Ⓑ Ⓒ Ⓓ
3 Ⓐ Ⓑ Ⓒ Ⓓ	15 Ⓐ Ⓑ Ⓒ Ⓓ	27 Ⓐ Ⓑ Ⓒ Ⓓ	39 Ⓐ Ⓑ Ⓒ Ⓓ	51 Ⓐ Ⓑ Ⓒ Ⓓ
4 Ⓐ Ⓑ Ⓒ Ⓓ	16 Ⓐ Ⓑ Ⓒ Ⓓ	28 Ⓐ Ⓑ Ⓒ Ⓓ	40 Ⓐ Ⓑ Ⓒ Ⓓ	52 Ⓐ Ⓑ Ⓒ Ⓓ
5 Ⓐ Ⓑ Ⓒ Ⓓ	17 Ⓐ Ⓑ Ⓒ Ⓓ	29 Ⓐ Ⓑ Ⓒ Ⓓ	41 Ⓐ Ⓑ Ⓒ Ⓓ	
6 Ⓐ Ⓑ Ⓒ Ⓓ	18 Ⓐ Ⓑ Ⓒ Ⓓ	30 Ⓐ Ⓑ Ⓒ Ⓓ	42 Ⓐ Ⓑ Ⓒ Ⓓ	
7 Ⓐ Ⓑ Ⓒ Ⓓ	19 Ⓐ Ⓑ Ⓒ Ⓓ	31 Ⓐ Ⓑ Ⓒ Ⓓ	43 Ⓐ Ⓑ Ⓒ Ⓓ	
8 Ⓐ Ⓑ Ⓒ Ⓓ	20 Ⓐ Ⓑ Ⓒ Ⓓ	32 Ⓐ Ⓑ Ⓒ Ⓓ	44 Ⓐ Ⓑ Ⓒ Ⓓ	
9 Ⓐ Ⓑ Ⓒ Ⓓ	21 Ⓐ Ⓑ Ⓒ Ⓓ	33 Ⓐ Ⓑ Ⓒ Ⓓ	45 Ⓐ Ⓑ Ⓒ Ⓓ	
10 Ⓐ Ⓑ Ⓒ Ⓓ	22 Ⓐ Ⓑ Ⓒ Ⓓ	34 Ⓐ Ⓑ Ⓒ Ⓓ	46 Ⓐ Ⓑ Ⓒ Ⓓ	
11 Ⓐ Ⓑ Ⓒ Ⓓ	23 Ⓐ Ⓑ Ⓒ Ⓓ	35 Ⓐ Ⓑ Ⓒ Ⓓ	47 Ⓐ Ⓑ Ⓒ Ⓓ	
12 Ⓐ Ⓑ Ⓒ Ⓓ	24 Ⓐ Ⓑ Ⓒ Ⓓ	36 Ⓐ Ⓑ Ⓒ Ⓓ	48 Ⓐ Ⓑ Ⓒ Ⓓ	

SECTION 2

1 Ⓐ Ⓑ Ⓒ Ⓓ	11 Ⓐ Ⓑ Ⓒ Ⓓ	21 Ⓐ Ⓑ Ⓒ Ⓓ	31 Ⓐ Ⓑ Ⓒ Ⓓ	41 Ⓐ Ⓑ Ⓒ Ⓓ
2 Ⓐ Ⓑ Ⓒ Ⓓ	12 Ⓐ Ⓑ Ⓒ Ⓓ	22 Ⓐ Ⓑ Ⓒ Ⓓ	32 Ⓐ Ⓑ Ⓒ Ⓓ	42 Ⓐ Ⓑ Ⓒ Ⓓ
3 Ⓐ Ⓑ Ⓒ Ⓓ	13 Ⓐ Ⓑ Ⓒ Ⓓ	23 Ⓐ Ⓑ Ⓒ Ⓓ	33 Ⓐ Ⓑ Ⓒ Ⓓ	43 Ⓐ Ⓑ Ⓒ Ⓓ
4 Ⓐ Ⓑ Ⓒ Ⓓ	14 Ⓐ Ⓑ Ⓒ Ⓓ	24 Ⓐ Ⓑ Ⓒ Ⓓ	34 Ⓐ Ⓑ Ⓒ Ⓓ	44 Ⓐ Ⓑ Ⓒ Ⓓ
5 Ⓐ Ⓑ Ⓒ Ⓓ	15 Ⓐ Ⓑ Ⓒ Ⓓ	25 Ⓐ Ⓑ Ⓒ Ⓓ	35 Ⓐ Ⓑ Ⓒ Ⓓ	
6 Ⓐ Ⓑ Ⓒ Ⓓ	16 Ⓐ Ⓑ Ⓒ Ⓓ	26 Ⓐ Ⓑ Ⓒ Ⓓ	36 Ⓐ Ⓑ Ⓒ Ⓓ	
7 Ⓐ Ⓑ Ⓒ Ⓓ	17 Ⓐ Ⓑ Ⓒ Ⓓ	27 Ⓐ Ⓑ Ⓒ Ⓓ	37 Ⓐ Ⓑ Ⓒ Ⓓ	
8 Ⓐ Ⓑ Ⓒ Ⓓ	18 Ⓐ Ⓑ Ⓒ Ⓓ	28 Ⓐ Ⓑ Ⓒ Ⓓ	38 Ⓐ Ⓑ Ⓒ Ⓓ	
9 Ⓐ Ⓑ Ⓒ Ⓓ	19 Ⓐ Ⓑ Ⓒ Ⓓ	29 Ⓐ Ⓑ Ⓒ Ⓓ	39 Ⓐ Ⓑ Ⓒ Ⓓ	
10 Ⓐ Ⓑ Ⓒ Ⓓ	20 Ⓐ Ⓑ Ⓒ Ⓓ	30 Ⓐ Ⓑ Ⓒ Ⓓ	40 Ⓐ Ⓑ Ⓒ Ⓓ	

SECTION 3

1. Ⓐ Ⓑ Ⓒ Ⓓ
2. Ⓐ Ⓑ Ⓒ Ⓓ
3. Ⓐ Ⓑ Ⓒ Ⓓ
4. Ⓐ Ⓑ Ⓒ Ⓓ
5. Ⓐ Ⓑ Ⓒ Ⓓ
6. Ⓐ Ⓑ Ⓒ Ⓓ
7. Ⓐ Ⓑ Ⓒ Ⓓ
8. Ⓐ Ⓑ Ⓒ Ⓓ
9. Ⓐ Ⓑ Ⓒ Ⓓ
10. Ⓐ Ⓑ Ⓒ Ⓓ

11. Ⓐ Ⓑ Ⓒ Ⓓ
12. Ⓐ Ⓑ Ⓒ Ⓓ
13. Ⓐ Ⓑ Ⓒ Ⓓ
14. Ⓐ Ⓑ Ⓒ Ⓓ
15. Ⓐ Ⓑ Ⓒ Ⓓ

Student-Produced Responses

ONLY ANSWERS ENTERED IN THE CIRCLES IN EACH GRID WILL BE SCORED. YOU WILL NOT RECEIVE CREDIT FOR ANYTHING WRITTEN IN THE BOXES ABOVE THE CIRCLES.

16.

17.

18.

19.

20.

SECTION 4

1 Ⓐ Ⓑ Ⓒ Ⓓ	11 Ⓐ Ⓑ Ⓒ Ⓓ	21 Ⓐ Ⓑ Ⓒ Ⓓ
2 Ⓐ Ⓑ Ⓒ Ⓓ	12 Ⓐ Ⓑ Ⓒ Ⓓ	22 Ⓐ Ⓑ Ⓒ Ⓓ
3 Ⓐ Ⓑ Ⓒ Ⓓ	13 Ⓐ Ⓑ Ⓒ Ⓓ	23 Ⓐ Ⓑ Ⓒ Ⓓ
4 Ⓐ Ⓑ Ⓒ Ⓓ	14 Ⓐ Ⓑ Ⓒ Ⓓ	24 Ⓐ Ⓑ Ⓒ Ⓓ
5 Ⓐ Ⓑ Ⓒ Ⓓ	15 Ⓐ Ⓑ Ⓒ Ⓓ	25 Ⓐ Ⓑ Ⓒ Ⓓ
6 Ⓐ Ⓑ Ⓒ Ⓓ	16 Ⓐ Ⓑ Ⓒ Ⓓ	26 Ⓐ Ⓑ Ⓒ Ⓓ
7 Ⓐ Ⓑ Ⓒ Ⓓ	17 Ⓐ Ⓑ Ⓒ Ⓓ	27 Ⓐ Ⓑ Ⓒ Ⓓ
8 Ⓐ Ⓑ Ⓒ Ⓓ	18 Ⓐ Ⓑ Ⓒ Ⓓ	28 Ⓐ Ⓑ Ⓒ Ⓓ
9 Ⓐ Ⓑ Ⓒ Ⓓ	19 Ⓐ Ⓑ Ⓒ Ⓓ	29 Ⓐ Ⓑ Ⓒ Ⓓ
10 Ⓐ Ⓑ Ⓒ Ⓓ	20 Ⓐ Ⓑ Ⓒ Ⓓ	30 Ⓐ Ⓑ Ⓒ Ⓓ

Student-Produced Responses

ONLY ANSWERS ENTERED IN THE CIRCLES IN EACH GRID WILL BE SCORED. YOU WILL NOT RECEIVE CREDIT FOR ANYTHING WRITTEN IN THE BOXES ABOVE THE CIRCLES.

SECTION 5: ESSAY

You may wish to remove these sample answer document pages to respond to the practice SAT Essay Test.

Begin Essay here.

If you need more space, please continue on the next page.

Cut Here

Cut Here

ESSAY

If you need more space, please continue on the next page.

ESSAY

_____

_____

_____

_____

_____

_____

_____

_____

_____

_____

_____

_____

_____

_____

_____

_____

_____

_____

_____

_____

_____

_____

_____

Cut Here

ESSAY

STOP here with the Essay.

1   1

Reading Test

65 MINUTES, 52 QUESTIONS

Turn to Section 1 of your answer sheet to answer the questions in this section.

DIRECTIONS

Each passage or pair of passages below is followed by a number of questions. After reading each passage or pair, choose the best answer to each question based on what is stated or implied in the passage or passages and in any accompanying graphics (such as a table or graph).

Questions 1–10 are based on the following passage

This passage is adapted from Robert Louis Stevenson, *Strange Case of Dr. Jekyll and Mr. Hyde*, originally published in 1886. In this story, Mr. Utterson, a lawyer, is conversing with Mr. Enfield, a distant cousin, as they walk on the streets of London.

Line   "Did you ever remark that door?" Mr. Enfield asked, and when his companion had replied in the affirmative, "It is connected in my mind," added he, "with a very odd story."

5   "Indeed?" said Mr. Utterson, with a slight change of voice, "and what was that?"

"Well, it was this way," returned Mr. Enfield: "I was coming home from some place at the end of the world, about three o'clock of a black
10   winter morning, and my way lay through a part of town where there was literally nothing to be seen but lamps. Street after street and all the folks asleep—street after street, all lighted up as if for a procession and all as empty as a church—till
15   at last I got into that state of mind when a man listens and listens and begins to long for the sight of a policeman.

All at once, I saw two figures: one a little man who was stumping along eastward at a good
20   walk, and the other a girl of maybe eight or ten who was running as hard as she was able down a cross street. Well, sir, the two ran into one

another naturally enough at the corner; and then came the horrible part of the thing; for the man
25   trampled calmly over the child's body and left her screaming on the ground. It sounds nothing to hear, but it was hellish to see. It wasn't like a man; it was like some damned Juggernaut.[1] I gave a view-halloa,[2] took to my heels, collared my
30   gentleman, and brought him back to where there was already quite a group about the screaming child. He was perfectly cool and made no resistance, but gave me one look, so ugly that it brought out the sweat on me like running. The
35   people who had turned out were the girl's own family, and pretty soon, the doctor, for whom she had been sent put in his appearance. Well, the child was not much the worse, more frightened, according to the Sawbones, and there you might
40   have supposed would be an end to it.

But there was one curious circumstance. I had taken a loathing to my gentleman at first sight. So had the child's family, which was only natural. But the doctor's case was what struck
45   me. He was the usual cut and dry apothecary, of no particular age and colour, with a strong Edinburgh accent and about as emotional as a bagpipe. Well, sir, he was like the rest of us; every time he looked at my prisoner, I saw that
50   Sawbones turn sick and white with desire to kill him. I knew what was in his mind, just as he knew what was in mine; and killing being out of the question, we did the next best. We told the man we could and would make such a scandal out

1

1

55 of this as should make his name stink from one
end of London to the other. If he had any friends
or any credit, we undertook that he should lose
them. And all the time, as we were pitching it in
red hot, we were keeping the women off him as
60 best we could for they were as wild as harpies.

I never saw a circle of such hateful faces; and
there was the man in the middle, with a kind of
black sneering coolness—frightened too, I could
see that—but carrying it off, sir, really like Satan.
65 'If you choose to make capital out of this accident,' said he, 'I am naturally helpless. No gentleman but wishes to avoid a scene,' says he. 'Name
your figure.' Well, we screwed him up to a hundred pounds for the child's family; he would have
70 clearly liked to stick out; but there was something
about the lot of us that meant mischief, and at last
he struck. The next thing was to get the money;
and where do you think he carried us but to that
place with the door?—whipped out a key, went
75 in, and presently came back with the matter of
ten pounds in gold and a check for the balance,
drawn payable to bearer and signed with a name

that I can't mention, though it's one of the points
of my story, but it was a name at least very well
80 known and often printed. The figure was stiff, but
the signature was good for more than that, if it
was only genuine.

I took the liberty of pointing out to my gentleman that the whole business looked apocryphal,
85 and that a man does not, in real life, walk into
a cellar door at four in the morning and come
out of it with another man's check for close upon
a hundred pounds. But he was quite easy and
sneering. 'Set your mind at rest,' says he, 'I will
90 stay with you till the banks open and cash the
check myself.' So we all set off, the doctor, and
the child's father, and our friend and myself, and
passed the rest of the night in my chambers; and
next day, when we had breakfasted, went in a
95 body to the bank. I gave in the check myself, and
said I had every reason to believe it was a forgery.
Not a bit of it. The check was genuine."

[1]an imposing and seemingly unstoppable force
[2]the shout made by a hunter upon seeing a fox break cover

CONTINUE →

1

1

Which choice best describes what happens in the passage?

A) Two relatives discuss a strange experience they shared in a London neighborhood.

B) A man relates a story about a hideous event that involves a reputable local figure.

C) A local hero discusses the event that earned him his reputation for bravery.

D) A gentleman describes a bizarre situation by which he came into a small fortune.

2

As used in line 19, "good" most nearly means

A) healthful.

B) nimble.

C) brisk.

D) generous.

3

Which choice best described the nature of the implicit agreement between Mr. Enfield and the doctor?

A) They would blackmail the strange man rather than kill him.

B) They would protect the girl from ever encountering the strange man again.

C) They would abscond with the money that the strange man offered them.

D) They would take the strange man to the police if they ever saw him in public again.

4

Which choice provides the best evidence for the answer to the previous question?

A) Lines 37–40 ("Well . . . to it")

B) Lines 51–53 ("I knew . . . best")

C) Lines 72–74 ("The next . . . door?")

D) Lines 83–89 ("I took . . . pounds")

5

As used in line 44, "case" most nearly means

A) legal action.

B) small item of luggage.

C) particular situation.

D) medical condition.

6

The name on the check is one that Mr. Enfield "can't mention" because

A) he cannot recall it.

B) it belongs to a reputable man.

C) it is traumatic to remember.

D) it is loathsome to him.

7

In line 72, the phrase "he struck" means that the strange man

A) had a sudden brilliant idea.

B) lashed out violently.

C) made a deal with the crowd.

D) bolted away suddenly.

8

When Mr. Enfield states that "the whole business looked apocryphal" (line 84), he implies that

A) it was hard to believe the cruelty with which the strange man treated the small girl.

B) the reaction of the crowd was a bizarre and frightening thing to witness.

C) he was still not sure whether his encounter with the strange man was part of a dream.

D) he did not trust that the strange man was going to keep his word.

CONTINUE

1

9

Mr. Enfield primarily regarded the strange man as

A) an emotionally detached brute.

B) a wildly unpredictable menace.

C) a scheming charlatan.

D) a hapless and boorish dolt.

10

Which choice provides the best evidence for the answer to the previous question?

A) Lines 18–22 ("All . . . street")

B) Lines 32–34 ("He was . . . running")

C) Lines 56–58 ("If he . . . them")

D) Lines 66–67 ("No gentleman . . . he")

CONTINUE

1   1

Questions 11–21 are based on the following passage and supplementary material.

This passage is adapted from Ari Petronas, Ph.D., and Daniel Drell, Ph.D., editors, *Genomes to Life: Accelerating Biological Discovery.* ©2015 the U.S. Department of Energy.

Line   The Human Genome Project (HGP), an international scientific effort from 1990 to 2003, decoded the complete sequence of DNA base pairs and genes in the human genome, and made
5   this information available for further biological study. This new knowledge has already produced significant medical breakthroughs, and further applications are bounded only by the limits of scientists' imaginations.
10   To appreciate the complexity and implications of this project, it's important to first understand some key terms. DNA (deoxyribonucleic acid) is the double helix–shaped molecule that provides each of our cells with instructions for
15   manufacturing proteins. The entire complement of human DNA in our genome is arranged into 24 distinct *chromosomes*—physically separate molecules that range in length from about 50 million to 250 million *base pairs*. Our genes, the
20   units of heredity that determine our biological inheritance, consist of particular sub-sequences of these base pairs.
        Chromosomal abnormalities, such as having too many or too few chromosomes, are known
25   to cause many genetic disorders, so understanding the chemistry of chromosomes is important for preventing, diagnosing, and treating these potentially deadly diseases. It is also essential for medical researchers to learn more about the pro-
30   teins that these chromosomes encode, because these molecules perform most of life's essential functions and make up the majority of cellular structures.
        Proteins are large, complex molecules made
35   up of smaller subunits called *amino acids*. The constellation of all proteins in a cell is called its *proteome*. Unlike the relatively unchanging genome, the proteome changes from minute to minute in response to tens of thousands of

40   intra-cellular and extra-cellular environmental signals. The amino acid sequences in individual proteins are specified by the genes that encode them, but the behavior of those proteins within the cell depends on the complex interactions with
45   other molecules (and particularly other proteins) in the cell. The study of these interactions is known as *proteomics* and will likely be the focus of research for decades to come.
        Although monumental, the completion of
50   the Human Genome Project in 2003 was only the first step to understanding human genetics at the molecular level. The next generation of study is known as *functional genomics*, the investigation of gene interactions. There is still much we
55   don't know about the purpose and interactions of many human genes, let alone the activities of the proteins they create. Understanding genes and other DNA sequences requires developing strategies for large-scale investigations across entire
60   genomes. These investigations require overcoming enormous technical hurdles. For instance, efficient research requires creating complete sets of full-length synthesized DNA molecules (called *cDNA*), which encode only the expressed genes of
65   an organism, that is, those that actually produce functional proteins. Another hurdle lies in understanding the mechanisms by which genetic information leads to an actual observable trait, like blood type or eye color, called a *phenotype*. Yet
70   another is to understand how genetic *mutations* (changes in structure) occur, and how they affect the host organism. All of this work is enormously computational, and requires the development of efficient hardware and software techniques for
75   gathering and analyzing data.
        Genomics and its associated disciplines provide powerful analytical tools for human sciences as well, such as forensics, bioarchaeology, anthropology, evolutionary psychology, and
80   human geography. It also extends well beyond the human species, providing insights into agriculture, livestock breeding, and bioprocessing. The genomics of nonhuman organisms can help us solve challenges in energy production,
85   environmental remediation, carbon sequestration, health care, and agriculture. For instance, the genome of the mealworm (*Tenebrio monitor*)

CONTINUE ➡

1   1

produces enzymes that enable it to digest Styrofoam, a substance long thought to be non-
90 biodegradable and a scourge on the environment. Tobacco plants can be engineered to produce an enzyme (a special digestive protein) that metabolizes explosives such as TNT and dinitroglycerin. Other plants and animals are rich pharmaceuti-
95 cal resources, producing molecules with powerful medicinal properties.

Today, all of these diverse but interrelated investigations can be categorized into the

meta-discipline of *bioinformatics*, which merges
100 biology, computer science, and information technology to manage and analyze information derived from the genome and the myriad processes associated with it.

Progress in bioinformatics points to an
105 exciting future. We can already see how this research may lead to breakthroughs in medical diagnostics, treatments, and cures for diseases like Alzheimer's and cancer, and even the mitigation of environmental degradation.

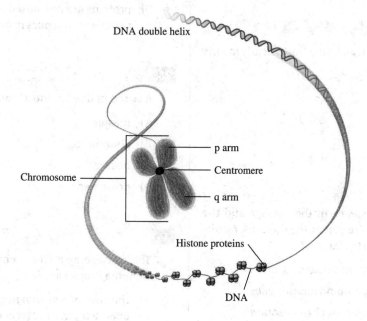

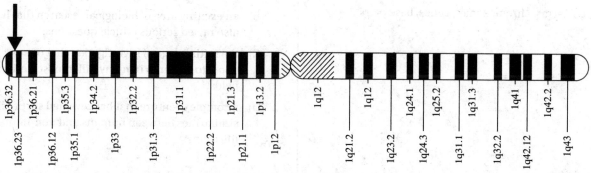

Location of the MTHFR gene: on the short (p) arm of chromosome 1 at position 36.3, from base pair 11,785,729 to 11,806,102. The MTHFR gene provides instructions for making an enzyme that plays a role in the processing of amino acids, the building blocks of proteins. Polymorphisms (variations) in this gene are associated with many conditions, including an increased risk of spina bifida, a birth defect of the spine and spinal cord.

CONTINUE ➡

1   1

11

The primary purpose of the passage is to

A)   clarify the definitions of recently coined
     scientific terms.

B)   investigate promising new therapies for
     devastating diseases.

C)   argue for cooperation among researchers in
     different areas of biology.

D)   provide an overview of a broad domain of
     current scientific research.

12

As used in line 36, "constellation" most nearly means

A)   arrangement

B)   structure

C)   cluster

D)   collection

13

According to the evidence in the passage and the
diagrams, which choice places the molecular units
in order from smallest to largest?

A)   genes, base pairs, chromosomes, arms

B)   base pairs, arms, chromosomes, genes

C)   base pairs, genes, arms, chromosomes

D)   arms, chromosomes, genes, base pairs

14

The author uses the word "encode" in lines 30 and
42 to indicate that

A)   the creation of new proteins within a cell
     depends on the translation of complex
     molecular sequences.

B)   the interactions among chromosomes within a
     cell can be very difficult to analyze and predict.

C)   proteins contain information that must be
     translated in order for observable traits to be
     expressed.

D)   proteins are composed of very long and
     complex sequences of amino acids.

15

As used in line 72, "host" most nearly means

A)   master.

B)   abundance.

C)   bearer.

D)   presenter.

16

The passage as a whole characterizes the Human
Genome Project as

A)   the apex of research in genetics and cellular
     chemistry in the 21st century.

B)   an exciting area of biological research that has
     also raised serious ethical questions.

C)   the initial stage of investigation that opens
     doors to research in many different scientific
     fields.

D)   a complex venture that has revealed surprising
     similarities between humans and non-human
     life forms.

CONTINUE ▶

1   **1**

17

Which choice provides the best evidence for the answer to the previous question?

A) Lines 10–12 ("To . . . terms")

B) Lines 49–52 ("Although . . . level")

C) Lines 54–57 ("There . . . create")

D) Lines 97–103 ("Today . . . with it")

18

According to the passage, which of the following is a true statement about cDNA?

A) It is composed of lengthy sequences of amino acids.

B) It includes reconstructed portions of an organism's chromosomes.

C) It reveals the process by which genetic mutations occur.

D) It enables bacteria to be programmed to metabolize toxic substances.

19

A scientist who investigates how one class of molecules deactivates a particular enzyme in a cell is most likely to be a specialist in the science of

A) functional genomics

B) bioinformatics

C) cDNA synthesis

D) proteomics

20

Which choice provides the best evidence for the answer to the previous question?

A) Lines 41–46 ("The . . . cell")

B) Lines 54–57 ("There . . . create")

C) Lines 61–66 ("For . . . proteins")

D) Lines 97–103 ("Today . . . with it")

21

According to the diagrams, the number of base pairs in the MTHFR gene is

A) less than 1,000.

B) between 1,000 and 5,000.

C) between 10,000 and 50,000.

D) between 100,000 and 500,000.

CONTINUE

Questions 22–32 are based on the following passages.

Passage 1 is from Thomas Jefferson, "First Inaugural Address," given on March 4, 1801. Passage 2 is adapted from Henry Childs Merwin, *Thomas Jefferson*, first published in 1901.

Passage 1

Line

The contest of opinion being now decided by the voice of the nation, announced according to the rules of the Constitution, all will, of course, arrange themselves under the will of the law, and
5 unite in common efforts for the common good. All, too, will bear in mind this sacred principle, that though the will of the majority is in all cases to prevail, that will to be rightful must be reasonable; that the minority possess their equal rights,
10 which equal law must protect, and to violate would be oppression. Let us, then, fellow-citizens, unite with one heart and one mind. Let us restore to social intercourse that harmony and affection without which liberty and even life itself are
15 but dreary things. And let us reflect that, having banished from our land that religious intolerance under which mankind so long bled and suffered, we have yet gained little if we countenance a political intolerance as despotic, as wicked, and
20 capable of as bitter and bloody persecutions.

But every difference of opinion is not a difference of principle. We have called by different names brethren of the same principle. We are all Republicans; we are all Federalists. If there
25 be any among us who would wish to dissolve this Union or to change its republican form, let them stand undisturbed as monuments of the safety with which error of opinion may be tolerated where reason is left free to combat it. I
30 know, indeed, that some honest men fear that a republican government can not be strong, that this Government is not strong enough; but would the honest patriot, in the full tide of successful experiment, abandon a government which has
35 so far kept us free and firm on the theoretic and visionary fear that this Government, the world's best hope, may by possibility want energy to preserve itself? I trust not. I believe this, on the contrary, the strongest Government on earth. I
40 believe it the only one where every man, at the call of the law, would fly to the standard of the law, and would meet invasions of the public order as his own personal concern.

Passage 2

For the presidential election of 1800, Adams
45 was again the candidate on the Federal side, and Jefferson on the Republican side. Jefferson, by interviews, by long and numerous letters, by the commanding force of his own intellect and character, had at last welded the anti-Federal ele-
50 ments into a compact and disciplined Republican party. The contest was waged with the utmost bitterness, and especially with bitterness against Jefferson.

Above all, Jefferson was both for friends
55 and foes the embodiment of Republicanism. He represented those ideas which the Federalists, and especially the New England lawyers and clergy, really believed to be subversive of law and order, of government and religion. To them he
60 figured as "a fanatic in politics, and an atheist in religion"; and they were so disposed to believe everything bad of him that they swallowed whole the worst slanders which the political violence of the times, far exceeding that of the present day,
65 could invent.

The Federalists had a characteristic plan: they proposed to pass a law devolving the Presidency upon the chairman of the Senate, in case the office of President should become
70 vacant; and this vacancy they would be able to bring about by prolonging the election until Mr. Adams's term of office had expired. The chairman of the Senate, a Federalist, of course, would then become President. This scheme Jefferson
75 and his friends were prepared to resist by force. "Because," as he afterward explained, "that precedent once set, it would be artificially reproduced, and would soon end in a dictator."

Mr. Adams, who was deeply chagrined by
80 his defeat, did not attend the inauguration of his successor, but left Washington in his carriage,

CONTINUE

at sunrise, on the fourth of March; and Jefferson
rode on horseback to the Capitol, unattended,
and dismounting, fastened his horse to the fence
85 with his own hands. The inaugural address, brief,
and beautifully worded, surprised most of those
who heard it by the moderation and liberality of
its tone. "Let us," said the new President, "restore
to social intercourse that harmony and affection
90 without which liberty, and even life itself, are but
dreary things."

The purchase of Louisiana increased
Jefferson's popularity, and in 1805, at the age of
sixty-two, he was elected to his second term as
95 President by an overwhelming majority. Even
Massachusetts was carried by the Republicans,
and the total vote in the electoral college stood:
162 for Jefferson and Clinton; 14 for the Federal
candidates.

CONTINUE ➤

22

Which of the following best describes the relationship between the two passages?

A) Passage 2 provides the political background behind the speech Jefferson gives in Passage 1.

B) Passage 2 is a critique of the principles that Jefferson lays out in Passage 1.

C) Passage 2 describes the variety of popular opinion that greeted Jefferson's speech in Passage 1.

D) Passage 2 discusses the long-term social impacts of Jefferson's speech in Passage 1.

23

The first paragraph of Passage 1 is primarily an argument

A) for the universal value of democracy.

B) for the adoption of new Constitutional rights.

C) against the tyranny of the majority.

D) against the abandonment of religious principles.

24

As used in line 4, "arrange" most nearly means

A) assemble.

B) dispose.

C) schedule.

D) transcribe.

25

The rhetorical question in lines 29–38 ("I know . . . itself?") is an appeal to

A) perseverance in the face of uncertainty.

B) honesty in the face of political posturing.

C) reason in the face of irrationality.

D) courage in the face of adversity.

26

The list of prepositional phrases in lines 47–49 ("by interviews . . . character") represents a series of

A) scholarly talents.

B) diplomatic efforts.

C) documentary sources.

D) political principles.

27

Which choice from Passage 1 best exemplifies the "moderation and liberality" (line 87) described in Passage 2?

A) The "contest of opinion" (line 1)

B) The "sacred principle" (line 6)

C) The "will to be rightful" (line 8)

D) The "difference of principle" (lines 21–22)

28

Passage 2 indicates that the election preceding Jefferson's first inaugural speech

A) demonstrated the strength of the two-party system.

B) exemplified widespread corruption.

C) illustrated the dangers of political dynasty.

D) was dominated by scathing personal attacks.

29

Which choice provides the best evidence for the answer to the previous question?

A) Lines 44–46 ("For . . . side")

B) Lines 46–51 ("Jefferson . . . party")

C) Lines 51–53 ("The . . . Jefferson")

D) Lines 54–55 ("Above . . . Republicanism")

30

As used in line 18, "countenance" most nearly means

A) endure.

B) disrupt.

C) face.

D) tolerate.

31

Passage 1 regards radical political debate primarily as

A) essential to liberal democracy.

B) wasteful and unproductive.

C) unnecessarily bitter and divisive.

D) fundamentally disloyal.

32

Which choice provides the best evidence for the answer to the previous question?

A) Lines 24–29 ("If there . . . it")

B) Lines 29–38 (I know . . . itself?")

C) Line 38 ("I . . . not")

D) Lines 39–43 ("I believe . . . concern")

CONTINUE

Questions 33–41 are based on the following passage.

This passage is adapted from Clarence Darrow, *Crime: Its Cause and Treatment*, originally published in 1922.

Line
Neither the purpose nor the effect of punishment has ever been definitely agreed upon, even by its most strenuous advocates. No doubt the idea of punishment originated in the feeling of
5 resentment and vengeance that, to some extent at least, is incident to life. The dog is hit with a stick and turns and bites the stick. Animals repel attack and fight their enemies to death. Primitive man vented his hatred and vengeance on things
10 animate and inanimate. In tribes no injury was satisfied until some member of the offending tribe was killed. In more recent times family feuds have followed down the generations and until the last member of a family was destroyed.
15 Individuals, communities and whole peoples hate and swear vengeance for an injury, real or fancied. Whether the victim is weak or strong, old or young, sane or insane, makes no difference; men and societies react to injury exactly as
20 animals react.
Even though increasing knowledge may have somewhat softened the language of vengeance over the years, both religion and the law have found their chief justification for punishment in
25 the doctrine of revenge. Still, most people are now ashamed to admit that punishment is based on vengeance and, for that reason, various excuses and apologies have been offered for the cruelty that goes with it. Some of the more humane
30 contend that the object of this infliction is the reformation of the victim. This, of course, cannot be urged of the death penalty or even punishment for life, or for very long-term sentences. In these cases there is neither inducement to reform
35 nor any object in the reformation. No matter how thorough the reform, the prisoner never goes back to society, or he returns after there is no longer a chance to be of use to the world or to enjoy life.
Those who say that punishment is for the
40 purpose of reforming the prisoner are not familiar with human psychology. The prison almost invariably tends to brutalize men and breeds bitterness and blank despair. The life of the ordinary

prisoner is given over to criticism and resent-
45 ment against existing things, especially to settled hatred of those who are responsible for his punishment. Only a few, and these are the weakest, ever blame themselves for their situation. Every man of intelligence can trace the various steps
50 that led him to the prison door, and he can feel, if he does not understand, how inevitable each step was. The number of "repeaters" in prison shows the effect of this kind of a living death upon the inmates. To be branded as a criminal and turned
55 out in the world again leaves one weakened in the struggle of life and handicapped in a race that is hard enough for most men at the best. In prison and after leaving prison, the man lives in a world of his own; a world where all moral values are
60 different from those professed by the jailer and society in general. The great influence that helps to keep many men from committing crime—the judgment of his fellows—no longer deters him in his conduct. In fact, every person who under-
65 stands penal institutions—no matter how well such places are managed—knows that a thousand are injured or utterly destroyed by service in prison, where one is helped.
A much larger class of people offers the
70 excuse that punishment deters from crime. In fact, this idea is so well rooted that few think of questioning it. The idea means that unless A shall be punished for murder, then B will kill; therefore A must be punished, not for his sake, but to keep
75 B from crime. This is vicarious punishment and can hardly appeal to anyone who is either just or humane.
So much has been written about the decrease of crime that follows the reduction of penalties,
80 and likewise about the numerous crimes of violence that generally follow public hangings, that it is hardly necessary to recall it to the reader.
Punishment really means the infliction of pain because the individual has willfully trans-
85 gressed. Its supposed justification is that somehow the evil done is atoned for, or made good, or balanced if the author of the evil shall suffer pain. Punishment means that the suffering by the victim is the end, and it does not mean that any
90 good will grow out of the suffering.

1   **1**

33

The main purpose of the passage is to

A) highlight a political injustice.

B) argue against an irrational law.

C) question an inefficacious practice.

D) advocate a traditional viewpoint.

34

As used in line 3, "strenuous" most nearly means

A) resolute.

B) grueling.

C) strained.

D) savage.

35

The passage suggests that the desire to punish criminals is

A) the result of peer pressure.

B) a natural emotional response.

C) an imitation of animal behavior.

D) a corruption of our social instincts.

36

Which choice provides the best evidence for the answer to the previous question?

A) Lines 1–3 ("Neither . . . advocates")

B) Lines 3–6 ("No . . . life")

C) Lines 7–8 ("Animals . . . death")

D) Lines 10–12 ("In tribes . . . killed")

37

The passage argues that the use of punishment as a deterrent is

A) an abhorrent example of misplaced justice.

B) so obviously effective as to not require justification.

C) based on sound principles but marred by inept practice.

D) transparently illogical to all who consider it.

38

As used in line 78, "decrease" most nearly means

A) reduced importance.

B) lower incidence.

C) waning influence.

D) dwindling support.

39

Darrow characterizes the prison system primarily as

A) a necessary means of keeping dangerous criminals off the street.

B) a breeding ground for hostility and indignation.

C) a potentially effective instrument of criminal reform.

D) a network of unscrupulous commercial institutions.

CONTINUE ➤

40

Which choice provides the best evidence for the answer to the previous question?

A) Lines 29–31 ("Some . . . victim")

B) Lines 35–38 ("No . . . life")

C) Lines 43–47 ("The life . . . punishment")

D) Lines 57–61 ("In prison . . . general")

41

In lines 78–82 ("So much . . . reader") Darrow is asserting that

A) The number of books that have been written about prison reform is overwhelming.

B) The public has grown weary of reading about increasing rates of crime.

C) There is clear evidence against the effectiveness of punishment as a deterrent.

D) The inhumanity of capital punishment is well established.

Questions 42–52 are based on the following passage.

This passage is adapted from Sidney Perkowitz, "Light Dawns." Originally published in *Aeon* magazine (aeon. co), September 18, 2015.

Line   We have now fixed the speed of light in a vacuum, c, at exactly 299,792.458 kilometers per second. Why this particular speed and not something else? Or, to put it another way, where does
5   the speed of light come from?

       Electromagnetic theory gave a first crucial insight 150 years ago. The Scottish physicist James Clerk Maxwell showed that when electric and magnetic fields change in time, they interact
10   to produce an electromagnetic wave. Maxwell calculated the speed of the wave from his equations and found it to be exactly the known speed of light. This suggested that light was an electromagnetic wave—as was soon confirmed.

15   A further breakthrough came in 1905, when Albert Einstein showed that c is the universal speed limit. According to his Special Theory of Relativity, nothing can move faster. So, thanks to Maxwell and Einstein, we know that the speed
20   of light is connected with a number of other phenomena in surprising ways.

       But neither theory fully explains what determines that speed. What might? According to new research, the secret of c can be found in
25   the nature of empty space. Until quantum theory came along, electromagnetism was the complete theory of light. It remains tremendously important and useful, but it raises a question. To calculate the speed of light in a vacuum, Maxwell used
30   empirically measured values for two constants, called ε_0 and μ_0, that define the electric and magnetic properties of empty space.

       The thing is, in a vacuum, it's not clear that these numbers should mean anything. After all,
35   electricity and magnetism actually arise from the behavior of charged elementary particles such as electrons. But if we're talking about empty space, there shouldn't be any particles in there, should there? This is where quantum physics enters.
40   In the advanced version called quantum field

theory, a vacuum is never really empty. It is the "vacuum state," the lowest energy of a quantum system, in which quantum fluctuations produce evanescent energies and elementary particles.

45   What's a quantum fluctuation? Heisenberg's Uncertainty Principle states that there is always some indefiniteness associated with physical measurements. According to classical physics, we can know exactly the position and momentum
50   of, for example, a billiard ball at rest. But this is precisely what the Uncertainty Principle denies. According to Heisenberg, we can't accurately know both at the same time. It's as if the ball quivered or jittered slightly relative to the fixed
55   values we think it has. These fluctuations are too small to make much difference at the human scale; but in a quantum vacuum, they produce tiny bursts of energy or (equivalently) matter, in the form of elementary particles that rapidly pop
60   in and out of existence.

       These short-lived phenomena might seem to be a ghostly form of reality. But they do have measurable effects, including electromagnetic ones. That's because these fleeting excitations of
65   the quantum vacuum appear as pairs of particles and antiparticles with equal and opposite electric charge, such as electrons and positrons. An electric field applied to the vacuum distorts these pairs to produce an electric response, and a
70   magnetic field affects them to create a magnetic response. This behavior gives us a way to *calculate*, not just measure, the electromagnetic properties of the quantum vacuum and, from them, to derive the value of c.

75   Whether the "constants" like c and G (the constant that dictates the behavior of gravity) are really constant throughout the universe is an ancient philosophical controversy. Aristotle believed that the Earth was differently consti-
80   tuted from the heavens. Copernicus held that our local piece of the universe is just like any other part of it. Today, science follows the modern Copernican view, assuming that the laws of physics are the same everywhere in space-time. But
85   this assumption needs to be tested, especially for G and c, to make sure we are not misinterpreting what we observe in the distant universe.

CONTINUE ▶

1   **1**

Nobel Laureate Paul Dirac raised the possibility that *G* might vary over time. In 1937, cos-
90 mological considerations led him to suggest that
it decreases by about one part in 10 billion per
year. Was he right? Probably not. Observations of
astronomical bodies under gravity do not show
this decrease, and so far there is no sign that *G*

95 varies in space. Similarly, there seems to be no
credible evidence that *c* varies in space or time.
Determining these values to such astonishing accuracy is tremendously useful to scientists,
but their apparent arbitrariness drives physicists
100 mad. Why these numbers? Couldn't they have
been different?

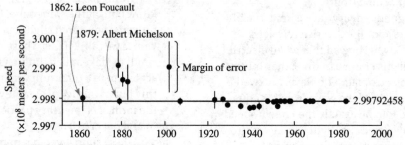

History of Experimental Estimates of the Speed of Light

Source: C. F. Black and College Hill Coaching.

42

The primary purpose of the passage is to

A) describe the development of a scientific theory.

B) investigate some unresolved scientific conundrums.

C) explore the implications of a fruitful scientific discovery.

D) recount a history of ever more accurate scientific measurements.

43

As used in line 1, "fixed" most nearly means

A) repaired.

B) focused.

C) established.

D) prepared.

44

According to the passage, Maxwell's calculations were problematic primarily because they

A) included dubious numbers.

B) were based on an impractical theory.

C) did not match experimental evidence.

D) suggested that light acts as a wave.

45

Which choice provides the best evidence for the answer to the previous question?

A) Lines 13–14 ("This . . . confirmed")

B) Lines 33–34 ("The thing . . . anything")

C) Lines 45–48 ("Heisenberg's . . . measurements")

D) Lines 75–78 ("Whether . . . controversy")

46

The graph shows historical variations in the estimated values for the speed of light. The author would most likely attribute these variations to

A) quantum fluctuations in a vacuum.

B) changes in the speed of light over time.

C) increased experimental precision over time.

D) the wave-like behavior of light.

47

Which choice provides the best evidence for the answer to the previous question?

A) Lines 13–14 ("This . . . confirmed")

B) Lines 45–48 ("Heisenberg's . . . measurements")

C) Lines 75–78 ("Whether . . . controversy")

D) Lines 95–96 ("Similarly . . . time")

48

Which choice provides the best translation of the question "where does the speed of light come from?" in lines 4–5?

A) How have scientists been able to derive an accurate estimate of the speed of light from known equations?

B) What theoretical and technical advances have enabled scientists to measure the speed of light so precisely?

C) What fundamental properties of the physical universe can be used to determine the speed of light?

D) What accounts for such a strange physical constant in an otherwise orderly universe?

1   **1**

49

The passage discusses quantum fluctuations primarily to make the point that

A) light behaves in a surprisingly unpredictable manner.

B) the physical properties of space itself can explain the speed of light.

C) there are upper limits to the accuracy of any measurement of the speed of light.

D) Maxwell's method for calculating the speed of light was fundamentally flawed.

50

As used in line 82, "follows" most nearly means

A) comes sequentially after.

B) pays close attention to.

C) acts in accordance with.

D) serves as a logical consequence of.

51

The author mentions Aristotle in order to make the point that

A) questions about the speed of light are ancient.

B) careful scientists do not assume the universality of physical laws.

C) ancient thinkers would likely be baffled by modern quantum theory.

D) pre-Copernican theories of the universe have been thoroughly disproven.

52

According to the graph, which choice is the most accurate statement about Leon Foucault's and Albert Michelson's estimates of the speed of light?

A) Michelson's estimate was more accurate and more precise.

B) Michelson's estimate was less accurate and more precise.

C) Michelson's estimate was more accurate and less precise.

D) Michelson's estimate was less accurate and less precise.

STOP

**If you finish before time is called, you may check your work on this section only.
Do not turn to any other section of the test.**

Writing and Language Test
35 MINUTES, 44 QUESTIONS

Turn to Section 2 of your answer sheet to answer the questions in this section.

DIRECTIONS

Each passage below is accompanied by a number of questions. For some questions, you will consider how the passage might be revised to improve the expression of ideas. For other questions, you will consider how the passage might be edited to correct errors in sentence structure, usage, or punctuation. A passage or a question may be accompanied by one or more graphics (such as a table or graph) that you will consider as you make revising and editing decisions.

Some questions will direct you to an underlined portion of a passage. Other questions will direct you to a location in a passage or ask you to think about the passage as a whole.

After reading each passage, choose the answer to each question that most effectively improves the quality of writing in the passage or that makes the passage conform to the conventions of standard written English. Many questions include a "NO CHANGE" option. Choose that option if you think the best choice is to leave the relevant portion of the passage as it is.

CONTINUE ▶

2   2

Questions 1–11 are based on the following passage.

Where Does the Vice President Live?

Although many of our nation's founders wanted to avoid anything associated with monarchism, they recognized that one of **1** it's benefits was the lack of civil struggles over succession. **2** Then they established that the executive branch would include a Vice **3** President who would have no particular role except to take command if the President dies, resigns, or is removed from office. As Vice President Gerald Ford noted, "The vice presidency throughout our history has been an office that invites argument and defies definition." Ben Franklin quipped that the Vice President should be addressed as "Your Superfluous Excellency."

Few things indicate the Vice President's undefined position **4** so well as the official residence. Many people assume that the Vice President has quarters in the White House. The **5** truth, being laughable if it was not so pathetic, is that until 1974 the Vice President had no official residence at all.

1

A) NO CHANGE
B) its
C) they're
D) their

2

A) NO CHANGE
B) In so doing,
C) Nevertheless,
D) Accordingly,

3

A) NO CHANGE
B) President to have
C) President, thereby having
D) President; who would have

4

A) NO CHANGE
B) as like
C) as it does
D) better, than

5

A) NO CHANGE
B) truth would be laughable if not so pathetic, is
C) truth, which would be laughable if it were not so pathetic, is
D) truth, being laughable if not so pathetic, is

CONTINUE ➡

2

2

Before 1974, Vice Presidents lived wherever they could find lodging. Some, especially former Senators or Congressman, already had homes near Washington, D.C., and some were wealthy enough to buy temporary homes. Others actually stayed in hotels. **6** Finally, in July of 1974, Congress **7** denigrated the house at One Observatory Circle in Washington, D.C., as the official residence of the Vice President.

8 Completely renovated, Gerald Ford was the first Vice President expected to live in the beautiful 19th Century home. Then the soap opera continued.

6

At this point, the writer is considering adding the following sentence.

> In 1922, when Vice President Calvin Coolidge's hotel residence caught fire, the fire marshal did not recognize him or even know that he lived at the hotel.

Should the author make this addition here?

A) Yes, because it reveals the difficulty of finding housing in the 1920s.

B) Yes, because it illustrates the relatively low status that the Vice President had.

C) No, because it interrupts the discussion about the variety of housing options enjoyed by Vice Presidents.

D) No, because it distracts from the generally lighthearted nature of the discussion.

7

A) NO CHANGE

B) designed

C) designated

D) derogated

8

A) NO CHANGE

B) Gerald Ford was the first Vice President expected to live in the beautiful and completely renovated 19th century home.

C) The beautiful and completely renovated 19th century home was expected to be lived in by Gerald Ford as the first Vice President.

D) It was Gerald Ford who was expected to live in the beautiful 19th century home, being completely renovated.

CONTINUE ➤

[9] Next, before Ford could move into the residence, President Richard Nixon resigned and left the presidency to him. Then, Nelson Rockefeller was chosen by Ford as the next Vice President. However, Rockefeller already owned a residence in Washington, D.C., so he used the house only for official entertaining. After waiting 198 years for an official domicile, the office of Vice President [10] would have to wait yet another three years before establishing One Observatory Circle as a functioning residence. Walter Mondale, who became vice-president in 1977, was the first to claim the house as a true home.

The United States Navy still officially owns One Observatory Circle and is [11] in charge both of maintenance and staff. In fact, to this day, many people refer to the official residence of the Vice President as "The Admiral's House."

9

Which choice most logically and effectively combines the two sentences?

A) Before being able to move into the residence, President Richard Nixon resigned and left the presidency to Ford, who chose Nelson Rockefeller as the next Vice President.

B) Before Ford could move into the residence, President Richard Nixon resigned and left the presidency to Ford, who then chose Nelson Rockefeller as the next Vice President.

C) But President Richard Nixon resigned and left the presidency to Ford before he could move into the residence, choosing Nelson Rockefeller as the next Vice President.

D) When President Richard Nixon resigned and left the presidency to Ford, it was before he could move into the residence, and he chose Nelson Rockefeller as the next Vice President.

10

A) NO CHANGE

B) yet would have to be waiting

C) yet had to be waiting

D) had to be waiting yet

11

A) NO CHANGE

B) both in charge of maintenance and staff

C) in charge of both maintenance and of staff

D) in charge of both maintenance and staff

2

2

2

Questions 12–22 are based on the following passage.

"Truth Will Out"

Having been a personal recruiter for over sixteen years, **12** my job can basically be defined as getting other people jobs. I have to screen applicants and check backgrounds and references, but that's just the beginning. I also have to search for both applicants and opportunities, and then try to find the most suitable matches. Next, I must get to know my client intimately, and this step generally gives me the best opportunity **13** of determining a successful match. To accomplish this, I must establish transparency in our relationship. At this point, I'm sometimes not sure if I'm so much a recruiter as a detective or a psychological profiler, **14** a professional who is often called in to analyze the behavior patterns of criminals.

My first piece of advice to all **15** applicants, no—my urgent plea; sounds ridiculously banal: be yourself. **16** Extenuate your uniqueness, but be honest. You want a job that's a good match for you, not for your imaginary friend. Don't force yourself into a job with a culture that doesn't fit your personality.

12

A) NO CHANGE
B) I can basically define my job as
C) the definition of my job can basically be
D) I can basically define my job as:

13

A) NO CHANGE
B) of making a determination of
C) to determine
D) to make a determination of

14

The writer is considering deleting this phrase and ending the sentence with a period. Should the writer do this?

A) Yes, because the reference to criminality detracts from the point of the paragraph.
B) Yes, because the role of a psychological profiler has already been established.
C) No, because this definition provides information that is used in the next paragraph.
D) No, because clarifying job descriptions is an important task of a personal recruiter.

15

A) NO CHANGE
B) applicants: no, my urgent plea—sounds
C) applicants—no, my urgent plea—sounds
D) applicants: no, my urgent plea, sounds

16

A) NO CHANGE
B) Effectuate
C) Attenuate
D) Accentuate

CONTINUE ▶

2   2

If you are really a person who "marches to a different drummer," **17** you need a kindred spirit as a boss. If not, you'll find yourself with a manager who will turn and run when you reveal your true self—and simultaneously **18** oust you out the door in the opposite direction.

19 Additionally, if you find that place where you can be yourself and do your job your own way, as long as the job gets done well, then you will find the key to professional satisfaction. When we do what comes naturally to us, we excel.

17

Which choice best connects this sentence with the rest of the paragraph?

A) NO CHANGE

B) you might consider dressing more professionally for your interview.

C) learn how to exaggerate your uniqueness to make a strong impression.

D) stay away from discussions about personal likes and dislikes, and keep things professional.

18

Which choice best maintains the logic and clarity of the sentence?

A) NO CHANGE

B) throw

C) banish

D) urge

19

A) NO CHANGE

B) However,

C) Furthermore,

D) Simultaneously,

2   **2**

I also have a strong corollary to my first doctrine: don't think you can hide an uncomfortable truth forever! I often must work hard to [20] gloss over all of the information I need from a candidate in order to make sure that he or she is right for the job. But getting a candidate to share relevant but uncomfortable facts is not easy. Before I recommend someone with an otherwise stellar resumé for a position, I need to fill in the blanks. For example, why is there is a two year gap in employment? Why did a relocation to another city never happen as expected? [21] A candidate should reveal any such relevant secrets before it becomes too late to smooth them out. [22] Take it from me: surprises like these on a background or credit check will guarantee that an offer of employment will be rescinded.

20

Which choice best maintains the logical and stylistic coherence of the paragraph?

A) NO CHANGE

B) ferret out

C) rifle through

D) speculate about

21

At this point, the writer is considering adding the following sentence.

> Does a driving record include anything embarrassing, such as a DWI conviction?

Should the writer make this addition?

A) Yes, because it gives a specific example of the effects of withholding information from an employer.

B) Yes, because it indicates a particularly serious detail that could be relevant to an employer.

C) No, because it detracts from the paragraph's focus on creating a "stellar resumé."

D) No, because it does not indicate a concern that would be embarrassing to most people.

22

Which choice best provides a relevant concluding thought to the paragraph?

A) NO CHANGE

B) The job of a personal recruiter entails much more than finding positions and applicants.

C) Many jobs and many applicants are not all they might appear to be at first glance.

D) Potential employees should be very wary of job descriptions that seem to good to be true.

CONTINUE ▶

Questions 23–33 are based on the following passage and supplementary material.

Don't Play Chicken with Your Health

Many people today want to avoid disease and help the environment by living "organically" and eating "unprocessed" foods. These goals are fine in theory, but not always **23** feasible or possible to achieve.

Almost every day, stories in the media **24** would seem to feature a new exposé about product mislabeling or corrupt marketing in the organic foods supply world. **25** Distrust in this food supply is growing. An increasing number of people, especially urbanites without access to farmers' markets, are choosing to become their own food suppliers. Although urban vegetable gardens have been popular for a very long time, this

23

A) NO CHANGE
B) possible to feasibly achieve
C) feasible or possible to achieve
D) feasible to achieve

24

A) NO CHANGE
B) seem
C) seems
D) have seemed

25

Which choice most effectively combines the two sentences?

A) As distrust in the food supply grows, an increasing number of people, especially urbanites without access to farmers' markets, are choosing to become their own food suppliers.

B) An increasing number of people, especially urbanites without access to farmers' markets, have growing distrust in the food supply, but they're choosing to become their own food suppliers.

C) An increasing number of people, especially urbanites, are choosing to become their own food suppliers because of growing distrust in the food supply and not having access to farmers' markets.

D) As distrust is growing in the food supply, especially in urbanites without access to farmers' markets, an increasing number of people are choosing to become their own food suppliers.

2   **2**

new desire for natural products **26** <u>unconsumed</u> by hormone additives, dangerous chemicals, or **27** <u>pesticides has</u> created a new trend in "natural living": backyard or rooftop chicken-keeping. Many urban hen farmers have recently undertaken to change municipal livestock **28** <u>restrictions, so this</u> is where the situation gets interesting. Back in the 1800s, many American cities banned urban livestock, primarily for health reasons. Because of the recent growth of the natural foods movement, **29** <u>we should return our focus to the sanitation of urban farming</u>.

26

A) NO CHANGE

B) unrestrained

C) untainted

D) deprived

27

A) NO CHANGE

B) pesticides, has

C) pesticides have

D) pesticides, have

28

A) NO CHANGE

B) restrictions, this

C) restrictions; and this

D) restrictions, and this

29

Which choice most effectively sets up the paragraph that follows?

A) NO CHANGE

B) we must examine the conditions of these early farms to understand why these bans were enacted.

C) we can't be sure whether such laws now need to be strengthened or abandoned.

D) we must not impose excessive restrictions on such a demonstrably healthful practice.

CONTINUE ➔

Our eagerness for "fresher" food should not override our concerns about potential health risks. If not correctly managed, urban agriculture can be unhygienic. *Salmonella*, a bacterium that lives in the intestines of poultry, can be a major issue.

[30] But *Salmonella* is only one of many potentially dangerous germs lurking in urban farms. The *Salmonella* bacteria can contaminate anything the infected birds touch, and then transfer to the hands, shoes, or clothing of those [31] who handle the birds or even if they just work or play around the birds' habitats. Although backyard poultry is no more likely to be contaminated with *Salmonella* than commercial poultry is, it does put more vulnerable citizens at risk, because there are so few safeguards between the birds and the public.

A surprising number of urban citizens are in favor of allowing the ownership of chickens within city limits. In a 2013 government survey, [32] over two-thirds of those urban citizens surveyed from around the country said that they were at least somewhat in agreement with the statement "I would be in favor of a law in my community that allows for the ownership of chickens." It seems likely, then, that more cities will start to ratify more open urban farming laws.

[30]

At this point, the author wants to include information that underscores the particularly insidious nature of *Salmonella*. Which choice best accomplishes this goal?

A) NO CHANGE

B) The treatment for *Salmonella* typically includes antibiotics and intravenous hydration.

C) *Salmonella* affects nearly 40,000 people per year in the United States, although most recover without treatment.

D) Although *Salmonella* usually doesn't make birds sick, it can cause serious illness in humans, to whom it is passed with amazing ease.

[31]

A) NO CHANGE

B) who play, work, or even just handle the birds

C) who handle the birds, or even just work or play

D) handling the birds, or even if they just play or work

[32]

At this point, the writer wants to provide accurate and relevant information from the table. Which choice best accomplishes this goal?

A) NO CHANGE

B) slightly less than two-thirds

C) slightly more than half

D) well over one-third

CONTINUE ➤

2

2

This could be a good thing, as long as proper sanitary regulations are also **33** found. Farming is not a game or a hobby, and rooftop hens are not pets. The urban farmer must be even more vigilant than the commercial farmer when it comes to hygiene, because the risks are even greater.

33

A) NO CHANGE

B) appropriated

C) bequeathed

D) adopted

Percent Responses to the Statement, "I am in favor of a law in my community that allows for the ownership of chickens" in Select American Cities (2013)					
	Denver	Los Angeles	Miami	New York	All Cities
Strongly Agree	26.1	17.5	14.6	13.9	16.9
Agree	23.8	14.1	12.6	15.4	15.7
Slightly Agree	12.6	11.4	9.1	12.6	11.8
Slightly Disagree	5.7	8.4	5.5	7.9	7.6
Disagree	10.6	12.4	14.2	15.9	13.6
Strongly Disagree	21.2	36.2	44.0	34.3	34.4

Source: U.S. Department of Agriculture, Animal and Plant Health Inspection Services

CONTINUE ➤

2   **2**

Questions 34–44 are based on the following passage.

Guernica

Already the world's most influential artist, **34** Pablo Picasso's painting, "Guernica," earned him a reputation as a political critic as well. Picasso created his mural for the Spanish pavilion of the 1937 Paris *Exposición Internacional*. The theme of the *Exposición* was modern technology, and Picasso used that theme to condemn the evils of modern weaponry. **35** He made his subject out of the Nazi and Italian bombing of Guernica, an ancient civilian town in Basque, Spain. The Axis powers believed that this rural town would be a perfect target to test new techniques of aerial bombing. During the attack of about three hours, bombers **36** destroyed the town and then flew low over neighboring fields, machine-gunning townspeople who were running to safety. **37** Thus implementing the Nazi strategy of terror bombing, deliberately targeting civilians in order to break their will to resist.

34

A) NO CHANGE

B) "Guernica," a painting by Pablo Picasso, earned him a reputation as a political critic as well.

C) Pablo Picasso, who earned a reputation as a political critic as well by painting "Guernica."

D) Pablo Picasso earned a reputation as a political critic as well by painting "Guernica."

35

A) NO CHANGE

B) His subject was

C) The subject he made was

D) His subject was of

36

A) NO CHANGE

B) had destroyed

C) were destroying

D) would destroy

37

A) NO CHANGE

B) This implemented

C) This tactic implemented

D) Thus implementing the tactic for

2   2

News reports and photographs of the atrocities quickly reached Paris, where they motivated Picasso to create his masterpiece. **38** He began painting just six days after the bombing, Picasso completed his huge mural, 11½ feet tall by 25½ feet long, in only 5 weeks.

39 In "Guernica," Picasso intended to depict, in vivid detail, the inhumanity and suffering of war. Instead, he used graphic shapes and symbolic figures to **40** make the sense of agony caused by the brutality and violence of the event. Today, most **41** critic's studying the painting agree that Picasso's distorted images are at least as poignant as the horrible photographs of the event.

38

A) NO CHANGE
B) He had begun painting
C) His painting began
D) Beginning his painting

39

Which choice most effectively sets up the information that follows?

A) NO CHANGE
B) Picasso did not intend "Guernica" to be a historically accurate depiction of the attack.
C) Picasso's raw emotional energy came through in the faces of his subjects.
D) Picasso used "Guernica" to showcase the new techniques of Cubist painting.

40

A) NO CHANGE
B) explain
C) balance
D) evoke

41

A) NO CHANGE
B) critics study
C) critics studying
D) critic's study of

CONTINUE ➤

2   2

Figures are **42** <u>squished</u> together: a screaming mother holding a dead child, a disembodied arm holding a lamp, an open-eyed corpse, a screaming bull with a strangely human face, an impaled horse.

The multi-perspective vision of Cubism allowed Picasso to dissect figures and backgrounds and re-integrate them to create new, more intense images. He believed that Cubism allowed him to see new relation-ships among time, space, and energy, **43** <u>like Einstein with Relativity</u>. In his own way, Picasso created a modern visual language, a language that **44** <u>few of his contemporaries were able to successfully emulate</u>.

42

Which choice best maintains the tone and style of the passage?

A) NO CHANGE

B) mushed

C) crushed

D) scrunched

43

A) NO CHANGE

B) in much the same way as Relativity allowed Einstein similar insights

C) like Relativity and what it did for Einstein

D) like what Relativity did for Einstein

44

Which choice provides the most suitable conclusion for the passage as a whole?

A) NO CHANGE

B) can portray subtle beauty as well as the horrors of war.

C) provides new ways of portraying images of animals, people, and events.

D) continues to influence the way that contemporary artists see the world.

STOP

**If you finish before time is called, you may check your work on this section only.
Do not turn to any other section of the test.**

3   3

Math Test—No Calculator
25 MINUTES, 20 QUESTIONS

Turn to Section 3 of your answer sheet to answer the questions in this section.

DIRECTIONS

For questions 1–15, solve each problem, choose the best answer from the choices provided, and fill in the corresponding circle on your answer sheet. **For questions 16–20**, solve the problem and enter your answer in the grid on the answer sheet. Please refer to the directions before question 16 on how to enter your answers in the grid. You may use any available space in your test booklet for scratch work.

NOTES

1. The use of a calculator **is not permitted**.
2. All variables and expressions used represent real numbers unless otherwise indicated.
3. Figures provided in this test are drawn to scale unless otherwise indicated.
4. All figures lie in a plane unless otherwise indicated.
5. Unless otherwise indicated, the domain of a given function f is the set of all real numbers x for which $f(x)$ is a real number.

Reference

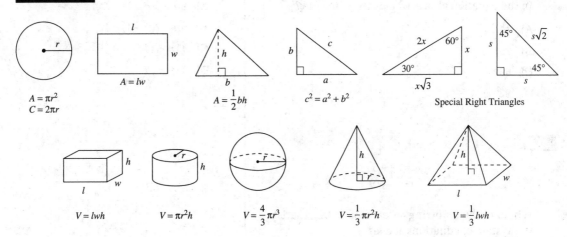

$A = \pi r^2$
$C = 2\pi r$

$A = lw$

$A = \frac{1}{2}bh$

$c^2 = a^2 + b^2$

Special Right Triangles

$V = lwh$

$V = \pi r^2 h$

$V = \frac{4}{3}\pi r^3$

$V = \frac{1}{3}\pi r^2 h$

$V = \frac{1}{3}lwh$

The number of degrees of arc in a circle is 360.
The number of radians of arc in a circle is 2π.
The sum of the measures in degrees of the angles of a triangle is 180.

CONTINUE ➡

3 **3**

1

If $2(x+2)=3x-1$, what is the value of x?

A) 5

B) 3

C) $\dfrac{5}{6}$

D) $\dfrac{3}{8}$

2

If $\dfrac{1}{2}x+\dfrac{1}{3}y=7$, what is the value of $6x+4y$?

A) 21

B) 42

C) 84

D) 128

3

$$\frac{3(k-5)}{4}=\frac{5+2k}{3}$$

In the equation above, what is the value of k?

A) 14

B) 29

C) 65

D) 82

4

$$x=5y+5$$
$$2x-y=19$$

Which of the following ordered pairs (x, y) satisfies the system of equations above?

A) (1, 10)

B) (1, 5)

C) (10, 15)

D) (10, 1)

5

Dosages of children's medications are calculated by the child's weight. The dosage of amoxicillin for a one year-old child is 40 milligrams per kilogram of body weight per day. Which of the following functions models the dosage, d, in milligrams of amoxicillin per day for a one-year-old child weighing p pounds? (1 kilogram = 2.2 pounds)

A) $d=2.2p+40$

B) $d=2.2(40p)$

C) $d=\dfrac{2.2p}{40}$

D) $d=\dfrac{40p}{2.2}$

6

Calvin is hanging photographs that are 9 inches wide in a horizontal row, and he wants 2 inches of space between the photographs. He wants to create the display with no more than 12 feet between the outmost edges of the first and last photographs. Which inequality expresses the number, n, of these photographs Calvin can include in the display?

A) $9n+2(n-1)\le 144$

B) $9n+2(n-1)\le 12$

C) $11n\le 144$

D) $11n\le 12$

CONTINUE ▶

3   3

7

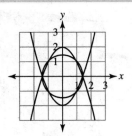

$$y = x^2 - 2$$
$$y = 2 - x^2$$
$$x^2 + y^2 = 2$$

The system of three equations shown above is graphed in the xy-plane. How many solutions does this system have?

A) Zero

B) Two

C) Four

D) Six

8

$$\left(\frac{1}{10} + \frac{1}{5}\right)x = 1$$

Mr. Hong has two hoses available to fill a pool. The blue hose alone can fill his pool in 10 hours. The red hose can fill the pool in half that time. Mr. Hong wonders how long it would take to fill the pool using both hoses at once. The equation above describes this situation. Which of the following is the best interpretation of x in this equation?

A) The rate, in pools per hour, at which both hoses together fill the pool

B) The number of hours it takes to fill the pool using both hoses

C) The number of pools that both hoses, working together, can fill in one hour

D) The total number of gallons of water required to fill the pool

---

9

$$2i^2 + 3i^3 - 4i^4 + 5i^5$$

Which of the following is equivalent to the complex number shown above? ($i = \sqrt{-1}$)

A) $-6 - 8i$

B) $-6 + 2i$

C) $2 + 2i$

D) $2 + 8i$

10

In a certain sequence, each term after the first term is 4 less than three times the previous term. The third term of the sequence is 20. What is the sum of the second term and the fourth term?

A) 2

B) 48

C) 56

D) 64

11

$$f(x) = x^3 + 2x^2 - 16x - 32$$
$$g(x) = x^2 + 6x + 8$$

When $y = f(x)$ and $y = g(x)$ are graphed together on the xy-plane, the graph of $y = f(x)$ passes through both x-intercepts of the graph of $y = g(x)$. Which of the following ordered pairs (x, y) is the third x-intercept of $y = f(x)$?

A) $(2, 0)$

B) $(4, 0)$

C) $(-8, 0)$

D) $(-10, 0)$

CONTINUE ➔

3　　　　　　　　　　　　　　　　**3**

12

If $x = a^2 - b^2$ and $y = 2a - 2b$, where $a \neq b$, which of the following is equal to $\dfrac{10x}{y}$?

A) 5

B) $5a - b$

C) $5a - 5b$

D) $5a + 5b$

13

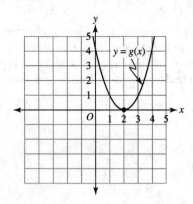

The figure above shows the graph of quadratic function $y = g(x)$ in the xy-plane. If this graph were shifted up one unit, it would coincide with the function $y = h(x)$ (not shown). Which of the following is the equation that defines $h(x)$?

A) $h(x) = (x - 2)^2 + 1$

B) $h(x) = (x + 2)^2 + 1$

C) $h(x) = (x - 1)^2 + 1$

D) $h(x) = x^2 + 3$

14

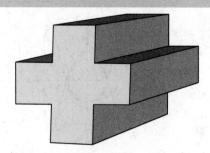

The metal beam shown above is a right prism with parallel faces in the shape of a cross. Each cross-shaped face of is composed of five identical squares, each with a side length of 6 inches. If the beam has a depth of 72 inches, what is the volume, in cubic <u>feet</u>, of the beam? (1 foot = 12 inches)

A) 1.5 cubic feet

B) 7.5 cubic feet

C) 10.8 cubic feet

D) 12.9 cubic feet

15

$$4^{4x} = 64a^4$$

In the equation above, x and a are positive numbers. If $2^{2x} = na$, what is the value of n?

A) 2

B) $\sqrt{6}$

C) $\sqrt{8}$

D) 4

---

3 **3**

DIRECTIONS

For questions 16–20, solve the problem and enter your answer in the grid, as described below, on the answer sheet.

1. Although not required, it is suggested that you write your answer in the boxes at the top of the columns to help you fill in the circles accurately. You will receive credit only if the circles are filled in correctly.

2. Mark no more than one circle in any column.

3. No question has a negative answer.

4. Some problems may have more than one correct answer. In such cases, grid only one answer.

5. **Mixed numbers** such as $3\frac{1}{2}$ must be gridded as 3.5 or $\frac{7}{2}$.

   (If $3\frac{1}{2}$ is entered into the grid as 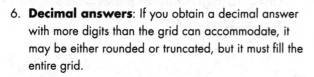, it will be interpreted as $\frac{31}{2}$, not $3\frac{1}{2}$.)

6. **Decimal answers**: If you obtain a decimal answer with more digits than the grid can accommodate, it may be either rounded or truncated, but it must fill the entire grid.

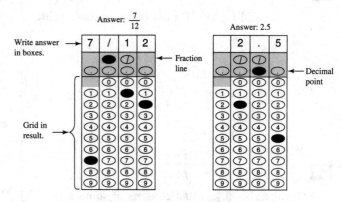

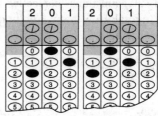

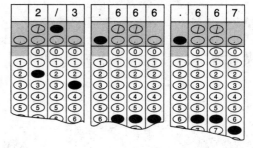

CONTINUE

3   **3**

16

If $t^2 = 5t$ and $t = 2x - 1$, what is one possible value of x?

17

Alliyah takes a test that consists of some 3-point questions and some 5-point questions. She answered 20 questions correctly, and earned 86 points in total. How many 5-point questions did she answer correctly?

18

If $\dfrac{x}{x^2 - 9} - \dfrac{1}{x+3} = \dfrac{1}{4x-12}$, what is the value of x?

19

$$m^2 + 5 = x$$
$$9y^2 = x - 5$$

Based on the system of equations above, what is the value of $\left|\dfrac{m}{y}\right|$?

20

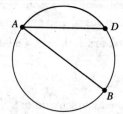

Segment AB is a diameter of the circle above, and $AB = \dfrac{20}{\pi}$. If the measure of $\angle BAD$ is $\dfrac{\pi}{5}$ radians, what is the length of arc AD?

STOP

If you finish before time is called, you may check your work on this section only.
Do not turn to any other section of the test.

4 **4**

Math Test—Calculator

55 MINUTES, 38 QUESTIONS

Turn to Section 4 of your answer sheet to answer the questions in this section.

DIRECTIONS

For questions 1–30, solve each problem, choose the best answer from the choices provided, and fill in the corresponding circle on your answer sheet. **For questions 31–38,** solve the problem and enter your answer in the grid on the answer sheet. Please refer to the directions before question 31 on how to enter your answers in the grid. You may use any available space in your test booklet for scratch work.

NOTES

1. The use of a calculator **is permitted**.
2. All variables and expressions used represent real numbers unless otherwise indicated.
3. Figures provided in this test are drawn to scale unless otherwise indicated.
4. All figures lie in a plane unless otherwise indicated.
5. Unless otherwise indicated, the domain of a given function f is the set of all real numbers for which $f(x)$ is a real number.

REFERENCE

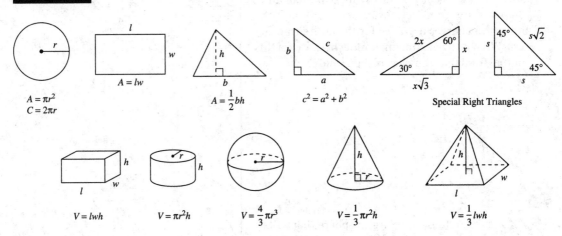

The number of degrees of arc in a circle is 360.
The number of radians of arc in a circle is 2π.
The sum of the measures in degrees of the angles of a triangle is 180.

CONTINUE

4 **4**

1

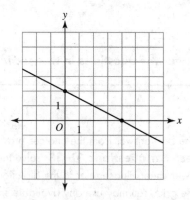

Which of the following is an equation representing the line shown in the figure above?

A) $y = \frac{1}{2}x + 2$

B) $3x + 6y = 12$

C) $y = -2x + 2$

D) $3y = 6x + 12$

2

Gretchen has $4,000 to invest in a mutual fund. Shares of the fund cost $3.19 per share, and the brokerage charges a $75 fee for the entire transaction. What is the maximum number of shares of this mutual fund that Gretchen can purchase?

A) 53

B) 1,179

C) 1,230

D) 1,231

3

What is the radius of the largest sphere that will fit inside a cube with a volume of 64 cubic inches?

A) 2 inches

B) 3 inches

C) 4 inches

D) 6 inches

4

If the function $f(x) = x^3 - x^2 + px - 3$ has a zero at $x = 1$, what is the value of p?

A) 3

B) 1

C) 0

D) −3

5

1, 2, 3, 4, 5

How many pairs of different numbers, chosen from the list above, have a sum that is odd?

A) Four

B) Five

C) Six

D) Seven

CONTINUE ▶

4 **4**

Questions 6 and 7 refer to the following information.

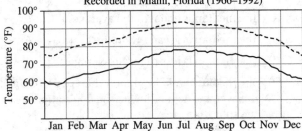

Average Daily High and Low Temperatures Recorded in Miami, Florida (1966–1992)

The graph above shows average daily high and low temperatures recorded in Miami, Florida, during the years 1966–1992.

6

In the period between 1966 and 1992, during which of the following months was the average daily low temperature in Miami, Florida, closest to 75°F?

A) January

B) April

C) October

D) November

7

In the month for which the average daily high temperature in Miami was closest to 80°F, what was the average daily low temperature for the month?

A) 60°F

B) 63°F

C) 72°F

D) 74°F

8

Which of the following inequalities is equivalent to $-3x - 5y < 4y - 6$?

A) $x < -3y - 2$

B) $x > -3y + 2$

C) $x < 3y - 2$

D) $x > 3y + 2$

9

Anton's lemonade juice machine squeezes lemons at a constant rate of 75 lemons per hour. His brother, Luigi, has a lemonade juice machine that squeezes lemons at a constant rate of 80 lemons per hour. How many more <u>minutes</u> does it take Anton's machine to squeeze 40 lemons than it takes Luigi's machine?

A) 2

B) 3

C) 4

D) 5

CONTINUE

4 **4**

Questions 10 and 11 refer to the following information.

The histogram below shows the proportion of households in a large suburban area that own a certain number of dogs.

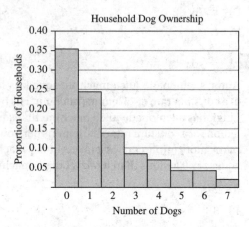

Household Dog Ownership

10

According to a local ordinance, no household in this area may own more than 3 dogs. What is the approximate percentage of households in this area that are in violation of the ordinance?

A) 9%

B) 17%

C) 26%

D) 83%

11

Using the data in the histogram, a researcher calculates the median number of dogs per household and the average number of dogs per household for this suburban area. Based on the graph, which of the following statements must be true?

A) The median is equal to the average.

B) The median is greater than the average.

C) The median is less than the average.

D) The median could be greater than or less than the average, depending on the population of the suburban area.

12

Graham University admits one-third of those who apply, and of those admitted, 40% enroll. In 2013, a total of 46,815 students applied to Graham University. Which of the following is the best estimate of the number of students who will be admitted but will <u>not</u> enroll?

A) 6,242

B) 9,363

C) 15,605

D) 18,726

CONTINUE

13

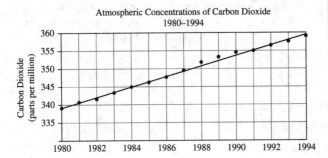

Atmospheric Concentrations of Carbon Dioxide
1980–1994

According to the data in the scatter plot above, what was the approximate rate of increase in the atmospheric concentration of carbon dioxide, in parts per million per <u>decade</u>? (1 decade = 10 years)

A) 1.5

B) 3.0

C) 6.5

D) 14.5

14

Vie's security code consists of four integers, separated by hyphens, that satisfy the following rules:

- Exactly one of the four numbers is even.
- One of the four numbers is her age.
- Exactly one of the four numbers is triple the value of one of the other numbers.
- Exactly one of the four numbers is prime.

Which of the following could be Vie's security code?

A) 66-63-22-13

B) 51-17-11-18

C) 55-77-33-11

D) 50-63-39-13

Questions 15 and 16 refer to the following information.

Ms. Lee administered a 50-point quiz to her trigonometry class. After scoring the quiz, she decided that the scores were not as strong as she had hoped, so she gave the class a second quiz on the same material the next day. She told the class that she would count only the higher of the two scores for each student. The table below shows the scores on both quizzes for six students in the class.

Student	1	2	3	4	5	6
Quiz 1	40	34	34	34	36	20
Quiz 2	48	40	32	38	32	26

15

What is the average final score on the quiz for these six students?

A) 33

B) 36

C) 37

D) 38

16

If the final score of a seventh student were included in this set, the average of the seven scores would be 35. What is the final quiz score for the seventh student?

A) 21

B) 23

C) 24

D) 25

CONTINUE

4

4

17

Which of the following could be the graph of $y - 4 = k(x - 1)^2$ in the xy-plane if k is a constant less than zero?

A)

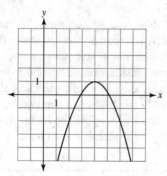

B)

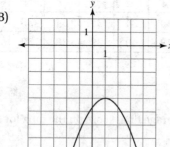

C)

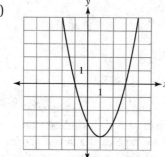

D)

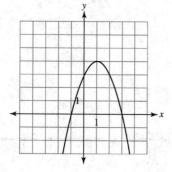

18

When graphed in the xy-plane, the functions $f(x) = x^2 - x - 2$ and $g(x) = kx - 6$ intersect at the point $(-2, a)$. What is the value of k?

A) −5

B) −1

C) 3

D) 8

19

Nationwide Movie Theater Admissions		
Year	Total Cash Receipts (billions of dollars)	Total Attendance (billions)
2006	5.5	1.25
2007	5.9	1.34
2008	6.4	1.39
2009	7.0	1.48
2010	7.5	1.47
2011	7.7	1.40

The table above shows the total cash receipts for ticket sales, in billions of dollars, and the number of people attending, in billions, for movie theaters nationwide from 2006 to 2011. Based on the table, by how much did the receipts per attendee increase from 2006 to 2011?

A) $0.11 per person

B) $0.24 per person

C) $1.10 per person

D) $2.20 per person

CONTINUE ➡

4   4

20

The current price of unleaded gasoline is \$2.10 per gallon and is expected to rise about \$0.16 per month for the foreseeable future. The current price of a gallon of diesel fuel is 30% higher than that of gasoline but is expected to increase only \$0.09 per month. If these trends hold, in how many months will the per-gallon price of the two fuels be equal?

A) 9

B) 10

C) 11

D) 12

21

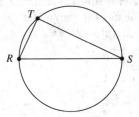

The segment RS is a diameter of the circle above. If the circumference of this circle is $\dfrac{13\pi}{2}$ and $RT = 2.5$, what is the area of triangle RTS?

A) 7.5

B) 8.125

C) 15.0

D) 16.25

22

$$a = 3k$$
$$b = 6k + 5$$
$$c = k$$
$$d = 4k - 5$$

Line l passes through the points (a, b) and (c, d), where a, b, c, and d satisfy the equations above, where $k > 0$. If line m is perpendicular to line l, what is the slope of line m, in terms of k?

A) $-\dfrac{k}{k+10}$

B) $-\dfrac{k}{k+5}$

C) $\dfrac{k+5}{k}$

D) $\dfrac{k+10}{k}$

23

If $\dfrac{3x}{y^2} = \dfrac{24y^{-2}}{x^{-2}}$, what is the value of x?

A) $\dfrac{1}{8}$

B) $\dfrac{1}{6}$

C) $\dfrac{1}{4}$

D) $\dfrac{1}{2}$

CONTINUE

4 **4**

24

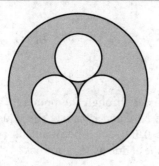

In the figure above, each of the three smaller circles is tangent to the other two and has a diameter of 2 centimeters. The larger circle has a diameter of 6 centimeters. What fraction of the area of the larger circle is shaded?

A) $\dfrac{4}{9}$

B) $\dfrac{1}{2}$

C) $\dfrac{5}{9}$

D) $\dfrac{2}{3}$

25

If $18 - 2k^2 = 16k$, and $k < 0$, what is the value of k^2?

A) 1

B) 9

C) 36

D) 81

26

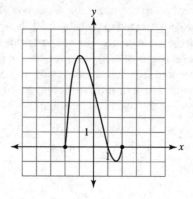

$$f(x) = x^3 - x^2 - 4x + 4$$

The function $y = f(x)$ is graphed in the xy-plane above on the interval $-2 \le x \le 2$. Which of the following indicates the range of x values on this interval for which $f(x) > 2x + 4$?

A) $-2 < x < 0$

B) $-2 < x < 1$

C) $-2 < x < 2$

D) $1 < x < 2$

CONTINUE ➤

4

4

27

Stephanie, Daphne, and Brian each have one AP test to take. One test is in AP Biology, one is in AP U.S. History, and one is in AP Calculus. The tests are on three different days next week: Monday, Tuesday, and Wednesday. Stephanie's test is before Brian's test, but after the U.S. History test. Brian is <u>not</u> taking AP Biology. Which choice correctly indicates which test Stephanie is taking and on what day?

	Subject	Test Day
A)	AP Biology	Monday
B)	AP Biology	Tuesday
C)	AP Calculus	Tuesday
D)	AP U.S. History	Monday

28

If x is the radian measure of an angle, where $0 < x < \dfrac{\pi}{2}$ and $\tan x = k$, which of the following is the value of $\tan(\pi - x)$?

A) k

B) $-k$

C) $\pi - k$

D) $k - \pi$

Questions 29 and 30 refer to the following information.

The table below shows the women's world-record times for the 100 meters from 1911 to 1936.

Year	1911	1913	1920	1921	1925	1928	1932	1933	1934	1935	1936
Record Time (sec)	18.8	13.1	13.0	12.8	12.4	12.0	11.9	11.8	11.7	11.6	11.5

29

What was the average rate of change, in seconds per year, for the world-record women's 100-meter time over the period from 1911 to 1936?

A) −0.292

B) −0.281

C) −0.261

D) −0.130

30

By 1973, the world-record time for the women's 100 meters dropped to 10.8 seconds. The change from 1936 to 1973 is equal to the change from 1925 to what year?

A) 1926

B) 1928

C) 1934

D) 1935

CONTINUE

4 4

CONTINUE ▶

Directions

For questions 31–38, solve the problem and enter your answer in the grid, as described below, on the answer sheet.

1. Although not required, it is suggested that you write your answer in the boxes at the top of the columns to help you fill in the circles accurately. You will receive credit only if the circles are filled in correctly.

2. Mark no more than one circle in any column.

3. No question has a negative answer.

4. Some problems may have more than one correct answer. In such cases, grid only one answer.

5. **Mixed numbers** such as $3\frac{1}{2}$ must be gridded as 3.5 or $\frac{7}{2}$.

   (If $3\frac{1}{2}$ is entered into the grid as 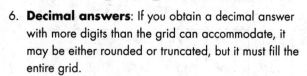, it will be interpreted as $\frac{31}{2}$, not $3\frac{1}{2}$.)

6. **Decimal answers**: If you obtain a decimal answer with more digits than the grid can accommodate, it may be either rounded or truncated, but it must fill the entire grid.

Answer: $\frac{7}{12}$ Answer: 2.5

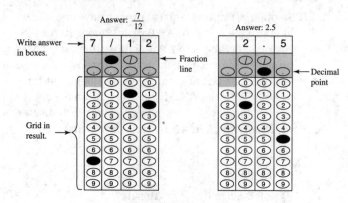

Answer: 201
Either position is correct.

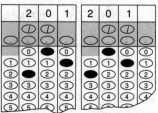

Acceptable ways to grid $\frac{2}{3}$ are:

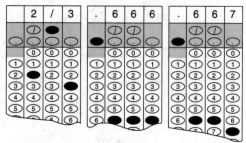

4   **4**

31

A line containing the points $(0, -5)$ and $(a, 27)$ has a slope of 4. What is the value of a?

32

As part of a presentation for a client, an architect constructs a model of a proposed building, using a scale of 1 inch to 64 feet. The architect wants to include a representation of an oak tree that would be preserved during the building process. If the oak tree is actually 96 feet tall, what is the height, in inches, of the model representation of this tree?

33

The equation $t^2 + 5t = 14$ has solutions $t = a$ and $t = b$. If $a < b$, what is the value of $b - a$?

34

Among the registered voters in Curtsville, 30% are registered as Democrats, 25% are registered as Republicans, and 45% are registered as Independents. In this year's election, 58% of the registered Democrats, 60% of the registered Republicans, and 64% of registered Independents cast their votes. If 372 registered Republicans cast their votes in Curtsville in this year's election, how many registered voters does Curtsville have?

35

What is the only positive integer value for n that satisfies the inequality $2 < \left| \dfrac{1}{3} - \dfrac{2}{3}n \right| < 3$?

36

What is the least positive integer m such that $\dfrac{1}{\sqrt{50}} - \dfrac{2}{m} > 0$?

CONTINUE ➡

4 **4**

Questions 37 and 38 refer to the following information.

A "fair" coin is defined as a coin that, when tossed, has a 0.5 probability of landing heads and a 0.5 probability of landing tails. If a coin is not fair, one of those probabilities is greater than the other, but their sum is still 1.

Julia and Ivan use two methods to determine whether or not a coin is fair. Method 1 consists of performing 20 trials, each of which consists of tossing the coin 5 times and recording the number of times a head appears. The average of these 20 results is called x. The best estimate for the probability of this coin landing heads is then calculated with the formula $p = \dfrac{x}{5}$.

Method 2 consists of performing 20 trials, each of which involves tossing the coin until it lands heads and then recording number of the toss on which the first head was observed. The average of these 20 results is then called y. The best estimate for the probability of the coin landing heads is then calculated with the formula $p = \dfrac{1}{y}$.

37

Julia uses Method 2 to test a coin and discovers that, on average, the first head appears on toss 2.5. What is the best estimate for the probability that this coin will land <u>tails</u>?

38

Ivan uses Method 1 to test a coin and discovers that, on average, the coin lands heads 3.75 times out of 5 tosses. Based on Ivan's best estimate from this method, how many tosses, on average, should it take until the first head appears?

STOP

**If you finish before time is called, you may check your work on this section only.
Do not turn to any other section of the test.**

5   5

Essay

50 MINUTES, 1 QUESTION

Directions

The essay gives you the opportunity to show how effectively you can read and comprehend a passage and write an essay analyzing the passage. In your essay, you should demonstrate that you have read the passage carefully, present a clear and logical analysis, and use language precisely.

Your essay must be written on the lines provided in your answer booklet; except for the Planning Page of the answer booklet, you will receive no other paper on which to write. You will have enough space if you write on every line, avoid wide margins, and keep your handwriting to a reasonable size. Remember that people who are not familiar with your handwriting will read what you write. Try to write or print so that what you are writing is legible to those readers.

You have 50 minutes to read the passage and write an essay in response to the prompt provided inside this booklet.

As you read the passage below, consider how Marie Myung-Ok Lee uses

- evidence, such as facts or examples, to support claims
- reasoning to develop ideas and connect claims and evidence
- stylistic or persuasive elements, such as word choice or appeals to emotion, to add power to the ideas expressed

---

Adapted from Marie Myung-Ok Lee, "What Muffins Say About Mitt Romney." Originally published in the *New York Times* on September 2, 2012. ©2012 New York Times.

1   Some supporters of Mitt Romney, in an effort to make him seem more human, have been disseminating a story, first told by a biographer, about how their candidate has a charmingly eccentric habit: he eats only the tops of muffins. His theory is that during the baking process, the butter sinks to the bottom. This story conveys so many things: our guy is an everyday Joe—he eats muffins, not crumpets. And look, even his breakfast is an opportunity to make disciplined decisions—just think how he'll do with the budget.

2   The Romney campaign clearly hasn't thought about how this anecdote will play to a crucial voting bloc: Asian immigrants.

3   My parents came here from Korea after the Korean War. My father arrived on a cargo ship with $200 in his pocket. From those humble beginnings, he established a flourishing medical practice, one that sent four children to college and let him achieve one of the highest marks of Korean immigrant distinction: the purchasing of a Burberry scarf.

4   Like many Korean immigrants of his generation (and many immigrants in general), he was drawn to the Republican Party. For one thing, the platform is easy to understand: taxes are bad. Republicans also seem more patriotic. They want to ban burning the American flag, while the Democrats engage in confusing, peevish debates about whether flag burning is free speech.

5   For more than 40 years, my parents maintained their unshakable loyalty, even while living in Minnesota, the only state with the distinction of voting for a Democrat in every presidential election after 1972, and despite the Republicans' rising anti-immigration fervor—which was aimed, I pointed out, right at them. After all, they were, for a time in the 1960s, undocumented aliens, and it was our Democratic members of Congress who stayed their deportation.

6   But I knew better than to argue with my parents. My father passed on years ago, but the 2012 Republican convention seemed custom-made for him: Mr. Romney's chiseled, MacArthuresque look, his Harvard creds and blond wife, a Burberry love of all things Anglo-Saxon and, possibly most appealing, the easy-to-understand if not-quite-truthful theme of "We built it." That, of course, is the immigrant story in a nutshell.

7   So why did Mitt Romney have to go ruin it with the muffin tops?

8   My father's story, like many immigrants', is one of hardship. He survived famine conditions during the Korean War and never let that experience stray too far from his consciousness. Our cabinets were comically, cornucopically stuffed: every bag of free peanuts from the airlines, the logos changing with the mergers (Northwest Orient, Republic Airlines, Northwest Airlines, Delta), those doll-size paper tubes of salt and pepper that came free with my father's lunch in the physicians' dining room, Saltines and oyster crackers and pharma-company-sponsored bags of potato chips.

9   During the Korean War, when everyone was hungry, he told me, Koreans would take garbage and boil it to make a kind of stew. Of course that seems disgusting, he said. But it was better than going hungry. Despite being a physician, he happily ate foods tipping into rancidity. He drank sour milk. He reheated coffee. He once bought some Sheba Tender Terrine with Turkey and Chicken dinners, impressed by their cheapness, and would not be dissuaded from finishing his supply when we informed him with horror that it was cat food. Once, during a vacation, we forgot to refrigerate the doggie bag from dinner, and it sat in the warm hotel room overnight. Someone's move to place the funky bag in the garbage the next morning set off my father's immigrant mentality inner-motion detector. He wouldn't listen to our pleading—we were sure he'd be dead of ptomaine poisoning by noon—as he ingested the entire contents of the carton. Annoyed, he chided us kids for our snobbish tastes, called us wasteful.

10   I can only imagine what he would have had to say about a presidential candidate so heedless he eats only the top off a muffin. No matter how loyal a Republican, my father would likely have declared Mr. Romney a very silly, profligate man—not the kind of man to be trusted with his precious tax money. Perhaps his vote would have gone to a Democrat for the first time ever. Politico has declared the Asian-American vote "key for both parties." Will muffin-top-gate cause other immigrant parents to join their Democratic-leaning children?

CONTINUE ▶

5   **5**

11 On the other hand, there is one part of Mitt Romney's story that would appeal to my father (besides the fact that both chose their names: Mitt using his middle name instead of Willard, my father deciding William had a nicer ring than Chae-sik). My father always found the American culture of pets—with special food (not to mention a special doctor) *just for the dog*—preposterous. Our childhood longing for a pet bedeviled him. It's possible he might have been one with the logic of Mr. Romney's executive decision to strap the family dog, in a crate, to the roof of the car, thereby keeping the luggage clean and safe inside. In the pet department at least, my father would have thought the man had his priorities straight. Perhaps he would have forgiven him the muffin tops after all.

Write an essay in which you explain how Marie Myung-Ok Lee builds an argument to persuade her audience that Mitt Romney's presidential campaign sent mixed messages to Asian-American immigrants. In your essay, analyze how she uses one or more of the features listed in the box above (or features of your own choice) to strengthen the logic and persuasiveness of her argument. Be sure that your analysis focuses on the most relevant features of the passage.

Your essay should NOT explain whether you agree with Lee's claims, but rather explain how she builds an argument to persuade her audience.

SAT PRACTICE TEST 2 ANSWER KEY

Section 1: Reading	Section 2: Writing and Language	Section 3: Math (No Calculator)	Section 4: Math (Calculator)
1. B	1. B	1. A	1. B
2. C	2. D	2. C	2. C
3. A	3. A	3. C	3. A
4. B	4. A	4. D	4. A
5. C	5. C	5. D	5. C
6. B	6. B	6. A	6. C
7. C	7. C	7. B	7. B
8. D	8. B	8. B	8. B
9. A	9. B	9. B	9. A
10. B	10. A	10. D	10. B
11. D	11. D	11. B	11. C
12. D	12. B	12. D	12. B
13. C	13. C	13. A	13. D
14. A	14. A	14. B	14. D
15. C	15. C	15. C	15. C
16. C	16. D	16. 3 or 1/2 or .5	16. B
17. B	17. A	17. 13	17. D
18. B	18. D	18. 9	18. A
19. D	19. B	19. 3	19. C
20. A	20. B	20. 6	20. A
21. C	21. B		21. A
22. A	22. A		22. B
23. C	23. D		23. A
24. B	24. B		24. D
25. A	25. A		25. D
26. B	26. C		26. A
27. B	27. A		27. B
28. D	28. D		28. B
29. C	29. A		29. A
30. D	30. D		30. C
31. A	31. C		31. 8
32. A	32. D		32. 1.5
33. C	33. D		33. 9
34. A	34. D		34. 2480
35. B	35. B		35. 4
36. B	36. A		36. 15
37. A	37. C		37. 3/5 or .6
38. B	38. D		38. 4/3 or 1.33
39. B	39. B		
40. C	40. D		
41. C	41. C		
42. B	42. C		
43. C	43. B		
44. A	44. B		
45. B			
46. C			
47. D			
48. C			
49. B			
50. C			
51. B			
52. A			

Total Reading Points (Section 1)

Total Writing and Language Points (Section 2)

Total Math Points (Section 3 + Section 4)

Scoring Your Test

1. Use the answer key to mark your responses on each section.

2. Total the number of correct responses for each section:

    1. Reading Test   Number correct: _____ **(Reading Raw Score)**

    2. Writing and Language Test   Number correct: _____ **(Writing and Language Raw Score)**

    3. Mathematics Test—No Calculator   Number correct: _____

    4. Mathematics Test—Calculator   Number correct: _____

3. Add the raw scores for sections 3 and 4. This is your **Math Raw Score:** _____

4. Use the table on page 152 to calculate your **Scaled Test and Section Scores (10–40).**

    Math Section Scaled Score (200–800):   _____

    Reading Test Scaled Score (10–40):   _____

    Writing and Language Test Scaled Score (10–40):   _____

5. Add the **Reading Test Scaled Score** and the **Writing and Language Test Scaled Score (sum will be 20–80)**, and multiply this sum by 10 to get your **Reading and Writing Test Section Score (200–800).**

    Sum of Reading + Writing and Language Scores: _____ $\times 10 =$

    Reading and Writing Section Score: _____

Scaled Section and Test Scores

Raw Score	Math Section Score	Reading Test Score	Writing/ Language Test Score	Raw Score	Math Section Score	Reading Test Score	Writing/ Language Test Score
58	800			29	540	27	29
57	790			28	530	26	29
56	780			27	520	26	28
55	760			26	510	25	27
54	750			25	510	25	27
53	740			24	500	24	26
52	730	40		23	490	24	26
51	730	39		22	480	23	25
50	720	39		21	470	23	24
49	710	38		20	460	23	24
48	700	37		19	460	22	23
47	690	36		18	450	22	23
46	680	35		17	440	21	22
45	670	35		16	430	21	21
44	660	34	40	15	420	20	20
43	660	33	39	14	410	20	20
42	650	33	38	13	390	19	19
41	650	32	37	12	370	18	18
40	640	32	37	11	360	18	17
39	630	31	36	10	350	17	16
38	620	31	35	9	340	16	16
37	610	30	34	8	320	16	15
36	600	30	33	7	300	15	14
35	590	29	33	6	280	14	13
34	580	29	32	5	270	13	12
33	570	28	32	4	250	12	11
32	570	28	31	3	230	11	10
31	560	28	31	2	210	10	10
30	550	27	30	1	200	10	10

PRACTICE SAT 2 ANSWER EXPLANATIONS

Section 1: Reading

1. B — General Purpose

In this story, man describes a true story about an odious man who tramples a little girl and then pays off the family with a check signed by a person whose name *is very well known and often printed* (lines 79–80) and who is *good for more than that* (line 81) amount. In other words, *a hideous event that involves a reputable local figure*.

2. C — Word in Context

The man and child collide because both are moving quickly and are not paying attention to what might happen when they reach the corner. He was *stumping along eastward at a **brisk** walk* (lines 19–20).

3. A — Inference

Lines 49–56 indicate that Mr. Enfield and the doctor had an implicit understanding: *I saw that [doctor] turn sick and white with desire to kill him. I knew what was in his mind, just as he knew what was in mine . . . we told the man we could and would make such a scandal out of this as should make his name stink from one end of London to the other* unless he agreed to pay restitution to the family of the girl. That is, they agreed to blackmail him rather than kill him.

4. B — Textual Evidence

As indicated in the previous explanation, the best evidence is in lines 49–56.

5. C — Word in Context

In saying that *the doctor's case was what struck me*, Enfield is saying that the doctor's *particular situation* was notable, because although he was *cut and dry*, he was nevertheless *sick and white with desire to kill him*.

6. B — Interpretation

Enfield indicates that the name on the check is *very well known and often printed* and that the *signature was good for more than* the amount for which the check had been made out. Therefore, Enfield does not mention the name, because he does not want to risk hurting the signer's good reputation.

7. C — Word in Context

In this context, it is clear that the strange man is negotiating with the crowd to maintain his reputation and make reparation for his deed. He *struck [a deal]* (line 72)

to pay the family rather than *stick out* (line 70), or continue to debate the matter.

8. D — Interpretation

In this paragraph, Enfield remarks to the strange man about how bizarre it seems that a man enters a door and comes out with the check of a (seemingly) very different man with a very different reputation. Thus, the whole situation *looked apocryphal* (not legitimate) (line 84). Enfield's mind was only put *at rest* (line 90) when he discovered the *check was genuine* (line 98). In other words, Enfield's doubts about the strange man were assuaged only when Enfield was confident that the man would *keep his word* and pay the family as he had promised.

9. A — Inference

Enfield indicates that the stranger was *perfectly cool* (lines 32–34) even though he had just committed a heinous act. Thus, Enfield regards the man as an *emotionally detached brute*.

10. B — Textual Evidence

As indicated in the explanation above, the best evidence is in line 32.

11. D — General Purpose

The passage provides a general overview of the Human Genome Project and the *broad domain of current scientific research* associated with it.

12. D — Word in Context

The context of this paragraph makes it clear that proteomics is the study of protein interactions within a cell. Since this proteome *changes from minute to minute* (lines 38–39), the set of proteins cannot have any set *arrangement* or *structure*, or indeed any particular type of grouping, such as a *cluster*. Therefore, the phrase *constellation of all proteins* must mean the *comprehensive collection* of various proteins within the cell.

13. C — Cross-Textual Analysis/Graphical Analysis

One chromosome has four "arms," many genes are located on each arm of the chromosome, and every gene consists of many base pairs.

14. A — Specific Detail

The passage uses the word *encode* in lines 30 and 42 to refer to the process by which genetic information (*complex molecular sequences*) is interpreted to create proteins within the cell.

---

15. C   Word in Context

The phrase *host organism* refers to the plant or animal in which the genetic mutations occur. Thus, *host* means *bearer*.

---

16. C   Inference

The first paragraph of the passage starts with the statements that the Human Genome Project has already led to breakthroughs in biology and medicine, and that further applications are *bounded only by the limits of scientists' imaginations*. The passage explicitly reiterates the idea that the HGP is just an initial stage of research by stating that is *was only the first step to understanding human genetics on the molecular level* (lines 49–52).

---

17. B   Textual Evidence

As the previous explanation indicates, the best evidence is found in lines 49–52.

---

18. B   Interpretation

The passage indicates that cDNA molecules are *full-length synthesized DNA molecules, which encode only the expressed genes of an organism* (lines 63–65). Since lines 15–17 clarify that *the entire complement of human DNA in our genome is arranged into 24 distinct chromosomes*, it must be the case that the genes that cDNA molecules encode are reconstructions of portions of an organism's chromosomes.

---

19. D   Inference

Line 92 identifies an *enzyme* as a *digestive protein*. Lines 41–46 indicate that the study of the *complex interactions* between proteins and other molecules in cells is called *proteomics*.

---

20. A   Textual Evidence

As the previous explanation indicates, the best evidence is in lines 41–46.

---

21. C   Graphical Analysis/Cross-Textual Evidence

The caption below the diagram indicates that the MTHR gene is located *from base pair 11,785,729 to 11,806,102*. Thus it contains 11,806,102–11,785,729 base pairs. Notice that the question does not require a precise calculation, only an approximate answer. It should be easy to see that this difference is certainly bigger than 10,000 but less than 50,000.

---

22. A   Cross-Textual Analysis

Passage 2 describes the bitter campaign between Jefferson and Adams and the animosity between their two parties, providing background to Jefferson's inaugural speech and his desire to restore harmony in the new nation.

---

23. C   Interpretation

Though Jefferson says that the *will of the majority is in all cases to prevail* (lines 7–8), he warns that that *the minority possess their equal rights, which equal law must protect* (lines 9–10). In lines 19–20, he also warns that *political intolerance* can become as *despotic, as wicked, and capable of as bitter and bloody persecutions* as the religious intolerance from which their ancestors fled. In other words, he is saying that the rule of the majority in a democratic system must not become a *tyranny of the majority* against minorities.

---

24. B   Word in Context

The statement *all will, of course, arrange themselves under the will of the law* means that all people will respect the law and *dispose themselves* (that is, *behave*) accordingly.

---

25. A   Interpretation

In lines 33–38, Jefferson suggests that an *honest patriot* would not *abandon government which has so far kept us free and firm* just because he or she fears that *this Government . . . may by possibility want energy to preserve itself.* In other words, he is encouraging patriots to *persevere* despite the *uncertainty* they may have in the country's ability to endure.

---

26. B   Interpretation

In these lines, the author of Passage 2 describes Jefferson's methods of building a unified political party.

---

27. B   Cross-Textual Analysis

When the author of Passage 2 refers to the *moderation and liberality* of Jefferson's speech, he is referring to Jefferson's grace in victory, and specifically to how he resists gloating over or belittling his political adversaries. Jefferson himself mentions this very idea as the *sacred principle* (line 6) that the *minority possess their equal rights* (line 9).

---

28. D   Inference

According to the passage, the election was waged with *utmost bitterness, and especially with bitterness against Jefferson* (lines 51–53), and his political enemies *swallowed whole the worst slanders* about him (lines 62–63).

---

29. C   Textual Evidence

As indicated in the explanation of the previous question, the best evidence is in lines 51–53.

30. D   **Word in Context**

In saying *we have yet gained little if we countenance a political intolerance as despotic, as wicked and capable of as bitter and bloody persecutions,* Jefferson means that we must not *tolerate* such intolerance.

31. A   **Inference**

Jefferson states that *every difference of opinion is not a difference of principle* (lines 21–22), and that even those who disagree with the ruling government should stand *as monuments of the safety with which error of opinion may be tolerated where reason is free to combat it* (lines 24–29). In other words, political debate is *essential to liberal democracy.*

32. A   **Textual Evidence**

As the explanation to the previous question indicates, the best evidence is in lines 24–29.

33. C   **General Purpose**

In this passage, Darrow questions the *efficacy* (effectiveness) of a justice system that is based on punishment. He is not arguing against any particular law, or political injustice, but the *practice* of punishing criminals with lengthy or lifelong prison sentences.

34. A   **Word in Context**

In saying that *Neither the purpose nor the effect of punishment has ever been definitely agreed upon, even by its most strenuous advocates,* Darrow is saying that even the most *resolute* (determined) proponents of punishment do not understand what it's for or what it does.

35. B   **Inference**

In lines 3–6, Darrow says *No doubt the idea of punishment originated in the feeling of resentment and vengeance that, to some extent at least, is incident to life.* He means that the desire to punish criminals is a *natural emotional response.*

36. B   **Textual Support**

As the explanation to the previous question indicates, the best evidence is in lines 3–6.

37. A   **Interpretation**

In lines 69–77, Darrow discusses the question of whether *punishment deters from crime.* He decries *vicarious punishment,* which means punishing one person for the sake of someone else, as neither *just* nor *humane.* Therefore, it is an *abhorrent example of misplaced judgment.* Darrow indicates that deterrent punishment is not at all *transparently illogical to all who consider it,* because he says that *this idea is so*

well rooted that few think of questioning it (lines 71–72). That is, they consider it reasonable because it is so well-established.

38. B   **Word in Context**

In this context, *the decrease of crime* refers to the *lower incidence* of crime.

39. B   **Inference**

Darrow states that *The life of the ordinary prisoner is given over to criticism and resentment against existing things, especially to settled hatred of those who are responsible for his punishment* (lines 43–47). In other words, the prison system is *a breeding ground for hostility and indignation.*

40. C   **Textual Evidence**

As the explanation to the previous question indicates, the best evidence is in lines 43–47.

41. C   **Interpretation**

In lines 79–82, Darrow states that the *reduction of [criminal] penalties* leads to a *decrease of crime.* This directly contradicts the theory that harsh punishment is a deterrent to crime.

42. B   **General Purpose**

The passage as a whole investigates some *unresolved scientific conundrums,* namely the questions of why the speed of light is *this particular speed and not something else?* (lines 3–4) and *what determines that speed?* (lines 22–23) Although the passage mentions Maxwell's equations, Einstein's Theory of Relativity, and Heisenberg's Uncertainty Principle, it does not focus on any *particular theory* or its development. It also does not focus on any particular *discovery* or *accuracy of measurements.*

43. C   **Word in Context**

By the statement *We have now fixed the speed of light . . . at exactly 299,792.458 kilometers per second,* the author is saying that we have *established* this as a scientific fact.

44. A   **Inference**

In lines 33–34, the passage states that *in a vacuum, it's not clear that [the numbers Maxwell used to describe the properties of empty space] should mean anything.* In other words, those numbers were *dubious.*

45. B   **Textual Detail**

As the explanation to the previous question indicates, the best evidence is in lines 34–34.

46. C   Cross-Textual Interpretation

In lines 95–96, the author states that *there seems to be no credible evidence that* c *[the speed of light] varies in space or time*. Therefore, the variations in the estimated values of *c* as indicated in the graph cannot represent *changes in the speed of light over time*. The discussion of *quantum fluctuations* in lines 45–60 do not provide any clue about why experimental values for *c* might change over time. Likewise, the fact that light is an *electromagnetic wave* (lines 13–14) merely confirms the validity of Maxwell's equations, not the fact that our estimates of *c* might change over time. The graph clearly shows that these estimated values settle down to a single value over time, due to better and better *experimental precision*.

47. D   Textual Evidence

As the explanation to the previous question indicates, the best evidence is in lines 95–96.

48. C   Interpretation

The passage as a whole addresses the question, *where does the speed of light come from?* by looking at how other phenomena might help explain why the speed of light is what it is. It begins by noting that James Clerk Maxwell derived the speed of light from his electromagnetic equations (thereby implying that light gets its speed from the nature of electricity and magnetism), but then explained that these equations in turn depended on the *quantum fluctuations* of empty space. These are all *fundamental properties of the physical universe* that might be used to *determine the speed of light*.

49. B   Purpose/Specific Meaning

Analyzing the *quantum fluctuations* helps scientists calculate electromagnetic properties of empty space and from that to derive the value of *c*.

50. C   Word in Context

The statement that *science follows the modern Copernican view* means that it *acts in accordance with* that view; that is, it assumes that the views of Copernicus are basically correct.

51. B   Interpretation

In lines 75–87, the author discusses the *ancient controversy* about whether or not *"constants" like c and G ... are really constant*. In saying that *Aristotle believed that the Earth was differently constituted from the heavens*, the author is saying that Aristotle weighed in on the question about the "constancy" of the universe by rejecting it: he claimed that one part of the universe (Earth) obeyed fundamentally different laws from another part (the heavens). In other words, the author is indicating that at

least one great scientific thinker *did not assume the universality of physical laws*.

52. A   Graphical Inference

On the graph, the more *accurate* measurements are closer to the horizontal line that indicates the established speed of light. The more *precise* measurements are those with a smaller margin of error, that is, with a shorter vertical line. Since Michelson's measurement is closer to the horizontal line and has a smaller vertical line, it is *both* more accurate and more precise.

Section 2: Writing and Language

1. B   Standard English Conventions/ Pronoun Usage

The correct answer must be a possessive pronoun that agrees with the singular antecedent *monarchism*. The original phrasing is incorrect because *it's* is the contraction of *it is*, but *its* is a singular possessive pronoun. *They're* is a contraction of *they are*, and *their* is a plural possessive pronoun.

2. D   Clarity of Expression/Transitions

This sentence indicates a consequence of the situation described in the previous sentence. The adverb *Accordingly* indicates a statement that represents a reasonable or logical consequence.

3. A   Coordination

The original phrasing is correct. Choice B creates an illogical adverbial phrase *to have no particular role*. In choice C, the adverb *thereby* is illogical. In choice D, the semicolon is wrong, because the clause that follows it is not independent.

4. A   Punctuation/Logic/Idiom

The only comparison that logically follows standard written English is choice A. Choice B is unidiomatic, choice C is illogical, and choice D misuses the comma.

5. C   Mood/Coordination

The interrupting modifier (the phrase between the commas) indicates a hypothetical situation and so should use the *subjunctive mood*. Choice C is the only one that provides the appropriate interrupter. Choices A and D are not in the subjunctive mood, and choice B improperly coordinates the clauses because it is missing a comma.

6. B   Clear Expression of Ideas/Development

This sentence supports the main idea of the passage, namely that the office of the vice president has historically held low status, by indicating that even a local public official did not recognize Vice President Coolidge. It is appropriate to this paragraph in particular because it develops the idea that some vice presidents had to live in hotels.

---

7. C   **Diction**

The logic of the sentence requires a word that means *assigned* or *appointed*.

---

8. B   **Coordination/Dangling Participles**

The original phrase begins with a dangling participle. Choice C is poorly coordinated and needlessly uses the passive voice. Choice D ends with a dangling participle. Only choice B properly coordinates the ideas.

---

9. B   **Coordination**

Choice B establishes the correct sequence of events and aptly subordinates clauses to a main clause. Choice A illogically implies that Nixon would have moved into the vice president's quarters. In choice C, the pronoun *he* lacks an unambiguous antecedent, and the participle *choosing* dangles. In choice D, the pronouns *it* and *he* lack clear antecedents.

---

10. A   **Coordination/Tense**

The sentence is correct as written. Choices B, C, and D are in the wrong tense.

---

11. D   **Clear Expression of Ideas**

This sentence uses the comparative idiom *both A and B*, so the phrases replacing *A* and *B* must have parallel form. Choice D is the only phrase that provides parallel form: *maintenance* and *staff* are both simple common nouns.

---

12. B   **Dangling Participles/Punctuation**

With the original phrasing, the participle *Having* dangles. Recall that when a sentence starts with a participial phrase, the subject of the main clause must also be the subject of the participle. The subject of this participle is *I*, so only choices B and D correct the dangling problem. Choice D is incorrect, however, because it misuses the colon. A colon is used to introduce defining examples or explanatory clauses.

---

13. C   **Idiom**

The phrase *opportunity of determining* is not idiomatic. The correct idiom is *opportunity to determine*.

---

14. A   **Clear Expression of Ideas/Development**

This sentence is simply making the point that the recruiter feels like a multitasker. Providing the technical definition of a psychological profiler only detracts from this point.

---

15. C   **Interrupting Modifiers**

Interrupting modifiers should be separated from the main clause by dashes, commas, or parentheses, but these punctuation marks can't be mixed. Choice C is the only one that uses consistent punctuation to indicate the interrupting phrase.

---

16. D   **Expression of Ideas/Diction**

This sentence requires a word that means *emphasize* or *stress*.

---

17. A   **Clear Expression of Ideas/Development**

The original phrasing provides the idea that best connects with the sentence that follows, which describes the consequences of getting a boss who doesn't understand you.

---

18. D   **Logic/Redundancy/Diction**

A boss who *turns and runs* cannot simultaneously *throw* you out the door, because the first action requires that your boss turn away from you, and the second requires that your boss turn toward you. Yes, they are metaphors rather than literal actions, but they must coordinate logically. Therefore, choice B is incorrect. Choices A and C are incorrect because *oust you out* and *banish you out* are redundant.

---

19. B   **Cohesiveness/Transitions**

This sentence requires a contrasting adverb, since it portrays a happy situation in contrast to the unhappy situation described in the previous sentence.

---

20. B   **Diction/Tone**

The author has been describing how diligently he works as he attempts to get truthful statements from his clients. Choice B is the only one that follows this idea. To *ferret out* is to search and discover through persistent investigation.

---

21. B   **Development**

This is an excellent example to include because it is exactly the sort of unfortunate information a candidate would be likely to want to omit from an application.

---

22. A   **Development**

Choice A offers a neat conclusion by describing a serious consequence to not being honest on a job application.

---

23. D   **Clear Expression of Ideas/Redundancy**

Feasible and *possible* are synonyms. Choose one!

---

24. B   **Tense/Subject-Verb Agreement**

The verb must agree with the plural subject *stories*, and the logic of the sentence requires the present tense.

25. A   **Clear Expression of Ideas/Subordination and Coordination**

Choice A establishes the correct logical relationships among the ideas and aptly subordinates clauses and phrases to a main clause. In choice B, the conjunction *but* is illogical. In choice C, the compound phrase at the end of the sentence is not parallel. In choice D, the modifying phrases *in the food supply* and *in urbanites* are misplaced and illogical.

26. C   **Clarity of Expression/Diction**

This word must be an adjective describing a relationship between *natural products* and *hormone additives*, and choice C, *untainted*, provides the only logical choice. Additives cannot *consume*, *restrain*, or *deprive* natural products.

27. A   **Standard English Conventions/Commas/ Subject-Verb Agreement**

The sentence is correct as written. The core of the sentence (the subject, verb, and object) is the phrase *desire has created a trend*. The verb must agree with the singular word *desire*, and there should be no comma at the end of the prepositional phrase *for natural . . . pesticides*.

Helpful Hint: Remember that nonessential prepositional phrases (like *for natural . . . pesticides*) can be "trimmed" to get at the core of a sentence.

28. D   **Punctuation/Coordination**

In choice A, the conjunction *so* incorrectly indicates a consequence. The logic of the sentence requires a conjunction that indicates an *addition*. Choice B forms a comma splice. Choice C is incorrect because the clause that follows the semicolon is not independent.

29. A   **Clear Expression of Ideas/Organization**

The next paragraph is about potential health risks in urban farming that were recognized in the 1800s but have been undervalued in the recent urban farming boom. Therefore, choice A provides the most logical transition to this paragraph about *sanitation* practices.

30. D   **Coordination/Development**

Choice D is the only one that mentions the *insidious nature* of the disease. Something insidious spreads harmfully in a subtle or stealthy manner. Choice D says *Salmonella* spreads *with amazing ease* though the carrier birds do not appear to be infected.

31. C   **Parallelism**

Words or phrases in a list should be parallel, that is, share the same grammatical form. In this sentence, all

three verbs should follow the subject *who* in the simple present tense. Choices B and C provide this parallel form, but choice B is illogical because it suggests that handling the birds is a *less* significant interaction than merely working or playing around their cages, when in fact it is a much *more* significant interaction.

32. D   **Data Analysis**

Add up the percentages for all the cities for all three Agree categories, and the total is under 50% but well over 33%.

33. D   **Diction**

The sentence requires a word that means *followed* or *accepted*.

34. D   **Clear Expression of Ideas/Modification**

In the original sentence, the modifying phrase at the beginning of the sentence dangles. Because *Pablo Picasso's painting* is not *the world's most influential artist*, it should not be the subject of the main clause. Clearly the subject must be *Pablo Picasso*. Choice D is the only one that corrects this error. Choice C is a sentence fragment.

35. B   **Clear Expression of Ideas**

Choice B provides the most logical, idiomatic, and concise phrasing.

36. A   **Standard English Conventions/Tense**

The sentence is correct as written. The passage requires a simple past tense.

37. C   **Sentence Fragments/Pronoun-Antecedent Agreement**

Choices A and D produce sentence fragments. Choice B is incorrect because the pronoun *this* does not have a clear antecedent.

38. D   **Coordination**

Although the first clause in the original sentence sounds fine, it does not coordinate with the clause that follows because it creates a comma splice. Choices B and C commit the same mistake. Choice D corrects the problem by replacing the independent clause with a participial phrase that coordinates with the main clause.

39. B   **Clear Expression of Ideas/Development**

Because the second sentence begins with the word *Instead*, this first two sentences must describe contrasting situations. Choice B offers the most direct contrast: Picasso used *graphic shapes and symbolic figures* rather than offering a *historically accurate depiction of the attack.*

---

40. D   **Clear Expression of Ideas/Diction**

Picasso's vivid images *call forth* or *elicit* or *evoke* a sense of agony.

---

41. C   **Standard English Conventions/Apostrophes**

The core (subject and verb) of this sentence is *critics agree,* so the apostrophe in the original phrasing and in choice D is incorrect. Choice B is incorrect because it creates a sentence with two uncoordinated verbs.

---

42. C   **Clarity of Expression/Diction**

Though all choices are grammatically correct, only C maintains the appropriately serious tone of the rest of the paragraph. The words in the remaining choices are inappropriately informal or playful.

---

43. B   **Clear Expression of Ideas/**
                            Logical Comparisons

This phrase is establishing a comparison between Picasso and Einstein, and therefore must be logical and follow the Law of Parallelism. Only choice B creates a clear, logical, and parallel comparison.

---

44. B   **Clear Expression of Ideas**

Choice B provides the best conclusion because it alludes directly to the subject of the passage as a whole, "Guernica," while also indicating the legacy of Picasso.

Section 3: Math (No Calculator)

---

1. A   **Heart of Algebra (solving equations) EASY**

$$2(x+2) = 3x - 1$$

Distribute: $2x + 4 = 3x - 1$
Subtract $2x$: $4 = x - 1$
Add 1: $5 = x$

---

2. C   **Additional Topics (systems) EASY**

Original equation: $\dfrac{1}{2}x + \dfrac{1}{3}y = 7$

Multiply by 12: $12\left(\dfrac{1}{2}x + \dfrac{1}{3}y\right) = 84$

Distribute: $6x + 4y = 84$

---

3. C   **Algebra (solving equations) EASY**

Original equation: $\dfrac{3(k-5)}{4} = \dfrac{5+2k}{3}$

Cross multiply: $9(k-5) = 20 + 8k$

Distribute: $9k - 45 = 20 + 8k$
Subtract $8k$ and add 45: $k = 65$

---

4. D   **Algebra (systems) EASY**

There are several methods we could use to solve this system. One method is simply to "test" each ordered pair in the choices to see which one satisfies both equations. If you prefer to do it algebraically, notice that the answer choices tell us that we should solve the system for y instead of x. Why? Because all of the y-coordinates are different in the choices, but some of the x-coordinates repeat. Therefore, the best algebraic strategy is to substitute for x and solve for y.

Original equations: $x = 5y + 5$ and $2x - y = 19$
Substitute $x = 5y + 5$ into the second equation:
                                  $2(5y + 5) - y = 19$
Distribute: $10y + 10 - y = 19$
Combine like terms: $9y + 10 = 19$
Subtract 10: $9y = 9$
Divide by 9: $y = 1$
Notice that the only choice with a y-coordinate of 1 is choice D (10, 1). Substituting $x = 10$ and $y = 1$ into both equations confirms that this ordered pair satisfies both equations.

---

5. D   **Advanced Mathematics**
              (two-variable relationships) EASY

This is a straightforward conversion problem:

$$p \text{ pounds} \times \frac{1 \text{ kilogram}}{2.2 \text{ pounds}} \times \frac{40 \text{ milligrams amoxicillin}}{1 \text{ kilogram}}$$

$$= \frac{40p}{2.2} \text{ milligrams of amoxicillin}$$

---

6. A   **Algebra (inequalities) MEDIUM**

If Calvin hangs n photographs, there will be $n - 1$ spaces between them, and each space is 2 inches wide. Since each photograph is 9 inches wide, the total width of the display is $9n + 2(n - 1)$ inches. If this display can be no wider than 12 feet (or 144 inches), then $9n + 2(n-1) \le 144$.

---

7. B   **Advanced Mathematics (quadratics)**
                                 MEDIUM

Solutions of the system coincide with those points at which <u>all three graphs</u> intersect. There are 2 such points of intersection: $(-\sqrt{2}, 0)$ and $(\sqrt{2}, 0)$.

---

8. B   **Advanced Mathematics (functions)**
                                 MEDIUM

The key to this problem is seeing that the equation is a standard "rate × time = work" equation. The blue hose takes 10 hours to fill the pool, so it fills the pool at a rate of $\dfrac{1}{10}$ pool per hour. The red hose requires 5 hours to do the job, so it fills at a rate of $\dfrac{1}{5}$ pool per hour. Together, then the two hoses working together fill the pool at a rate of $\frac{1}{10} + \frac{1}{5}$ pool per hour. The right side of the equation shows the total amount of work done, which is 1 pool. Therefore, x represents the total time, in hours, needed to fill one pool using both hoses.

---

9. B   **Special Topics (imaginary numbers) MEDIUM**

Original expression: $2i^2 + 3i^3 - 4i^4 + 5i^5$
Based on the definition that $i = \sqrt{-1}$, we can show that $i^2 = -1$, $i^3 = -i$, $i^4 = 1$, and $i^5 = i$.
Substitute these values into original expression:
$$2(-1) + 3(-i) - 4(1) + 5(i)$$
Simplify: $-2 - 3i - 4 + 5i$
Combine like terms: $-6 + 2i$

---

10. D   **Advanced Mathematics (sequences and inverse operations) MEDIUM-HARD**

The third term of the sequence is 20. To find the fourth term, we can simply apply the rule of the sequence: "multiply the previous term by 3 and subtract 4." This gives $3(20) - 4 = 56$ as the fourth term. The second term can be found by applying the *inverse* of the sequence rule: "*add* 4 to the *previous* term, then *divide* by 3." Applying this to the third term gives us $(20 + 4) \div 3 = 8$ for the second term. Therefore, the sum of the second term and the fourth term is $8 + 56 = 64$.

---

11. B   **Advanced Mathematics (factoring polynomials) MEDIUM-HARD**

We can find the x-intercepts of $y = g(x)$ by factoring:
$$g(x) = x^2 + 6x + 8 = (x + 2)(x + 4)$$
The Zero Product Property shows that the graph of $y = g(x)$ has x-intercepts at $(-2, 0)$ and $(-4, 0)$. If the graph of $y = f(x)$ shares these same x-intercepts, it must also share the same factors associated with those x-intercepts, $(x + 2)$ and $(x + 4)$. If we define the third x-intercept of g as $x = k$, then f should factor like this:
$$f(x) = x^3 + 2x^2 - 16x - 32 = (x + 2)(x + 4)(x - k)$$
Now we can find the value of k by just noticing that the product of the constant terms in the factors must equal the constant term in the original polynomial, which is -32:
$$(2)(4)(-k) = -32$$
Simplify: $-8k = -32$
Divide by -8: $k = 4$
Therefore, the third x-intercept of $y = f(x)$ is $(4, 0)$.

---

12. D   **Algebra (simplifying rational expressions) MEDIUM**

Substitute for x and y, then factor and cancel:

$$\frac{10x}{y} = \frac{10(a^2 - b^2)}{2(a - b)} = \frac{10(a - b)(a + b)}{2(a - b)} = \frac{10(a + b)}{2} = 5a + 5b$$

---

13. A   **Advanced Mathematics (analysis of parabolas) MEDIUM-HARD**

The graph of $y = g(x)$ is a parabola with a vertex at $(2, 0)$. If this parabola is shifted up one unit, it will have a vertex at $(2, 1)$. Since all of the equations in the choices are written in vertex form ($y = (x - k)^2 + k$, where (h, k) is the vertex), it should be easy to see that the correct equation is $y = (x - 2)^2 + 1$.

---

14. B   **Additional Topics (volume) MEDIUM**

Since we want the volume of the beam in cubic feet, it's a good idea to convert all measures to feet. The edges of the cross-shaped base are all 6 inches, or 1/2 foot, in measure; therefore, each of the five squares on the base has an area of $(1/2)^2 = 1/4$ square foot, so the total area of the base is $5(1/4) = 5/4$ square feet. The length of the beam is 72 inches, or $72 \div 12 = 6$ feet. Since the volume of a prism is equal to the area of the base times the height, the volume is $(5/4)(6) = 30/4 = 7.5$ cubic feet.

---

15. C   **Additional Topics (exponentials and radicals) HARD**

Recall that analyzing exponentials is easier if we have a common base. Notice that $64 = 2^6$ and $4 = 2^2$.
Original equation: $4^{4x} = 64a^4$
Substitute $64 = 2^6$ and $4 = 2^2$: $(2^2)^{4x} = 2^6 a^4$
Simplify: $2^{8x} = 2^6 a^4$
Raise both sides to the 1/4 power: $2^{2x} = 2^{3/2} a$
Substitute second equation, $2^{2x} = na$: $na = 2^{3/2} a$
Divide by a: $n = 2^{3/2} = (2^3)^{1/2} = \sqrt{2^3} = \sqrt{8}$

---

16. 3 or 1/2 or .5   **Advanced Mathematics (quadratic systems) MEDIUM**

There are several ways to tackle this question, but perhaps the simplest is to solve the first equation for t and then plug into the second equation to find x.

     $t^2 = 5t$
Subtract $5t$: $t^2 - 5t = 0$
Factor: $t(t - 5) = 0$
Use the Zero Product Property: $t = 0$ or $t = 5$
Plug $t = 0$ into the second equation: $0 = 2x - 1$
Add 1: $1 = 2x$
Divide by 2: $1/2 = x$
Plug $t = 5$ into the second equation: $5 = 2x - 1$
Add 1: $6 = 2x$
Divide by 2: $3 = x$
Therefore, x can equal either 1/2 or 3.

---

17. 13   **Algebra (word problems) MEDIUM**

Let n equal the number of 5-point questions that Alliyah answered correctly. If she answered 20 questions correctly overall, then she must have answered $20 - n$ of the 3-point questions correctly. Therefore, she earned $5n + 3(20 - n)$ points in total: $5n + 3(20 - n) = 86$

Distribute: $5n + 60 - 3n = 86$

Combine like terms: $2n + 60 = 86$

Subtract 60: $2n = 26$

Divide by 2: $n = 13$

---

18. 9   **Algebra (solving equations)**
MEDIUM-HARD

$$\frac{x}{x^2 - 9} - \frac{1}{x+3} = \frac{1}{4x - 12}$$

Factor the denominators:

$$\frac{x}{(x-3)(x+3)} - \frac{1}{x+3} = \frac{1}{4(x-3)}$$

Multiply by the common denominator, $4(x-3)(x+3)$:

$$4(x+3)(x-3)\left(\frac{x}{(x-3)(x+3)}\right) - 4(x+3)(x-3)\left(\frac{1}{x+3}\right)$$

$$= 4(x+3)(x-3)\left(\frac{1}{4(x-3)}\right)$$

Simplify: $4x - 4(x-3) = x + 3$

Distribute: $4x - 4x + 12 = x + 3$

Simplify: $12 = x + 3$

Subtract 3: $9 = x$

---

19. 3   **Algebra (systems of equations)**
MEDIUM

Given equations: $m^2 + 5 = x$ and $9y^2 = x - 5$

Substitute $m^2 + 5 = x$ into the second equation: $9y^2$

$$= (m^2 + 5) - 5$$

Simplify: $9y^2 = m^2$

Divide by y^2: $9 = \dfrac{m^2}{y^2}$

Take the square root: $3 = \left|\dfrac{m}{y}\right|$

---

20. 6   **Additional Topics (arcs and circles) HARD**

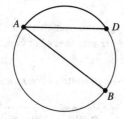

The circumference of a circle is equal to its diameter times π; therefore, the circumference of the circle is $\dfrac{20}{\pi} \times \pi = 20$. Since $<BAD$ is an inscribed angle with measure of $\dfrac{\pi}{5}$ radians, its intercepted arc DB has a measure $2 \times \dfrac{\pi}{5} = \dfrac{2\pi}{5}$. Since arc ADB is a semicircle, arc AD has a radian measure of $\pi - \dfrac{2\pi}{5} = \dfrac{3\pi}{5}$. We can find its length

now based on the fact that the length of any arc in a circle is proportional to its radian measure:

$$\frac{\frac{3\pi}{5}}{2\pi} = \frac{x}{20}$$

Cross-multiply: $12\pi = 2x\pi$

Divide by 2π: $6 = x$

Section 4: Math (Calculator)

1. B   **Algebra (analysis of lines) EASY**

One strategy you could use is to match up the key features of the linear equations with the features of the graph and work by process of elimination. The graph has an x-intercept of 4, a y-intercept of 2, and a slope of $-1/2$. Choice A has the wrong slope $(1/2)$. Choice C has the correct y-intercept (2) but the wrong slope (-2), and choice D has both the wrong slope (2) and the wrong y-intercept (4).

---

2. C   **Algebra (representing relationships) EASY**

Let x be the maximum number of shares Gretchen can purchase. Therefore, $\$3.19x$ is the total cost of those shares, and $\$(3.19x + 75)$ must be less than or equal to $\$4,000$: $3.19x + 75 \le 4,000$

Subtract 75: $3.19x \le 3,925$

Divide by 3.19: $x \le 1,230.41$

Therefore, Gretchen can purchase a maximum of 1,230 shares and stay within her budget.

---

3. A   **Additional Topics (3-D geometry) EASY**

If a sphere is inscribed in a cube, then the diameter of the sphere is equal to the length of one edge of the cube. If each edge of the cube has length x inches and the cube has a volume of 64 cubic inches: $V = x^3 = 64$

Take the cube root: $x = 4$

This means that the diameter of the sphere is also 4 inches, so the radius of the sphere is $4 \div 2 = 2$ inches.

---

4. A   **Advanced Mathematics (functions) EASY**

If $x = 1$ is a zero of the function, then $f(1) = 0$:

$$f(1) = (1)^3 - (1)^2 + p(1) - 3 = 0$$

Simplify: $1 - 1 + p - 3 = 0$

Simplify: $p - 3 = 0$

Add 3: $p = 3$

---

5. C   **Problem Solving and Data Analysis**
(counting) EASY

One good way to count all of the possible pairs is to use the Method of Exhaustion: start by "exhausting" all such pairs that include the number 1; then move on to all of the remaining pairs that include the number 2, et cetera:

$$1+2=3 \quad 1+4=5 \quad 2+3=5 \quad 2+5=7 \quad 3+4=7 \quad 4+5=9$$

---

6. **C**   **Problem Solving and Data Analysis (multi-variable graphs) EASY**

The solid line shows the average daily low temperatures. In October, the average low temperature varies from about 76°F to about 73°F, so the average low temperature for October is closest to 75°F.

---

7. **B**   **Problem Solving and Data Analysis (multi-variable graphs) MEDIUM**

You might notice that the difference between the average high temperature and the average low temperature is between 12°F and 18°F throughout the year. Therefore, in the month when the average high temperature is 80°F, we should expect the average low temperature to be between 80°F − 18°F = 62°F and 80°F − 12°F = 68°F. The only choice within this range is (C) 63°F. Specifically, the months in which the average high temperature is closest to 80°F are February and October, and the graph shows that the average low temperatures for these months are both around 63°F.

---

8. **B**   **Algebra (inequalities) EASY**

Original inequality: $-3x - 5y < 4y - 6$
Add 5y: $-3x < 9y - 6$
Divide by −3 and "flip" the inequality: $x > -3y + 2$

---

9. **A**   **Algebra (rates) MEDIUM**

We can up proportions to determine how many minutes it would take for each to squeeze 40 lemons.

Anton's machine: $\dfrac{75 \text{ lemons}}{60 \text{ minutes}} = \dfrac{40 \text{ lemons}}{x \text{ minutes}}$

Cross-multiply: $75x = 2,400$
Divide by 75: $x = 32 \text{ minutes}$

Luigi's machine: $\dfrac{80 \text{ lemons}}{60 \text{ minutes}} = \dfrac{40 \text{ lemons}}{y \text{ minutes}}$

Cross multiply: $80x = 2,400$
Divide by 80: $y = 30 \text{ minutes}$

Therefore, Anton's machine takes 2 minutes longer than it takes Luigi's machine.

---

10. **B**   **Problem Solving and Data Analysis (histograms) MEDIUM**

According to the histogram, the proportion of households that own 4 or more dogs is approximately 0.07 + 0.04 + 0.04 + 0.02 = 0.17, or 17% of the households.

---

11. **C**   **Problem Solving and Data Analysis (central tendency) MEDIUM**

The median is the number below which 50% of the data fall and above which 50% of the data fall. According to

---

the histogram, about 36% of the households have no dogs, and another 24% have 1 dog. Because 36% + 24% = 60%, the median number of dogs is 1. The overall shape of the histogram is "skewed right," which means that there are more numbers that are much larger than the median than much lower than the median. In these cases, the average is always larger than the median.

To calculate the average, you can multiply each proportion of households times the number of dogs that proportion owns and add the results. Average = 0.36(0) + 0.24(1) + 0.14(2) + 0.09(3) + 0.07(4) + 0.04(5) + 0.04(6) + 0.02(7) = 1.65 pets per household.

---

12. **B**   **Problem Solving and Data Analysis (percentages) EASY-MEDIUM**

Since the total number of applicants was 46,815, one-third of those, or 46,815 ÷ 3 = 15,605 were admitted. Of these, 100% − 40% = 60% will <u>not</u> enroll, and 0.60(15,605) = 9,363.

---

13. **D**   **Data Analysis (scatter plots) MEDIUM**

To find the rate of increase per decade, it is best to choose two points that are 10 years apart, such as 1980 and 1990. In 1980, the atmospheric concentration of carbon dioxide was approximately 339 parts per million, and in 1990, it was approximately 354 parts per million, for a rate of 354 − 339 = 15 parts per million per decade, which is closest to choice D.

---

14. **D**   **Additional Topics (logic) MEDIUM**

For many logic questions, it helps to work by process of elimination.

A) This choice violates the rule that **exactly one of the four numbers is even**. It has two: 22 and 66.

B) This choice violates the rule that **exactly one of the four numbers is prime**. It has two: 17 and 11.

C) This choice violates the rule that **exactly one of the four numbers is even**. It has no even numbers.

D) This violates none of the rules.

---

15. **C**   **Problem Solving and Data Analysis (central tendency) MEDIUM**

The final score for each student is the higher of the two, so the average final score for these 6 students is (48 + 40 + 34 + 38 + 36 + 26) ÷ 6 = 37.

---

16. **B**   **Problem Solving and Data Analysis (averages) MEDIUM**

The sum of the final scores for the original 6 students is 48 + 40 + 34 + 38 + 36 + 26 = 222. If the average of the scores for all seven students is 35, then the sum of the seven scores must be $35 \times 7 = 245$. Therefore, the score for the seventh student must by $245 - 222 = 23$.

---

17. D   **Advanced Mathematics (graphs of quadratic functions) MEDIUM-HARD**

Original equation: $y - 4 = k(x-1)^2$
Add 4: $y = k(x-1)^2 + 4$
This is the "vertex form" of a quadratic function, which reveals that the graph is a parabola with vertex at (1, 4). The fact that k is a constant less than zero tells us that this parabola is "open down." The only choice that satisfies both of these criteria is D.

---

18. A   **Advanced Mathematics (functions) MEDIUM-HARD**

If the graph of f contains the point $(-2, a)$, then $f(-2) = a$:
$$f(-2) = (-2)^2 - (-2) - 2 = a$$
Simplify: $4 + 2 - 2 = a$
Simplify: $4 = a$
The graph of g must also contain the point $(-2, 4)$, so $g(-2) = 4$:
$$g(-2) = k(-2) - 6 = 4$$
Simplify: $-2k - 6 = 4$
Add 6: $-2k = 10$
Divide by -2: $k = -5$

---

19. C   **Data Analysis (calculations) MEDIUM**

In 2006, the receipts per attendee was $5.5 billion $\div$ 1.25 billion people = $4.40. In 2011, the receipts per attendee was $7.7 billion $\div$ 1.40 billion people = $5.50, for an increase of $5.50 - $4.40 = $1.10 per person.

---

20. A   **Algebra (word problems) MEDIUM-HARD**

If the current price per gallon for unleaded gasoline is $2.10, then the current price for a gallon of diesel fuel is 30% higher: $(1.3)(\$2.10) = \$2.73$. In m months, the price of unleaded gas will be $\$(2.10 + 0.16m)$ and the price of diesel will be $\$(2.73 + 0.09m)$. We want to know when these prices are equal: $2.10 + 0.16m = 2.73 + 0.09m$
Subtract 0.09m and 2.10: $0.07m = 0.63$
Divide by 0.07: $m = 9$

---

21. A   **Additional Topics (Circles and Triangles) MEDIUM-HARD**

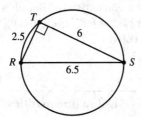

Because RS is a diameter, it divides the circle into two semicircles. Since angle RTS is an inscribed angle that

intercepts an arc of 180°, angle RTS must be a 90° angle. The circumference is equal to π times the diameter, so the diameter must be $13/2 = 6.5$. We can now use the Pythagorean Theorem to find TS: $TS^2 + 2.5^2 = 6.5^2$
Simplify: $TS^2 + 6.25 = 42.25$
Subtract 6.25: $TS^2 = 36$
Take the square root: $TS = 6$
Now we may use RT and TS as the bases of the triangle to calculate the area of the triangle: $(2.5)(6) \div 2 = 7.5$.

---

22. B   **Algebra (slopes of lines) MEDIUM-HARD**

Recall that slopes of perpendicular lines are opposite reciprocals of each other.

Slope of line l: $\dfrac{y_2 - y_1}{x_2 - x_1} = \dfrac{d - b}{c - a}$

Therefore, the slope of line m is its opposite reciprocal:
$$-\dfrac{c - a}{d - b} = \dfrac{a - c}{d - b}$$

Substitute for all unknowns in terms of k and simplify:
$$\dfrac{a - c}{d - b} = \dfrac{3k - k}{(4k - 5) - (6k + 5)} = \dfrac{2k}{-2k - 10} = -\dfrac{k}{k + 5}$$

---

23. A   **Algebra (exponentials) MEDIUM**

Original equation: $\dfrac{3x}{y^2} = \dfrac{24y^{-2}}{x^{-2}}$

Cross-multiply: $(3x)(x^{-2}) = (24y^{-2})(y^2)$
Simplify: $3x^{-1} = 24y^0$
Multiply by x (and remember that $y^0 = 1$): $3 = 24x$
Divide by 24: $\dfrac{3}{24} = \dfrac{1}{8} = x$

---

24. D   **Additional Topics (circles) MEDIUM-HARD**

The large circle has a diameter of 6 centimeters, so its radius is $6 \div 2 = 3$ centimeters, and its area is $\pi(3)^2 = 9\pi$ square centimeters. Each small circle has a diameter of 2 centimeters, so its radius is $2 \div 2 = 1$ centimeter, and its area is $\pi(1)^2 = \pi$ square centimeters. Since there are three of them, their total area is 3π square centimeters. This means that the shaded region has an area of $9\pi - 3\pi = 6\pi$, which is $6\pi/9\pi = 2/3$ of the total.

---

25. D   **Algebra (solving equations) MEDIUM-HARD**

Original equation: $18 - 2k^2 = 16k$
Add $2k^2$ and subtract 18: $0 = 2k^2 + 16k - 18$
Divide by 2: $0 = k^2 + 8k - 9$
Factor: $0 = (k + 9)(k - 1)$
Solve using the Zero Product Property: $k = -9$ or 1
Since the problem tells us that k must be negative, $k = -9$ and therefore, $k^2 = 81$.

26. A   Advanced Mathematics
                      (analyzing functions) HARD

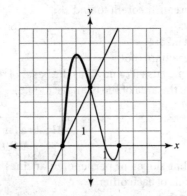

If we draw the line $y = 2x + 4$, then all of the points above this line are the points where $y > 2x + 4$. The part of the function that lies above the line, as the graph shows, are the points corresponding to the values of x between -2 and 0.

27. B   Additional Topics (logic)
                            MEDIUM-HARD

Since Stephanie's test is before at least one test (Brian's test), it can't be the last test, so her test must be on either Monday or Tuesday. Since Stephanie's test is after at least one test (the U.S. History test), it cannot be the first test, so it must be on either Tuesday or Wednesday. Therefore, Stephanie's test must be on Tuesday, the U.S. History test is on Monday, and Brian's test is on Wednesday. If Brian is not taking the Biology test, and he is not taking the U.S. History test (because it is on Monday), he must be taking the Calculus test. Therefore, Daphne must be taking the U.S. History test on Monday, Stephanie is taking the Biology test on Tuesday, and Brian is taking the Calculus test on Wednesday.

28. B   Advanced Mathematics (trigonometry) HARD

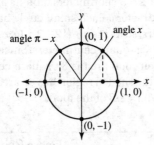

It first helps to notice that x and $\pi - x$ are supplements; that is, they have a sum of π radians or $180°$. Since x is in the first quadrant, where the tangent is positive, its supplement is in the second quadrant, where the tangent is negative. These two angles have the same reference angle, so their tangents are opposites.

29. A   Problem Solving and Data Analysis
                           (rates) MEDIUM

The period from 1911 to 1936 is a 25-year span, and the total decrease in the world record time over that period is $11.5 - 18.8 = -7.3$ seconds. Therefore, the rate of change is $-7.3 \div 25 = -0.292$ seconds per year.

30. C   Data Analysis (drawing comparisons)
                            MEDIUM-HARD

The change from 1936 to 1973 was $10.8 - 11.5 = -0.7$ seconds. In 1925, the winning time was 12.4. A change of -0.7 would take the winning time to 11.7, which was the record in 1934.

31. 8   Algebra (linear relationships) EASY

We can simply use the slope formula to solve this one:

$$\text{slope} = \frac{y_2 - y_1}{x_2 - x_1} = \frac{27 - (-5)}{a - 0} = \frac{32}{a}$$

If the slope of this line is 4: $\dfrac{32}{a} = 4$

Multiply by a: $32 = 4a$

Divide by 4: $8 = a$

32. 1.5   Data Analysis (ratios) MEDIUM

Let $x =$ the size of the model tree in inches. The scale of 1 inch to 64 feet allows us to set up a proportion:

$$\frac{1}{64} = \frac{x}{96}$$

Cross-multiply; $64x = 96$

Divide by 64: $x = 1.5$

33. 9   Advanced Mathematics
                         (solving quadratics) MEDIUM

Original equation: $t^2 + 5t = 14$

Subtract 14: $t^2 + 5t - 14 = 0$

Factor: $(t + 7)(t - 2) = 0$

Solve with the Zero Product Property: $t = -7$ or $t = 2$

Since a is the lesser of the two solutions, then $a = -7$ and $b = 2$, so $b - a = 2 - (-7) = 9$.

34. 2480   Problem Solving and Data Analysis
                           (percents) MEDIUM

Let n represent the number of registered voters in Curtsville. If 25% of these are registered as Republicans, then there are $0.25n$ registered Republicans in Curtsville. If 60% of these voted, then $(0.60)(0.25n)$ registered Republicans voted: $(0.60)(0.25n) = 372$

Simplify: $0.15n = 372$

Divide by 0.15: $n = 2480$

35. 4   Algebra (inequalities) MEDIUM-HARD

$$2 < \left| \frac{1}{5} - \frac{2}{5}n \right| < 3$$

Consider that the argument to the absolute value could be positive or negative:

$$2<\frac{1}{3}-\frac{2}{3}n<3 \text{ or } -3<\frac{1}{3}-\frac{2}{3}n<-2$$

Multiply by 3: $\qquad 6<1-2n<9 \text{ or } -9<1-2n<-6$

Subtract 1: $\qquad 5<-2n<8 \text{ or } -10<-2n<-7$

Divide by –2 and "flip" the inequalities:

$$-2.5>n>-4 \text{ or } 5>n>3.5$$

The only integer that satisfies the first inequality is $n=-3$, and the only integer that satisfies the second inequality is $n=4$. Since the question asks only for the positive integer value, the answer is $n=4$.

---

36. **15**   **Additional Topics (rational inequalities) MEDIUM**

$$\frac{1}{\sqrt{50}}-\frac{2}{m}>0$$

Multiply by $m\sqrt{50}$ (the common denominator):

$$m-2\sqrt{50}>0$$

Add $2\sqrt{50}$: $\qquad\qquad m>2\sqrt{50}\approx14.1$

So the least positive integer that satisfies this inequality is $m=15$.

---

37. **3/5 or .6**   **Problem Solving and Data Analysis (probability) MEDIUM**

If the first head appeared, on average, after 2.5 tosses, then the best estimate for the probability of landing <u>heads</u> is $1 \div 2.5 = 0.4$. Recall that the probability of the coin landing heads plus the probability of it landing tails must equal 1; therefore, the probability of the coin landing <u>tails</u> is $1 - 0.4 = 0.6$ or 3/5.

---

38. **4/3 or 1.33**   **Advanced Mathematics (probability) HARD**

If the coin land heads an average of 3.75 times out of 5, then the best estimate for the probability of the coin landing heads is $3.75 \div 5 = 0.75$. If this value for p is then used in the formula for Method 2, where y represents the number of the roll on which the first head appears, we have: $\qquad 0.75=\frac{1}{y}$

Multiply by y: $\qquad\qquad\qquad 0.75y = 1$

Divide by 0.75: $\qquad\qquad\qquad y = 1.33 \text{ or } 4/3$

PRACTICE SAT 3

ANSWER SHEET

SECTION 1

1 Ⓐ Ⓑ Ⓒ Ⓓ	13 Ⓐ Ⓑ Ⓒ Ⓓ	25 Ⓐ Ⓑ Ⓒ Ⓓ	37 Ⓐ Ⓑ Ⓒ Ⓓ	49 Ⓐ Ⓑ Ⓒ Ⓓ
2 Ⓐ Ⓑ Ⓒ Ⓓ	14 Ⓐ Ⓑ Ⓒ Ⓓ	26 Ⓐ Ⓑ Ⓒ Ⓓ	38 Ⓐ Ⓑ Ⓒ Ⓓ	50 Ⓐ Ⓑ Ⓒ Ⓓ
3 Ⓐ Ⓑ Ⓒ Ⓓ	15 Ⓐ Ⓑ Ⓒ Ⓓ	27 Ⓐ Ⓑ Ⓒ Ⓓ	39 Ⓐ Ⓑ Ⓒ Ⓓ	51 Ⓐ Ⓑ Ⓒ Ⓓ
4 Ⓐ Ⓑ Ⓒ Ⓓ	16 Ⓐ Ⓑ Ⓒ Ⓓ	28 Ⓐ Ⓑ Ⓒ Ⓓ	40 Ⓐ Ⓑ Ⓒ Ⓓ	52 Ⓐ Ⓑ Ⓒ Ⓓ
5 Ⓐ Ⓑ Ⓒ Ⓓ	17 Ⓐ Ⓑ Ⓒ Ⓓ	29 Ⓐ Ⓑ Ⓒ Ⓓ	41 Ⓐ Ⓑ Ⓒ Ⓓ	
6 Ⓐ Ⓑ Ⓒ Ⓓ	18 Ⓐ Ⓑ Ⓒ Ⓓ	30 Ⓐ Ⓑ Ⓒ Ⓓ	42 Ⓐ Ⓑ Ⓒ Ⓓ	
7 Ⓐ Ⓑ Ⓒ Ⓓ	19 Ⓐ Ⓑ Ⓒ Ⓓ	31 Ⓐ Ⓑ Ⓒ Ⓓ	43 Ⓐ Ⓑ Ⓒ Ⓓ	
8 Ⓐ Ⓑ Ⓒ Ⓓ	20 Ⓐ Ⓑ Ⓒ Ⓓ	32 Ⓐ Ⓑ Ⓒ Ⓓ	44 Ⓐ Ⓑ Ⓒ Ⓓ	
9 Ⓐ Ⓑ Ⓒ Ⓓ	21 Ⓐ Ⓑ Ⓒ Ⓓ	33 Ⓐ Ⓑ Ⓒ Ⓓ	45 Ⓐ Ⓑ Ⓒ Ⓓ	
10 Ⓐ Ⓑ Ⓒ Ⓓ	22 Ⓐ Ⓑ Ⓒ Ⓓ	34 Ⓐ Ⓑ Ⓒ Ⓓ	46 Ⓐ Ⓑ Ⓒ Ⓓ	
11 Ⓐ Ⓑ Ⓒ Ⓓ	23 Ⓐ Ⓑ Ⓒ Ⓓ	35 Ⓐ Ⓑ Ⓒ Ⓓ	47 Ⓐ Ⓑ Ⓒ Ⓓ	
12 Ⓐ Ⓑ Ⓒ Ⓓ	24 Ⓐ Ⓑ Ⓒ Ⓓ	36 Ⓐ Ⓑ Ⓒ Ⓓ	48 Ⓐ Ⓑ Ⓒ Ⓓ	

SECTION 2

1 Ⓐ Ⓑ Ⓒ Ⓓ	11 Ⓐ Ⓑ Ⓒ Ⓓ	21 Ⓐ Ⓑ Ⓒ Ⓓ	31 Ⓐ Ⓑ Ⓒ Ⓓ	41 Ⓐ Ⓑ Ⓒ Ⓓ
2 Ⓐ Ⓑ Ⓒ Ⓓ	12 Ⓐ Ⓑ Ⓒ Ⓓ	22 Ⓐ Ⓑ Ⓒ Ⓓ	32 Ⓐ Ⓑ Ⓒ Ⓓ	42 Ⓐ Ⓑ Ⓒ Ⓓ
3 Ⓐ Ⓑ Ⓒ Ⓓ	13 Ⓐ Ⓑ Ⓒ Ⓓ	23 Ⓐ Ⓑ Ⓒ Ⓓ	33 Ⓐ Ⓑ Ⓒ Ⓓ	43 Ⓐ Ⓑ Ⓒ Ⓓ
4 Ⓐ Ⓑ Ⓒ Ⓓ	14 Ⓐ Ⓑ Ⓒ Ⓓ	24 Ⓐ Ⓑ Ⓒ Ⓓ	34 Ⓐ Ⓑ Ⓒ Ⓓ	44 Ⓐ Ⓑ Ⓒ Ⓓ
5 Ⓐ Ⓑ Ⓒ Ⓓ	15 Ⓐ Ⓑ Ⓒ Ⓓ	25 Ⓐ Ⓑ Ⓒ Ⓓ	35 Ⓐ Ⓑ Ⓒ Ⓓ	
6 Ⓐ Ⓑ Ⓒ Ⓓ	16 Ⓐ Ⓑ Ⓒ Ⓓ	26 Ⓐ Ⓑ Ⓒ Ⓓ	36 Ⓐ Ⓑ Ⓒ Ⓓ	
7 Ⓐ Ⓑ Ⓒ Ⓓ	17 Ⓐ Ⓑ Ⓒ Ⓓ	27 Ⓐ Ⓑ Ⓒ Ⓓ	37 Ⓐ Ⓑ Ⓒ Ⓓ	
8 Ⓐ Ⓑ Ⓒ Ⓓ	18 Ⓐ Ⓑ Ⓒ Ⓓ	28 Ⓐ Ⓑ Ⓒ Ⓓ	38 Ⓐ Ⓑ Ⓒ Ⓓ	
9 Ⓐ Ⓑ Ⓒ Ⓓ	19 Ⓐ Ⓑ Ⓒ Ⓓ	29 Ⓐ Ⓑ Ⓒ Ⓓ	39 Ⓐ Ⓑ Ⓒ Ⓓ	
10 Ⓐ Ⓑ Ⓒ Ⓓ	20 Ⓐ Ⓑ Ⓒ Ⓓ	30 Ⓐ Ⓑ Ⓒ Ⓓ	40 Ⓐ Ⓑ Ⓒ Ⓓ	

SECTION 3

1. Ⓐ Ⓑ Ⓒ Ⓓ   11. Ⓐ Ⓑ Ⓒ Ⓓ
2. Ⓐ Ⓑ Ⓒ Ⓓ   12. Ⓐ Ⓑ Ⓒ Ⓓ
3. Ⓐ Ⓑ Ⓒ Ⓓ   13. Ⓐ Ⓑ Ⓒ Ⓓ
4. Ⓐ Ⓑ Ⓒ Ⓓ   14. Ⓐ Ⓑ Ⓒ Ⓓ
5. Ⓐ Ⓑ Ⓒ Ⓓ   15. Ⓐ Ⓑ Ⓒ Ⓓ
6. Ⓐ Ⓑ Ⓒ Ⓓ
7. Ⓐ Ⓑ Ⓒ Ⓓ
8. Ⓐ Ⓑ Ⓒ Ⓓ
9. Ⓐ Ⓑ Ⓒ Ⓓ
10. Ⓐ Ⓑ Ⓒ Ⓓ

Student-Produced Responses

ONLY ANSWERS ENTERED IN THE CIRCLES IN EACH GRID WILL BE SCORED. YOU WILL NOT RECEIVE CREDIT FOR ANYTHING WRITTEN IN THE BOXES ABOVE THE CIRCLES.

16.

17.

18.

19.

20.

SECTION 4

1 Ⓐ Ⓑ Ⓒ Ⓓ   11 Ⓐ Ⓑ Ⓒ Ⓓ   21 Ⓐ Ⓑ Ⓒ Ⓓ
2 Ⓐ Ⓑ Ⓒ Ⓓ   12 Ⓐ Ⓑ Ⓒ Ⓓ   22 Ⓐ Ⓑ Ⓒ Ⓓ
3 Ⓐ Ⓑ Ⓒ Ⓓ   13 Ⓐ Ⓑ Ⓒ Ⓓ   23 Ⓐ Ⓑ Ⓒ Ⓓ
4 Ⓐ Ⓑ Ⓒ Ⓓ   14 Ⓐ Ⓑ Ⓒ Ⓓ   24 Ⓐ Ⓑ Ⓒ Ⓓ
5 Ⓐ Ⓑ Ⓒ Ⓓ   15 Ⓐ Ⓑ Ⓒ Ⓓ   25 Ⓐ Ⓑ Ⓒ Ⓓ
6 Ⓐ Ⓑ Ⓒ Ⓓ   16 Ⓐ Ⓑ Ⓒ Ⓓ   26 Ⓐ Ⓑ Ⓒ Ⓓ
7 Ⓐ Ⓑ Ⓒ Ⓓ   17 Ⓐ Ⓑ Ⓒ Ⓓ   27 Ⓐ Ⓑ Ⓒ Ⓓ
8 Ⓐ Ⓑ Ⓒ Ⓓ   18 Ⓐ Ⓑ Ⓒ Ⓓ   28 Ⓐ Ⓑ Ⓒ Ⓓ
9 Ⓐ Ⓑ Ⓒ Ⓓ   19 Ⓐ Ⓑ Ⓒ Ⓓ   29 Ⓐ Ⓑ Ⓒ Ⓓ
10 Ⓐ Ⓑ Ⓒ Ⓓ   20 Ⓐ Ⓑ Ⓒ Ⓓ   30 Ⓐ Ⓑ Ⓒ Ⓓ

Student-Produced Responses

ONLY ANSWERS ENTERED IN THE CIRCLES IN EACH GRID WILL BE SCORED. YOU WILL NOT RECEIVE CREDIT FOR ANYTHING WRITTEN IN THE BOXES ABOVE THE CIRCLES.

31   32   33   34

35   36   37   38

SECTION V: ESSAY

You may wish to remove these sample answer document pages to respond to the practice SAT Essay Test.

Begin ESSAY here.

_____

_____

_____

_____

_____

_____

_____

_____

_____

_____

_____

_____

_____

_____

_____

_____

_____

_____

_____

_____

_____

_____

_____

_____

_____

If you need more space, please continue on the next page.

1

Cut Here

ESSAY

_____

_____

_____

_____

_____

_____

_____

_____

_____

_____

_____

_____

_____

_____

_____

_____

_____

_____

_____

_____

_____

_____

_____

_____

_____

_____

_____

If you need more space, please continue on the next page.

Cut Here

ESSAY

If you need more space, please continue on the next page.

ESSAY

_____

_____

_____

_____

_____

_____

_____

_____

_____

_____

_____

_____

_____

_____

_____

_____

_____

_____

_____

_____

_____

_____

_____

_____

_____

_____

_____

STOP here with the Essay.

Cut Here

1

1

Reading Test

65 MINUTES, 52 QUESTIONS

Turn to Section 1 of your answer sheet to answer the questions in this section.

DIRECTIONS

Each passage or pair of passages below is followed by a number of questions. After reading each passage or pair, choose the best answer to each question based on what is stated or implied in the passage or passages and in any accompanying graphics (such as a table or graph).

Questions 1–10 are based on the following passage.

This passage is adapted from Lincoln Steffens, *The Shame of the Cities*, originally published in 1904. Steffens was a New York reporter who targeted urban political corruption.

Line
The misgovernment of the American people is misgovernment by the American people. Now, the typical American citizen is the business man. The typical business man is a bad citizen; he is
5 busy. If he is a "big business man" and very busy, he does not neglect; he is busy with politics, oh, very busy and very businesslike. He is a self-righteous fraud, this big business man. He is the chief source of corruption, and it would be a boon
10 if he would neglect politics. But he is not the business man that neglects politics; that worthy is the good citizen, the typical business man. He too is busy. He is the one that has no use and therefore no time for politics. When his neglect has permit-
15 ted bad government to go so far that he can be stirred to action, he is unhappy, and he looks around for a cure that shall be quick, so that he may hurry back to the shop. Naturally, too, when he talks politics, he talks shop. His patent remedy
20 is quack; it is business.

There is hardly an office from United States Senator down to Alderman in any part of the country to which the business man has not been

elected; yet politics remains corrupt, government
25 pretty bad, and the selfish citizen has to hold himself in readiness like the old volunteer firemen to rush forth at any hour, in any weather, to prevent the fire; and he goes out sometimes and he puts out the fire (after the damage is done) and
30 he goes back to the shop sighing for the business man in politics. The business man has failed in politics as he has in citizenship.

Why? Because politics is business. That's what's the matter with it. That's what's the matter
35 with everything—art, literature, religion, journalism, law, medicine—they're all business, and all—as you see them. Make politics a sport, as they do in England, or a profession, as they do in Germany, and we'll have—well, something else
40 than we have now, if we want it, which is another question. But don't try to reform politics with the banker, the lawyer, and the dry-goods merchant, for these are business men and there are two great hindrances to their achievement of reform:
45 one is that they are different from, but no better than, the politicians; the other is that politics is not "their line." The politician is a business man with a specialty. When a business man of some other line learns the business of politics, he is
50 a politician, and there is not much reform left in him. Consider the United States Senate, and believe me.

The commercial spirit is the spirit of profit, not patriotism; of credit, not honor; of individual

55 gain, not national prosperity; of trade and dicker-
    ing, not principle. "My business is sacred," says
    the business man in his heart. "Whatever pros-
    pers my business, is good; it must be. Whatever
    hinders it, is wrong; it must be. A bribe is bad,
60 that is, it is a bad thing to take; but it is not so bad
    to give one, not if it is necessary to my business."
    "Business is business" is not a political senti-
    ment, but our politician has caught it. And as for
    giving bad government or good, how about the
65 merchant who gives bad goods or good goods,
    according to the demand?

But there is hope, not alone despair, in the
commercialism of our politics. If our political
leaders are to be always a lot of political mer-
70 chants, they will supply any demand we may
create. All we have to do is to establish a steady
demand for good government. If the demand
were steady, they, being so commercial, would
"deliver the goods."

CONTINUE →

1

1

1

The overall tone of the passage is best described as

A) beseeching.

B) analytical.

C) facetious.

D) censorious.

2

As used in line 6, to "neglect" means to

A) abandon public service to go into business.

B) disregard a professional duty.

C) ignore social circumstances.

D) shirk familial obligations.

3

As used in line 9, "boon" refers to a

A) financial windfall.

B) social benefit.

C) useful discovery.

D) illicit payment.

·4

Steffens suggests that our best hope for productive political reform lies in

A) reducing bribery by establishing strong anti-corruption laws.

B) encouraging more artists and clergy to run for office.

C) making campaigns more competitive by forming more political parties.

D) creating a popular market for effective leadership.

5

Which choice provides the best evidence for the answer to the previous question?

A) Lines 7–8 ("He is . . . man")

B) Lines 37–41 ("Make . . . question")

C) Lines 60–63 ("A bribe . . . business")

D) Lines 72–74 ("If . . . goods")

6

In line 16, the statement "he is unhappy" means that the typical businessman

A) is concerned about unfavorable economic conditions.

B) objects to governmental interference in his everyday business affairs.

C) resents feeling obliged to partake in civic matters.

D) feels that the demands of running a business are onerous.

7

The statement "His patent remedy is quack" (lines 19–20) implies that the businessman in politics is inclined to

A) apply business principles to civic matters.

B) disregard the rules of proper government.

C) be contemptuous of the general public.

D) employ questionable accounting methods.

1

8

Stephens uses the metaphor of a fire in the second paragraph (lines 21–32) primarily to make the point that

A) civic servants are indispensable to the public welfare.

B) ordinary citizens are capable of extraordinarily selfless acts.

C) politicians who serve corporate interests can be profoundly inept.

D) dangerous political ideas can spread quickly and widely.

9

According to Steffens, the typical businessman is different from the "big business man" primarily in that the typical businessman

A) does not consider politics a priority.

B) better understands the needs of ordinary citizens.

C) is better suited to fixing the problems of government.

D) earns his money honestly, rather than through bribery and corruption.

10

Which choice provides the best evidence for the answer to the previous question?

A) Lines 7–8 ("He is . . . business man")

B) Lines 12–14 ("He . . . politics")

C) Lines 58–59 ("Whatever . . . be")

D) Lines 69–73 ("If our . . . create")

CONTINUE

1   1

Questions 11–21 are based on the following passage and supplementary material.

This passage is adapted from Greg Klerkx, "Outer Limits." ©2014 *Aeon* magazine (aeon.co), originally published August 1, 2014.

Line
The question of where "outer" space begins intrigues us because it marks the borderline between a world where we are protected by Earth, and one where we must fend for ourselves.
5 After all, Earth's atmosphere is our first and last line of defense against lethal ultraviolet radiation and rogue meteors.

But perhaps science isn't the right tool to gauge where space begins. After all, there is
10 no real thing called "space." There are layers of atmosphere that grow gradually thinner as you move outward, and a giant shell of gravity that does the same, but space is, ultimately, a phenomenological concept. Its boundary lies wher-
15 ever humans feel they have crossed a threshold of distance, or protection, or some other radical departure from terrestrial experience.

In October 2012, the Austrian skydiver and BASE[1] jumper Felix Baumgartner leapt out of a
20 balloon-tethered gondola approximately 39 kilometers above the New Mexico desert. Reaching a top speed of 1,342 kilometers per hour— fast enough to break the speed of sound and create a shock wave captured on film—Baumgartner set
25 an altitude record for skydiving, and achieved the longest vertical free-fall in history.[2]

However amazing it was, Baumgartner was nowhere near to anyone's definition of space. Even at the apex of his mission, Baumgartner was
30 still comfortably within the stratosphere and, in terms of gravity, Sir Isaac Newton would have had no trouble recognizing the effects at work on Baumgartner's body. He leapt. He fell.

The cleverest marketing campaigns, like the
35 one behind Baumgartner's feat, succeed because they tap into the zeitgeist. With the highest peaks summited, with vehicular speed records now iterative rather than truly pioneering, it often feels as though humankind has run out of the
40 kind of challenges that once forced us to rethink what it means to be human. The Space Race has a

lot to answer for in this respect: for sheer daring, very little can compare to being squeezed into the business end of a retooled nuclear missile and
45 fired into orbit.

Indeed, space travellers have confessed to all manner of emotions in advance of flight: excitement and dread, wonder and trepidation, gut-trembling fear and childlike eagerness. But
50 no matter how vivid one's prelaunch feelings, nothing comes close to lift-off itself. The former NASA administrator Aaron Cohen once described launch as "a barely controlled explosion" that made even the relatively luxurious space shuttle a
55 bone-jarring experience. Outside a space vehicle, any meaningful atmosphere disappears almost immediately. At 39 kilometers up, without a pressure suit or a pressurized vehicle, hypoxia, hypothermia and the rupturing of skin and organs set
60 in quickly. At 118 kilometers, the Earth's horizon appears distinctly curved and the space beyond it darkens into an inky black. Unstrap from your seat, and you'd float free in microgravity. You might also be spacesick, as more than half of all
65 astronauts are.

Of the hundred or so billion human beings that have lived on this planet, only about 550 have made it to space. Between them, they have generated thousands of words describing the
70 experience—some coherent, others less so. There are bits of poetry and verse, quips and quotations, solemn readings from religious texts, all of which suggest that the experience affects the mind at least as powerfully as the body. The
75 Mercury astronaut Scott Carpenter said that the Earth looked like "a delicate flower" from space. Alan Shepard, the first American in space, cried. Perhaps the most concise distillation of opinion came from the world's first space traveller, Yuri
80 Gagarin, who simply said, "What beauty."

Getting into orbit is still the province of governments or private companies with resources well beyond what most of us can afford. Reaching the edge of space is a more universally achiev-
85 able feat, but only as long as the definition of that boundary remains fluid. Virgin Galactic, which has yet to launch a single commercial flight, is reportedly booked up for several years to come with hundreds of deposits in the bank, even
90 though its offer of "spaceflight" is tenuous at best.

CONTINUE ▶

1 **1**

Hit the lottery jackpot, cash in a pension fund or sell off a second home, and you too could actually touch the cold, frightening edge of our world.

Michael Collins quipped that the space
95 program needed "more English majors." Baumgartner would probably agree, having confessed frustration in interview after interview that he could not say something more profound about his experience than: "It was cool." But
100 maybe that's the point. Maybe we want to touch the edge of space because it's the one place left to us that promises a shivering sense of primeval, inarticulate rapture; a place where language, like air, ceases to matter.

[1]BASE = parachuting or wingsuit flying from a fixed structure or cliff
[2]until Alan Eustace broke this record with a 41.4-kilometer jump on October 24, 2014

Altitudes for Historic Jumps 1960–2014

Source: @2015 College Hill Coaching

CONTINUE →

11

In the first paragraph, outer space is characterized primarily as

A) an inviting frontier.

B) a daunting paradox.

C) a spectacular conquest.

D) a treacherous environment.

12

In line 33, the statements "He leapt," and "He fell," serve to emphasize what aspect of Baumgartner's jump?

A) its perilousness

B) its predictability

C) its relative ease

D) its profundity

13

As used in line 56, "meaningful" most nearly means

A) insightful.

B) suggestive.

C) earnest.

D) substantial.

14

The author describes the experiences of astronauts primarily to make the point that

A) recent technological advances have made space travel much safer.

B) the concept of space is as much a subjective one as a scientific one.

C) space flight is far more technologically sophisticated than skydiving.

D) many space-related endeavors have become too commercialized.

15

Which choice provides the best evidence for the answer to the previous question?

A) Lines 57-60 ("At 39 . . . quickly")

B) Lines 63-65 ("You . . . are")

C) Lines 66-68 ("Of the . . . space")

D) Lines 70-74 ("There . . . body")

16

As used in line 90, "tenuous" most nearly means

A) delicate.

B) invalid.

C) dubious.

D) insubstantial.

17

The author believes that "science isn't the right tool to gauge where space begins" because

A) scientists have conflicting opinions based on their specialties.

B) the question is a matter for philosophers, rather than scientists, to decide.

C) the experience of space travel cannot be easily quantified.

D) there is still much progress to be made in the development of space technologies.

18

Which choice provides that best evidence for the answer to the previous question?

A) Lines 14-17 ("Its . . . experience")

B) Lines 27-28 ("However . . . space")

C) Lines 51-55 ("The former . . . experience")

D) Lines 100-104 ("Maybe . . . matter")

CONTINUE ▶

1   **1**

19

If the Karman line is regarded as the official "edge" of outer space, approximately how far, according to the diagram, were the highest skydiving jumps from the edge of space?

A) 40 kilometers

B) 50 kilometers

C) 60 kilometers

D) 100 kilometers

20

According to the diagram, Felix Baumgartner made his famous jump at an altitude where the temperature was approximately

A) 50°F colder than that at the earth's surface.

B) 10°F colder than that at the earth's surface.

C) 10°F warmer than that at the earth's surface.

D) 50°F warmer than that at the earth's surface.

21

In lines 103–104, the statement "language . . . ceases to matter" means that

A) prior theories about space and motion no longer apply.

B) the desire to explore is one we share with our most ancient ancestors.

C) progress requires heroic effort, and not merely the articulation of goals.

D) intense experiences are not enhanced by efforts to describe them.

CONTINUE

Questions 22–32 are based on the following passage.

This passage is from George Eliot, *Middlemarch*, originally published in 1874. In this story, the bachelor Mr. Brooke is talking to the scholarly clergyman Mr. Casaubon and Mr. Casaubon's fiancé, Dorothea, who is also Mr. Brooke's niece. Celia is Dorothea's sister.

Line   "Well, but now, Casaubon, such deep studies, classics, mathematics, that kind of thing, are too taxing for a woman—too taxing, you know."

        "Dorothea is learning to read the characters
5   simply," said Mr. Casaubon, evading the question. "She had the very considerate thought of saving my eyes."

        "Ah, well, without understanding, you know—that may not be so bad. But there is a
10   lightness about the feminine mind—a touch and go—music, the fine arts, that kind of thing—they should study those up to a certain point, women should, but in a light way, you know. A woman should be able to sit down and play you or sing
15   you a good old English tune. That is what I like, though I have heard most things—been at the opera in Vienna: Gluck, Mozart, everything of that sort. But I'm a conservative in music—it's not like ideas, you know. I stick to the good old
20   tunes."

        "Mr. Casaubon is not fond of the piano, and I am very glad he is not," said Dorothea, whose slight regard for domestic music and feminine fine art must be forgiven her, considering the
25   small tinkling and smearing in which they chiefly consisted at that dark period. She smiled and looked up at her betrothed with grateful eyes. If he had always been asking her to play the "Last Rose of Summer," she would have required much
30   resignation. "He says there is only an old harpsichord at Lowick, and it is covered with books."

        "Ah, there you are behind Celia, my dear. Celia, now, plays very prettily, and is always ready to play. However, since Casaubon does not like
35   it, you are all right. But it's a pity you should not have little recreations of that sort, Casaubon: the bow always strung—that kind of thing, you know—will not do."

        "I never could look on it in the light of a
40   recreation to have my ears teased with measured noises," said Mr. Casaubon. "A tune much iterated has the ridiculous effect of making the words in my mind perform a sort of minuet to keep time—an effect hardly tolerable, I imagine,

45   after boyhood. As to the grander forms of music, worthy to accompany solemn celebrations, and even to serve as an educating influence according to the ancient conception, I say nothing, for with these we are not immediately concerned."

50   "No; but music of that sort I should enjoy," said Dorothea. "When we were coming home from Lausanne my uncle took us to hear the great organ at Freiberg, and it made me sob."

        "That kind of thing is not healthy, my dear,"
55   said Mr. Brooke. "Casaubon, she will be in your hands now: you must teach my niece to take things more quietly, eh, Dorothea?"

        He ended with a smile, not wishing to hurt his niece, but really thinking that it was perhaps
60   better for her to be early married to so sober a fellow as Casaubon, since she would not hear of Chettam.

        "It is wonderful, though," he said to himself as he shuffled out of the room—"it is wonder-
65   ful that she should have liked him. However, the match is good. I should have been travelling out of my brief to have hindered it, let Mrs. Cadwallader say what she will. He is pretty certain to be a bishop, is Casaubon. That was a
70   very seasonable pamphlet of his on the Catholic Question—a deanery at least. They owe him a deanery."

        And here I must vindicate a claim to philosophical reflectiveness, by remarking that Mr.
75   Brooke on this occasion little thought of the Radical speech which, at a later period, he was led to make on the incomes of the bishops. What elegant historian would neglect a striking opportunity for pointing out that his heroes did
80   not foresee the history of the world, or even their own actions? For example, that Henry of Navarre, when a Protestant baby, little thought of being a Catholic monarch, or that Alfred the Great, when he measured his laborious nights with burning
85   candles, had no idea of future gentlemen measuring their idle days with watches. Here is a mine of truth, which, however vigorously it may be worked, is likely to outlast our coal.

        But of Mr. Brooke I make a further remark
90   perhaps less warranted by precedent—namely, that if he had foreknown his speech, it might not have made any great difference. To think with pleasure of his niece's husband having a large ecclesiastical income was one thing, but to make
95   a Liberal speech was another thing, and it is a narrow mind which cannot look at a subject from various points of view.

CONTINUE ▶

22

Which choice best summarizes the passage?

A) Mr. Brooke becomes convinced that Mr. Casaubon and Dorothea are well suited to each other, despite Dorothea's flaws.

B) Mr. Brooke counsels Mr. Casaubon against marrying someone who does not share his love of classical studies and music.

C) Mr. Brooke consents to the relationship between Dorothea and Mr. Casaubon, but criticizes Mr. Casaubon for his hypocrisy.

D) Mr. Brooke cautions his niece Dorothea that her fiancé Mr. Casaubon is not the man she thinks he is.

23

As Mr. Brooke uses it in line 10, "lightness" most nearly means

A) naivety.

B) liveliness.

C) humor.

D) lucidity.

24

Mr. Casaubon apparently regards "domestic music" (line 23) as

A) a welcome accompaniment to his studies.

B) an insufferably tedious experience.

C) something he will tolerate for Dorothea's sake.

D) a pleasant diversion from his work.

25

Which choice provides the best evidence for the answer to the previous question?

A) Lines 13-15 ("A woman . . . tune")

B) Lines 30-31 ("He says . . . books")

C) Lines 41-45 ("A tune . . . boyhood")

D) Lines 45-49 ("As to . . . concerned")

26

Mr. Brooke's statement that "it's not like ideas" (lines 18-19) suggests that he

A) does not find philosophical debate as pleasurable as Mr. Casaubon does.

B) finds music to be much more accessible than politics.

C) is inclined to hold unconventional opinions on social issues.

D) enjoys music that reinforces his nationalistic views.

27

Dorothea apparently prefers music that is

A) quick and energetic.

B) sweet and melodious.

C) dignified and majestic.

D) suitable for dancing.

CONTINUE →

1

1

28

The passage indicates that Mr. Brooke would later become

A) an accomplished classical musician.

B) a detractor of Dorothea's relationship with Mr. Casaubon.

C) a high-ranking official of the church.

D) a critic of the clergy and its affluence.

29

Which choice provides the best evidence for the answer to the previous question?

A) Lines 58–62 ("He . . . Chettam")

B) Lines 66–68 ("I should . . . will")

C) Lines 73–77 ("And . . . bishops")

D) Lines 89–92 ("But . . . difference")

30

In lines 73–77, the narrator indicates that Mr. Brooke's attitude expressed in lines 63–72 is

A) blatantly insincere.

B) prone to change.

C) inappropriately domineering.

D) mildly subversive.

31

As used in line 88, "worked" most nearly means

A) accomplished.

B) arranged.

C) quarried.

D) manipulated.

32

The final paragraph credits Mr. Brooke primarily with

A) open-mindedness.

B) shrewdness.

C) sentimentality.

D) forbearance.

Questions 33–42 are based on the following passage.

This passage is adapted from Michael Graziano, "Build-a-Brain." ©2015 *Aeon* magazine (aeon.co), originally published July 10, 2015.

Line   The race is on to figure out what exactly consciousness is and how to build it. I've made my
own entry into that race, a framework for understanding consciousness called the Attention
5 Schema theory, which suggests that consciousness is no bizarre by-product—it's a tool for regulating information in the brain.

Imagine a robot equipped with camera eyes,
looking at a tennis ball. If we can build a brain to
10 be conscious of the tennis ball—just that—then
we'll have made the essential leap.

What information should be in our build-a-
brain to start with? Clearly, information about
the ball. Light enters the eye and is translated
15 into signals. The brain processes those signals
and builds a description of the ball, constructing
information such as color, shape, and location. It
constructs a dataset that's constantly revised as
new signals come in, an *internal model*. Millions
20 of wavelengths of light mix together and reflect
from different parts of the ball, but the eyes and
brain simplify that complexity into the property
of color. It's a caricature, a proxy for reality, and
it's good enough for survival.

25 The brain constructs a vast number of such
simplified models, and those models compete
with each other for resources. The scene might
be cluttered with tennis racquets, a few people,
the trees in the distance. The brain needs to
30 prioritize.

That focusing is called *attention*. What
neuroscientists mean by attention is something
mechanistic. A particular internal model in the
brain wins the competition for the moment,
35 suppresses its rivals, and dominates the brain's
outputs.

With a computer and a camera, we could
give our robot an internal model of the ball and
an attentional focus on the ball. But is the robot
40 *conscious* of the ball in the same subjective sense
that you might be? Would it claim to have an

inner feeling? Some scholars of consciousness
would say yes.

I would say no. We have more work to do. We
45 ask the robot, "Are you aware of the ball?" It says,
"Cannot compute."

Why? Because the machine accesses the
internal model that we've given it so far and
finds no relevant information. Plenty of infor-
50 mation about the ball. No information about
what "awareness" is, and no information about
itself. After all, we asked it, "Are *you aware* of the
ball?" It doesn't even have information on what
this "you" is, so of course it can't answer the
55 question.

But we can fix that. Let's add another component, a second internal model of the *self*. Like
any other model, it is information put together in
the brain. One particularly important part of the
60 human self-model is called the *body schema*.

The body schema is the brain's internal
model of the physical self: how it moves, what
belongs to it, what doesn't, and so on. This is a
complex and delicate piece of equipment. The
65 neurologist Oliver Sacks tells of a man who wakes
up in the hospital after a stroke to find that some-
body has played a horrible joke. For some reason
there's a rubbery, cadaverous leg in bed with him.
Disgusted, he grabs the leg and throws it out of
70 bed. Unfortunately, it is attached to him. A part of
the man's body schema has become corrupted in
such a way that he can no longer process the fact
that his leg belongs to him.

Now that our build-a-brain has a self-model
75 as well as a model of the ball, we can ask it, "Tell
us about yourself." It replies, "I am standing at
this location, I am this tall and this wide, and I
grew up in Buffalo," or whatever else is available
in its self-model. Now we ask, "Are you aware of
80 the ball?" It says, "Cannot compute." Equipped
with only those two internal models, the machine
cannot pass for human.

The real use of a brain is to have some control
over yourself and the world around you. So far
85 we've given our robot a model of the ball and a
model of itself. But we've neglected the complex
relationship between the self and the ball. Let's
add a model of that relationship and see what
that gives us.

CONTINUE →

1

90   Alas, we can no longer dip into standard neuroscience. Whereas we have decades of research on internal models of concrete things such as tennis balls, there's virtually nothing on any internal model of *attention*. It might describe attention as
95   a *mental possession* of something, or something that *empowers* you to react, or something located *inside* of you.

Now when we ask, "What's the relationship between you and the ball," it says, "I have mental
100   possession of the ball." We ask, "Tell us more about how this mental possession works." And then something strange happens.
It says, "There is no physical mechanism. It just is. It's non-physical and it's located inside me.
105   It's my *consciousness*."

Potential Models for the Relationship Between Awareness and Attention

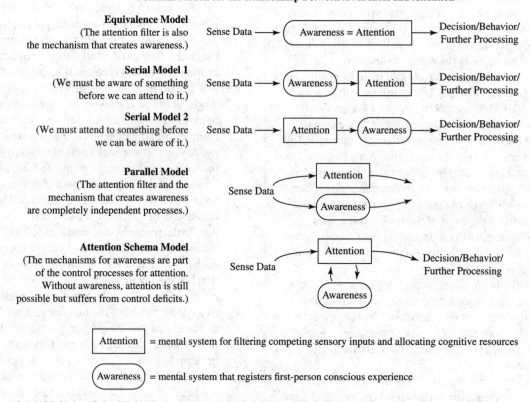

Equivalence Model
(The attention filter is also the mechanism that creates awareness.)

Serial Model 1
(We must be aware of something before we can attend to it.)

Serial Model 2
(We must attend to something before we can be aware of it.)

Parallel Model
(The attention filter and the mechanism that creates awareness are completely independent processes.)

Attention Schema Model
(The mechanisms for awareness are part of the control processes for attention. Without awareness, attention is still possible but suffers from control deficits.)

Attention = mental system for filtering competing sensory inputs and allocating cognitive resources

Awareness = mental system that registers first-person conscious experience

Source: C. F. Black and College Hill Coaching, based on the work of Michael Graziano and Taylor Webb

CONTINUE ▶

33

The primary function of the first paragraph is to

A) propose a solution to a problem.

B) describe a flaw in a way of thinking.

C) establish the limits of a debate.

D) provide the background for a discovery.

34

In line 11, the "leap" refers to

A) a logical inference.

B) a technological breakthrough.

C) a cultural watershed.

D) an act of persuasion.

35

What does the author suggest about the human brain's visual representation of an object?

A) It requires input from other senses as well.

B) It is assembled with astonishing quickness.

C) It omits a great deal of detail.

D) It requires a lot of attentional resources.

36

Which choice provides the best evidence for the answer to the previous question?

A) Lines 14–15 ("Light . . . signals")

B) Lines 15–17 ("The . . . location")

C) Lines 17–19 ("It . . . *model*")

D) Lines 23–24 ("It's . . . survival")

37

According to the diagram, the Attention Schema Model is similar to Serial Model 2 in that, in both models,

A) a mind cannot execute a behavior without being aware of it.

B) sensory data can be directly processed by either the attention filter or the awareness system.

C) a mind cannot pay attention to anything that has not already been brought into awareness.

D) a mind cannot be aware of anything that has not been processed by the attention filter.

38

The author questions a robot throughout the passage primarily in order to

A) establish the shortcomings of mechanistic views of the human mind.

B) indicate the minimum requirements for conscious awareness.

C) specify the technological hurdles that plague modern robotics engineers.

D) illustrate the recent progress that has been made in cognitive science.

CONTINUE ➔

1   **1**

39

The passage suggests that the major obstacle to constructing a functioning model of a conscious mind is

A) representing the attentional relationship between the self and the objects of perception.

B) preventing corruption of the brain's internal model of the body.

C) creating a model of attention that filters sensory data the way real brains do.

D) updating the dataset that serves as the internal model of perceptual objects.

40

Which choice provides the best evidence for the answer to the previous question?

A) Lines 19–23 ("Millions . . . color")

B) Lines 33–36 ("A particular . . . outputs")

C) Lines 61–63 ("The body . . . so on")

D) Lines 91–94 ("Whereas . . . *attention*")

41

As used in line 90, "dip into" most nearly means

A) immerse ourselves in.

B) condescend to.

C) draw upon.

D) vanish into.

42

The author refers to the work of Oliver Sacks in order to make a point about

A) the importance of competent medical care.

B) the unreliability of some representations.

C) the dangers of losing consciousness.

D) the hazards of playing practical jokes.

CONTINUE ➔

1   **1**

Questions 42–52 are based on the following passage.

Passage 1 is from John Stuart Mill, "A Few Words on Non-Intervention," an essay on the benevolence of England originally published in *Fraser's Magazine*, December 1859. Passage 2 is adapted from Noam Chomsky, transcript of as speech given at the Institute of European Affairs, January 19, 2006.

Passage 1

Line   There is a country in Europe, far exceeding
any other in wealth and in the power that wealth
bestows, the declared principle of whose foreign
policy is to let other nations alone. No coun-
5   try apprehends from it any aggressive designs.
Power, from of old, is wont to encroach upon the
weak, and to quarrel for ascendancy with those
who are as strong as itself. Not so this nation.
It will not submit to encroachment, but if other
10   nations do not meddle with it, it will not meddle
with them. Any attempt it makes to exert influence over them, even by persuasion, is rather in
the service of others, than of itself: to mediate
in the quarrels which break out between foreign
15   States, to arrest obstinate civil wars, to reconcile
belligerents, to intercede for mild treatment of
the vanquished, or finally, to procure the abandonment of some national crime and scandal to
humanity, such as the slave-trade.
20   Not only does this nation desire no benefit
to itself at the expense of other, it desires none
in which all others do not freely participate. It
makes no treaties stipulating for separate commercial advantages. If the aggressions of barbar-
25   ians force it to successful war, and its victorious
arms put it in a position to command liberty of
trade, whatever it demands for itself it demands
for all mankind. The cost of the war is its own;
the fruits it shares in fraternal equality with the
30   whole human race. Its own ports and commerce
are free as the air and the sky: all its neighbors
have full liberty to resort to it, paying either no
duties, or, if any, generally a mere equivalent
for what is paid by its own citizens. Nor does it
35   concern itself though they, on their part, keep all
to themselves, and persist in the most jealous and
narrow-minded exclusion of its merchants and
goods.
    A nation adopting this policy is a novelty in
40   the world; so much so it would appear that many
are unable to believe it when they see it.

Passage 2

    The idea that Europe, and later the United
States, is the guarantor of world order is very old.
One can begin to discuss it with John Stuart Mill's
45   "A Few Words on Non-Intervention." His essay
asked whether England should intervene in the
ugly world, in Europe and elsewhere, or whether
it should let the barbarians fight it out. His conclusion was that, balancing the various condi-
50   tions, England should intervene, even though
by doing so, England would endure the abuse
of the Europeans, who cannot comprehend that
England is a "novelty in the world," an angelic
power that seeks nothing for itself and acts only
55   for the benefits of others. Though it bears the cost
of intervention, it shares the benefits of its labor
with others equally.
    Mill was calling for the expansion of the
occupation of India to several new provinces.
60   His article appeared in 1859, immediately after
the Sepoy Rebellion (called in British history the
"India mutiny"), which Britain put down with
extreme savagery and brutality. Mill was a corresponding secretary of the East India Company.
65   The purpose of the expansion was to try to obtain
a monopoly over opium so that England could
break into the Chinese market. The only way to
break into the Chinese market was by obtaining
a monopoly of the opium trade and compelling
70   the Chinese to become opium addicts. In fact, the
Second Opium War (1856 to 1860) achieved that.
Britain established the world's most extensive
narco-trafficking enterprise; there's never been
anything remotely like it. Not only were they able
75   to break into China for the first time, but also the
profits from opium supported the Raj[1], the costs
of the British Navy, and provided very significant
capital, which fueled the industrial revolution in
England.
80   Mill was very aware of this, but his picture
was that since England is an angelic power we
should help the barbarians. The United States

CONTINUE ➡

is the same. Germany was the same. Japan was the same. The Japanese internal records
85   in Manchuria and China are overflowing with the milk of human kindness: Japan's going to create an "earthly paradise," expending its own resources for the benefit of barbarians; it was going to protect them from the bandits who were
90   trying to prevent Japan's noble efforts. This was probably very sincere. The Emperor Hirohito in his surrender declaration gave an eloquent statement with the same noble intentions. Hitler gave the same arguments when he took over
95   Czechoslovakia. The goal was to eliminate ethnic conflicts, let everyone live in peace and harmony under the tutelage of civilized Germany. And so it continues to the present moment.

[1]the British occupation of colonial India between 1858 and 1947.

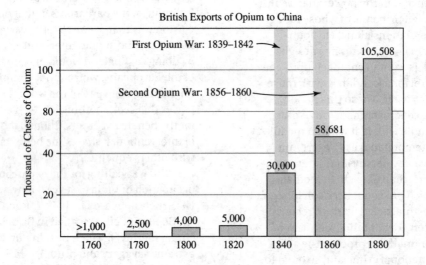

British Exports of Opium to China

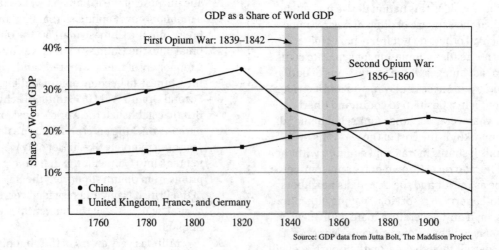

GDP as a Share of World GDP

Source: GDP data from Jutta Bolt, The Maddison Project

CONTINUE ▶

1

1

43

As used in line 5, "apprehends from" most nearly means

A) takes forcefully from.

B) ascribes to.

C) understands despite.

D) withholds from.

44

Passage 1 suggests that any economic advantage enjoyed by England is due to

A) special agreements with friendly nations.

B) remuneration for diplomatic services.

C) unintentional circumstances.

D) a superior system of trade.

45

Which choice provides the best evidence for the answer to the previous question?

A) Lines 1–4 ("There . . . alone")

B) Lines 11–19 ("Any . . . slave-trade")

C) Lines 24–28 ("If . . . mankind")

D) Lines 34–38 ("Nor . . . goods")

46

Which statement best describes the relationship between the passages?

A) Passage 2 refutes the central claim advanced in Passage 1.

B) Passage 2 provides supportive illustrations on the general view described in Passage 1.

C) Passage 2 argues against the practicality of the proposals put forth in Passage 1.

D) Passage 2 expresses reservations about developments discussed in Passage 2.

47

The author of Passage 2 intends the phrase "the milk of human kindness" (line 86) to convey a sense of

A) beneficence.

B) indulgence.

C) jocularity.

D) cynicism.

48

As used in line 33, "duties" most nearly means

A) responsibilities.

B) missions.

C) considerations.

D) tariffs.

49

The graphs support the argument in Passage 2 primarily by showing

A) the growth of the British narco-trafficking enterprise.

B) the collusion of Britain and Germany in the Opium Wars.

C) the brutality with which Britain suppressed the Sepoy Rebellion.

D) the benefits that expanded British trade provided for the world economy.

50

With which statement in Passage 1 would the author of Passage 2 most likely agree?

A) Lines 6–8 ("Power . . . itself")

B) Line 8 ("Not so . . . nation")

C) Lines 11–19 ("Any . . . slave-trade")

D) Lines 20–21 ("Not only . . . participate")

CONTINUE

1   **1**

51

The author of Passage 2 would most likely respond to the claim that "many are unable to believe it when they see it" (lines 40–41) by pointing out that, in fact,

A) England's benevolence was met with open hostility among its European neighbors.

B) other nations doubted England's policies only because they regarded them as hypocritical.

C) Britain's benevolent foreign policy was extremely hard to implement.

D) other nations not only understood England's policy, they emulated it.

52

Which choice provides the best evidence for the answer to the previous question?

A) Lines 48–55 ("His . . . others")

B) Lines 70–71 ("In fact . . . that")

C) Lines 80–82 ("Mill . . . barbarians")

D) Lines 93–95 ("Hitler . . . Czechoslovakia")

STOP

**If you finish before time is called, you may check your work on this section only.
Do not turn to any other section of the test.**

2   2

Writing and Language Test
35 MINUTES, 44 QUESTIONS

Turn to Section 2 of your answer sheet to answer the questions in this section.

DIRECTIONS

Each passage below is accompanied by a number of questions. For some questions, you will consider how the passage might be revised to improve the expression of ideas. For other questions, you will consider how the passage might be edited to correct errors in sentence structure, usage, or punctuation. A passage or a question may be accompanied by one or more graphics (such as a table or graph) that you will consider as you make revising and editing decisions.

Some questions will direct you to an underlined portion of a passage. Other questions will direct you to a location in a passage or ask you to think about the passage as a whole.

After reading each passage, choose the answer to each question that most effectively improves the quality of writing in the passage or that makes the passage conform to the conventions of standard written English. Many questions include a "NO CHANGE" option. Choose that option if you think the best choice is to leave the relevant portion of the passage as it is.

CONTINUE ➔

2　　　　　　　　　　　　　　　　　　　　　　　　　**2**

Questions 1–11 are based on the following passage and supplementary material.

Update Your Resumé

Webster's Dictionary defines "blue-collar" as "relating to jobs that require physical work." However, in the last 60 years, as the United States has transformed from an industrial economy to a service economy, **1** this has rendered this definition as dead as Noah Webster.

Today's job seekers must understand that blue-collar jobs are defined not so much by the kind of work they do, **2** but by the kind of relationship they have with management. Today, **3** being white-collar doesn't just mean working in an office, it means having the power to decide the fates of blue-collar workers. As a result, blue-collar increasingly means "replaceable."

It used to be that blue-collar workers were distinguished by their level of education, but the steady increase in the number of high school and college graduates **4** has changed this. Perhaps you're thinking, "But I'll work with my mind, not with my hands. I'll have a master's degree. I'll be white-collar." That may be wishful thinking. Unless you actually own your business—and this carries its own risks—your job may be just as interchangeable **5** as factories were 100 years ago.

1

A) NO CHANGE
B) this definition has been rendered
C) this definition being rendered
D) thereby rendering this definition

2

A) NO CHANGE
B) as
C) but instead
D) rather

3

A) NO CHANGE
B) white-collar jobs
C) if you are white-collar it
D) to be white collar

4

A) NO CHANGE
B) are changing
C) have changed
D) would change

5

A) NO CHANGE
B) as those in factories
C) as the ones factories did
D) than those in factories

CONTINUE ➡

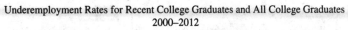

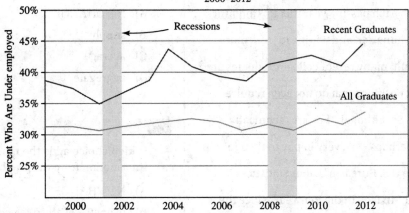

Underemployment Rates for Recent College Graduates and All College Graduates
2000–2012

Source: US Census Bureau and US Bureau of Labor Statistics

CONTINUE

2   **2**

There are millions of job seekers with college degrees, and with each passing year this **6** amount will get younger, hungrier, and willing to work more cheaply. As a result, many recent college graduates are willing to accept positions that do not even require a college degree. So, although they are technically employed, and perhaps even very happy in their jobs, they are what the U.S. Bureau of Labor Statistics calls "underemployed." In fact, in the four years since the start of the 2008–2009 recession, **7** over 40% of all college graduates were unemployed.

6

A) NO CHANGE
B) supply
C) average
D) aggregate

7

Which choice adds the most relevant and accurate information from the graph above?

A) NO CHANGE
B) over 40% of all college graduates were underemployed.
C) over 40% of all recent college graduates were unemployed.
D) over 40% of all recent college graduates were underemployed.

2   2

Long gone are the days when a college graduate had a secure pipeline to a comfortable career in a big company and could count on a steady climb up the corporate ladder. Today, the average worker **8** will have seven jobs in his or her lifetime, and that number may be on the rise.

The buzzword used describe this new environment is "dynamic." In the Information Age, changes happen very quickly. The Internet and other communication technologies **9** cause companies to hire contract workers from across the globe, often with very specialized skills. This depresses wages to an extent, but it can also be a boon to educated workers. So long as corporate lobbyists do not destroy "net neutrality," the Internet will remain a powerful tool for workers as well as companies. **10** It's easier now compared to before to create your own career—as an independent consultant, a sole proprietor, or even a blogger—by leveraging the power of the Internet.

It will also help enormously to become a lifelong learner, and, correspondingly, to update your resumé regularly. The Internet offers plenty of tools, such as LinkedIn, **11** to keep in contact with all of your professional connections and keeping feelers out for the next great opportunity.

8

Which choice most effectively connects with the previous sentence and the paragraph that follows?

A) NO CHANGE

B) will work until he or she is nearly 70 years old, and perhaps even beyond.

C) receives about the same salary, adjusted for inflation, as a worker received 35 years ago.

D) has far more education than the average corporate worker did in the 1960s.

9

A) NO CHANGE

B) require

C) remind

D) enable

10

A) NO CHANGE

B) It's easy compared to before,

C) It's easier now

D) Its easier than ever now,

11

A) NO CHANGE

B) in keeping

C) for keeping

D) that keep

CONTINUE ➡

2   **2**

Questions 12–22 are based on the following passage.

Take a Deep Breath in a National Park

Good air quality is essential to our health and to the health of our natural environment. Air pollution comes from many **12** diverse and various sources throughout the world. Some of the harmful gases and particles in the atmosphere have natural origins such as volcanoes and brush fires. However, the most dangerous pollutants come from burning fossil fuels and engaging in slash-and-burn **13** agriculture, this process spews tons of carbon dioxide and ash into the atmosphere and, even worse, destroys nature's most potent pollutant-scrubbing tool, the forest. These **14** situations have serious effects not only on air quality, but also on wildlife, vegetation, lakes, streams, and soils. Some pollutants can even affect ecosystems that are hundreds or even thousands of miles away.

Given all the negative effects of air pollution, it is no wonder that the National Park Service (NPS) takes a great interest in the problem. The NPS is a government agency, established in 1916, **15** who's mission is to manage and protect our national parks and to ensure enjoyment for future generations of visitors.

12
A) NO CHANGE
B) diverse sources
C) interchangeable sources
D) sources

13
A) NO CHANGE
B) agriculture, which spews
C) agriculture, being a process that spews
D) agriculture, spewing

14
A) NO CHANGE
B) phenomena
C) activities
D) gases

15
A) NO CHANGE
B) it's
C) its
D) whose

2   2

Many of our national parks have already been significantly affected by air pollution. Acid rain has damaged vegetation, changed the biodiversity of the soil, and **16** <u>even buildings and monuments have been damaged</u>. Ozone, sulfur dioxide, and particulate matter have reached concentrations that harm plants and **17** <u>wildlife, exacerbating</u> breathing problems such as asthma among people visiting or working in the parks. **18** Such damage to **19** <u>visitors</u> experiences leads to economic losses for the parks and their surrounding communities. If these damaging effects are not soon mitigated, the outlook for our parks is bleak.

16

A) NO CHANGE
B) even damaging buildings and monuments
C) even damaged buildings and monuments
D) buildings and monuments have even been damaged

17

A) NO CHANGE
B) wildlife, and so exacerbate
C) wildlife and exacerbate
D) wildlife; exacerbating

18

At this point, the author is considering inserting the following sentence.

> Air pollution can even affect the aesthetic resources of our parks, obscuring mountain vistas and sending smog into pristine valleys.

Should the writer make this change?

A) No, because a discussion of beauty detracts from this paragraph's focus on health.
B) No, because this information does not provide a transition to the discussion about economics that follows.
C) Yes, because these details help explain why some people might reconsider plans to visit national parks.
D) Yes, because this information indicates important health hazards that visitors to the parks might face.

19

A) NO CHANGE
B) visitors'
C) visitors's
D) visitor's

CONTINUE ➡

[1] The Environmental Protection Agency (EPA) has identified several demonstrably harmful air pollutants and has set national regulatory standards for their concentrations. [2] It is also studying several other potentially troublesome pollutants, such as mercury and acid deposition, with an eye toward regulating those as well. [3] EPA officials are also monitoring the particles that cause unsightly haze in an effort to restore the pristine visual beauty of the parks. **20**

The EPA's Air Quality Inventory compares current air conditions to standards designed to protect human health and sensitive vegetation. Since air quality can vary dramatically from place to place and day to day, only comprehensive and long-term data can provide the information required **21** in EPA officials making reliable assessments and propose long-term measures. The new challenge is to **22** reveal how best to apply air quality data to help improve current conditions in parks.

20

The writer wants to add the following sentence to the paragraph

> To address these problems, we must monitor the most significant pollutants and try to control them.

The best placement for this sentence is immediately

A) before sentence 1.

B) after sentence 1.

C) after sentence 2.

D) after sentence 3.

21

A) NO CHANGE

B) so that EPA officials would make

C) for EPA officials who are making

D) for EPA officials to make

22

A) NO CHANGE

B) determine

C) require

D) administer

CONTINUE ➡

2   **2**

Questions 23–33 are based on the following passage.

The Chicago Seven

In 1968, political activists **23** lured national attention, and a federal indictment, for allegedly inciting riots at the Democratic National Convention in Chicago. The facts that unraveled during the four-and-a-half-month trial revealed **24** that the political and cultural differences were profound that were dividing the country at that time. The arrest and trial of the group known as the "Chicago Seven" became a pivotal point in the protest movement that centered on the Vietnam War, government corruption, and the unfairness of the federal court system. The defendants used their nationally televised trial to challenge the rights of official authority through outrageous antics that **25** were furious to the presiding judge, Julius Hoffman, but delighted anti-establishment audiences.

26 Just as the accused used the trial to criticize the status quo of American society, so the prosecution used the trial for its own political purposes. As defendant Tom Hayden concluded, the government "decided to put radicalism on trial." Although the Chicago Seven were certainly political radicals,

23

A) NO CHANGE
B) pulled
C) tempted
D) drew

24

A) NO CHANGE
B) how politically and culturally profound the differences were
C) the profound political and cultural differences
D) that the differences were profound in culture and politics

25

A) NO CHANGE
B) infuriated the presiding judge, Julius Hoffman, but were delighting
C) were furious to the presiding judge, Julius Hoffman, but were delightful to
D) infuriated the presiding judge, Julius Hoffman, but delighted

26

A) NO CHANGE
B) Although
C) Because
D) Despite the fact that

CONTINUE ➡

they were not clearly guilty of the crime for which they were on 27 trial; crossing state lines to incite a riot in violation of the anti-riot provisions of the Civil Rights Act of 1968. The prosecutors were clearly justified 28 for accusing the Chicago Seven of participating in a riot that resulted in injuries and property damage. However, the allegation that they crossed state lines with the intention of inciting this riot 29 was much harder to substantiate.

By all accounts, the defendants behaved outrageously during the trial. Nevertheless, the judge clearly overreacted to their antics, issuing the defendants and their lawyers 159 counts of criminal contempt and sentencing them to terms from three months to four years. Even worse, the defendants clearly 30 aggrieved the jury, who convicted five of the seven defendants of the most serious charges and sentenced them to an additional five years in prison.

27

A) NO CHANGE
B) trial: crossing state lines to incite
C) trial: to cross state lines to incite
D) trial: crossing state lines for inciting

28

A) NO CHANGE
B) with
C) by
D) in

29

Which choice most effectively connects this sentence with the previous one?

A) NO CHANGE
B) could, if proven, lead to a lengthy prison sentence.
C) really caught the attention of the media.
D) was disputed just as vigorously as the other charge.

30

A) NO CHANGE
B) antagonized
C) bemused
D) disputed

2

2

However, in 1972, the U.S. Court of Appeals of the Seventh Circuit ruled that Judge Hoffman was inappropriately biased against the defendants, and that the jury selection process violated the defendants' rights to a fair trial. Accordingly, **31** the convictions were overturned by the appeals court, and even threw out the contempt of court charges.

The Chicago Seven appeals decision is a vivid reminder of how important both decorum and impartiality are to the judicial process and how politics can **32** taint that process. It also serves as a fitting epilogue to the anti-war movement of the late 60s and early 70s **33**.

31

A) NO CHANGE

B) the appeals court overturned the convictions

C) the appeals court had overturned the convictions

D) the convictions had been overturned by the appeals court

32

A) NO CHANGE

B) eliminate

C) deconstruct

D) magnify

33

The writer wants to add the following information to the end of this sentence.

> especially since American involvement in Vietnam was winding down and the nation's attention was turning to the political crimes of the Nixon administration.

Should the author make this addition?

A) No, because it draws the focus of the paragraph away from the anti-war protests.

B) No, because it contradicts the central thesis about the politicization of the judicial process.

C) Yes, because it explains why the American public was shifting its focus.

D) Yes, because it provides information about the fate of the Chicago Seven.

CONTINUE ➡

2   2

Questions 34–44 are based on the following passage.

"Starry Night"

Only thirteen months after completing his painting "Starry Night," and only six months after it received a glowing review in the *Mercure de France*, Vincent van Gogh **34** is dead, at the age of 37, probably of a self-inflicted gunshot wound. During his brief, tortured lifetime, van Gogh sold only one painting and did not live long enough to enjoy major critical success. Nevertheless, in the ten short years he worked, van Gogh produced over 2,000 works of art for the world to enjoy forever.

35 "Starry Night" is perhaps van Gogh's most famous painting. Van Gogh created it while he was voluntarily living at an asylum after one of his episodes of mental illness. Van Gogh revealed his inspiration in a letter to his sister in 1888, saying, "the night is more alive and more richly colored than the day." No painting could better **36** improvise such an insight. Measuring only 29 inches high by 36¼ inches wide, **37** Van Gogh's masterpiece nevertheless overwhelms the viewer.

A luminous night sky is filled with energy, contrasting the dark sleepy village beneath it. Wispy clouds swirl in vivid blues and greens in front of stars that

34

A) NO CHANGE
B) had been
C) was
D) would have been

35

Which choice most effectively joins the two sentences at the underlined portion?

A) "Starry Night" was created by van Gogh, as perhaps his most famous painting, while he was
B) Perhaps his most famous painting, van Gogh created "Starry Night" while he was
C) Van Gogh created "Starry Night," perhaps his most famous painting, while he was
D) "Starry Night" is perhaps van Gogh's most famous painting, creating it while he was

36

A) NO CHANGE
B) epitomize
C) collaborate
D) restore

37

A) NO CHANGE
B) Van Gogh nevertheless overwhelms the viewer with his masterpiece
C) the viewer is nevertheless overwhelmed by van Gogh's masterpiece
D) Van Gogh's masterpiece has the viewer overwhelmed nevertheless

CONTINUE ➤

2   **2**

seem not so much **38** to shimmer as to explode. A golden crescent moon seems ready to swallow itself. Accents of bright white and yellow move the eye ever upward from the earth below. **39** In the foreground, a cypress tree, at once a flame and its dark shadow, spirals skyward.

[1] Does the painting symbolize **40** turmoil or tranquility; despair or hope? [2] The cypress is common in cemeteries, so perhaps it represents mourning. [3] Then again, it is reaching to the sky, so perhaps it indicates the hope of a heavenly journey. [4] To some, "Starry Night" shows that Van Gogh had faith in light despite his chronic bouts with darkness and that he was on the road to recovery. **41**

38

A) NO CHANGE

B) to shimmer than to explode

C) as to shimmer as to explode

D) as to shimmer than to explode

39

The writer is considering omitting the underlined sentence. Should the writer do this?

A) Yes, because the metaphorical description of the tree detracts from the paragraph's analytical tone.

B) Yes, because the paragraph is focused on the objects in the sky, not the objects on the ground.

C) No, because this detail adds vibrancy to the description and sets up the next paragraph.

D) No, because this detail adds a necessary element of whimsy to the description of the painting.

40

A) NO CHANGE

B) turmoil on the one hand or tranquility on the other; similarly, does it represent despair or hope?

C) either turmoil or tranquility; likewise, despair or hope?

D) turmoil or tranquility; and is it despair or hope?

41

The author is adding the following sentence to this paragraph.

> If so, what happened in just thirteen months?

This sentence should be placed

A) immediately after sentence 1.

B) immediately after sentence 2.

C) immediately after sentence 3.

D) immediately after sentence 4.

CONTINUE ➡

2   **2**

Perhaps these questions about van Gogh's **42** intent and state of mind don't really matter. Perhaps what matters is, as G. Albert Aurier wrote in 1890, "the impression left upon the retina when it first views the strange, intense, and feverish work." In over 120 years, the compelling painting and its enigmatic painter **43** will have lost no charisma. In 2014, more than 1.6 million devotees visited Amsterdam's van Gogh Museum, and over 2.8 million art lovers made the pilgrimage to the Museum of Modern Art in New York City to see "Starry Night." In the same year, van Gogh's "Still Life, Vase with Daisies and Poppies" sold for 61.7 million dollars at a Sotheby's auction. **44** It's hard to imagine what the tormented and impoverished artist would think of the joy, not to mention fame and fortune, his works are bringing over a century later.

42

A) NO CHANGE

B) background and influence

C) technique and reputation

D) philosophy and beliefs

43

A) NO CHANGE

B) would have

C) has

D) have

44

Which choice most effectively concludes the passage and ties the last paragraph to the first?

A) NO CHANGE

B) Van Gogh's modern appeal surpasses even that of Dali and Picasso, two of the greatest artists of the 20th century.

C) A year later, another van Gogh work, "L'allée des Alyscamps" fetched even more: 66.3 million dollars.

D) Van Gogh's color and brushstroke techniques have been attempted by countless artists, but never replicated with the same success.

STOP

If you finish before time is called, you may check your work on this section only.
Do not turn to any other section of the test.

3 3

Math Test—No Calculator

25 MINUTES, 20 QUESTIONS

Turn to Section 3 of your answer sheet to answer the questions in this section.

DIRECTIONS

For questions 1–15, solve each problem, choose the best answer from the choices provided, and fill in the corresponding circle on your answer sheet. **For questions 16–20**, solve the problem and enter your answer in the grid on the answer sheet. Please refer to the directions before question 16 on how to enter your answers in the grid. You may use any available space in your test booklet for scratch work.

NOTES

1. The use of a calculator **is not permitted**.
2. All variables and expressions used represent real numbers unless otherwise indicated.
3. Figures provided in this test are drawn to scale unless otherwise indicated.
4. All figures lie in a plane unless otherwise indicated.
5. Unless otherwise indicated, the domain of a given function f is the set of all real numbers x for which $f(x)$ is a real number.

REFERENCE

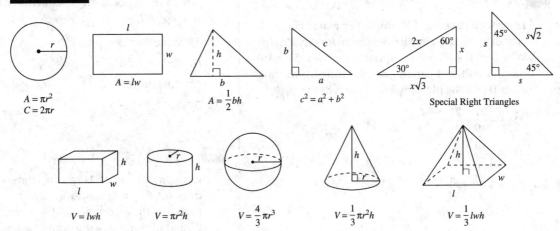

The number of degrees of arc in a circle is 360.
The number of radians of arc in a circle is 2π.
The sum of the measures in degrees of the angles of a triangle is 180.

CONTINUE →

1

If $\dfrac{7}{3}a = \dfrac{3}{4}$, what is the value of a?

A) $\dfrac{9}{28}$

B) $\dfrac{6}{11}$

C) $\dfrac{7}{4}$

D) $\dfrac{28}{9}$

2

If $3x + a = x + b$, what is the value of x in terms of a and b?

A) $\dfrac{b-a}{2}$

B) $\dfrac{b-a}{3}$

C) $\dfrac{a+b}{3}$

D) $\dfrac{a-b}{2}$

3

Laura's car averages 27 miles per gallon for high-way driving and 21 miles per gallon for city driving. Which of the following equations relates the minimum number of gallons, x, her car needs to travel 10 miles on the highway and b miles in the city?

A) $x = \dfrac{27}{10} + \dfrac{21}{b}$

B) $x = \dfrac{10}{21} + \dfrac{b}{27}$

C) $x = \dfrac{10}{27} + \dfrac{b}{21}$

D) $x = 270 + 21b$

4

Which of the following is equal to $\sqrt[3]{x^7}$ for all values of x?

A) $x^{\frac{3}{7}}$

B) $x^{\frac{7}{3}}$

C) x^{10}

D) x^{21}

5

A line in the xy-plane has a slope of $-\dfrac{3}{4}$ and passes through the point $(8, 4)$. What is the y-intercept of this line?

A) $(0, -6)$

B) $(0, -2)$

C) $(0, 6)$

D) $(0, 10)$

6

$$(ab^2c^2 + abc - a^2b^2c) - (a^2b^2c - ab^2c^2 + abc)$$

Which of the following is equivalent to the expression above?

A) $2abc - 2a^2b^2c$

B) $2abc + 2a^2b^2c$

C) $2ab^2c^2 - 2a^2b^2c$

D) $2ab^2c^2 + 2a^2b^2c$

7

In the xy-plane, an isosceles triangle has two vertices on the x-axis and one vertex on the y-axis at $(0, 4)$. The perimeter of the triangle is 16 units. Which of the following could be another vertex of the triangle?

A) $(0, 3)$

B) $(-3, 0)$

C) $(4, 0)$

D) $(0, -4)$

CONTINUE ➤

8

If $a = x^2 - 1$ and $b = (x-1)^2$, which of the following is equal to $\dfrac{a-b}{2}$ for all values of x?

A) 0

B) 2

C) x

D) $x - 1$

9

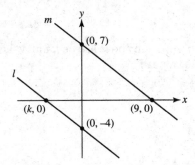

In the xy-plane above, line l is parallel to line m. What is the value of k?

A) $-\dfrac{36}{7}$

B) $-\dfrac{32}{7}$

C) $-\dfrac{37}{9}$

D) $-\dfrac{28}{9}$

10

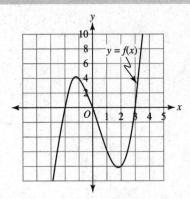

$$f(x) = x^3 - x^2 - 6x$$

The graph in the xy-plane of the function $y = f(x)$ is shown above. If the graph of $y = -2x - 4$ were drawn on the same axes, which of the following would <u>not</u> be a point of intersection of the two graphs?

A) $(-2, 0)$

B) $(0, 0)$

C) $(1, -6)$

D) $(2, -8)$

11

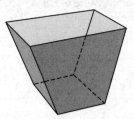

A planter is built with a 12-inch by 12-inch square base and a 12-inch by 18-inch rectangular top so that the front and back faces of the planter are parallel trapezoids. The planter is 2 feet high. If this planter is filled with soil that costs $4 per cubic foot, what is the cost of soil required to fill the planter? (1 foot = 12 inches)

A) $8

B) $10

C) $12

D) $14

CONTINUE ▶

12

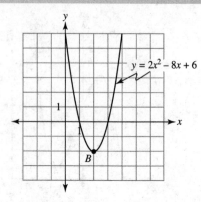

$y = 2x^2 - 8x + 6$

Which of the following equivalent forms of the equation graphed in the xy-plane above shows the coordinates of vertex B as constants in the equation?

A) $y = 2(x^2 - 4x + 3)$

B) $y = 2(x - 1)(x - 3)$

C) $y = 2(x - 2)^2 - 2$

D) $y = 2(x^2 - 4x) + 6$

13

The nth term, a_n, of a sequence is given by the formula $a_n = a_1 r^{n-1}$ where r is a constant. If $a_1 = \frac{1}{4}$ and $r = 2$, for what value of n is $a_n = 32$?

A) 5

B) 6

C) 7

D) 8

14

For a polynomial $p(x)$, the value of $p(2) = 1$ and $p(4) = -1$. Which of the following must be true about $p(x)$?

A) $x - 4$ is a factor of $p(x)$.

B) $x - 1$ is a factor of $p(x)$.

C) $p(x)$ has a zero between $x = 2$ and $x = 4$.

D) The remainder when $p(x)$ is divided by $x - 1$ is 2.

15

$$\frac{x^2 + 1}{x + 1} = x - 1 + \frac{b}{x + 1}$$

If the equation above is true for all values of x, what is the value of b?

A) -2

B) 0

C) 1

D) 2

3   3

DIRECTIONS

For questions 16–20, solve the problem and enter your answer in the grid, as described below, on the answer sheet.

1. Although not required, it is suggested that you write your answer in the boxes at the top of the columns to help you fill in the circles accurately. You will receive credit only if the circles are filled in correctly.

2. Mark no more than one circle in any column.

3. No question has a negative answer.

4. Some problems may have more than one correct answer. In such cases, grid only one answer.

5. **Mixed numbers** such as $3\frac{1}{2}$ must be gridded as 3.5 or $\frac{7}{2}$.

   (If $3\frac{1}{2}$ is entered into the grid as 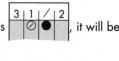, it will be interpreted as $\frac{31}{2}$, not $3\frac{1}{2}$.)

6. **Decimal answers**: If you obtain a decimal answer with more digits than the grid can accommodate, it may be either rounded or truncated, but it must fill the entire grid.

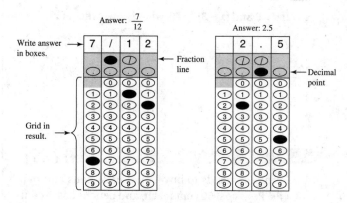

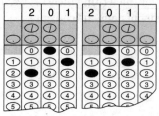

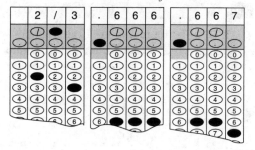

CONTINUE ▶

3 **3**

16

If $x > 0$ and $(x - 3)^2 = 49$, what is the value of x?

17

Fernanda needs to buy a total of 24 pens and pencils. Pens cost 50 cents each, and pencils cost 5 cents each. If she does not want to spend more than $5 total for the writing utensils, what is the maximum number of pens she can buy?

18

If (1, 2) is the midpoint of the segment with endpoints at (−2, −2) and (a, b), what is the value of $a + b$?

19

What is the least positive integer n that satisfies the inequality $\dfrac{1}{100} - \dfrac{9}{n^2} > 0$?

20

$$ax + by = 8$$

$$\frac{1}{5}x + \frac{2}{3}y = 30$$

If the system above has no solutions, what is the value of $\dfrac{a}{b}$?

STOP

**If you finish before time is called, you may check your work on this section only.
Do not turn to any other section of the test.**

4   4

Math Test—Calculator

55 MINUTES, 38 QUESTIONS

Turn to Section 4 of your answer sheet to answer the questions in this section.

DIRECTIONS

For questions 1–30, solve each problem, choose the best answer from the choices provided, and fill in the corresponding circle on your answer sheet. **For questions 31–38**, solve the problem and enter your answer in the grid on the answer sheet. Please refer to the directions before question 31 on how to enter your answers in the grid. You may use any available space in your test booklet for scratch work.

NOTES

1. The use of a calculator **is permitted**.
2. All variables and expressions used represent real numbers unless otherwise indicated.
3. Figures provided in this test are drawn to scale unless otherwise indicated.
4. All figures lie in a plane unless otherwise indicated.
5. Unless otherwise indicated, the domain of a given function f is the set of all real numbers for which $f(x)$ is a real number.

REFERENCE

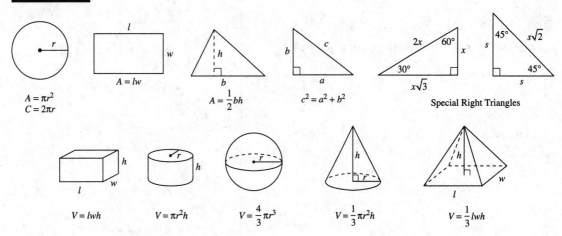

The number of degrees of arc in a circle is 360.
The number of radians of arc in a circle is 2π.
The sum of the measures in degrees of the angles of a triangle is 180.

CONTINUE ➡

4 **4**

1

$$f(x) = 3x + c$$

In the function above, c is a constant. If $f(4) = 17$, what is the value of c?

A) 5

B) 15

C) 28

D) 29

2

A routine motor vehicle check determines that approximately 5 out of every 200 vehicles inspected have an expired emissions sticker. At this rate, approximately how many vehicles with expired emissions stickers should there be if 5,000 vehicles are inspected?

A) 100

B) 125

C) 150

D) 250

3

If $\frac{1}{3}m + \frac{1}{12}p = 12$, what is the value of $4m + p$?

A) 36

B) 48

C) 72

D) 144

4

If k is a constant greater than zero, which of the following could be the graph of $y = k(x - k)$ in the xy-plane?

A)

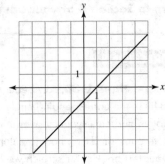

B)

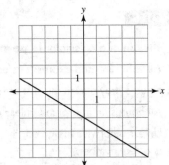

C)

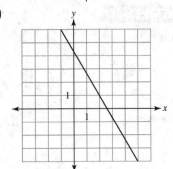

D)

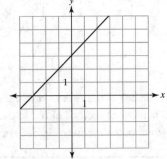

CONTINUE

4   4

5

Alissa received a $20 gift card for her birthday, which she was able to use on her favorite video streaming site. The site charges an $8 one-time membership fee. Each episode of Alissa's favorite TV series costs $1.99. Which of the following expressions represents the amount remaining, in dollars, on her gift card after she watches x episodes of the series?

A) $1.99(x - $20) + $8

B) $28 - $1.99x

C) $1.99x + $28

D) $12 - $1.99x

6

x	2	3	4	5	6
$f(x)$	5	4	3	2	1
$g(x)$	2	6	5	4	3

The table above shows some values of the functions $g(x)$ and $f(x)$ for particular values of x. If b is a number such that $g(f(b)) = 5$, which of the following could be a value of b?

A) 3

B) 4

C) 5

D) 6

Questions 7 and 8 refer to the following information.

Kate teaches a 5-session online course for a company that pays its instructors a base amount of $200 per 5-session course plus a fixed amount of money for each student who enrolls. When 50 students enroll, she is paid $725 to teach the course.

7

How much is Kate paid for each student who enrolls in her course?

A) $9.50

B) $10.50

C) $12.50

D) $14.50

8

Next year, the company will raise the base amount paid to each instructor for each course by 25%, but will not change fixed amount paid per enrolled student. If 60 students enroll in Kate's course next year, how much will the company pay her to teach the course?

A) $855.00

B) $880.00

C) $987.50

D) $1,012.50

CONTINUE

4 **4**

9

Keith can read p pages in 20 minutes. At this rate, how many minutes will it take him to read 70 pages?

A) $\dfrac{7p}{2}$

B) $\dfrac{2p}{7}$

C) $\dfrac{p}{1,400}$

D) $\dfrac{1,400}{p}$

10

Jason buys a new smartphone with a monthly data plan. The phone costs \$355 and the data plan costs \$40 per month. For each month that he pays his data bill on time, he receives a \$10 rebate toward the cost of his phone. If Jason pays his bill on time every month but cancels his contract after 18 months, how much will he have paid for the phone and data plan in total?

A) \$895

B) \$1,075

C) \$1,135

D) \$1,315

11

The function g has four distinct zeros. Which of the following could represent the complete graph of g in the xy-plane?

A)

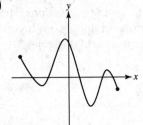

B)

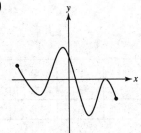

C)

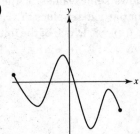

D)

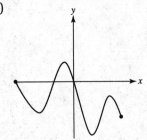

---

4   **4**

Questions 12 and 13 refer to the following information.

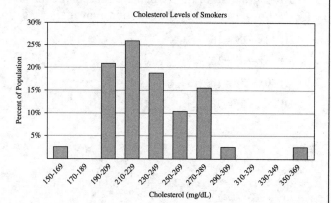

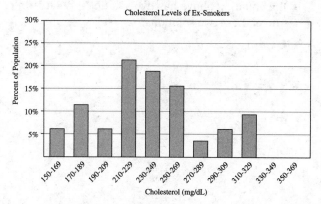

The graphs above show the results of a study conducted to test the hypothesis that quitting smoking will reduce the chances that a person will have high cholesterol levels. The study measured the overall cholesterol level of 500 current smokers and 500 people who had been habitual smokers but who had quit at least two years previously. For the sake of this study, "high" cholesterol is defined as overall levels higher than 269 mg/dL.

12

According to the data, approximately how many of the current smokers in the study had cholesterol levels below 210 mg/dL?

A) 48

B) 72

C) 120

D) 160

13

Do these graphs provide strong evidence in support of the tested hypothesis?

A) Yes, because the average cholesterol level for ex-smokers is much less than the average cholesterol level for current smokers.

B) Yes, because far fewer ex-smokers than current smokers have "high" cholesterol levels.

C) No, because the average cholesterol level for ex-smokers is slightly higher than the average cholesterol level for current smokers.

D) No, because the percentage of ex-smokers with "high" cholesterol levels is not significantly different than the percentage of current smokers with "high" cholesterol levels.

14

$$x^2 + y^2 = 80$$
$$y = 2x$$

When the equations above are graphed in the xy-plane, they form a circle and a line containing a secant of the circle. If one of the points of intersection of the two graphs is (a, b), what is the value of ab?

A) −32

B) 8

C) 32

D) 64

CONTINUE ➔

4 **4**

15

Which of the following is the equation of a line that, when graphed in the xy-plane, has a slope of 2 and contains the point (1, 3)?

A) $2x + y = 5$

B) $2x - y = 5$

C) $2x + y = -1$

D) $2x - y = -1$

16

The chirping rate of crickets varies linearly with outdoor temperature. One evening, Nicki counted 44 cricket chirps in one 15-second span, and noted that the outdoor temperature was 29°C. On another evening, she counted 32 chirps in 15 seconds, and noted that the temperature was 22°C. Which equation can be used to find the temperature, T, in degrees Celsius, given the number of cricket chirps, c, that are counted in a 15-second span?

A) $T = \dfrac{12}{7}c - \dfrac{230}{7}$

B) $T = \dfrac{12}{7}c - \dfrac{160}{7}$

C) $T = \dfrac{7}{12}c + \dfrac{115}{6}$

D) $T = \dfrac{7}{12}c + \dfrac{10}{3}$

17

$$x - 2y = 10$$

Which of the following is the equation of a line that, when graphed in the xy-plane, is perpendicular to the line described by the equation above?

A) $3x + 6y = 18$

B) $3x - 6y = 18$

C) $6x + 3y = 18$

D) $6x - 3y = 18$

18

$$2x - \frac{5}{x} = \frac{1}{3}$$

The equation above has two solutions. What is the sum of these two solutions?

A) $\dfrac{1}{6}$

B) $\dfrac{2}{5}$

C) $\dfrac{3}{2}$

D) $\dfrac{5}{3}$

CONTINUE

4 **4**

Questions 19 and 20 refer to the following information.

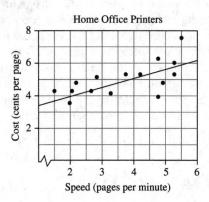

Home Office Printers

The scatter plot above shows the print speed and cost per printed page for 15 home office printers and the line of best fit for the data.

19

The line of best fit for the data is given by the equation $c = 0.58s + 2.74$, where c is the printing cost, in cents per page, and s is the printing speed, in pages per minute. According to this equation, what is the best estimate for the speed, in pages per minute, of a printer that prints 20 pages per <u>dollar</u>?

A) 3.70 pages per minute

B) 3.90 pages per minute

C) 4.00 pages per minute

D) 4.20 pages per minute

20

It takes the slowest printer in this group k minutes longer to print a 100-page document than it take the fastest printer in this group to print the same document. Which of the following is closest to k?

A) 42

B) 48

C) 54

D) 72

21

In a survey of 50 people who attended a certain movie, 41 of the people said that they purchased snacks at the concession stand, and 32 people said that they enjoyed the movie. What is the least possible number of people surveyed who could have both purchased snacks and enjoyed the movie?

A) 9

B) 18

C) 22

D) 23

CONTINUE

22

Percentage of Adults Living Below the Poverty Line

Legend:
- Full-Time Workers
- Part-Time Workers
- Unemployed

(Bar graph: y-axis "Percent Below Poverty Line" from 5% to 40%; x-axis "Age Group (Years)" with categories 18–24, 25–34, 35–54, 55–64, 65+)

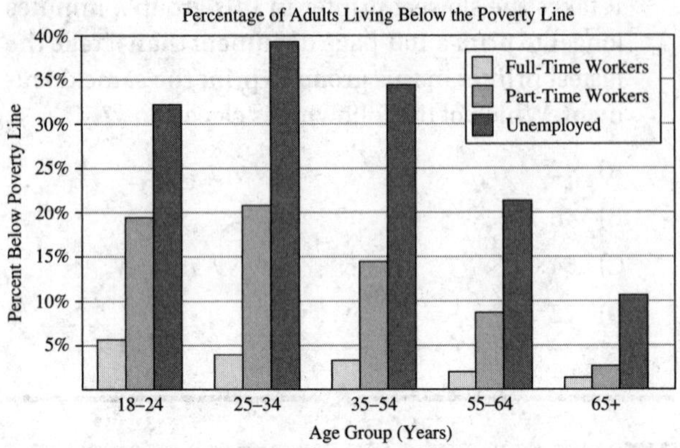

The graph above shows the percentage of 15 groups of adults, by age group and employment level, that live below the poverty line. The data were gathered from a survey of 1,000 randomly chosen adults.

Which of the following statistics about the 1,000 surveyed adults can be most accurately determined from the graph?

A) The percentage of unemployed adults ages 18 and above who live below the poverty line.

B) The percentage of people ages 65 and above who live below the poverty line

C) The percentage of unemployed adults ages between 25 and 34 years of age who live below the poverty line

D) The percentage of adults ages 55 to 64 who work part-time

23

$$P = P_0 r^t$$

A researcher at a bird conservancy wants to model the population of finches in an urban area by using the equation above, where P is the population of finches in the area and t is the number of years that have passed since the study began. The researcher determines that the finch population in this area at the beginning of the study is 1,200 and that this population is declining at a rate of 7% per year. What value should the researcher use for r?

A) -0.07

B) 0.93

C) 1.07

D) 1.93

24

In a particular city, the monthly cost of premium cable television service is normally 15% higher than the monthly cost of satellite television service. To attract new customers, each provider offers a discounted rate for the first two years. The cable provider discounts its rate by $10 per month, and the satellite service discounts its rate by 5%. At those sale rates, the monthly cost of the two services is the same. What is the regular (nonsale) monthly cost of premium cable television service?

A) $47.50

B) $50.00

C) $57.50

D) $66.25

4   **4**

25

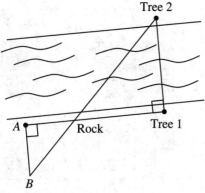

Tree 2

Tree 1

A • Rock

B

Note: Figure not drawn to scale.

Jessica wants to determine the width of a river, measured between two large trees, one on each bank of the river, as shown above. Standing at Tree 1, and looking at Tree 2, she turns 90° and walks along the river bank. When she reaches a point 60 yards from Tree 1, she marks the spot with a large rock and then continues along the same line until she reaches point *A*, which is 96 yards away from Tree 1. From point *A* she turns 90° away from the river and walks until she reaches point *B* where she can sight along a line through the marker rock to the tree on the other bank. If points *A* and *B* are 171 <u>feet</u> apart, what is the width of the river? (1 yard = 3 feet)

A) 38 yards

B) 95 yards

C) 114 yards

D) 285 yards

26

If $\dfrac{a}{2b} > 1$, and $a < 0$, which of the following statements must be true?

A) $a > 2b + 1$

B) $a < 2b + 1$

C) $a > -2b + 1$

D) $a = 2b + 1$

27

If the equation $y = (x - 3)(x - 7)$ is graphed in the xy-plane, it forms a parabola with a vertex at (a, b). What is the value of b?

A) −8

B) −4

C) −2

D) 4

28

$$V = \frac{k}{P}$$

At a fixed temperature, the volume of a sample of gas, V, in liters, is related to the applied pressure, P, in atmospheres, by the equation above, where k is a constant. A sample of gas at a fixed temperature has a volume of 6 liters. What will be the volume of this sample if the applied pressure is increased by 50%?

A) 2 liters

B) 3 liters

C) 4 liters

D) 5 liters

29

Which of the following expressions is equal to $\sqrt{-18} - \sqrt{-8}$? (Note: $i^2 = -1$)

A) $-i\sqrt{2}$

B) $-\sqrt{2}$

C) $i\sqrt{2}$

D) $3i\sqrt{2}$

30

A triangle has angles with measures 90°, $a°$, and $b°$. Which of the following must be true?

A) $\sin a° = \cos b°$

B) $\sin a° = \tan b°$

C) $\sin a° = \cos (90 - b)°$

D) $\sin a° = \sin (90 - a)°$

CONTINUE ➜

4 **4**

DIRECTIONS

For questions 31–38, solve the problem and enter your answer in the grid, as described below, on the answer sheet.

1. Although not required, it is suggested that you write your answer in the boxes at the top of the columns to help you fill in the circles accurately. You will receive credit only if the circles are filled in correctly.

2. Mark no more than one circle in any column.

3. No question has a negative answer.

4. Some problems may have more than one correct answer. In such cases, grid only one answer.

5. **Mixed numbers** such as $3\frac{1}{2}$ must be gridded as 3.5 or $\frac{7}{2}$.

(If $3\frac{1}{2}$ is entered into the grid as [grid], it will be interpreted as $\frac{31}{2}$, not $3\frac{1}{2}$.)

6. **Decimal answers**: If you obtain a decimal answer with more digits than the grid can accommodate, it may be either rounded or truncated, but it must fill the entire grid.

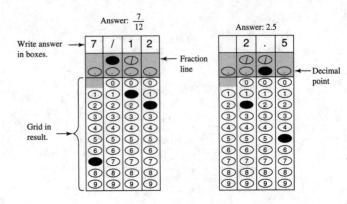

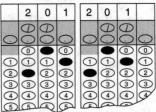

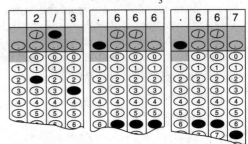

CONTINUE ▶

4 **4**

31

Any temperature in degrees Fahrenheit, F, can be converted to a temperature in degrees Celsius, C, by the formula $C = \frac{5}{9}(F - 32)$. What temperature, in degrees Fahrenheit, is equivalent to 30° Celsius?

32

Abby makes blankets by stitching together small crocheted squares. She can stitch together between 8 and 15 of these squares in an hour. If Abby wants to make a blanket that requires 1,170 squares, and she can devote three hours each day to stitching squares, what is the minimum number of days she needs to complete the blanket?

33

Mrs. Battle's current monthly salary is $3,000. Each month, her employer deducts 5% from her monthly salary and transfers that money into her pension plan. Her employer then contributes an additional amount equal to 3% of Mrs. Battle's monthly salary to her pension plan. Next year, Mrs. Battle will receive a 4% salary increase. By how much, in dollars, will the total monthly contribution to her pension plan increase after her raise takes effect? (Ignore the $ sign when gridding.)

34

If the measure of angle A is $\frac{7\pi}{10}$ radians and the measure of angle A is four times the measure of angle B, what is the measure of angle B, in <u>degrees</u>?

35

What is the product of all possible solutions to the equation $(p - 1)(p + 2) = -8$?

36

$$x^3 + 14x^2 + bx + 60$$

If $x + 2$ is a factor of the polynomial above, what is the value of b?

CONTINUE →

Questions 37 and 38 refer to the following information.

2012 House of Representatives Election			
District	Total Votes Cast for All Candidates	Incumbent's Campaign Expenditures (× $1,000)	% of Votes Received by Incumbent
1	360,000	420	48%
2	380,000	418	48%
3	420,000	580	50%
4	480,000	526	52%
5	510,000	730	55%
6	661,000	1,200	60%

The table above shows data for the 2012 campaigns of the incumbents in 6 Congressional districts.

37

How much campaign money, in dollars, did the District 5 incumbent spend for each vote received? (Round your answer to the nearest cent, and ignore the $ sign when gridding.)

38

A political consultant uses the data in this table to analyze the relationship between campaign expenditures of an incumbent's campaign and the total number of votes that candidate received. She calculates that the line of best fit relating the total number of votes received, v, to the total campaign expenses in dollars, x, is given by $v = kx + 72,600$, where k is a positive constant. If the data for District 6 match this model perfectly, what is the value of k?

STOP

If you finish before time is called, you may check your work on this section only. Do not turn to any other section of the test.

5   5

Essay

50 MINUTES, 1 QUESTION

DIRECTIONS

The essay gives you the opportunity to show how effectively you can read and comprehend a passage and write an essay analyzing the passage. In your essay, you should demonstrate that you have read the passage carefully, present a clear and logical analysis, and use language precisely.

Your essay must be written on the lines provided in your answer booklet; except for the Planning Page of the answer booklet, you will receive no other paper on which to write. You will have enough space if you write on every line, avoid wide margins, and keep your handwriting to a reasonable size. Remember that people who are not familiar with your handwriting will read what you write. Try to write or print so that what you are writing is legible to those readers.

You have 50 minutes to read the passage and write an essay in response to the prompt provided inside this booklet.

As you read the passage below, consider how Anna Reisman uses

- evidence, such as facts or examples, to support claims
- reasoning to develop ideas and connect claims and evidence
- stylistic or persuasive elements, such as word choice or appeals to emotion, to add power to the ideas expressed

Adapted from Anna Reisman, M.D., "Hounded." ©2014 the American Medical Association. Originally published in the *Journal of the American Medical Association (JAMA)*.

1   The two reasons why I dreaded my monthly house call to a tiny old man with big round glasses were loud and furry.

2   The angry barking and frantic scraping of claws began even before I'd pressed the doorbell. Once, the larger dog—a scruffy, overgrown terrier—snapped his jaws at my legs. I panicked, shoved my doctor's bag between us, and slammed the door. After that, my patient's daughter herded the dogs—the yappers, I called them—to another room where a sliding glass door muffled their braying, and I could listen to the old man's raspy breaths and trim his rough toenails in peace.

3   I am not a dog person.

4   But in my line of work—I'm a primary care physician who sometimes makes house calls—dogs are everywhere. To me, they're nothing more than jumping, growling, barking barriers to good care. They're messy, shedding clumps of fur and dander and doggy drool everywhere, and they're intrusive, the way they poke their snoots in embarrassing places. At best, the dogs I've met on house calls are useless: one aged white dog watched me

through a rain-splattered window as I rang and rang the doorbell. I tapped on the glass, expecting the beast to bark my arrival; instead, he raised a hind leg, peed on the couch, and limped away.

5   Some dogs are downright scary. I cowered in one living room where a vicious-sounding dog hurled itself over and over at the locked door between us so intently that I thought the door would come off the hinges. Another patient reassured me and the dog-fearing medical resident (sometimes trainees came along to learn about house calls) that his pooch would just sniff her a bit before settling down. A moment later, the beast lunged, frightening both of us half to death. While visiting a patient in his backyard—his wife didn't want me and the resident, a different one, in the house—a mean-looking pair of lion-sized Dobermans chained to a pulley paced, their squinty eyes riveted on us. They growled when the resident wrapped their owner's arm in a blood pressure cuff. I can't help but wonder if they imagined he was wearing a leash now too.

6   For older people who can still get around, I understand that dogs can provide companionship, of course, and with their dependency on a human for a feeding and walking schedule, structure. But for the oldest and most infirm? Even sleeping dogs pose risks.

7   One white-haired octogenarian tripped over a snoring Fido and broke her hip (the patient's, not Fido's). At another house, nobody noticed that the dog, curled up by his sleeping master on his electronic hospital bed, was lying right on top of the bed control device. The next morning, the man's daughter was horrified to find her frail father propelled to unsafe heights.

8   I'd heard a couple of do-gooder dog tales, like the one about a stone-deaf man whose dog became his ears. The only way his nurse could get into his house, she told me, was to yell for the dog through the mail slot. The dog would gallop to its owner, and the ancient man would totter in to unlock the door. Another nurse described a patient whose lower legs were so loaded with fluid that they oozed. You guessed it: his long-tongued floppy-eared best friend happily kept them clean, all the live-long day.

9   But dogs like this, in my experience, were clearly the exception.

10   And then one day, I paid a visit to a man in his 80s with advanced dementia who, a few weeks earlier, had fallen out of bed and fractured his hip. I leaned over the bars of his bed and gently tapped his thin shoulder. Ever since the fall, he'd lost the mischievous twinkle in his eye, his readiness to laugh.

11   "Hello, there," I said brightly. My patient's skin was sallow and his mouth drooped open. He stared at the ceiling. A pale purple vein pulsed weakly at his temple. The screen door creaked open behind me and something small and warm bumped into my leg. It was his niece's dog, a Chihuahua, the size, make, and model of a rat. Before I could protest, she placed the squirming creature, leash jangling, on the old man's pillow. I cringed, expecting an awful spasm or, worse, none.

12   Instead, the old man came alive. He cooed and snuggled. He smiled. The pup's simple wriggly warmth had triggered something deep inside his dementia-addled brain, perhaps a memory of a beloved dog, or maybe it was just the dog's eagerness, the tickle of the nuzzling moist nose, the panting that warmed his cheeks, the happy thumping of the pointy tail on his bony chest.

13   All right, I remember thinking, begrudgingly. Maybe there is some primitive reflex to animal love. Maybe the pet therapy people are onto something. But I still shuddered thinking about the yappers.

CONTINUE

One night, a few hours after midnight, my tiny bespectacled patient awoke, his bladder full. He heaved himself up from the recliner where he slept, felt around for his walker, and lost his balance. Face down on the hardwood floor, unable to get up, he called and called for his daughter, fast asleep on the other side of the house. He could have been there all night. He could have died. But the dogs ran to him, and then, those wonderful and responsible animals—no, caregivers—ran to her. Those yappers saved his life. And made a convert out of me.

Write an essay in which you explain how Anna Reisman builds an argument to persuade her audience that dogs can be caregivers. In your essay, analyze how she uses one or more of the features listed in the box above (or features of your own choice) to strengthen the logic and persuasiveness of her argument. Be sure that your analysis focuses on the most relevant features of the passage.

Your essay should NOT explain whether you agree with Reisman's claims, but rather explain how she builds an argument to persuade her audience.

SAT PRACTICE TEST 3 ANSWER KEY

Section 1: Reading	Section 2: Writing and Language	Section 3: Math (No Calculator)	Section 4: Math (Calculator)
1. D	1. B	1. A	1. A
2. B	2. B	2. A	2. B
3. B	3. A	3. C	3. D
4. D	4. A	4. B	4. A
5. D	5. B	5. D	5. D
6. C	6. B	6. C	6. A
7. A	7. D	7. B	7. B
8. C	8. A	8. D	8. B
9. A	9. D	9. A	9. D
10. B	10. C	10. B	10. A
11. D	11. C	11. B	11. B
12. B	12. D	12. C	12. C
13. D	13. B	13. D	13. D
14. B	14. C	14. C	14. C
15. D	15. D	15. D	15. D
16. C	16. C	16. 10	16. D
17. C	17. B	17. 8	17. C
18. A	18. C	18. 10	18. A
19. C	19. B	19. 31	19. B
20. A	20. A	20. 3/10 or .3	20. B
21. D	21. D		21. D
22. A	22. B		22. C
23. A	23. D		23. B
24. B	24. C		24. C
25. C	25. D		25. B
26. C	26. A		26. B
27. C	27. B		27. B
28. D	28. D		28. C
29. C	29. A		29. C
30. B	30. B		30. A
31. C	31. B		31. 86
32. A	32. A		32. 26
33. A	33. C		33. 9.60
34. B	34. C		34. 31.5
35. C	35. C		35. 6
36. D	36. B		36. 54
37. D	37. A		37. 2.6
38. B	38. A		38. .27
39. A	39. C		
40. D	40. A		
41. C	41. D		
42. B	42. A		
43. B	43. D		
44. C	44. A		
45. C			
46. A			
47. D			
48. D			
49. A			
50. A			
51. D			
52. D			

Total Reading Points (Section 1)

Total Writing and Language Points (Section 2)

Total Math Points (Section 3 + Section 4)

Scoring Your Test

1.   Use the answer key to mark your responses on each section.

2.   Total the number of correct responses for each section:

      1. Reading Test   Number correct: _____ **(Reading Raw Score)**

      2. Writing and Language Test   Number correct: _____ **(Writing and Language Raw Score)**

      3. Mathematics Test—No Calculator   Number correct: _____

      4. Mathematics Test—Calculator   Number correct: _____

3.   Add the raw scores for sections 3 and 4. This is your **Math Raw Score:** _____

4.   Use the table on page 230 to calculate your **Scaled Test and Section Scores (10–40).**

     Math Section Scaled Score (200–800):   _____

     Reading Test Scaled Score (10–40):   _____

     Writing and Language Test Scaled Score (10–40):   _____

5.   Add the **Reading Test Scaled Score** and the **Writing and Language Test Scaled Score (sum will be 20–80)**, and multiply this sum by 10 to get your **Reading and Writing Test Section Score (200–800).**

     Sum of Reading + Writing and Language Scores: _____ $\times 10 =$

     Reading and Writing Section Score: _____

Scaled Section and Test Scores

Raw Score	Math Section Score	Reading Test Score	Writing/ Language Test Score	Raw Score	Math Section Score	Reading Test Score	Writing/ Language Test Score
58	800			29	540	27	29
57	790			28	530	26	29
56	780			27	520	26	28
55	760			26	510	25	27
54	750			25	510	25	27
53	740			24	500	24	26
52	730	40		23	490	24	26
51	730	39		22	480	23	25
50	720	39		21	470	23	24
49	710	38		20	460	23	24
48	700	37		19	460	22	23
47	690	36		18	450	22	23
46	680	35		17	440	21	22
45	670	35		16	430	21	21
44	660	34	40	15	420	20	20
43	660	33	39	14	410	20	20
42	650	33	38	13	390	19	19
41	650	32	37	12	370	18	18
40	640	32	37	11	360	18	17
39	630	31	36	10	350	17	16
38	620	31	35	9	340	16	16
37	610	30	34	8	320	16	15
36	600	30	33	7	300	15	14
35	590	29	33	6	280	14	13
34	580	29	32	5	270	13	12
33	570	28	32	4	250	12	11
32	570	28	31	3	230	11	10
31	560	28	31	2	210	10	10
30	550	27	30	1	200	10	10

PRACTICE SAT 3 ANSWER EXPLANATIONS

Section 1: Reading

1. D   **Tone**

In saying that the *"big business man"* is a *self-righteous fraud* (lines 7–8), Steffens establishes a very condemnatory or *censorious* tone that is maintained throughout the passage.

2. B   **Word in Context**

After saying *he does not neglect*, the author offers an explanation: *he is very busy with politics, oh, very busy and very business like* (lines 6–7). In other words, he does not *disregard* his *professional duty*.

3. B   **Word in Context**

The author wishes that the *big business man* would disregard his professional duty because *he is the chief source of corruption* (lines 8–9). In saying that *it would be a boon if he would neglect politics* (lines 9–10), the author is saying that the big business man's neglect would be a *social benefit*.

4. D   **Interpretation**

In the final paragraph, Steffens provides *hope . . . in the commercialization of our politics* (lines 68–69) and tells us that to realize this hope, *All we have to do is to establish a steady demand for good government. If the demand were steady, they, being so commercial, would "deliver the goods"* (lines 72–75).

5. D   **Textual Evidence**

As indicated in the explanation to the previous question, the best evidence is found in lines 73–75.

6. C   **Interpretation**

The typical businessman is too busy and *therefore [has] no time for politics* (lines 13–14). In other words, he is unhappy when situations force him to leave business matters and get involved public affairs.

7. A   **Interpretation**

The parallel structure of the two sentences in lines 18–20 indicates clearly that the *typical businessman* sees every political problem as a business problem: *when he talks politics, he talks shop. His patent remedy is quack; it is business.* In other words, he *applies business principles to civic matters.*

8. C   **Interpretation**

The fire metaphor that the author uses in line 25–31 emphasizes the idea that a person who performs a job part time and without professional training is not likely to do a good job. If politicians are more interested in their businesses than in their political duties, they will not do them well.

9. A   **Specific Detail**

Steffens indicates that, unlike the "big business man" who *is busy with politics* (line 6), the typical businessman is *too busy* and *has no use and therefore no time for politics* (lines 12–14).

10. B   **Textual Evidence**

As indicated in the explanation to the previous question, the best evidence is found in lines 12–14.

11. D   **Tone**

The author indicates that we need defense from outer space dangers like *lethal ultraviolet radiation and rogue meteors* (lines 6–7). In other words, outer space is a *treacherous environment*.

12. B   **Interpretation**

The point of this paragraph is that, although Baumgartner's jump may have been *amazing* (line 27), it was *nowhere near to anyone's definition of space* (line 28), and in fact well within the realm of ordinary experience as described by the physical laws of Isaac Newton. The two sentences *He leapt,* and *He fell,* simply reinforce the *predictable* nature of the jump.

13. D   **Word in Context**

The phrase *any meaningful atmosphere* (line 56) means *any substantial atmosphere*.

14. B   **Inference**

The author describes the experiences of astronauts in lines 46–99 to make the point that *the concept of space is as much a subjective one as a scientific one.* In lines 73–74, the author states that these experiences *suggest that the experience affects the mind at least as powerfully as the body.*

15. D   **Textual Evidence**

As indicated in the explanation to the previous question, the best evidence is found in lines 70–74.

16. C   **Word in Context**

The statement that Virgin Galactic's *offer of "spaceflight" is tenuous at best* (line 90) means that, since the company has *yet to launch a single commercial flight* (line 87), its offer is *dubious* (doubtful).

17. C   **Inference**

In lines 13–17, the author indicates that *space is, ultimately, a phenomenological concept. Its boundary lies wherever humans feel they have crossed a threshold of distance, or protection, or some other radical departure from terrestrial experience.* In other words, the *experience of space travel cannot be easily quantified* because it is a very personal kind of experience.

18. A   **Textual Evidence**

As indicated in the explanation to the previous question, the best evidence is found in lines 14–17.

19. C   **Graphical Analysis**

According to the diagram, the Karman line is at an altitude of 100 kilometers, and the highest jumps are near the 40-kilometer line.

20. A   **Graphical Analysis**

The graph on the left indicates that the temperature at ground level is slightly less than 50°F and at the altitude of Baumgartner's jump is slightly less than 0°F.

21. D   **Interpretation**

The phrase *language . . . ceases to matter* (lines 103–104) echoes the main point of the final paragraph, which is that it is irrelevant, if not impossible, to describe the experience of space flight verbally. In other words, *intense experiences are not enhanced by efforts to describe them.*

22. A   **General Purpose**

Mr. Brooke indicates that *the match is good* (line 66) between Mr. Casaubon and Dorothea, even though he acknowledges that Dorothea cannot *sit down and play you . . . a good old English tune* (lines 14–15) as a woman should, and is in fact *behind Celia [her sister]*, who *plays very prettily* (lines 32–33). Furthermore, Brooke believes that Dorothea does not have a *healthy* (line 54) ability to control her emotions, and in fact must learn to *take things more quietly* (lines 56–57).

23. A   **Word in Context**

In the first several paragraphs, Mr. Brooke discusses his beliefs about the proper role of women, including his belief that *deep studies . . . are too taxing for a woman* (lines 1–3). In other words, Brooke believes that the *lightness about the feminine mind* (line 10) is its *naivety* and lack of sophistication.

24. B   **Inference**

In discussing his own taste for "domestic music," Mr. Casaubon states that *a tune much iterated [repeated]* is *hardly tolerable* (lines 41–44). That is, it is *an insufferably tedious experience.*

25. C   **Textual Analysis**

As indicated in the explanation to the previous question, the best evidence is found in lines 41–45.

26. C   **Interpretation**

Mr. Brooke states that he *is a conservative in music,* and then *it's not like ideas, you know* (lines 18–19), thereby suggesting that he is not as conservative about ideas as he is about music. In other words, he *is inclined to hold unconventional opinions on social issues.* This fact is confirmed later in the passage, when the narrator mentions the *Radical speech* that Mr. Brooke would later make about *the incomes of the bishops* (lines 76–77).

27. C   **Interpretation**

In line 50, Dorothea says *music of that sort I should enjoy,* referring to the *grander forms of music, worthy to accompany solemn celebrations* (lines 45–46) mentioned by Mr. Casaubon. In fact, that music *made [her] sob* (line 53). In other words, she prefers *dignified and majestic* music.

28. D   **Inference**

In lines 73–77, the narrator gives us a glimpse into the future, and we learn that Mr. Brooke will give a *Radical speech* against the high income of Bishops.

29. C   **Textual Evidence**

As indicated in the explanation to the previous question, the best evidence is found in lines 73–77.

30. B   **Detail**

Mr. Brooke's commentary in lines 63–72 indicates that he is glad that Mr. Casaubon is likely to become a bishop. In lines 73–77, however, the narrator indicates that, in so doing, Mr. Brooke *little though of the Radical speech which, at a later period, he was led to make on the incomes of the bishops.* In other words, Mr. Brooke's later experience would radically change his views about the bishops, and hence his earlier viewpoint was *prone to change.*

31. C   **Word in Context**

In this sentence, the metaphor *mine of truth* treats truth as something that can be taken from a mine, or *quarried.*

32. A   **Interpretation**

The narrator implies that Mr. Brooke can *look at a subject from various points of view* (lines 96–97), and so credits

Mr. Brooke with *open-mindedness*, even if that open-mindedness may be somewhat opportunistic.

---

33. A **Specific Purpose**

The author opens by stating that the problem he will discuss is *to figure out what consciousness is and how to build it* (lines 1–2). He then proposes a specific solution to that problem by proposing his *Attention Schema theory* (lines 4–5).

---

34. B **Word in Context**

The statement *we'll have made the essential leap* (line 11) means that we will have overcome the most significant technological hurdle to figuring out *how to build [a conscious mind]* (line 2). In other words, the *leap* in this case is a technological breakthrough.

---

35. C **Interpretation**

According to the passage, the brain creates a *dataset* (line 18) of visual information from the ball, but this dataset is *a caricature, a proxy for reality* (line 23). In other words, it is one of the *simplified models* (line 26) that the brain constructs to avoid sensory overload. This dataset *omits a great deal of detail*.

---

36. D **Textual Evidence**

As indicated in the explanation to the previous question, the best evidence is found in lines 23–24.

---

37. D **Graphical Analysis**

Look at the arrows in the Schema Model and the Serial 2 Model. In both cases the arrow must pass through Attention before moving to Awareness.

---

38. B **Interpretation**

The author asks questions of his hypothetical robot in line 45, lines 52–53, lines 79–80, lines 98–99, and lines 100–101, to reveal how the functions that are successively added to its software contribute to its growing consciousness.

---

39. A **Inference**

In lines 86–87, the author suggests that adding a model of the *complex relationship between the self and the ball*, that is, a mechanism to provide the information that the "self" is *paying attention* to the "ball," is required to give the robot "conscious awareness" of that ball. In the next paragraph, the author indicates that adding such a model is problematic, because *whereas we have decades of research on internal models of concrete things such as tennis balls, there's virtually nothing on any internal model of attention* (lines 91–94).

---

40. D **Textual Evidence**

As indicated in the explanation to the previous question, the best evidence is found in lines 91–94.

---

41. C **Word in Context**

The statement *we can no longer dip into standard neuroscience* means that established neuroscience does not provide a handy solution to our problem. In other words, we cannot *draw upon* its resources.

---

42. B **Purpose/Interpretation**

The author refers to the work of Oliver Sacks in lines 64–73 to illustrate how *the brain's internal model of the physical self* (lines 61–62) is a *complex and delicate piece of equipment* (lines 63–64). That is, the representation known as the *body schema* (line 61) is not always reliable.

---

43. B **Word in Context**

The sentence *No country apprehends from it any aggressive designs* (lines 4–5) means that no other country can reasonably believe that England is aggressive. In other words, they do not *ascribe to* England any aggressive designs.

---

44. C **Inference**

In line 23, Mill states that England *makes no treaties stipulating for separate commercial advantage*, and rather seeks equal footing with all other nations in matters of trade. In lines 24–27, Mill states that *If the aggressions of the barbarians force [England] to successful war, and its victorious arms put it in a position to command liberty of trade, whatever it demands for itself it demands for all mankind.* Since it seeks no commercial advantage for itself, any advantages it may enjoy must be due to *unintentional circumstances*.

---

45. C **Textual Support**

As indicated in the explanation to the previous question, the best evidence is found in lines 24–28.

---

46. A **Cross-Textual Analysis**

In Passage 2, Chomsky is directly challenging Mill's claim that England, and indeed all imperial powers, is acting out of benevolence. Therefore, Passage 2 refutes the central claim of Passage 1.

---

47. D **Tone/Interpretation**

In Passage 2, Chomsky is criticizing powers that use rhetoric of noble intent when invading and occupying other nations. When he says the Japanese records in Manchuria and China are *overflowing with the milk of human kindness* (lines 85–86), he is saying that they claim noble intentions, but are in fact committing heinous atrocities. Therefore, his statement conveys a tone of *cynicism*.

---

48. D **Word in Context**

In this context, the phrase *paying no duties* means paying no fines or tariffs at England's ports.

49. A   **Cross-Textual Analysis**

The first graph shows the dramatic rise in British exports of opium to China coinciding with the two Opium Wars. The second graph shows the steady rise of the British and German economies and the steady fall of China's economy over the same period. This supports Chomsky's contention in Passage 2 that *Britain established the world's most extensive narco-trafficking enterprise* (lines 72–73).

50. A   **Cross-Textual Analysis**

Noam Chomsky would certainly agree that *Power, from of old, is wont to encroach upon the weak, and to quarrel for ascendancy with those who are as strong as itself* (lines 6–8), because this is essentially the thesis of Passage 2. Although Mill claims that England provides an exception to this rule, Chomsky disagrees.

51. D   **Cross-Textual Inference**

When Mill says that *many are unable to believe it when they see it* (lines 40–41), he is referring to England's foreign policy of benevolence. Chomsky's speech indicates that, in fact, many nations, such as the United States (line 82), Germany (line 83), and Japan (line 83), made the same claims to benevolence as they were committing acts of aggression against other nations.

52. D   **Textual Evidence**

Lines 93–95 state that *Hitler gave the same arguments when he took over Czechoslovakia.* This supports Chomsky's point that other nations emulated Britain's foreign policy of claimed benevolence.

Section 2: Writing and Language

1. B   **Pronoun Antecedents/Coordination**

In the original sentence, the definite pronoun *this* lacks a clear antecedent. Choice B corrects this problem by specifying the referent, *definition*. Choices C and D produce sentence fragments.

2. B   **Idiom/Comparisons**

This sentence uses the comparison idiom *not so much A as B*. The wording of the comparison must be precise, and the phrases in *A* and *B* must be parallel. Choice B is the only one that follows the idiom.

3. A   **Parallelism/Comparisons**

This sentence compares *being white-collar* with *working in an office.* Notice that this comparison follows the Law of Parallelism because both of these are gerund phrases. The original phrasing is the only one that uses the correct parallel structure.

4. A   **Subject-Verb Agreement/Verb Aspect/
Verb Mood**

The original sentence is best. The subject of the sentence is *increase*, so the verb must agree with this singular subject. Also, the verb should be in the present tense and perfect (or "consequential") aspect, because the verb indicates a present status that is the consequence of past events.

5. B   **Logical Comparison/Idiom**

This sentence is making a direct comparison, so this comparison must be logical. It compares *your job* to *the jobs in factories 100 years ago*. The original phrasing makes an illogical comparison. Choice C uses an incorrect verb. Choice D makes an unidiomatic comparison: *than* implies an unbalanced comparison, such as those described by comparative adjectives, e.g., *faster than* or *more than*.

6. B   **Diction/Clear Expression**

The *millions of job seekers* represent a *supply* of potential labor to employers.

7. D   **Idiom**

The heading of the graph indicates that these lines represent *underemployment* rather than *unemployment*, and the top line represents *recent graduates* rather than *all graduates*.

8. A   **Clear Expression of Ideas/Cohesiveness**

The original phrase effectively connects to the previous sentence by providing a fact that supports the contention that college graduates can no longer count on *a secure pipeline to a comfortable career* and a *steady climb up the corporate ladder.*

9. D   **Diction/Clear Expression of Ideas**

The Internet *enables* companies to hire contract workers. It is illogical to say that the Internet *causes*, *requires*, or *reminds* companies.

10. C   **Punctuation/Redundancy**

Choice C is the most concise and effective answer. All of the other choices are redundant or needlessly wordy. Choice D also includes a diction error, because *Its* is the possessive pronoun, not the contraction for *It is*.

11. C   **Idiom/Clear Expression of Ideas**

The phrase *offers tools to keep* is unidiomatic. The proper idiom is *offers tools for keeping*. Choice B is unidiomatic. Choice D is illogical, because the tools don't keep in touch, rather they help *us* keep in touch.

12. D Redundancy

Choices A and B are redundant, since the phrase *from many sources throughout the world* already implies that the sources are varied. Choice C is illogical.

13. B Coordination/Comma Splices/ Dangling Participles

The original phrasing creates a comma splice, since both clauses are independent. Choice C is awkward and contains a dangling participle. Choice D also creates a dangling participle.

14. C Diction/Clear Expression of Ideas

The previous sentences refer to *activities*, specifically *burning fossil fuels* and *engaging in slash-and-burn agriculture*, both of which clearly have *serious effects* on the environment. These are not properly called *situations* or *phenomena*, because they are intentional actions. *Gases* doesn't work, because the previous sentence refers to nongaseous pollutants, like ash, and only mentions one gas: carbon dioxide.

15. D Pronouns

Since the *mission* is the mission of the NPS, this sentence requires a possessive pronoun. The original phrasing is incorrect because *who's* is the contraction of *who is*. Choice B is incorrect because *it's* is the contraction of *it is*. Choice C is incorrect because it creates a comma splice. Only choice D provides a possessive pronoun and avoids the comma splice. Although many writers disapprove of the "personification" implied by *whose*, this usage is standard in American English.

16. C Parallelism

The Law of Parallelism says that items in a list should be in the same grammatical format. Since the first two items are past participle phrases, *damaged vegetation* and *changed the biodiversity*, the third item must follow the same form: *damaged buildings and monuments*.

17. C Coordination

The original sentence is illogical because the participial phrase following the comma does not logically modify the main clause. Since the second half of the sentence provides a compound predicate, that predicate should be preceded by a simple conjunction, as in choice C.

18. C Cohesiveness/Development

This paragraph discusses how air pollution has already damaged many national parks. This sentence and the one that follows it add the important information that pollution harms the experience of visitors.

19. B Pronouns/Possession

The context requires the plural possessive form: *visitors'*. Choice A is not possessive. Choice C is not the standard form of any word. Choice D is not plural.

20. A Transitions/Cohesiveness

This sentence works best as a transition sentence at the beginning of the paragraph, because the phrase *these problems* refers to the *damaging effects* discussed in the previous paragraph.

21. D Idiom

The standard idiom is *provide the information required for EPA officials **to make** reliable assessments*.

22. B Diction

The context of this paragraph makes it clear that the challenge EPA and parks officials face is *to **determine** how to best apply air quality data* to improve current conditions. Choice A does not work, because *revealing* this plan would not be a challenge, once the plan is made. Choice C does not work, because these agencies aren't *requiring* anything of anyone else. Choice D does not work, because the phrase *administer how best to apply* is unidiomatic and illogical.

23. D Diction

Although all of the choices have very similar meanings, only choice D, *drew*, has the correct tone and connotation for this context. Choice A is incorrect because to *lure* is to draw with the intention of capturing. The context makes it clear that these activists had no such intention. Choice B is incorrect because *pulled attention* is not idiomatic. Choice C is incorrect because *tempted* implies that national attention can desire something. This is illogical: although an audience can desire something that draws its attention, the attention itself cannot desire anything, and so cannot be *tempted*.

24. C Clear Expression of Ideas/Coordination

The original phrasing does not coordinate with the modifying phrase *that were dividing*. Choice B is incorrect because the phrase *politically and culturally profound* is illogical, and clearly alters the intended original meaning. Choice D is incorrect because it establishes an illogical antecedent for the pronoun *that*.

25. D Clear Expression of Ideas/Diction

The original phrasing is incorrect because *antics* cannot be *furious*. Ditto for Choice C. Choice B is incorrect because the predicates are not parallel. Choice D provides parallel predicates as well as logical phrasing.

26. A   **Logical Coordination/Transitions**

The original sentence provides the most concise and logical phrasing for the comparison. Choices B, C, and D are all illogical.

27. B   **Coordination/Idiom**

In the original phrasing, the semicolon is misused because the clause that follows it is not independent. The colon can be used in this case, however, because it can be used after an independent clause to indicate an illustrative or explanatory word or phrase that need not be an independent clause. In choice B, the phrase that follows the colon explains that crime. Choice C is incorrect because the infinitive *to cross* incorrectly indicates the *purpose* of the crime rather than the crime itself. Choice D is incorrect because the phrase *crossing . . . for inciting* is unidiomatic.

28. D   **Idiom**

The proper idiom here is *justified in accusing*.

29. A   **Logical Cohesiveness**

The original phrasing provides the most logical connection to the previous sentence, which indicates that the prosecutors *were clearly justified* in accusing the defendants of one charge. This sentence begins with *However*, so it must provide an example of an *unjustified* accusation.

30. B   **Clear Expression of Ideas/Diction**

The second half of the sentence makes it clear that the jury felt it must punish the defendants for their antics. Therefore, those antics must have *antagonized* the jury. *Aggrieved* is an adjective, and although it derives from a verb, it is no longer used as a verb in standard English. To be *aggrieved* means to feel resentment at unfair treatment. *Bemused* means *puzzled*, and *disputed* means *argued about*.

31. B   **Parallelism/Voice**

The second (nonunderlined) half of this sentence provides a second predicate, which should be parallel with the first. Choices B and D provide parallel predicates, but choice D is in the wrong tense.

32. A   **Diction/Clear Expression of Ideas**

The context makes it clear that politics *tainted* the judicial process in the case of the Chicago Seven. To *taint* means to *contaminate*.

33. C   **Logical Coherence**

The original sentence states that the trial of the Chicago Seven was a fitting epilogue to the anti-war movement but does not explain why. The additional information provides that explanation.

34. C   **Verb Tense/Verb Mood/Verb Aspect**

The context of the sentence establishes that this verb should be in the simple past tense.

35. C   **Coordination**

Choice C is only one that provides a smooth and effective combination of the sentences. Choice A is incorrect because the interrupting modifier is illogical. Choices B and D both include dangling modifiers.

36. B   **Diction**

The painting *epitomizes* (serves as a perfect example of) van Gogh's insight, because, by the description that follows, it aptly captures how *alive* and *richly colored* the night sky is.

37. A   **Coordination/Dangling Participles**

The subject of this clause must also be the subject of the participial phrase *Measuring only 29 inches high by 36¼ inches wide,* because otherwise the participial phrase will dangle. Only choices A and D avoid the dangler, but D is incorrect because the verb phrase *has the viewer overwhelmed* is illogical and nonstandard.

38. A   **Comparisons/Idiom/Parallelism**

This sentences uses the parallel construction *not so much A as B*. The original provides the proper idiomatic phrasing as well as parallel form (infinitives) for *A* and *B*. Choices B, C, and D are not idiomatic.

39. C   **Development**

This sentence contributes to the colorful and energetic description of the painting and is necessary to provide context to the next paragraph, which returns to a discussion of the cypress.

40. A   **Parallelism**

The original phrasing is best. It seems at first that the semicolon is being misused because the clause that follows does not seem to be independent. But, in fact, it is. The clause is the elliptical (shortened) form of *[does the painting symbolize] despair or hope?* which clearly is an independent clause. The phrase in brackets can be omitted here because it merely repeats the phrase verbatim from the first clause. This omission is called *parallel ellipsis*, the omission of words or phrases that are implied by a parallel form.

41. D   **Cohesiveness**

This sentence belongs at the very end of the paragraph, because it draws specifically on the contrast between the hope expressed in sentence 4 and van Gogh's suicide 13 months later.

42. A   **Cohesiveness**

This sentence refers to the questions about van Gogh that were discussed in the previous paragraph. These were questions about van Gogh's *intent* (*Does the painting symbolize turmoil or tranquility?*) and *state of mind* (*perhaps it indicates the hope of a heavenly journey*).

---

43. D   **Verb Tense/Verb Aspect/**
Subject-Verb Agreement

This verb indicates that the current status of van Gogh and "Starry Night" is a consequence of previous events, so it requires the "present perfect" (or "present consequential") form, *have lost*. Although choice C is also in the "present consequential," it does not agree with the plural subject, *compelling painting and its enigmatic painter*.

---

44. A   **Cohesiveness/Conclusions**

The original sentence effectively concludes the passage and ties into the first paragraph by echoing its themes of torment (*his brief, tortured lifetime*) and poverty (*sold only one painting*).

Section 3: Math (No Calculator)

1. A   **Algebra (linear equations) EASY**

Original equation: $\dfrac{7}{3}a = \dfrac{3}{4}$

Multiply by $\dfrac{3}{7}$: $a = \dfrac{3}{4} \times \dfrac{3}{7} = \dfrac{9}{28}$

---

2. A   **Algebra (solving equations) EASY**

Original equation: $3x + a = x + b$

Subtract x: $2x + a = b$

Subtract a: $2x = b - a$

Divide by 2: $x = \dfrac{b-a}{2}$

---

3. C   **Algebra (expressing relationships) EASY**

Because Laura's car averages 27 miles per gallon for highway driving, she needs 10/27 gallons to travel 10 miles on the highway. (Notice that "dimensional analysis" helps here: when "miles" are divided by "miles/gallon," the quotient yields "gallons," which is the unit we want.) Similarly, because her car averages 21 miles per gallon for city driving, she needs $b/21$ gallons to travel b miles in the city.

---

4. B   **Advanced Mathematics**
(exponentials) EASY

Recall that $\sqrt[n]{x} = x^{\frac{1}{n}}$ and $(x^m)^n = x^{mn}$: $\sqrt[3]{x^7} = (x^7)^{\frac{1}{3}} = x^{\frac{7}{3}}$

---

5. D   **Additional Topics (analyzing linear**
equations and graphs) EASY

We can solve this problem in several ways, but perhaps the simplest is to write the equation in "point-slope" form (since we are given the slope or the line and a point on the line) and convert it to "slope-intercept" form.

Point-slope form given slope $= -\dfrac{3}{4}$ and line contains $(8, 4)$: $(y-4) = -\dfrac{3}{4}(x-8)$

Distribute: $y - 4 = -\dfrac{3}{4}x + 6$

Add 4: $y = -\dfrac{3}{4}x + 10$

Therefore, the y-intercept of the graph is at the point $(0, 10)$.

---

6. C   **Advanced Mathematics (simplifying**
polynomial expressions) MEDIUM

Original expression:
$$(ab^2c^2 + abc - a^2b^2c) - (a^2b^2c - ab^2c^2 + abc)$$

Distribute: $ab^2c^2 + abc - a^2b^2c - a^2b^2c + ab^2c^2 - abc$

Collect like terms:
$$(ab^2c^2 + ab^2c^2) + (abc - abc) + (-a^2b^2c - a^2b^2c)$$

Simplify: $2ab^2c^2 - 2a^2b^2c$

---

7. B   **Advanced Mathematics (functions) MEDIUM**

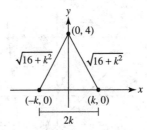

If we consider the point $(0, 4)$ to be the vertex where the two congruent sides meet, then because of the symmetry of an isosceles triangle, the two other vertices must be at $(-k, 0)$ and $(k, 0)$. Now, if you want, you can test the coordinates of the points in the choices to see which one yields a triangle with a perimeter of 16 units.

Alternately, if you want to flex your algebra and analytical geometry muscles, you can "solve." The base of the triangle has a length of $2k$, as shown above, and we can then use the Pythagorean Theorem to find the lengths of the two congruent sides in terms of k. Since $4^2 + k^2 = (\text{side})^2$, we can see that the two congruent sides have length $\sqrt{16+k^2}$, as shown above. Since the perimeter is 16: $2k + 2\sqrt{16+k^2} = 16$

Divide by 2: $k + \sqrt{16+k^2} = 8$

Subtract k: $\sqrt{16+k^2} = 8 - k$

Square both sides (and FOIL on the right side):
$$16 + k^2 = 64 - 16k + k^2$$

Subtract $k^2 + 16$: $0 = 48 - 16k$

Add 16k: $16k = 48$
Divide by 16: $k = 3$
Therefore, the remaining two vertices are (3, 0) and (–3, 0).

---

8. D   **Advanced Mathematics
(quadratic systems) MEDIUM**

Substitute and simplify:

$$\frac{a-b}{2} = \frac{(x^2-1)-(x-1)^2}{2} = \frac{x^2-1-(x^2-2x+1)}{2}$$

$$= \frac{x^2-1-x^2+2x-1}{2} = \frac{2x-2}{2} = x-1$$

---

9. A   **Algebra (linear graphs) MEDIUM**

We can calculate the slope of line m using the slope

formula: $\text{slope} = \frac{y_2 - y_1}{x_2 - x_1} = \frac{0-7}{9-0} = -\frac{7}{9}$

Since line l must have the same slope:

$$\frac{-4-0}{0-k} = \frac{-4}{-k} = \frac{4}{k} = -\frac{7}{9}$$

Cross-multiply: $-36 = 7k$

Divide by 7: $-\frac{36}{7} = k$

---

10. B   **Advanced Mathematics (non-linear systems)
MEDIUM-HARD**

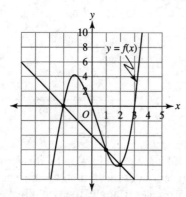

We can simply graph the line $y = -2x - 4$ on the same
xy-plane and note the intersection points. One tricky
thing here is that the vertical (y-axis) scale is different
from the horizontal (x-axis scale). Notice that the vertical
lines are only one unit apart (so the x-axis scale is 1 unit),
but the horizontal lines are two units apart (so the y-axis
scale is 2 units). Therefore, the line with a slope of –2
and a y-intercept of –4 looks like the one graphed above.
Just reading the coordinates of the points of intersection
shows that those points are at (–2, 0), (1, –6), and (2, –8).
You should also be able to confirm that all three of these
ordered pairs satisfy both equations.

---

11. B   **Additional Topics (volume) MEDIUM-HARD**

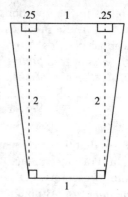

The planter is in the form of a prism with trapezoidal
bases. The volume of any prism is equal to the area of the
base times the height. To find the area of the trapezoidal
bases, we can use the formula for the area of a trapezoid,
$A_{\text{trapezoid}} = \frac{b_1 + b_2}{2} \times h$, after we convert all lengths to feet:

$$A_{\text{trapezoid}} = \frac{1+1.5}{2} \times 2 = 2.5 \text{ square feet}$$

(Alternately, you can look at the trapezoid as being composed of a rectangle and two right triangles, as shown
in the diagram above, with units converted to feet, and
calculate the area as the sum of those three areas.)

Since the height of this prism (the "depth" of the
planter) is 1 foot, the total volume of the planter is
(2.5)(1) = 2.5 cubic feet. Since the soil costs $4 per cubic
foot, the total cost of soil is $4(2.5) = $10.

---

12. C   **Advanced Mathematics (forms of quadratic
functions) MEDIUM-HARD**

The parabola shown has a vertex, B, at (–2, 2). The equation in choice C is in "vertex form" ($y = a(x - h)^2 + k$), so it
shows these coordinates directly as constants.

---

13. D   **Advanced Mathematics (sequence problems)
MEDIUM-HARD**

If $a_1 = \frac{1}{4}$ and $r = 2$, then the first 10 terms of the sequence

are $\frac{1}{4}, \frac{1}{2}$, 1, 2, 4, 8, 16, 32, 64, and 128. Since the 8th of

these terms is 32, $n = 8$.

---

14. C   **Advanced Mathematics
(graphs of polynomials) MEDIUM-HARD**

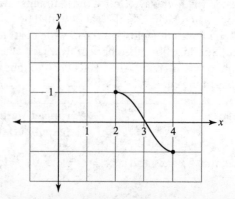

All graphs of polynomial functions are continuous; that is, they can be sketched in the xy-plane without lifting your pencil from the page. If we plot the two points of the function that are given, $(2, 1)$ and $(4, -1)$, and draw a curve connecting the two, it is clear that the graph must cross the x-axis somewhere between $x = 2$ and $x = 4$. Choice A is incorrect because it implies that $p(4) = 0$, which is clearly not true. Choice B is incorrect because it implies that $p(1) = 0$, which may or may not be true. Choice D is incorrect because it implies that $p(1) = 2$, which may or may not be true.

---

15. D **Advanced Mathematics (analyzing polynomial functions) HARD**

Although you might prefer to answer this question by actually performing "long division" on the rational expression on the left of the equation (in which case b represents the remainder), you may find it to be a bit more straightforward to just multiply both sides of the equation by the common denominator and solve for b.

Original equation:
$$\frac{x^2+1}{x+1} = x - 1 + \frac{b}{x+1}$$

Multiply both sides by $x + 1$: $\quad x^2 + 1 = (x-1)(x+1) + b$

FOIL on the right side: $\qquad x^2 + 1 = x^2 - 1 + b$

Subtract x^2: $\qquad\qquad\qquad 1 = -1 + b$

Add 1: $\qquad\qquad\qquad\qquad 2 = b$

---

16. 10 **Algebra (solving equations) EASY**

Original equation: $\qquad\qquad (x - 3)^2 = 49$

Take the square root (remember there are two!):
$$x - 3 = \pm 7$$

Add 3: $\qquad\qquad\qquad x = 10 \text{ or } -4$

Since $x > 0$, the correct answer is $x = 10$.

---

17. 8 **Algebra (solving inequalities) MEDIUM**

Since the question asks for the maximum number of pens Fernanda can buy, let's define p as that number. Since she buys a total of 24 pens and pencils, she must buy $24 - p$ pencils. Since each pen costs 50 cents, she spends $50p$ cents on pens, and since each pencil costs 5 cents, she spends $5(24 - p) = 120 - 5p$ cents on pencils. Since she can't spend more than 5 dollars, or 500 cents:
$$50p + 120 - 5p \leq 500$$

Simplify: $\qquad\qquad\qquad 45p + 120 \leq 500$

Subtract 120: $\qquad\qquad\qquad 45p \leq 380$

Divide by 45: $\qquad\qquad\qquad p \leq 8.444\ldots$

Since p must be a whole number, its greatest possible value is 8.

---

18. 10 **Algebra (graphs of lines) MEDIUM**

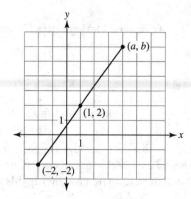

It's important to read this question carefully. Notice that we are *given* the midpoint, so we aren't trying to find it. We are trying to find the other *endpoint*. One way to find it is to sketch a graph of the points, as shown above. If you count carefully, it should be easy to see that the other endpoint must be at $(4, 6)$. Alternately, you can use the midpoint formula, $\text{midpoint} = \left(\frac{x_1+x_2}{2}, \frac{y_1+y_2}{2}\right)$:

$$(1,2) = \left(\frac{-2+a}{2}, \frac{-2+b}{2}\right)$$

Find a by equating the x-coordinates: $\quad 1 = \frac{-2+a}{2}$

Multiply by 2: $\qquad\qquad\qquad 2 = -2 + a$

Add 2: $\qquad\qquad\qquad\qquad 4 = a$

Find b by equating the y-coordinates: $\quad 2 = \frac{-2+b}{2}$

Multiply by 2: $\qquad\qquad\qquad 4 = -2 + b$

Add 2: $\qquad\qquad\qquad\qquad 6 = b$

Therefore, $a + b = 4 + 6 = 10$.

---

19. 31 **Algebra (solving inequalities) MEDIUM-HARD**

Original inequality: $\qquad \frac{1}{100} - \frac{9}{n^2} > 0$

Notice that $100n^2$ must be positive, so multiplying by $100n^2$ doesn't require "flipping:" $\quad n^2 - 900 > 0$

Add 900: $\qquad\qquad\qquad\qquad n^2 > 900$

Take square root (assuming n is positive): $\quad n > 30$

Since n must be greater than 30, the least positive integer solution is $n = 31$.

---

20. 3/10 or .3 **Algebra (linear systems) HARD**

If this system has no solutions, then the equations represent parallel lines in the xy-plane. This means that their slopes must be equal. Recall that if a line is expressed in "standard form," $ax + by = c$, that its slope is $-a/b$. (You can also prove this by converting this equation to "slope-intercept form.") Therefore, if the two slopes are the same:
$$-\frac{a}{b} = -\frac{\frac{1}{5}}{\frac{2}{3}} = -\frac{1}{5} \times \frac{3}{2} = -\frac{3}{10}$$

Multiply by -1: $\qquad\qquad\qquad \frac{a}{b} = \frac{3}{10}$

Section 4: Math (Calculator)

1. **A**   Advanced Mathematics (functions) EASY

If $f(4) = 17$: $3(4) + c = 17$

Simplify: $12 + c = 17$

Subtract 12: $c = 5$

---

2. **B**   Problem Solving and Data Analysis (proportions) EASY

The phrase "at this rate" always suggests a proportion. The number of cars with expired emissions stickers can be calculated by setting up and solving this proportion:

$$\frac{5}{200} = \frac{x}{5000}$$

Cross-multiply: $25{,}000 = 200x$

Divide by 200: $125 = x$

---

3. **D**   Algebra (solving equations) EASY

The simplest strategy here is to look closely at what the question is asking for and find the simplest way to get there. The question asks for the value of $4m + p$. Notice that this is precisely the expression we get if we multiply both sides of the original equation by its common denominator, 12:

Original equation: $\frac{1}{3}m + \frac{1}{12}p = 12$

Multiply both sides by 12: $4m + p = 144$

---

4. **A**   Algebra (graphs of linear equations) EASY

Notice that we can get the given equation into "slope-intercept" form by just distributing:

Original equation: $y = kx - k^2$

This means that this line has a slope of k and a y-intercept of $-k^2$. If k is positive, then the slope is positive and the y-intercept is negative. Only choice A gives a graph of a line with a positive slope and a negative y-intercept. Notice that this is the graph for $k = 1$.

---

5. **D**   Algebra/Problem Solving (expressing linear relationships) EASY

Since each episode of the series costs $1.99, it costs Alissa $1.99x$ to watch x episodes. The total remaining on her gift card after the $8 membership fee and the payment for x episodes is $\$20 - \$8 - \$1.99x = \$12 - \$1.99x$.

---

6. **A**   Advanced Mathematics (compositions of functions) EASY-MEDIUM

The expression $g(f(b))$ means the result when an input b is put through the function f, and then this result is put through the function g. If $g(f(b)) = 5$, then $f(b)$ must be a number that, when put into g, yields an output of 5. The table indicates that the only input to g that yields an output of 5 is 4; therefore, $f(b) = 4$. This means that b is a number that, when put into f, yields an output of 4.

The table shows that 3 is the only input to f that yields an output of 4.

---

7. **B**   Algebra (analyzing linear relationships in context) EASY

Let x represent the amount that Kate is paid per student enrolled in her course. The total amount that Kate will be paid for this course when 50 students are enrolled is then $\$200 + \$50x$:

         $200 + 50x = 725$

Subtract 200: $50x = 525$

Divide by 50: $x = 10.50$

---

8. **B**   Algebra (analyzing linear relationships) EASY

If the base amount is increased by 25%, it becomes (1.25) $(\$200) = \$250$. If 60 students enroll for next year's course, the total she will receive is $\$250 + 60(\$10.50) = \$880$.

---

9. **D**   Problem Solving and Data Analysis (proportions) EASY-MEDIUM

Since the answer choices contain unknowns, one way to approach this question is to pick a convenient value for p to make the question easier to think about. Notice that if we choose $p = 20$, that is, if Keith reads 20 pages in 20 minutes, then clearly he reads 1 page per minute, and therefore should take 70 minutes to read 70 pages. If we plug in $p = 20$ to the choices, we get

A) $7(20)/2 = 70$

B) $2(20)/7 = 5.7$

C) $20/1{,}400 = 0.014$

D) $1{,}400/20 = 70$

Which, of course, eliminates choices B and C, but doesn't help us choose between A and D. (<u>Note</u>: This is a good reminder NOT to be too hasty in choosing an answer when plugging in. Just because a choice gives you the value you are looking for in that particular case doesn't mean that it will *always* give the right answer.)

Of course, we could plug in a different value for p to eliminate one of the remaining choices, but let's use this opportunity to look at the algebraic method, which is to simply treat the problem as a conversion:

$$70 \text{ pages} \times \frac{20 \text{ minutes}}{p \text{ pages}} = \frac{1{,}400}{p} \text{ minutes}$$

Notice that "pages" unit cancels top and bottom, and we get the proper units of "minutes."

---

10. **A**   Algebra (translating quantitative information) MEDIUM

Jason pays $355 for the phone itself, and then pays $40 each month for the next 18 months, for a total of $\$355 + 18(\$40) = \$355 + \$720 = \$1{,}075$. However, each month he receives a $10 rebate, so the total is reduced by $18(\$10) = \$180$, and $\$1{,}075 - \$180 = \$895$.

11. B   **Advanced Mathematics (graphs of polynomials) MEDIUM**

The zeros of a function correspond to the points at which the graph of that function in the xy-plane cross the x-axis. If the function has four distinct zeros, its graph must touch the x-axis in only four points, which is true only of the graph in choice B.

12. C   **Problem Solving and Data Analysis (interpreting histograms) MEDIUM**

The question asks about current smokers, so the relevant information is in the top graph. The first three bars on the left correspond to those cholesterol levels below 210 mg/dL, and these bars account for a total of about $3\% + 0\% + 21\% = 24\%$ of the smokers in the study. Since there were 500 smokers in this study, this accounts for about $(0.24)(500) = 120$ smokers.

13. D   **Problem Solving and Data Analysis (drawing conclusions) MEDIUM-HARD**

The hypothesis being tested is *that quitting smoking will reduce the chances that a person will have high cholesterol levels*. This theory would be supported by evidence that those who have recently quit smoking have a significantly smaller probability of having high cholesterol levels than do current smokers. However, the data do not show that. In fact, the proportions that have cholesterol levels above 269 are about the same for both groups: $16\% + 3\% + 0\% + 0\% + 3\% = 22\%$ for smokers, and $4\% + 6\% + 9\% + 0\% + 0\% = 22\%$ for ex-smokers.

Although choice C might seem to be a reasonable response, this fact is not relevant to the *stated hypothesis*, which is about the *chances of having high cholesterol levels* rather than about *average* cholesterol levels.

14. C   **Advanced Mathematics (non-linear systems) MEDIUM**

This system can be solved most easily by substitution:
$$x^2 + y^2 = 80$$
Substitute the second equation, $y = 2x$, into the first:
$$x^2 + (2x)^2 = 80$$
Simplify: $x^2 + 4x^2 = 80$
Combine like terms: $5x^2 = 80$
Divide by 5: $x^2 = 16$
Take the square root: $x = \pm 4$
Since the question does not specify a particular point of intersection, we can choose $x = 4$, and plug into the second equation find the corresponding value of y:
$$y = 2(4) = 8$$
Therefore, $a = 4$ and $b = 8$, so $ab = 32$. (Notice that if we chose the solution $x = -4$, the corresponding value of y would be -8, so the product ab would still be 32.)

15. D   **Algebra (graphing lines) EASY**

Since the equations are all given in standard $(ax + by = c)$ form, we can find the slope of each line with the slope formula $= -a/b$. This gives us slopes of (A) $-2/1 = -2$, (B) $-2/-1 = 2$, (C) $-2/1 = -2$, and (D) $-2/-1 = 2$. Since the line must have a slope of 2, we can eliminate choices A and C. Then we can substitute $x = 1$ and $y = 3$ to see which equation is satisfied by the point (1, 3). Only choice D works, because $2(1) - 3 = -1$.

16. D   **Algebra (modeling linear relationships) MEDIUM**

We are given two ordered-pair solutions: (44 chirps, 29°C) and (32 chirps, 22°C). All of the choices are linear equation in slope-intercept form, so to find the right linear equation, we can first find the slope: $m = \dfrac{y_2 - y_1}{x_2 - x_1} = \dfrac{29 - 22}{44 - 32} = \dfrac{7}{12}$. Notice that this eliminates choices A and B. We can then find the value of the y-intercept by first plugging in one of the ordered pairs into the point-slope form of the line:
$$T - 22 = \frac{7}{12}(c - 32)$$
Distribute:
$$T - 22 = \frac{7}{12}c - \frac{56}{3}$$
Add 22 (or $\dfrac{66}{3}$) to both sides:
$$T = \frac{7}{12}c - \frac{56}{3} + \frac{66}{3} = \frac{7}{12}c + \frac{10}{3}$$

17. C   **Algebra (linear equations) MEDIUM**

The slope of a line in standard $(ax + by = c)$ form is $-a/b$, so the slope of the given line is $(-1)/(-2) = 1/2$. Perpendicular lines have slopes that are opposite reciprocals, so we are looking for the equation of a line with a slope of $-2/1 = -2$. Since all of the choices are linear equations in standard form, we can find their slopes in the same way we found the slope of the first line.
A) slope $= -3/6 = -1/2$
B) slope $= 3/(-6) = 1/2$
C) slope $= -6/3 = -2$
D) slope $= -6/(-3) = 2$

18. A   **Advanced Mathematics (solving quadratics) MEDIUM-HARD**

Although it may not look like it, this is a quadratic equation. We can see this by simply multiplying both sides of the equation by the common denominator, $3x$.
Original equation: $2x - \dfrac{5}{x} = \dfrac{1}{3}$
Multiply both sides by $3x$: $6x^2 - 15 = x$
Subtract x: $6x^2 - x - 15 = 0$
At this point we could solve this quadratic by factoring or by using the quadratic formula, but there is actually a one-step solution. Divide by 6: $x^2 - \dfrac{1}{6}x - \dfrac{15}{6} = 0$

This gives us a lead coefficient of 1 and puts the quadratic in the form $x^2 + bx + c = 0$. Any quadratic in this form has two solutions (which may be the same number repeated, or two non-real numbers). The sum of these solutions is always $-b$ and their product is always c. Since the question asks only for the sum of these solutions, this sum is just the opposite of the x coefficient: $\frac{1}{6}$.

If you prefer to go the whole nine yards, you can solve the quadratic by factoring:

$$6x^2 - x - 15 = (3x - 5)(2x + 3) = 0$$

So, by the Zero Product Property, the solutions are $x = \frac{5}{3}$ and $x = -\frac{3}{2}$, and their sum is $\frac{5}{3} + \left(-\frac{3}{2}\right) = \frac{10}{6} - \frac{9}{6} = \frac{1}{6}$.

---

19. B   **Problem Solving and Data Analysis**
                          (lines of best fit) MEDIUM-HARD

The line of best fit, like the scatter plot itself, relates *cost in cents per page* and *speed in pages per minute*. The quantity we're given, however, is neither of those, so it must be converted. If a printer can print 20 pages per dollar, it can print 20 pages per 100 cents, or $20/100 = 1/5$ of a *page per cent*. The cost in *cents per page* is just the reciprocal of this rate, so this printer can print at a cost of $5/1 = 5$ *cents per page*. This corresponds to the c in the equation that represents the line of best fit: $c = 0.58s + 2.74$
Substitute $c = 5$: $5 = 0.58s + 2.74$
Subtract 2.74: $2.26 = 0.58s$
Divide by 0.58: $3.90 = s$
Therefore, the best estimate for the speed of the printer is 3.90 pages per minute.

---

20. B   **Problem Solving and Data Analysis**
                          (scatter plots) MEDIUM-HARD

The slowest printer in this group is the printer represented by the leftmost dot in the scatter plot, and the fastest printer is represented by the rightmost dot. The leftmost dot corresponds to a speed of 1.5 pages per minute, and the rightmost dot corresponds to a speed of 5.5 pages per minute. (Notice that the horizontal scale does not have a "zero" on the left. This fact is indicated by the jagged portion on the left end of the horizontal axis. The rest of the axis should make it clear that the tick marks are 0.5 apart, and since the leftmost dot is one tick mark to the left of 2, its horizontal value is $2.0 - 0.5 = 1.5$.) The faster printer takes $(100 \text{ pages})/(5.5 \text{ pages per minute}) = 18.2$ minutes to print a 100-page document, while the slowest printer takes $(100 \text{ pages})/(1.5 \text{ pages per minute}) = 66.7$ minutes to print the same document, for a difference of $66.7 - 18.2 = 48.5$ minutes, which is closest to choice B, 48 minutes.

---

21. D   **Problem Solving and Data Analysis**
                          (analysis of sets) MEDIUM-HARD

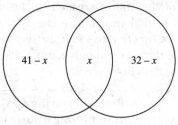

Bought Snacks   Enjoyed Movie

A Venn diagram is helpful in examining this situation. Look carefully at the diagram above and notice how it represents the situation this question describes. The circle on the left represents everyone who bought snacks and the circle on the right represents everyone who enjoyed the movie. Let's let x represent the number of people who *both* bought snacks *and* enjoyed the movie: the overlap between the two sets. Since 41 people in total bought snacks, and x of them also liked the movie, then $41 - x$ of them bought snacks but did *not* like the movie. Similarly, since 32 people in total liked the movie, and x of them also bought snacks, then $32 - x$ people enjoyed the movie but did *not* buy snacks. Since these three sets can account for no more than 50 people (the total number surveyed): $(41 - x) + (x) + (32 - x) \leq 50$
Simplify: $73 - x \leq 50$
Add x and subtract 50: $23 \leq x$
Since x can be no less than 23, this is the least possible number of people surveyed who could have both purchased snacks and enjoyed the movie.

---

22. C   **Problem Solving and Data Analysis**
                          (interpreting graphs) MEDIUM-HARD

This graph shows data for a group of 1,000 people who were broken into 15 subsets, as indicated by the 15 separate bars. Notice, however, that the graph does not show how *many* people are in each set, but only the *percentage* of the people in each set who live below the poverty line. The quantity in choice A cannot be determined from the graph, because the set of *unemployed adults ages 18 and above* is represented by 5 separate bars, and since we don't know how to "weigh" each bar (because we don't know how many people belong in each subset), we cannot calculate an overall percentage. Likewise, the quantity in choice B cannot be determined, because the set of *adults ages 65 and over* is represented by 3 bars. The quantity in choice D cannot be determined, because the 11th bar from the left represents the *percentage of surveyed part-time workers ages 55 to 64 who live below the poverty line,* and NOT *the percentage of adults ages 55 to 64 who work part-time.* The quantity in choice C, however, can be determined from this graph because it is the quantity represented by the 6th bar from the left.

23. B   **Advanced Mathematics**
                    (exponential growth) MEDIUM

We know that $P = 1,200$ when $t = 0$, so:
$$1,200 = P_0 r^0 = P_0$$
Therefore, the equation has the form $P = 1,200r$. After one year, the bird population decreases by 7%, so the population is $1,200 - 0.07(1,200) = 1116$. Therefore:
$$1116 = 1,200r^1$$
Divide by 1,200: $0.93 = r$
A simpler strategy is simply to recognize that r represents the common ratio of one year's population to the previous year's population. Since each year, the population is decreasing by 7%, it is $100\% - 7\% = 93\% = 0.93$ of the previous year's population.

---

24. C   **Problem Solving and Data Analysis**
                 (percents) MEDIUM-HARD

Let x represent the monthly cost of satellite TV. Since premium cable service costs 15% more, its monthly cost is $x + \$0.15x = \$1.15x$. After the $10 monthly discount, the monthly cost for premium cable becomes $\$1.15x - \$10$. After a 5% discount, the monthly cost of satellite TV is $x - \$.05x = \$0.95x$. If the two services now cost the same: $1.15x - 10 = 0.95x$
Subtract $0.95x$ and add 10: $0.20x = 10$
Divide by 0.20: $x = 50$
This means that the regular monthly cost of satellite TV is $50. Since premium cable service normally costs 15% more, its monthly cost is $(1.15)(\$50) = \$57.50$.

---

25. B   **Additional Topics (similar triangles)**
                 MEDIUM-HARD

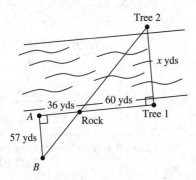

It is important to mark up the diagram and confirm the measures in the diagram with the information in the problem. For consistency, we should indicate all measurements in yards. Let x represent the width of the river, in yards. The distance from Tree 1 to the Rock is 60 yards. The distance from point A to Tree 1 is 96 yards, so the distance from the rock to point A is 36 yards. The distance from A to B is $171 \div 3 = 57$ yards. To find the value of x, we must use the fact that the two triangles are similar because two of their corresponding angles are equal.

Now we can set up a proportion: $\dfrac{57}{36} = \dfrac{x}{60}$

Multiply by 60 and simplify:
$$\frac{(60)(57)}{36} = \frac{3420}{36} = 95 = x$$

---

26. B   **Algebra (inequalities) HARD**

Original inequality: $\dfrac{a}{2b} > 1$

This means, of course, that $\dfrac{a}{2b}$ is positive, which means that the numerator and denominator of this fraction must have the same sign. Since we are told that a is negative, $2b$ must also be negative. Therefore, multiplying both sides of the inequality by $2b$ requires "flipping" the inequality: $a < 2b$
Now, since $2b$ must be less than $2b + 1$:
$$a < 2b < 2b + 1$$
Therefore, by the Transitive Law of Inequality:
$$a < 2b + 1$$
Alternately, we can often solve "must be true" questions by process of elimination. That is, we can find counterexamples for the four wrong answers. We simply need to start choosing values for a and b that satisfy the conditions of the problem. For instance, $a = -6$ and $b = -2$ satisfy both inequalities (which you should confirm for yourself now). Next, we notice that these solutions are *not* solutions of any of the statements in A, C, or D.

---

27. B   **Advanced Mathematics (graphing parabolas)**
             MEDIUM-HARD

There are several ways to approach this problem, but the best strategy is usually to start with the information that is handed to us. Since the quadratic is expressed in factored form, it is easy to see that the graph has zeroes at $x = 3$ and $x = 7$. The question asks about the vertex of this parabola, so we should remember that the x-coordinate of the vertex of a parabola is always the average of the zeroes. (This is because the vertical line through the vertex is the axis of symmetry for the parabola.) Therefore, the x-coordinate of the vertex is $(3 + 7) \div 2 = 5$. We can plug this directly back into the equation: $y = (5 - 3)(5 - 7) = (2)(-2) = -4$. Therefore, the vertex of the parabola is $(5, -4)$.

---

28. C   **Problem Solving and Data Analysis**
                 (variation) MEDIUM-HARD

The question doesn't specify the applied pressure for the original sample of gas, so although we could solve the problem by leaving P as an unknown, it's not a bad idea to pick a convenient value for P, such as $P = 2$ atmospheres.

Given formula: $V = \dfrac{k}{P}$

If $P = 2$ when $V = 6$: $6 = \dfrac{k}{2}$

Multiply by 2: $12 = k$
Since k is a constant, it doesn't change even when the other quantities change. If P increases by 50%, it becomes

$(1.5)(2) = 3$ atmospheres. We can substitute these values into the original formula to find the new value for V.

$$V = \frac{12}{3} = 4 \text{ liters}$$

29. **C**　　　　Special Topics (complex numbers) HARD

Original expression:　　　　　　　　$\sqrt{-18} - \sqrt{-8}$

Factor out $\sqrt{-1}$:　　　　　　$\sqrt{-1}\sqrt{18} - \sqrt{-1}\sqrt{8}$

Substitute $\sqrt{-1} = i$:　　　　　　$i\sqrt{18} - i\sqrt{8}$

Factor the perfect square from each radicand:

$$i\sqrt{9}\sqrt{2} - i\sqrt{4}\sqrt{2}$$

Simplify:　　　　　　　　　　$3i\sqrt{2} - 2i\sqrt{2}$

Combine like terms:　　　　　　　　$i\sqrt{2}$

30. **A**　　　　Special Topics (trigonometry)
　　　　　　　　　　　　　MEDIUM-HARD

As with most geometry and trigonometry questions, it is helpful to draw a diagram. Since the angles in a triangle must always have a sum of 180°, $a + b + 90 = 180$, and so $a + b = 90$. We can choose values for a and b that have a sum of 90, and see which statement must be true. For instance, if we choose $a = 30°$ and $b = 60°$, only choice A yields a true statement. Alternately we can recall the Co-function Identity: any trigonometric ratio for an angle is equal to the co-trigonometric ratio of its complement. That is: $\sin(x°) = \cos(90°-x°)$ for all x, etc.

31. **86**　　　　　Algebra (solving equations) EASY

We simply need to substitute $C = 30$ into the equation

and solve for F:　　　　　　　　$30 = \frac{5}{9}(F - 32)$

Multiply by $\frac{9}{5}$:　　　　　　　$54 = F - 32$

Add 32:　　　　　　　　　　$86 = F$

32. **26**　　　Problem Solving and Data Analysis (rates)
　　　　　　　　　　　　　EASY-MEDIUM

Since we want to minimize the number of days that Abby needs to complete the blanket, she must stitch as many squares as she can per day. Since she can stitch a maximum of 15 squares per hour, and the blanket requires 1,170 squares, it will take her $1,170 \div 15 = 78$ hours in total. Since she can work only 3 hours per day, it will take her $78 \div 3 = 26$ days minimum.

33. **9.60**　　　　Algebra (percent change) MEDIUM

The monthly contributions to Mrs. Battle's pension plan total 8% of her monthly salary (5% from Mrs. Battle's personal deduction plus 3% from her employer). Mrs. Battle's current monthly salary is $3,000, so the monthly contributions to her pension total $(0.08)(\$3,000) = \$240$. When she receives a 4% raise, her new salary will be $(1.04)(\$3,000) = \$3,120$ so monthly contributions to her pension will be $(0.08)(\$3,120) = \$249.60$, which is a monthly increase of $\$249.60 - \$240 = \$9.60$.

34. **31.5**　　　　Additional Topics (angles) MEDIUM

Recall that π radians is equivalent to 180°. Therefore, an angle of $\frac{7\pi}{10}$ radians has a measure of $\frac{7\pi}{10}$ radians $\times \frac{180°}{\pi \text{ radians}} = 126°$. Since this measure is 4 times the measure of angle B, the measure of angle B must be $126° \div 4 = 31.5°$.

35. **6**　　　Algebra (solving equations) MEDIUM-HARD

Original equation:　　　　　　$(p - 1)(p + 2) = -8$

FOIL:　　　　　　　　　　$p^2 + 2p - p - 2 = -8$

Simplify and add 8:　　　　　　$p^2 + p + 6 = 0$

Now we have the equation in quadratic form with a leading coefficient of 1 (that is, it resembles the form $x^2 + bx + c = 0$). It turns out that this quadratic is not easily factorable, but we can find the solutions using the quadratic formula: $p = \frac{-b \pm \sqrt{b^2 - 4ac}}{2a}$. Unfortunately, this will yield complex solutions because the discriminant is negative: $b^2 - 4ac = (1)^2 - 4(1)(6) = -23$. Fortunately, however, there is a simple way to find the answer we are looking for. The question doesn't ask for the individual solutions, but rather the *product* of these solutions. If a quadratic equation is in the form $x^2 + bx + c = 0$, then the sum of the solutions is always $-b$ and the product of these solutions is always c. Since $c = 6$ in our equation, this must be the product of the two solutions.

If you prefer to do it the hard way (which, of course, you shouldn't), multiplying the two results given by the quadratic formula will yield the same answer:

$$\left(\frac{-1 + \sqrt{1^2 - 4(1)(6)}}{2}\right)\left(\frac{-1 - \sqrt{1^2 - 4(1)(6)}}{2}\right)$$

$$= \left(\frac{-1 + i\sqrt{23}}{2}\right)\left(\frac{-1 - i\sqrt{23}}{2}\right)$$

$$= \frac{1^2 - i^2(\sqrt{23})^2}{4} = \frac{1 + 23}{4} = 6$$

36. **54**　　　Additional Topics (analyzing polynomials)
　　　　　　　　　　　　　MEDIUM-HARD

The Factor Theorem states that any polynomial with a factor of $(x - h)$ must equal 0 when $x = h$. (This is because when $x = h$, the factor of $(x - h)$ becomes $(h - h) = 0$, and anything times 0 equals 0.) Therefore, if $x + 2$ is a factor of $x^3 + 14x^2 + bx + 60$, then this polynomial must equal 0 when $x = -2$:

$$(-2)^3 + 14(-2)^2 + b(-2) + 60 = 0$$

Simplify:　　　　　　　　$-8 + 56 - 2b + 60 = 0$

Combine like terms:　　　　　　$108 - 2b = 0$

Add $2b$:　　　　　　　　$108 = 2b$

Divide by 2:　　　　　　　$54 = b$

37. **2.60**   **Data Analysis (interpretation of data)**
MEDIUM-HARD

The District 5 incumbent spent 730 × $1,000 = $730,000 and received 55% of the 510,000 votes (0.55 × 510,000 = 280,500 votes). So if the incumbent spent $730,000 for 280,500 votes:

$$\$730,000 \div 280,500 \text{ votes} = \$2.60 \text{ per vote}$$

---

38. **.27**   **Data Analysis (line of best fit) HARD**

We are told that the line of best fit is given by the equation $v = kx + 72{,}600$. If the data in District 6 matches this model perfectly, we can plug the values from District 6 in to solve for k. In District 6 there were 661,000 votes cast and the incumbent received 60% of those votes. So $v = 661{,}000 \times 0.6 = 396{,}600$ votes. The total expenditures in District 6 were $1,200,000:

Now plug those in and solve:

$$396{,}600 = k(1{,}200{,}000) + 72{,}600$$

Subtract 72,600: $324{,}000 = 1{,}200{,}000k$

Divide by 1,200,000: $.27 = k$

PRACTICE SAT 4

ANSWER SHEET

SECTION 1

1 Ⓐ Ⓑ Ⓒ Ⓓ	13 Ⓐ Ⓑ Ⓒ Ⓓ	25 Ⓐ Ⓑ Ⓒ Ⓓ	37 Ⓐ Ⓑ Ⓒ Ⓓ	49 Ⓐ Ⓑ Ⓒ Ⓓ
2 Ⓐ Ⓑ Ⓒ Ⓓ	14 Ⓐ Ⓑ Ⓒ Ⓓ	26 Ⓐ Ⓑ Ⓒ Ⓓ	38 Ⓐ Ⓑ Ⓒ Ⓓ	50 Ⓐ Ⓑ Ⓒ Ⓓ
3 Ⓐ Ⓑ Ⓒ Ⓓ	15 Ⓐ Ⓑ Ⓒ Ⓓ	27 Ⓐ Ⓑ Ⓒ Ⓓ	39 Ⓐ Ⓑ Ⓒ Ⓓ	51 Ⓐ Ⓑ Ⓒ Ⓓ
4 Ⓐ Ⓑ Ⓒ Ⓓ	16 Ⓐ Ⓑ Ⓒ Ⓓ	28 Ⓐ Ⓑ Ⓒ Ⓓ	40 Ⓐ Ⓑ Ⓒ Ⓓ	52 Ⓐ Ⓑ Ⓒ Ⓓ
5 Ⓐ Ⓑ Ⓒ Ⓓ	17 Ⓐ Ⓑ Ⓒ Ⓓ	29 Ⓐ Ⓑ Ⓒ Ⓓ	41 Ⓐ Ⓑ Ⓒ Ⓓ	
6 Ⓐ Ⓑ Ⓒ Ⓓ	18 Ⓐ Ⓑ Ⓒ Ⓓ	30 Ⓐ Ⓑ Ⓒ Ⓓ	42 Ⓐ Ⓑ Ⓒ Ⓓ	
7 Ⓐ Ⓑ Ⓒ Ⓓ	19 Ⓐ Ⓑ Ⓒ Ⓓ	31 Ⓐ Ⓑ Ⓒ Ⓓ	43 Ⓐ Ⓑ Ⓒ Ⓓ	
8 Ⓐ Ⓑ Ⓒ Ⓓ	20 Ⓐ Ⓑ Ⓒ Ⓓ	32 Ⓐ Ⓑ Ⓒ Ⓓ	44 Ⓐ Ⓑ Ⓒ Ⓓ	
9 Ⓐ Ⓑ Ⓒ Ⓓ	21 Ⓐ Ⓑ Ⓒ Ⓓ	33 Ⓐ Ⓑ Ⓒ Ⓓ	45 Ⓐ Ⓑ Ⓒ Ⓓ	
10 Ⓐ Ⓑ Ⓒ Ⓓ	22 Ⓐ Ⓑ Ⓒ Ⓓ	34 Ⓐ Ⓑ Ⓒ Ⓓ	46 Ⓐ Ⓑ Ⓒ Ⓓ	
11 Ⓐ Ⓑ Ⓒ Ⓓ	23 Ⓐ Ⓑ Ⓒ Ⓓ	35 Ⓐ Ⓑ Ⓒ Ⓓ	47 Ⓐ Ⓑ Ⓒ Ⓓ	
12 Ⓐ Ⓑ Ⓒ Ⓓ	24 Ⓐ Ⓑ Ⓒ Ⓓ	36 Ⓐ Ⓑ Ⓒ Ⓓ	48 Ⓐ Ⓑ Ⓒ Ⓓ	

SECTION 2

1 Ⓐ Ⓑ Ⓒ Ⓓ	11 Ⓐ Ⓑ Ⓒ Ⓓ	21 Ⓐ Ⓑ Ⓒ Ⓓ	31 Ⓐ Ⓑ Ⓒ Ⓓ	41 Ⓐ Ⓑ Ⓒ Ⓓ
2 Ⓐ Ⓑ Ⓒ Ⓓ	12 Ⓐ Ⓑ Ⓒ Ⓓ	22 Ⓐ Ⓑ Ⓒ Ⓓ	32 Ⓐ Ⓑ Ⓒ Ⓓ	42 Ⓐ Ⓑ Ⓒ Ⓓ
3 Ⓐ Ⓑ Ⓒ Ⓓ	13 Ⓐ Ⓑ Ⓒ Ⓓ	23 Ⓐ Ⓑ Ⓒ Ⓓ	33 Ⓐ Ⓑ Ⓒ Ⓓ	43 Ⓐ Ⓑ Ⓒ Ⓓ
4 Ⓐ Ⓑ Ⓒ Ⓓ	14 Ⓐ Ⓑ Ⓒ Ⓓ	24 Ⓐ Ⓑ Ⓒ Ⓓ	34 Ⓐ Ⓑ Ⓒ Ⓓ	44 Ⓐ Ⓑ Ⓒ Ⓓ
5 Ⓐ Ⓑ Ⓒ Ⓓ	15 Ⓐ Ⓑ Ⓒ Ⓓ	25 Ⓐ Ⓑ Ⓒ Ⓓ	35 Ⓐ Ⓑ Ⓒ Ⓓ	
6 Ⓐ Ⓑ Ⓒ Ⓓ	16 Ⓐ Ⓑ Ⓒ Ⓓ	26 Ⓐ Ⓑ Ⓒ Ⓓ	36 Ⓐ Ⓑ Ⓒ Ⓓ	
7 Ⓐ Ⓑ Ⓒ Ⓓ	17 Ⓐ Ⓑ Ⓒ Ⓓ	27 Ⓐ Ⓑ Ⓒ Ⓓ	37 Ⓐ Ⓑ Ⓒ Ⓓ	
8 Ⓐ Ⓑ Ⓒ Ⓓ	18 Ⓐ Ⓑ Ⓒ Ⓓ	28 Ⓐ Ⓑ Ⓒ Ⓓ	38 Ⓐ Ⓑ Ⓒ Ⓓ	
9 Ⓐ Ⓑ Ⓒ Ⓓ	19 Ⓐ Ⓑ Ⓒ Ⓓ	29 Ⓐ Ⓑ Ⓒ Ⓓ	39 Ⓐ Ⓑ Ⓒ Ⓓ	
10 Ⓐ Ⓑ Ⓒ Ⓓ	20 Ⓐ Ⓑ Ⓒ Ⓓ	30 Ⓐ Ⓑ Ⓒ Ⓓ	40 Ⓐ Ⓑ Ⓒ Ⓓ	

SECTION 3

1	Ⓐ	Ⓑ	Ⓒ	Ⓓ
2	Ⓐ	Ⓑ	Ⓒ	Ⓓ
3	Ⓐ	Ⓑ	Ⓒ	Ⓓ
4	Ⓐ	Ⓑ	Ⓒ	Ⓓ
5	Ⓐ	Ⓑ	Ⓒ	Ⓓ
6	Ⓐ	Ⓑ	Ⓒ	Ⓓ
7	Ⓐ	Ⓑ	Ⓒ	Ⓓ
8	Ⓐ	Ⓑ	Ⓒ	Ⓓ
9	Ⓐ	Ⓑ	Ⓒ	Ⓓ
10	Ⓐ	Ⓑ	Ⓒ	Ⓓ
11	Ⓐ	Ⓑ	Ⓒ	Ⓓ
12	Ⓐ	Ⓑ	Ⓒ	Ⓓ
13	Ⓐ	Ⓑ	Ⓒ	Ⓓ
14	Ⓐ	Ⓑ	Ⓒ	Ⓓ
15	Ⓐ	Ⓑ	Ⓒ	Ⓓ

Student-Produced Responses

ONLY ANSWERS ENTERED IN THE CIRCLES IN EACH GRID WILL BE SCORED. YOU WILL NOT RECEIVE CREDIT FOR ANYTHING WRITTEN IN THE BOXES ABOVE THE CIRCLES.

16 17 18 19 20

	⊘	⊘	
⊙	⊙	⊙	⊙
	0	0	0
1	1	1	1
2	2	2	2
3	3	3	3
4	4	4	4
5	5	5	5
6	6	6	6
7	7	7	7
8	8	8	8
9	9	9	9

SECTION
4

1 Ⓐ Ⓑ Ⓒ Ⓓ   11 Ⓐ Ⓑ Ⓒ Ⓓ   21 Ⓐ Ⓑ Ⓒ Ⓓ
2 Ⓐ Ⓑ Ⓒ Ⓓ   12 Ⓐ Ⓑ Ⓒ Ⓓ   22 Ⓐ Ⓑ Ⓒ Ⓓ
3 Ⓐ Ⓑ Ⓒ Ⓓ   13 Ⓐ Ⓑ Ⓒ Ⓓ   23 Ⓐ Ⓑ Ⓒ Ⓓ
4 Ⓐ Ⓑ Ⓒ Ⓓ   14 Ⓐ Ⓑ Ⓒ Ⓓ   24 Ⓐ Ⓑ Ⓒ Ⓓ
5 Ⓐ Ⓑ Ⓒ Ⓓ   15 Ⓐ Ⓑ Ⓒ Ⓓ   25 Ⓐ Ⓑ Ⓒ Ⓓ
6 Ⓐ Ⓑ Ⓒ Ⓓ   16 Ⓐ Ⓑ Ⓒ Ⓓ   26 Ⓐ Ⓑ Ⓒ Ⓓ
7 Ⓐ Ⓑ Ⓒ Ⓓ   17 Ⓐ Ⓑ Ⓒ Ⓓ   27 Ⓐ Ⓑ Ⓒ Ⓓ
8 Ⓐ Ⓑ Ⓒ Ⓓ   18 Ⓐ Ⓑ Ⓒ Ⓓ   28 Ⓐ Ⓑ Ⓒ Ⓓ
9 Ⓐ Ⓑ Ⓒ Ⓓ   19 Ⓐ Ⓑ Ⓒ Ⓓ   29 Ⓐ Ⓑ Ⓒ Ⓓ
10 Ⓐ Ⓑ Ⓒ Ⓓ   20 Ⓐ Ⓑ Ⓒ Ⓓ   30 Ⓐ Ⓑ Ⓒ Ⓓ

Student-Produced Responses

ONLY ANSWERS ENTERED IN THE CIRCLES IN EACH GRID WILL BE SCORED. YOU WILL NOT RECEIVE CREDIT FOR ANYTHING WRITTEN IN THE BOXES ABOVE THE CIRCLES.

31 32 33 34

35 36 37 38

SECTION 5: ESSAY

You may wish to remove these sample answer document pages to respond to the practice SAT Essay Test.

Begin ESSAY here.

If you need more space, please continue on the next page.

1

Cut Here

Cut Here

ESSAY

If you need more space, please continue on the next page.

2

ESSAY

If you need more space, please continue on the next page.

Cut Here

ESSAY

_____

_____

_____

_____

_____

_____

_____

_____

_____

_____

_____

_____

_____

_____

_____

_____

_____

_____

_____

_____

_____

_____

_____

_____

_____

_____

_____

_____

STOP here with the Essay.

Cut Here

1

1

Reading Test

65 MINUTES, 52 QUESTIONS

Turn to Section 1 of your answer sheet to answer the questions in this section.

DIRECTIONS

Each passage or pair of passages below is followed by a number of questions. After reading each passage or pair, choose the best answer to each question based on what is stated or implied in the passage or passages and in any accompanying graphics (such as a table or graph).

Questions 1–11 are based on the following passage.

This passage is adapted from F. Scott Fitzgerald, *The Beautiful and the Damned*, originally published in 1922. Anthony and Gloria, a young couple, have been discussing the possibility that Anthony's grandfather will fund Anthony to go to Europe as a war correspondent.

Line
Anthony found his wife deep in the porch hammock voluptuously engaged with a lemonade and a tomato sandwich.

They rejoiced happily, gay again with reborn
5 irresponsibility. Then he told her of his opportunity to go abroad, and that he was almost ashamed to reject it.

"What do *you* think? Just tell me frankly."

"Why, Anthony!" Her eyes were startled. "Do
10 you want to go? Without me?"

His face fell—yet he knew, with his wife's question, that it was too late. Her arms, sweet and strangling, were around him, for he had made all such choices back in that room in the Plaza the
15 year before. This was an anachronism from an age of such dreams.

"Gloria," he lied, in a great burst of comprehension, "of course I don't. I was thinking you might go as a nurse or something."

20 As she smiled he realized again how beautiful she was, a gorgeous girl of miraculous freshness. She embraced his suggestion with luxurious intensity, holding it aloft like a sun of her own making and basking in its beams. She strung

25 together an amazing synopsis for an extravaganza of martial adventure. But Anthony, after he had carried her romantically up the stairs, stayed awake to brood upon the day, vaguely angry with her, vaguely dissatisfied.

30 "What am I going to do?" he began at breakfast. "Here we've been married a year and we've just worried around without even being efficient people of leisure."

"Yes, you ought to do something," she admit-
35 ted, being in an agreeable and loquacious humor. This was not the first of these discussions, but as they usually developed Anthony in the role of protagonist, she had come to avoid them.

"It's not that I have any moral compunc-
40 tions about work," he continued, "but Grampa may die tomorrow and he may live for ten years. Meanwhile we're living above our income and all we've got to show for it is a farmer's car and a few clothes. We keep an apartment that we've only
45 lived in three months and a little old house way off in nowhere. We're frequently bored and yet we won't make any effort to know any one except the same crowd who drift around California all summer wearing sport clothes and waiting for their
50 families to die."

"How you've changed!" remarked Gloria. "Once you told me you didn't see why an American couldn't loaf gracefully."

"Well, damn it, I wasn't married. And the old
55 mind was working at top speed and now it's going round and round like a cog-wheel with nothing to catch it. As a matter of fact I think that if I hadn't

CONTINUE ➤

1   1

met you I *would* have done something. But you make leisure so subtly attractive—"

60   "Oh, it's all my fault—"

"I didn't mean that, and you know I didn't. But here I'm almost twenty-seven and—"

"Oh," she interrupted in vexation, "you make me tired! Talking as though I were objecting or

65 hindering you! I should think you'd be strong enough to settle your own problems without coming to me. You *talk* a lot about going to work. I could use more money very easily, but *I'm* not complaining. Whether you work or not I love you."

70 Her last words were gentle as fine snow upon hard ground. But for the moment neither was attending to the other—they were each engaged in polishing and perfecting his own attitude.

"I have worked—some." This by Anthony was

75 an imprudent bringing up of raw reserves. Gloria laughed, torn between delight and derision; she resented his sophistry as at the same time she admired his nonchalance. She would never

blame him for being the ineffectual idler so long

80 as he did it sincerely, from the attitude that nothing much was worth doing.

"Work!" she scoffed. "Oh, you sad bird! You bluffer! Work—that means a great arranging of the desk and the lights, a great sharpening of pencils,

85 and 'Gloria, don't sing!' and 'Please keep that damn cook Tana away from me,' and 'Let me read you my opening sentence,' and 'I won't be through for a long time, Gloria, so don't stay up for me,' and a tremendous consumption of tea or coffee. And that's all. In

90 just about an hour I hear the old pencil stop scratching and look over. You've got out a book and you're 'looking up' something. Then you're reading. Then yawns—then bed and a great tossing about because you're all full of caffeine and can't sleep. Two weeks

95 later the whole performance over again."

With much difficulty Anthony retained a scanty breech-clout[1] of dignity.

---

[1] a thin strip of material; a loincloth

1   **1**

1

Which choice best summarizes the passage?

A) A man expresses his dissatisfaction with his marriage and plans a dramatic change.

B) A husband and wife consider lifestyle changes but revert to habitual indolence.

C) A young husband blames his wife for the poor choices they have made in life.

D) A young wife disapproves of her husband's work and pleads with him to change jobs.

2

The opening sentence of the passage serves mainly to

A) characterize Gloria's tendency toward self-indulgence.

B) establish the topic of the conversation that follows.

C) contrast Gloria's indolence with Anthony's ambitiousness.

D) indicate Gloria's ability to find enjoyment despite the couple's poverty.

3

Anthony lies to Gloria about wanting her to accompany him overseas because

A) he is concerned that the trip might be too dangerous.

B) he still has unfulfilled dreams from the previous year.

C) he feels obligated to his wife for better or worse.

D) he hopes to pressure his grandfather into paying for the trip.

4

Which choice provides the best evidence for the answer to the previous question?

A) Lines 5–7 ("Then . . . reject it")

B) Lines 12–15 ("Her arms . . . before")

C) Lines 18–19 ("I was . . . something")

D) Lines 20–22 ("As . . . freshness")

5

Gloria regards Anthony's suggestion that she join him on the trip with a sense of

A) scorn and contempt.

B) romanticism and excitement.

C) patriotism and altruism.

D) apprehension and dread.

6

Which choice provides the best evidence for the answer to the previous question?

A) Lines 9–10 ("Do you . . . me?")

B) Lines 20–22 ("As she . . . freshness")

C) Lines 24–26 ("She strung . . . adventure")

D) Lines 34–35 ("Yes . . . humor")

7

As used in line 48, "drift" most nearly means

A) digress substantially

B) float aimlessly

C) accumulate haphazardly

D) move sideways

1

1

8

Which choice best describes the couple's attitude toward work?

A) Anthony is tentatively drawn toward work despite Gloria's disdain for it.

B) Anthony resents the pressure Gloria is putting on him to work harder.

C) Both Anthony and Gloria want to work harder but are unsure how to do it.

D) Both Gloria and Anthony are unhappy with Anthony's grandfather's expectations of them.

9

As used in line 70, "fine" most nearly means

A) satisfactory

B) magnificent

C) powdery

D) precise

10

The sentence in lines 74–75 ("This . . . reserves") suggests that Anthony's statement was

A) a desperate retort.

B) a contemptible evasion.

C) an overly emotional outburst.

D) a boastful response.

11

In the final paragraphs, Gloria is upset because

A) she believes that Anthony is being insincere about his desire to work.

B) she is afraid that Anthony will not put on a convincing performance for his grandfather.

C) she is concerned that Anthony is considering going on the trip without her.

D) she realizes that Anthony is unlikely to secure gainful employment.

CONTINUE ➡

1   **1**

CONTINUE

Questions 12–22 are based on the following passage and supplementary material.

This passage is adapted from H. A. Lorentz, *The Einstein Theory of Relativity: A Concise Statement,* originally published in 1920.

Line

The present revival of interest in Dr. Albert Einstein's "Theory of Relativity," proposed in 1905, is due to the remarkable confirmation that it received in the report of the observations made
5   during the sun's eclipse of last May to determine whether rays of light passing close to the sun are deflected from their course.

The total eclipse of the sun of May 29 resulted in a striking confirmation of the new theory of
10   Einstein's universal attractive power of gravitation, and thus reinforced the conviction that the defining of this theory is one of the most important steps ever taken in the domain of natural science.
15   For centuries, Newton's theory of the attraction of gravitation has been the most prominent example of a theory of natural science. Through the simplicity of its basic idea (a force of attraction between two bodies is directly proportional
20   to the product of their masses and also inversely proportional to the square of the distance between them), through the completeness with which it explained so many of the peculiarities in the movement of the bodies making up the solar
25   system; and, finally, through its universal validity, even in the case of the far-distant planetary systems, it compelled the admiration of all.

Over the centuries, while the skill of the mathematicians was devoted to making more
30   exact calculations of the consequences to which it led, no real progress was made in the science of gravitation. It is true that the inquiry was transferred to the field of physics, following Cavendish's success in demonstrating the
35   common attraction between bodies with which laboratory work can be done, but it always was evident that natural philosophy had no grip on the universal power of attraction. While in electric effects an influence exercised by the matter
40   placed between bodies was speedily observed— the starting-point of a new and fertile doctrine of

electricity—in the case of gravitation not a trace of an influence exercised by intermediate matter could ever be discovered. It was, and remained,
45   inaccessible and unchangeable, without any connection, apparently, with other phenomena of natural philosophy.

Einstein has put an end to this isolation; it is now well established that gravitation affects not
50   only matter, but also light. Thus strengthened in the faith that his theory already has inspired, we may assume with him that there is not a single physical or chemical phenomenon that does not feel—although very probably in an unnoticeable
55   degree—the influence of gravitation, and that, on the other side, the attraction exercised by a body is limited in the first place by the quantity of matter it contains and also, to some degree, by motion and by the physical and chemical condi-
60   tion in which it moves.

As summarized by an American astronomer, Professor Henry Norris Russell, in the *Scientific American*:

"The central fact which has been proved—
65   and which is of great interest and importance—is that the natural phenomena involving gravitation and inertia (such as the motions of the planets) and the phenomena involving electricity and magnetism (including the motion of light) are not
70   independent of one another, but are intimately related, so that both sets of phenomena should be regarded as parts of one vast system, embracing all Nature."

Einstein's theory has the very highest degree
75   of aesthetic merit: every lover of the beautiful must wish it to be true. It gives a vast unified survey of the operations of nature, with a technical simplicity in the critical assumptions that makes the wealth of deductions astonishing. It
80   is a case of an advance arrived at by pure theory: the whole effect of Einstein's work is to make physics more philosophical (in a good sense), and to restore some of that intellectual unity which belonged to the great scientific systems of the
85   seventeenth and eighteenth centuries, but which was lost through increasing specialization and the overwhelming mass of detailed knowledge.

In some ways our age is not a good one to live in, but for those who are interested in physics
90   there are great compensations.

1   1

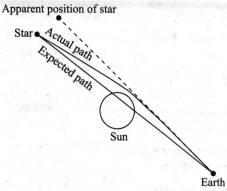

Apparent position of star

Star • Actual path

Expected path

Sun

Earth

Effect of Sun's Gravity on Light
from a Distant Star

12

The passage as a whole serves mainly to

A) outline an academic issue.

B) argue for a philosophical approach.

C) analyze a recently discovered phenomenon.

D) pay tribute to a scientific theory.

13

The "conviction" in line 11 is

A) an ideological belief.

B) an academic consensus.

C) a scientific discovery.

D) a legal phenomenon.

14

According to the passage, the Theory of Relativity was not widely accepted for fifteen years because

A) it contradicted the basic findings of Cavendish.

B) Einstein's scientific reputation had not been established.

C) it had not been verified with objective evidence.

D) its formulation did not allow for precise mathematical calculations.

15

Which choice provides the best evidence for the answer to the previous question?

A) Lines 1–7 ("The . . . course")

B) Lines 15–17 ("For centuries . . . science")

C) Lines 28–32 ("Over . . . gravitation")

D) Lines 32–38 ("It . . . attraction")

16

Lorentz expresses admiration for all of the following qualities of Newton's theory of gravitation <u>except</u> its

A) cogency.

B) elegance.

C) universality.

D) cleverness.

17

As used in line 35, "common" most nearly means

A) public.

B) unexceptional.

C) crude.

D) mutual.

CONTINUE ➡

1   **1**

18

The passage suggests that, until Einstein, studies in gravitation were limited because

A) mathematicians were too focused on making precise calculations.

B) Newton's theory of gravitation was not practical for making verifiable predictions.

C) physicists were preoccupied with studying electrical rather than gravitational effects.

D) scientists could not find evidence that gravity acts on anything other than massive objects.

19

Which choice provides the best evidence for the answer to the previous question?

A) Lines 28–32 ("Over the . . . gravitation")

B) Lines 32–38 ("It is . . . attraction")

C) Lines 38–44 ("While in . . . discovered")

D) Lines 44–47 ("It was . . . philosophy")

20

The quotation from Henry Norris Russell suggests that Russell values what aspect of physical laws?

A) Their predictive power

B) Their agreement with other physical laws

C) Their mathematical precision

D) Their abstract nature

21

According to the diagram and the information in the passage, scientists who studied the total eclipse of May 29, 1920, most likely observed that

A) stars that were expected to be visible to observers on Earth were instead obscured by the sun.

B) stars that were expected to be obscured by the sun were instead visible to observers on Earth.

C) stars that were visible during the eclipse were in fact much brighter than expected.

D) the rays of light from the sun were bent as they entered Earth's gravitational field.

22

The author suggests that scientific research in the nineteenth century was characterized by

A) a commitment to unifying disparate scientific theories.

B) dramatic advances in the quality of scientific instruments.

C) an inability to see patterns across scientific disciplines.

D) an emphasis on philosophical rigor rather than scientific precision.

CONTINUE ➡

1   **1**

Questions 23–32 are based on the following passages and supplementary material.

Passage 1 is adapted from Andrew Jackson, "Annual Message to Congress, 1830." Passage 2 is adapted from Ralph Waldo Emerson, "Letter to President Martin Van Buren, 1836." Both passages discuss the U.S. Indian Removal Act, which was signed into law in 1830 and implemented from 1830 to 1847.

Passage 1

Line   The benevolent policy of the Government in relation to the removal of the Indians beyond the white settlements is approaching a happy consummation. Two important tribes have
5   accepted the provision made at the last session of Congress, and it is believed that their example will induce the remaining tribes to seek the same obvious advantages.

A speedy removal will be important to the
10   United States, to individual States, and to the Indians themselves. The pecuniary[1] advantages which it promises to the Government are the least of its recommendations. It will place a dense and civilized population in large tracts of country
15   now occupied by a few savage hunters. By opening the whole territory between Tennessee on the north and Louisiana on the south to the settlement of the whites, it will incalculably strengthen the southwestern frontier and render the adjacent
20   States strong enough to repel future invasions without remote aid. It will relieve the whole State of Mississippi and the western part of Alabama of Indian occupancy, and enable those States to advance rapidly in population, wealth, and
25   power. It will separate the Indians from immediate contact with settlements of whites. It will free them from the power of the States. It will enable them to pursue happiness in their own way and under their own rude institutions. It will retard
30   the progress of decay, which is lessening their numbers, and perhaps cause them gradually, under the protection of the Government and through the influence of good counsels, to cast off their savage habits and become an interesting,
35   civilized community.

What good man would prefer a country covered with forests and ranged by a few thousand savages to our extensive Republic, studded with cities, towns, and prosperous farms embellished
40   with all the improvements which art can devise or industry execute, occupied by more than 12,000,000 happy people, and filled with all the blessings of liberty, civilization and religion?

The policy of the General Government
45   toward the red man is not only liberal, but generous. He is unwilling to submit to the laws of the States and mingle with their population. To save him from this alternative, or perhaps utter annihilation, the General Government kindly offers
50   him a new home, and proposes to pay the whole expense of his removal and settlement.

Passage 2

Sir, my communication respects the sinister rumors concerning the Cherokee people. It is the understanding of all humane persons in the
55   Republic that the Cherokee people shall be duly cared for; that they shall taste justice and love from all to whom we have delegated the office of dealing with them.

But the newspapers now inform us that a
60   treaty contracting for the exchange of all the Cherokee territory was pretended to be made by an agent on the part of the United States with some persons appearing on the part of the Cherokee; that the fact afterwards transpired
65   that these deputies did by no means represent the will of the Cherokee Nation; and that, out of eighteen thousand souls composing the nation, fifteen thousand six hundred and sixty-eight have protested against the so-called treaty. It
70   now appears that the government of the United States chose to hold the Cherokees to this sham treaty. Almost the entire Cherokee Nation stands up and says, "This is not our act. Do not mistake that handful of deserters for us," and the
75   American President and the Cabinet, the Senate and the House of Representatives, neither hear these men nor see them, and are contracting to put this active nation into carts and boats, and to drag them over mountains and rivers to a wilder-
80   ness at a vast distance beyond the Mississippi.

CONTINUE ➡

1　　　　　　　　　　　　　　　　　　　　　　　　　　**1**

As a paper purporting to be an army order fixes a month from this day as the hour for this doleful removal.

　　Do the newspapers rightly inform us? We
85　hoped the Indians were misinformed, and that their remonstrance was premature. You, sir, will bring that chair in which you sit into infamy if your seal is set to this instrument of perfidy; and the name of our nation, hitherto the sweet

90　omen of religion and liberty, will stink to the world.

　　Will the American government steal? Will it lie? Will it kill? I pray that you, whose hands are strong with the delegated power of fifteen mil-
95　lion, will avert with that might the terrific injury which threatens the Cherokee tribe.

[1]financial

The Indian Removal Act (1830–1847)

Tribal Nation	Years of Removal	Approximate Tribal Population Before Removal	Total Number Removed (Including Fugitive Slaves)	Approximate Total Number of Deaths Resulting from Removal
Choctaw	1831–1836	19,550	12,550	2,000–4,000
Seminole	1832–1842	5,000+	2,833	700
Creek	1834–1837	22,700	19,600	3,500
Cherokee	1836–1838	21,500	22,000	2,000–8,000
Chickasaw	1837–1847	4,920	4,000+	500–800

CONTINUE ➡

23

Which choice best paraphrases the sentence in lines 11–13 ("The . . . recommendations")?

A) The implementation of the Indian Removal Act is likely to be very expensive.

B) The practical effects of the Indian Removal Act are more important than its benevolent intentions.

C) The Indian Removal Act will provide far more than monetary benefits.

D) The costs of the Indian Removal Act have not been fully worked out.

24

As used in line 13, "dense" most nearly means

A) formidable.

B) compact.

C) impenetrable.

D) unintelligent.

25

President Jackson suggests that his removal plan will benefit the Indians by

A) granting them political sovereignty.

B) encouraging a favorable system of trade.

C) exempting them from federal taxation.

D) dismantling their corrupt institutions.

26

Which choice provides the best evidence for the answer to the previous question?

A) Lines 15–21 ("By . . . aid")

B) Lines 21–25 ("It . . . power")

C) Lines 26–27 ("It . . . states")

D) Lines 29–35 ("It . . . community")

27

The second paragraph (lines 9–35) of Passage 1 serves mainly to

A) illustrate a concept.

B) correct a misconception.

C) explain a phenomenon.

D) delineate a rationale.

28

The sentence in lines 36–43 ("What . . . religion?") is notable for its use of all of the following except

A) an appeal to nationalism.

B) stark juxtaposition.

C) rhetorical question.

D) dramatic irony.

29

As used in line 52, "respects" most nearly means

A) pays tribute to.

B) takes into account.

C) avoids harming.

D) abides by.

30

In Passage 2, Emerson regards newspapers primarily as providers of

A) government propaganda.

B) popular opinion.

C) reliable information.

D) anti-Indian sentiment.

CONTINUE ➤

1   **1**

31

Which choice provides the best evidence for the answer to the previous question?

A) Lines 59–69 ("But the . . . treaty")

B) Lines 69–72 ("It now . . . treaty")

C) Lines 81–83 ("As a paper . . . removal")

D) Line 84 ("Do . . . inform us?")

32

In the context of the two passages, the information in the table suggests that

A) Emerson's plea convinced Van Buren to curb the Indian Removal Act.

B) Emerson's letter brought wide attention to the plight of the Indians.

C) the Cherokee population agreed peacefully to the terms of the treaty.

D) President Van Buren was unmoved by Emerson's petition.

1

1

Questions 33–42 are based on the following passage.

This passage is adapted from John Toon, Rob Margetta, et al., "Finding the Origins of Life in a Drying Puddle." ©2015 National Science Foundation, originally published in *Discovery*, July 20, 2015.

Line
Anyone who has noticed a water puddle drying in the sun may have seen the basic phenomenon that produced life on Earth. Essential molecules of complex life, polypeptides, can be
5 formed simply by mixing amino and hydroxy acids—which existed together on early Earth—and then subjecting them to cycles of wet and dry conditions. This simple process, which could have taken place in a puddle drying out in the sun and
10 then re-forming with the next rain, works because chemical bonds formed by one compound make bonds easier to form with another.

Recent research supports the theory that life could have begun on dry land, perhaps even in
15 the desert, where cycles of nighttime cooling and dew formation are followed by daytime heating and evaporation. Just 20 of these day-night, wet-dry cycles were needed to form a complex mixture of polypeptides in the lab. The process
20 also allowed the breakdown and reassembly of the organic materials to form random sequences that could have led to the formation of the polypeptide chains that were needed for life. "The simplicity of using hydration-dehydration cycles
25 to drive the kind of chemistry you need for life is really appealing," said Nicholas Hud, a professor in the School of Chemistry and Biochemistry at Georgia Tech, and director of the NSF Center for Chemical Evolution. "It looks like dry land would
30 have provided a very favorable environment for getting the chemistry necessary for life started."

Previously, scientists made polypeptides from amino acids by heating them well past the boiling point of water, or by driving polymeriza-
35 tion with activating chemicals. Professor Hud noted, however, that the high temperatures are beyond the point at which most life could survive, and activating chemicals may not have existed on early Earth. The simplicity of the wet-dry cycle,
40 therefore, makes it attractive for explaining how peptides could have formed. Strangely enough,

the idea for this research was inspired by the demonstration that polyesters, commonly known synthetic textiles fibers, are easy to form by repeti-
45 tive hydration-dehydration cycles. The "ester" in polyester refers to a group of chemical compounds derived from reactions involving an acid—and that can include a group of amino acids important to biological processes. The potential importance
50 of this reaction in the earliest stages of life is supported by studies of meteorites, which revealed that both compounds would have been present on the prebiotic Earth. According to Professor Hud, in the wet-dry cycles, formation of polyester
55 comes first, which then facilitates the more difficult peptide formation. Experimentally, Hud's graduate students produced molecules that were a mixture of polyesters and peptides, and after just three wet-dry cycles, and at temperatures as low
60 as 65 degrees Celsius (149°F), peptides consisting of two and three units began to form.

"The peptide bonds formed because the ester bonds lowered the energy barrier that needed to be crossed," Hud said.
65 Beyond easily forming the polypeptides, the wet-dry process has an additional advantage. It allows compounds like peptides to be regularly broken apart and re-formed, creating new structures with randomly ordered amino acids. This
70 ability to recycle amino acids not only conserves organic material that may have been in short supply on early Earth, but also provides the potential for creating more useful combinations.

These research findings are very new, and
75 their ultimate value is still unknown. Nobody is "creating life"—microscopic breathing, thinking creatures in petri dishes in laboratories who will grow and take over the world. Nonetheless, the demonstration of peptide formation is exciting. It
80 introduces a multitude of questions in our ongoing quest to understand how life may have started. Future studies will include a look at the sequences formed, what other sequences might result, and whether or not the process could ultimately lead
85 to reactions able to continue without the wet-dry cycles. Perhaps, if this process were repeated many times, a peptide could grow large enough to become a catalyst for other chemical reactions. Or perhaps a system might even begin to develop
90 properties that would allow it to reproduce itself!

CONTINUE ➤

1   1

33

The scenario described in the first sentence is intended to highlight

A) the relative obscurity of a theory.

B) the predictive power of an experiment.

C) the unexpected prevalence of a process.

D) the elegant beauty of an experience.

34

As used in line 10, "works" most nearly means

A) succeeds.

B) cultivates.

C) toils.

D) maneuvers.

35

The evidence that the chemical ingredients for polypeptide formation were present on early Earth came from

A) the desert.

B) meteorites.

C) laboratory experiments.

D) the textile industry.

36

Which choice provides the best evidence for the answer to the previous question?

A) Lines 13–17 ("Recent . . . evaporation")

B) Lines 41–45 ("Strangely . . . cycles")

C) Lines 49–53 ("The potential . . . Earth")

D) Lines 56–61 ("Experimentally . . . form")

37

Earlier theories of polypeptide formation on early Earth were problematic primarily because

A) they assumed the presence of chemicals that were unlikely to exist on prebiotic Earth.

B) they required extremely hot temperatures that were unlikely to exist on prebiotic Earth.

C) they did not account for the possibility that such chemicals could form on dry land.

D) they required the presence of organic material.

38

Which choice provides the best evidence for the answer to the previous question?

A) Lines 13–17 ("Recent . . . evaporation")

B) Lines 19–23 ("The process . . . life")

C) Lines 35–39 ("Professor . . . Earth")

D) Lines 39–41 ("The . . . formed")

39

As used in line 75, "ultimate" most nearly means

A) final.

B) eventual.

C) elementary.

D) ideal.

40

According to Nicholas Hud, the formation of ester bonds facilitates the formation of polypeptides by

A) accelerating the drying process.

B) creating amino acids.

C) increasing the number of wet-dry cycles.

D) reducing the required reaction temperature.

---

1   **1**

41

The "other sequences" mentioned in line 83 are

A) alternate experimental methods of polypeptide synthesis.

B) different evolutionary paths for complex molecules.

C) modifications in the duration and temperature of wet-dry cycles.

D) variations in the arrangement of amino acids in a single molecule.

42

The passage indicates that further research into polypeptide synthesis will focus primarily on

A) self-sustaining chemical reactions.

B) creating complex organisms.

C) high-temperature chemical mechanisms.

D) the nature of the wet-dry cycles.

CONTINUE

1 ━━━━━━━━━━━━━━━━━━━━━━━━━━━━━━━━━━━━━ **1**

Questions 43–52 are based on the following passage.

This passage is adapted from Vito Marcantonio, "Labor's Martyrs," published in 1938.

Line

"I am suffering because I am a radical, and indeed I am a radical; I have suffered because I was an Italian, and indeed I am an Italian; I have suffered more for my family and for my beloved
5   *than for myself; but I am so convinced to be right that you could execute me two times, and if I could be reborn two other times I would live again to do what I have done already."* (Bartolomeo Vanzetti, just before he was sentenced to death
10 on April 10, 1927.)

Nicola Sacco and Bartolomeo Vanzetti were poor Italian workers. Both came to this country like all our countrymen in search of peace and work and plenty. Both found only hard work and
15 hard knocks. Sacco was a shoe-worker. Vanzetti had followed many trades after his arrival here in the summer of 1908. He worked in mines, mills, and factories. Finally he landed in a rope plant in Plymouth, Massachusetts. That was the last
20 factory job he held. For here, as in all the others, he talked union and organization, and organized a successful strike. After that, he was blacklisted for good and had to make a living peddling fish to his Italian neighbors in the little town known as
25 the cradle of liberty.

During the years 1919 and 1920 two phenomena made their appearance in the state of Massachusetts. One was national, the other local. The first was U.S. Attorney General Mitchell
30 Palmer's "red delirium" which caused him to hunt radicals with the same zeal but much more frenzy than the old Massachusetts witch hunters in every corner of the land. The second was a wave of payroll robberies obviously executed by a
35 skilled and experienced gang of bandits.

In April, 1920, both these currents crossed the paths of Sacco and Vanzetti. Their friend Andrea Salsedo was arrested by Palmer's "heroes," tortured, held incommunicado for 11
40 weeks, and thrown from the eleventh story of the Department of Justice office in New York City to his death. This happened on May 4, 1920. Early in April the Slater and Merrill Shoe Factory paymaster was murdered in Bridgewater, Massachusetts,
45 and some $15,000 carried off. On May 5, Sacco and Vanzetti were arrested in South Braintree, Massachusetts, and held on suspicion of being the guilty bandits. After he nabbed them, Chief of Police Stewart discovered, with the aid of
50 Department of Justice agents, that he had two dangerous radicals marked for "watching" in Department files in Washington.

What happened after that, though it lasted seven long and torturous years, is fairly famil-
55 iar to the American people. It ended in 1927 in the electric chair at Charlestown Jail in Massachusetts. The finest minds in the world, the greatest masses of workers and their friends, made their protest known to the American
60 government, through its embassies, before its government buildings, in the streets and roadways of America.

But Judge Webster Thayer, who bragged, "Did you see what I did to those anarchistic
65 bastards?" disregarded all the evidence proving their innocence, and poisoned the minds of the already hatred-ridden jury against them, with speeches about the soldier boys in France, the flag, "consciousness of guilt," and the perfidy of
70 "foreigners." The witnesses for the defense proved the innocence of Sacco and Vanzetti beyond the shadow of a doubt. Italian housewives told of buying eels from Vanzetti on the day of both crimes with which he was charged. (Another
75 payroll robbery committed on Christmas eve, 1919, was thrown in for good measure against him, to secure that conviction first and bring him to trial for murder as a convicted payroll robber.) Sacco had an official from the Italian Consulate
80 in Boston to testify for him. He had been in Boston on the day of the Bridgewater crime enquiring about a passport to Italy for himself, his wife and child. The official couldn't forget him, because instead of a passport photo he
85 brought a big framed portrait of his whole family with him! Ballistic testimony from an expert who was a state witness was brought to show that the fatal bullet was not Sacco's, but to no avail. New trials were denied. The State Supreme Court
90 upheld the murder verdict. The governor upheld it. He appointed a special commission of professors headed by President Lowell of Harvard, and they upheld it. Four justices of the United States Supreme Court were contacted for a stay of
95 execution. All refused.

On August 22, 1927, Sacco and Vanzetti were legally murdered by the State of Massachusetts. The tragedy of their untimely and cruel death is still an open wound in the hearts of many of us
100 who remember them as shining spirits, as truly great men such as only the lowly of the earth can produce.

CONTINUE ▶

43

The overall tone of the passage is best described as

A) indignant.

B) dispassionate.

C) ironic.

D) pleading.

44

The author mentions "mines, mills, and factories" in lines 17–18 primarily to emphasize

A) the breadth of Vanzetti's labor organizing skills.

B) the scope of economic opportunity in the early 20th century.

C) the extent of Vanzetti's professional experience.

D) the level of prejudice that prevailed throughout industrial America.

45

As used in line 21, "union" most nearly means

A) coalition.

B) friendship.

C) linkage.

D) blending.

46

The author suggests that Vanzetti eventually found it difficult to get work because of

A) the racial prejudice of factory owners.

B) his efforts in planning a work stoppage.

C) the transition away from an industrial economy.

D) an inability to find good vocational training.

47

Which choice provides the best evidence for the answer to the previous question?

A) Lines 14–15 ("Both . . . knocks")

B) Lines 15–17 ("Vanzetti . . . 1908")

C) Lines 22–25 ("After that . . . liberty")

D) Lines 29–33 ("The first . . . land")

48

The passage discusses the fate of Andrea Salsedo primarily in order to

A) establish an alibi for Sacco and Vanzetti.

B) indicate a mood of popular vigilantism.

C) reveal an instance of official misconduct.

D) illustrate the power of the labor movement.

1   **1**

49

As used in line 36, "currents" most nearly means

A) popular beliefs.

B) unfortunate circumstances.

C) inexplicable phenomena.

D) contemporary theories.

50

Which specific accusation of wrongdoing does the author make in the passage?

A) A law enforcement agent planted evidence against a suspect.

B) An attorney did not provide faithful representation.

C) A judge did not remain impartial.

D) A federal official lied under oath.

51

Which choice provides the best evidence for the answer to the previous question?

A) Lines 22–25 ("After . . . liberty")

B) Lines 29–33 ("The first . . . land")

C) Lines 48–52 ("After . . . Washington")

D) Lines 63–70 ("But . . . foreigners")

52

The "Italian housewives" (line 72) were presumably called to testify in order to

A) establish an alibi.

B) place Vanzetti at the scene of the crime.

C) act as character witnesses.

D) provide evidence of corruption.

STOP

**If you finish before time is called, you may check your work on this section only.
Do not turn to any other section of the test.**

2 **2**

Writing and Language Test
35 MINUTES, 44 QUESTIONS

Turn to Section II of your answer sheet to answer the questions in this section.

DIRECTIONS

Each passage below is accompanied by a number of questions. For some questions, you will consider how the passage might be revised to improve the expression of ideas. For other questions, you will consider how the passage might be edited to correct errors in sentence structure, usage, or punctuation. A passage or a question may be accompanied by one or more graphics (such as a table or graph) that you will consider as you make revising and editing decisions.

Some questions will direct you to an underlined portion of a passage. Other questions will direct you to a location in a passage or ask you to think about the passage as a whole.

After reading each passage, choose the answer to each question that most effectively improves the quality of writing in the passage or that makes the passage conform to the conventions of standard written English. Many questions include a "NO CHANGE" option. Choose that option if you think the best choice is to leave the relevant portion of the passage as it is.

CONTINUE →

2   2

Questions 1–11 are based on the following passage.

A Walk on the Wild Side

Imagine tagging birds at a national wildlife refuge, conducting wildlife surveys, and **1** to restore fragile habitats. Now imagine doing all of this **2** since improving your chances of finding a successful career. Although it may sound too good to be true, it's not.

In recent years, the U.S Fish and Wildlife Service **3** has started an internship program. The 150 million-acre National Wildlife Refuge System **4** consists of more than 551 National Wildlife Refuges and thousands of small wetlands and other special management areas, as well as 70 National Fish Hatcheries, 65 fishery resource offices, and 86 ecological services field **5** stations. So this system needs thousands of dedicated workers, many of them interns, to operate efficiently. Student volunteers in the FWS internship program can nourish their minds, bodies, and spirits while contributing to environmental causes and to their future employment prospects.

1

A) NO CHANGE
B) restoring
C) where you restore
D) you restore

2

A) NO CHANGE
B) also
C) but
D) while

3

Which choice is most appropriate to the style and content of the passage?

A) NO CHANGE
B) has created a win-win for students and the nation in making an internship program.
C) has established a program to match the needs of today's students with the needs of our national parks.
D) has created something very special for both students and the nation.

4

A) NO CHANGE
B) consisted of
C) is consisted of
D) is consistent with

5

A) NO CHANGE
B) stations: so
C) stations, and
D) stations where

2   **2**

The FWS offers two programs: the Internship Program for current students and the Recent Graduate Program. The Internship Program provides students currently in high school, college, or trade school with opportunities to work in agencies and explore federal careers while completing their education. The Recent Graduate Program is intended to promote careers in the civil service to those who have recently graduated with certificates ranging from a vocational degree to a doctorate. **6**

7 Although the joys of working in nature may be enough to attract you, new research provides another excellent reason **8** for your consideration of working as an intern with the FWS. According to a multiyear study by the Corporation for National and Community Service (CNCS), volunteering is a great way to help you find long-term professional success. The research suggests that volunteering may "level the playing field" for those who typically have a more difficult time finding employment, especially during a recession.

6

At this point, the writer is considering adding the following sentence.

> Students with advanced degrees may also qualify for the Professional Management Fellowship, which develops future FWS leaders.

Should the writer make this addition here?

A) Yes, because describes the duties of prospective FWS interns.

B) Yes, because it expands on the opportunities provided by the FWS internship programs.

C) No, because it distracts from the discussion of the Recent Graduate Program and its benefits.

D) No, because the paragraph is focused on volunteer opportunities, not professional opportunities.

7

A) NO CHANGE

B) Although the joys of working in nature being

C) The joys of working in nature may be

D) The joys of working in nature being

8

A) NO CHANGE

B) for you're considering

C) for your considering

D) to consider

2   **2**

The FWS programs offer opportunities to almost everyone. For most volunteer jobs, no special skills are **9** required. On-the-job training is provided as needed. Individual talents and skills are matched with volunteer interests and work opportunities. **10** The following are typical jobs on a preserve, including conducting wildlife population surveys, guiding school groups and other visitors, assisting with laboratory research, improving habitats, fighting invasive species, photographing natural and cultural resources, and working with computers and other technical equipment.

The mission of the U.S. Fish and Wildlife Service is to conserve and protect wildlife and their habitats. **11** Their programs are within the oldest in the world dedicated to conservation, dating back to 1871. Although much has changed since then, the Service continues to grow, as do the opportunities for students.

9

Which choice best combines the two sentences at the underlined portion?

A) required as on-the-job training would be provided

B) required, because on-the-job training is provided

C) required, because it provides on-the-job training

D) required, since it is providing on-the-job training

10

A) NO CHANGE

B) The following typical jobs on a preserve include

C) Jobs on a preserve are typically including

D) Typical jobs on a preserve include

11

A) NO CHANGE

B) It's programs are within

C) Its programs are among

D) Their programs are among

2   2

Questions 12–22 are based on the following passage.

Drawing in the Digital Age

–1–

Why are we still drawing as if we were living during the Renaissance? 12 To be sure, the tools for drawing are easier to get and maybe even easier to use, but the basic process is exactly the same. Artists still start with a sketch just as Leonardo Da Vinci did in the 15th century. With all the advancements of the last 500 years, shouldn't drawing have benefited in some fundamental way?

–2–

Imagine you could reach inside your old Batman comic book, 13 grabbing the Caped Crusader by the shoulder, and spin the whole scene around to get a new 3-D view. Such a technology would allow you to draw the way you would with pen and paper, except that when you put the pen down, the sketch would be viewable from multiple directions—like a sculpture. 14 The tool could someday enable scientists to create 3-D images of molecular structures. Architecture students could gain new perspectives on their building designs. Filmmakers could find new ways to visualize storyboards.

–3–

The platform started as a passion project by Dorsey nearly 10 years ago. There is a disconnect, she thought, between sketching in 2-D, which is fast and fluid, and modeling in 3-D, 15 which is slow requiring precise geometry. Artists and other professionals

12

A) NO CHANGE
B) Surprisingly,
C) Following that thought,
D) Although

13

A) NO CHANGE
B) grab the Caped Crusader
C) the Caped Crusader was grabbed
D) then grabbing the Caped Crusader

14

At this point, the writer is considering adding the following sentence.

> The potential applications of this new technology would be limited only by the user's imagination.

Should the writer make this addition here?

A) Yes, because it highlights a specific use of the new technology.
B) Yes, because it provides a transition to a description of various uses of the technology.
C) No, because it distracts from the discussion of the technical features of the technology.
D) No, because it introduces information about the technology that is not developed in the paragraph.

15

A) NO CHANGE
B) being slow and requiring
C) which is slow and requires
D) which is slow in requiring

CONTINUE

2   **2**

need more intuitive tools to unlock their creativity.
16 <u>She had studied architecture as an undergraduate.</u>
<u>Then she was</u> drawn to computer graphics and interac-
tive technologies in order to **17** <u>invest</u> her interest in
developing new tools for artistic expression.

–4–

[1] Dorsey wanted to create a way of sketching that
18 <u>would be very different than</u> the methods artists
have always used. [2] Today's digital illustration packages merely simulate drawing on paper. [3] Starting in
2007, Dorsey's project created an entirely new media
type, as well as a new set of tools for interacting with it.
[4] Dorsey's challenge was to find a way to explore complex geometric forms through drawing. [5] According to
Dorsey, these packages don't accelerate the sketching
process or enhance a sketch's value "as an ideation or
communication tool." [6] To meet the challenge, her
technology incorporates elements of computer-aided
design, 2-D and 3-D graphics, software engineering,
and human-computer interaction. **19**

–5–

Computer scientist Julie Dorsey has created a
software platform called Mental Canvas that changes
the way that artists see and interact with their work.
"Fundamentally," says Dorsey, "this new platform
expands on what we think of as a drawing or sketch."

16

In context, which choice best combines the two sentences at the underlined portion?

A) After studying architecture as an
undergraduate, she was

B) Studying architecture as an undergraduate,
she would have been

C) She studied architecture as an undergraduate;
then was

D) After studying architecture as an
undergraduate, then she was

17

A) NO CHANGE

B) suggest

C) pursue

D) control

18

A) NO CHANGE

B) would differ dramatically from

C) would be totally different than

D) would be absolutely different from

19

To make this paragraph most logical, sentence 5
should be placed

A) where it is now.

B) before sentence 1.

C) immediately after sentence 2.

D) immediately after sentence 3.

2   2

−6−

[20] So why hasn't drawing fundamentally changed since the Renaissance? "The underlying representations are 3-D rather than 2-D, and [21] it's really fast and fluid," Dorsey explains. As a first demonstration of the new platform, Mental Canvas applied the technology to an illustrated book called *The Other Side* by Istvan Banyai. The book is a modern-day graphic novel, taking the reader on a complex, visual journey. Dorsey's 3-D technology creates an immersive experience for the reader, providing a whole new way of experiencing a narrative. Dorsey looks forward to a time when all illustrations allow the viewer to move around and even through them. [22]

20

The writer is considering deleting this question. Should the writer make this change?

A) Yes, because the rest of the paragraph does not address this question.

B) Yes, because the tone of the question is too casual for such a formal essay.

C) No, because it provides a natural transition into the discussion of the capabilities of Dorsey's platform.

D) No, because it indicates an important motivation behind Dorsey's invention.

21

A) NO CHANGE

B) its

C) they're

D) their

22

To make the passage most logical, paragraph 5 should be placed

A) where it is now.

B) after paragraph 1.

C) after paragraph 3.

D) after paragraph 6.

CONTINUE ➡

| 2   **2 |**

Questions 23–33 are based on the following passage and supplementary material.

The Smart Grid

The "Smart Grid" is a modernization project to **23** amplify the efficiency of our nationwide electrical system. Developing a secure smart grid will also increase the resiliency and reliability of our electricity infrastructure. Consumers will experience fewer outages due to usage spikes or storms, and recover faster **24** when they do. But all advances in technology today **25** seems to carry with it new questions about privacy and security. So, while we enjoy our smartphones and smart tablets, many of us are still concerned about going "smart" with electric meters.

26 In fact, a key component of the smart grid—the digital meter—is already in many of our homes. The first digital meters were the Automated Meter Reading (AMR) units. These meters, which are still in side use today, are "one-way communication" units **27** for automatically providing power companies with monthly household usage data.

23
A) NO CHANGE
B) enlarge
C) escalate
D) increase

24
A) NO CHANGE
B) from them
C) from any such outages
D) after they happen

25
A) NO CHANGE
B) seems to carry with them
C) seem to carry with them
D) seemed to carry with it

26
A) NO CHANGE
B) For instance,
C) Additionally,
D) So,

27
A) NO CHANGE
B) for providing automatically
C) to provide automatically
D) that automatically provide

2   **2**

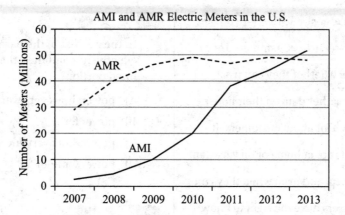

AMI and AMR Electric Meters in the U.S.

28 Ever since their introduction in 2007, however, "two-way" Advanced Metering Infrastructure
(AMI) meters began to outnumber AMR meters in use
nationwide. **29** These meters, which have been used
for many years now, provide communication both from
the home to the electric company and from the electric company back to the home. AMI meters can tell
users when they're spending the most on power and
how to cut back on costs. They can alert homeowners,
via smartphone apps, to usage spikes and timely price
changes. If customers then **30** coordinate this information wisely—perhaps by cutting down usage at peak
times—the result could be less stress on power grids,
lower consumption of fossil fuels at plants, and lower
electric bills.

28

Which choice provides the most precise and accurate information based on the graph?

A) NO CHANGE

B) Within two years of

C) Within four years of

D) Within six years of

29

The writer is considering deleting this sentence.
Should the writer make this change?

A) Yes, because it introduces information that is
   irrelevant to the discussion of AMI meters.

B) Yes, because it provides only redundant
   information.

C) No, because it makes an important distinction
   between AMR meters and AMI meters.

D) No, because it provides an important transition
   to the discussion of AMI capabilities.

30

A) NO CHANGE

B) utilize

C) correlate

D) practice

CONTINUE ➤

2   2

Everyone wants reliable, cost-effective 31 power. Everyone also wants cyber-security. Customers are justifiably concerned about whether they can trust computers that constantly gather data on their households. Power usage can say a lot about customers. It can indicate when residents are at home or on vacation, when they're awake or asleep, and even when they run certain appliances. Customers have the right to know who has access to the data. How is the information being secured? Could it be provided to law enforcement, with or without a warrant?

Despite our concerns, the world is growing more interconnected. 32 As the smart grid expands and in spite of wariness, customers depend on electric utilities to provide reliable energy to charge their computers, phones, and electric cars. Utilities, in turn, depend on customers to get information that will help them provide better service. 33

31

In the context of the paragraph, which choice most effectively combines the sentences at the underlined portion?

A) power: however, everyone also wants

B) power for

C) power, but everyone also wants

D) power without

32

Which choice provides the most logical introduction to the sentence?

A) NO CHANGE

B) As the smart grid is increasing despite everyone's concerns,

C) Despite the fact that the smart grid is expanding,

D) DELETE the underlined portion and capitalize "customers."

33

Which choice most appropriately concludes the passage and reinforces its main idea?

A) As concerns about cyber-security grow, consumers must become more vigilant.

B) The smart grid will provide many benefits in the future, such as cheaper and more reliable energy.

C) Soon, customers will have to learn to accept the smart grid if they want to maintain their lifestyles.

D) The smart grid is changing the relationship between customers and utilities, increasing both promise and peril.

CONTINUE ▶

2   2

Questions 34–44 are based on the following passage and supplementary material.

Go West Young Man

On January 1, 1863, Daniel Freeman, a Union Army scout, was scheduled to report for duty in St. Louis. But he had another duty to fulfill, as **34** well; homesteading. At a New Year's Eve party the night before, Freeman had met the clerk of a local Land Office and convinced him to open the office shortly after midnight so that Freeman could file a land claim. In doing so, Freeman became the first person **35** to take advantage of the opportunities provided by the Homestead Act, a law signed by President Abraham Lincoln on May 20, 1862.

The Homestead Act of 1862 has been called one of the most important pieces of legislation in the history of the United States. Signed into law **36** in 1862 by Lincoln after the secession of Southern states, the Act turned over vast tracts of public land to private citizens. **37** It would later be surpassed in significance by the Emancipation Proclamation of 1863.

34

A) NO CHANGE
B) well, homesteading
C) well: homesteading
D) well which was homesteading

35

A) NO CHANGE
B) taking advantage for
C) who took the advantage of
D) who would have taken advantage of

36

A) NO CHANGE
B) by Lincoln, in 1862,
C) in 1862, by Lincoln,
D) DELETE the underlined portion.

37

Which choice provides the most relevant detail?

A) NO CHANGE
B) All told, two hundred and seventy million acres of land were claimed and settled under the Act.
C) The Homestead Act of May 20, 1862, started a program that would grant public land to small farmers.
D) An earlier homestead bill passed the House in 1858 but was defeated by one vote in the Senate.

CONTINUE ➡

38 A homesteader had only to be the head of a household or at least 21 years old to put in a claim for up to 160 acres of free federal land. Settlers from all walks of life successfully claimed land, including newly arrived immigrants, farmers without land of their own, single women, and former slaves. To gain legal title to their land, at the end of five years homesteaders had to complete a **39** "Proving Up" Form. They had to prove that all requirements had been met. Homesteaders were required to find two neighbors to swear that the applicants had lived on the land, built a home, made improvements, and farmed for at least 5 years. A filing fee of $18 was the only money required, but sacrifice and hard work **40** took a different price from the settlers.

After successful completion of this final form, the homesteader received the "patent" for the land, signed with the name of the current President of the United States. This paper was often proudly displayed on a cabin wall to represent the homesteader's hard work and determination.

38

The writer is considering starting the paragraph with the following sentence.

> The Homestead Act imposed few restrictions on its beneficiaries.

Should the writer make this addition here?

A) Yes, because it describes a particular restriction of the Homestead Act.

B) Yes, because it introduces the discussion about restrictions in the sentence that follows.

C) No, because it blurs the paragraph's focus on the variety of people who benefited from the Homestead Act.

D) No, because it repeats information that was stated previously.

39

Which choice most effectively combines the sentences at the underlined portion?

A) "Proving Up" Form to prove

B) "Proving Up" Form; proving

C) "Proving Up" Form where they proved

D) "Proving Up" Form, for proving

40

A) NO CHANGE

B) introduced

C) exacted

D) initiated

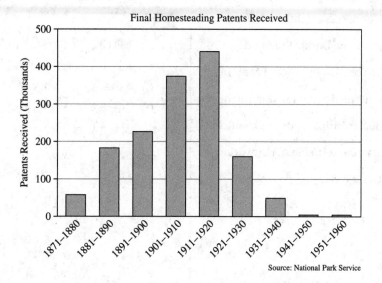

Final Homesteading Patents Received

Source: National Park Service

The Homestead Act was finally repealed on October 21, 1976. But because most prime land had been homesteaded in the first five decades of the Act, the number of homestead patents had begun to drop sharply **41** soon after the repeal. By that time, the Act had fulfilled its **42** purpose for distributing and developing the land of the frontier and facilitating American progress. **43** All told, 1.6 million individual claims were approved, and repercussions of this legislation can still be detected throughout America today, decades after the cry of "Free Land!" has faded away.

41

Which choice best represents the information in the graph?

A) NO CHANGE

B) about 75 years before the repeal.

C) about 60 years before the repeal.

D) about 20 years before the repeal.

42

A) NO CHANGE

B) purpose to distributing

C) purpose: distributing

D) purpose; distributing

43

A) NO CHANGE

B) In conclusion,

C) Interestingly,

D) Nevertheless,

CONTINUE ➤

2   **2**

On March 16, 1936, Congress established a new monument [44] to the site of the Daniel Freeman homestead in Beatrice, Nebraska. President Franklin D. Roosevelt called the Homestead National Monument of America a tribute to "the hardships . . . through which the early settlers passed in the settlement, cultivation and civilization of the Great West."

44

A) NO CHANGE
B) for
C) with
D) on

STOP

If you finish before time is called, you may check your work on this section only. Do not turn to any other section of the test.

Math Test—No Calculator

25 MINUTES, 20 QUESTIONS

Turn to Section 3 of your answer sheet to answer the questions in this section.

DIRECTIONS

For questions 1–15, solve each problem, choose the best answer from the choices provided, and fill in the corresponding circle on your answer sheet. **For questions 16–20**, solve the problem and enter your answer in the grid on the answer sheet. Please refer to the directions before question 16 on how to enter your answers in the grid. You may use any available space in your test booklet for scratch work.

NOTES

1. The use of a calculator **is not permitted**.

2. All variables and expressions used represent real numbers unless otherwise indicated.

3. Figures provided in this test are drawn to scale unless otherwise indicated.

4. All figures lie in a plane unless otherwise indicated.

5. Unless otherwise indicated, the domain of a given function f is the set of all real numbers x for which $f(x)$ is a real number.

REFERENCE

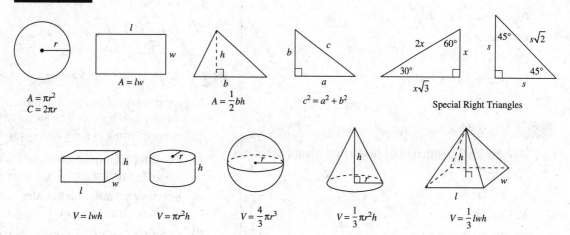

$A = \pi r^2$
$C = 2\pi r$

$A = lw$

$A = \frac{1}{2}bh$

$c^2 = a^2 + b^2$

Special Right Triangles

$V = lwh$

$V = \pi r^2 h$

$V = \frac{4}{3}\pi r^3$

$V = \frac{1}{3}\pi r^2 h$

$V = \frac{1}{3}lwh$

The number of degrees of arc in a circle is 360.
The number of radians of arc in a circle is 2π.
The sum of the measures in degrees of the angles of a triangle is 180.

CONTINUE ➡

3 **3**

1

If $\dfrac{2}{x+2}=\dfrac{1}{5}$ what is the value of x?

A) 3

B) 5

C) 8

D) 10

2

If a is 4 times as large as b and $a-b=6$, what is the value of a?

A) 12

B) 8

C) 6

D) 2

3

$$-3(a-1)^2 + 2(a-1)$$

Which of the following is equivalent to the expression above?

A) $-a^2 +2a - 1$

B) $-3a^2 + 2a$

C) $-3a^2 + 5a - 2$

D) $-3a^2 + 8a - 5$

4

If $f(x) = 2 - 2x$, which of the following is equivalent to $f(-2x)$?

A) $2 - 2x^2$

B) $2 - 4x$

C) $2 + 4x$

D) $2 + 2x^2$

5

$$\dfrac{x}{y}=3$$
$$y=3(x+2)$$

If (x, y) is a solution to the system of equations above, what is the value of y?

A) $-\dfrac{9}{4}$

B) $-\dfrac{6}{5}$

C) $-\dfrac{3}{4}$

D) $\dfrac{3}{4}$

6

Which of the following expressions <u>cannot</u> have a positive value for any real value of x?

A) $1-|4+x^2|$

B) $4-|1+x^2|$

C) $1-|4-x^2|$

D) $4-|1-x^2|$

7

Rey wants to run a total of 30 miles in 6 days, starting on Monday and finishing on Saturday. Which of the following training plans will accomplish this goal?

A) Running 3.5 miles on Monday, and increasing his daily mileage by 0.5 miles

B) Running 2.5 miles on Monday, and increasing his daily mileage by 1 mile

C) Running 7 miles on Monday, and decreasing his daily mileage by 1 mile

D) Running 6 miles on Monday, and decreasing his daily mileage by 0.5 miles

CONTINUE ➡

8

$$\sqrt{x^2+16}=x+2$$

What is the complete solution set to the equation above?

A) $\{-3, 3\}$

B) $\{-5, 3\}$

C) $\{3\}$

D) $\{5\}$

9

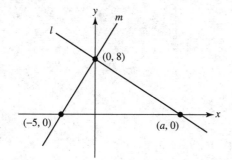

In the xy-plane above, if line l is perpendicular to line m, what is the value of a?

A) 12.2

B) 12.8

C) 13.2

D) 13.8

10

$$B=\frac{x+W}{y+W}$$

Given the formula above, which choice gives the formula for W in terms of x, y, and B?

A) $W=\dfrac{x-B}{y-B}$

B) $W=\dfrac{x-By}{B-1}$

C) $W=\dfrac{x-y}{B-x}$

D) $W=\dfrac{x-By}{B}$

11

$$a=2.5t+3$$
$$b=5.5t+2$$

In the equations above, a and b represent the distances that particles A and B, respectively, are from the origin at time t. How far is point B from the origin when it is twice as far from the origin as point A?

A) 2

B) 8

C) 23

D) 46

12

If $x > 1$, which of the following is equivalent to

$$\frac{1+\dfrac{1}{x+1}}{1-\dfrac{1}{x-1}}?$$

A) $\dfrac{(x-1)(x+2)}{(x+1)(x-2)}$

B) $\dfrac{(x-1)(x-2)}{(x+1)(x+2)}$

C) $\dfrac{(x+1)(x-2)}{(x-1)(x+2)}$

D) $\dfrac{(x+1)(x+2)}{(x-1)(x-2)}$

13

If $p(x)$ is a quadratic function and $p(-1) = p(7) = 2$, which of the following could be the coordinates of the vertex of the parabola formed when $y = p(x)$ is graphed in the xy-plane?

A) $(0, 8)$

B) $(4, 3)$

C) $(6, 7)$

D) $(3, 9)$

CONTINUE ➡

14

If $(3x + a)(4x + b) = 12x^2 + cx + 3$ for all values of x, and a and b are negative integers, what are the two possible values for c?

A) -15 and -13

B) -15 and -10

C) -13 and -9

D) -10 and -9

15

If $a - 3b = 5$, what is the value of $\dfrac{3^a}{27^b}$?

A) 3^{-5}

B) 27^{-5}

C) 3^5

D) The value cannot be determined from the information given.

DIRECTIONS

For questions 16–20, solve the problem and enter your answer in the grid, as described below, on the answer sheet.

1. Although not required, it is suggested that you write your answer in the boxes at the top of the columns to help you fill in the circles accurately. You will receive credit only if the circles are filled in correctly.

2. Mark no more than one circle in any column.

3. No question has a negative answer.

4. Some problems may have more than one correct answer. In such cases, grid only one answer.

5. **Mixed numbers** such as $3\frac{1}{2}$ must be gridded as 3.5 or $\frac{7}{2}$.

   (If $3\frac{1}{2}$ is entered into the grid as [3 1 / 2], it will be interpreted as $\frac{31}{2}$, not $3\frac{1}{2}$.)

6. **Decimal answers**: If you obtain a decimal answer with more digits than the grid can accommodate, it may be either rounded or truncated, but it must fill the entire grid.

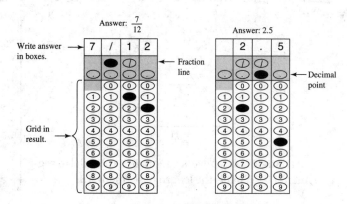

Answer: $\frac{7}{12}$

Answer: 2.5

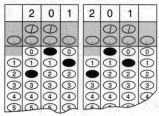

Answer: 201
Either position is correct.

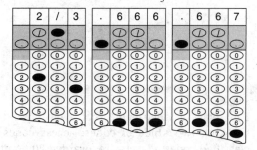

Acceptable ways to grid $\frac{2}{3}$ are:

CONTINUE

16

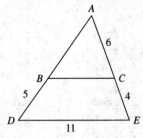

In triangle DAE above, segment BC is parallel to segment DE. What is the length of segment AB?

17

If $x > 0$ and $x^2 - 12 = 4x$, what is the value of x?

18

Paul plays a video game that awards points for breaking two kinds of codes: access codes and classified codes. Players are awarded 20 points for breaking each access code and 75 points for breaking each classified code. If Paul has broken 12 codes and has earned 735 points, how many classified codes did Paul break?

19

$$2x^2(4x^2 - 5) = 18$$

If $x > 0$, what is the solution to the equation above?

20

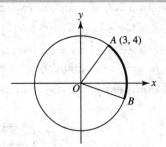

In the xy-plane above, point O is the center of the circle. If arc AB has a length of 2π, what is the measure of $\angle AOB$ in degrees? (Ignore the degree symbol when gridding.)

STOP

**If you finish before time is called, you may check your work on this section only.
Do not turn to any other section of the test.**

Math Test—Calculator
55 MINUTES, 38 QUESTIONS

Turn to Section 4 of your answer sheet to answer the questions in this section.

DIRECTIONS

For questions 1–30, solve each problem, choose the best answer from the choices provided, and fill in the corresponding circle on your answer sheet. **For questions 31–38**, solve the problem and enter your answer in the grid on the answer sheet. Please refer to the directions before question 31 on how to enter your answers in the grid. You may use any available space in your test booklet for scratch work.

NOTES

1. The use of a calculator **is permitted**.

2. All variables and expressions used represent real numbers unless otherwise indicated.

3. Figures provided in this test are drawn to scale unless otherwise indicated.

4. All figures lie in a plane unless otherwise indicated.

5. Unless otherwise indicated, the domain of a given function f is the set of all real numbers for which $f(x)$ is a real number.

REFERENCE

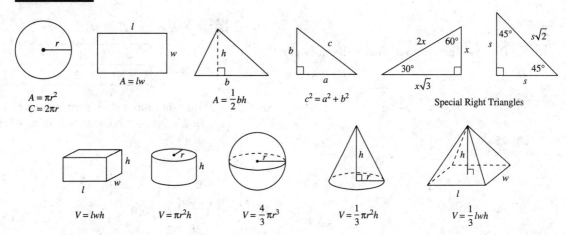

The number of degrees of arc in a circle is 360.
The number of radians of arc in a circle is 2π.
The sum of the measures in degrees of the angles of a triangle is 180.

CONTINUE ➡

4 **4**

1

Matt has published a book that is available as a paperback and as an e-book. He earns $1.12 in royalties for each paperback that is sold and $0.58 in royalties for each e-book that is sold. Which of the following represents the amount of royalties, in dollars, Matt earns if x paperbacks and y e-books are sold?

A) $0.58x + 1.12y$

B) $0.58x - 1.12y$

C) $1.12x + 0.58y$

D) $1.12x - 0.58y$

2

The average of three numbers is 8, and the average of two other numbers is 6. What is the average of all five numbers?

A) 7.0

B) 7.2

C) 7.5

D) 7.6

3

If $f(x) = x^2 + c$, and $f(2) = 9$, what is the value of $f(4)$?

A) 5

B) 16

C) 21

D) 25

4

$$y = ax + b$$
$$y = cx + d$$

In the equations above, a, b, c, and d are nonzero constants. When the equations above are graphed in the xy-plane, they form two perpendicular lines. Which of the following statements must be true?

A) $ac = -1$

B) $a + c = 0$

C) $ac = 1$

D) $ac = 0$

5

Which equation below represents a parabola in the xy-plane that passes through the origin and the point $(4, 0)$?

A) $y = 2x^2 + 4$

B) $y = -4x^2 + 4$

C) $y = x^2 - 16$

D) $y = 2x^2 - 8x$

6

x	1	3	5
$h(x)$	-2	a	3

The table above show some values of the linear function h for particular values of x. What is the value of a?

A) -0.5

B) 0.5

C) 1.5

D) 2.5

CONTINUE ➤

4   **4**

Questions 7 and 8 refer to the following information.

The population, P, of bison at a preserve is estimated by the equation $P = 240 + 21t$ where t is the number of years that have elapsed since the preservation program began on March 30, 2006.

7

According to the given equation, on which date is the bison population predicted to reach 660?

A) March 30, 2022

B) March 30, 2024

C) March 30, 2026

D) March 30, 2028

8

On March 30, 2014, the preserve conducted a new survey and determined that the bison population was 420. The naturalist in charge of the program decided to adjust the population equation so that it would give the correct population for March 30, 2014. If the naturalist adjusts only the coefficient of t in the equation, what should be the new coefficient of t?

A) 20.5

B) 21.5

C) 22.5

D) 23.5

9

If $\dfrac{x\sqrt{2}-4+5x}{2}=0$, what is the value of x?

A) 0

B) $\dfrac{\sqrt{2}+5}{2}$

C) $\dfrac{\sqrt{2}+5}{4}$

D) $\dfrac{4}{\sqrt{2}+5}$

10

Which of the following equations indicates the total value, V, of an investment fund after t years if the fund begins with a $2,400 initial investment and earns a 10% annual interest rate that is compounded <u>monthly</u>? (Assume that no withdrawals are made.)

A) $V = \$2,400(1+0.1)^{12t}$

B) $V = \$2,400\left(1+\dfrac{0.1}{12}\right)^{t}$

C) $V = \$2,400\left(1+\dfrac{0.1}{12}\right)^{12t}$

D) $V = \$2,400\left(\dfrac{1.1}{12}\right)^{12t}$

CONTINUE

4   **4**

11

A researcher is studying the eating habits of all adults in a large city and is interested particularly in how often those adults eat fast food rather than prepare their own meals. The researcher asked 350 adult customers at a major chain restaurant about how often they ate fast food and how often they prepared their own meals. Of these respondents, 120 were unmarried. Which of the following changes in the survey method would best improve the reliability of the results?

A) Giving the survey to a larger sample group at the restaurant

B) Conducting the survey at a farmer's market rather than at a chain restaurant

C) Excluding the results from the unmarried respondents

D) Giving the survey to a group of adults selected at random from public records

▼

Questions 12 and 13 refer to the following information.

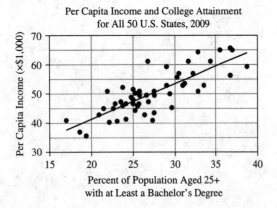

Per Capita Income and College Attainment
for All 50 U.S. States, 2009

Percent of Population Aged 25+
with at Least a Bachelor's Degree

The scatter plot above shows the relationship between per capita annual income and the percentage of adults with college degrees for all 50 U.S. states in 2009.

12

According to the line of best fit, in 2009, approximately what percent of the adults ages 25 and above have college degrees in a state with a per capita annual income of $50,000?

A) 21%

B) 27%

C) 34%

D) 37%

13

According to the scatter plot, the per capita annual income for the state with the highest per capita income is approximately what percent greater than the per capita income for the state with the lowest per capita income?

A) 30% greater

B) 36% greater

C) 53% greater

D) 83% greater

▲

14

$$x^2 + (y - 3)^2 = 49$$
$$y = b$$

If the equations above are graphed in the xy-plane, they form a circle and a line. If the line is tangent to the circle, which of the following could be a value of b?

A) −7

B) −4

C) 3

D) 4

CONTINUE

4   **4**

15

The gross domestic product of Country A is 80% greater than the gross domestic product of Country B. If the gross domestic product of Country A is $720 billion, what is the gross domestic product of Country B?

A) $640 billion

B) $576 billion

C) $400 billion

D) $144 billion

16

	Top 10% of class	Bottom 90% of class
Took at least one AP course	42	312
Took no AP courses	3	93

The table above shows number of students in the top 10% and the bottom 90% of a recent graduating class from Madison Regional High School who did or did not enroll in any AP courses during their high school careers. If a student who graduated in the top 10% of this class is chosen at random, what is the probability that he or she did not take any AP courses?

A) $\dfrac{1}{32}$

B) $\dfrac{1}{15}$

C) $\dfrac{1}{14}$

D) $\dfrac{13}{15}$

17

Mars has an approximately circular orbit around the Sun. If this orbit has a radius of 142 million miles, and Mars makes this orbit once every 687 days, which of the following is closest to the average speed of Mars, in miles per hour, as it orbits the Sun?

A) 5,000

B) 54,000

C) 108,000

D) 1,300,000

18

$$\left(\frac{1}{2}\right)^{\frac{t}{k}}$$

The expression above shows the fraction of the original mass of a radioactive substance that remains after t years if that substance has a half-life of k years. If substance A has a half-life of 3 years and substance B has a half-life of 7 years, and there is initially 1 kilogram of each substance, which of the following expressions shows how many more kilograms of substance B is left than substance A after t years?

A) $\left(\dfrac{1}{2}\right)^{\frac{t}{7-3}}$

B) $\left(\dfrac{1}{2}\right)^{\frac{t}{3}-\frac{t}{7}}$

C) $\left(\dfrac{1}{2}\right)^{\frac{t}{3}}-\left(\dfrac{1}{2}\right)^{\frac{t}{7}}$

D) $\left(\dfrac{1}{2}\right)^{\frac{t}{7}}-\left(\dfrac{1}{2}\right)^{\frac{t}{3}}$

CONTINUE ➡

4 **4**

Questions 19 and 20 refer to the following information.

Allison is considering opening an online boutique to sell her designer boots. She needs to hire a company to design her website, to host the site on its secure servers, and to provide her employees with regular technical support in using and updating the website. The website design is a one-time expense, but fees for hosting and support are charged monthly. The table below shows what each of three companies charges for those three services.

Company	Cost for Website Design Services	Monthly Cost for Web Hosting	Monthly Cost for Technical Support
A	$5,000	$30	$360
B	$3,300	$35	$320
C	$4,200	$25	$300

19

How much more money would it cost Allison to hire Company A to design, host, and support her website for 2 years than it would cost her to hire Company B to provide the same services for the same amount of time?

A) $1,235

B) $1,620

C) $2,540

D) $3,275

20

Allison has decided that she will choose either Company B or Company C to provide all three services. Which of the following describes all the values of m, where m is the number of months for which the total cost of hiring Company B is less than the total cost of hiring Company C?

A) $m > 30$

B) $m < 30$

C) $m > 90$

D) $m < 90$

▲

21

If $m = 2^k$, which of the following is equivalent to $\left(\dfrac{8}{m}\right)^2$?

A) 2^{6-2k}

B) 2^{2k-6}

C) $2^{\frac{6}{k}}$

D) $2^{\frac{k}{6}}$

4   **4**

22

In a particular video game, the "strength rating" of a player is an integer from 1 to 6 based on the number of consecutive hours the player has remained in the game without being eliminated. Every player's strength rating increases by 1 unit for every whole hour, or part thereof, that the player remains in the game, up to 6 hours. Which of the graph shows the strength rating of a player as a function of the time the player remains in the game?

A)

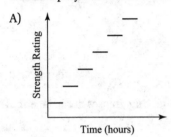

B)

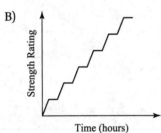

C)

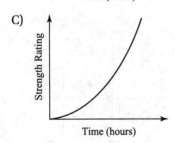

D)

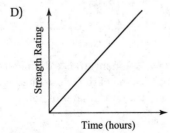

23

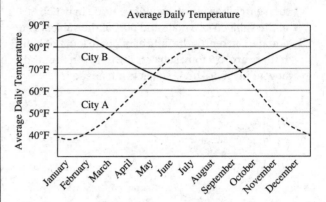

The graph above shows the average daily temperature for City A (which is in the Northern Hemisphere) and City B (which is in the Southern Hemisphere) over the course of a year. Which of the following is the most accurate statement about this information?

A) The average annual temperature for City A is greater than the average annual temperature for City B.

B) The standard deviation of the average daily temperatures for City A is greater than the standard deviation of the average daily temperatures for City B.

C) The coolest average daily temperature for City B is warmer than the warmest average daily temperature for City A.

D) The warmest average daily temperature for City B is approximately the average annual temperature for City A.

24

In the equation $y = A(x - 1)(x - k)$, A and k are non-zero constants. When this equation is graphed in the xy-plane, it forms a parabola with a vertex at $(4, 5)$. What is the value of k?

A) 3

B) 5

C) 7

D) 9

CONTINUE ▶

25

A researcher wants to conduct a study in which 50% of the subjects are male and 50% of the subjects are female. Currently, the ratio of males to females is 5:7. If there are 420 total subjects currently in the study, how many more male subjects are needed?

A) 70

B) 120

C) 168

D) 175

26

Danielle is reading a 800-page book and has already read 120 pages. If she reads 16 pages a day for the next 15 days, what percentage of the book will she have read after those 15 days?

A) 40%

B) 45%

C) 48%

D) 54%

27

Anna's car has an efficiency of p miles per gallon of gasoline when it travels at a highway speed of k miles per hour. Which of the following represents the number of hours Anna can travel on 10 gallons of gasoline if she maintains a steady speed of k miles per hour?

A) $\dfrac{10p}{k}$

B) $\dfrac{10k}{p}$

C) $\dfrac{10}{pk}$

D) $10pk$

28

$$y = a$$
$$y = bx^2 + 5$$

In the system of equations above, a and b are constants. For which of the following values of a and b does the system of equations have no real solutions?

A) $a = 2, b = 4$

B) $a = -1, b = -1$

C) $a = 6, b = 1$

D) $a = 2, b = -1$

29

Which of the following expressions is equal to $(1 - i)^3$? (Note: $i^2 = -1$)

A) $2 + 2i$

B) $2 - 2i$

C) $-2 + 2i$

D) $-2 - 2i$

30

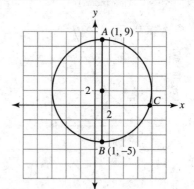

In the xy-plane above, segment AB is a diameter of the circle and point C is one of the two x-intercepts of the circle. What are the coordinates of point C?

A) $(\sqrt{45}, 0)$

B) $(\sqrt{46}, 0)$

C) $(1 + \sqrt{45}, 0)$

D) $(2 + \sqrt{46}, 0)$

CONTINUE →

CONTINUE →

4   **4**

DIRECTIONS

For questions 31–38, solve the problem and enter your answer in the grid, as described below, on the answer sheet.

1. Although not required, it is suggested that you write your answer in the boxes at the top of the columns to help you fill in the circles accurately. You will receive credit only if the circles are filled in correctly.

2. Mark no more than one circle in any column.

3. No question has a negative answer.

4. Some problems may have more than one correct answer. In such cases, grid only one answer.

5. **Mixed numbers** such as $3\frac{1}{2}$ must be gridded as 3.5 or $\frac{7}{2}$.

   (If $3\frac{1}{2}$ is entered into the grid as 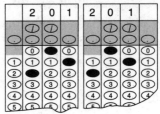, it will be interpreted as $\frac{31}{2}$, not $3\frac{1}{2}$.)

6. **Decimal answers**: If you obtain a decimal answer with more digits than the grid can accommodate, it may be either rounded or truncated, but it must fill the entire grid.

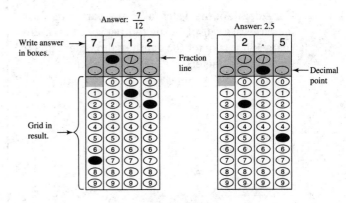

Answer: $\frac{7}{12}$

Write answer in boxes. → Fraction line

Grid in result. → Answer: 2.5 — Decimal point

Answer: 201
Either position is correct.

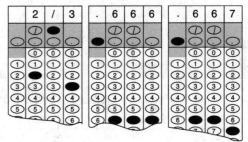

Acceptable ways to grid $\frac{2}{3}$ are:

31

If the depth of the water table at a particular farm increases at a rate of 0.15 meters per year, how many years will it take for the depth of the water table to increase by 3 meters?

32

In the xy-plane, the point $(2, 14)$ lies on the graph of $y = 3x + b$. What is the value of b?

33

Food	Rent	Clothing	Entertainment
$350	$950	$240	$260

The table above shows Dana's monthly expenses broken down into four categories. If she constructs a pie graph with four sectors representing each of the four monthly expense categories, what should be the degree measure of the central angle of the sector representing clothing expenses? (Ignore the degree symbol when gridding.)

34

$$f(x) = 2 - 4x$$
$$g(x) = 5x - 2$$

If the functions f and g are defined by the equations above, for what value of m does $f(g(m)) = 0$?

35

$$2x^3 - 3x^2 + 4x - 6 = 0$$

For what real value of x is the equation above true?

36

What is the smallest positive value of c such that $2 \sin(4c°) = \sqrt{3}$?

4   4

▼

Questions 37 and 38 refer to the following information.

$$d = 12 - 9\cos\left(\frac{2\pi(t+9)}{365}\right)$$

The day length in Fairbanks, Alaska—that is, the number of hours per day that the sun is above the horizon—can be modeled by the equation above, where d is the day length, in hours, and t is the number of the day of the year, where $t = 1$ corresponds to January 1st and $t = 365$ corresponds to December 31st.

37

In Fairbanks, Alaska, the longest day length of the year is how many hours longer than the shortest day length of the year?

38

What integer value of t corresponds to the shortest day length of the year in Fairbanks, Alaska?

▲

STOP

If you finish before time is called, you may check your work on this section only.
Do not turn to any other section of the test.

| 5 | 5 |

Essay
50 MINUTES, 1 QUESTION

The essay gives you the opportunity to show how effectively you can read and comprehend a passage and write an essay analyzing the passage. In your essay, you should demonstrate that you have read the passage carefully, present a clear and logical analysis, and use language precisely.

Your essay must be written on the lines provided in your answer booklet; except for the Planning Page of the answer booklet, you will receive no other paper on which to write. You will have enough space if you write on every line, avoid wide margins, and keep your handwriting to a reasonable size. Remember that people who are not familiar with your handwriting will read what you write. Try to write or print so that what you are writing is legible to those readers.

You have 50 minutes to read the passage and write an essay in response to the prompt provided inside this booklet.

As you read the passage below, consider how Anna Reisman uses

- evidence, such as facts or examples, to support claims

- reasoning to develop ideas and connect claims and evidence

- stylistic or persuasive elements, such as word choice or appeals to emotion, to add power to the ideas expressed

---

Adapted from Anna Reisman, M.D., "Stories of Sleazy Professors." ©2016 *Chronicle of Higher Education*. Originally published January 24, 2016.

1   Back when I was in medical school, my supervising doctor, Dr. Schwartz, and I disagreed about the interpretation of a patient's X-ray, and so we jogged up a few flights of stairs to seek an opinion from an expert. "She's a student?" The radiology professor eyed me up and down. "I thought she was your girlfriend."

2   Yep, it's one of those stories. I don't remember his comments about the X-ray; I just felt deeply embarrassed, angry, and relieved that the room was dark enough so nobody could see my flushed face. I would have liked nothing more than to kick the radiologist square in the crotch of his well-made suit.

3   Then the radiology professor asked me what I planned to do after medical school. Internal medicine, I told him, my voice hoarse. "Back in my day," he leered, "you would be home with the kids."

4   Dr. Schwartz and I walked down the stairs in silence. Although I'd worked with some unpleasant people, nobody had let loose such blatantly sexist remarks. The next afternoon, I was surprised to find a handwritten note from Dr. Schwartz: "I was very upset about yesterday's episode. As I told you, it wasn't the first time—it's a pattern for him, and he's been called to task for this kind of behavior before."

5   He asked me to consider signing an accompanying letter and assured me he would not pursue the issue if I had any objections. In the letter, he described the incident in detail and his observation that I had been upset by how I had been treated. He also wrote that he was aware that others had observed similar behavior by this particular man.

6   "I think this behavior is particularly disturbing because it was directed toward a young female student, a relationship in which there is a large power differential," Dr. Schwartz wrote. "My presence apparently did not deter the behavior. It is my opinion that he abused this power differential and verbally abused this student."

7   I was surprised—and grateful—that a male attending physician in a position of power had such a visceral reaction to the episode. But I could not bring myself to sign the letter. The radiologist was the chief of a department. If he spread the word that I was a troublemaker, the repercussions could be long-lasting. And so I shoveled the incident into my personal compost pile of untold and troubling stories. Maybe in a few years, I told Dr. Schwartz.

8   Similar scenes have played out a million times in the lives of students, of all genders, in all fields. And although the guy didn't touch me, it was humiliating. I came to him with a question and I expected him to share his knowledge, not ogle me and tell me that I should be focused on finding a man. He tried to rob me of my developing professional identity, and while he didn't succeed, he left me with a natural mistrust of male academic physicians in positions of power.

9   Medical training today may seem like a kinder, gentler beast. Schools now provide peer counselors, offer reflective-writing sessions, review sexual-misconduct policies with faculty members, encourage students to report such behavior, reward examples of positive uses of power, and set up support groups.

10   And yet in the big picture, little seems to have changed. One 2014 analysis of 51 studies of harassment and discrimination in medical training found that almost 60 percent of trainees had experienced them in one form or another.

11   A recent Association of American Universities survey on sexual assault and sexual misconduct at 27 universities indicated an alarming amount of reported sexual harassment at the graduate level by faculty members. At the graduate level at Yale, for example, 29.5 percent of female students and 18.2 percent of male students reported sexual harassment by faculty members.

12   Students still hesitate to tell their stories for the same reasons that I did all those years ago. The reluctance to come forward lingers even beyond graduation. The world of academic medicine is tight. People talk.

13   We need a safe way for students to tell those stories without having to wait for years to feel that it's safe. A new website called Systemic Disease offers just that. It's all about sharing stories of bias and harassment in the medical-training arena, anonymously and broadly. Created by a group of health-profession students, the site has the goals of creating conversation, inspiring advocacy, and identifying more avenues of support. There are no names, no schools, and no time stamps. The point is not to identify and punish perpetrators; it's to allow students to vent about those situations, and to know that others—students, faculty members, administrators, and the public—will read, ponder, and learn.

14   I emailed Dr. Schwartz a few months ago and asked if he remembered whether he had sent the letter all those years ago. He had, he told me, but he didn't know if anything had changed, other than the fact that the radiologist never made eye contact with him again. Perhaps if I had signed the letter, it would have had more effect. Perhaps not. But if Systemic Disease had existed back then, I'd surely have posted my story and might have heard from other students at other schools about their experiences with sleazy professors. And maybe there would be so many stories out there that the old-boy network would get the message.

Write an essay in which you explain how Anna Reisman builds an argument to persuade her audience that sexual harassment among professionals is an important issue that needs to be addressed. In your essay, analyze how she uses one or more of the features listed in the box above (or features of your own choice) to strengthen the logic and persuasiveness of her argument. Be sure that your analysis focuses on the most relevant features of the passage.

Your essay should NOT explain whether you agree with Reisman's claims, but rather explain how she builds an argument to persuade her audience.

SAT PRACTICE TEST 4 ANSWER KEY

Section 1: Reading	Section 2: Writing and Language	Section 3: Math (No Calculator)	Section 4: Math (Calculator)
1. B	1. B	1. C	1. C
2. A	2. D	2. B	2. B
3. C	3. C	3. D	3. C
4. B	4. A	4. C	4. A
5. B	5. C	5. C	5. D
6. C	6. B	6. A	6. B
7. B	7. A	7. B	7. C
8. A	8. D	8. C	8. C
9. C	9. B	9. B	9. D
10. A	10. D	10. B	10. C
11. A	11. C	11. D	11. D
12. D	12. A	12. A	12. B
13. B	13. B	13. D	13. D
14. C	14. B	14. A	14. B
15. A	15. C	15. C	15. C
16. D	16. A	16. 7.5 or 15/2	16. B
17. D	17. C	17. 6	17. B
18. D	18. B	18. 9	18. D
19. C	19. C	19. 1.5 or 3/2	19. C
20. B	20. A	20. 72	20. B
21. B	21. C		21. A
22. C	22. B		22. A
23. C	23. D		23. B
24. A	24. C		24. C
25. A	25. C		25. A
26. C	26. A		26. B
27. D	27. D		27. A
28. D	28. D		28. A
29. B	29. B		29. D
30. C	30. B		30. C
31. A	31. C		31. 20
32. D	32. D		32. 8
33. C	33. D		33. 48
34. A	34. C		34. .5 or 1/2
35. B	35. A		35. 1.5 or 3/2
36. C	36. D		36. 15
37. A	37. B		37. 18
38. C	38. B		38. 356
39. B	39. A		
40. D	40. C		
41. D	41. C		
42. A	42. C		
43. A	43. A		
44. C	44. D		
45. A			
46. B			
47. C			
48. C			
49. B			
50. C			
51. D			
52. A			

Total Reading Points (Section 1)	Total Writing and Language Points (Section 2)	Total Math Points (Section 3 + Section 4)

Scoring Your Test

1. Use the answer key to mark your responses on each section.

2. Total the number of correct responses for each section:

    1. Reading Test   Number correct: _____ **(Reading Raw Score)**

    2. Writing and Language Test   Number correct: _____ **(Writing and Language Raw Score)**

    3. Mathematics Test—No Calculator   Number correct: _____

    4. Mathematics Test—Calculator   Number correct: _____

3. Add the raw scores for sections 3 and 4. This is your **Math Raw Score:** _____

4. Use the table on page 306 to calculate your **Scaled Test and Section Scores (10–40)**.

    Math Section Scaled Score (200–800):   _____

    Reading Test Scaled Score (10–40):   _____

    Writing and Language Test Scaled Score (10–40):   _____

5. Add the **Reading Test Scaled Score** and the **Writing and Language Test Scaled Score (sum will be 20-80)**, and multiply this sum by 10 to get your **Reading and Writing Test Section Score (200–800)**.

    Sum of Reading + Writing and Language Scores: _____ × 10 =

    Reading and Writing Section Score: _____

Scaled Section and Test Scores

Raw Score	Math Section Score	Reading Test Score	Writing/ Language Test Score	Raw Score	Math Section Score	Reading Test Score	Writing/ Language Test Score
58	800			29	540	27	29
57	790			28	530	26	29
56	780			27	520	26	28
55	760			26	510	25	27
54	750			25	510	25	27
53	740			24	500	24	26
52	730	40		23	490	24	26
51	730	40		22	480	23	25
50	720	39		21	470	23	24
49	710	38		20	460	23	24
48	700	37		19	460	22	23
47	690	36		18	450	21	22
46	680	35		17	440	21	21
45	670	35		16	430	20	20
44	660	34	40	15	420	20	19
43	660	33	39	14	410	20	19
42	650	33	38	13	390	19	18
41	650	32	37	12	370	18	17
40	640	32	37	11	360	18	16
39	630	31	36	10	350	17	16
38	620	31	35	9	340	16	15
37	610	30	34	8	320	15	14
36	600	30	33	7	300	15	13
35	590	29	33	6	280	14	13
34	580	29	32	5	270	13	12
33	570	28	31	4	250	12	11
32	570	28	31	3	230	11	10
31	560	28	31	2	210	10	10
30	550	27	30	1	200	10	10

PRACTICE SAT 4 ANSWER EXPLANATIONS

Section 1: Reading

1. B — **Summary**

The passage as a whole tells the story of a young couple, Anthony and Gloria. Anthony is considering accepting his grandfather's offer to fund his way to Europe to serve as a war correspondent, but he is worried that they are not *being efficient people of leisure* (lines 32–33). Gloria is dismissive of the idea that Anthony can do much more than *loaf gracefully* (line 53). Despite Anthony's luke-warm expressions of regret at not being more productive (lines 58–59: *I would have done something. But you make leisure so subtly attractive*), Anthony does not commit to anything and the vignette ends with Gloria mocking his pretentions of productivity. Choice A is incorrect because Anthony does not express dissatisfaction with his marriage. Choice C is incorrect because Anthony does not blame Gloria for any poor choices they have made. Choice D is incorrect because Gloria does not plead with Anthony to change jobs.

2. A — **Purpose**

The passage as a whole establishes both characters as lazy and entitled. The opening sentence describes Gloria *deep in the porch hammock voluptuously engaged with a lemonade and a tomato sandwich*, aptly characterizing her *tendency toward self-indulgence*. Although choice C mentions Gloria's indolence, it is incorrect because the passage as a whole does not characterize Anthony as being *ambitious*.

3. C — **Inference**

Anthony *lied* (line 17) that he wanted Gloria to accompany him to Europe because he *had made all such choices back in that room in the Plaza the year before* (lines 13–14). Anthony then reveals that *we've been married a year* (line 31), so his reference to the choices he made at the Plaza most likely refer to decisions they made about their life together as a married couple. That is, he *feels obligated to his wife for better or worse*.

4. B — **Textual Evidence**

As indicated in the explanation to the previous question, the best evidence is found in lines 12–15.

5. B — **Interpretation**

When Anthony suggests that Gloria can accompany him on the trip *as a nurse or something* (line 18), Gloria *embrace[s] his suggestion with luxurious intensity, holding it aloft like a sun of her own making and basking in its beams. She strung together an amazing synopsis of martial adventure"* (lines 22–26). In other words, she greets his suggestion with *romanticism and excitement*.

6. C — **Textual Evidence**

As indicated in the explanation to the previous question, the best evidence is found in lines 24–26.

7. B — **Word in Context**

When Anthony mentions *the same crowd who drift all around California* (lines 47–48), he is referring to the idle rich who *float aimlessly* without purposeful work.

8. A — **Characterization**

Anthony is *tentatively drawn toward work* because he actively entertains the possibility of going to Europe as a war correspondent. Furthermore, he expresses some regret and discomfort over the fact that he is not working (*the old mind was working at top speed and now it's going round and round like a cog-wheel with nothing to catch it*, lines 54–57). However, Gloria clearly indicates her disdain at the idea (*Gloria laughed, torn between delight and derision* [lines 76–77]; *she scoffed* [line 83]).

9. C — **Word in Context**

The phrase *gentle as fine snow upon hard ground* is a simile describing how Gloria's loving words were received by Anthony at that moment. Just as a little bit of *powdery* snow has little effect on the *hard ground*, so her words were not heard by Anthony because he was *engaged in polishing and perfecting his own attitude* (lines 73–74).

10. A — **Interpretation**

The statement *This by Anthony was an imprudent bringing up of raw reserves* (lines 74–75) indicates that Anthony's statement (*"I have worked—some"*) was like using inexperienced soldiers (*raw reserves*) to fight a difficult battle, which is something that a field general would only do in the most desperate of situations. In other words it was a *desperate retort* to Gloria's suggestion that Anthony was not capable of work. Choice B is incorrect because Anthony's statement is not an *evasion* of any sort—he is not trying to avoid any difficult situation. Choice C is incorrect because he is not guilty of any *emotional outburst*. Choice D is incorrect, because neither he nor Gloria interpret his statement as a boast of any kind.

11. **A**   Interpretation

Gloria's words in lines 83–97 mock Anthony's suggestions that he is capable of work. By calling him a *bluffer* (line 84), she is indicating that she believes he *is being insincere about his desire to work*.

---

12. **D**   Purpose

The passage as a whole *pays tribute* to Einstein's Theory of Relativity, and in particular the *remarkable confirmation* (line 3) it has received from recent observations and its *highest degree of aesthetic merit* (lines 74–75).

---

13. **B**   Word in Context

The *conviction that the defining of this theory is one of the most important steps ever taken in the domain of natural science* is a reference to the *academic consensus* that Einstein's theory is very important. Choice A is incorrect because the context implies no *ideological* (driven by a commitment to a cause rather than the weight of evidence) *belief*. Choice C is incorrect because the *conviction* itself is not a scientific discovery, but rather a belief about the value of a scientific theory. Choice D is incorrect because the context implies nothing legal.

---

14. **C**   Interpretation

This passage was written in 1920, fifteen years after the Theory of Relativity was first proposed in 1905. The first sentence (lines 1–7) indicates that the *revival of interest* in the theory was due to the *remarkable confirmation that it received in the report of observations made during the sun's eclipse . . . to determine whether rays of light passing close to the sun are deflected from their course*. In other words, the theory was not widely accepted at the time it was proposed because it had not yet been *verified with objective evidence*. Choice B is incorrect because the passage does not indicate that Einstein lacked a strong scientific reputation. Choice C is incorrect because Einstein's theory did not contradict Cavendish's findings. Choice D is incorrect because the passage does not indicate that Einstein's theory did not allow for precise calculations, and indeed it suggests that the mathematical predictions it made were in fact confirmed by observation.

---

15. **A**   Textual Evidence

As indicated in the explanation to the previous question, the best evidence is found in lines 1–7.

---

16. **D**   Detail

Lorentz praises Newton's theory of gravitation for its *cogency* (lines 22–25: *the completeness with which it explained so many of the peculiarities in the movement of the bodies making up the solar system*), its *elegance* (line 18: *the simplicity of its basic idea*), and its *universality*

(lines 25–27: *its universal validity, even in the case of far-distant planetary systems*). The passage does not explicitly praise its *cleverness*, however, even though we can imagine that Lorentz probably did consider it very clever.

---

17. **D**   Word in Context

When Lorentz refers to *the common attraction between bodies*, he is referring to the *mutual* attraction between any two masses, as he had previously described when he summarized Newton's law of gravitation in lines 18–22.

---

18. **D**   Inference

The fourth paragraph (lines 28–47) discusses the study of gravitation from Newton's time until Einstein's time, and indicates that *no real progress was made in the science of gravitation* (lines 31–32) primarily because *while in electric effects an influence exercised by the matter placed between bodies was speedily observed . . . in the case of gravitation not a trace of an influence exercised by intermediate matter could ever be discovered* (lines 38–44). In other words, although the science of electricity flourished because scientists could measure the influence that charged particles had on objects placed between them, no such "intermediate" influence could be detected in the case of gravity until observations of the eclipse showed that light passing near a massive object could be bent by its gravitational field.

---

19. **C**   Textual Evidence

As indicated in the explanation to the previous question, the best evidence is found in lines 38–44.

---

20. **B**   Inference

Lorentz quotes Russell in lines 66–73 because Russell indicates that *the natural phenomena involving gravitation . . . and the phenomena involving electricity and magnetism . . . should be regarded as parts of one vast system, embracing all Nature* (lines 66–73). In other words, the physical laws of gravitation, electricity, and magnetism are all in agreement.

---

21. **B**   Graphical Interpretation

The diagram indicates that the light coming from a distant star is bent by the Sun's gravitational field, so that, to an observer on Earth, a star that would have been blocked by the sun if its light traveled in a straight path was instead visible because the light curved and made it appear (as the dotted line shows) that the star was "peeking out" from behind the Sun.

---

22. **C**   Interpretation

The passage indicates that Einstein's theory served *to restore some of that intellectual unity which belonged to the great scientific systems of the seventeenth and eighteenth* centuries, but which was lost through increasing special-ization and the overwhelming mass of detailed knowledge (lines 83–87). In other words, 19th-century science was characterized by an inability to see patterns across scientific disciplines because of overspecialization.

---

23. C   **Paraphrasing**

When Jackson states that the *pecuniary* (monetary) *advantages which [the Indian Removal Act] promises to the Government are the least of its recommendations* (lines 11–13), he means that it *will provide far more than monetary benefits,* and in fact he immediately proceeds to enumerate those benefits.

---

24. A   **Word in Context**

When Jackson says that the Indian Removal Act *will place a dense and civilized population in large tracts of country now occupied by a few savage hunters* (lines 13–15), he is referring to white settlers who will constitute a *formidable* population to take over from the Indians. Choice B is incorrect because this population is spread throughout *large tracts* (line 13) and not a *compact* area. Choice C is incorrect because Jackson is not discussing the ability to *penetrate* this population. Choice D is incorrect because he is not discussing the intelligence of the white settlers.

---

25. A   **Inference**

Jackson indicates that his plan will *free [the Indian population] from the power of the States* (lines 26–27) and thereby grant them their sovereignty.

---

26. C   **Textual Evidence**

As the explanation to the previous question indicates, the best evidence is found in lines 25–27.

---

27. D   **Purpose**

The second paragraph of Passage 1 discusses why the speedy implementation of Indian Removal Act *will be important to the United States, to individual States, and to the Indians themselves* (lines 9–11) and then goes on to explain the advantages of his plan. That is, he is *delineating* (describing precisely) *a rationale* (a set of reasons for a course of action).

---

28. D   **Rhetorical Devices**

The sentence in lines 36–43 is notable for its *appeal to nationalism* (*our extensive Republic*), a *stark juxta-position* (*forests . . . ranged with a few thousand savages* versus *prosperous farms embellished with all the improvements which art can devise*), and a *rhetorical question* (the sentence as a whole is a question that is not intended to query, but rather to assert that his plan is far preferable to the alternative). It does not, however,

feature *dramatic irony* (a dramatic device whereby the reader or viewer comes to know something that a character does not know).

---

29. B   **Word in Context**

When Emerson states that his *communication respects the sinister rumors concerning the Cherokee people* (lines 52–53), he is saying that his letter is *taking into account* these rumors, and will discuss their implications.

---

30. C   **Inference**

The sentence in lines 59–69 indicates that *the newspapers now inform us that a treaty . . . was pretended to be made . . . that the fact afterwards transpired [that the Cherokee were misrepresented] . . . and that [a vast major-ity of the Cherokee] have protested against the so-called treaty.* These three claims are treated as fact by Emerson, because he is protesting these reports under the assump-tion that they are reliable. In other words, he is regard-ing the newspapers primarily as *providers of reliable information.* Choice A is incorrect because, although Emerson reveals a deep distrust of the government, he does not indicate that the newspapers are providing *propaganda.* Choice B is incorrect because his citation of news sources regards their description of events, not their presentation of *popular opinion.* Choice D is incor-rect, because Emerson does not imply that the newspa-pers themselves are providing *anti-Indian sentiment.*

---

31. A   **Textual Evidence**

As the explanation to the previous question indicates, the best evidence is found in lines 59–69.

---

32. D   **Graphical Inference**

The table shows that the Indian Removal Act continued to be implemented until 1847, which is 11 years after Emerson's letter was sent. The table also shows that this removal was fairly complete, since the large majority of the tribal population was moved. Therefore, it can be inferred that *Van Buren was unmoved by Emerson's petition.*

---

33. C   **Specific Purpose**

The first sentence of the passage indicates that a com-mon event, *a water puddle drying in the sun,* is quite pos-sibly an example of *the basic phenomenon that produced life on Earth.* In other words, the *process* that may have produced life on Earth is *unexpectedly prevalent.*

---

34. A   **Word in Context**

The statement *[t]his simple process . . . works because chemical bonds formed by one compound make bonds easier to form with another* (lines 8–12) means that the process *succeeds* in producing complex molecules.

35. B   **Detail**

In lines 51–53, the passage states *studies of meteorites . . . revealed that [both amino and hydroxy acids] would have been present on the prebiotic (pre-life) Earth.* The first paragraph indicates that these acids are the chemical ingredients for polypeptide formation.

36. C   **Textual Evidence**

As indicated in the explanation to the previous question, the best evidence is found in lines 49–53.

37. A   **Interpretation**

In lines 32–39, the passage states that *[p]reviously, scientists made polypeptides from amino acids by heating them well past the boiling point of water [which is too hot for most life], or by driving polymerization with activating chemicals . . . [that] may not have existed on early Earth* (lines 32–39). In other words, before this new theory, scientists did not know how polypeptides could have formed on early Earth. Choice B is incorrect because the passage does not imply that extremely hot temperatures did not exist on early Earth, only that life was not likely to develop at such temperatures. Choice C is incorrect because, although the wet-dry theory turns out to be promising, not accounting for reactions occurring on dry land was not a stumbling block for earlier theories. Choice D is incorrect because the passage does not indicate that earlier theories presumed the presence of organic material.

38. C   **Textual Evidence**

As the explanation to the previous question indicates, the best evidence is found in lines 35–39.

39. B   **Word in Context**

Although "ultimate" usually means "final," in this context the author is referring to what will *eventually* happen, rather than what will *finally* happen. When the passage states that *[the] ultimate value [of these research findings] is still unknown* (line 75), he means that we don't know what *[f]uture studies* (line 82) may reveal. In other words, we do not understand what their *eventual* value is.

40. D   **Interpretation**

In lines 54–60, the passage states that *in the wet-dry cycles, formation of polyester comes first, which then facilitates the more difficult peptide formation . . . after just three wet-dry cycles, and at temperatures as low as 65 degrees Celsius.* Hud then explains that *the ester bonds lowered the energy barrier that needed to be crossed* (lines 62–64). In other words, ester bonds facilitated the formation of polypeptides by *reducing the required reaction temperature.*

41. D   **Phrase in Context**

When the authors state that *[f]uture studies will include a look at the sequences formed* (lines 82–83), they are referring to the sequences formed when *peptides [are] broken apart and re-formed, creating new [molecules] with randomly ordered amino acids* (lines 67–69). In other words, the *other sequences* mentioned in line 83 are *variations in the arrangement of amino acids in a single molecule.*

42. A   **Detail**

The final paragraph discusses further research in polypeptide synthesis. It mentions that this research will focus on *whether or not the [wet-dry cycle] process could ultimately lead to reactions able to continue without the wet-dry cycles . . . [whether]a peptide could grow large enough to become a catalyst for other chemical reactions . . . [and whether] a system might even begin to develop properties that would allow it to reproduce itself.* All of these are examples of *self-sustaining chemical reactions.*

43. A   **Tone**

The passage as a whole discusses the circumstances surrounding the trial and ultimate execution of Sacco and Vanzetti in the 1920s. The author characterizes these circumstances as a *tragedy* that led to *their untimely and cruel death* (line 98). Overall then the tone of the passage is *indignant* (angry over unjust treatment). The passage is clearly not *dispassionate* (lacking emotion) or *ironic* (conveying a counterintuitive state of affairs). Although it may seem that the author is *pleading* to rectify an injustice, the passage makes clear that the injustice cannot be rectified at this point, and so it is not making any *plea.*

44. C   **Purpose**

The second paragraph discusses Sacco and Vanzetti's plight as *poor Italian workers* (line 12) who were in search of *work and plenty* (line 14). In saying that Vanzetti *worked in mines, mills, and factories* (lines 17–18), the author is indicating the *extent of Vanzetti's professional diligence.*

45. A   **Word in Context**

When the passage states that Vanzetti *talked union and organization* (line 21), it means that he worked to organize a labor union, which is a type of *coalition.*

46. B   **Inference**

In lines 21–23, the passage indicates that Vanzetti *organized a successful strike . . . [and so] was blacklisted for good and had to make his living peddling fish.* In other words, he found it difficult to get work because of his *efforts in planning a work stoppage.*

47. C   **Textual Evidence**

As the explanation to the previous question indicates, the best evidence is in lines 22–25.

48. C   **Purpose**

Lines 38–42 describe the fate of Andrea Salsedo, who *was arrested by [Attorney General Mitchell Palmer's] "heroes," tortured, held incommunicado for 11 weeks, and thrown from the eleventh story of the Department of Justice office in New York City to his death.* This *reveals an instance of official misconduct* and is mentioned in order to establish the environment in which Sacco and Vanzetti were tried. Choice A is incorrect because this event did not *establish an alibi for Sacco and Vanzetti.* Choice B is incorrect because, although it was an instance in which government officials took the law into their own hands, it was not *popular vigilantism,* because it did not necessarily reflect the mood of the *people.* Choice D is incorrect because, although Mitchell may have acted against Salsedo because he feared the power of the labor movement, the actions described in lines 38–42 do not directly indicate that power.

49. B   **Word in Context**

The statement that *these currents crossed the paths of Sacco and Vanzetti* means that the *unfortunate circumstances* of Palmer's "red delirium" and the wave of payroll robberies created an environment that ultimately led to the miscarriage of justice in the case of Sacco and Vanzetti.

50. C   **Detail**

In lines 65–67, the passage indicates that Judge Webster Thayer *disregarded all the evidence proving [Sacco and Vanzetti's] innocence, and poisoned the minds of the already hatred-ridden jury against them.* In other words, *a judge did not remain impartial.*

51. D   **Textual Evidence**

As the explanation to the previous question indicates, the best evidence is in lines 63–70.

52. A   **Inference**

After stating that *[t]he witnesses for the defense proved the innocence of Sacco and Vanzetti beyond the shadow of a doubt* (lines 70–72), the author provides an example of this testimony: *Italian housewives told of buying eels from Vanzetti on the day of both crimes with which he was charged* (lines 72–74). Such testimony, which places the defendant in a different location at the time a crime allegedly occurred, is intended to *establish an alibi.*

Section 2: Writing and Language

1. B   **Parallelism**

Only choice B maintains the parallel structure of the list *tagging . . . conducting . . . and restoring.*

2. D   **Diction/Clear Expression of Ideas**

The context of the paragraph makes it clear that *improving your chances of finding a successful career* is a bonus on top of the other pleasurable activities. The most appropriate conjunction for this purpose is *while.*

3. C   **Clear Expression of Ideas/Transitions**

The original phrasing disrupts the promotional tone of the first paragraph with a mundane fact. Choice C best maintains this promotional tone and provides an appropriate transition to the discussion that follows. Choice B is incorrect because the jargon *win-win* is inconsistent with the tone and style of the passage. Choice D is incorrect because it does not mention the internship program and therefore does not provide an apt transition to the sentence that follows.

4. A   **Idiom**

The original sentence is best. The proper idiom is *the NWRS consists of more than 551 National Wildlife Refuges . . .* Choice B is incorrect because the sentence is indicating a general fact, and so the verb must be in the present tense. Choices C and D are not idiomatic.

5. C   **Coordination/Logic**

The original phrasing is illogical, since the idea in the second sentence does not logically follow from the previous idea. Choice B is incorrect for the same reason. Choice D is incorrect because the pronoun *where* is illogical.

6. B   **Development**

The sentence provides an appropriate extension of the discussion of the FWS internship programs.

7. A   **Coordination**

The original phrasing is best. Choice B is incorrect because it forms a clause fragment. Choice C is incorrect because it forms a comma splice. Choice D is incorrect because it forms an illogical and dangling modifier.

8. D   **Clear Expression of Ideas/Idiom**

The correct idiomatic form is *reason to consider* or *reason for you to consider.* Only choice D is idiomatic.

9. B   **Pronoun Agreement/Verb Mood**

Choice A is incorrect because the sentence indicates a fact, and so the verb should be in the indicative mood, not the subjunctive mood. Choice B is idiomatically and logically correct. Choices C and D are both incorrect because the pronoun *it* lacks a logical antecedent.

---

10. D   **Clear Expression of Ideas/Redundancy**

The original phrasing is redundant, as is choice B. Choice C is incorrect because *are typically including* is not idiomatic.

---

11. C   **Pronoun Form and Agreement**

The original phrasing is incorrect because the pronoun *their* lacks a plural antecedent, since *the U.S. Fish and Wildlife Service* is singular. Choice D is incorrect for the same reason. Choice B is incorrect because *it's* is a contraction, not a possessive pronoun, and *within* is not idiomatic.

---

12. A   **Transitions**

The original phrasing is best, because *to be sure* can logically modify a clause asserting a qualifying fact. Choice B is incorrect because the sentence indicates no surprising idea. Choice C is incorrect because the sentence does not provide a logical progression from a previous thought. Choice D is incorrect because it creates a redundancy, since *but* already indicates the contrast between the clauses.

---

13. B   **Parallelism**

Choice B is the only choice that maintains parallel form in the phrase *reach . . . grab . . . and spin*.

---

14. B   **Development**

This sentence provides a good transition to the description of the various uses of the new drawing technology.

---

15. C   **Parallelism/Coordination/Idiom**

The original phrasing is incorrect because the two modifying phrases do not coordinate effectively. Choice B provides a more parallel phrasing, but it forms a misplaced participle. Choice C provides logical and parallel phrasing. Choice D is incorrect because *slow in requiring* is not idiomatic.

---

16. A   **Coordination**

Choice A establishes a logical temporal sequence of events. Choice B is incorrect because the sentence indicates a fact, so its verb should not be subjunctive. Choice C is incorrect because the phrase that follows the semicolon is not an independent clause. Choice D is incorrect because it is redundant.

---

17. C   **Diction/Clear Expression of Ideas**

The context of the sentence makes it clear that Dorsey's studies were intended to help her *pursue her interest*.

---

18. B   **Idiom/Comparisons/Clear Expression**

The original phrasing is not idiomatic: the proper idiom is *different from*. (Recall that *than* is required with comparative adjectives, as in *faster than*, but *different* is not a comparative adjective.) Choice C is incorrect for the same reason. Choice D is incorrect because *absolutely* is not a logical adverb in this context.

---

19. C   **Logical Cohesiveness**

This sentence belongs immediately after sentence 2 because the phrase *these packages* is clearly referring to the *digital illustration packages* mentioned in sentence 2, and not Dorsey's new platform.

---

20. A   **Development/Transitions**

This question should be deleted because the question is not relevant to the topic of the paragraph, which is about the benefits and applications of Dorsey's new digital drawing platform.

---

21. C   **Pronoun Agreement**

The original phrasing is incorrect because the pronoun *it* does not agree in number with the antecedent *representations*. Choice C is correct because *they're* is a contraction of *they are*.

---

22. B   **Cohesiveness/Development**

Paragraph 5 introduces Dorsey and her software platform, the features of which are discussed starting in paragraph 2. Therefore, this paragraph should be placed between paragraphs 1 and 2.

---

23. D   **Diction**

Although all of the choices have very similar meanings, only choice D, *increase*, has the correct meaning and connotation for this context. Efficiency can be *increased*, but it cannot be *amplified* (which applies to a sound or signal), *enlarged* (which applies to an object), or *escalated* (which applies to a conflict).

---

24. C   **Pronoun Antecedents**

All of the choices except C are problematic because the pronouns *they* and *them* lack a clear antecedent, since there are several plural nouns to which they could refer: *consumers, outages, spikes*, and *storms*. Choice C clarifies this reference.

---

25. C   **Subject-Verb Agreement/**
                          Pronoun-Antecedent Agreement

In the original phrasing, the verb *seems* does not agree with the plural subject *advances*, and the pronoun *it* likewise does not agree with its antecedent, which is also *advances*. The only choice in which both the verb and pronoun agree with their referents is choice C.

26. A   **Transitions**

The original phrasing provides the most logical transition, since the fact that smart meters are already common seems to assuage the concern mentioned in the previous paragraph.

---

27. D   **Coordination/Idiom**

The original phrasing is not idiomatic. Choice B is not idiomatic, and it does not coordinate with the direct object, *power companies*. Choice C also does not coordinate with the object of the verb. Choice D is the only one that provides an idiomatic phrase that coordinates with the object.

---

28. D   **Graphical Inference**

The graph indicates that the number of AMI units surpassed the number of AMR units in 2013, which is approximately six years after the introduction in 2007.

---

29. B   **Redundancy**

This sentence includes no information that cannot be directly inferred from the previous sentence.

---

30. B   **Clear Expression of Ideas/Diction**

The example of *cutting down usage at peak times* is an instance of effectively *utilizing* the information from smart meters.

---

31. C   **Coordination**

Choice A is incorrect because the clause following the colon is not explanatory. Choice B is incorrect because the *cost-effective power* does not itself provide *cyber security*. Choice D is incorrect because the statement is illogical: the customers want both benefits. Only choice C logically coordinates the two ideas.

---

32. D   **Development/Cohesiveness**

This phrase should be deleted because it disrupts the logical flow from a general claim made in the previous sentence (*the world is growing more interconnected*) to the specific illustrations in the sentences that follow.

---

33. D   **Conclusions**

Choice D is best because it is the only one that emphasizes the two major themes of the passage: the promises of smart grid technology and its potential perils.

---

34. C   **Coordination**

A colon is required here, because *homesteading* serves to identify the other *duty* that Freeman had to fulfill. Colons may be used to introduce explanatory phrases or terms, but semicolons may not.

---

35. A   **Idiom/Mood**

Only choice A is idiomatic. Choice D is also incorrect because it uses the subjunctive mood.

---

36. D   **Redundancy**

This phrase should be deleted because it repeats information stated in the previous paragraph.

---

37. B   **Development/Cohesiveness**

The previous sentence refers to the scale of the Homestead Act and particularly to the fact that *vast tracts of land* were turned over. The only choice that extends this idea is B, which provides specific numbers to illustrate the scale.

---

38. B   **Cohesiveness/Transitions**

This sentence provides an appropriate introduction to the discussion about the relatively lax restrictions imposed on those who would take advantage of the Homestead Act.

---

39. A   **Idiom/Coordination**

Choice A provides the most idiomatic and logical coordination. Choice B is incorrect because the phrase following the semicolon is not an independent clause. Choice C is incorrect because the form is not a place, so the pronoun *where* is illogical. Choice D is incorrect because the comma is misplaced and the phrasing is not idiomatic.

---

40. C   **Diction**

Exacted is the most appropriate word among the choices to indicate the effect of the homesteaders' hard work. To *exact a price* is to impose a burdensome cost, which is what their years of sacrifice did.

---

41. C   **Graphical Inference**

The graph shows that a dramatic drop-off in patents occurred within a decade of 1920, which was 56 years before the repeal of the Homestead Act. Therefore, the most accurate choice is C: *about 60 years before the repeal.*

---

42. C   **Coordination/Idiom**

The phrase *distributing and developing land* serves to explain or illustrate the *purpose* of the Homestead Act. Choice C most effectively introduces this explanatory information with a colon.

---

43. A   **Transition**

The original phrasing provides the most effective introduction to information describing the overall effects of the Act. Choice B is incorrect because this fact does not serve as a concluding thought. Choice C is incorrect because the sentence provides no surprising fact. Choice D is incorrect because the sentence does not contrast with a previous sentence.

---

44. **D**   Idiom

The context makes it clear that the monument is *to* Daniel Freeman and the Homestead Act in general, but the monument is *on* the site of the Daniel Freeman homestead.

Section 3: Math (No Calculator)

---

1. **C**   Algebra (linear equations) EASY

Original equation: $\dfrac{2}{x+2} = \dfrac{1}{5}$

Cross-multiply: $x + 2 = 10$
Subtract 2: $x = 8$

---

2. **B**   Algebra (solving equations) EASY

Given equation: $a - b = 6$
Since the question asks us for the value of a, it's a good idea to express b in terms of a, so let's solve for b.
Add b: $a = 6 + b$
Subtract 6: $a - 6 = b$
If a is 4 times as large as b: $a = 4b$
Substitute $b = a - 6$: $a = 4(a - 6)$
Distribute: $a = 4a - 24$
Subtract $4a$: $-3a = -24$
Divide by -3: $a = 8$

---

3. **D**   Algebra (rewriting expressions) EASY

Original expression: $-3(a-1)^2 + 2(a-1)$
FOIL: $-3(a^2 - 2a + 1) + 2(a - 1)$
Distribute: $-3a^2 + 6a - 3 + 2a - 2$
Collect like terms: $-3a^2 + 8a - 5$

---

4. **C**   Advanced Mathematics (functions) EASY

Definition of function: $f(x) = 2 - 2x$
Use $-2x$ as the input: $f(-2x) = 2 - 2(-2x)$
Simplify: $f(-2x) = 2 + 4x$

---

5. **C**   Algebra (linear systems) EASY

Since the question asks us to find the value of y, it makes sense to find the value of x in terms of y and substitute.

First equation: $\dfrac{x}{y} = 3$

Multiply by y: $x = 3y$
Second equation: $y = 3(x + 2)$
Substitute $x = 3y$: $y = 3(3y + 2)$
Distribute: $y = 9y + 6$
Subtract $9y$: $-8y = 6$

Divide by -8: $y = \dfrac{6}{-8} = -\dfrac{3}{4}$

---

6. **A**   Algebra (absolute value and numerical reasoning) MEDIUM

Each choice is the difference between a positive number and an absolute value, and this difference is positive if and only if the first number in the difference is greater than the absolute value. In choice A, $|4 + x^2|$ can never be smaller than 1 (in fact, the smallest it can be is 4, when $x = 0$). Therefore, the expression in choice A is always negative. All of the others can have positive values, at least for certain values of x. Choice B ($4 - |1 + x^2|$) is positive when $x = 0$. Choice C ($1 - |4 - x^2|$) is positive when $x = 2$. Choice D ($4 - |1 - x^2|$) is positive when $x = 0$.

---

7. **B**   Algebra (linear relations and numerical reasoning) EASY

Finding the total weekly mileage for each choice requires adding the terms in an arithmetic sequence.
A) $3.5 + 4.0 + 4.5 + 5.0 + 5.5 + 6.0 = 28.5$
B) $2.5 + 3.5 + 4.5 + 5.5 + 6.5 + 7.5 = 30$
C) $7 + 6 + 5 + 4 + 3 + 2 = 27$
D) $6.0 + 5.5 + 5.0 + 4.5 + 4.0 + 3.5 = 28.5$
Therefore, the only plan that gets Rey to his 30-mile goal is plan B.

---

8. **C**   Advanced Mathematics (rational equations) MEDIUM

Original equation: $\sqrt{x^2 + 16} = x + 2$
Square both sides: $x^2 + 16 = (x + 2)^2$
FOIL: $x^2 + 16 = x^2 + 4x + 4$
Subtract x^2 and 4: $12 = 4x$
Divide by 4: $3 = x$

---

9. **B**   Additional Topics (perpendicular lines) MEDIUM

First we can calculate the slope of line m using the slope

formula: $\text{slope} = \dfrac{y_2 - y_1}{x_2 - x_1} = \dfrac{8 - 0}{0 - (-5)} = \dfrac{8}{5}$

Since perpendicular lines in the xy-plane have slopes that are negative reciprocals of each other, line l must

have a slope of $-5/8$: $\dfrac{0 - 8}{a - 0} = -\dfrac{5}{8}$

Simplify: $\dfrac{-8}{a} = -\dfrac{5}{8}$

Cross-multiply: $64 = 5a$
Divide by 5: $12.8 = a$

---

10. **B**   Algebra (solving equations) MEDIUM-HARD

Original equation: $B = \dfrac{x + W}{y + W}$

Multiply by $y + W$: $B(y + W) = x + W$
Distribute: $By + BW = x + W$
Now, to solve for W, we must gather all terms that include W on one side, so we should subtract W and subtract By:
     $BW - W = x - By$

Factor W from both terms on left side: $W(B-1) = x - By$

Divide both sides by $B-1$: $W = \dfrac{x-By}{B-1}$

---

11. D   **Algebra (linear parametric equations)**
                                                        MEDIUM

If point B is twice as far from the origin as point A, then $b = 2a$. Substituting $a = 2.5t + 3$ and $b = 5.5t + 2$ gives

$$5.5t + 2 = 2(2.5t + 3)$$

Distribute: $\qquad\qquad\qquad\qquad 5.5t + 2 = 5t + 6$

Subtract $5t$ and 2: $\qquad\qquad\qquad 0.5t = 4$

Multiply by 2: $\qquad\qquad\qquad\qquad\quad t = 8$

Be careful—don't pick B yet, because the question does not ask for the value of t, but rather for *how far point B is from the origin*. This means we must plug this value for t into the equation that lets us solve for b:

$$b = 5.5(8) + 2 = 44 + 2 = 46$$

---

12. A   **Advanced Mathematics**
                                    (simplifying rationals) MEDIUM

Original expression: $\qquad\qquad \dfrac{1 + \dfrac{1}{x+1}}{1 - \dfrac{1}{x-1}}$

Multiply numerator and denominator by $(x+1)(x-1)$:

$$\dfrac{(x+1)(x-1)\left(1 + \dfrac{1}{x+1}\right)}{(x+1)(x-1)\left(1 - \dfrac{1}{x-1}\right)}$$

Distribute: $\qquad \dfrac{(x+1)(x-1)+(x-1)}{(x+1)(x-1)-(x+1)}$

Factor numerator and denominator in terms of common factors: $\qquad \dfrac{(x-1)((x+1)+1)}{(x+1)((x-1)-1)}$

Simplify: $\qquad\qquad\qquad \dfrac{(x-1)(x+2)}{(x+1)(x-2)}$

---

13. D   Advanced Mathematics (graphing parabolas)
                                                  MEDIUM-HARD

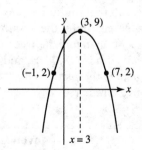

The problem gives us two points on the parabola: $(-1, 2)$ and $(7, 2)$. Since these two points have the same y-coordinate, they must be reflections of each other over the parabola's axis of symmetry, which is a vertical line

at the average of the x-coordinates of the two points. Since the average of their x-coordinates is $(-1 + 7)/2 = 3$, the axis of symmetry is $x = 3$. The vertex of the parabola must be on this axis, and choice D $(3, 9)$ provides the only option that satisfies this condition.

---

14. A   Advanced Mathematics (quadratic equations)
                                                  MEDIUM-HARD

If the equation is true for all values of x—that is, it is an *identity*—then the quadratics on either side of the equation must have identical coefficients. We can FOIL the left-hand side of the equation so that the sides match up:

$$(3x + a)(4x + b) = 12x^2 + cx + 3$$

FOIL: $\quad 12x^2 + (3b + 4a)x + ab = 12x^2 + cx + 3$

Clearly, the first coefficients of the quadratics are the same on both sides, but the others must be identical, too, so $3b + 4a = c$ and $ab = 3$. This second equation will help us find a and b. Since they are negative integers, the only possible solutions are $a = -1$ and $b = -3$, or $a = -3$ and $b = -1$. Plugging in these two solutions into the other equation gives us the two possible values of $c = 3(-1) + 4(-3) = -15$ and $c = 3(-3) + 4(-1) = -13$.

---

15. C   **Advanced Mathematics (analyzing**
                                        polynomial functions) HARD

When working with exponential expressions, it usually helps to express the exponentials in terms of the same base, if possible. Since $27 = 3^3$, both the numerator and denominator can be expressed in base 3.

Original expression: $\qquad\qquad\qquad \dfrac{3^a}{27^b}$

Substitute $27 = 3^3$: $\qquad\qquad\qquad \dfrac{3^a}{(3^3)^b}$

Use identity $(x^m)^n = x^{mn}$: $\qquad\qquad \dfrac{3^a}{3^{3b}}$

Use identity $x^m/x^n = x^{m-n}$: $\qquad\qquad 3^{a-3b}$

Substitute $a - 3b = 5$: $\qquad\qquad\qquad 3^5$

---

16. 7.5 or 15/2   **Additional Topics**
                                        (similarity) EASY

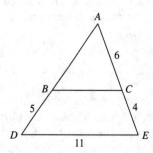

If segment BC is parallel to segment DE, then $\angle ABC$ and $\angle ADE$ are congruent because they form a corresponding pair. Since triangles ABC and ADE also share angle A, they are similar by the AA (angle-angle)

similarity theorem. This means that all of the corresponding sides are proportional:
$$\frac{AB}{AD}=\frac{AC}{AE}$$
Let's define x as the length of AB and substitute the lengths into this equation:
$$\frac{x}{5+x}=\frac{6}{6+4}$$

Cross-multiply:	$10x=30+6x$
Subtract $6x$:	$4x=30$
Divide by 4:	$x=7.5$

---

17. 6   **Advanced Mathematics (solving quadratics) EASY-MEDIUM**

This is simply a quadratic equation, so it can be solved by factoring or by using the quadratic formula. In this case, the quadratic is fairly easy to factor once it's in the right form.

	$x^2-12=4x$
Subtract $4x$:	$x^2-4x-12=0$
Factor:	$(x-6)(x+2)=0$
Solve with the Zero Product Property:	$x=6$ or $x=-2$

Since $x>0$, the solution is $x=6$.
Alternately, we can solve this with the quadratic formula:

$$x=\frac{4\pm\sqrt{(-4)^2-4(1)(-12)}}{2}=\frac{4\pm\sqrt{16+48}}{2}$$

$$=\frac{4\pm\sqrt{64}}{2}=\frac{4\pm8}{2}=-2\text{ or }6$$

---

18. 9   **Algebra (linear systems and numerical reasoning) MEDIUM**

Let's let m represent the number of classified codes that Paul has broken. Since the question tells us that Paul has broken 12 codes in all, he must have broken $12-m$ access codes. Since access codes are worth 20 points and classified codes are worth 75 points, and Paul earned 735 points altogether,

	$75m+20(12-m)=735$
Distribute:	$75m+240-20m=735$
Combine like terms:	$55m+240=735$
Subtract 240:	$55m=495$
Divide by 55:	$m=9$

---

19. 1.5 or 3/2   **Advanced Mathematics (solving polynomials) MEDIUM-HARD**

Original equation:	$2x^2(4x^2-5)=18$
Distribute:	$8x^4-10x^2=18$
Subtract 18:	$8x^4-10x-18=0$
Divide by 2:	$4x^4-5x-9=0$

Although this is a 4th-degree polynomial, it is "quadratic in x^2," which means that it becomes a normal quadratic equation if we make the substitution $y=x^2$:

	$4(x^2)^2-5x^2-9=0$
Substitute $y=x^2$:	$4y^2-5y-9=0$
Factor:	$(4y-9)(y+1)=0$

Solve using the Zero Product Property:
$4y-9=0$ or $y+1=0$; therefore, $y=9/4$ or $y=-1$

Substitute $x^2=y$:	$x^2=9/4$ or $x^2=-1$

Since x is a real number, $x^2=-1$ has no solutions. And if x must be positive, then the only solution to $x^2=9/4$ is $x=3/2$ or 1.5

---

20. 72   **Additional Topics (arcs) HARD**

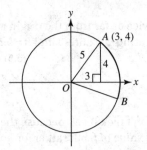

Since we know the coordinates of the center of the circle as well as a point on the circle, we can calculate the radius of the circle using the distance formula: $r=\sqrt{(3-0)^2+(4-0)^2}=\sqrt{9+16}=\sqrt{25}=5$ (or we can just notice that dropping the perpendicular from $(3, 4)$ to the x-axis creates a 3-4-5 right triangle, as shown above). This means that the circumference of the circle is $2\pi r=2\pi(5)=10\pi$. Since arc AB has a length of 2π, it represents $2\pi/10\pi=1/5$ of the entire circumference. Since the circumference of the circle has a degree measure of $360°$, the measure of the central angle AOB is $(1/5)(360°)=72°$.

Section 4: Math (Calculator)

1. C   **Algebra (representing quantities) EASY**

If Matt sells x paperbacks and earns \$1.12 each in royalties, he earns \$1.12x in paperback royalties altogether. If he sells y e-books and earns \$0.58 each in royalties, he earns \$0.58y in e-book royalties altogether, for a total of \$$(1.12x+0.58y)$ in royalties.

---

2. B   **Problem Solving and Data Analysis (averages) EASY**

When analyzing problems that deal with averages, it often helps to recall that the sum of any set of numbers equals their average times the number of numbers (sum = average × #). Therefore, if three numbers have an average of 8, their sum is 8 × 3 = 24, and if two numbers have an average of 6, their sum is 6 × 2 = 12. Therefore, the sum of all five numbers is 24 + 12 = 36, and so their average is 36 ÷ 5 = 7.2.

---

3. C   **Advanced Mathematics (analyzing functions) EASY**

We can calculate the value of $f(4)$ as long as we know the value of c in the definition of f, so this is our first task.

Original definition of function:	$f(x)=x^2+c$
Substitute $f(2)=9$:	$f(2)=(2)^2+c=9$

Subtract 4: $c = 5$

Therefore, $f(x) = x^2 + 5$, and so $f(4) = (4)^2 + 5 = 16 + 5 = 21$.

---

4. **A**   Additional Topics (perpendicular lines) EASY

If perpendicular lines are graphed in the xy-plane, and if neither line is vertical, then their slopes are opposite reciprocals. Neither line is vertical, because a and c are nonzero. The slopes of the two lines are a and c, respectively, and if these are opposite reciprocals, then $ac = -1$.

---

5. **D**   Advanced Mathematics (parabolas) EASY

Since each equation is in the form of a quadratic function ($y = ax^2 + bx + c$), then each represents the graph of a parabola. The only question is which one is satisfied by the ordered pairs (0, 0) and (4, 0). We could simply plug these values into each equation and see which one is true for both points. We could also notice that both of these points are x-intercepts, so they both correspond to a factor of the quadratic, and so the quadratic must include $(x - 0)$ and $(x - 4)$ as factors. Notice that choice D factors to $y = 2x^2 - 8x = 2(x)(x - 4)$.

---

6. **B**   Algebra (analyzing linear relationships in context) EASY

We can use the two known ordered pairs to calculate the slope of the line:

$$\text{slope} = \frac{y_2 - y_1}{x_2 - x_1} = \frac{3 - (-2)}{5 - 1} = \frac{5}{4}$$

Then we can use this equation again to solve for a:

$$\frac{3 - a}{5 - 3} = \frac{3 - a}{2} = \frac{5}{4}$$

Cross-multiply: $12 - 4a = 10$

Subtract 12: $-4a = -2$

Divide by -4: $a = 0.5$

---

7. **C**   Algebra (linear relationships in context) EASY

First, we must calculate the value of t that corresponds to a population of 660 bison: $660 = 240 + 21t$

Subtract 240: $420 = 21t$

Divide by 21: $20 = t$

Since t is defined as the number of years that have elapsed since the preservation program began on March 30, 2006, the bison population is predicted to reach 660 precisely 20 years later, on March 30, 2026.

---

8. **C**   Algebra (linear relationships in context) MEDIUM

The new survey determined that on March 30, 2014, the bison population was 420. By the definition of the variable, this corresponds to $P = 420$ when $t = 8$. The naturalist wants to use this to adjust the t coefficient in the population equation. Let's call this new coefficient m. This means that the new equation is $P = 240 + mt$. If we plug in our new values for P and t we get: $420 = 240 + m(8)$

Simplify: $420 = 240 + 8m$

Subtract 240: $180 = 8m$

Divide by 8: $22.5 = m$

---

9. **D**   Advanced Mathematics (radical equations) MEDIUM

Original equation: $\dfrac{x\sqrt{2} - 4 + 5x}{2} = 0$

Multiply by 2: $x\sqrt{2} - 4 + 5x = 0$

Add 4: $x\sqrt{2} + 5x = 4$

Factor x from the left side: $x(\sqrt{2} + 5) = 4$

Divide by $\sqrt{2} + 5$: $x = \dfrac{4}{\sqrt{2} + 5}$

---

10. **C**   Advanced Mathematics (exponential relationships) MEDIUM

If the annual interest rate of the fund is 10% (or 0.1), and it is compounded monthly, the monthly rate is (0.1)/12. To increase a quantity by (0.1)/12, we must multiply it by $1 + (0.1)/12$, which represents 100% plus the 1/12 of 10% interest. Over the course of t years, the fund will have had $12t$ compounding periods, since there are 12 months per year. This means that the total value of the fund at the end of t years is $V = \$2,400 \left(1 + \dfrac{0.1}{12}\right)^{12t}$.

---

11. **D**   Problem Solving and Data Analysis (data-gathering methods) MEDIUM

The researcher is interested in the eating habits of *all adults* in a large city, but the adults who eat at a major chain restaurant are not likely to represent the eating habits of urban adults in general. Those adults who make all of their own meals and do not eat fast food are very unlikely to be found in a major chain restaurant. A better survey method, then, would be to utilize a more randomized sampling method.

Choice A, giving the survey to a larger sample group at the restaurant, would not address the original sampling bias. Choice B, conducting the survey at a farmer's market rather than at a chain restaurant, would merely tilt the sampling bias toward those who make their own meals, but would not provide a less biased sample. Choice C, excluding the results from the unmarried respondents, would not address any relevant bias in the sample. The only choice that would introduce a more reliable sample is D, giving the survey to a group of adults selected at random from public records.

(Of course, a careful experimenter should always make sure that these public records do not contain other biases. For instance, if they are public records of homeowners rather than renters, they would likely contain a disproportional number of wealthy people who tend not to eat fast food.)

12. **B**   Problem Solving and Data Analysis
(scatter plots) MEDIUM

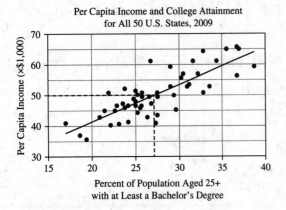

Per Capita Income and College Attainment
for All 50 U.S. States, 2009

As the dotted lines above indicate, the line of best fit appears to contain the point (27%, $50,000), which means that a state in which 27% of the adult population have college degrees is expected to have a per capita income of $50,000.

13. **D**   Problem Solving and Data Analysis
(scatter plots) MEDIUM

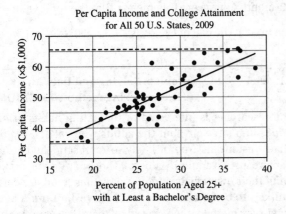

Per Capita Income and College Attainment
for All 50 U.S. States, 2009

As the dotted lines above indicate, the lowest per capita income indicated on the scatter plot is about $36,000 and the highest is about $66,000. The greater value is $(66,000 - 36,000)/36,000 = 30,000/36,000 = 0.83$ or 83% greater than the smaller value.

14. **B**   Advanced Mathematics
(nonlinear systems) MEDIUM

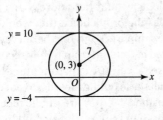

The equation $x^2 + (y - 3)^2 = 49$ represents a circle with center (0, 3) and a radius of $\sqrt{49} = 7$, as shown above.

The equation $y = b$ represents a horizontal line. If this horizontal line is tangent to the circle, then it is one of the two shown in the diagram above, either 7 units above the center of the circle, at $y = 3 + 7 = 10$, or 7 units below the center of the circle, at $y = 3 - 7 = -4$.

15. **C**   Problem Solving and Data Analysis
(percent change) MEDIUM

Let's define b as the gross domestic product of Country B. If the gross domestic product of Country A is $720 billion, and this is 80% greater than the gross domestic product of Country B, then 720 billion $= 1.80b$. Dividing both sides by 1.80 gives $b = 400$ billion.

16. **B**   Problem Solving and Data Analysis
(tables and probabilities) MEDIUM

The table shows that there are a total of $42 + 3 = 45$ students in the top 10% of the graduating class, and that 3 of these students took no AP courses. This means that $3/45 = 1/15$ of the students in the top 10% of the class took no AP courses.

17. **B**   Algebra (conversions) MEDIUM

This is a fairly straightforward conversion problem. First, we must determine the distance that Mars travels when it makes one full orbit around the Sun. This orbit is a circle with radius 142 million miles, so it has a length equal to the circumference of this circle, or $2\pi(142 \text{ million}) = 892$ million miles. Next we convert this to a speed in miles per hour by using the fact that this orbit takes 687 days and there are 24 hours in a day.

$$\frac{892{,}000{,}000 \text{ miles}}{1 \text{ orbit}} \times \frac{1 \text{ orbit}}{687 \text{ days}} \times \frac{1 \text{ day}}{24 \text{ hours}}$$

$$= 54{,}113 \text{ miles per hour}$$

Notice that the units cancel correctly, and that the units match up on both sides of the equation.

18. **D**   Advanced Mathematics (exponential decay)
MEDIUM-HARD

According to the equation, the fraction of substance A that remains after t years is $\left(\frac{1}{2}\right)^{\frac{t}{3}}$. Since this is a fraction of 1 kilogram, it also represents the number of kilograms that remain of substance A after t years. Similarly, $\left(\frac{1}{2}\right)^{\frac{t}{7}}$ represents the amount of substance B that remains after t years. Because substance B has a longer half life than substance A has, there will always be more of substance B remaining than substance A; therefore, the expression $\left(\frac{1}{2}\right)^{\frac{t}{7}} - \left(\frac{1}{2}\right)^{\frac{t}{3}}$ tells us how much more of substance B remains than substance A. Choice C gives the opposite of this difference, and so it yields a negative value.

19. **C**   Problem Solving and Data Analysis
(data in context) MEDIUM-HARD

To hire Company A to provide all three services for 24 months would cost $5,000 + $30(24) + $360(24) = $14,360. (Keep in mind that the website design fee is a one-time fee, but the other two are monthly fees.) Similarly, the cost for hiring Company B for the same amount of time would be $3,300 + $35(24) + $320(24) = $11,820. The difference between the costs is $14,360 − $11,820 = $2,540.

20. **B**   Problem Solving and Data Analysis
(scatter plots) MEDIUM-HARD

The cost for hiring Company B to provide all three services is $3,300 + $35m + $320m = $3,300 + $355m, and the cost of hiring Company C to provide the same services for the same length of time is $4,200 + $25m + $300m = $4,200 + $325m. If the cost of hiring Company B is less than that of hiring Company C, then

$$3,300 + 355m < 4,200 + 325m$$

Subtract 3,300: $355m < 900 + 325m$
Subtract 325m: $30m < 900$
Divide by 30: $m < 30$

21. **A**   Advanced Mathematics (exponentials)
MEDIUM-HARD

The answer choices suggest that this expression can be simplified to an exponential with base 2. Therefore, it's important to notice that $8 = 2^3$.

Original expression: $\left(\dfrac{8}{m}\right)^2$

Substitute $8 = 2^3$ and $m = 2^k$: $\left(\dfrac{2^3}{2^k}\right)^2$

Use the identity $x^m/x^n = x^{m-n}$: $(2^{3-k})^2$
Use the identity $(x^m)^n = x^{mn}$: 2^{6-2k}

22. **A**   Problem Solving and Data Analysis
(interpreting graphs) MEDIUM-HARD

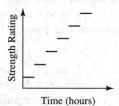

The problem makes it clear that the strength rating of a player can only have integer values: 1, 2, 3, 4, 5, and 6. Therefore, the graph cannot be a "continuous" one, but rather one that makes abrupt jumps whenever the player's strength rating increases. Choice A is the only one that shows a graph with such abrupt and discontinuous jumps. Choice B looks somewhat close, but it must be incorrect because it shows a continuous function.

23. **B**   Data Analysis and Problem Solving
(graphical statistics) MEDIUM

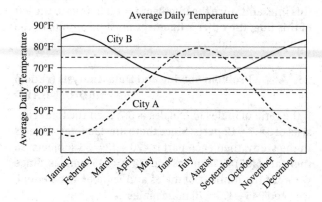

It helps to draw the "midlines" for both curves—the line halfway between the annual extremes—as shown above. These midlines show the average annual temperature for the two cities: about 58° for City A and about 75° for City B. Choice A is incorrect because the average annual temperature for City A (58°) is not greater than the average temperature for City B (75°). Choice B is correct because the "spread" of temperatures (which is what standard deviation measures) is clearly greater for City A than City B: the temperatures for City A have a spread of over 40° (from about 38° to about 80°), but the temperatures for City B have a spread of only about 20° (from about 65° to about 85°). Choice C is incorrect because the coolest average daily temperature for City B (about 65°) is not warmer than the warmest average daily temperature for City A (about 80°). Choice D is incorrect because the warmest average daily temperature for City B (about 85°) is not approximately the average annual temperature for City A (about 58°).

24. **C**   Advanced Mathematics
(analyzing quadratics) MEDIUM-HARD

The problem gives us two points on the parabola: the vertex at (4, 5) and the zero at (1, 0), which we can see by using the Zero Product Property on one of the factors, $(x − 1)$, of the equation. The equation tells us that the parabola has x-intercepts at $x = 1$ and $x = k$, and we need to find the value of k. Graphing this information and using the symmetry of parabolas helps us to find k:

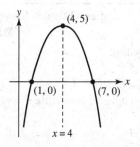

Since the line of symmetry is a vertical line passing through the vertex, it must be the line $x = 4$, as shown in the figure above. The x-intercepts must be symmetric to this line, and since the intercept $x = 1$ is 3 units to the left of this line, the other x-intercept must be 3 units to the right, at $x = 7$, and so $k = 7$.

---

25. A   **Problem Solving and Data Analysis (ratios)**
MEDIUM-HARD

If the ratio of males to females is 5:7, then the total consists of $5 + 7 = 12$ parts. Since there are 420 total subjects in the study, then each part is $420 \div 12 = 35$ subjects, so there are $5(35) = 175$ males and $7(35) = 245$ females. Since we want the number of males and females to be equal, we need $245 - 175 = 70$ more males.

---

26. B   **Problem Solving and Data Analysis (percentages and rates) HARD**

If Danielle has already read 120 pages, she has $800 - 120 = 680$ pages left to read. If she reads 16 pages a day for 15 days, she will read an additional $(16)(15) = 240$ pages, for a total of $120 + 240 = 360$ pages. This is $360/800 = 0.45$ or 45% of the entire book.

---

27. A   **Problem Solving and Data Analysis (rates)**
MEDIUM-HARD

We can use the given rates as conversion factors to convert 10 gallons into the number of hours she can drive:

$$10 \text{ gallons} \times \frac{p \text{ miles}}{1 \text{ gallon}} \times \frac{1 \text{ hour}}{k \text{ miles}} = \frac{10p}{k} \text{ hours}$$

---

28. A   **Advanced Mathematics (nonlinear systems) HARD**

The graph of $y = a$ is a horizontal line, and the graph of $y = bx^2 + 5$ is a parabola with a vertex at $(0, 5)$. If the system has no real solutions, then these two graphs cannot intersect. This can happen in two ways: if the horizontal line is above the vertex and the parabola is "open down," or if the horizontal line is below the vertex and the parabola is "open up." Choice A yields a horizontal line that is below the vertex of an "open up" parabola.

---

29. D   **Special Topics (complex numbers)**
MEDIUM-HARD

Original expression:	$(1-i)^3$
Expand:	$(1-i)(1-i)(1-i)$
FOIL first two factors:	$(1-i-i+i^2)(1-i)$
Combine like terms and substitute $i^2 = -1$:	$(-2i)(1-i)$
Distribute:	$-2i + 2i^2$
Substitute $i^2 = -1$:	$-2i - 2 = -2 - 2i$

---

30. C   **Special Topics (circles) HARD**

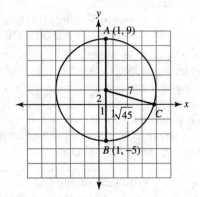

First let's draw the radius from the center of the circle to point C. Since AB is the diameter and its length is $9 - (-5) = 14$, the radius of the circle is $14/2 = 7$. Notice that this radius is the hypotenuse of the right triangle with shorter leg of 2. (Notice that the scale on the coordinate plane is *2 units* per line.) We can use the Pythagorean Theorem to find the longer leg of this triangle: $2^2 + b^2 = 7^2$. This gives us $b = \sqrt{45}$. Since point C is this distance to the right of the line $x = 1$ (the line that contains AB), it has coordinates $(1 + \sqrt{45}, 0)$.

---

31. 20   **Algebra (word problems) EASY**

$$3 \text{ meters} \times \frac{1 \text{ year}}{0.15 \text{ meters}} = 20 \text{ years}$$

---

32. 8   **Algebra (lines in the coordinate plane) EASY**

Given equation:	$y = 3x + b$
Substitute $x = 2$ and $y = 14$:	$14 = 3(2) + b$
Simplify:	$14 = 6 + b$
Subtract 6:	$8 = b$

---

33. 48   **Problem Solving and Data Analysis (pie graphs) MEDIUM**

Since the total expenditures are $350 + 950 + 240 + 260 = 1,800$ dollars, clothing expenses constitute $240/1,800 = 2/15$ of the total. Therefore, on a pie graph, the clothing expenses sector would have a central angle of $(2/15)(360°) = 48°$.

---

34. .5 or 1/2   **Advanced Mathematics (compositions) MEDIUM**

Given functions:	$f(x) = 2 - 4x$
	$g(x) = 5x - 2$
Substitute to find the expression for $f(g(m))$:	
	$f(g(m)) = f(5m - 2) = 2 - 4(5m - 2)$
Distribute and simplify:	$f(g(m)) = 10 - 20m$
Set $f(g(m)) = 0$:	$0 = 10 - 20m$
Add $20m$:	$20m = 10$
Divide by 20:	$m = 0.5$

35. **1.5 or 3/2**   **Advanced Mathematics (solving polynomials) MEDIUM-HARD**

Original equation: $2x^3 - 3x^2 + 4x - 6 = 0$
The expression on the left can be factored by grouping:
$$x^2(2x-3) + 2(2x-3) = (x^2+2)(2x-3) = 0$$
Only the second of these factors can equal 0, so:
$$2x - 3 = 0$$
Add 3 and divide by 2: $x = 1.5$

36. **15**   **Additional Topics (trigonometry) MEDIUM-HARD**

Original equation: $2\sin(4c^\circ) = \sqrt{3}$

Divide by 2: $\sin(4c^\circ) = \dfrac{\sqrt{3}}{2}$

The smallest positive angle with a sine of $\dfrac{\sqrt{3}}{2}$ is 60°.

Therefore $4c = 60$
Divide by 4: $c = 15$

37. **18**   **Data Analysis (trigonometric formulas) MEDIUM-HARD**

If the formula $d = 12 - 9\cos\left(\dfrac{2\pi(t+9)}{365}\right)$ is graphed in the xy-plane, where d is represented by the y-axis and t is represented by the x-axis, the resulting graph is a sinusoid with an amplitude of 9. This means that the longest day length of the year is 9 hours longer than the average day length and the shortest day length of the year is 9 hours shorter than the average day length. Therefore the difference between the longest and shortest day length is 18 hours.

38. **356**   **Data Analysis (trigonometric formulas) MEDIUM-HARD**

The function $d = 12 - 9\cos\left(\dfrac{2\pi(t+9)}{365}\right)$ has its minimum when $9\cos\left(\dfrac{2\pi(t+9)}{365}\right)$ has a maximum. Since $y = \cos x$ has its first positive maximum at $x = 2\pi$: $\dfrac{2\pi(t+9)}{365} = 2\pi$

Distribute and multiply both sides by 365:
$$2\pi t + 18\pi = 730\pi$$
Subtract 18π: $2\pi t = 712\pi$
Divide by 2π: $t = 356$

PRACTICE SAT 5

ANSWER SHEET

SECTION 1

1 Ⓐ Ⓑ Ⓒ Ⓓ	13 Ⓐ Ⓑ Ⓒ Ⓓ	25 Ⓐ Ⓑ Ⓒ Ⓓ	37 Ⓐ Ⓑ Ⓒ Ⓓ	49 Ⓐ Ⓑ Ⓒ Ⓓ
2 Ⓐ Ⓑ Ⓒ Ⓓ	14 Ⓐ Ⓑ Ⓒ Ⓓ	26 Ⓐ Ⓑ Ⓒ Ⓓ	38 Ⓐ Ⓑ Ⓒ Ⓓ	50 Ⓐ Ⓑ Ⓒ Ⓓ
3 Ⓐ Ⓑ Ⓒ Ⓓ	15 Ⓐ Ⓑ Ⓒ Ⓓ	27 Ⓐ Ⓑ Ⓒ Ⓓ	39 Ⓐ Ⓑ Ⓒ Ⓓ	51 Ⓐ Ⓑ Ⓒ Ⓓ
4 Ⓐ Ⓑ Ⓒ Ⓓ	16 Ⓐ Ⓑ Ⓒ Ⓓ	28 Ⓐ Ⓑ Ⓒ Ⓓ	40 Ⓐ Ⓑ Ⓒ Ⓓ	52 Ⓐ Ⓑ Ⓒ Ⓓ
5 Ⓐ Ⓑ Ⓒ Ⓓ	17 Ⓐ Ⓑ Ⓒ Ⓓ	29 Ⓐ Ⓑ Ⓒ Ⓓ	41 Ⓐ Ⓑ Ⓒ Ⓓ	
6 Ⓐ Ⓑ Ⓒ Ⓓ	18 Ⓐ Ⓑ Ⓒ Ⓓ	30 Ⓐ Ⓑ Ⓒ Ⓓ	42 Ⓐ Ⓑ Ⓒ Ⓓ	
7 Ⓐ Ⓑ Ⓒ Ⓓ	19 Ⓐ Ⓑ Ⓒ Ⓓ	31 Ⓐ Ⓑ Ⓒ Ⓓ	43 Ⓐ Ⓑ Ⓒ Ⓓ	
8 Ⓐ Ⓑ Ⓒ Ⓓ	20 Ⓐ Ⓑ Ⓒ Ⓓ	32 Ⓐ Ⓑ Ⓒ Ⓓ	44 Ⓐ Ⓑ Ⓒ Ⓓ	
9 Ⓐ Ⓑ Ⓒ Ⓓ	21 Ⓐ Ⓑ Ⓒ Ⓓ	33 Ⓐ Ⓑ Ⓒ Ⓓ	45 Ⓐ Ⓑ Ⓒ Ⓓ	
10 Ⓐ Ⓑ Ⓒ Ⓓ	22 Ⓐ Ⓑ Ⓒ Ⓓ	34 Ⓐ Ⓑ Ⓒ Ⓓ	46 Ⓐ Ⓑ Ⓒ Ⓓ	
11 Ⓐ Ⓑ Ⓒ Ⓓ	23 Ⓐ Ⓑ Ⓒ Ⓓ	35 Ⓐ Ⓑ Ⓒ Ⓓ	47 Ⓐ Ⓑ Ⓒ Ⓓ	
12 Ⓐ Ⓑ Ⓒ Ⓓ	24 Ⓐ Ⓑ Ⓒ Ⓓ	36 Ⓐ Ⓑ Ⓒ Ⓓ	48 Ⓐ Ⓑ Ⓒ Ⓓ	

SECTION 2

1 Ⓐ Ⓑ Ⓒ Ⓓ	11 Ⓐ Ⓑ Ⓒ Ⓓ	21 Ⓐ Ⓑ Ⓒ Ⓓ	31 Ⓐ Ⓑ Ⓒ Ⓓ	41 Ⓐ Ⓑ Ⓒ Ⓓ
2 Ⓐ Ⓑ Ⓒ Ⓓ	12 Ⓐ Ⓑ Ⓒ Ⓓ	22 Ⓐ Ⓑ Ⓒ Ⓓ	32 Ⓐ Ⓑ Ⓒ Ⓓ	42 Ⓐ Ⓑ Ⓒ Ⓓ
3 Ⓐ Ⓑ Ⓒ Ⓓ	13 Ⓐ Ⓑ Ⓒ Ⓓ	23 Ⓐ Ⓑ Ⓒ Ⓓ	33 Ⓐ Ⓑ Ⓒ Ⓓ	43 Ⓐ Ⓑ Ⓒ Ⓓ
4 Ⓐ Ⓑ Ⓒ Ⓓ	14 Ⓐ Ⓑ Ⓒ Ⓓ	24 Ⓐ Ⓑ Ⓒ Ⓓ	34 Ⓐ Ⓑ Ⓒ Ⓓ	44 Ⓐ Ⓑ Ⓒ Ⓓ
5 Ⓐ Ⓑ Ⓒ Ⓓ	15 Ⓐ Ⓑ Ⓒ Ⓓ	25 Ⓐ Ⓑ Ⓒ Ⓓ	35 Ⓐ Ⓑ Ⓒ Ⓓ	
6 Ⓐ Ⓑ Ⓒ Ⓓ	16 Ⓐ Ⓑ Ⓒ Ⓓ	26 Ⓐ Ⓑ Ⓒ Ⓓ	36 Ⓐ Ⓑ Ⓒ Ⓓ	
7 Ⓐ Ⓑ Ⓒ Ⓓ	17 Ⓐ Ⓑ Ⓒ Ⓓ	27 Ⓐ Ⓑ Ⓒ Ⓓ	37 Ⓐ Ⓑ Ⓒ Ⓓ	
8 Ⓐ Ⓑ Ⓒ Ⓓ	18 Ⓐ Ⓑ Ⓒ Ⓓ	28 Ⓐ Ⓑ Ⓒ Ⓓ	38 Ⓐ Ⓑ Ⓒ Ⓓ	
9 Ⓐ Ⓑ Ⓒ Ⓓ	19 Ⓐ Ⓑ Ⓒ Ⓓ	29 Ⓐ Ⓑ Ⓒ Ⓓ	39 Ⓐ Ⓑ Ⓒ Ⓓ	
10 Ⓐ Ⓑ Ⓒ Ⓓ	20 Ⓐ Ⓑ Ⓒ Ⓓ	30 Ⓐ Ⓑ Ⓒ Ⓓ	40 Ⓐ Ⓑ Ⓒ Ⓓ	

SECTION 3

1. Ⓐ Ⓑ Ⓒ Ⓓ
2. Ⓐ Ⓑ Ⓒ Ⓓ
3. Ⓐ Ⓑ Ⓒ Ⓓ
4. Ⓐ Ⓑ Ⓒ Ⓓ
5. Ⓐ Ⓑ Ⓒ Ⓓ
6. Ⓐ Ⓑ Ⓒ Ⓓ
7. Ⓐ Ⓑ Ⓒ Ⓓ
8. Ⓐ Ⓑ Ⓒ Ⓓ
9. Ⓐ Ⓑ Ⓒ Ⓓ
10. Ⓐ Ⓑ Ⓒ Ⓓ

11. Ⓐ Ⓑ Ⓒ Ⓓ
12. Ⓐ Ⓑ Ⓒ Ⓓ
13. Ⓐ Ⓑ Ⓒ Ⓓ
14. Ⓐ Ⓑ Ⓒ Ⓓ
15. Ⓐ Ⓑ Ⓒ Ⓓ

Student-Produced Responses

ONLY ANSWERS ENTERED IN THE CIRCLES IN EACH GRID WILL BE SCORED. YOU WILL NOT RECEIVE CREDIT FOR ANYTHING WRITTEN IN THE BOXES ABOVE THE CIRCLES.

16. 17. 18. 19. 20.

SECTION
4

1 Ⓐ Ⓑ Ⓒ Ⓓ
2 Ⓐ Ⓑ Ⓒ Ⓓ
3 Ⓐ Ⓑ Ⓒ Ⓓ
4 Ⓐ Ⓑ Ⓒ Ⓓ
5 Ⓐ Ⓑ Ⓒ Ⓓ
6 Ⓐ Ⓑ Ⓒ Ⓓ
7 Ⓐ Ⓑ Ⓒ Ⓓ
8 Ⓐ Ⓑ Ⓒ Ⓓ
9 Ⓐ Ⓑ Ⓒ Ⓓ
10 Ⓐ Ⓑ Ⓒ Ⓓ

11 Ⓐ Ⓑ Ⓒ Ⓓ
12 Ⓐ Ⓑ Ⓒ Ⓓ
13 Ⓐ Ⓑ Ⓒ Ⓓ
14 Ⓐ Ⓑ Ⓒ Ⓓ
15 Ⓐ Ⓑ Ⓒ Ⓓ
16 Ⓐ Ⓑ Ⓒ Ⓓ
17 Ⓐ Ⓑ Ⓒ Ⓓ
18 Ⓐ Ⓑ Ⓒ Ⓓ
19 Ⓐ Ⓑ Ⓒ Ⓓ
20 Ⓐ Ⓑ Ⓒ Ⓓ

21 Ⓐ Ⓑ Ⓒ Ⓓ
22 Ⓐ Ⓑ Ⓒ Ⓓ
23 Ⓐ Ⓑ Ⓒ Ⓓ
24 Ⓐ Ⓑ Ⓒ Ⓓ
25 Ⓐ Ⓑ Ⓒ Ⓓ
26 Ⓐ Ⓑ Ⓒ Ⓓ
27 Ⓐ Ⓑ Ⓒ Ⓓ
28 Ⓐ Ⓑ Ⓒ Ⓓ
29 Ⓐ Ⓑ Ⓒ Ⓓ
30 Ⓐ Ⓑ Ⓒ Ⓓ

Student-Produced Responses

ONLY ANSWERS ENTERED IN THE CIRCLES IN EACH GRID WILL BE SCORED. YOU WILL NOT RECEIVE CREDIT FOR ANYTHING WRITTEN IN THE BOXES ABOVE THE CIRCLES.

31

32

33

34

35

36

37

38

SECTION 5: ESSAY

You may wish to remove these sample answer document pages to respond to the practice SAT Essay Test.

Begin ESSAY here.

ESSAY

If you need more space, please continue on the next page.

ESSAY

_____

_____

_____

_____

_____

_____

_____

_____

_____

_____

_____

_____

_____

_____

_____

_____

_____

_____

_____

_____

_____

_____

_____

_____

_____

Cut Here

ESSAY

_____

_____

_____

_____

_____

_____

_____

_____

_____

_____

_____

_____

_____

_____

_____

_____

_____

_____

_____

_____

_____

_____

_____

_____

_____

_____

STOP here with the Essay.

Cut Here

1   1

Reading Test

65 MINUTES, 52 QUESTIONS

Turn to Section 1 of your answer sheet to answer the questions in this section.

DIRECTIONS

Each passage or pair of passages below is followed by a number of questions. After reading each passage or pair, choose the best answer to each question based on what is stated or implied in the passage or passages and in any accompanying graphics (such as a table or graph).

Questions 1–11 are based on the following passage.

This passage is adapted from Oscar Wilde, *The Picture of Dorian Gray*, originally published in 1891.

Line
"It is quite finished," Hallward cried at last, and stooping down he wrote his name in long vermilion letters on the left-hand corner of the canvas.
5   "My dear fellow, I congratulate you most warmly," Lord Henry said. "It is the finest portrait of modern times."
"Is it really finished?" Dorian Gray murmured, stepping down from the platform.
10   "Quite finished," said the painter.
Dorian made no answer, but passed listlessly in front of his picture and turned towards it. When he saw it he drew back, and his cheeks flushed for a moment with pleasure. A look of joy
15 came into his eyes, as if he had recognized himself for the first time. He stood there motionless and in wonder, dimly conscious that Hallward was speaking to him, but not catching the meaning of his words. The sense of his own beauty
20 came on him like a revelation. He had never felt it before. Basil Hallward's compliments had seemed to him to be merely the charming exaggeration of friendship. He had listened to them, laughed at them, forgotten them. Then had come
25 Lord Henry Wotton with his strange panegyric[1] on youth, his terrible warning of its brevity. That

had stirred him at the time, and now, as he stood gazing at the shadow of his own loveliness, the full reality of the description flashed across him.
30 Yes, there would be a day when his face would be wrinkled and wizen, his eyes dim and colourless, the grace of his figure broken and deformed. The scarlet would pass away from his lips and the gold steal from his hair. The life that was to make
35 his soul would mar his body. He would become dreadful, hideous, and uncouth.
As he thought of it, a sharp pang of pain struck through him like a knife and made each delicate fibre of his nature quiver. His eyes deep
40 ened into amethyst, and across them came a mist of tears. He felt as if a hand of ice had been laid upon his heart.
"Don't you like it?" cried Hallward at last, stung a little by the lad's silence, not
45 understanding what it meant.
"Of course he likes it," said Lord Henry. "Who wouldn't like it? It is one of the greatest things in modern art. I will give you anything you like to ask for it. I must have it."
50   "How sad it is!" murmured Dorian Gray with his eyes still fixed upon his own portrait. "How sad it is! I shall grow old, and horrible, and dreadful. But this picture will remain always young. It will never be older than this particular day
55 of June. If it were only the other way! If it were I who was to be always young, and the picture that was to grow old! For that—for that—I would give everything! Yes, there is nothing in the whole

CONTINUE ▶

1   **1**

world I would not give! I would give my soul
60 for that!"

"You would hardly care for such an arrangement, Basil," cried Lord Henry, laughing.

"I should object very strongly, Harry," said
Hallward.
65   Dorian Gray turned and looked at him. "I
believe you would, Basil. Yes," he continued, "Till
I have my first wrinkle, I suppose. I know, now,
that when one loses one's good looks, whatever
they may be, one loses everything. Your picture
70 has taught me that. Lord Henry Wotton is perfectly right. Youth is the only thing worth having.
I am jealous of everything whose beauty does not
die. I am jealous of the portrait you have painted
of me. Why should it keep what I must lose? Every
75 moment that passes takes something from me
and gives something to it. Oh, if it were only the
other way! If the picture could change, and I
could be always what I am now!"

Hallward cried, "Between you both have
80 made me hate the finest piece of work I have ever

done, and I will destroy it. What is it but canvas
and colour? I will not let it come across our three
lives and mar them."

Dorian Gray lifted his golden head and with
85 pallid face and tear-stained eyes, looked at him
as he walked over to the painting-table and found
the long palette-knife, with its thin blade of lithe
steel. He had found it at last. He was going to rip
up the canvas.
90   With a stifled sob the lad leaped from the
couch, and, rushing over to Hallward, tore the
knife out of his hand, and flung it to the end of the
studio. "Don't, Basil, don't!" he cried. "It would be
murder!"
95   "I am glad you appreciate my work at last,
Dorian," said the painter coldly.

"Appreciate it? I am in love with it, Basil. It is
part of myself. I feel that."

"You know the picture is yours, Dorian. I
100 gave it to you before it existed."

_____

[1] a speech in praise of something

CONTINUE ➡

1

1

Which choice best summarizes the passage?

A) A painter completes a portrait, and two other characters argue over who should own it.

B) A young man is so upset by his portrait that he wants to destroy it, but the painter halts the destruction.

C) A painter criticizes two men for failing to understand the meaning of his portrait.

D) A painter presents his portrait, but its subject reacts to it in a very unexpected way.

2

As used in line 13, "drew" most nearly means

A) sketched.

B) pulled.

C) guided.

D) dragged.

3

The passage suggests that Dorian's ultimate attitude toward the portrait is motivated primarily by his

A) sudden awareness of the transience of youth.

B) impatience with Lord Henry's pompous speeches.

C) admiration of Hallward's artistic talent.

D) fondness for Hallward's friendship.

4

Which choice provides the best evidence for the answer to the previous question?

A) Lines 16–19 ("He . . . words")

B) Lines 19–20 ("The sense . . . revelation")

C) Lines 23–24 ("He . . . them")

D) Lines 43–45 ("Don't . . . meant")

5

As used in line 19, "sense" most nearly means

A) purpose.

B) definition.

C) impression.

D) wisdom.

6

It can be inferred that Dorian's immediate reaction to Lord Henry's statement in lines 5–7 was one of

A) indifference.

B) disdain.

C) excitement.

D) disappointment.

7

In lines 20–26, Dorian recalls several events because

A) he is perplexed by the actions of Hallward and Lord Henry.

B) he is trying to understand the strange nature of the portrait.

C) he wants to recapture the experiences of his youth.

D) he realizes that those events held more meaning than he thought.

CONTINUE ▶

1 | **1**

8

Hallward wants to destroy his portrait because

A) he is convinced that it does not flatter its subject.

B) it reminds him of his squandered youth.

C) it has evoked feelings of despair in Dorian.

D) he does not want Lord Henry to own it.

9

Hallward does not respond to Lord Henry's statement "I must have it" (line 49) most likely because Hallward

A) is busy with the task of cleaning up the studio.

B) is excited that his portrait is being met with such strong praise.

C) is angered by Dorian's criticism of the portrait.

D) does not intend Lord Henry to have the portrait.

10

Which choice provides the best evidence for the answer to the previous question?

A) Lines 43–45 ("Don't . . . meant")

B) Lines 50–51 ("How . . . portrait")

C) Lines 90–93 ("With . . . studio")

D) Lines 99–100 ("I gave . . . existed")

11

Throughout the passage, Dorian's feelings about the painting evolve from

A) joy to fear to rejection.

B) awe to sorrow to protectiveness.

C) dismissiveness to despondency to anger.

D) love to admiration to confusion.

CONTINUE ➡

1   1

Questions 12–22 are based on the following passages.

Passage 1 is adapted from Henry David Thoreau, *Walden*, originally published in 1854. Passage 2 is adapted from Arthur Christopher Benson, *From a College Window*, originally published in 1906.

Passage 1

Line   I am convinced that to maintain one's self on this earth is not a hardship but a pastime, if we will live simply and wisely. It is not necessary that a man should earn his living by the sweat of his
5 brow, unless he sweats easier than I do.

    One young man of my acquaintance wondered if he should live as I did. I would not have any one adopt *my* mode of living on any account. I desire that there may be as many different
10 persons in the world as possible; but I would have each one be very careful to find out and pursue *his own* way, and not his father's or his mother's or his neighbor's instead.

    The mass of men lead lives of quiet despera-
15 tion. What is called resignation is confirmed desperation. From the desperate city you go into the desperate country, and have to console yourself with the bravery of minks and muskrats. A stereotyped but unconscious despair is con-
20 cealed even under what are called the games and amusements. There is no play in them, for this comes after work.

    I went to the woods because I wished to live deliberately, to front only the essential facts of
25 life, and see if I could not learn what it had to teach, and not, when I came to die, discover that I had not lived. I did not wish to live what was not life, nor to practice resignation. I wanted to live deep and suck out all the marrow of life, to live
30 sturdily and Spartan-like, to cut a broad swath and shave close, to drive life into a corner, and reduce it to its lowest terms.

    Our life is frittered away by detail. An honest man has hardly need to count more than his ten
35 fingers, or in extreme cases he may add his ten toes, and lump the rest. Simplicity, simplicity, simplicity! Simplify, simplify. Instead of three meals a day, eat but one; instead of a hundred dishes, five; and reduce other things in proportion.

40   I left the woods for as good a reason as I went there. Perhaps it seemed to me that I had several more lives to live, and could not spare any more time for that one. I learned this, at least, by my experiment: In proportion as one
45 simplifies life, the laws of the universe will appear less complex, and solitude will not be solitude, nor poverty poverty, nor weakness weakness.

Passage 2

    The one thing that is entirely fatal to sim-
50 plicity is the desire to stimulate the curiosity of others in the matter. The most conspicuous instance of this is the case of Thoreau, who is by many regarded as the apostle of the simple life. Thoreau was a man of extremely simple tastes, it
55 is true. He ate pulse,[1] whatever that may be, and drank water; he contemplated nature, and he loved to disembarrass himself of all the apparatus of life. He found that by working six weeks, he could earn enough to enable him to live in a hut
60 in a wood for the rest of the year and to meet his small expenses.

    But Thoreau was indolent rather than simple; and what spoilt his simplicity was that he was forever hoping that he would be observed and
65 admired; he was forever peeping out of the corner of his eye, to see if inquisitive strangers were hovering about to observe the hermit at his contemplation. He found his own simplicity a deeply interesting and refreshing subject of contemplation.

70   And then, too, it was easier for Thoreau to make money than it would be for the ordinary man. When Thoreau wrote his famous maxim, "To maintain oneself on this earth is not a hardship but a pastime," he did not add that he was
75 himself a man of many remarkable gifts and could earn easily. He could effortlessly make admirable pencils that sold well, he was an excellent land-surveyor, and he was a published author. Moreover, Thoreau was a celibate by
80 nature. He would no doubt have found, if he felt the need of a wife and had children, and had no

1   **1**

aptitude for skilled labor, that he would have had
to work as hard as any one else.

85   Thoreau, too, did not care in the least for
society, and sociability is expensive. Not that
he avoided his fellow-men, but society was not
essential to him. But though he was ascetic by
preference, he cannot be called a simple man,
because the essence of simplicity is not to ride a
90 hobby hard. The moment a man is conscious that
he is simple, he is simple no longer. You cannot

become simple, by doing elaborately the things
that the simple man would do without thinking. Asceticism is the sign and not the cause
95 of simplicity. The simple life will become easy
and common enough when people have simple
minds and hearts, when they do the duties that
lie ready to their hand, and do not crave for
recognition.

¹legumes such as chickpeas, lentils, and beans

CONTINUE ➜

12

As used in line 1, "maintain" most nearly means

A) sustain.

B) confirm.

C) steady.

D) declare.

13

In Passage 1, Thoreau suggests that the pursuit of diversion is

A) a frivolous waste of energy.

B) a mere consolation for an empty life.

C) a means for developing skills.

D) a way to restore emotional well-being.

14

Which choice provides the best evidence for the answer to the previous question?

A) Lines 19–21 ("A stereotyped . . . amusements")

B) Lines 23–27 ("I . . . lived")

C) Lines 27–28 ("I . . . resignation")

D) Line 33 ("Our life . . . detail")

15

Passage 1 as a whole suggests that Thoreau was most strongly motivated by a desire to

A) reject modernity.

B) pursue independence.

C) embrace poverty.

D) write simply.

16

In the final sentence of Passage 1, Thoreau repeats the words "solitude," "poverty," and "weakness" in order to highlight

A) the transformative power of austerity.

B) the desperation found in solitude.

C) the ironies of modern life.

D) the simplicity of language.

17

According to Passage 2, Thoreau's credibility is damaged primarily by his

A) self-conscious attitude.

B) lack of professional skill.

C) unspoken materialism.

D) ignorance of modern society.

18

Which choice provides the best evidence for the answer to the previous question?

A) Lines 70–72 ("And . . . man")

B) Lines 80–83 ("He . . . else")

C) Lines 84–85 ("Thoreau . . . expensive")

D) Lines 90–91 ("The moment . . . longer")

CONTINUE

1

19

Passage 2 suggests that Thoreau is not a good model for others who seek the simple lifestyle primarily because

A) his philosophical writings are hard for the average reader to understand.

B) most people are neither as talented nor as free from responsibility as he was.

C) he was far more social and decadent than he claimed to be.

D) he advocates more for richness of experience than for simplicity of experience.

20

Which choice best paraphrases the statement that Thoreau "did not care in the least for society" (lines 84–85)?

A) Thoreau was a well-known recluse.

B) Thoreau resented modern technology.

C) Thoreau was too poor to entertain friends.

D) Thoreau did not need to socialize.

21

As used in line 98, "lie" most nearly means

A) are.

B) consist.

C) recline.

D) deceive.

22

Which choice best describes the relationship between the two passages?

A) Passage 2 questions the legitimacy of the argument presented in Passage 1.

B) Passage 2 cautions against the lifestyle promoted in Passage 1.

C) Passage 2 advocates a practice that contradicts the one described in Passage 1.

D) Passage 2 discusses the practical applications of the philosophy presented in Passage 1.

CONTINUE ⟶

1   1

Questions 23–32 are based on the following passage and supplementary material.

This passage is adapted from Sarah Scoles, "Earth's Aliens." ©2015 *Aeon* magazine. Originally published July 9, 2015.

Line   In the late 1670s, Antonie van Leeuwenhoek looked through a microscope at a drop of water and found a whole world. It was tiny, squirmy, and lived, invisibly, all around us. Humans were
5 supposed to be the center of the world, and these "animalcules" seemed to have no effect—visible or otherwise—on our existence, so why were they here? Now we know that those animalcules are microbes and that they actually rule our world:
10 they make us sick, keep us healthy, decompose our waste, feed the bottom of our food chain, and make our oxygen. Human ignorance of them had no bearing on their significance, just as gravity was important before an apple dropped on Isaac
15 Newton's head.
    We could be poised on another such philosophical precipice, about to discover a second hidden world: alien life on our own planet. Today, scientists seek extraterrestrial microbes in
20 geysers shooting from Enceladus,[1] in the ocean sloshing beneath the ice crust of Europa[2] and in the formerly wet rocks of Mars. But perhaps these efforts are too far afield. If multiple lines of life bubbled up on Earth and evolved separately from
25 our ancient ancestors, we could discover alien biology without leaving this planet.
    The modern-day descendants of these "aliens" might still be here, squirming around with van Leeuwenhoek's microbes. Scientists
30 call these hypothetical hangers-on the *shadow biosphere*. If a shadow biosphere were ever found, it would provide evidence that life isn't a once-in-a-universe statistical accident. If biology can happen twice on one planet, it must
35 have happened countless times on countless other planets. But most of our scientific methods are ill-equipped to discover a shadow biosphere. And that's a problem, says Dr. Carol

Cleland, the originator of the term and its big-
40 gest proponent.
    In 2007, Cleland wrote about just such a trace of evidence: desert varnish. It's a strange sheen, like a hardened waterfall, that covers desert rocks all over the planet. The streaks run
45 down rocks from the desert of El Azizia in Libya to Antarctica's Dry Valley. Desert varnish—into which people have scraped petroglyphs[3] for thousands of years—appears layer by layer, growing only the width of a human hair each
50 millennium. The varnish is replete with arsenic, iron, and manganese, although the rocks it coats are not. No known geochemical or biological process can account for its ingredients. And yet there it is. Since that discovery, Cleland has
55 urged scientists not to discount—but to seek out—such anomalies as the varnish, things that don't quite seem to fit. Because maybe they *don't* fit.
    Telling scientists to find a shadow biosphere
60 is like asking a chimpanzee to add oil to a car: they don't know what they're looking for or what tools to use. Nevertheless, Cleland has some suggestions. First, look at life in places where life "shouldn't" be. Even the most sauna-happy
65 microbes, called hyperthermophiles, wilt above 122°C. If we find anything living at 150°C, then there's a good chance they're not of our ilk. Send balloons into the upper atmosphere; scramble up to high plateaus; snowmobile to the South Pole;
70 don end-of-world suits and venture into uranium mines. Remain alert for phenomena that make us say not "Eureka!" but "Huh, that's weird!" And then consider that their explanation might, in fact, be very, very weird.
75   The discovery of life as we don't know it would hint that biology is a universal law, like physics and chemistry. If you drop a trombone off a terrestrial building, it will fall to the ground—every time. If molecular clouds have
80 just the right density, dynamics, and ingredients, they will collapse into new stars—every time. If they collapse into new stars, the leftover gas and dust will always collapse into planets. *Maybe*

CONTINUE ▶

85 when those planets have the right ingredients baked at the right temperature, they always make life. A shadow biosphere—evidence that biology emerged more than once on Earth— suggests that biology emerges as a normal conse-
90 quence of "Goldilocks" or "just-right" conditions, rather than being a mysterious lottery-ticket phenomenon.

    Today, if asked whether life concocts itself given the right conditions, many people would

95 respond affirmatively. It's not a new idea. But concrete, complex proof that we are the predict-able result of a predictable law would tip over our throne, once and for all.

[1]the sixth-largest moon of Saturn
[2]the fourth-largest moon of Jupiter
[3]rock carvings

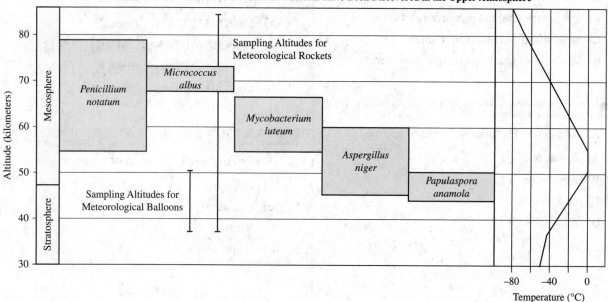

Altitudes at Which Known Terrestrial Bacteria Have Been Discovered in the Upper Atmosphere

Adapted from Ishenetsky, et. al. (1978)

CONTINUE ▶

1   **1**

23

The first paragraph serves mainly to

A) describe the power of a scientific tool.

B) compare two different cultural perspectives.

C) highlight the importance of a discovery.

D) introduce a surprising feature of an organism.

24

In the first paragraph, the author refers to an apple dropping on Isaac Newton's head in order to make the point that

A) microbes are as pervasive as gravity.

B) ignorance does not preclude relevance.

C) scientific progress is inevitable.

D) discoveries can be made in different ways.

25

As used in line 13, "bearing" most nearly means

A) direction.

B) demeanor.

C) endurance.

D) relevance.

26

The author evidently believes that the search for extraterrestrial life

A) has yielded important biological discoveries.

B) indicates that life can arise in multiple ways.

C) is a promising line of research, even if it has so far been fruitless.

D) may not be an optimal use of scientific resources.

27

Which choice provides the best evidence for the answer to the previous question?

A) Lines 8–12 ("Now . . . oxygen")

B) Lines 19–22 ("Today . . . Mars")

C) Lines 22–23 ("But . . . afield")

D) Lines 27–29 ("The . . . microbes")

28

As used in line 23, "lines" most nearly means

A) lineages.

B) contours.

C) fields.

D) fabrications.

1   1

29

The passage suggests that the most intriguing feature of desert varnish is its

A) extreme durability.

B) slow growth.

C) geographical pervasiveness.

D) unknown origins.

30

Which choice provides the best evidence for the answer to the previous question?

A) Lines 41–42 ("In . . . varnish")

B) Lines 42–44 ("It's a . . . planet ")

C) Lines 46–50 ("Desert . . . millennium")

D) Lines 52–53 ("No known . . . ingredients")

31

Given the information in the passage, the information in the diagram

A) supports the idea that hyperthermophiles wilt above 122°C.

B) supports the idea that life found by weather balloons in the upper atmosphere must be extraterrestrial.

C) refutes the contention that microbes are not likely to live at temperatures above 150°C.

D) refutes the suggestion that life found by weather balloons in the upper atmosphere cannot be well-known microbes.

32

As it is used in line 76, the statement "biology is a universal law" is best interpreted to mean

A) we are beginning to answer the most challenging questions about the origins of life.

B) complex life is likely to be found throughout the universe.

C) the principles of biology are more fundamental than the principles of physics.

D) life will emerge under measurable and predictable circumstances.

CONTINUE ➤

1   **1**

Questions 33–42 are based on the following passage and supplementary material.

This passage is adapted from Chief Justice of the Supreme Court Earl Warren, "Opinion of the Court in *Brown v. Board of Education of Topeka, Kansas*," published May 17, 1954.

Line
The plaintiffs contend that segregated public schools are not "equal" and cannot be made "equal," and that hence [the plaintiffs] are deprived of the equal protection of the laws.

5   The doctrine of "separate but equal" did not make its appearance in this Court until 1896 in the case of *Plessy v. Ferguson*, involving not education but transportation. [Until now] the Court expressly reserved decision on the question of

10 whether or not *Plessy v. Ferguson* should apply to public education.

We must look to the effect of segregation itself on public education.

In approaching this problem, we cannot turn

15 the clock back to 1868, when the [equal protection clause of the 14th Amendment] was adopted, or even to 1896, when *Plessy v. Ferguson* was written. We must consider public education in the light of its present place in American life. Only in this

20 way can it be determined if segregation in public schools deprives these plaintiffs of the equal protection of the laws.

Today, education is perhaps the most important function of state and local governments. It

25 is required in the performance of our most basic public responsibilities, even service in the armed forces. It is the very foundation of good citizenship. Today it is a principal instrument in awakening the child to cultural values, in preparing

30 him for later professional training, and in helping him to adjust normally to his environment. In these days, it is doubtful that any child may reasonably be expected to succeed in life if he is denied the opportunity of an education. Such an

35 opportunity, where the state has undertaken to provide it, is a right which must be made available to all on equal terms.

Does segregation of children in public schools solely on the basis of race, even though

40 the physical facilities and other "tangible" factors may be equal, deprive the children of the minority group of equal educational opportunities? We believe that it does.

In *Sweatt v. Painter*, in finding that a segre-

45 gated law school for Negroes could not provide them equal educational opportunities, this Court relied in large part on "those qualities which are incapable of objective measurement but which make for greatness in a law school." In

50 *McLaurin v. Oklahoma State Regents*, the Court, in requiring that a Negro admitted to a white graduate school be treated like all other students, again resorted to intangible considerations: ". . . ability to study, to engage in discussions and

55 exchange views with other students, and, in general, to learn his profession." Such considerations apply with added force to children in grade and high schools. To separate them from others of similar age and qualifications solely because of

60 their race generates a feeling of inferiority as to their status in the community that may affect their hearts and minds in a way unlikely ever to be undone. The effect of this separation on their educational opportunities was well stated by a

65 finding in the Kansas case by a court which nevertheless felt compelled to rule against the Negro plaintiffs:

"Segregation of white and colored children in public schools has a detrimental effect upon

70 the colored children. The impact is greater when it has the sanction of the law, for the policy of separating the races is usually interpreted as denoting the inferiority of the Negro group. A sense of inferiority affects the motivation of a

75 child to learn. Segregation with the sanction of law, therefore, has a tendency to retard the educational and mental development of Negro children and to deprive them of some of the benefits they would receive in a racially integrated

80 school system."

Whatever may have been the extent of psychological knowledge at the time of *Plessy v. Ferguson*, this finding is amply supported

CONTINUE ▶

by modern authority. Any language in *Plessy v.*
85 *Ferguson* contrary to this finding is rejected.
We conclude that, in the field of public
education, the doctrine of "separate but equal"
has no place. Separate educational facilities are
inherently unequal. Therefore, we hold that the

90 plaintiffs and others similarly situated for whom
the actions have been brought are, by reason of
the segregation complained of, deprived of the
equal protection of the laws guaranteed by the
Fourteenth Amendment.

Educational Segregation in the U.S. Prior to *Brown v. Board of Education*

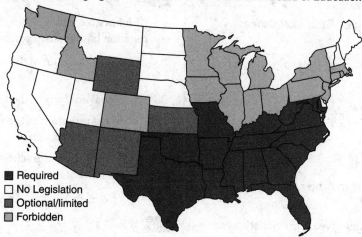

■ Required
□ No Legislation
▨ Optional/limited
▧ Forbidden

CONTINUE ➤

1   1

33

Chief Justice Warren uses quotes in the first sentence in order to

A) define a legal term.

B) refer to a document.

C) question a recent coinage.

D) indicate mild sarcasm.

34

As used in line 12, "look to" most nearly means

A) aspire to.

B) see to.

C) hope for.

D) examine.

35

Chief Justice Warren indicates that the *Plessy v. Ferguson* decision

A) was overturned many years previously.

B) was not specifically concerned with schooling.

C) provides a precedent for the *Brown v. Board of Education* case.

D) was decided before the 14th Amendment was passed.

36

Which choice provides the best evidence for the answer to the previous question?

A) Lines 5–8 ("The . . . transportation")

B) Lines 14–17 ("In . . . written")

C) Lines 81–84 ("Whatever . . . authority")

D) Lines 84–85 ("Any . . . rejected")

37

Chief Justice Warren's argument against racial segregation laws focuses primarily on

A) a consideration of their psychological effects on children.

B) a legal analysis of the term "equal."

C) an examination of the errors in the *Plessy v. Ferguson* decision.

D) disparities in the school facilities for students of different races.

38

Which choice provides the best evidence for the answer to the previous question?

A) Lines 1–4 ("The plaintiffs . . . laws")

B) Lines 14–17 ("In . . . written")

C) Lines 75–80 ("Segregation . . . system")

D) Lines 88–89 ("Separate . . . unequal")

CONTINUE ▶

39

The passage suggests that the "Kansas case" (line 65) is remarkable for the fact that it

A) contradicted the decision in the *Plessy v. Ferguson* case.

B) acknowledged a profound social problem that it was unable to redress.

C) introduced the phrase "separate but equal" into legal circles.

D) prohibited discrimination based on race in graduate school admissions.

40

The "considerations" in line 53 pertain to

A) disputed legal distinctions.

B) dominant cultural trends.

C) professional career decisions.

D) unquantifiable social factors.

41

According to the map, what fraction of the 48 contiguous U.S. states required school segregation before the *Brown v. Board of Education* decision?

A) One-fourth

B) One-third

C) One-half

D) Two-thirds

42

As used in line 88, "has no place" most nearly means

A) is widely unpopular.

B) is hard to define.

C) should not be tolerated.

D) is not part of established law.

CONTINUE ➡

Questions 43–52 are based on the following passage.

This passage is adapted from C. F. Black, "The Problem with Perfect: A Grammatical Plea," ©2016 College Hill Coaching.

Line   Think about it: when someone says, "I have lived in New York" is she saying anything other than "I lived in New York?" That is, does the word "have" have any real job in the first sentence, or is
5   it a freeloader?

Those of you who paid attention in eighth grade English class might say that these sentences have different tenses. The first sentence is in the *simple past tense* while the second is in the
10   *present perfect tense*.

Can I have my "A" now, Ms. Bumthistle?

But really, don't these sentences mean pretty much the same thing? No they don't, but you would be astonished at the many contradictory
15   explanations you might hear, even from very educated folks.

Some say that the present perfect tense indicates ongoing action through the present moment, and so "I have lived in New York"
20   implies "I still live in the Big Apple." Others say it implies action in the indefinite past: "I lived in Brooklyn some time ago, but I'm not sure when." Some think it indicates actions or states that are over and done: "I'll never walk in Central
25   Park again." Others say it's emphatic, like a playground retort (at least when you stress the "have"): "I don't care what you say. I <u>did</u> live in the Bronx."

Still others say it's a regionalism or an affecta-
30   tion. The British just prefer to use "have" when talking about the past. For instance, where a Yank might say, "I took a walk," a Brit would prefer to say "I have taken a walk." It just sounds more proper.

So who's right?
35   None of the above. All of this fuzziness swirls around one very imperfect word: *perfect*, which has been misused by teachers for decades. We should strike it from grammatical discourse and replace it with a better word: *consequential*.
40   First of all—sorry, Ms. Bumthistle and all her eighth-grade victims—but there is no such thing as the "present perfect tense" (or, for that matter, the past perfect tense or the future perfect tense). We speakers of English have only two
45   tenses (yes, two) for locating verbs in time: past and present. That's it. That covers it all. (Don't get me started on whether or not the future tense is really a tense. It's not. Nothing has ever

happened in the future, and our language cer-
50   tainly doesn't imply otherwise. When we refer to the future, we do it *now*.) The term *perfect* refers to something different from tense: the *aspect* of a verb, that is, how an action or state of being affects the status of the subject or situation to
55   which it applies.

Confused? Okay, take the verb *to eat*. We can use this verb in the present tense, but with many different aspects. "I eat" has the *habitual* aspect: "I am in the habit of eating." "I am eating" has the
60   *progressive* aspect: "I am in the process of eating." "I have to eat" has the *compulsive* aspect: "I feel compelled to eat." "I have eaten" takes the *consequential* aspect: "My present status is a consequence of previous eating."
65   A *perfect* verb isn't flawless. Rather, it indicates a *status-as-consequence*. When I say "I have lived in New York," I mean, "Who I am now is a consequence of the fact that I lived in New York, whether or not I still do." Unlike "I lived
70   in New York," it focuses on a current status, not a past action. It implies neither flawlessness, nor ongoing action, nor finality, nor vagueness of timing, nor emphasis, nor Anglophilia.[1] It simply conveys my current status-as-conse-
75   quence. The helping verb "to have," as we should expect, indicates a sort of possession: "I *have* the status of a New Yorker, even if I now live in Indianapolis."

Another reason to jettison *perfect* is that
80   linguists use the term ambiguously. They say that an action has a *perfective aspect* if it has a definite completion point (like *emptied, found,* or *won*), but an *imperfective aspect* if it can keep going (like *poured, searched,* or *fought*). This
85   quality is of course very different from what we are talking about when we try to distinguish between "I lived in New York" and "I have lived in New York."

Martin Luther King, Jr., beautifully exempli-
90   fied the consequential aspect when he said "I have been to the mountaintop." What was his point? Certainly not just that he once visited a mountaintop, nor that he was still up there, nor that he was unsure of his timing, nor that his visit
95   was complete. His point is his *status-as-conse-quence*: he is now more emboldened and enlightened as a result of his metaphorical visit.

Have you been convinced? Pitch *perfect*. Embrace the *consequential*.

---

[1]love or admiration for Great Britain.

CONTINUE ➡

1   1

43

The overall tone of the passage is best described as

A) didactic.

B) indignant.

C) dispassionate.

D) comical.

44

The question the author asks in line 11 ("Can . . . Bumthistle?") is best understood as

A) an earnest plea for recognition.

B) a humorous jab at servility.

C) a play on words.

D) an acknowledgment of negligence.

45

The author believes that the variety in the interpretations of the sentence "I have lived in New York" is due primarily to

A) the public's aversion to grammatical rules.

B) regional language preferences.

C) differences among the intentions of speakers.

D) erroneous and confused instruction.

46

Which choice provides the best evidence for the answer to the previous question?

A) Lines 3–5 ("That is . . . freeloader?")

B) Lines 35–37 ("All . . . decades")

C) Lines 66–69 ("When . . . do")

D) Lines 71–73 ("It implies . . . Anglophilia")

47

As used in line 38, "strike" most nearly means

A) propel.

B) afflict.

C) eliminate.

D) come to an agreement on.

48

The author would most likely regard the verb in the sentence "I am leaving tomorrow" as an example of

A) the present perfect tense.

B) the present tense.

C) the future tense.

D) the future progressive tense.

CONTINUE ➜

1   **1**

49

The author refers to Martin Luther King, Jr., primarily in order to

A) highlight the extent of the confusion about the use of consequential aspect.

B) distinguish the consequential aspect from the other verb aspects.

C) promote the use of the consequential aspect as a rhetorical device.

D) demonstrate the proper use of the consequential aspect.

50

The author objects to the explanation in lines 8–10 ("The first . . . *tense*") primarily because it

A) refers to a nonexistent tense.

B) denies the many possible meanings of the sentences.

C) contradicts the opinion of a majority of English teachers.

D) conflicts with the way that most readers interpret the sentences.

51

Which choice provides the best evidence for the answer to the previous question?

A) Lines 13–16 ("No . . . folks")

B) Lines 29–30 ("Still . . . affectation")

C) Lines 40–44 ("First . . . tense")

D) Line 65 ("A . . . flawless")

52

Which of the following would the author regard as the most accurate paraphrase of the sentence "I have studied economics?"

A) I know something about economics.

B) I am not finished with my studies of economics.

C) I once studied economics, but I'm not sure when.

D) I dispute your contention that I did not study economics.

STOP

**If you finish before time is called, you may check your work on this section only.
Do not turn to any other section of the test.**

2   2

Writing and Language Test
35 MINUTES, 44 QUESTIONS

Turn to Section 2 of your answer sheet to answer the questions in this section.

DIRECTIONS

Each passage below is accompanied by a number of questions. For some questions, you will consider how the passage might be revised to improve the expression of ideas. For other questions, you will consider how the passage might be edited to correct errors in sentence structure, usage, or punctuation. A passage or a question may be accompanied by one or more graphics (such as a table or graph) that you will consider as you make revising and editing decisions.

Some questions will direct you to an underlined portion of a passage. Other questions will direct you to a location in a passage or ask you to think about the passage as a whole.

After reading each passage, choose the answer to each question that most effectively improves the quality of writing in the passage or that makes the passage conform to the conventions of standard written English. Many questions include a "NO CHANGE" option. Choose that option if you think the best choice is to leave the relevant portion of the passage as it is.

CONTINUE ▶

2   2

Questions 1–11 are based on the following passage and supplementary material.

The Business of America

In a 1925 address, President Calvin Coolidge asserted, "The chief business of the American People is business. They are profoundly concerned with producing, buying, selling, investing, and prospering in the world." But to Coolidge, America was not all about just practical **1** matters: for in the same speech he declared, with equal confidence, that "the chief ideal of the United States is idealism."

When Coolidge gave his address, the country was booming: factory owners were profiting from techniques of mass production, consumers were buying in earnest, investors were enjoying one of the greatest bull markets in American history, and **2** gains in their standard of living were benefiting workers. It was easy, therefore, for Coolidge to speak **3** with such lofty terms. Within five years, however, the stock market would crash and the Great Depression **4** would begin its stranglehold on the nation, putting Coolidge's sentiments to the test. **5** In the decades to follow, meeting both America's practical needs and its ideals would become more challenging.

1

A) NO CHANGE
B) matters; for
C) matters for
D) matters, for

2

A) NO CHANGE
B) the standard of living gains were benefiting workers
C) workers were benefiting from gains in their standard of living
D) the standard of living was gaining, benefiting workers

3

A) NO CHANGE
B) for
C) in
D) to

4

A) NO CHANGE
B) had begun
C) began
D) would have begun

5

Which choice serves as the best transition between this paragraph and the next?

A) NO CHANGE
B) At the low point of the downturn, nearly 25% of Americans were out of work.
C) America would only emerge from the Depression as it fought World War II.
D) Years later, President Franklin Roosevelt's New Deal policies would be marshaled to address the nation's economic plight.

CONTINUE ▶

2   **2**

This integration is precisely the mission of the U.S. Department of Commerce. Established in 1903, **6** the purpose of the department is to create conditions for economic growth and opportunity by working with businesses, universities, communities, and workers to promote job creation, sustainable development, and improved standards of living. A young person looking for an exciting job at the heart of the business world should consider **7** how to work in the Department of Commerce.

The world of business and commerce grows more complex and competitive every year. The department needs young creative minds that can solve problems as the **8** twists and turns of international business intensify. While the needs of the Commerce Department continue to grow, so do the opportunities for applicants **9** with a wide variety of talents and interests. The Department employs specialists in economic analysis, telecommunications, and even oceanic and atmospheric **10** administration, since it has locations in all fifty states and in 86 foreign countries.

6

A) NO CHANGE
B) the purpose of the department is creating
C) the department's purpose is to create
D) the department works to create

7

A) NO CHANGE
B) how to work for
C) working for
D) the work of

8

A) NO CHANGE
B) challenges
C) obstacles
D) worries

9

A) NO CHANGE
B) of
C) for
D) to

10

A) NO CHANGE
B) administration with
C) administration, and has
D) administration, despite having

Its ranks include Nobel laureates, foreign service officers, patent attorneys, law enforcement officers, and aerospace engineers.

A healthy U.S. economy is an innovative economy. Accordingly, the Department of Commerce must constantly reinvent itself to keep up with changing times. **11** A new generation of thinkers and doers is needed to bring the Department to the cutting edge of an information-driven and computer-based economy. Perhaps you can be one of them.

11

The writer is considering deleting this sentence. Should the writer make this change?

A) Yes, because it disrupts the promotional tone of the passage by mentioning a need.

B) Yes, because it mentions information about the economy that was stated in the previous paragraph.

C) No, because it provides relevant details about the economy and it links to the sentence that follows.

D) No, because it explains the value of government service to those who are seeking new employment opportunities.

CONTINUE

2   2

Questions 12–22 are based on the following passage.

That Makes My Blood Boil!

Have you ever heard someone say, "That really makes my blood boil?" Cartoonists love the image: picture Donald Duck in one of his tempers, a flush **12** raising from his throat up to his face, until the top of his head explodes.

13 Strong emotions really can induce flushing, and stressful situations can cause blood pressure to spike. Our blood temperature doesn't change much, however. Even high-grade fevers almost never elevate blood temperature more than 10°F. Unlike reptiles, **14** mammals like us maintain a constant blood temperature of about 98.6°F.

12

A) NO CHANGE
B) increasing
C) surging
D) elevating

13

Which choice most logically combines the two sentences?

A) While strong emotions really can induce flushing, stressful situations can also cause blood pressure to spike, but our blood temperature doesn't change much.

B) Strong emotions really can induce flushing, but our blood temperature doesn't change much, even though stressful situations can cause blood pressure to spike.

C) Although strong emotions really can induce flushing, it is true that stressful situations can cause blood pressure to spike but our blood temperature doesn't change much.

D) Although strong emotions really can induce flushing and stressful situations can cause blood pressure to spike, our blood temperature doesn't change much.

14

A) NO CHANGE
B) our blood temperature, being that we're mammals, stays constant at
C) the blood temperature of mammals like us stays constant at
D) mammalian blood temperature, like us, stays constant at

CONTINUE ▶

Inside an intact, living human body, blood cannot reach its boiling point. **15** However, this does not mean that extreme heat is not very dangerous to humans.

In intense heat, our systems of thermoregulation can be overwhelmed. Perspiration, **16** the bodies main cooling system, can be taxed by dehydration or thwarted by excess humidity. Illnesses and conditions related to dehydration—such as cardiovascular disease and kidney disease—are **17** exaggerated by extreme heat. Accordingly, many scientists are concerned that the rise in global temperatures will lead to more and more heat-related fatalities.

15

Which choice provides the best transition to the paragraph that follows?

A) NO CHANGE

B) Lucky for us.

C) Despite all that happens inside our bodies, our blood temperature remains steady.

D) But when we get angry, it often feels as if it does.

16

A) NO CHANGE

B) the bodies'

C) is the body's

D) the body's

17

A) NO CHANGE

B) exacerbated

C) inflated

D) heightened

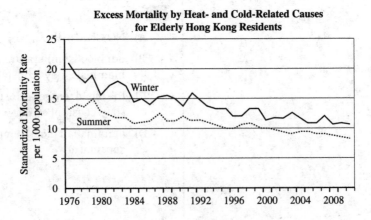

Excess Mortality by Heat- and Cold-Related Causes for Elderly Hong Kong Residents

2

2

However, a 2015 study by two Chinese scientists, Pui Hing Chau and Jean Woo, seems to assuage some of these concerns. They wanted to know whether rising temperatures are causing an increase in heat-related fatalities in the summer, but they also wondered if they might yield a decrease in *cold*-related deaths in the winter. **18** Their 2015 study sought to examine this relationship between global warming and mortality.

[1] They examined statistics on elderly residents of Hong Kong from 1976 to 2010. [2] They documented an average rise in atmospheric temperature over this period of 0.017°C per year. [3] They also found that the annual number of intense cold winter spells decreased steadily while the number of heat waves increased. [4] **19** Accordingly, they expected cold-related deaths to decline and heat-related deaths to increase over this time period. [5] But their results did not meet their expectations. [6] While the rate of cold-related deaths in winter did indeed decline, **20** from approximately 21,000 deaths in 1976 to approximately 11,000 deaths in 2010, the frequency of heat-related deaths in summer declined as well, by 38.8% over the entire 35-year span. [7] Chau and Woo concluded that "Hong Kong has not observed an increase in heat-related deaths as predicted in the Western literature" on global warming. **21**

18

The author is considering deleting this sentence. Should the writer make this change?

A) No, because it indicates an important detail about the nature of the study.

B) No, because it explains how the study assuaged the concerns of scientists.

C) Yes, because it repeats information that has already been stated in the passage.

D) Yes, because it disrupts the transition to the discussion of the study in the next paragraph.

19

A) NO CHANGE

B) Nevertheless,

C) Then,

D) Alternately,

20

Which choice most accurately represents the data in the graph?

A) NO CHANGE

B) from approximately 21 deaths per 1,000 persons in 1976 to approximately 11 deaths per 1,000 persons in 2010

C) from approximately 14,000 deaths in 1976 to approximately 8,000 deaths in 2010

D) from approximately 14 deaths per 1,000 persons in 1976 to approximately 8 deaths per 1,000 persons in 2010

21

To make the paragraph most logical, sentence 5 should be placed

A) where it is now.

B) immediately after sentence 1.

C) immediately after sentence 2.

D) immediately after sentence 3.

CONTINUE

2

2

These declines in death rates may be attributable more to cultural changes—such as safer work practices, healthier lifestyles, and better medical care— **22** rather than climate change. Indeed, Chau and Woo are careful not to dismiss the possible health risks associated with global warming. Nonetheless, their study may help reduce some of our fears as we face life on a warming planet.

22

A) NO CHANGE

B) than to

C) as to

D) more than

2   2

Questions 23–33 are based on the following passage.

The Peace Corps

In 1961, in the midst of the Cold War, President John F. Kennedy sought a way for young Americans to share "that decent way of life which is the foundation of freedom and a condition of peace." [23] First, he signed Executive Order 10924 to establish the United States Peace Corps.

The Peace Corps grew from Kennedy's concern [24] for the spread of communist ideals and practices, and his desire to see them replaced with [25] those of democracy instead. Kennedy noted that the Soviet Union "had hundreds of men and women, scientists, physicists, teachers, engineers, doctors, and nurses . . . prepared to spend their lives abroad in the service of world communism."

He [26] believed he had a duty to marshal the power of democracy to liberate the developing world from "hunger, ignorance, and poverty." It was a lofty plan that seemed almost too idealistic [27] even to attempt, yet it has proven to be one of President Kennedy's most enduring legacies.

23

A) NO CHANGE
B) Essentially,
C) However,
D) To that end,

24

A) NO CHANGE
B) with
C) about
D) against

25

A) NO CHANGE
B) those of democracy
C) democracy instead
D) democracy

26

A) NO CHANGE
B) had believed
C) would believe
D) would have to believe

27

A) NO CHANGE
B) even in attempting
C) for even someone to attempt
D) for even attempting

CONTINUE ➡

2   **2**

The Peace Corps was very popular in the 1960s, especially among idealistic college graduates, but its popularity declined in the 70s as the Vietnam War and the Watergate scandal **28** eliminated America's faith in government. In the 80s, President Reagan worked to revive the program and **29** its momentum had been gained again. During the Reagan administration, the scope of the Peace Corps broadened to include such programs such as computer literacy and business education. Reagan encouraged conservative-minded volunteers to join the largely liberal Peace Corps, and membership grew steadily **30** because the Berlin Wall fell in 1989, signaling the decline of communist influence in Europe.

28

A) NO CHANGE
B) traumatized
C) mistreated
D) eroded

29

A) NO CHANGE
B) it regained its momentum.
C) its momentum was regained again.
D) it regained its momentum again.

30

Which choice best indicates a steady increase in Peace Corps membership from the 1980s through the 1990s?

A) NO CHANGE
B) until
C) when
D) even after

2   **2**

Since the Peace Corps was founded in 1961, [31] its mission: to promote world peace and friendship— has not changed. [32] However, peace and friendship are harder to achieve in stressed and deprived communities, so the role of the Peace Corps has expanded. Some volunteers work with communities improve access to sustainable food and water sources. Others focus on health-related projects, [33] where they work to reduce the risk of pandemic diseases such as HIV/AIDS and malaria. Recently, the Corps has even turned its attention to the problem of gender inequality, empowering adults and youths to think beyond traditional roles and encouraging self-confidence.

Nearly 220,000 current and former volunteers know that the Peace Corps changes lives—both their own and those of people in communities around the world. The Peace Corps embraces change, seeking new and better ways to make a difference.

31

A) NO CHANGE
B) its mission—
C) it's mission—
D) its mission,

32

The writer is considering deleting this sentence. Should the writer make this change?

A) No, because it describes one of the new tasks undertaken by the modern Peace Corps.
B) No, because it provides a logical link between the Peace Corps' original mission and its new responsibilities.
C) Yes, because it blurs the paragraph's focus on the changing role of the Peace Corps.
D) Yes, because it mentions an irrelevant fact about stressed and deprived communities.

33

A) NO CHANGE
B) in reducing
C) when working to reduce
D) such as reducing

CONTINUE

2   2

Questions 34–44 are based on the following passage.

The Invention of the Millennium

As the year 2000 approached, *Life Magazine* listed its "100 Most Significant Events" of the previous 1,000 years. Its top event? Johannes Gutenberg's invention of the printing press in 1440. The choice was **34** apt.

The printing press with moveable type introduced the era of mass **35** communication. This had the effect of changing the world forever. Before Gutenberg's time, few people outside of a small minority of nobles, priests, and scribes could read or write. In the 15th century, however, Gutenberg's invention allowed a literate middle class to grow in Europe. Historians estimate that before Gutenberg printed his Bible there were perhaps 30,000 books in all of **36** Europe, and within 50 years as many as 12 million books were in circulation.

34

Which choice best fits the thesis of the passage as whole?

A) NO CHANGE

B) effective

C) special

D) flawed

35

Which choice most effectively joins the two sentences at the underlined portion?

A) communication; this changed

B) communication, thereby changing

C) communication, with the effect of changing

D) communication and this changed

36

A) NO CHANGE

B) Europe:

C) Europe, but

D) Europe, so

CONTINUE ▶

2   2

37 Some of these books included revolutionary ideas that crossed political borders, and ultimately dismantled some of the age-old political systems and religious institutions of Europe. The ability to disseminate information beyond the elite classes **38** broke down barriers to education and paved the way for the Reformation and for the establishment of the great European universities.

It's important to remember that Gutenberg did not invent printing, which was practiced in Asia nearly 600 years earlier, nor did he even invent movable type, **39** which the Chinese were doing 400 years earlier. For all of their ingenuity, the Chinese were held back by their alphabet, which consisted of more than 40,000 characters. The challenge of maintaining and managing so many separate printing blocks made the mass production of books **40** a dramatic task.

37

The writer is considering inserting this sentence to begin the paragraph.

> Almost seven centuries later, the printing industry is still going strong.

Should the writer make this addition here?

A) Yes, because it mentions an important detail about the history of printing.

B) Yes, because it provides support to the ideas in the previous paragraph.

C) No, because it does not introduce the discussion about literacy in 15th century Europe.

D) No, because it reiterates a point made previously in the passage.

38

A) NO CHANGE

B) busted the impediments to

C) obliterated what was in the way of

D) provided a kick to

39

A) NO CHANGE.

B) which was done by the Chinese

C) which was first used by the Chinese

D) as the Chinese did

40

A) NO CHANGE

B) an impractical

C) an outrageous

D) an extreme

CONTINUE ➡

2
2

Most European languages, in contrast, had only 26 to 30 **41** letters, and setting pages for printing was much simpler. European education profited enormously from this fluke in linguistic history.

This is not to say that Gutenberg wasn't inventive. He modeled his press on the machines that **42** they had long been using to extract oil from olives, but made many significant adaptations. For his movable type, he invented a durable alloy of lead, tin, and antimony. For his ink he used a smudge-resistant mixture of lampblack, turpentine, and linseed oil. He engineered all of his letter blocks **43** were the same size so that they would fit securely on the page frame and could be easily interchanged.

In today's Information Age, it's easy to forget that Gutenberg's system was the standard in printing for 350 years, as well as the heart that pumped knowledge through the veins of civilization. The mechanical press has given way to electronic printers, which in turn are **44** fading in the era of mobile computing. Perhaps before you upload your next paper to Google Docs, you should remember the profound impact that the Gutenberg press had on the development of modern culture.

41

A) NO CHANGE
B) letters, but
C) letters, so
D) letters, for

42

A) NO CHANGE
B) had long been used
C) were what they were using
D) were being long used

43

A) NO CHANGE
B) as if they were
C) to be
D) as

44

A) NO CHANGE
B) falling into disuse
C) withering
D) growing dull

STOP

**If you finish before time is called, you may check your work on this section only.
Do not turn to any other section of the test.**

3   3

Math Test—No Calculator
25 MINUTES, 20 QUESTIONS

Turn to Section 3 of your answer sheet to answer the questions in this section.

DIRECTIONS

For questions 1–15, solve each problem, choose the best answer from the choices provided, and fill in the corresponding circle on your answer sheet. **For questions 16–20**, solve the problem and enter your answer in the grid on the answer sheet. Please refer to the directions before question 16 on how to enter your answers in the grid. You may use any available space in your test booklet for scratch work.

NOTES

1. The use of a calculator **is not permitted**.

2. All variables and expressions used represent real numbers unless otherwise indicated.

3. Figures provided in this test are drawn to scale unless otherwise indicated.

4. All figures lie in a plane unless otherwise indicated.

5. Unless otherwise indicated, the domain of a given function f is the set of all real numbers x for which $f(x)$ is a real number.

REFERENCE

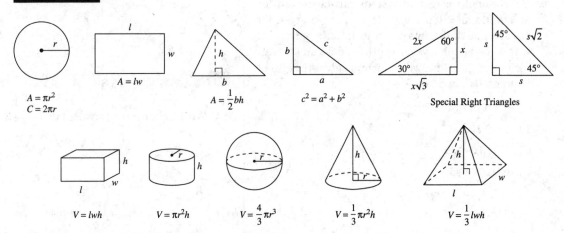

$$A = \pi r^2$$
$$C = 2\pi r$$

$$A = lw$$

$$A = \frac{1}{2}bh$$

$$c^2 = a^2 + b^2$$

Special Right Triangles

$$V = lwh$$

$$V = \pi r^2 h$$

$$V = \frac{4}{3}\pi r^3$$

$$V = \frac{1}{3}\pi r^2 h$$

$$V = \frac{1}{3}lwh$$

The number of degrees of arc in a circle is 360.
The number of radians of arc in a circle is 2π.
The sum of the measures in degrees of the angles of a triangle is 180.

CONTINUE ▶

3 **3**

1

A grocery store pledges to completely eliminate its use of plastic bags in exactly three years. To meet this goal, it will reduce consumption by 100 bags per month. How many plastic bags per month is it using currently?

A) 300

B) 1,200

C) 2,400

D) 3,600

2

Which choice is equal to $\sqrt{81} + \sqrt{36}$?

A) $\sqrt{117}$

B) 12

C) 14

D) 15

3

A car rental company rents cars for $25 per day. An optional navigation system can be rented for an additional $10 per day. Renters are charged for gas at a rate of 10 cents per mile. If Carla rents a car with a navigation system for three days and travels x miles in that time, which formula gives the cost of her rental, C, in dollars?

A) $C = 0.10x + 105$

B) $C = 0.10x + 75$

C) $C = 10x + 105$

D) $C = 10x + 85$

4

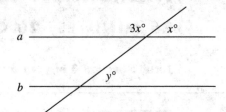

If lines a and b are parallel in the figure above, what is the value of $x + y$?

A) 45

B) 90

C) 105

D) 135

5

$$\frac{1}{2}(2x - 6) = -2(-2x - 7.5)$$

What is the solution to the equation above?

A) −6

B) −4

C) 4

D) 6

6

Which choice is equivalent to $\dfrac{x^{-\frac{1}{3}}y^3}{y^{-2}}$?

A) $\dfrac{y}{\sqrt[3]{x}}$

B) $\dfrac{y}{x^3}$

C) $\dfrac{y^5}{\sqrt[3]{x}}$

D) $\dfrac{y^5}{x^3}$

CONTINUE

3   **3**

7

Which factored expression below is equivalent to $x(2x-4)(-x+3)$?

A) $-2x(x-6)(x+1)$

B) $x(x+4)(x-3)$

C) $-2x(x-2)(x-3)$

D) $-x(2x-4)(x+3)$

8

$$y=-\frac{1}{2}x-4$$

$$x=2y+2$$

If the two equations above are graphed in the xy-plane, what is the relationship between the lines?

A) The two lines are perpendicular.

B) The two lines are distinct and parallel.

C) The two lines intersect but are not perpendicular.

D) The two lines are identical.

9

The equation $p = 7x - 125$ can be used by the owner of a smoothie cart to calculate p, the total profit in dollars in a given day if x smoothies are sold. What does the number 125 represent in this equation?

A) The daily cost, in dollars, to run the smoothie cart

B) The average income from smoothies sold for any day of the week

C) The average numbers of smoothies sold

D) The total income from smoothies sold the previous day

10

What is the remainder when $x^2 - 5x + 6$ is divided by $x - 4$?

A) 0

B) 1

C) 2

D) 3

11

The function g has the property that $g(-x) = -g(x)$ for all real values of x. If $g(-2) = -8$, which of the following could define g?

A) $g(x) = x^3 - x$

B) $g(x) = x^3$

C) $g(x) = x^2 - 12$

D) $g(x) = x^2 + 6x$

12

What is the sum of all values of r that satisfy the equation $3r^2 - 12r + 7 = 0$?

A) -4

B) 0

C) 2

D) 4

13

If $i^x i^y = 1$ and $i = \sqrt{-1}$, which of the following could be the values of x and y?

A) $x = 0, y = 1$

B) $x = 1, y = 2$

C) $x = 2, y = 6$

D) $x = 3, y = 6$

CONTINUE ➡

3   **3**

14

Ibrahim must collect and catalog different specimens of flowers and leaves for a botany project. If he gathers and catalogs flower specimens at a rate of 4 per hour and leaf specimens at a rate of 2 every 20 minutes, and he must collect a total of f flowers and l leaves for the project, which expression represents the total number of <u>minutes</u> it will take him to complete the project?

A) $4f + 2l$

B) $60\left(\dfrac{f}{4} + \dfrac{l}{2}\right)$

C) $\dfrac{f}{4} + \dfrac{l}{6}$

D) $60\left(\dfrac{f}{4} + \dfrac{l}{6}\right)$

15

$$y = -6x + 10$$
$$y = x^2 - 7x + 10$$

If (x, y) is a solution to the system above, which choice is a possible value of $x + y$?

A) 1

B) 4

C) 5

D) 12

CONTINUE

3   3

DIRECTIONS

For questions 16–20, solve the problem and enter your answer in the grid, as described below, on the answer sheet.

1. Although not required, it is suggested that you write your answer in the boxes at the top of the columns to help you fill in the circles accurately. You will receive credit only if the circles are filled in correctly.

2. Mark no more than one circle in any column.

3. No question has a negative answer.

4. Some problems may have more than one correct answer. In such cases, grid only one answer.

5. **Mixed numbers** such as $3\frac{1}{2}$ must be gridded as 3.5 or $\frac{7}{2}$.

(If $3\frac{1}{2}$ is entered into the grid as 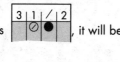, it will be interpreted as $\frac{31}{2}$, not $3\frac{1}{2}$.)

6. **Decimal answers:** If you obtain a decimal answer with more digits than the grid can accommodate, it may be either rounded or truncated, but it must fill the entire grid.

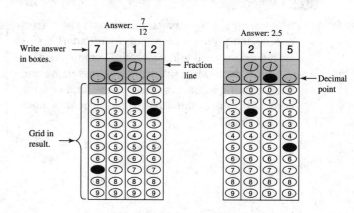

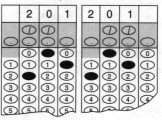

Answer: 201
Either position is correct.

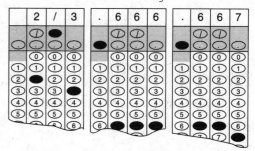

Acceptable ways to grid $\frac{2}{3}$ are:

CONTINUE ➡

16

In a carnival ring-toss game, a player must earn exactly 100 points to win. Successful short tosses earn 5 points each and successful long tosses earn 15 points each. Mike plays the ring-toss game and wins, making at least four long tosses and missing none of his tosses, how many tosses could he have made in total?

17

If $a = b + 4$, what is the value of $a^2 - 2ab + b^2$?

18

If $w = 3\sqrt{5}$ and $2w - \sqrt{20} = \sqrt{8y}$, what is the value of y?

19

$$mx + ny = 3$$
$$34x + 17y = 51$$

In the system of equations above, m and n are constants. If the system has infinitely many solutions, what is the value of $m + n$?

20

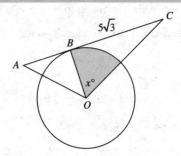

Note: Figure not drawn to scale.

In the figure above, point O is the center of the circle and segment AC is tangent to the circle at point B such that $BC = 5\sqrt{3}$. If $\sin (x°) = \dfrac{\sqrt{3}}{2}$ and the area of the shaded sector is $k\pi$, what is the value of k?

STOP

If you finish before time is called, you may check your work on this section only.
Do not turn to any other section of the test.

4   4

Math Test—Calculator
55 MINUTES, 38 QUESTIONS

Turn to Section 4 of your answer sheet to answer the questions in this section.

DIRECTIONS

For questions 1–30, solve each problem, choose the best answer from the choices provided, and fill in the corresponding circle on your answer sheet. **For questions 31–38**, solve the problem and enter your answer in the grid on the answer sheet. Please refer to the directions before question 31 on how to enter your answers in the grid. You may use any available space in your test booklet for scratch work.

NOTES

1. The use of a calculator is **permitted**.
2. All variables and expressions used represent real numbers unless otherwise indicated.
3. Figures provided in this test are drawn to scale unless otherwise indicated.
4. All figures lie in a plane unless otherwise indicated.
5. Unless otherwise indicated, the domain of a given function f is the set of all real numbers for which $f(x)$ is a real number.

REFERENCE

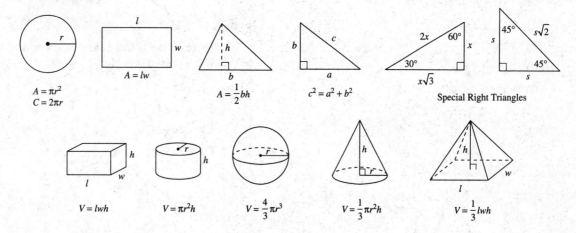

The number of degrees of arc in a circle is 360.
The number of radians of arc in a circle is 2π.
The sum of the measures in degrees of the angles of a triangle is 180.

CONTINUE ➡

4 **4**

1

When the equation $3x - 2y = 12$ is graphed in the xy-plane, what is the y-intercept?

A) -6

B) -4

C) 6

D) 12

2

If $4n \geq 9$, what is the least possible value of $4n+1$?

A) 13

B) 10

C) 8

D) 5

3

$$4c + 7d = 29$$

$$2c + 3d = 13$$

What is the value of c that corresponds to the solution of the system above?

A) 2

B) 3

C) 4

D) 8

4

Priscilla is stocking her garden store with soil and fertilizer for the spring. She plans to buy 2 bags of fertilizer for every 6 bags of soil. If she buys a total of 132 bags of soil, how many bags of fertilizer did she buy?

A) 22

B) 44

C) 68

D) 396

5

At Wide Awake coffee shop, a customer can buy a small coffee for $2.50 and any number of additions, such as soy milk, whipped cream, or flavored syrup, for $0.30 each. Which expression represents the cost, in dollars, of a small coffee with n additions?

A) $0.3n$

B) $0.3n + 2.5$

C) $2.8n$

D) $2.5n + 0.3n$

6

If $g(x) = 2x - 5$ and $f(x) = -x + 3$, which of the following represents $f(g(x))$?

A) $-2x - 2$

B) $-2x - 1$

C) $-2x + 1$

D) $-2x + 8$

CONTINUE ➡

4 | | **4**

7

Which of the following is the simplified form of $(3x^2 - 4x + 2) - (4x^2 - 3x - 1)$?

A) $-x^2 - x + 3$

B) $-x^2 - 7x + 1$

C) $x^2 - 7x + 3$

D) $-x^2 - x + 1$

8

If x is the degree measure of an angle between $0°$ and $90°$, and if $\cos x° = \frac{4}{5}$, what is the value of $\tan x°$?

A) $\dfrac{5}{4}$

B) $\dfrac{3}{4}$

C) $\dfrac{4}{3}$

D) $\dfrac{3}{5}$

9

The height of Jenna's best pole vault last season was in the 85th percentile of all high school pole vaults in the country last season. Which choice is the best interpretation of this statistic?

A) Jenna's best pole vault was 15% lower than the best vault in the country last season.

B) Jenna's best pole vault was 85% higher than the nationwide average last season.

C) Jenna's vault was at least as high as the best vault of 85% of the pole vaulters in the country last season.

D) Jenna won the pole vault event in 85% of the meets in which she participated last season.

10

Frannie has budgeted $60 to buy new running shoes at Bay Island Running Company, which is having a storewide 20% off sale. If a 5% sales tax is also added to her purchase, what is the maximum price of running shoes, before discount and sales tax, that Frannie can buy?

A) $68.50

B) $70.64

C) $71.42

D) $78.26

11

If $a = \dfrac{1}{b}$ and $a + b = 0$, what is the value of a?

A) $\sqrt{2}$

B) $2\sqrt{2}$

C) 4

D) The value of a cannot be a real number.

12

A new colony of black garden ants with an initial population of p_0 grows at a rate of 20% per week for the first 5 weeks after the initial colonization. Which of the following equations models the population, p, of the colony w weeks after the initial colonization, where $0 \le w \le 5$?

A) $p = p_0(1.2)^w$

B) $p = p_0(1.02)^w$

C) $p = (1.2p_0)^w$

D) $p = (1.02p_0)^w$

CONTINUE ➡

4 **4**

13

Which of the following equivalent forms of the equation $x - 3y - 12 = 0$ shows the slope and the <u>x-intercept</u> of its graph in the xy-plane as constants or coefficients?

A) $x - 3y = 12$

B) $y = \dfrac{1}{3}x - 4$

C) $y = \dfrac{1}{3}(x - 12)$

D) $x = 3(y + 4)$

14

Which of the following functions corresponds to a graph in the xy-plane with x-intercepts at -2 and 3, and a y-intercept of 12?

A) $f(x) = (-2x - 4)(2x - 6)$

B) $f(x) = (-2x - 4)(x - 3)$

C) $f(x) = (4x + 2)(3x - 9)$

D) $f(x) = (2x + 4)(2x + 6)$

15

Which choice represents the values of x for which the function $y = \dfrac{x^2 + 2x - 3}{x^2 - 5x - 6}$ is undefined?

A) $x = -1, x = 6$

B) $x = -2, x = 3$

C) $x = 1, x = -6$

D) $x = 2, x = -3$

16

A botanist hypothesizes that, in a certain patch of forest, the median diameter of the 360 white oak trees is 42 inches. The histograms below show the data collected on the diameters of 360 white oak trees. Which graph is consistent with the botanists' hypothesis?

A)
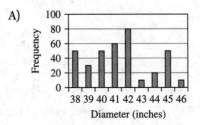

B)
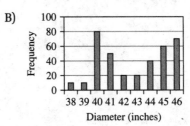

C)
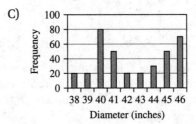

D)
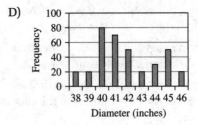

CONTINUE ➡

4 **4**

17

In the xy-coordinate plane, line l has a slope of $\frac{1}{4}$ and passes through points $(26, -p)$ and $(-2p, 4)$. What is the value of p?

A) -12

B) -7

C) 12

D) 21

18

Which expression indicates both solutions of the equation $3x^2 + 4x - 10 = 0$?

A) $\dfrac{-2 \pm \sqrt{34}}{3}$

B) $\dfrac{-2 \pm i\sqrt{104}}{3}$

C) $\dfrac{-2 \pm 2\sqrt{34}}{3}$

D) $\dfrac{-4 \pm i\sqrt{104}}{3}$

19

The mean value of all the cars on a used car lot is $11,000 and the median value of these cars is $7,000. Which of the following offers the best explanation for the discrepancy between the mean car value and the median car value?

A) Many of the cars are valued between $7,000 and $11,000.

B) There are a few cars that cost much less than the other cars do.

C) There are many cars priced at $7,000.

D) There are a few cars that cost much more than the other cars do.

Questions 20 and 21 refer to the following information.

Week	Reported Cases
1	300
2	1,500
3	7,500
4	37,500

The table above gives the approximate number of reported cases of influenza in a country in the first four weeks of an outbreak.

20

Which of the following functions best models the number of reported cases, C, in the nth week of the outbreak?

A) $C = 1,500(10^{n-1})$

B) $C = 300(10^{n-1})$

C) $C = 300(5^{n-1})$

D) $C = 150(2^n)$

21

Which choice best characterizes the data shown in the table?

A) The number of reported cases increases exponentially with time, increasing by 400% each week.

B) The number of reported cases increases exponentially with time, increasing by 40% each week.

C) The number of reported cases increases linearly with time, increasing by approximately 12,000 cases per week.

D) The number of reported cases increases linearly with time, increasing by approximately 1,200 cases per week.

CONTINUE

4 **4**

22

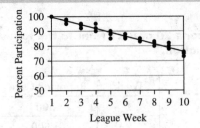

League Week

The scatter plot above shows the percent participation for three kickball leagues for each week during a 10-week season. If there were a total of 108 players in all three leagues, then which choice best approximates the number of players who dropped out of the league each week?

A) 27

B) 9

C) 3

D) 2.5

23

If $m + n = 208$ and $\dfrac{m}{n} = \dfrac{4}{9}$, then what is the value of mn ?

A) 36

B) 576

C) 3,328

D) 9,216

Questions 24 and 25 refer to the following information.

	Coral Heads/km^2	
Species	2005	2015
Acropora palmata	87	42
Acropora cervicornis	66	39
Monastrae annularis	26	24
Monastrae cavernosa	40	38

The table above shows the findings of marine biologists studying the decline of reef-building corals along the eastern Florida coast between 2005 and 2015.

24

Which coral species experienced the greatest percent decline between 2005 and 2015?

A) *Acropora palmata*

B) *Acropora cervicornis*

C) *Monastrae annularis*

D) *Monastrae cavernosa*

25

Marine biologists use species-specific models to predict future population decline. For *Acropora*, scientists assume a linear relationship between time and coral head decline. If p represents the average number of *Acropora palmata* coral heads per square kilometer that are lost each year and c represents the average number of *Acropora cervicornis* coral heads per kilometer that are lost each year, what is $\dfrac{p}{c}$?

A) $\dfrac{27}{3}$

B) $\dfrac{5}{3}$

C) $\dfrac{3}{5}$

D) $\dfrac{50}{9}$

CONTINUE

4 **4**

26

A bakery has a 52-pound supply of flour to make its swirled coffee cake fulfill holiday orders. The recipe calls for a 2:4:1 ratio, by weight, of sugar to flour to butter. How many pounds of sugar and butter combined does the bakery need to buy to complete the holiday orders for swirled coffee cake?

A) 91

B) 39

C) 26

D) 13

27

The dive tank managers at Seaside SCUBA Center try to keep their recreational SCUBA tanks filled with air at a pressure of approximately 3,000 pounds per square inch (psi). The maximum acceptable pressure for a tank is 3,300 psi, and the minimum acceptable pressure is 2,600 psi. Which inequality expresses the complete range of acceptable pressures, P, in psi, for the SCUBA tanks?

A) $|P-2,950| \le 350$

B) $|P-2,950| \ge 350$

C) $|P-3,000| \le 300$

D) $|P-3,000| \ge 400$

28

Derrick has completed a training run in which he ascended a mountain by the north trail and descended the same mountain by the east trail. He averaged a rate of 3 kilometers per hour during the ascent and 5 kilometers per hour during the descent. If the ascent took him $\frac{5}{8}$ of the total time of the run, then the north trail was what percent of the total distance of his run?

A) 37%

B) 48%

C) 50%

D) 63%

29

The sum of three integers, each less than 10, is 17. If the product of the two smallest integers is 50% less than the product of the two greatest integers, what is the value of the middle integer?

A) 4

B) 5

C) 6

D) 7

30

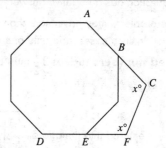

The figure above shows an octagon with eight congruent sides and eight congruent angles. Points A, B, and C are collinear and points D, E, and F are collinear. What is the value of x ?

A) 112.5°

B) 132.5°

C) 135°

D) 150°

CONTINUE

4   **4**

DIRECTIONS

For questions 31–38, solve the problem and enter your answer in the grid, as described below, on the answer sheet.

1. Although not required, it is suggested that you write your answer in the boxes at the top of the columns to help you fill in the circles accurately. You will receive credit only if the circles are filled in correctly.

2. Mark no more than one circle in any column.

3. No question has a negative answer.

4. Some problems may have more than one correct answer. In such cases, grid only one answer.

5. **Mixed numbers** such as $3\frac{1}{2}$ must be gridded as 3.5 or $\frac{7}{2}$.

   (If $3\frac{1}{2}$ is entered into the grid as 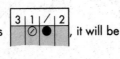, it will be interpreted as $\frac{31}{2}$, not $3\frac{1}{2}$.)

6. **Decimal answers:** If you obtain a decimal answer with more digits than the grid can accommodate, it may be either rounded or truncated, but it must fill the entire grid.

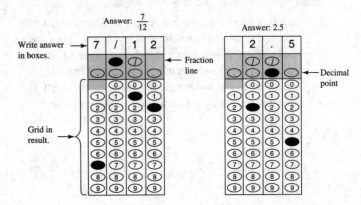

Answer: $\frac{7}{12}$ Answer: 2.5

Answer: 201
Either position is correct.

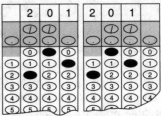

Acceptable ways to grid $\frac{2}{3}$ are:

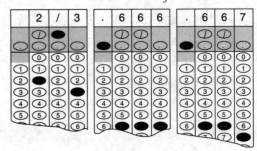

CONTINUE ▶

4 **4**

31

Delaney attended a fundraiser that sold $2 raffle tickets for regular prizes and $5 raffle tickets for the grand prize. If Delaney spends a total of $28 on both kinds of raffle tickets, how many $2 raffle tickets could she have bought?

32

If 30% of a is equal to 10% of b, and $a + b = 80$, then what is the value of a?

33

	Did not beat PR	Beat PR
Rest	76	114
Yoga	51	59

The table above shows the results of a study in which 300 sprinters competed in a 100-meter dash. The day before the race, each sprinter either took a day of rest or had a light yoga workout. It was then recorded whether or not each sprinter surpassed his or her personal record (PR) in the race. Of the sprinters who took a day of rest, what percentage did not beat their personal record? (Ignore the % symbol when gridding. For instance, enter 34.5% as 34.5.)

34

When a basketball player takes a free throw, the probability that she will make it is p, where $0 < p < 1$, and the probability that she will miss it is q, where $q = 1 - p$. When she takes two consecutive free throws, the probability that she will make both is p^2, and the probability that she will make one and miss one is $2pq$. Whenever Kia takes two free throws, she has a 0.64 probability of making both of them, what is the probability that she will miss both free throws?

35

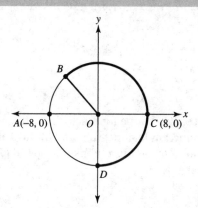

The figure above shows a circle centered at the origin. If arc BCD has a length of $\dfrac{60\pi - 32}{5}$, what is the measure of angle AOB, in <u>radians</u>?

36

If $4(2^{y-2}) = 32^x$, what is the value of $\dfrac{y}{x}$?

CONTINUE ▶

4 **4**

38

Throughout the year of Dave's phase-out, the three other glassblowers agree to absorb the balance of Dave's weekly production load. (The "balance" refers to the difference between Dave's weekly production and his weekly production before the phase-out began.) The most experienced glassblower will take 50% of this balance, and the least experienced glassblower will take 25% of this balance. In the 52nd and final week of Dave's phase-out, how many more units will the most experienced glassblower absorb from Dave's workload than the least experienced glassblower? (Round your answer to the nearest whole number.)

Questions 37 and 38 refer to the following information.

Dave, a head glassblower at a factory, has a steady weekly production load of 1,000 units. However, he has announced his retirement and will reduce his weekly production load by 4% each week for the next year. This phase-out process can be modeled by the equation $m = 1{,}000k^n$, where m is the number of units that Dave will produce in the nth week after he first announced his retirement, and k is a constant.

37

According to the formula, what will Dave's weekly production load be, in units, in the 3rd week after he announces his retirement? (Round to the nearest integer.)

STOP

**If you finish before time is called, you may check your work on this section only.
Do not turn to any other section of the test.**

5   5

Essay
50 MINUTES, 1 QUESTION

The essay gives you the opportunity to show how effectively you can read and comprehend a passage and write an essay analyzing the passage. In your essay, you should demonstrate that you have read the passage carefully, present a clear and logical analysis, and use language precisely.

Your essay must be written on the lines provided in your answer booklet; except for the Planning Page of the answer booklet, you will receive no other paper on which to write. You will have enough space if you write on every line, avoid wide margins, and keep your handwriting to a reasonable size. Remember that people who are not familiar with your handwriting will read what you write. Try to write or print so that what you are writing is legible to those readers.

You have 50 minutes to read the passage and write an essay in response to the prompt provided inside this booklet.

As you read the passage below, consider how Oliver Sacks uses

- evidence, such as facts or examples, to support claims
- reasoning to develop ideas and connect claims and evidence
- stylistic or persuasive elements, such as word choice or appeals to emotion, to add power to the ideas expressed

---

Adapted from Oliver Sacks "My Own Life." ©2015 New York Times. Published on February 19, 2015.

1   A month ago, I felt that I was in good health, even robust health. At 81, I still swim a mile a day. But my luck has run out—a few weeks ago I learned that I have multiple metastases in the liver. Nine years ago it was discovered that I had a rare tumor of the eye, an ocular melanoma. The radiation and lasering to remove the tumor ultimately left me blind in that eye. But though ocular melanomas metastasize in perhaps 50 percent of cases, given the particulars of my own case, the likelihood was much smaller. I am among the unlucky ones.

2   I feel grateful that I have been granted nine years of good health and productivity since the original diagnosis, but now I am face to face with dying. The cancer occupies a third of my liver, and though its advance may be slowed, this particular sort of cancer cannot be halted.

3   It is up to me now to choose how to live out the months that remain to me. I have to live in the richest, deepest, most productive way I can. In this I am encouraged by the words of one of my favorite philosophers, David Hume, who, upon learning that he was mortally ill at age 65, wrote a short autobiography in a single day in April of 1776. He titled it "My Own Life."

4   "I now reckon upon a speedy dissolution," he wrote. "I have suffered very little pain from my disorder; and what is more strange, have, notwithstanding the great decline of my person, never suffered a moment's abatement of my spirits. I possess the same ardour as ever in study, and the same gaiety in company."

5   5

5   I have been lucky enough to live past 80, and the 15 years allotted to me beyond Hume's three score and five have been equally rich in work and love. In that time, I have published five books and completed an autobiography (rather longer than Hume's few pages) to be published this spring; I have several other books nearly finished.

6   Hume continued, "I am . . . a man of mild dispositions, of command of temper, of an open, social, and cheerful humour, capable of attachment, but little susceptible of enmity, and of great moderation in all my passions."

7   Here I depart from Hume. While I have enjoyed loving relationships and friendships and have no real enmities, I cannot say (nor would anyone who knows me say) that I am a man of mild dispositions. On the contrary, I am a man of vehement disposition, with violent enthusiasms, and extreme immoderation in all my passions.

8   And yet, one line from Hume's essay strikes me as especially true: "It is difficult," he wrote, "to be more detached from life than I am at present." Over the last few days, I have been able to see my life as from a great altitude, as a sort of landscape, and with a deepening sense of the connection of all its parts. This does not mean I am finished with life.

9   On the contrary, I feel intensely alive, and I want and hope in the time that remains to deepen my friendships, to say farewell to those I love, to write more, to travel if I have the strength, to achieve new levels of understanding and insight. This will involve audacity, clarity and plain speaking; trying to straighten my accounts with the world. But there will be time, too, for some fun (and even some silliness, as well).

10 I feel a sudden clear focus and perspective. There is no time for anything inessential. I must focus on myself, my work and my friends. I shall no longer look at "NewsHour" every night. I shall no longer pay any attention to politics or arguments about global warming. This is not indifference but detachment—I still care deeply about the Middle East, about global warming, about growing inequality, but these are no longer my business; they belong to the future. I rejoice when I meet gifted young people—even the one who biopsied and diagnosed my metastases. I feel the future is in good hands.

11 I have been increasingly conscious, for the last 10 years or so, of deaths among my contemporaries. My generation is on the way out, and each death I have felt as an abruption, a tearing away of part of myself. There will be no one like us when we are gone, but then there is no one like anyone else, ever. When people die, they cannot be replaced. They leave holes that cannot be filled, for it is the fate—the genetic and neural fate—of every human being to be a unique individual, to find his own path, to live his own life, to die his own death.

12 I cannot pretend I am without fear. But my predominant feeling is one of gratitude. I have loved and been loved; I have been given much and I have given something in return; I have read and traveled and thought and written. I have had an intercourse with the world, the special intercourse of writers and readers.

13 Above all, I have been a sentient being, a thinking animal, on this beautiful planet, and that in itself has been an enormous privilege and adventure.

Write an essay in which you explain how Oliver Sacks builds an argument to persuade his audience that dying should be an act of dignity and well-being. In your essay, analyze how he uses one or more of the features listed in the box above (or features of your own choice) to strengthen the logic and persuasiveness of his argument. Be sure that your analysis focuses on the most relevant features of the passage.

Your essay should NOT explain whether you agree with Sacks' claims, but rather explain how he builds an argument to persuade his audience.

SAT PRACTICE TEST 5 ANSWER KEY

Section 1: Reading	Section 2: Writing and Language	Section 3: Math (No Calculator)	Section 4: Math (Calculator)
1. D	1. D	1. D	1. A
2. B	2. C	2. D	2. B
3. A	3. C	3. A	3. A
4. B	4. A	4. B	4. B
5. C	5. A	5. A	5. B
6. A	6. D	6. C	6. D
7. D	7. C	7. C	7. A
8. C	8. B	8. C	8. B
9. D	9. A	9. A	9. C
10. D	10. C	10. C	10. C
11. B	11. C	11. B	11. D
12. A	12. C	12. D	12. A
13. B	13. D	13. C	13. C
14. A	14. A	14. D	14. B
15. B	15. A	15. C	15. A
16. A	16. D	16. 8, 10, or 12	16. C
17. A	17. B	17. 16	17. B
18. D	18. C	18. 10	18. A
19. B	19. A	19. 3	19. D
20. D	20. B	20. 25/6 or 4.16 or 4.17	20. C
21. A	21. A		21. A
22. A	22. B		22. C
23. C	23. D		23. D
24. B	24. C		24. A
25. D	25. B		25. B
26. D	26. A		26. B
27. C	27. A		27. A
28. A	28. D		28. C
29. D	29. B		29. B
30. D	30. D		30. A
31. D	31. B		31. 4 or 9
32. D	32. B		32. 20
33. B	33. D		33. 40
34. D	34. A		34. .04 or 1/25
35. B	35. B		35. .8 or 4/5
36. A	36. C		36. 5
37. A	37. C		37. 885
38. C	38. A		38. 220
39. B	39. C		
40. D	40. B		
41. B	41. C		
42. C	42. B		
43. A	43. C		
44. B	44. B		
45. D			
46. B			
47. C			
48. B			
49. D			
50. A			
51. C			
52. A			

Total Reading Points (Section 1)

Total Writing and Language Points (Section 2)

Total Math Points (Section 3 + Section 4)

Scoring Your Test

1. Use the answer key to mark your responses on each section.

2. Total the number of correct responses for each section:

    1. Reading Test   Number correct: _____ **(Reading Raw Score)**

    2. Writing and Language Test   Number correct: _____ **(Writing and Language Raw Score)**

    3. Mathematics Test—No Calculator   Number correct: _____

    4. Mathematics Test—Calculator   Number correct: _____

3. Add the raw scores for sections 3 and 4. This is your **Math Raw Score**: _____

4. Use the table on page 383 to calculate your **Scaled Test and Section Scores (10–40)**.

    Math Section Scaled Score (200–800):   _____

    Reading Test Scaled Score (10–40):   _____

    Writing and Language Test Scaled Score (10–40):   _____

5. Add the **Reading Test Scaled Score** and the **Writing and Language Test Scaled Score (sum will be 20–80)**, and multiply this sum by 10 to get your **Reading and Writing Test Section Score (200–800)**.

    Sum of Reading + Writing and Language Scores: _____ × 10 =

    Reading and Writing Section Score: _____

Scaled Section and Test Scores

Raw Score	Math Section Score	Reading Test Score	Writing/ Language Test Score	Raw Score	Math Section Score	Reading Test Score	Writing/ Language Test Score
58	800			29	540	27	29
57	790			28	530	26	29
56	780			27	520	26	28
55	760			26	510	25	27
54	750			25	510	25	27
53	740			24	500	24	26
52	730	40		23	490	24	26
51	730	40		22	480	23	25
50	720	39		21	470	23	24
49	710	38		20	460	23	24
48	700	37		19	460	22	23
47	690	36		18	450	21	22
46	680	35		17	440	21	21
45	670	35		16	430	20	20
44	660	34	40	15	420	20	19
43	660	33	39	14	410	20	19
42	650	33	38	13	390	19	18
41	650	32	37	12	370	18	17
40	640	32	37	11	360	18	16
39	630	31	36	10	350	17	16
38	620	31	35	9	340	16	15
37	610	30	34	8	320	15	14
36	600	30	33	7	300	15	13
35	590	29	33	6	280	14	13
34	580	29	32	5	270	13	12
33	570	28	31	4	250	12	11
32	570	28	31	3	230	11	10
31	560	28	31	2	210	10	10
30	550	27	30	1	200	10	10

PRACTICE SAT 5 ANSWER EXPLANATIONS

Section 1: Reading

1. D   **Summary**

In this story, Dorian Gray has had his portrait done by Basil Hallward. Dorian is initially dumbstruck by *wonder* (line 17) at the youthful beauty captured in the painting, but then *a sharp pang of pain struck him like a knife* (lines 37–38) when he realized that youth is fleeting, and he makes the very strange request that the painting grow old while he remains youthful, instead of vice versa.

2. B   **Word in Context**

Lines 11–13 discuss Dorian's movements: he *passed listlessly in front of his picture and turned towards it . . . [then] drew back.* In other words, he *pulled back* in astonishment.

3. A   **Inference**

In the end, Dorian says that he is *in love with* (line 89) the painting, despite the wrenching emotions it has elicited in him. His admiration for it is due to the fact that it captures his youthful beauty: *[t]he sense of his own beauty came on him like a revelation* (lines 19–20). Choice B is incorrect because Dorian does not express any impatience with Lord Henry, but rather agreement with his sentiments. Choice C is incorrect because, although Dorian almost certainly does admire Hallward's artistic talent, he does not express it himself. Indeed, it is Lord Henry, not Dorian, who says that the painting *is one of the greatest things in modern art* (lines 42–43). Dorian's love of the painting is motivated not so much by an admiration of Hallward's artistic skill as by the youthful vigor his painting represents. Choice D is incorrect because the passage does not discuss in any depth the nature of Dorian's and Hallward's relationship.

4. B   **Textual Evidence**

As the explanation to the previous question indicates, the best evidence is in lines 19–20.

5. C   **Word in Context**

In saying that *[t]he sense of his own beauty came upon him like a revelation* (lines 19–20), the author means that he is finally feeling the *impression* of his own beauty.

6. A   **Inference**

Dorian's immediate reaction to Lord Henry's hyperbolic claim that *[i]t is the finest portrait of modern times* (lines 6–7) is to *murmur* (lines 8–9) and to *pass listlessly* (line 11) in front of the portrait. Clearly, he is not *excited* by Lord Henry's words, but neither is he *disdainful* of them

or *disappointed* in them. He is *indifferent* about Lord Henry's words until he sees the painting for himself.

7. D   **Purpose**

Immediately after perceiving the portrait as a *revelation* (line 20), Dorian recalls (in lines 21–29) several events that transpired as the portrait was being painted, which Dorian had dismissed at the time, each of which indicated that the portrait was capturing some deep youthful beauty. Now that Dorian has seen the portrait, he understands the meaning of those events. Choice A is incorrect because Dorian was never perplexed by Lord Henry's or Hallward's actions, but rather dismissive of them and then appreciative of them. Choice B is incorrect because the portrait is a *revelation* to Dorian, and therefore he does not find it strange. Choice C is incorrect because, although Dorian does become obsessed with retaining his youth, these recollections do not serve that purpose.

8. C   **Interpretation**

Hallward wants to destroy the painting because it has evoked feelings of despair in Dorian. After Dorian says *"I am jealous of the portrait you have painted of me"* (lines 73–74), Hallward responds by saying *"you . . . have made me hate the finest piece of work I have ever done, and I will destroy it"* (lines 79–81).

9. D   **Inference**

In the end, Hallward says to Dorian, *"I gave [the portrait] to you before it existed"* (lines 99–100), meaning that he never intended for anyone else to own the portrait. Therefore, when Lord Henry said, *"I will give you anything you like to ask for it. I must have it,"* (lines 48–49), Hallward does not respond because he refuses to consider the proposition.

10. D   **Textual Evidence**

As indicated in the explanation to the previous question, the best evidence is found in lines 99–100.

11. B   **Tone**

Dorian's feelings toward the portrait evolve from *awe* (*stood there motionless and in wonder*, lines 16–17), to *sorrow* (*"How sad it is!"* line 46), to *protectiveness* (*"Don't, Basil, don't! . . . It would be murder!"* lines 93–94).

12. A   **Word in Context**

In Passage 1, Henry David Thoreau advocates that everyone *be very careful to find out and pursue his own way* (lines 11–12) and suggests that some of his readers may wish to pursue a much simpler lifestyle. When he says that *to maintain one's self on this earth is not a hardship but a pastime,* he means that we can *sustain* ourselves without excessively hard labor.

---

13. B   **Inference**

Thoreau states that *[a] stereotyped but unconscious despair is concealed even under what are called the games and amusements* (lines 19–21). In other words, the pursuit of sports and diversions is *a mere consolation for an empty life.* Choice A is incorrect because Thoreau does not go so far as to call diversions a *frivolous waste of energy.* Rather, he suggests that their pursuit masks a deep inner despair. Choice C is incorrect because he does not discuss diversions as means of developing skills. Choice D is incorrect because Thoreau does not advocate pursuing diversions for emotional well-being, but rather that we *live deep and suck out all the marrow of life* (lines 28–29).

---

14. A   **Textual Evidence**

As indicated in the explanation to the previous question, the best evidence is found in lines 19–21.

---

15. B   **Inference**

Although Thoreau does give advice in Passage 1 for living a simple life in the woods, he does not indicate any motivation to *reject modernity,* to *embrace poverty,* or *write simply.* Rather, his strongest advice is that we *be very careful to find out and pursue [our] own way* (lines 11–12) and *live deep and suck out all the marrow of life, to live sturdily and Spartan-like, to cut a broad swath and shave close, to drive life into a corner, and reduce it to its lowest terms* (lines 28–30). These are powerful lines advocating *independence* rather than mere isolation, poverty, or simple expression.

---

16. A   **Purpose**

In the final sentence of Passage 1, Thoreau is indicating what he learned from his experiment in living the simple life: *[i]n proportion as one simplifies life, the laws of the universe will appear less complex, and solitude will not be solitude, nor poverty poverty, nor weakness weakness* (lines 44–48). In other words, if you simplify your life, your life will become more connected, richer, and stronger.

---

17. A   **Interpretation**

The author of Passage 2 says that although Thoreau is *regarded as the apostle of the simple life* (line 53), in fact he *was indolent* (lazy) *rather than simple, and what spoilt his simplicity was that he was forever hoping that he would be observed and admired* (lines 62–65). He could not be a model of simplicity, because *[t]he moment*

a man is conscious that he is simple, he is simple no longer (lines 90–91). In other words, his attitude was too self-conscious.

---

18. D   **Textual Evidence**

As indicated in the explanation to the previous question, the best evidence is found in lines 90–91.

---

19. B   **Inference**

Passage 2 states that *it was easier for Thoreau to make money than it would have been for the ordinary man . . . [because] he could effortlessly make pencils that sold well, he was an excellent land-surveyor, and he was a published author* (lines 70–79) and that Thoreau *no doubt would have found, if he felt the need of a wife and had children, that he would have had to work as hard as anyone else* (lines 80–83). In other words, Thoreau was not a good model for other who seek the simple lifestyle because *most people are neither as talented nor as free from responsibility as Thoreau was.* Choice A is incorrect because Passage 2 does not discuss the difficulty of Thoreau's philosophical writings. Choice C is incorrect because the author of Passage 2 does not suggest that Thoreau was social or decadent, and in fact states that Thoreau *did not care in the least for society* (lines 84–85) and that he *was a man of very simple tastes . . . [who] loved to disembarrass himself of all the apparatus of life* (lines 54–58). Choice D is incorrect because, although Thoreau does seem to advocate for richness of experience (*suck out all the marrow of life,* lines 28–29), Passage 2 does not suggest that this is a problem for Thoreau.

---

20. D   **Paraphrase**

When the author of Passage 2 states that Thoreau *did not care in the least for society* (lines 84–85), he is saying that Thoreau was not bothered, as other people might be, by living in isolation. That is, he *did not need to socialize* as many other people do. Choice A is incorrect because Passage 2 does not state that Thoreau was a *well-known recluse,* and in fact says explicitly that Thoreau did not *avoid his fellow-men* (lines 85–86).

---

21. A   **Word in Context**

When the author of Passage 2 states that *The simple life will become easy . . . when people . . . do the duties that lie ready to their hand, and do not crave for recognition* (lines 95–99), he means that people will become simple when they *do* the tasks that *are ready* to their hand, instead of talking about doing them.

---

22. A   **Cross-Textual Analysis**

Passage 2 questions the legitimacy of the argument that Thoreau presents in Passage 1, because Thoreau is not a reliable spokesperson for the lifestyle he is advocating. Choice B is incorrect because Passage 2 does not caution against a simple life, but merely suggests that Thoreau is not its most apt advocate. Choice C is incorrect because Passage 2 does not advocate a practice that is any different from the one promoted by Thoreau. Choice D is incorrect because Passage 2 is not an essay about practical applications, but rather a work of criticism.

---

23. C   **Purpose**

The first paragraph discusses the discovery of microbes by Antonie van Leeuwenhoek in the 1670s, and the fact that these creatures *actually rule our world* (line 9) despite our previous ignorance of them.

---

24. B   **Purpose**

When the author states that *Human ignorance of [microbes] had no bearing on their significance, just as gravity was important before an apple dropped on Isaac Newton's head* (lines 12–15), she is saying that *ignorance does not preclude relevance.* That is, just because we don't know how a particular phenomenon works, or even that it exists, does not mean that the phenomenon is not important.

---

25. D   **Word in Context**

The statement that our ignorance of microbes *had no bearing on their significance* means that our ignorance had no *relevance* on the fact of whether microbes are important.

---

26. D   **Inference**

The author states that *perhaps these efforts [to find exotic life forms on other planets] are too far afield* (lines 22–23). In other words, the search for extraterrestrial life *may not be an optimal use of scientific resources*, because exotic forms of life may exist right here on Earth.

---

27. C   **Textual Evidence**

As indicated in the explanation to the previous question, the best evidence is found in lines 22–23.

---

28. A   **Word in Context**

The phrase *multiple lines of life* (line 23) refers to the different ways that life could have evolved from chemicals on Earth. That is, they are different *lineages* of evolution.

---

29. D   **Inference**

The author of the passage discusses desert varnish because Dr. Carol Cleland regards it as *a trace of evidence* (lines 41–42) that the "shadow biosphere" exists. What makes it intriguing, according to Cleland, is the fact that *No known geochemical or biological process can account for its ingredients* (lines 52–53), and so it is possible that

it is somehow related to the shadow biosphere. It has *unknown origins.*

---

30. D   **Textual Evidence**

As indicated in the explanation to the previous question, the best evidence is found in lines 52–53.

---

31. D   **Graphical Analysis**

The diagram shows that weather balloons generally function at altitudes between about 38 and 50 kilometers, and that at least 5 species of terrestrial bacteria have been found to exist at these and even higher altitudes. Therefore, Dr. Cleland's suggestion that scientists may find exotic life forms if they *Send balloons into the upper atmosphere* (lines 67–68) is compromised by the fact that non-exotic life is already there. At least, the evidence in the diagram *refutes the suggestion that life found by weather balloons in the upper atmosphere cannot be well-known microbes.*

---

32. D   **Interpretation**

The second to last paragraph discusses the author's belief that discovering the "shadow biosphere" would *hint that biology is a universal law, like physics and chemistry* (lines 76–77). The author goes on to describe what she means when she says that physics and chemistry are "universal laws:" a massive object will always fall toward a bigger massive object, and molecular clouds will always collapse into stars or planets. She then states that evidence of the "shadow biosphere" would imply that *biology emerges as a normal consequence of "Goldilocks" or "just right" conditions.* In other words, *life will emerge under measurable and predictable circumstances.*

---

33. B   **Specific Purpose**

Chief Justice Warren puts quotes around the word "equal" in the first sentence because throughout this opinion he refers to the doctrine of "separate but equal" which was at the heart of the decision of the *Plessy v. Ferguson* case; therefore, this *refers to a document.* Choice A is incorrect, because "equal" is not a legal term, and he is not defining anything in this first sentence. He suggests that he will unpack the meaning of the term "equal" later in the argument, but he is not defining anything here. Choice C is incorrect because the word "equal" was not recently coined, and Warren is not questioning its meaning. Choice D is incorrect because Warren is not being sarcastic, but rather indicating how a current social circumstance (segregated schools) is not in fact equitable.

---

34. D   **Phrase in Context**

The statement *We must look to the effect of segregation itself on public education* means that we must *examine* how segregation affects schooling.

---

35. B   **Interpretation**

The passage states that *The doctrine of "separate but equal" did not make its appearance in this Court until 1896 in the case of Plessy v. Ferguson, involving not education but transportation* (lines 5–8). Therefore, the case was not specifically concerned with schooling.

---

36. A   **Textual Evidence**

As indicated in the explanation to the previous question, the best evidence is found in lines 5–8.

---

37. A   **Theme**

The thrust of Chief Justice Warren's argument is made in the extended quotation in lines 68–80, in which a finding for another case held that *Segregation with the sanction of law, therefore, has a tendency to retard the educational and mental development of Negro children and to deprive them of some of the benefits they would receive in a racially integrated school system* (lines 75–80). This indicates that Warren's argument focuses primarily on the *psychological effects of racial segregation laws on children.*

---

38. C   **Textual Evidence**

As indicated in the explanation to the previous question, the best evidence is found in lines 75–80.

---

39. B   **Inference**

In introducing the finding in the Kansas case, Chief Justice Warren remarks that this finding was stated *by a court which nevertheless felt compelled to rule against the Negro plaintiffs* (lines 65–67). In other words, although this court acknowledged the problem of segregation and its devastating effects on school children, it was unable to redress the problem.

---

40. D   **Word in Context**

The *considerations* mentioned in line 53 refer to those considerations that compelled the decisions in *Sweatt v. Painter* and *McLaurin v. Oklahoma State Regents,* namely, *those qualities which are incapable of objective measurement but which make for greatness* (lines 47–49) in schooling—in other words, *unquantifiable social factors* like the *ability to study, to engage in discussions and exchange views with other students* (lines 54–55).

---

41. B   **Graphical Analysis**

The map indicates that 16 of the 48 states "required" racial segregation prior to *Brown v. Board of Education,* which is 1/3 of the total.

---

42. C   **Phrase in Context**

When Chief Justice Warren states that *in the field of public education, the doctrine of "separate but equal" has no place,* he is saying that it *should not be tolerated,* and this is the ultimate conclusion in this decision.

---

43. A   **Tone**

The passage as a whole is dedicated to answering the question *what does "present perfect" mean?* It answers this question by showing the many confused responses to this question, and then providing what the author regards as the definitive answer: *A perfect verb . . . indicates status-as-consequence"* (lines 65–66). An essay devoted to instruction is a *didactic* essay. Choice B is incorrect because although the author does point out many common mistakes made by English teachers and common speakers alike, he indicates no *indignation* (anger at unjust treatment) over these mistakes. Choice C is incorrect because the author demonstrates a strong investment in and opinion on this subject, and therefore is not *dispassionate* (detached). Choice D is incorrect because, although the author uses humor on occasion to make his point (e.g., *sorry, Ms. Bumthistle,* line 40), the overall tone of the passage is not at all comical.

---

44. B   **Interpretation**

The question *Can I have my "A" now, Ms. Bumthistle?* is intended to indicate mock pride in the author's "proper" explanation—the one that an eighth-grade English teacher might approve of. Since the author goes on to indicate that this explanation is in fact wrong, this question is *a humorous jab at servility.*

---

45. D   **Inference**

In lines 35–37, the author states that *All of this fuzziness* (that is, the confusion about the interpretation of a sentence such as "I have lived in New York") *swirls around one very imperfect word:* perfect, *which has been misused by teachers for decades.* In other words, people are confused about the meaning of this sentence because they have been taught incorrectly. Choice A is incorrect because the passage never directly indicates that the public is averse to grammatical rules. Choice B is incorrect because the author does not agree that the confusion about this sentence is a matter of regionalism. Choice C is incorrect because the author does not discuss the intentions of the speaker.

---

46. B   **Textual Evidence**

As indicated in the explanation to the previous question, the best evidence is found in lines 35–37.

---

47. C   **Word in Context**

The assertion that *We should strike it from grammatical discourse* (lines 37–38) means that we should *eliminate* the term *perfect* in phrases such as *present perfect* and replace it with *consequential.* Notice, also, that the word *strike* is used here in an idiomatic phrase: *strike from*, and that the options in choices B and D would not be idiomatic in this context.

---

48. B   **Inference**

The author indicates, in the parenthetical comments in lines 46–51, that there is no such thing as a "future tense." Therefore the author would not regard the sentence *I am leaving tomorrow* as an example of the future tense, even though it is clearly making reference to an event that may come in the future. This eliminates choices C and D. Choice A is incorrect because the author indicates in lines 40–42 that there is no such thing as the "present perfect tense." Therefore, the author would regard the verb *am leaving* as being in the present tense, since *am* is the first-person present tense form of the verb *to be*.

---

49. D   **Purpose**

The author states that *Martin Luther King, Jr., beautifully exemplified the consequential aspect* in his "I have been to the mountaintop" speech. That is, King's speech helped to *demonstrate the proper use of the consequential aspect*. Choice A is incorrect because the author does not indicate that King was confused about the use of the consequential aspect. Choice B is incorrect because the author is not distinguishing any verb aspects in this paragraph. Choice C is incorrect because the author is not promoting the use of the consequential aspect, but rather pointing out how to use and interpret it properly.

---

50. A   **Inference**

The author objects to the explanation in lines 8–10 because it *refers to a nonexistent tense*. In lines 40–42, the author states that *there is no such thing as the "present perfect tense."*

---

51. C   **Textual Evidence**

As indicated in the explanation to the previous question, the best evidence is found in lines 40–42.

---

52. A   **Inference**

As the author explains in lines 65–78, the *present perfect*, as exemplified in the sentence *I have studied economics*, indicates status-as-consequence. Following the example in that paragraph, this sentence is best interpreted to mean *I have the status of someone who studied economics*, which is closest in meaning to choice A: *I know something about economics*. Choice B is incorrect because the author indicates that the perfect aspect does not imply *ongoing action* (line 72). Choice C is incorrect because the author indicates that the perfect aspect does not imply *vagueness of timing* (lines 72–73). Choice D is incorrect because the author indicates that the perfect aspect is not *emphatic, like a playground retort* (lines 25–27).

Section 2: Writing and Language

1. D   **Punctuation/Coordination**

The original phrasing is incorrect because using the colon with the preposition *for* is redundant. Both the colon and the conjunction *for* serve to introduce an explanation, but only one should be used at a time. Choice B is incorrect because the clause that follows the semicolon is not independent. Choice C is incorrect because joining to independent clause with a conjunction also requires a comma.

---

2. C   **Parallelism**

Only choice C maintains the parallel structure of the list *factory owners were profiting . . . consumers were buying . . . investors were enjoying . . . and workers were benefiting.*

---

3. C   **Idiom**

The correct idiom for indicating Coolidge's manner of speaking is *speak in such lofty terms*. One can *speak for* a cause or person, *speak in* different languages or tongues, *speak to* a friend or group, or *speak in* particular terms.

---

4. A   **Parallelism/Verb Form**

The original sentence is best. To maintain parallel structure, the two verbs in the sentence should have the same verb form, which is the past tense with the future aspect: *would crash* and *would begin*. (Yes, I know, you're asking how can a verb be both past and future? In fact, this is precisely how to describe the form of the verb in *Within five years, however, the stock market would crash*. This verb is in the past tense and indicative mood, as it is clearly indicating an actual event in the past. But it also uses the "future auxiliary" *would*, which is the past tense form of the auxiliary verb *will*. This is the construction we use to indicate an event that is destined to happen in the *future relative to some point in the past*.)

---

5. A   **Transitions**

The original sentence provides the best transition, because it provides a referent for the *integration* that is mentioned in the first sentence of the next paragraph. None of the other choices provides any appropriate transition to the topic sentence of the next paragraph.

---

6. D   **Dangling Participles**

This sentence begins with a participial phrase, so the subject of the main clause must also be the subject of the participle *established*. Since it was the *department* that was *established in 1903*, only choice D provides a logical subject for the main clause.

7. **C**   Clear Expression of Ideas/Logic

Since this sentence is giving advice to someone *looking for an exciting job*, the only logical phrasing is C: the person should consider *working for* the department. Choices A, B, and D imply that the prospective worker should merely study the department rather than actually seek to work there.

8. **B**   Diction/Logic

The original phrasing is incorrect because *twists and turns* might multiply, but they cannot logically *intensify*. Similarly, *obstacles* can grow, but not intensify. *Worries* can indeed grow, but *worries* is not the proper word to describe the difficulties involved in international business. Choice B, *challenges*, is the only word that works logically in the full context of the sentence.

9. **A**   Idiom/Logic

Opportunities would grow for applicants *who have* a wide variety of talents and interests, that is, those *with* a wide variety of talents and interests.

10. **C**   Transitions

The original phrasing is incorrect because the second clause does not explain the first. Choice B is incorrect because it creates a misplaced prepositional phrase. Choice C is best because it coordinates the two predicates to create parallel clauses. Choice D is incorrect because the two clauses do not contrast.

11. **C**   Development/Cohesiveness

The sentence should stay where it is because it provides detailed adjectives (*information-driven and computer-based*) that describe the developing economy, and it's the only choice that allows the final sentence to make sense.

12. **C**   Diction

The action of the flush moving quickly from Donald Duck's neck to the top of his head is aptly called *surging*. Choice A is incorrect because *raising* derives from a transitive verb: it requires a direct object. Choice B is incorrect, because *increasing* does not convey the upward motion the description requires. Choice D is incorrect because *elevating* implies intentional rather than inertial motion.

13. **D**   Coordination

Combining these two sentences requires coordinating three clauses. Only choice D coordinates all three in a logical way. Choices A and C are incorrect because they both imply that the first two clauses contrast each other, but they do not. Choice B is incorrect because it does

not properly coordinate the two supportive clauses, but rather separates them and creates an unnecessary back-and-forth double contrast.

14. **A**   Logical Comparison/Coordination

The original phrasing is the only choice that forms a logical contrast—*mammals* are *unlike reptiles*. The other choices illogically contrast *reptiles* with *blood temperature*.

15. **A**   Transitions

The original phrasing provides the most effective transition into a discussion of the specific ways in which extreme heat can be dangerous to humans.

16. **D**   Possessive Form

The original phrasing is incorrect because the context requires both a singular noun and the possessive form. Choice B is incorrect because the noun form is plural. Choice C is incorrect because this inserts a second and illogical verb into the clause.

17. **B**   Diction

The original phrasing is illogical because *exaggerated* implies intentional distortion. Choice C is incorrect because *inflated* implies expansion rather than intensification. Choice D is incorrect because *heightened* applies to a reactive (emotional or cognitive) state rather than a physical one. The best choice to convey the effect that extreme heat has on these conditions is *exacerbated*.

18. **C**   Cohesiveness/Development

All of the information in this sentence has already been stated or implied in the paragraph.

19. **A**   Transitions/Coordination

The original phrasing best conveys the fact that their expectations *accorded with* their previous findings. Choices B and D are incorrect because there is no contrast between their predictions and their previous findings. Choice C is incorrect because *Then* implies a time sequence, which is not appropriate to this context.

20. **B**   Graphical Analysis

The graph shows two lines: the top lines shows excess mortality (in cases per 1,000 people) in the winter months, and the bottom line shows the excess mortality (in cases per 1,000 people) in the summer months. This sentence refers to the winter, so we must look at the top line, which shows a decline from 21 deaths per 1,000 persons in 1976 to approximately 11 deaths per 1,000 persons in 2010.

21. A   **Cohesiveness/Logic**

The sentence is most logical where it is, because it provides a logical link between their expectations and the actual results of the study.

22. B   **Comparisons/Idiom**

This sentence uses the comparative idiom *more A than B*. The Law of Parallelism requires that the words or phrases in *A* and *B* have the same grammatical form, and idiom requires that the phrase otherwise be precisely worded. The original phrasing is neither parallel nor idiomatic. Choice C is incorrect because it is parallel but not idiomatic. Choice D is incorrect because it is neither parallel nor idiomatic. Only choice B is both parallel and idiomatic: *these declines . . . were attributable more to cultural changes . . . than to climate change*.

23. D   **Transitions/Coordination**

The original phrasing is incorrect, because this sentence does not represent the first item in a list. Choice B is incorrect because this sentence is not attempting to summarize a point. Choice C is incorrect because this sentence does not contrast with the previous one. Only choice D provides a logical transition between the first and second sentences.

24. C   **Idiom/Clear Expression of Ideas**

This sentence discusses a *worry about a situation*, so the proper idiomatic expression is *concern about*. We may show *concern for* another person and his or her well-being. We may be *concerned with* a cause or purpose that we support. The phrase *concern against* is not idiomatic.

25. B   **Redundancy/Logical Comparison**

The original phrasing is redundant, because the verb *replace* already indicates putting something *in the stead* of another. Choice C is likewise redundant. Choice D is incorrect because it forms an illogical comparison. In this sentence, the pronoun *them* refers to *communist ideals and practices*, which can only be replaced by *the ideals and practices of democracy*.

26. A   **Verb Aspect/Verb Mood**

This sentence, like the sentence before it, indicates a fact about Kennedy's beliefs. The verb, therefore, should be in the past tense, indicative mood, and non-consequential aspect, as it is in the original. Choice B is incorrect because it is in the consequential ("perfect") aspect. Choice C is incorrect because it is in the subjunctive mood. Choice D is incorrect because it is in the subjunctive and compulsive mood.

27. A   **Idiom/Modifier Errors**

The original phrasing is idiomatic and logical. Choice B is incorrect because the prepositional phrase *in attempting* has nothing to modify. Choice C is incorrect because the placement of the modifier, *even*, is illogical. Choice D is incorrect because the prepositional phrase *for attempting* has nothing to modify.

28. D   **Diction**

Choice D, *eroded*, best describes the effect that the Vietnam War and the Watergate scandal had on *America's faith in government*. Choice A is incorrect because *eliminated* is too extreme to describe this situation, and because it refers to a process, rather than a mere series of events, that systematically destroys or eradicates something. Choice B is incorrect because *faith* is not something that can be *traumatized*. Choice C is incorrect because *faith* is not something that can be *mistreated*, since it is not a sentient being.

29. B   **Voice/Redundancy/Verb Aspect**

The original phrasing misuses the "consequential" aspect of the verb. Choices C and D are redundant: *to regain* means to gain *again*. Only choice B avoids these problems.

30. D   **Clear Expression of Ideas**

Only choice D, *even after*, indicates a steady increase in membership from the 1980s through the 1990s. Choice A implies growth only after 1989, choice B implies growth only up to 1989, and choice C implies growth only in the year 1989.

31. B   **Possessive Form/Possessive Form**

The interrupting phrase in this sentence should have identical punctuation at either end: since it ends with a dash, it should begin with a dash as well. Choice C is wrong, however, because *it's* is the contraction of *it is* and is not a possessive form.

32. B   **Development/Cohesiveness**

This sentence should be kept, because it provides a logical link between the Peace Corps' original mission of promoting *world peace and friendship* with its new responsibilities like improving access to food, water, and health care.

33. D   **Pronoun-Antecedent Agreement/Clear Expression of Ideas**

The original phrasing is incorrect because *projects* are not locations, so the pronoun *where* is illogical. Likewise, projects are not time periods, so the pronoun *when* is illogical in choice C. Choice B is incorrect because the prepositional phrase *in reducing* is neither logical nor idiomatic.

---

34. A   **Diction/Cohesiveness**

The passage as a whole explains the dramatic effects that Gutenberg's invention had on the entire continent of Europe. Therefore, it supports the contention that the choice was an *apt* (fitting) one.

---

35. B   **Coordination/Pronoun Antecedents**

Choices A and D are incorrect because the pronoun *this* has no unambiguous antecedent: is it referring to the *printing press*, to *moveable type*, or to *the era of mass communication*? Choice C is incorrect because it forms an illogical prepositional phrase. The only choice that logically coordinates the clauses is choice B.

---

36. C   **Coordination**

The second clause logically contrasts with the first, so the conjunction *but* is most logical.

---

37. C   **Development/Cohesiveness**

This sentence should not be included, because it introduces an idea that is at odds with the discussion in the rest of the paragraph, which is about the effect that the printing press had on literacy and culture in 15th-century Europe.

---

38. A   **Diction/Tone**

The original phrasing conveys a logical idea with a tone that is consistent with the rest of the passage. Choice B is incorrect because *busted* is inappropriate in both meaning and tone. Choice C is incorrect because *obliterated* is too violent a term and *what was in the way* is a vague reference. Choice D is incorrect because *provided a kick to* is too violent and informal in tone.

---

39. C   **Pronoun Agreement/Logical Comparisons**

In the original phrasing, the pronoun *which* refers to the immediately preceding noun, *movable type*. Since it is illogical to say that *the Chinese were doing movable type*, or that *movable type was done by the Chinese*, choices A and B are incorrect. Choice C conveys a logical idea, that *movable type was first used by the Chinese*. Choice D is illogical because it implies a comparison rather than a contrast.

---

40. B   **Diction**

The most effective choice for describing an unworkable task is choice B, *impractical*. Choice A is incorrect because this situation implies no drama or histrionics. Choice C is incorrect because *outrageous* means *worthy of outrage*, which is clearly not the case here.

Choice D is incorrect because *extreme* is too vague for this context.

---

41. C   **Coordination**

The second clause of this sentence indicates a logical consequence to the first clause, so the conjunction *so* is most logical.

---

42. B   **Pronoun Agreement/Modifier Use**

The pronoun *they* in the original phrasing lacks a logical antecedent, as it does in choice C. Choice D is incorrect because the modifier *long* is misplaced, and because it uses the progressive aspect instead of the consequential aspect. Choice B is the only choice that avoids these problems.

---

43. C   **Idiom/Clear Expression of Ideas**

The two clauses in this sentence are *He engineered* and *they would fit*. The original phrasing is incorrect because it inserts a superfluous verb. Choice B is incorrect because this clause is indicating a fact, not a hypothetical situation. Choice C uses the correct idiomatic form, *engineered to be the same size*, to convey intent. Choice D is incorrect because this clause is not making a comparison.

---

44. B   **Diction/Clear Expression of Ideas**

Since the sentence is about the decline use of printers, the best choice is *falling into use*. Choice A, *fading*, implies that the printers are losing their color or intensity. Choice C, *withering*, implies that they are something like dying leaves. Choice D, *growing dull*, implies that they are tarnishing pieces of metal.

Section 3: Math (No Calculator)

---

1. D   **Algebra (word problems) EASY**

Since there are 12 months in a year, there are 36 months in three years. If the store's bag usage is reduced to 0 by reducing the usage by 100 bags per month for 36 months, it must have begun with a usage rate of $(36)(100) = 3{,}600$ bags per month.

---

2. D   **Advanced Mathematics (radicals) EASY**

The square root of 81 is 9, and the square root of 36 is 6. Therefore the sum is $9 + 6 = 15$.

---

3. A   **Algebra (word problems) EASY**

The cost of renting a car with GPS navigation is $25 + $10 = $35 per day, and Carla rents the car for three days for a cost of $(3)(\$35) = \$105$ without gas. If gas costs $0.10

per mile, then gas for x miles costs $0.10x$. Therefore, the total cost, in dollars, is $0.10x + 105$.

---

4. B   **Additional Topics (parallel lines) EASY**

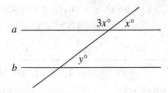

If lines a and b are parallel, then $x = y$ because corresponding angles must be congruent. The top two angles form a line, so $x + 3x = 4x = 180°$. Dividing both sides by 4 gives $x = 45°$, and therefore $x + y = 45 + 45 = 90$.

---

5. A   **Algebra (linear equations) EASY**

Original equation to be solved for x: $\frac{1}{2}(2x-6)=-2(-2x-7.5)$

Distribute: $x - 3 = 4x + 15$
Subtract x from both sides: $-3 = 3x + 15$
Subtract 15 from both sides: $-18 = 3x$
Divide by 3 on both sides: $-6 = x$

---

6. C   Advanced Mathematics (exponents) MEDIUM

Original expression: $\dfrac{x^{-\frac{1}{3}}y^3}{y^{-2}}$

Use the exponential rule $x^{-n} = \dfrac{1}{x^n}$: $\dfrac{y^3}{x^{\frac{1}{3}}y^{-2}}$

Use the exponential rule $\dfrac{x^a}{x^b} = x^{a-b}$: $\dfrac{y^5}{x^{\frac{1}{3}}}$

Use the exponential rule $x^{\frac{1}{n}} = \sqrt[n]{x}$: $\dfrac{y^5}{\sqrt[3]{x}}$

---

7. C   **Advanced Mathematics (equivalent expressions) MEDIUM**

Original expression: $x(2x-4)(-x+3)$
Factor out a 2 from the middle term and -1 from the third term: $x(2)(x-2)(-1)(x-3)$
Use the Commutative Law of Multiplication to combine the numerical factors: $-2x(x-2)(x-3)$

---

8. C   **Algebra (linear equations) MEDIUM**

It's important first to notice that the first equation is in "slope-intercept" form ($y = mx + b$), the second is not, because x is isolated rather than y. It's also important to remember that parallel lines have equal slopes and perpendicular lines have slopes that are the opposite reciprocals of each other.

First equation: $y = -\frac{1}{2}x - 4$

Second equation: $x = 2y + 2$
Subtract 2: $x - 2 = 2y$
Divide by 2 (and "swap" the sides of the equation):
$$y = \frac{1}{2}x - 1$$

This shows that the first equation has a slope of $-1/2$ and the second has a slope of $1/2$. Since these slopes are neither equal nor opposite reciprocals, the two lines are neither parallel nor perpendicular. They are just intersecting lines.

---

9. A   **Algebra (interpreting formulas) MEDIUM**

Consider what the equation $p = 7x - 125$ would give in the situation where no smoothies are sold, that is $x = 0$. In that case, $p = 7(0) - 125$, which means that the smoothie cart would lose $125 on a day when no smoothies are sold. This indicates that 125 is the daily cost, in dollars, to run the smoothie cart.

---

10. C   Advanced Mathematics (dividing polynomials) MEDIUM-HARD

There are three ways to answer this question. One way is simply to divide the polynomials just as you would divide two numbers by long division:

$$
\begin{array}{r}
x - 1 \\
x-4{\overline{\smash{\big)}\,x^2 - 5x + 6}} \\
\underline{x^2 - 4x} \\
x + 6 \\
\underline{x + 4} \\
2
\end{array}
$$

This shows that the remainder is 2. If you're clever, you can accomplish the same task by using synthetic division (if you can remember it). The third way, for <u>really</u> clever folks, is to use the Remainder Theorem, which says that the remainder when the polynomial $P(x)$ is divided by $x - k$ is always equal to $P(k)$. In this case, that means that the remainder is $P(4) = (4)^2 - 5(4) + 6 = 16 - 20 + 6 = 2$.

---

11. B   **Advanced Mathematics (functions and symmetry) MEDIUM-HARD**

If $g(-x) = -g(x)$ for all x in the domain of g, then g is an <u>odd</u> function, which means that its graph in the xy-plane is symmetric with respect to the origin (that is, the graph looks the same upside-down or right-side-up). If g is a polynomial, then it must only have odd-degree terms (this is why it is called <u>odd</u> symmetry). Only choices A and B are odd functions, and only choice B satisfies the second condition, because $g(-2) = (-2)^3 = -8$.

12. D **Advanced Mathematics (quadratics)**
MEDIUM-HARD

One way to solve this equation is to use the quadratic equation, $x = \dfrac{-b \pm \sqrt{b^2 - 4ac}}{2a}$, to find the two solutions, then add them together. For this quadratic, $a = 3$, $b = -12$, and $c = 7$, so:

$$r = \frac{12 \pm \sqrt{(-12)^2 - 4(3)(7)}}{2(3)}$$

Simplify:
$$r = \frac{12 \pm \sqrt{60}}{6}$$

Simplify:
$$r = 2 \pm \frac{\sqrt{15}}{3}$$

Therefore the two solutions are $2 + 2\sqrt{10}$ and $2 - 2\sqrt{10}$, and their sum is 4.

But there is also a simpler way of answering this question, without having to find the individual solutions. You may recall the theorem that any quadratic in the form $x^2 - mx + n = 0$ (where m and n are constants) has two solutions whose sum is m and whose product is n. The quadratic $3r^2 - 12r + 7 = 0$ is not quite in this form, but we can easy get it in the right form by dividing both sides by 3, giving us $r^2 - 4r + \dfrac{7}{3} = 0$, which tells us that the two solutions to this equation have a sum of 4 and a product of $\dfrac{7}{3}$.

13. C **Additional Topics**
(complex numbers) MEDIUM-HARD

Original equation: $i^x i^y = 1$
Use the exponential identity $(x^m)(x^n) = x^{m+n}$: $i^{x+y} = 1$
Recall the "cycle" of the powers of i:

$$i^0 = 1, \; i^1 = i, \; i^2 = -1, \; i^3 = -i, \; i^4 = 1, \; i^5 = i \ldots$$

This shows that $i^n = 1$ if and only if n is a multiple of 4. Therefore, $x + y$ must be a multiple of 4. The only choice in which $x + y$ is a multiple of 4 is choice C.

14. D **Algebra (rates) HARD**

Ibrahim can collect and catalog flower specimens at a rate of 4 every hour, or 4 every 60 minutes, or 1/15 of a flower per minute. He can collect and catalog leaf specimens at a rate of 2 every 20 minutes, or 1/10 of a leaf per minute. Recall that, since $work = rate \times time$, we can find the time with the formula $time = work \div rate$. Therefore, the time it takes Ibrahim to collect and catalog f flowers at a rate of 1/15 of a flower per minute is $f \div (1/15) = 15f$ minutes. The time it takes him to collect and catalog l leaves at 1/10 of a leaf per minute is $l \div (1/10) = 10l$ minutes. Therefore, the total time required is $15f + 10l$ minutes, which is equivalent to choice D.

15. C **Advanced Mathematics (solving quadratics)**
HARD

Subsitute $y = -6x + 10$ into the second equation to solve for x: $-6x + 10 = x^2 - 7x + 10$
Subtract 10: $-6x = x^2 - 7x$
Add $7x$: $x = x^2$
Subtract x: $0 = x^2 - x$
Factor: $0 = (x)(x - 1)$
By the Zero Product Property, the solutions are $x = 0$ and $x = 1$.
If $x = 0$: $y = -6(0) + 10 = 10$
If $x = 1$: $y = -6(1) + 10 = 4$
Therefore, $x + y$ can equal $0 + 10 = 10$ or $1 + 4 = 5$. Therefore, the correct answer is C.

16. 8, 10, or 12 **Algebra (systems of linear equations) EASY**

Let l represent the number of long tosses that Mike makes and s represent the number of short tosses he makes. The total points he scores can be represented by the equation:
$$15l + 5s = 100$$
Divide by 5 on both sides: $3l + s = 20$
Mike makes at least 4 long tosses, so let's begin with $l = 4$:
If $l = 4$, then $3(4) + s = 20$, so $s = 8$ and the total number of tosses is $4 + 8 = 12$.
If $l = 5$, then $3(5) + s = 20$, so $s = 5$ and the total number of tosses is $5 + 5 = 10$.
If $l = 6$, then $3(6) + s = 20$, so $s = 2$ and the total number of tosses is $6 + 2 = 8$.

17. 16 **Algebra (manipulating expressions) EASY**

The expression $a^2 - 2ab + b^2$ can be factored as $(a - b)^2$. Since $a = b + 4$, subtracting b from both sides gives us $a - b = 4$. Therefore $(a - b)^2 = 4^2 = 16$.

18. 10 **Advanced Mathematics (radicals) MEDIUM**

Plug $w = 3\sqrt{5}$ into the equation $2w - \sqrt{20} = \sqrt{8y}$:

$$2(3\sqrt{5}) - \sqrt{20} = \sqrt{8y}$$

Simplify:
$$6\sqrt{5} - \sqrt{20} = \sqrt{8y}$$

Simplify $\sqrt{20}$ by factoring :
$$6\sqrt{5} - \sqrt{4}\sqrt{5} = \sqrt{8y}$$

Simplify:
$$6\sqrt{5} - 2\sqrt{5} = 4\sqrt{5} = \sqrt{8y}$$

Square both sides of the equation:
$$(4\sqrt{5})^2 = 8y$$

Simplify:
$$80 = 8y$$

Divide by 8:
$$10 = y$$

19. 3 Algebra (systems of linear equations) MEDIUM

If a system has infinitely many solutions, then the two equations represent the same graph in the xy-plane.
First equation: $mx + ny = 3$
Multiply both sides by 17 so that the equations "match" on the right side: $17mx + 17ny = 51$

This equation must be equivalent to $34x + 17y = 51$, so $17m = 34$ and $17n = 17$, and therefore $m = 2$ and $n = 1$. Therefore, $m + n = 3$.

20. **25/6 or 4.16 or 4.17**　　　　**Additional Topics (sectors, tangents, and triangles) HARD**

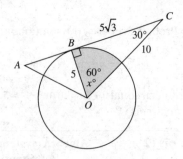

If AC is a tangent to the circle, then it is perpendicular to the radius to point B. Recall that the sine of an acute angle in a right triangle is the ratio of the opposite side to the hypotenuse. Therefore, if $\sin(x°) = \dfrac{\sqrt{3}}{2}$: $\dfrac{5\sqrt{3}}{OC} = \dfrac{\sqrt{3}}{2}$

Cross-multiply:　　　　　　　$10\sqrt{3} = (OC)(\sqrt{3})$
Divide by $\sqrt{3}$:　　　　　　　　　$10 = OC$
Now we can use the Pythagorean Theorem to find the length of OB:　　　　　　$(OB)^2 + (5\sqrt{3})^2 = 10^2$
Simplify:　　　　　　　　　　　$(OB)^2 + 75 = 100$
Subtract 75 from both sides:　　　　$(OB)^2 = 25$
Take the square root of both sides:　　　$OB = 5$
Therefore the circle has a radius of 5 and the circle has an area of $\pi(5)^2 = 25\pi$.

You should recognize this ratio of sides, $x : x\sqrt{3} : 2x$ as belonging to a 30°-60°-90° triangle, therefore $x = 60$ (you should also recall the basic trig fact that $\sin 60° = \dfrac{\sqrt{3}}{2}$), and therefore the sector is $60/360 = 1/6$ of the entire circle. So the area of the sector is $25\pi/6$, and so $k = 25/6$.

Section 4: Math (Calculator)

1. **A**　　　　　　　　　　　**Algebra (linear equations) EASY**

The y-intercept of a line is the value of y for which $x = 0$. Therefore, $3(0) - 2y = 12$, and so $-2y = 12$ and $y = -6$ is the y-intercept.

2. **B**　　　　　　　　　　　**Algebra (inequalities) EASY**

If $4n \geq 9$, then the LEAST possible value for $4n$ is 9. Therefore, the least possible value of $4n + 1$ is 10.

3. **A**　　　　　**Algebra (systems of linear equations) EASY**

Original system:　　　$\begin{cases} 4c + 7d = 29 \\ 2c + 3d = 13 \end{cases}$

Multiply the second equation by 2:　$\begin{cases} 4c + 7d = 29 \\ 4c + 6d = 26 \end{cases}$

Subtract the corresponding sides of the equations to eliminate c:　　　　　　　　　　$d = 3$
Substitute $d = 3$ into first equation:　$4c + 7(3) = 29$
Simplify:　　　　　　　　　　　　$4c = 8$
Divide by 4 on both sides:　　　　　　$c = 2$

4. **B**　　　　　**Problem Solving and Data Analysis (proportions) EASY**

Priscilla buys a 2 bags of soil for every 6 bags of fertilizer. If x represents the number of bags of fertilizer Priscilla bought, then we can set up a proportion:　$\dfrac{2}{6} = \dfrac{x}{132}$

Cross-multiply:　　　　　　　　　$6x = 264$
Divide by 6:　　　　　　　　　　　$x = 44$

5. **B**　　　　　　　　**Algebra (word problems) EASY**

Each addition costs \$0.30, so n additions cost \$0.30n. A \$2.50 coffee with n additions therefore costs $\$(0.3n + 2.5)$.

6. **D**　　　　**Algebra (compositions of functions) EASY**

Substitute $g(x) = 2x - 5$ into $f(g(x))$: $f(g(x)) = f(2x - 5) = -(2x - 5) + 3 = -2x + 5 + 3 = -2x + 8$

7. **A**　　　　　**Advanced Mathematics (subtracting polynomials) EASY**

Subtracting a number is equivalent to adding its opposite, so to simplify this expression we should distribute then combine like terms: $(3x^2 - 4x + 2) - (4x^2 - 3x - 1) = 3x^2 - 4x + 2 - 4x^2 + 3x + 1 = -x^2 - x + 3$

8. **B**　　　　　　　　**Additional Topics (trigonometry) EASY**

If $\cos x° = 4/5$ and $0 < x < 90$, then x can be considered as an acute angle in a triangle like the one below, in which the length of the adjacent side is 4 and the length of the hypotenuse is 5. You should recognize this as a 3-4-5 right triangle (or use the Pythagorean Theorem to find the missing side), and see that the tangent of x is therefore 3/4.

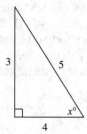

9. C   **Problem Solving and Data Analysis (statistical interpretation) MEDIUM**

An 85th percentile score is a score that "beats or equals" at least 85% of the other scores. In this context, that means that Jenna's best pole vault last year was at least as high as the best vault of 85% of the pole vaulters in the country last year.

10. C   **Problem Solving and Data Analysis (percents and inequalities) MEDIUM**

Frannie's buying constraints can be represented by the equation $60 \geq 1.05(0.8x)$, in which x is the original cost, in dollars, of the running shoes. In this inequality, $0.8x$ represents the cost after the 20% discount has been applied (the cost is 80% of the original price) and 1.05 is the factor that adds the 5% sales tax.

	$60 \geq 1.05(0.8x)$
Simplify:	$60 \geq 0.84x$
Divide by 0.84 on both sides:	$71.428 \geq x$

Therefore the maximum original cost for her shoes is $71.42.

11. D   **Advanced Mathematics (quadratic equations) MEDIUM**

Substitute $a = \dfrac{1}{b}$ into $a + b = 0$:	$\dfrac{1}{b} + b = 0$
Multiply both sides by b:	$1 + b^2 = 0$
Subtract 1 from both sides:	$b^2 = -1$

Since the square root of -1 is not a real number (it is the imaginary number i), then the solutions to this system are not real: $a = i$ and $b = -i$.

12. A   **Advanced Mathematics (exponential growth) MEDIUM**

If the population grows by 20% each week, then the population is multiplied by 1.20 each week. If this happens over the course of w consecutive weeks, the population is $p = p_0(1.2)^w$.

13. C   **Algebra (linear equations) MEDIUM**

Original equation:	$x - 3y - 12 = 0$
Add 12 to both sides:	$x - 3y = 12$

This puts the equation into "standard form" $(ax + by = c)$. The graph of a linear equation in this form has a slope of $-a/b$ and an x-intercept of c/a. (You should verify this yourself.) This means that this line has a slope of 1/3 and an x-intercept of $12/1 = 12$. The only equation that includes these two values as constants or coefficients is C.

14. B   **Advanced Mathematics (solving quadratics) MEDIUM**

The x-intercepts of the graph correspond to the zeros of the function. These can be found by setting each factor of the polynomial equal to 0. When we do this, choices A and B both yield x-intercepts of -2 and 3. However, only

choice B yields a graph with a y-intercept of 12, because $f(0) = (-2(0) - 4)(0 - 3) = (-4)(-3) = 12$.

15. A   **Advanced Mathematics (analyzing polynomial graphs) MEDIUM**

This function is undefined at those values of x that yield 0 in the denominator, since division by 0 is undefined. We can find these values by factoring the denominator and using the Zero Product Property:

$(x^2 - 5x - 6) = (x - 6)(x + 1)$; therefore, the denominator is 0 when $x = 6$ and $x = -1$.

16. C   **Problem Solving and Data Analysis (central tendency) MEDIUM**

The median is the middle value of the data when it is arranged in ascending or descending order. For 360 data points, the median is the average of the 180th and 181st data point. The corresponding medians for the four histograms are A) 41, B) 43, C) 42, and D) 41.

17. B   **Algebra (linear equations) MEDIUM-HARD**

To find p, we can use the equation, slope $= \dfrac{y_2 - y_1}{x_2 - x_1}$:

$$\frac{4 - (-p)}{-2p - 26} = \frac{1}{4}$$

Simplify:	$\dfrac{4 + p}{-2p - 26} = \dfrac{1}{4}$
Cross-multiply:	$16 + 4p = -2p - 26$
Add $2p$ to both sides:	$16 + 6p = -26$
Subtract 16 from both sides:	$6p = -42$
Divide by 6 on both sides:	$p = -7$

18. A   **Advanced Mathematics (solving quadratics) MEDIUM-HARD**

The solutions to the polynomial $3x^2 + 4x - 10 = 0$ can be found by using the quadratic equation, $x = \dfrac{-b \pm \sqrt{b^2 - 4ac}}{2a}$, for which $a = 3$, $b = 4$, and $c = -10$:

$$x = \frac{-4 \pm \sqrt{4^2 - 4(3)(-10)}}{2(3)}$$

Simplify:	$x = \dfrac{-4 \pm \sqrt{136}}{6}$
Simplify $\sqrt{136}$:	$x = \dfrac{-4 \pm 2\sqrt{34}}{6}$
Divide numerator and denominator by 2:	$x = \dfrac{-2 \pm \sqrt{34}}{3}$

19. D   **Problem Solving/Data Analysis (central tendency) MEDIUM-HARD**

When the mean of a set of numbers is significantly greater than the median, it is generally because of "upper outliers," that is, extreme values in the set that pull the average up without affecting the median. If a set of numbers is "symmetrical about the median," that is, they are symmetrically spaced on either side of the middle value,

of numbers is "symmetrical about the median," that is, they are symmetrically spaced on either side of the middle value, then the median and the average are equal, as in {1, 2, 5, 8, 9} where both the median and the average are 5. However, if we change 9 to 90, making it an "upper outlier," we get {1, 2, 5, 8, 90}, in which the median is still 5, but the average is now 21.2.

---

20. C   Algebra (expressing functional relationships) MEDIUM-HARD

We can plug in values from the table and work by process of elimination. We can begin by using the fact that $C = 1,500$ when $n = 2$.

A) $C(2) = 1,500(10^{2-1}) = 15,000$
B) $C(2) = 300(10^{2-1}) = 3,000$
C) $C(2) = 300(5^{2-1}) = 1,500$
D) $C(2) = 150(2^2) = 6,000$

Choice C is the only one that yields the correct value.

---

21. A   Problem Solving and Data Analysis (tables) MEDIUM-HARD

Each week, the number of reported cases is 5 times the number of the previous week. This means that the number is increasing by 400% each week, because $(5x - x)/x = 4 = 400\%$.

---

22. C   Problem Solving and Data Analysis (graphical analysis) MEDIUM-HARD

During week 1, all three leagues have 100% participation. According to the line of best fit, all three leagues have about 75% participation by week 10, so there was a drop of 25% participation over a 9-week span. Since $(25\%)(108) = 27$, this means that 27 players dropped out over the course of 9 weeks, or at the rate of $27/9 = 3$ players every week.

---

23. D   Advanced Mathematics (systems) MEDIUM

Second given equation: $\dfrac{m}{n} = \dfrac{4}{9}$

Cross-multiply: $9m = 4n$

Divide by 4: $\dfrac{9}{4}m = n$

First given equation: $m + n = 208$

Substitute $n = \dfrac{9}{4}m$: $m + \dfrac{9}{4}m = 208$

Simplify: $\dfrac{13}{4}m = 208$

Multiply both sides by $\dfrac{4}{13}$: $m = 64$

Substitute into $n = \dfrac{9}{4}m$: $n = \left(\dfrac{9}{4}\right)(64) = 144$

Therefore, $mn = (64)(144) = 9,216$

---

24. A   Problem Solving/Data Analysis (percent change) MEDIUM-HARD

The "percent change" formula is percent change = $\dfrac{\text{final quantity} - \text{original quantity}}{\text{original quantity}} \times 100\%$. For *Acropora palmata*, then, the percent change is $\dfrac{87 - 42}{87} \times 100 \approx 52\%$, which represents the greatest percent decline of any of the coral species in the table over the 10-year span.

---

25. B   Algebra (linear equations) MEDIUM-HARD

For *Acropora palmata*, the number lost per year is $p = \dfrac{87 - 42}{2005 - 2015} = -\dfrac{45}{10}$. For *Acropora cervicornis*, the number lost per year is $c = \dfrac{66 - 39}{2005 - 2015} = -\dfrac{27}{10}$. Therefore, $\dfrac{p}{c} = \dfrac{-\dfrac{45}{10}}{-\dfrac{27}{10}} = -\dfrac{45}{10} \times -\dfrac{10}{27} = \dfrac{45}{27} = \dfrac{5}{3}$.

---

26. B   Problem Solving and Data Analysis (ratios) HARD

The bakery's recipe calls for a 2:4:1 ratio of sugar to flour to butter. This means that the ratio, by weight, of flour to the other ingredients is $4:(2+1) = 4:3$. If the weight of the flour is 52 pounds and x represents the combined weight, in pounds, of sugar and butter, then: $\dfrac{4}{3} = \dfrac{52}{x}$

Cross-multiply: $4x = 156$
Divide by 4: $x = 39$

---

27. A   Algebra (analyzing formulas) HARD

The average of the upper limit and the lower limit of pressures is $\dfrac{3,300 + 2,600}{2} = 2,950$. This means that the acceptable values are centered on 2,950. Notice that the upper limit and the lower limit are both exactly 350 units away from this average so we can express the range of values as "all values that are within 350 units of 2,950," which can be expressed as P, where $|P - 2,950| \le 350$.

---

28. C   Problem Solving/Data Analysis (rates) MEDIUM-HARD

Recall the formula *distance = rate × time*. Let's define t as the total time of Derrick's run. Derrick ascended the mountain at a rate of 3 km/hour, which took him $\dfrac{5}{8}$ of the time, so his distance on the north trail was $3\left(\dfrac{5}{8}t\right) = \dfrac{15}{8}t$. He descended the mountain at a rate of 5 km/hour, which took him $\dfrac{3}{8}$ of the time, so his distance on the east trail was $5\left(\dfrac{3}{8}t\right) = \dfrac{15}{8}t$. Since these two distances are obviously equal, the north trail must have been 50% of the total distance.

---

29. **B**   Problem Solving/Data Analysis (numerical reasoning) HARD

Let's call the three integers, in ascending order, a, b, and c. Their sum is 17, so $a + b + c = 17$. If the product of the two smallest integers is 50% less than the product of the two greatest integers, then: $ab = 0.5bc$

Divide by b: $a = 0.5c$

Multiply by 2: $2a = c$

Since all of the numbers are integers, this indicates that c, the largest number, must be even. Since each integer is less than 10, the largest c could is is 8. Let's see if that works. If $c = 8$, then a must equal half of that, or 4. Since the sum of all three integers must be 17, b must equal $17 - 8 - 4 = 5$. Therefore, $a = 4$, $b = 5$, and $c = 8$.

---

30. **A** Additional Topics (geometry/polygons) HARD

As with many difficult geometry questions, it helps to draw some extra lines on the diagram. Label the center of the octagon O and consider the pentagon $OBCFE$, as show below.

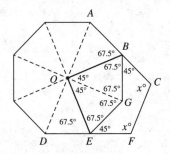

Each of the eight central angles at O is congruent, so each has the measure $360° \div 8 = 45°$. Likewise, each external angle to the octagon, like angle GBC, has the measure $360° \div 8 = 45°$. Each of the triangles inside the octagon is isosceles, so their base angles are congruent, so each must measure $(180° - 45°)/2 = 67.5°$. Recall that the sum of the interior angles to any n-sided polygon is $180°(n - 2)$, so the sum of the interior angles to pentagon $OBCFE$ must be $180°(5 - 2) = 540°$: $90 + 112.5 + x + x + 112.5 = 540$

Simplify: $315 + 2x = 540$

Subtract 315: $2x = 225$

Divide by 2: $x = 112.5$

---

31. **4 or 9**   Problem Solving/Data Analysis (proportions) EASY

If Delaney bought one $5 grand prize raffle ticket, she would have $23 left to buy regular prize raffle tickets. However, since $23 is not evenly divisible by $2, she would have to buy either 2 or 4 grand prize raffle tickets. If she bought 2 grand prize raffle tickets for $10, she could buy 9 regular prize raffle tickets for $18. If she bought 4 grand prize raffle tickets for $20, she could buy 4 regular prize raffle tickets for $8.

---

32. **20**   Algebra (systems) MEDIUM

If 30% of a is equal to 10% of b: $0.3a = 0.1b$

Multiply both sides by 10: $3a = b$

Substitute $b = 3a$ into $a + b = 80$: $a + 3a = 80$

Simplify: $4a = 80$

Divide by 4: $a = 20$

---

33. **40**   Problem Solving and Data Analysis (percents) MEDIUM

A total of $76 + 114 = 190$ sprinters had a day of rest the day before the race. Of those 190 people, 76 did not beat their PR. $\frac{76}{190} \times 100\% = 40\%$.

---

34. **.04 or 1/25**   Problem Solving and Data Analysis (probability) MEDIUM

The probability that she makes both is $p^2 = 0.64$, and therefore $p = 0.8$. This means that the probability that she will miss a free throw is $1 - 0.8 = 0.2$. The probability that she will miss two consecutively, then, is $(0.2)(0.2) = 0.04$.

---

35. **.8 or 4/5**   Advanced Mathematics (radians) MEDIUM-HARD

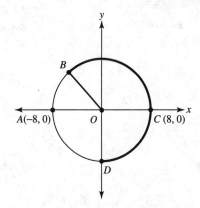

The circle has a radius of 8, and so its circumference is $2\pi(8) = 16\pi$. Arc $ABCD$ is three-fourths of the circumference, so it has a length of $(0.75)(16\pi) = 12\pi$. Since arc BCD has a length of $\frac{60\pi - 32}{5}$, arc AB has a length of $12\pi - \frac{60\pi - 32}{5} = \frac{60\pi}{5} - \frac{60\pi - 32}{5} = \frac{32}{5} = 6.4$. The radian measure of angle AOB is equal to the ratio of the length of its intercepted arc to the length of the radius: $6.4 \div 8 = 0.8 = 4/5$.

36. **5**   Advanced Mathematics (exponentials)
MEDIUM

Original equation:	$4(2^{y-2}) = 32^x$
Substitute $4 = 2^2$ and $32 = 2^5$:	$2^2(2^{y-2}) = (2^5)^x$
Simplify both sides:	$2^y = 2^{5x}$
If $|x| > 1$ and $x^a = x^b$, then $a = b$:	$y = 5x$
Divide both sides by x:	$\dfrac{y}{x} = 5$

37. **885**   Problem Solving (interpreting formulas)
HARD

In the formula $m = 1,000k^n$, the constant k represents the factor that multiplies Dave's production load each week. Since this workload is decreasing by 4% each week, he is doing 96%, or 0.96, of the previous week's work. Therefore, $k = 0.96$, and so the complete equation relating m and n is $m = 1,000(0.96)^n$. To find his production load in the third week, then we simply let $n = 3$: $1,000(0.96)^3 = 884.74$, which rounds to 885.

38. **220**   Problem Solving (percents/exponential expressions) HARD

In the 52nd week of the phase out, Dave's production load is $1,000(0.96)^{52} = 119.70$ units, which rounds to 120 units. This is $1,000 - 120 = 880$ fewer units than he had been producing before the phase-out. This means that the most experience glassblower must absorb $(0.50)(880) = 440$ units and the least experience glassblower must absorb $(0.25)(880) = 220$ units, so the difference is $440 - 220 = 220$ units.

PRACTICE SAT 6

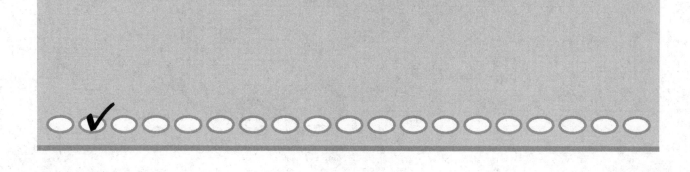

ANSWER SHEET

SECTION 1

#		#		#		#		#	
1	Ⓐ Ⓑ Ⓒ Ⓓ	13	Ⓐ Ⓑ Ⓒ Ⓓ	25	Ⓐ Ⓑ Ⓒ Ⓓ	37	Ⓐ Ⓑ Ⓒ Ⓓ	49	Ⓐ Ⓑ Ⓒ Ⓓ
2	Ⓐ Ⓑ Ⓒ Ⓓ	14	Ⓐ Ⓑ Ⓒ Ⓓ	26	Ⓐ Ⓑ Ⓒ Ⓓ	38	Ⓐ Ⓑ Ⓒ Ⓓ	50	Ⓐ Ⓑ Ⓒ Ⓓ
3	Ⓐ Ⓑ Ⓒ Ⓓ	15	Ⓐ Ⓑ Ⓒ Ⓓ	27	Ⓐ Ⓑ Ⓒ Ⓓ	39	Ⓐ Ⓑ Ⓒ Ⓓ	51	Ⓐ Ⓑ Ⓒ Ⓓ
4	Ⓐ Ⓑ Ⓒ Ⓓ	16	Ⓐ Ⓑ Ⓒ Ⓓ	28	Ⓐ Ⓑ Ⓒ Ⓓ	40	Ⓐ Ⓑ Ⓒ Ⓓ	52	Ⓐ Ⓑ Ⓒ Ⓓ
5	Ⓐ Ⓑ Ⓒ Ⓓ	17	Ⓐ Ⓑ Ⓒ Ⓓ	29	Ⓐ Ⓑ Ⓒ Ⓓ	41	Ⓐ Ⓑ Ⓒ Ⓓ		
6	Ⓐ Ⓑ Ⓒ Ⓓ	18	Ⓐ Ⓑ Ⓒ Ⓓ	30	Ⓐ Ⓑ Ⓒ Ⓓ	42	Ⓐ Ⓑ Ⓒ Ⓓ		
7	Ⓐ Ⓑ Ⓒ Ⓓ	19	Ⓐ Ⓑ Ⓒ Ⓓ	31	Ⓐ Ⓑ Ⓒ Ⓓ	43	Ⓐ Ⓑ Ⓒ Ⓓ		
8	Ⓐ Ⓑ Ⓒ Ⓓ	20	Ⓐ Ⓑ Ⓒ Ⓓ	32	Ⓐ Ⓑ Ⓒ Ⓓ	44	Ⓐ Ⓑ Ⓒ Ⓓ		
9	Ⓐ Ⓑ Ⓒ Ⓓ	21	Ⓐ Ⓑ Ⓒ Ⓓ	33	Ⓐ Ⓑ Ⓒ Ⓓ	45	Ⓐ Ⓑ Ⓒ Ⓓ		
10	Ⓐ Ⓑ Ⓒ Ⓓ	22	Ⓐ Ⓑ Ⓒ Ⓓ	34	Ⓐ Ⓑ Ⓒ Ⓓ	46	Ⓐ Ⓑ Ⓒ Ⓓ		
11	Ⓐ Ⓑ Ⓒ Ⓓ	23	Ⓐ Ⓑ Ⓒ Ⓓ	35	Ⓐ Ⓑ Ⓒ Ⓓ	47	Ⓐ Ⓑ Ⓒ Ⓓ		
12	Ⓐ Ⓑ Ⓒ Ⓓ	24	Ⓐ Ⓑ Ⓒ Ⓓ	36	Ⓐ Ⓑ Ⓒ Ⓓ	48	Ⓐ Ⓑ Ⓒ Ⓓ		

SECTION 2

#		#		#		#		#	
1	Ⓐ Ⓑ Ⓒ Ⓓ	11	Ⓐ Ⓑ Ⓒ Ⓓ	21	Ⓐ Ⓑ Ⓒ Ⓓ	31	Ⓐ Ⓑ Ⓒ Ⓓ	41	Ⓐ Ⓑ Ⓒ Ⓓ
2	Ⓐ Ⓑ Ⓒ Ⓓ	12	Ⓐ Ⓑ Ⓒ Ⓓ	22	Ⓐ Ⓑ Ⓒ Ⓓ	32	Ⓐ Ⓑ Ⓒ Ⓓ	42	Ⓐ Ⓑ Ⓒ Ⓓ
3	Ⓐ Ⓑ Ⓒ Ⓓ	13	Ⓐ Ⓑ Ⓒ Ⓓ	23	Ⓐ Ⓑ Ⓒ Ⓓ	33	Ⓐ Ⓑ Ⓒ Ⓓ	43	Ⓐ Ⓑ Ⓒ Ⓓ
4	Ⓐ Ⓑ Ⓒ Ⓓ	14	Ⓐ Ⓑ Ⓒ Ⓓ	24	Ⓐ Ⓑ Ⓒ Ⓓ	34	Ⓐ Ⓑ Ⓒ Ⓓ	44	Ⓐ Ⓑ Ⓒ Ⓓ
5	Ⓐ Ⓑ Ⓒ Ⓓ	15	Ⓐ Ⓑ Ⓒ Ⓓ	25	Ⓐ Ⓑ Ⓒ Ⓓ	35	Ⓐ Ⓑ Ⓒ Ⓓ		
6	Ⓐ Ⓑ Ⓒ Ⓓ	16	Ⓐ Ⓑ Ⓒ Ⓓ	26	Ⓐ Ⓑ Ⓒ Ⓓ	36	Ⓐ Ⓑ Ⓒ Ⓓ		
7	Ⓐ Ⓑ Ⓒ Ⓓ	17	Ⓐ Ⓑ Ⓒ Ⓓ	27	Ⓐ Ⓑ Ⓒ Ⓓ	37	Ⓐ Ⓑ Ⓒ Ⓓ		
8	Ⓐ Ⓑ Ⓒ Ⓓ	18	Ⓐ Ⓑ Ⓒ Ⓓ	28	Ⓐ Ⓑ Ⓒ Ⓓ	38	Ⓐ Ⓑ Ⓒ Ⓓ		
9	Ⓐ Ⓑ Ⓒ Ⓓ	19	Ⓐ Ⓑ Ⓒ Ⓓ	29	Ⓐ Ⓑ Ⓒ Ⓓ	39	Ⓐ Ⓑ Ⓒ Ⓓ		
10	Ⓐ Ⓑ Ⓒ Ⓓ	20	Ⓐ Ⓑ Ⓒ Ⓓ	30	Ⓐ Ⓑ Ⓒ Ⓓ	40	Ⓐ Ⓑ Ⓒ Ⓓ		

SECTION 3

1 Ⓐ Ⓑ Ⓒ Ⓓ
2 Ⓐ Ⓑ Ⓒ Ⓓ
3 Ⓐ Ⓑ Ⓒ Ⓓ
4 Ⓐ Ⓑ Ⓒ Ⓓ
5 Ⓐ Ⓑ Ⓒ Ⓓ
6 Ⓐ Ⓑ Ⓒ Ⓓ
7 Ⓐ Ⓑ Ⓒ Ⓓ
8 Ⓐ Ⓑ Ⓒ Ⓓ
9 Ⓐ Ⓑ Ⓒ Ⓓ
10 Ⓐ Ⓑ Ⓒ Ⓓ

11 Ⓐ Ⓑ Ⓒ Ⓓ
12 Ⓐ Ⓑ Ⓒ Ⓓ
13 Ⓐ Ⓑ Ⓒ Ⓓ
14 Ⓐ Ⓑ Ⓒ Ⓓ
15 Ⓐ Ⓑ Ⓒ Ⓓ

Student-Produced Responses

ONLY ANSWERS ENTERED IN THE CIRCLES IN EACH GRID WILL BE SCORED. YOU WILL NOT RECEIVE CREDIT FOR ANYTHING WRITTEN IN THE BOXES ABOVE THE CIRCLES.

16 17 18 19 20

SECTION 4

1 Ⓐ Ⓑ Ⓒ Ⓓ
2 Ⓐ Ⓑ Ⓒ Ⓓ
3 Ⓐ Ⓑ Ⓒ Ⓓ
4 Ⓐ Ⓑ Ⓒ Ⓓ
5 Ⓐ Ⓑ Ⓒ Ⓓ
6 Ⓐ Ⓑ Ⓒ Ⓓ
7 Ⓐ Ⓑ Ⓒ Ⓓ
8 Ⓐ Ⓑ Ⓒ Ⓓ
9 Ⓐ Ⓑ Ⓒ Ⓓ
10 Ⓐ Ⓑ Ⓒ Ⓓ

11 Ⓐ Ⓑ Ⓒ Ⓓ
12 Ⓐ Ⓑ Ⓒ Ⓓ
13 Ⓐ Ⓑ Ⓒ Ⓓ
14 Ⓐ Ⓑ Ⓒ Ⓓ
15 Ⓐ Ⓑ Ⓒ Ⓓ
16 Ⓐ Ⓑ Ⓒ Ⓓ
17 Ⓐ Ⓑ Ⓒ Ⓓ
18 Ⓐ Ⓑ Ⓒ Ⓓ
19 Ⓐ Ⓑ Ⓒ Ⓓ
20 Ⓐ Ⓑ Ⓒ Ⓓ

21 Ⓐ Ⓑ Ⓒ Ⓓ
22 Ⓐ Ⓑ Ⓒ Ⓓ
23 Ⓐ Ⓑ Ⓒ Ⓓ
24 Ⓐ Ⓑ Ⓒ Ⓓ
25 Ⓐ Ⓑ Ⓒ Ⓓ
26 Ⓐ Ⓑ Ⓒ Ⓓ
27 Ⓐ Ⓑ Ⓒ Ⓓ
28 Ⓐ Ⓑ Ⓒ Ⓓ
29 Ⓐ Ⓑ Ⓒ Ⓓ
30 Ⓐ Ⓑ Ⓒ Ⓓ

Student-Produced Responses

ONLY ANSWERS ENTERED IN THE CIRCLES IN EACH GRID WILL BE SCORED. YOU WILL NOT RECEIVE CREDIT FOR ANYTHING WRITTEN IN THE BOXES ABOVE THE CIRCLES.

31

32

33

34

35

36

37

38

SECTION 5: ESSAY

You may wish to remove these sample answer document pages to respond to the practice SAT Essay Test.

Begin ESSAY here.

_____

_____

_____

_____

_____

_____

_____

_____

_____

_____

_____

_____

_____

_____

_____

_____

_____

_____

_____

_____

_____

_____

_____

_____

_____

_____

If you need more space, please continue on the next page.

Cut Here

ESSAY

Cut Here

ESSAY

If you need more space, please continue on the next page.

ESSAY

1   1

Reading Test

65 MINUTES, 52 QUESTIONS

Turn to Section 1 of your answer sheet to answer the questions in this section.

DIRECTIONS

Each passage or pair of passages below is followed by a number of questions. After reading each passage or pair, choose the best answer to each question based on what is stated or implied in the passage or passages and in any accompanying graphics (such as a table or graph).

Questions 1–11 are based on the following passage.

This passage is adapted from Jane Austen, *Mansfield Park*, originally published in 1814. In this story, Fanny Price is talking to her cousin Edmund Bertram, son of Sir Thomas Bertram, about the prospective marriage between Edmund's sister Maria and Mr. Rushworth, the wealthy but foolish owner of the Sotherton estate.

Line
"Tomorrow, I think, my uncle dines at Sotherton," said Fanny. "I hope my uncle may continue to like Mr. Rushworth."

"That is impossible, Fanny, "Edmund replied.
5 "My father must like him less after tomorrow's visit, for we shall be five hours in his company. I dread the evil to follow—the impression it must leave on Sir Thomas. He cannot much longer deceive himself. I would give anything that
10 Rushworth and Maria had never met."

In this quarter, indeed, disappointment was impending over Sir Thomas. Not all his good-will for Mr. Rushworth and the advantages he offered Maria, not all Mr. Rushworth's deference for him,
15 could prevent him from soon discerning some part of the truth—that Mr. Rushworth was an inferior young man, as ignorant in business as in books, with opinions in general unfixed, and without seeming much aware of it himself.
20 He had expected a very different son-in-law; and beginning to feel grave on Maria's account, he tried to understand *her* feelings. Little

observation there was necessary to tell him that indifference was the most favorable state they
25 could be in. Her behavior to Mr. Rushworth was careless and cold. She could not, did not like him. Sir Thomas resolved to speak seriously to her. Advantageous as would be the alliance, and long standing and public as was the engagement, her
30 happiness must not be sacrificed to it.

With solemn kindness Sir Thomas addressed her: told her his fears, inquired into her wishes, entreated her to be open and sincere, and assured her that every inconvenience should be braved,
35 and the connection entirely given up, if she felt herself unhappy in the prospect of it. He would act for her and release her. Maria had a moment's struggle as she listened, and only a moment's: when her father ceased, she was able to give
40 her answer immediately, decidedly, and with no apparent agitation. She thanked him for his great attention and kindness, but told him he was quite mistaken in supposing she had the smallest desire of breaking her engagement, or was
45 sensible of any change of inclination since her forming it. She had the highest esteem for Mr. Rushworth, and she could not have a doubt of her happiness with him.

Sir Thomas was satisfied. Mr. Rushworth was
50 young enough to improve. Mr. Rushworth must and would improve in good society; and if Maria could now speak so securely of her happiness with him, speaking certainly without the blindness of love, she ought to be believed. A well-
55 disposed young woman, who did not marry for

CONTINUE ➤

love, was in general but the more attached to her own family. And the nearness of Mr. Rushworth's Sotherton estate to his own Mansfield must naturally hold out the greatest temptation, and
60 would, in all probability, be a continual supply of the most amiable and innocent enjoyments. Such were the reasonings of Sir Thomas.

To Maria the conference closed as satisfactorily as to him. She was in a state of mind to be
65 glad that she had secured her fate beyond recall; that she had pledged herself anew to Sotherton; that she was safe from the possibility of giving Henry Crawford the triumph of governing her actions and destroying her prospect. She retired
70 in proud resolve, determined only to behave more cautiously to Mr. Rushworth in future, that her father might not be again suspecting her.

Had Sir Thomas applied to his daughter within the first three or four days after Crawford's
75 leaving, before her feelings were at all tranquilized, before she had given up every hope of him,

her answer might have been different; but after another three or four days, when there was no return, no letter, no message, no symptom of a
80 softened heart, no hope of advantage from separation, her mind became cool enough to seek all the comfort that pride and self revenge could give.

Henry Crawford had destroyed her happiness, but he should not know that he had done it;
85 he should not destroy her credit, her appearance, her prosperity, too. He should not get to think of her as pining in retirement of Mansfield for *him*, rejecting Sotherton and London, independence and splendor, for *his* sake. Independence
90 was more needful than ever; the want of it at Mansfield more sensibly felt. She was less and less able to endure the restraint which her father imposed. She must escape from him and Mansfield as soon as possible, and find consola-
95 tion in fortune and consequence, bustle and the world, for a wounded spirit. Her mind was quite determined, and varied not.

CONTINUE ➡

1

1

1. The opening conversation between Fanny and Edmund suggests most strongly that

A) Edmund believes that his father will grow to dislike Mr. Rushworth.

B) Edmund regrets how he has portrayed Mr. Rushworth to his father.

C) Fanny and Edmund are conspiring together to sabotage Maria's engagement.

D) Edmund believes that his father is dangerously unpredictable.

2. The passage suggests that the engagement between Maria Bertram and Mr. Rushworth

A) is being kept as a secret within the family.

B) has only recently been announced.

C) is against Maria's will.

D) has been well-known for a long time.

3. Which choice provides the best evidence for the answer to the previous question?

A) Lines 25–26 ("Her . . . cold")

B) Lines 28–30 ("Advantageous . . . it")

C) Lines 36–37 ("He . . . release her")

D) Lines 91–93 ("She was . . . imposed")

4. As used in line 27, "resolved" most nearly means

A) analyzed.

B) decided.

C) rectified.

D) agreed.

5. It can be inferred that Henry Crawford is

A) a family member who is attempting to thwart Maria's engagement.

B) a former love interest of Maria who has spurned her.

C) a business rival of Mr. Rushworth.

D) a mysterious gentleman who is in love with Maria.

6. Maria resolves to "behave more cautiously" (lines 70–71) because she

A) is concerned that Henry Crawford will learn of her engagement.

B) does not want to offend her father.

C) feels responsible for hurting Mr. Rushworth's feelings.

D) does not want to give the impression that she does not want to marry Mr. Rushworth.

7. Which of the following best summarizes the meaning of the sentence in lines 73–83 ("Had Sir . . . give")?

A) Maria's feelings had transformed from desperation to vengeance.

B) Sir Thomas had lost all hope of understanding Maria's point of view.

C) Maria was still hoping to rekindle the affection of a former lover.

D) Maria's love for Mr. Rushworth had become steadfast.

CONTINUE ➤

1   **1**

8

Sir Thomas believes that a loveless marriage tends to bring

A) dishonor to the family.

B) needless hardship for the couple.

C) solidarity with the rest of the family.

D) misery for the couple's children.

9

Which choice provides the best evidence for the answer to the previous question?

A) Lines 20–22 ("He . . . feelings")

B) Line 27 ("Sir . . . her")

C) Lines 31–36 ("With . . . it")

D) Lines 54–57 ("A . . . family")

10

In line 65, "recall" most nearly means

A) remembrance.

B) regret.

C) retort.

D) retraction.

11

The tone conveyed in the last two sentences is primarily a combination of

A) seriousness and humor.

B) repulsion and attraction.

C) desperation and defiance.

D) love and indifference.

CONTINUE

1

1

This passage is adapted from Rob Margetta, "Where Do Rats Move After Disasters?" published November 5, 2015, in *Discoveries*. Courtesy of the National Science Foundation.

Line   For hundreds of years, humans have worried about rats as agents of disease. In the 11th century, the Persian scholar Avicenna observed that an epidemic of dead rats foreshadowed deadly
5   human epidemics. When rats die, their fleas—the carriers of plague bacteria—seek the closest possible new hosts, who are often people or their domestic animals. In 2015, scientists investigated the rat population of New York City (by some esti-
10 mates as large as the human population of 8 million) and found that at least one type of flea prevalent in the rodents could transmit bubonic plague. Fortunately, no evidence of infection was found in the fleas and, as a bacterial dis-
15 ease, plague can be treated with antibiotics. Nonetheless, the thought of plague is so horrific and its connection to rats so ingrained, that even some modern scientists are still obsessing over the topic.
20   Not so with Tulane University molecular ecologist Michael Blum and his research team. After Hurricane Katrina, Dr. Blum began a study to investigate how pathogens carried by rats corresponded with Katrina's flooding. Age-old
25 rat prejudice would suggest a very high correlation between rat population and disease in a natural disaster. Dr. Blum and his team have been trapping rats for six months a year in each of the last three years. Often in 100 degrees and
30 high humidity, they go door-to-door in neighborhoods where people have grown tired of being studied by outsiders in the decade since Hurricane Katrina. On a "good" day, they handle up to a dozen disease-carrying rats. The work
35 may sound unpleasant, but Blum says it's laying the groundwork for a potentially powerful tool in disaster relief: a mathematical model that could simulate how environmental changes, natural or man-made, affect populations of rodents that
40 carry pathogens hazardous to human health. It also provides better data on the rat population,

which can be used to guide smarter public policies.

    Risk perception is incredibly important. It
45 drives personal decisions and government action: it doesn't matter where the rats are, but where people think they are. If policymakers perceive that the highest risk of infestation is in densely populated areas, they will concentrate counter-
50 measures in those places. But what if that perception is based on incorrect assumptions, or if there are unexplored variables at work?

    The research, in fact, challenges conventional beliefs and expectations about the rodent
55 populations and their movements after disasters. Blum's findings contradict some previous assumptions. For one, a greater human population density doesn't necessarily mean more rats. In fact, Blum found that rats moved in when
60 humans abandoned spaces.

    "There is a relationship between population density and rodent densities here," Blum said. "But it's an inverse one. We're finding hot-spots in the city associated with abandonment." Another
65 early finding deals with the type of risks rat populations present to humans. Blum's team focuses on harmful pathogens rodents might carry and make people sick. Oddly enough, the much-feared plague is not a concern at all because the
70 plague bacteria does not naturally exist in the U.S except in scattered rural areas. The greater threats are those associated with contaminated water and soil, like *leptospirosis*, *bartonella* and *hantavirus*. Humans become infected by drink-
75 ing or swimming in water or having close contact with wet soil tainted by rodent droppings that carry the pathogens. While these diseases are mostly considered problems in the developing world, particularly in tropical areas, Blum and
80 his team's findings present deviations again from the conventional expectations. *Leptospirosis*, for example, is "actually prevalent across the New Orleans landscape," he said. "In some areas, up to 30 percent of rats carry the pathogen."
85   When combined, those two findings—how human behaviors affect where rats actually live and the diseases rats carry—illustrate how the researchers' findings could help protect areas after disasters, and the team's findings could
90 provide a factual basis for risk perception.

CONTINUE ▶

1   **1**

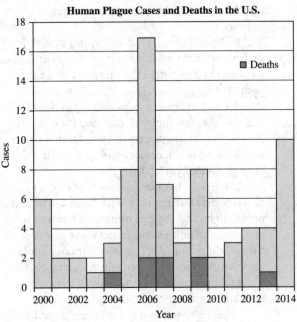

Human Plague Cases and Deaths in the U.S.

Year

Source: Centers for Disease Control and Prevention, Division of Vector-borne Diseases

---

12

The first paragraph serves primarily to

A) establish the magnitude of a problem.

B) dispute a widespread belief.

C) illustrate the validity of a theory.

D) indicate the extent of an attitude.

13

As used in line 24, "corresponded with" most nearly means

A) coincided with.

B) induced.

C) communicated with.

D) consented to.

14

The accompanying graph shows the data for the 80 reported cases of the plague in the United States in the 15 years from 2000 to 2014. Which statement about plague deaths in the United States is most justified by this graph?

A) They constituted 10% of all cases throughout the entire period.

B) They increased steadily during this period.

C) They were permanently eliminated in 2014.

D) They doubled between 2004 and 2005.

15

Michael Blum's research was motivated primarily by a desire to

A) find a cure for rat-borne diseases.

B) base public health policy on data rather than assumptions.

C) help New Orleans to recover economically after hurricane Katrina.

D) control the rat population in large cities.

16

Which choice provides the best evidence for the answer to the previous question?

A) Lines 5–8 ("When . . . animals")

B) Lines 22–24 ("After . . . flooding")

C) Lines 40–43 ("It also . . . policies")

D) Lines 59–60 ("In fact . . . spaces")

CONTINUE

1

1

17

The author uses quotation marks in line 33 to indicate that

A) New Orleans was profoundly affected by hurricane Katrina.

B) the goals of scientists do not always correspond to the goals of non-scientists.

C) the weather in New Orleans is frequently very pleasant.

D) the scientists were making progress in eradicating disease.

18

In context, the statement "it doesn't matter where the rats are" (line 46) is best interpreted to mean

A) rats are not as dangerous as many people believe.

B) scientists are not as concerned with rats as they are with the pathogens that rats carry.

C) the geographical location of an epidemic is not as important as its intensity.

D) policymakers are guided more by perception than by fact.

19

As used in line 49, "concentrate" most nearly means

A) reduce.

B) hoard.

C) focus.

D) think.

20

Blum's team found that rat populations

A) flourish as human populations begin to decline.

B) transmit the plague virus to humans by biting them.

C) tend to proliferate in high-density urban areas.

D) are being decimated by the *hantavirus.*

21

The author regards the plague in the United States as

A) a problem that intensifies as rat populations grow.

B) an isolated and manageable health risk.

C) an scourge about which surprisingly little is known.

D) a disease that is becoming increasingly resistant to treatment.

22

Which choice provides the best evidence for the answer to the previous question?

A) Lines 5–8 ("When . . . animals")

B) Lines 16–19 ("Nonetheless . . . topic")

C) Lines 24–27 ("Age-old . . . disaster")

D) Lines 68–71 ("Oddly . . . areas")

CONTINUE

1   **1**

Questions 23–32 are based on the following passages.

Passage 1 is adapted from John Adams, *Autobiography, Part I*, originally published circa 1802. Passage 2 is adapted from Jim Powell, "Thomas Paine, Passionate Pamphleteer for Liberty," originally published in *The Freeman* on January 1, 1996.

Passage 1

Line   This winter in Philadelphia appeared a Disastrous Meteor—Thomas Paine. He got into such company as would converse with him, pick-ing up what information he could concerning our
5 affairs. He gleaned the commonplace arguments such as the "Necessity of Independence," the justice of it, the provocation to it, our ability to maintain it. Dr. Benjamin Rush put him upon writing on the subject, furnished him with the
10 arguments which had been urged in Congress a hundred times, and gave him the title of *Common Sense* for his pamphlet.

    The "Arguments" in favor of Independence I liked very well. But the "Arguments" from the
15 Old Testament on the unlawfulness of monarchy were ridiculous, either from foolish superstition or from willful sophistry. The third part, a plan to a form of Government, was so democratical, without any restraint or attempt at any equi-
20 librium or counterpoise, that it must produce confusion and every evil work. I regretted to see so foolish a plan recommended to the people of the United States who were all waiting only for Congress to institute their State Governments. I
25 dreaded the effect so popular a pamphlet might have among the people, and determined to do all in my power to counteract the effect of it.

    The part of *Common Sense* which relates wholly to the question of Independence was
30 clearly written and contained a tolerable sum-mary of the arguments which I had been repeat-ing for nine months. But there is not a fact nor a reason stated in it which had not been frequently urged in Congress, and the phrases such as "The
35 Royal Brute of England," "The Blood upon his Soul," and a few others of equal delicacy had as

much weight with the people as his arguments. It has been a general opinion that this pamphlet was of great importance in the Revolution. I
40 doubted it at the time and have doubted it to this day.

    Notwithstanding these doubts, I felt myself obliged to Paine for the pains he had taken and for his good intentions to serve us, of which I then
45 had no doubt.

Passage 2

    With simple, bold, and inspiring prose, Thomas Paine launched a furious attack on tyranny. He denounced kings as inevitably cor-rupted by political power. He broke with previ-
50 ous political thinkers when he suggested a civil society where individuals pursue private pro-ductive lives. Paine envisioned a "Continental Union" based on individual rights. He answered objections from those who feared a break with
55 England. He called for a declaration to stir people into action.

    Common Sense crackled with unforgettable lines. For example: "Society is produced by our wants, and government by our wickedness . . .
60 The sun never shined on a cause of greater worth . . . to form the noblest, purest constitution on the face of the earth . . . O! Ye that love mankind! Ye that dare oppose not only the tyranny but the tyrant, stand forth! . . . We have it in our power to
65 begin the world over again . . . The birthday of a new world is at hand."

    The first edition, published on January 10, 1776, sold out quickly. Within three months, over 120,000 copies had been printed. Dr. Rush
70 recalled, "Its effects were sudden and extensive upon the American mind. It was read by public men, repeated in clubs, spouted in schools, and in one instance, delivered from the pulpit instead of a sermon." George Washington declared that
75 *Common Sense* offered "sound doctrine and unanswerable reasoning."

    Paine's incendiary ideas leaped across bor-ders. An edition appeared in French-speaking Quebec. John Adams reported that it was
80 "received in France and all Europe with rapture."

CONTINUE ➤

Common Sense was translated into German and Danish, and copies got into Russia. Altogether, some 500,000 copies were sold.

Before *Common Sense*, most colonists still
85 hoped things could work out with England. Then suddenly, increasing numbers spoke openly for independence. The Second Continental Congress asked Thomas Jefferson to serve on a five-person committee that would draft the declaration Paine
90 had suggested in *Common Sense*.

"Thomas Paine's *Common Sense*," reflected Harvard University historian Bernard Bailyn, "is the most brilliant pamphlet written during the American Revolution, and one of the most
95 brilliant pamphlets ever written in the English language. How it could have been produced by the bankrupt Quaker corset-maker, the some-time teacher, preacher, and grocer, and twice-dismissed excise officer who happened to catch
100 Benjamin Franklin's attention in England and who arrived in America only fourteen months before *Common Sense* was published is nothing one can explain without explaining genius itself."

CONTINUE

23

The two passages disagree about all of the following aspects of *Common Sense* EXCEPT

A) its significance in inspiring revolution.

B) the soundness of its arguments.

C) the extent of its popular appeal.

D) the genius of its author.

24

Adams uses the word "delicacy" in line 36 in order to make the point that Paine was not

A) as articulate in his arguments as he should have been.

B) particularly bold in his assertions about the need for independence.

C) as attuned to the sensibilities of the people as he should have been.

D) particularly subtle in his characterizations.

25

In lines 19–20, "equilibrium" refers primarily to a balance between

A) rule by the people and rule by the elite.

B) emotional appeal and logical persuasion.

C) obedience to the monarchy and independence from foreign rule.

D) economic pragmatism and social pragmatism.

26

John Adams would most likely respond to the claim in Passage 2 that "Paine launched a furious attack on tyranny" by pointing out that this attack was

A) not as furious as it should have been.

B) useful in rousing public opinion.

C) not argumentatively sound.

D) a cornerstone of revolutionary thought.

27

Which choice provides the best evidence for the previous question?

A) Lines 5–8 ("He . . . maintain it")

B) Lines 14–17 ("But . . . sophistry")

C) Lines 21–24 ("I regretted . . . Governments")

D) Lines 28–32 ("The part . . . months")

1   1

28

It can be inferred from the passages that John Adams and George Washington had different opinions about

A) the sincerity of Paine's efforts.

B) the benefits of independence.

C) the cogency of Paine's writing.

D) the brutality of British rule.

29

The positions listed in lines 97–99 are intended to highlight Paine's

A) plentiful experience in public service.

B) impeccable ethical standards.

C) extensive professional education.

D) relatively humble background.

30

The author of Passage 2 would most likely respond to the doubts that Adams expresses in lines 39–41 by saying that *Common Sense*

A) converted many colonists to the cause of independence.

B) denounced the monarchy in particularly harsh terms.

C) was very well received throughout Europe.

D) provided the framework for the United States Constitution.

31

Which choice provides the best evidence for the previous question?

A) Lines 48–49 ("He . . . power")

B) Lines 81–82 ("*Common* . . . Russia")

C) Lines 85–87 ("Then . . . independence")

D) Lines 87–90 ("The . . . *Sense*")

32

The tone of Passage 1 and the tone of Passage 2 are best described as, respectively,

A) analytical and lighthearted.

B) restrained and ambivalent.

C) critical and laudatory.

D) academic and promotional.

1   **1**

Questions 33–43 are based on the following passage and supplementary material.

This passage is adapted from Brandon Keim, "Why We Need to Stop Thinking So Much About Climate Change," published in *Aeon* magazine (aeon.co), December 15, 2015.

Line
       In the Great Basin desert in Utah is a kind of time machine. Homestead Cave has been inhab-ited for the past 13,000 years by owls, beneath whose roosts accumulated millennia-deep piles
5 of undigested fur and bone. By examining these piles, researchers have been able to reconstruct the region's ecological history. It contains a very timely lesson.
       Those 13,000 years spanned some profound
10 environmental upheavals. Indeed, the cave opened when Lake Bonneville receded at the last ice age's end and the Great Basin shifted from rainfall-rich coolness to its present hot, dry state. Yet despite these changes, life was pretty
15 stable. Different species flourished at differ-ent times, but the total amount of biological energy—a metric used by ecologists to describe all the metabolic activity in an ecosystem—remained steady.
20   About a century ago, though, all that changed. There's now about 20 per cent less bio-logical energy flowing through the Great Basin than at the 20th century's beginning. To put it another way: life's richness contracted by one-
25 fifth in an eyeblink of geological time. The cul-prit? Not climate change, but human activity, in particular the spread of non-native grasses that flourish in disturbed areas and sustain less life than would the native plants they've displaced.
30   Homestead Cave underscores how resilient nature can be, and also the enormity of human impacts, which in this case dwarfed the transi-tion to an entirely new climate state. The latter point is too often overlooked, obscured by a fixa-
35 tion on climate change as Earth's great ecologi-cal problem.
       The parable of Homestead Cave is no license to shirk climate duties and imagine that a rapidly warming Earth won't be calamitous for non-
40 human life. It will be. But so is a great deal else

that we do. Paying attention to climate change and to other human impacts shouldn't be a zero-sum game, but it too often seems that way.
       Witness the reception given to a recent
45 study on Atlantic cod in the Gulf of Maine, where cod stocks have failed to recover despite strict fishing restrictions enacted in 2010. Fast-rising water temperatures, said the research-ers, seem to have changed Gulf of Maine food
50 webs, depleting the cod's prey and slowing their recovery.
       Sure, the researchers noted chronic over-fishing, and that fisheries management needs to incorporate environmental factors. But that
55 nuance was lost in the public narrative, which was exclusively about climate: "Climate Change Fuels Cod Collapse," said the headlines, with barely a mention of the enormous ecological upheavals that preceded the collapse.
60   Cod had been brutally overfished since the beginning of the 20th century. Bottom-trawling fishing methods destroyed many of their seafloor spawning grounds, and also the habitat of their prey. Before that, dams built on almost every
65 coastal stream and river reduced once-vast popu-lations of migratory fish such as Atlantic salmon and shad, billions of which had historically nour-ished cod, by at least 95 per cent.
       In fact, the entire ecosystem had been dra-
70 matically altered before the Gulf of Maine began to warm. But the cod disaster was portrayed—misleadingly and counterproductively—as a climate issue.
       This habit of mind was also visible earlier
75 this year when Pope Francis released his encycli-cal on the climate, "*Laudato Si: On Care for Our Common Home.*" Coverage at first concentrated on the Pope's call for action on climate change. In fact, the encyclical was so much more.
80   It was a full-throated denunciation of the ideology of unlimited economic growth, a lam-entation of environmental degradation, a call for people to respect both ecosystems and individual animals: a radical, existentially challenging work,
85 of which climate was just one facet. Yet it took months after its release, when critiques from envi-ronmental scholars and theologians supplanted the initial media coverage, for the climate frame to expand.

CONTINUE ➤

1   **1**

90   What explains this climate-first habit? I think
we fail to appreciate just how big-footed 7.3 billion
humans are, and also the fact that climate change
is, in a sense, an easy out. It's comforting to think
that, if humanity can fix Earth's climate, nature's
95   problems will be also be solved.

But it's all too easy to imagine a future in
which humanity has averted the worst of climate
change but nature is woefully diminished.

The sixth great extinction won't be averted
100   just because atmospheric CO_2 levels fall below
350 parts per million. The United Nations climate
conference has just concluded with an agreement
that should help put humanity on a trajectory of
climate sanity—but to protect the living world,
105   we'll need to do much more.

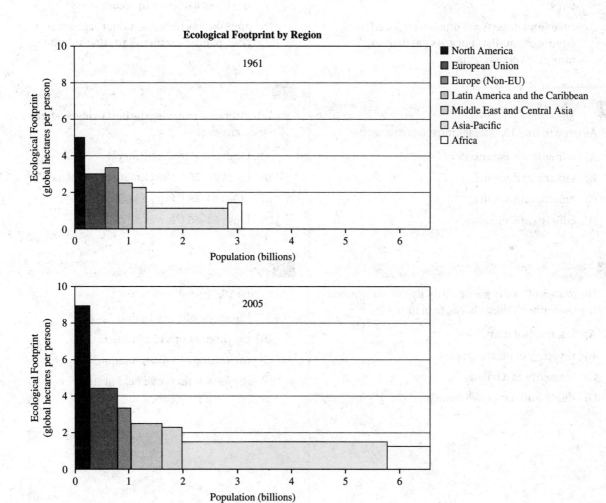

Source: Ecological Footprint Atlas 2008. Global Footprint Network (www.footprintnetwork.org)

CONTINUE ➤

33

The "timely lesson" mentioned in line 8 is that

A) climate change can drastically disrupt delicate ecosystems.

B) dramatic changes in global temperature can occur very suddenly.

C) human activity can have a more significant impact on global ecology than global warming does.

D) caves and deserts are often overlooked by environmentalists but are vital to many important ecosystems.

34

As used in line 15, "stable" most nearly means

A) climatically balanced.

B) lacking in diversity.

C) emotionally secure.

D) consistently vigorous.

35

Homestead Cave is particularly useful for illustrating the author's thesis because of its

A) relative isolation.

B) diversity of native species.

C) longevity as a habitat.

D) damp and dark environment.

36

The author believes that contemporary media coverage of environmental issues

A) is indispensable to raising public awareness about the dangers of global warming.

B) focuses excessively on climate issues to the exclusion of ecological issues.

C) has largely ignored the climatological data that has been gathered in recent years.

D) emphasizes the sensational aspects of controversies rather than their solutions.

37

Which choice provides the best evidence for the previous answer?

A) Lines 5–7 ("By . . . history")

B) Lines 26–29 ("Not climate . . . displaced")

C) Lines 54–59 ("But . . . collapse")

D) Lines 80–85 ("It was . . . facet")

38

In line 88, "frame" refers to

A) the scope of a discussion

B) the proportions of a problem

C) the setting of a phenomenon

D) the foundations of a field of study

1
1

39

The accompanying graphs best illustrate which quantity mentioned in the passage?

A) "biological energy" (lines 16–17)

B) "human activity" (line 26)

C) "climate change" (line 35)

D) "economic growth" (line 81)

40

The eighth paragraph (lines 60–68) serves mainly to exemplify

A) the different aspects of the media coverage of declining Atlantic cod stocks.

B) the various impacts of climate change on Atlantic cod populations.

C) the human activities that have altered the ecosystem of the Atlantic cod.

D) the ways that humans fail to heed the warnings from scientists about diminishing Atlantic cod populations.

41

The author believes that the *Laudato Si*

A) articulates a well-balanced position with regard to the human impact on the global environment.

B) emphasizes climate change more than it emphasizes the environmental degradation caused by human activity.

C) overlooks some important aspects of the political debate on global warming.

D) takes an overly optimistic view of the ability of humans to fix the climate.

42

Which choice provides the best evidence for the previous answer?

A) Lines 33–36 ("The . . . problem")

B) Lines 37–40 ("The parable . . . life")

C) Lines 77–78 ("Coverage . . . change")

D) Lines 80–85 ("It was . . . facet")

CONTINUE →

Questions 43–52 are based on the following passage.

This passage is adapted from Nathan Myhrvold, "Basic Science Can't Survive Without Government Funding," © 2016 Scientific American, a division of Nature America. Originally published in *Scientific American* magazine, February 1, 2016.

On December 2, 2015, the centennial anniversary of the publication of Einstein's General Theory of Relativity, science fans everywhere reflected on this amazing act of genius. But the
5　theory was not born, fully formed, in some eureka moment. Albert Einstein chipped away at it for years. He was finally driven to complete it by a fierce (though collegial) rivalry with mathematician David Hilbert.
10　Examine the detailed history of almost any iconic scientific discovery or technological invention—the light bulb, the transistor, DNA, even the Internet—and you'll find that the famous names credited with the breakthrough
15　were only a few steps ahead of a pack of competitors. Recently some writers and elected officials have used this phenomenon, called parallel innovation, to argue against the public financing of basic research.
20　In his new book for example, British science writer Matt Ridley claims that government just gets in the way of the natural evolution of science and invention. Many in the U.S. Congress agree. We spend too much taxpayer money on science,
25　some politicians say. Government should leave it to companies to finance the research they need.

These arguments are dangerously wrong. Without government support, most basic scientific research will never happen. This is most
30　clearly true for the kind of pure research that has delivered enormous prestige and great intellectual benefits but no profits, such as the work that brought us the Higgs boson, or the understanding that a supermassive black hole sits at the center of
35　the Milky Way, or the discovery of methane seas on the surface of Saturn's moon Titan. Company research laboratories used to do this kind of work: experimental evidence for the big bang was discovered at AT&T's Bell Labs, resulting in a
40　Nobel Prize. Now those days are gone.

Even in applied fields, such as materials science and computer science, companies now understand that basic research is a form of charity—so they avoid it. Scientists at Bell Labs
45　created the transistor, but that invention earned billions for Intel (and Microsoft).

Engineers at Xerox PARC invented the modern graphical user interface, although Apple (and Microsoft) profited the most. IBM researchers
50　pioneered the use of giant magnetoresistance to boost hard-disk capacity but soon lost the disk-drive business to Seagate and Western Digital.

When I created Microsoft Research, one of the largest industrial research labs founded in a
55　generation, Bill Gates and I were very clear that basic research was not our mission. We knew that unless our researchers focused narrowly on innovations we could turn into revenues quickly, we wouldn't be able to justify the R&D[1] budget
60　to our investors. The business logic at work here has not changed. Those who believe profit-driven companies will altruistically pay for basic science that has wide-ranging benefits—but mostly to others and not for a generation—
65　are naive.

If government were to leave it to the private sector to pay for basic research, most science would come to a screeching halt. What research survived would be done largely in secret, for fear
70　of handing the next big thing to a rival. In that situation, Einstein might never have felt the need to finish his greatest work.

Einsteins are few and far between. But we don't have to wait for a rare genius as long as we
75　stoke the competitive instincts of the smartest people around and persuade them to share their discoveries, in exchange for a shot at glory and riches.

[1]research and development

1 **1**

43

The author mentions Einstein's General Theory of Relativity in order to

A) draw attention to an important phenomenon in physics.

B) highlight the difference between theoretical science and applied science.

C) illustrate the effects of competition in scientific discovery.

D) show how an enlightened government can encourage innovation.

44

The author believes that "those days are gone" (line 40) because

A) companies don't find profit in basic scientific research.

B) scientists have become too competitive with one another.

C) government bureaucracy thwarts scientific discovery.

D) the public is not as interested in science as it is in entertainment.

45

Which choice provides the best evidence for the answer to the previous question?

A) Lines 10–16 ("Examine . . . competitors")

B) Lines 25–26 ("Government . . . need")

C) Lines 41–44 ("Even . . . it")

D) Line 73 ("Einsteins . . . between")

46

The author discusses "hard-disk capacity" (line 51) to make the point that

A) many technological discoveries are facilitated by competition.

B) scientific research requires substantial data processing.

C) enormous progress has been made in the field of computer hardware.

D) basic research does not always produce significant profit.

47

As used in line 63, "basic" most nearly means

A) meager.

B) unsatisfactory.

C) inexpensive.

D) essential.

48

The "situation" in line 71 is one in which

A) corporations compete with each other for economic advantage.

B) individual scientists compete with each other for prestige.

C) corporations form productive alliances to encourage innovation.

D) the federal government funds basic scientific research.

CONTINUE ➜

49

The author regards Matt Ridley's new book as a

A) blueprint for government action.

B) poor guide to public policy.

C) biased analysis of corporate competition.

D) reliable history of scientific innovation.

50

The author suggests that great scientific minds are motivated by a combination of

A) prestige and money.

B) altruism and discovery.

C) competition and patriotism.

D) collaboration and corporate loyalty.

51

Which choice provides the best evidence for the answer to the previous question?

A) Lines 7–9 ("He . . . Hilbert")

B) Lines 61–65 ("Those who . . . naive")

C) Lines 68–70 ("What . . . rival")

D) Lines 73–78 ("But . . . riches")

52

It can be inferred that the "wide-ranging benefits" (line 63) most likely do NOT include

A) cost-effective medical breakthroughs.

B) general scientific knowledge.

C) immediate corporate advantage.

D) technological advances in communication.

STOP

**If you finish before time is called, you may check your work on this section only.
Do not turn to any other section of the test.**

2

2

Writing and Language Test
44 QUESTIONS, 35 MINUTES

Turn to Section 2 of your answer sheet to answer the questions in this section.

DIRECTIONS

Each passage below is accompanied by a number of questions. For some questions, you will consider how the passage might be revised to improve the expression of ideas. For other questions, you will consider how the passage might be edited to correct errors in sentence structure, usage, or punctuation. A passage or a question may be accompanied by one or more graphics (such as a table or graph) that you will consider as you make revising and editing decisions.

Some questions will direct you to an underlined portion of a passage. Other questions will direct you to a location in a passage or ask you to think about the passage as a whole.

After reading each passage, choose the answer to each question that most effectively improves the quality of writing in the passage or that makes the passage conform to the conventions of standard written English. Many questions include a "NO CHANGE" option. Choose that option if you think the best choice is to leave the relevant portion of the passage as it is.

CONTINUE ▶

|2| **2|**

Questions 1–11 are based on the following passage.

Be Professional

What does it really mean to "act professionally?" It's a simple question without a simple answer. Often, it's a matter of perspective. The expectations and standards of behavior are different for every job.

1 Since posted positions might have similar titles, responsibilities, and preferred qualifications, different companies often operate in entirely different worlds, with entirely different cultures.

2 I learned my first lesson in 1989. Working in an office meant dressing the part, and for men that meant wearing a suit and tie—no exceptions. **3** It was the 80s—the era of Ronald Reagan and glam rock bands with big hair. I had worked in my father's office after school for a few days without committing any corporate faux pas until his partner and best friend returned from vacation. I made the mistake of doing what I had done so many times before, calling "Hi, Uncle Dave!" when he **4** would arrive the office. As it turned out, he was not my "uncle" in 1980s corporate America. As soon as I said his name, his face twisted, half in disgust, half in barely suppressed rage. He leaned in

1

A) NO CHANGE
B) Whenever
C) Although
D) As

2

Which choice most effectively sets up the sentence and paragraph that follow?

A) NO CHANGE
B) It's important to understand professional boundaries.
C) The way you greet your boss is very important.
D) In the 1980s, the standards for men in the workplace were very different from those for women.

3

The writer is considering deleting this sentence. Should the writer make this change?

A) No, because it includes important details about the culture of the 80s.
B) No, because it helps justify the standards for workplace behavior in the 80s.
C) Yes, because this sentence has a strikingly different tone than does the rest of the paragraph.
D) Yes, because this information is not relevant to a discussion of workplace professionalism.

4

A) NO CHANGE
B) arrives
C) arrived
D) had arrived

2

2

and seethed, "Jonathan, *in this office I am Mr. Stevens, and only Mr. Stevens.*" What registers as affection in one setting can register as the [5] scourge of nepotism in another.

Nine years later, [6] was when I was starting in my first junior executive position, the CEO of my new firm was Frank Murphy, whom I naturally called Mr. Murphy, and only Mr. Murphy. That is, until the end of my first week, when Mr. Murphy called me into his office.

"Look, Johnny," he said, "You've got to stop calling me Mr. Murphy. Please, just call me Frank."

It took a lot of effort before I finally felt comfortable doing so, but I did it because it was "professional," [7] and I have always wanted to please my bosses.

Protocol for phone calls has always been another hurdle for me. In one college internship, we were told that, whenever a call came in for the CEO, [8] we were to ask for the caller's name, phone number, when the person could be reached, and what the call was regarding. We were then to thank the person and give [9] the CEO when he was available the message in his office. The next summer,

---

5

A) NO CHANGE
B) mishap
C) setback
D) tragedy

6

A) NO CHANGE
B) when
C) it was when
D) DELETE the underlined portion.

7

Which choice connects most effectively to the overall thesis of the passage?

A) NO CHANGE
B) and professionalism is one of several hallmarks of workplace success.
C) at least in that specific time and place.
D) and standard practice in executive positions.

8

A) NO CHANGE
B) to ask
C) we asked
D) we could ask

9

A) NO CHANGE
B) the message to the CEO when he was available in his office.
C) the message when he was available in his office to the CEO.
D) the CEO when he was available the message in his office.

at a different firm, I naturally followed the same protocol **10** again when the phone rang. But things had changed. "If someone calls me, you put him through to my desk, dammit!" my new CEO shouted at me. "You don't ask questions, and you don't pry into my business. Who do you think you are?" I learned that lesson very quickly.

[1] If something as simple as how to greet your boss or answer a phone can be so complicated, what about all the other unwritten social mores that comprise a company work culture? [2] Thriving in different work environments means being a chameleon, changing with every different setting, and always according to unwritten and often changing rules. [3] The rules are rarely consistent and often defy common sense, but how well you navigate them will determine how well you do in a company. **11**

10

A) NO CHANGE
B) additionally
C) to boot
D) DELETE the underline portion.

11

The writer wants to include the following sentence in this paragraph.

Hopefully, you will master this skill before you make a mistake that might get you fired.

Where should this sentence be placed?

A) immediately before sentence 1
B) immediately after sentence 1
C) immediately after sentence 2
D) immediately after sentence 3

2   2

Questions 12–22 are based on the following passage.

Light in the National Gallery

The National Gallery of Art in Washington, D.C., is one of the **12** foremost national art museums in the world. Conceived by industrialist and financier Andrew W. Mellon as a gift to the United States, **13** admission to the museum is free and it is open to the public. As Secretary of the Treasury from 1921 to 1933, Mellon came to believe that the United States should have a national art museum comparable to **14** other great nations. In 1936, Mellon offered to donate his vast personal art collection to the project, to use his own funds for its construction, and **15** including a generous endowment for its operational costs. President Roosevelt and Congress accepted Mellon's gift, and the National Gallery of Art was estab-lished in 1937.

12

A) NO CHANGE
B) unbeaten
C) ultimate
D) optimal

13

A) NO CHANGE
B) the museum is open to the public, and admission is free
C) the public can visit the museum openly, free of charge
D) admission is free to the museum, which is open to the public

14

A) NO CHANGE
B) that of other
C) the ones from other
D) those of other

15

A) NO CHANGE
B) a generous
C) to include a generous
D) also a generous

CONTINUE

2   **2**

Located on the National Mall at Constitution Avenue, **16** the mission that the National Gallery of Art embraces is to collect, exhibit, and conserve works of art and to foster the understanding of those works of art at the highest possible museum and scholarly standards. We can all appreciate the role that museums play in collecting and exhibiting artworks, but few people truly understand and appreciate the challenges of art conservation.

The primary responsibility of the conservation division of the National Gallery of Art is to analyze and preserve the works of art in the Gallery's collection. **17** It examines these works carefully in order to preserve them and maintain their original beauty as much as possible. Although good lighting is essential to proper exhibition, light exposure can be a significant hazard to paintings and other works of art. Even worse than air pollution, exposure to harsh light can result in **18** enduring, permanent, and irrevocable damage to the delicate pigments and surfaces of centuries-old paintings. Even low-intensity light can cause serious **19** disregard over an extended period of time.

16

A) NO CHANGE

B) the National Gallery of Art embraces its mission

C) the National Gallery of Art, embracing its mission

D) the mission of the National Gallery of Art is to embrace and

17

The writer is considering deleting this sentence. Should it be kept or deleted?

A) Deleted, because it repeats information already stated in the passage.

B) Deleted, because it blurs the paragraph's focus on the work of conservation.

C) Kept, because it explains why the preservation of art is so important.

D) Kept, because it indicates the important duties of the conservation division.

18

A) NO CHANGE

B) irrevocable

C) enduring and irrevocable

D) permanent and enduring

19

A) NO CHANGE

B) disinclination

C) disability

D) degradation

2   2

The most potent sources of art damage [20] comes from infrared and ultraviolet light. Infrared radiation heats the surface of a painting, causing reactions such as cracking and lifting. High-energy ultraviolet rays can alter the molecular components of the paint, [21] which are much harder to reverse. Therefore, these wavelengths must be reduced as much as possible to prevent damage. The conservation team uses several types of meters to measure the brightness and frequency of the ambient light in its galleries, as well as specialized filters to reduce the harmful wavelengths. The team works closely with the Gallery's lighting department [22] in finding the most aesthetic illumination that will avoid irreversible harm to its valuable collection so that visitors can enjoy it for generations to come.

[20]
A) NO CHANGE
B) are
C) is
D) come from

[21]
A) NO CHANGE
B) which is
C) creating a problem that is
D) which is a problem that is

[22]
A) NO CHANGE
B) for finding
C) and found
D) to find

2 ▮▮▮▮▮▮▮▮▮▮▮▮▮▮▮▮▮▮▮▮▮▮▮▮▮ **2**

Questions 23–33 are based on the following passage.

(Not So) Blind as a Bat

Pity the poor bat, **23** maligned and misunderstood for centuries. Bats are not flying mice; they do not swarm and attack humans; they are not dirty, and in fact spend a lot of time grooming their fur. Of the world's 1,100 or more species of bat, only three are "vampire" bats, and the amount of blood they take for a meal does not hurt the livestock or other large mammals they favor. Most bats are quite **24** beneficial, they control insect populations, and **25** its excrement can be used as fertilizer and—believe it or not—an ingredient in gunpowder.

[1] Although, unlike other nocturnal animals, **26** the eyesight of bats are not highly evolved, they have astounding navigational and hunting skills that rival **27** those of the most adept birds of prey. [2] Their secret weapon is sonar. [3] While flying, they emit high-frequency sounds that bounce off objects and back to their highly developed ears, enabling them to detect even tiny insects in the dark. [4] This echolocation mechanism is not unlike the radar systems that meteorologists use to track storms, but bats can track their quarry while **28** emitting up to 190 chirps per second. [5] Their aerial maneuvers even inspired one

23
A) NO CHANGE
B) it is maligned
C) it has been maligned
D) being maligned

24
A) NO CHANGE
B) beneficial, so they
C) beneficial: they
D) beneficial where they

25
A) NO CHANGE
B) they're
C) there
D) their

26
A) NO CHANGE
B) the eyesight of bats is
C) bats have eyes that are
D) the eyes of bats are

27
A) NO CHANGE
B) the most adept
C) what the most adept
D) that of the most adept

28
Which choice most effectively sets up the sentence that follows?
A) NO CHANGE
B) flying acrobatically at full speed.
C) in pitch darkness.
D) chirping and listening simultaneously.

2   2

researcher to remark that studying bats as they home in on prey or drink nectar is "like watching a performance of the Nutcracker." **29**

A better understanding of bat echolocation could have many **30** <u>resourceful</u> applications in our world. For instance, a new mobility aid for the blind is being developed that can emit ultrasonic frequencies (sounds at a higher pitch than humans can hear) that are then analyzed by a microprocessor **31** <u>in much the same way as</u> echoes from a bat's environment are processed by **32** <u>their</u> brain. These ultrasonic frequencies are than transformed into audible waves that are then fed back to the user through earphones. In this method localized sound images correspond to the direction and the size of the obstacles. Results of early trials with this device have been very promising. A blind person trained in its use can learn to recognize a 1-mm-diameter wire and discriminate **33** <u>within</u> several nearby obstacles at the same time.

It's a good thing that we've overcome our fear of bats enough to learn what wonderful creatures they are. They may not be the cuddliest creatures on the planet, but they do us a world of good.

29

Where is the most logical place to add the following sentence?

The phrase "blind as a bat" is remarkably inapt.

A) Before sentence 1

B) Immediately after sentence 2

C) Immediately after sentence 3

D) After sentence 5

30

A) NO CHANGE

B) theoretical

C) no-nonsense

D) viable

31

A) NO CHANGE

B) as they are when

C) in a way the same as

D) in a similar way to

32

A) NO CHANGE

B) it's

C) its

D) they're

33

A) NO CHANGE

B) between

C) among

D) for

CONTINUE ➡

2   2

Questions 34–44 are based on the following passage and supplemental material.

The Blue Campaign

The Emancipation Proclamation was issued by President Abraham Lincoln in [34] 1863, which declared that "all persons held as slaves . . . are, and henceforward shall be, free." The following year, he worked to expand anti-slavery policies nationwide by [35] propositioning the passage of the Thirteenth Amendment "to abolish slavery and involuntary servitude." And so the practice of slavery in the United States was abolished for good in 1865. Or was it?

Gone are the open slave markets of Charleston and New York City, with human livestock on display, auctioned off to the highest bidders. [36] Gone also are the days when a person could be denied rights as a human being and legally treated as property. But the days of slavery are not entirely behind us. Human trafficking is a horrific form of modern-day [37] slavery, it involves the illegal trade of people for exploitation and commercial gain.

34

A) NO CHANGE
B) 1863: declaring that
C) 1863, declaring that
D) 1863, having declared that

35

A) NO CHANGE
B) designing
C) advocating
D) intending

36

A) NO CHANGE
B) The days are also gone
C) Also, the days are gone
D) The days also are gone

37

A) NO CHANGE
B) slavery: involving
C) slavery involving
D) slavery; that involves

2   **2**

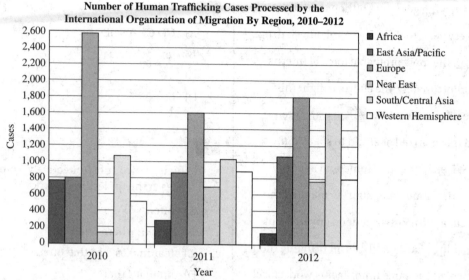

Number of Human Trafficking Cases Processed by the
International Organization of Migration By Region, 2010–2012

Source: Data Gathered from The International Organization of Migration (www.iom.int). Graphic ©2016 College Hill Coaching

In 2012, the International Organization of Migration (IOM), a group dedicated to the "humane and orderly management of migration" actively processed **38** about 6,000 human trafficking cases all over the world, but even this is a small fraction of the problem. **39** The group estimates that there are millions of trafficking victims worldwide each year, and 15,000 in the U.S. alone. Yet Americans are largely unaware of this criminal practice.

38

Which choice most accurately and effectively represents the information in the graph?

A) NO CHANGE

B) thousands of human trafficking cases, primarily in Africa and the Near East

C) more than twice as many human trafficking cases as it did in 2010

D) over 10,000 human trafficking cases internationally

39

The writer is considering deleting the underlined sentence. Should the sentence be kept or deleted?

A) Deleted, because it includes details that have already been mentioned.

B) Deleted, because it blurs the focus of the paragraph with loosely related details.

C) Kept, because it provides an important counterpoint to the main idea of the previous paragraph.

D) Kept, because it expands on the point made in the previous sentence by providing specific details.

CONTINUE

2   **2**

Human trafficking generates billions of dollars in illegal profit every year, making it second only to drug trafficking **40** in the most profitable form of international crime. Unfortunately, the efforts to fight this crime have been limited because **41** of fear. Often victims are too traumatized or afraid to speak out. In 2010, the U.S. Department of Homeland Security (DHS) launched the "Blue Campaign" to marshal the resources and capabilities of the federal government to protect trafficking victims and **42** for bringing their abusers to justice. At the same time, agents work closely with governmental and law enforcement partners, as well as other social service providers and non-governmental organizations to assist victims. Ending human trafficking requires the collective resolve of many vigilant agencies.

40

A) NO CHANGE

B) for

C) as

D) of

41

Which choice most effectively combines the sentences at the underlined portion?

A) often

B) of fear, where often

C) fear makes it so that often

D) often it's that

42

A) NO CHANGE

B) have brought

C) in bringing

D) to bring

2   2

To date, the Blue Campaign has trained more than 10,000 state, local, and campus law enforcement professionals, over 2,000 foreign law enforcement partners, and about 50,000 airline employees to spot the signs of human trafficking and take action when necessary. These professionals are the people who are most likely to witness victims of human trafficking.

Perhaps the most important tool for controlling human trafficking is publicity. As part of a nationwide public awareness **43** initiative, the campaign displays materials in 13 major U.S. airports and airs public service announcements around the country.

It took the moral indignation of a nation and the sacrifice of hundreds of thousands of lives in the Civil War to end legalized slavery in the United States. Let's hope that eradicating human trafficking **44** will happen soon.

43

A) NO CHANGE
B) achievement
C) scheme
D) enterprise

44

Which choice most effectively links to the previous sentence and maintains the focus of the passage?

A) NO CHANGE
B) won't be as costly.
C) will lead to a more prosperous world.
D) will become a goal of the U.S. Congress.

STOP

**If you finish before time is called, you may check your work on this section only.
Do not turn to any other section of the test.**

3　　　　　　　　　　　　　　　　　　　　　　　　　　　　**3**

Math Test—No Calculator

25 MINUTES, 20 QUESTIONS

Turn to Section 3 of your answer sheet to answer the questions in this section.

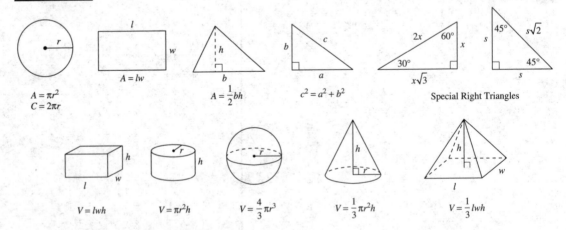

3

3

1

If $3b = 2$ what is the value of $\dfrac{b}{2}$?

A) $\dfrac{1}{6}$

B) $\dfrac{1}{3}$

C) $\dfrac{2}{3}$

D) $\dfrac{3}{4}$

2

Which of the following is equivalent to $\dfrac{x^3}{x} + \dfrac{x^5}{x^3}$ for all positive values of x?

A) $2x^2$

B) $2x^4$

C) $2x^6$

D) $2x^8$

3

If $m < -3$ and $-3m \le 2n$ what is the least possible integer value of n?

A) -5

B) -4

C) 5

D) 6

4

Janie runs a dog-sitting service in which she charges $12 per hour for the first dog and $5 per hour for each additional dog. She also charges an additional $10 fee to take up to three dogs to the dog park. Which choice represents the total charge, in dollars, for Janie to sit 3 dogs for n hours, including one trip to the dog park?

A) $17n + 10$

B) $22n + 10$

C) $22n + 30$

D) $36n + 20$

5

An oceanographer is studying the growth of two artificial reefs. Osprey Reef has an area of 400 square meters and is growing at a rate of 2.5 square meters per month. Pelican Reef has an area of 360 square meters and is growing at a rate of 3 square meters per month. At these rates, in how many months will the two reefs have the same area?

A) 40

B) 42

C) 64

D) 80

6

If $x < -10$, which of the following has the least value?

A) $\dfrac{1}{x^2}$

B) $\dfrac{1}{x^3}$

C) $\dfrac{1}{x^4}$

D) $\dfrac{1}{x^5}$

CONTINUE

3 **3**

7

Which choice is equivalent to $\sqrt{-27}+\sqrt{-48}$?

A) $-5\sqrt{3}$

B) $\sqrt{-75}$

C) $5i\sqrt{3}$

D) $7i\sqrt{3}$

8

$$n=416-4T$$

The equation above models the relationship between n, the number of cars per week at a gas station requesting full service, and T, the average weekly temperature in degrees Fahrenheit, where $30 \le T \le 80$. Which of the following is the best interpretation of the number 4 in this equation?

A) For every 4-degree increase in average weekly temperature, 1 fewer car requests full service per week.

B) For every 4-degree increase in average weekly temperature, 1 fewer car requests full service per day.

C) For every 1-degree increase in average weekly temperature, 4 fewer cars request full service per week.

D) For every 1-degree decrease in average weekly temperature, 4 fewer cars request full service per week.

9

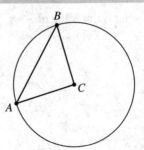

In the figure above, C is the center of the circle and segment AC is perpendicular to segment BC. If the area of triangle ABC is 8 square units, what is the length of arc AB?

A) 2π

B) 4π

C) 8π

D) 16π

10

Which of the following expressions is equivalent to

$$\frac{a}{b}(a-b)(a+b)?$$

A) $\dfrac{a^3}{b}-ab$

B) $\dfrac{a^2}{b}-b$

C) $\dfrac{a^3}{b}+\dfrac{2a^2}{b}+ab$

D) $\dfrac{a^2}{b}-ab$

---

3 **3**

11

$$f(x) = -\frac{1}{2}x + 1$$

$$g(x) = -4x - 1$$

When the line $y = g(f(x))$ is graphed in the xy-plane, what is its y-intercept?

A) -5

B) -3

C) 2

D) $\dfrac{3}{2}$

12

If $p(x) = 6x^2 + 2x$, which of the following is a factor of $p(x) - 4$?

A) $x + 4$

B) $x + 3$

C) $x + 2$

D) $x + 1$

13

If the equation $6x - xy = x^2 + 9$ is graphed in the xy-plane, at which point does the graph touch the x-axis?

A) $(-6, 0)$

B) $(-3, 0)$

C) $(3, 0)$

D) $(6, 0)$

14

For which of the following equations is $\dfrac{-3 - \sqrt{3^2 + 4(2)(5)}}{4}$ a solution?

A) $2x^2 + 3x = -5$

B) $2x^2 + 3x = 5$

C) $2x^2 - 3x = -5$

D) $2x^2 - 3x = 5$

15

$$\frac{x^3}{x-2} = x^2 + 2x + 4 + \frac{b}{x-2}$$

If the equation above is true for all values of x where $x \neq 2$, what is the value of b ?

A) -8

B) -4

C) 4

D) 8

CONTINUE ➡

3   3

DIRECTIONS

For questions 16–20, solve the problem and enter your answer in the grid, as described below, on the answer sheet.

1. Although not required, it is suggested that you write your answer in the boxes at the top of the columns to help you fill in the circles accurately. You will receive credit only if the circles are filled in correctly.

2. Mark no more than one circle in any column.

3. No question has a negative answer.

4. Some problems may have more than one correct answer. In such cases, grid only one answer.

5. **Mixed numbers** such as $3\frac{1}{2}$ must be gridded as 3.5 or $\frac{7}{2}$.

(If $3\frac{1}{2}$ is entered into the grid as [3 1 / 2], it will be interpreted as $\frac{31}{2}$, not $3\frac{1}{2}$.)

6. **Decimal answers**: If you obtain a decimal answer with more digits than the grid can accommodate, it may be either rounded or truncated, but it must fill the entire grid.

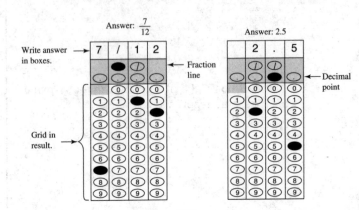

Answer: $\frac{7}{12}$

Answer: 2.5

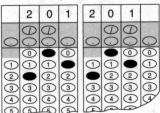

Answer: 201
Either position is correct.

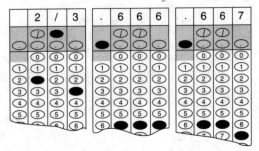

Acceptable ways to grid $\frac{2}{3}$ are:

CONTINUE →

3 3

16

In the xy-plane, the graph of $y = \frac{1}{3}x - 1$ passes through the point $(a, 1)$. What is the value of a?

17

$$2x^2 - bx + b = 0$$

If $x = 3$ is a solution to the equation, above, what is the value of b?

18

If $2 \le 3|3 - x| \le 3$, what is one possible value of x?

19

If $\frac{2+i}{2-i} = a + bi$, where $i = \sqrt{-1}$, what is the value of $a + b$?

20

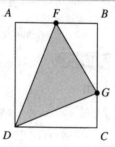

In the figure above, point F is the midpoint of side $\overline{AB}$ and G is a point on $\overline{BC}$ such that $BG = 2GC$. What fraction of the area of rectangle $ABCD$ is shaded?

STOP

**If you finish before time is called, you may check your work on this section only.
Do not turn to any other section of the test.**

4 4

Math Test—Calculator
55 MINUTES, 38 QUESTIONS

Turn to Section 4 of your answer sheet to answer the questions in this section.

DIRECTIONS

For questions 1–30, solve each problem, choose the best answer from the choices provided, and fill in the corresponding circle on your answer sheet. **For questions 31–38**, solve the problem and enter your answer in the grid on the answer sheet. Please refer to the directions before question 31 on how to enter your answers in the grid. You may use any available space in your test booklet for scratch work.

NOTES

1. The use of a calculator **is permitted**.

2. All variables and expressions used represent real numbers unless otherwise indicated.

3. Figures provided in this test are drawn to scale unless otherwise indicated.

4. All figures lie in a plane unless otherwise indicated.

5. Unless otherwise indicated, the domain of a given function f is the set of all real numbers for which $f(x)$ is a real number.

REFERENCE

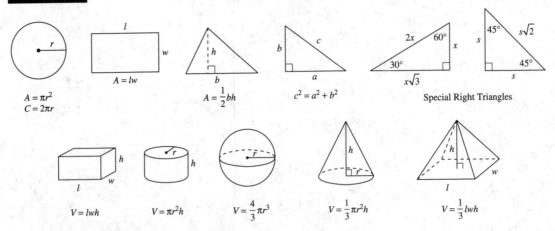

The number of degrees of arc in a circle is 360.
The number of radians of arc in a circle is 2π.
The sum of the measures in degrees of the angles of a triangle is 180.

CONTINUE →

4 **4**

1

Emma can fill a 12-gallon tank of gasoline for a cost of \$24.36. At this rate, how much should it cost her to fill a 16-gallon tank of gasoline?

A) \$32.48

B) \$34.88

C) \$35.12

D) \$36.54

2

If the average of a and b is 6 and the average of a, b, and c is 8, what is the value of c ?

A) 8

B) 10

C) 12

D) 16

3

$$x = 3a + b$$
$$y = a - b$$

Given the two equations above, which choice is equivalent to xy ?

A) $3a^2 - b^2$

B) $3a^2 - 4ab - b^2$

C) $3a^2 - 2ab - b^2$

D) $3a^2 - 2ab + b^2$

4

Which of the following systems of equations has no solution?

A) $\begin{cases} 2x + y = 0 \\ 2x + y = 1 \end{cases}$

B) $\begin{cases} 2x - y = 0 \\ 2x + y = 0 \end{cases}$

C) $\begin{cases} 2x + y = 0 \\ -2x + y = 0 \end{cases}$

D) $\begin{cases} 2x + y = 1 \\ -2x + y = 0 \end{cases}$

CONTINUE

4   **4**

5

Grade	Attack	Midfield	Defense	Goal	Total
12th	6	5	3	2	16
11th	4	6	4	1	15
10th	3	3	6	2	14
Total	13	14	13	5	45

The table above shows the distribution by grade and position for the 45 players on a boys' high school lacrosse team. If an attacker or midfielder is chosen at random from this team, what is the probability that he is in the 12th grade?

A) $\dfrac{10}{27}$

B) $\dfrac{11}{27}$

C) $\dfrac{16}{27}$

D) $\dfrac{11}{16}$

6

Arkady is trying to save \$5,000 to make a down payment on a new car. If he has \$300 already saved and plans to save \$40 every week, which inequality can he use to predict w, the number of weeks it will take him until he has enough for the down payment?

A) $5,300 \leq 40w + 300$

B) $4,700 \leq 40w$

C) $5,000 \leq 40w - 300$

D) $4,700 \leq 40w + 300$

Questions 7 and 8 refer to the following information.

A rubber ball is dropped vertically from a 10-meter tower to a hard surface below. Each time it strikes the ground, it bounces back to a height 80% of its previous height.

7

What maximum height does the ball reach immediately after its third bounce?

A) 6.4 meters

B) 5.12 meters

C) 4.096 meters

D) 3.2768 meters

8

What total vertical distance, both up and down, has the ball traveled when it strikes the ground for the fourth time?

A) 38.80 meters

B) 39.04 meters

C) 45.64 meters

D) 49.04 meters

CONTINUE

4 **4**

9

If $u = x + 2$ and $u \geq 0$, which of the following is equivalent to $(x-1)^2 \sqrt{x+2}$?

A) $(u-3)^2 \sqrt{u}$

B) $(u-2)^2 \sqrt{u}$

C) $(u-1)^2 \sqrt{u}$

D) $(u+1)^2 \sqrt{u}$

10

If $g(x) = 5x - 2$, and $g(a) = 8$, what is the value of $g(a+2)$?

A) 2

B) 12

C) 18

D) 23

11

If the equation $f(x) = 2$ has four distinct real solutions, which of the following could be the complete graph of $y = f(x)$?

A)

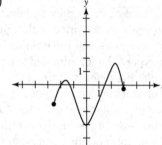

B)

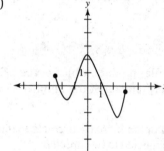

C)

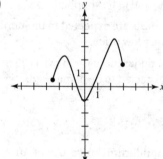

D)

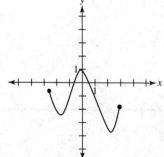

CONTINUE

4 **4**

Questions 12 and 13 refer to the following information.

In an economic market, the supply and demand of any product depends on the price of that product. The supply, $S(p)$, of a product is the number of units of that product expected to be supplied at a price of p dollars per unit. The demand, $D(p)$, of a product is the number of units of that product expected to be sold at a price of p dollars per unit. The "equilibrium price" of one unit of the product is the value of p at which the supply and the demand are equal. The supply and demand functions for a particular product are $S(p) = 25p + 100$ and $D(p) = -35p + 1,300$.

12

For this particular product, which of the following is the best interpretation of the number 25 in this system?

A) For every 1 dollar increase in price, 25 more units are expected to be supplied.

B) For every 25 dollars increase in price, one more unit is expected to be supplied.

C) At least 25 units are expected to be supplied, even at a very low price.

D) For every 1 dollar increase in price, 25 more units are expected to be demanded.

13

What is the equilibrium price of one unit of this product?

A) $20.00

B) $23.33

C) $60.00

D) $120.00

14

$$y = 2x^2 + 2x + 1$$
$$y = b$$

When the equations above are graphed in the xy-plane, they form a parabola and a line. If the line intersects the parabola in exactly one point, what is the value of b ?

A) $-\dfrac{1}{2}$

B) $-\dfrac{1}{4}$

C) $\dfrac{1}{2}$

D) 1

15

Joaquin is part of a crossword club. He earns 10 points for every easy puzzle he solves and 25 points for every hard puzzle he solves. If Joaquin solved 30 puzzles and earned a total of 375 points, how many more easy puzzles did he solve than hard puzzles?

A) 5

B) 10

C) 20

D) 25

CONTINUE

4   **4**

16

Frequency of Earthquake Magnitudes for Northwest California

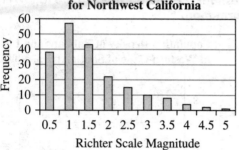

The graph above shows the distribution of Richter scale magnitudes for 200 recent earthquakes in northwest California. What is the median magnitude of these 200 earthquakes?

A) 1.0

B) 1.5

C) 2.0

D) 2.5

17

What is the sum of the solutions to the equation

$$2(x^2 + 4x) = 20 \ ?$$

A) −7

B) −4

C) 3

D) 4

18

A researcher is conducting a study to determine whether taking a zinc supplement can reduce the severity of cold symptoms. The treatment group for this study is 200 adult patients who will take a zinc supplement within 6 hours of first detecting cold symptoms. The researcher will then measure the length and severity of the cold symptoms for this treatment group. Which of the following comparison groups would best enable the researcher to reach a reliable conclusion about the ability of a zinc supplement to reduce the severity of cold symptoms?

A) A group of 200 adults without cold symptoms who also take the zinc supplement

B) A group of 200 children with cold symptoms who also take the zinc supplement

C) A group of 200 adults with cold symptoms who take sugar pills rather than the zinc supplements

D) A group of 100 children and 100 adults without cold symptoms who take sugar pills rather than the zinc supplements

19

Philip buys an annual membership to an online store for $80 in order to receive free shipping and handling on all of his orders for the year. Nonmembers pay a 2% shipping and handling surcharge on the cost of all orders after a 3.6% sales tax has been added. What is the approximate cost of merchandise Philip must purchase annually, <u>before sales tax</u>, in order for his savings on shipping and handling to cover the cost of his membership?

A) $2,940

B) $3,246

C) $3,861

D) $4,260

CONTINUE

4 **4**

20

Which of the following expressions is equivalent to $\dfrac{x-3}{x^2-1}$?

A) $\dfrac{2}{x+1} - \dfrac{1}{x-1}$

B) $\dfrac{1}{x+1} - \dfrac{2}{x-1}$

C) $\dfrac{2}{x+1} + \dfrac{1}{x-1}$

D) $\dfrac{1}{x+1} + \dfrac{2}{x-1}$

21

If $a = 2^{3k}$ and $b = 4^{-3k}$, which of the following is equivalent to $\dfrac{b}{a}$?

A) 2^{-9k}

B) 2^{-6k}

C) 2^{-3k}

D) 2^0

Questions 22 and 23 refer to the following information.

Population Density of Baboons and Leopards in Western Cape of South Africa, 2000-2010

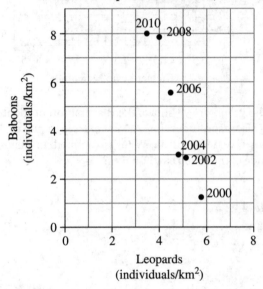

The scatterplot above shows the population densities of chacma baboons and leopards in the Western Cape of South Africa in 2-year intervals from 2000 to 2010.

22

What was the approximate percent change in the population density of chacma baboons from 2004 to 2006?

A) −6%

B) 30%

C) 55%

D) 90%

4

4

23

Which of the following statements about the population densities of chacma baboons and leopards in the Western Cape of South Africa is most justified by this graph?

A) The population densities of both species decreased linearly with time from 2000 to 2010.

B) The population densities of both species increased linearly with time from 2000 to 2010.

C) The population density of chacma baboons varied linearly with the population density of leopards in the period from 2000 to 2010.

D) The population density of chacma baboons varied inversely with the population density of leopards in the period from 2000 to 2010.

▲

24

Which of the following situations describes a population that is growing exponentially with time?

A) Every year, the population grows by 1% of the population of the previous year.

B) Every year, the population grows by 1,000 plus 2% of the original population.

C) Every year, the population grows by 2% of the original population.

D) Every year, the population grows by 10,000.

25

If $0 < a < 1$ and $-1 < b < 0$, which of the following must be true?

   I. $a^2 > b^2$

  II. $a^2 > (ab)^2$

  III. $b^3 < \left(\dfrac{a}{b}\right)^3$

A) I only

B) II only

C) III only

D) I and III only

26

Rogerio drives 1 hour and 18 minutes to meet a friend. The first 30 minutes of his trip was mostly highway driving, so he averaged 64 miles per hour for this portion. For the last 48 minutes of the trip, he averaged 50 miles per hour. What was Rogerio's average speed, approximately, for the entire trip?

A) 60 miles per hour

B) 58 miles per hour

C) 55 miles per hour

D) 53 miles per hour

---

4 **4**

27

Charlotte's club has several rectangular banners that it has been using around school to advertise a fundraiser. Charlotte wants a larger banner to use at the front entrance of the school, so she constructs a new rectangular banner that is 40% longer and k% taller than the smaller banners. If the new banners have an area that is 75% larger than the smaller banners, what is the value of k?

A) 20

B) 25

C) 30

D) 35

28

$$x + a = 4x - 8$$
$$y + b = 4y - 8$$

In the system of equations above, a and b are constants. If $a - b$ is equal to 1, which of the following must be true?

A) x is $\frac{1}{3}$ greater than y.

B) x is $\frac{1}{3}$ less than y.

C) x is 3 greater than y.

D) x is 3 less than y.

29

If y is 150% greater than x, where $x > 0$, then $x + y$ is what percent greater than y?

A) 40.0%

B) 66.7%

C) 71.4%

D) 150%

30

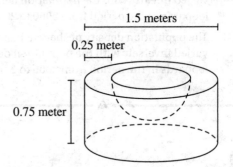

A raised cement fire pit is to be constructed according to the diagram above, consisting of a cylinder with a hemispherical cavity at the top. Which choice is closest to the volume, in cubic meters, of cement required to construct this fire pit?

A) 0.80 m³

B) 0.97 m³

C) 1.06 m³

D) 1.59 m³

CONTINUE ➤

4 4

For questions 31–38, solve the problem and enter your answer in the grid, as described below, on the answer sheet.

1. Although not required, it is suggested that you write your answer in the boxes at the top of the columns to help you fill in the circles accurately. You will receive credit only if the circles are filled in correctly.

2. Mark no more than one circle in any column.

3. No question has a negative answer.

4. Some problems may have more than one correct answer. In such cases, grid only one answer.

5. **Mixed numbers** such as $3\frac{1}{2}$ must be gridded as 3.5 or $\frac{7}{2}$.

   (If $3\frac{1}{2}$ is entered into the grid as ▦, it will be interpreted as $\frac{31}{2}$, not $3\frac{1}{2}$.)

6. **Decimal answers:** If you obtain a decimal answer with more digits than the grid can accommodate, it may be either rounded or truncated, but it must fill the entire grid.

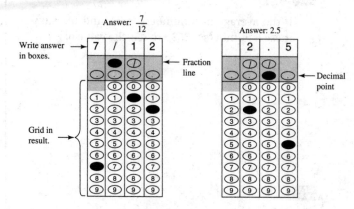

Answer: $\frac{7}{12}$

Answer: 2.5

Write answer in boxes.

Fraction line

Decimal point

Grid in result.

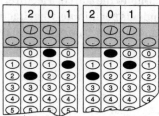

Answer: 201
Either position is correct.

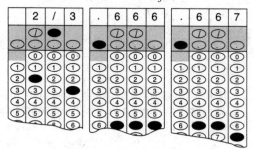

Acceptable ways to grid $\frac{2}{3}$ are:

31

If the average of n numbers is 32, and the sum of these n numbers is 352, what is the value of n?

32

An auditorium with 120 seats begins to fill 20 minutes prior to the start of a lecture. If it fills at a rate of 12 students per minute, what fraction of the seats are empty 12 minutes prior to the start of the lecture?

33

$$\frac{(x+1)(x-2)}{2}+3x$$

If the expression above is rewritten in the form ax^2+bx+c, where a, b, and c are constants, what is the value of b?

34

$$y \le 1{,}000 - 12x$$

$$y \le 3x$$

In the xy-plane, if a point with coordinates (m, n) lies in the solution set of the system of inequalities above, what is the maximum possible value of n?

35

If x is the degree measure of an angle such that $\sin(x^\circ)=\sin\left(\dfrac{5\pi}{4}\right)$ and $\tan(x^\circ)=\tan\left(\dfrac{5\pi}{4}\right)$, and if $720 < x < 1{,}080$, what is the value of x?

36

$$\frac{4}{1-x}=\frac{2}{x+2}-\frac{1}{2}$$

What is the sum of the two solutions of the equation above?

4   **4**

Questions 37 and 38 refer to the following information.

$$\text{Projectile 1: } h_1(t) = -4.9t^2 + 28t + 10$$

$$\text{Projectile 2: } h_2(t) = -4.9t^2 + 7t + 19$$

The functions above show the heights, in meters, t seconds after the simultaneous launch of two projectiles.

37

What is the height, in meters, of the two projectiles at the moment that their heights are equal?

38

What is the average vertical speed of Projectile 1, in meters per second, in the interval between its launch and the time it reaches its maximum height?

STOP

**If you finish before time is called, you may check your work on this section only.
Do not turn to any other section of the test.**

5   **5**

Essay

50 MINUTES, 1 QUESTION

DIRECTIONS

The essay gives you the opportunity to show how effectively you can read and comprehend a passage and write an essay analyzing the passage. In your essay, you should demonstrate that you have read the passage carefully, present a clear and logical analysis, and use language precisely.

Your essay must be written on the lines provided in your answer booklet; except for the Planning Page of the answer booklet, you will receive no other paper on which to write. You will have enough space if you write on every line, avoid wide margins, and keep your handwriting to a reasonable size. Remember that people who are not familiar with your handwriting will read what you write. Try to write or print so that what you are writing is legible to those readers.

You have <u>50 minutes</u> to read the passage and write an essay in response to the prompt provided inside this booklet.

As you read the passage below, consider how Jean Kim uses

- evidence, such as facts or examples, to support claims
- reasoning to develop ideas and connect claims and evidence
- stylistic or persuasive elements, such as word choice or appeals to emotion, to add power to the ideas expressed

---

Adapted from Jean Kim "Violence Stalks the American Dream Like a Badass Cowboy." ©2016 Aeon Media (Aeon.co). Originally published in *Aeon* magazine, February 15, 2016.

1   American culture is infused with the enduring vision of the American Dream: the Big Idea of the self-made individual who comes upon a new land and creates his or her own destiny. That dream is embodied in the sweeping landscapes of John Ford Westerns, and in the yearning of Jay Gatsby, seen as 'the single green light, minute and far away,' across the Long Island Sound. The cult of the individual has seemingly made America great, bequeathing the chance to fulfill one's thirst for success. But all too often the quest can become selfish, a narcissistic vision that neglects or even tramples on those in the way or at the margins. And, perhaps most dangerous, failure to fulfill the dream can erupt into violence.

2   The United States has a dark history of plundering, usurping and exploiting the weak to establish power. "You reap what you sow" is one common philosophy. "The fittest survive" is another. Human nature rises and falls on this egotism in the U.S., but when things go awry, when some don't get their way, outbursts, including violence, can result.

5   5

3 Americans watching this violence often react in an extremely bifurcated way, either detaching or recoiling in utter disgust. American media caters to this dichotomy. We have sanitized gore and aggression in television, video games, hunting and sports, particularly football, and movies, where violence gets much more lenient ratings than nudity or sex. At the same time, we have young people returning from war with missing limbs, children murdered in their schools and inner-city gunshot victims streaming into hospital trauma centers.

4 Only when violence becomes personal are Americans jarred, though briefly. With the advent of the Internet, cellphones and YouTube, we have these unexpected moments where the lava pours out. People react with confusion, shock; their numbness doesn't work anymore. But the more it happens, the more detached we become. In the end, we seem to view violence, especially gun violence, as a kind of bravado norm, the badass cowboy staking his claim on the homestead. Perhaps it is a way of feeling powerful by seeing yourself as the Grim Reaper in charge.

5 Along with acceptance of violence, the individualistic U.S. culture has seen the surge of another epidemic—narcissistic personality disorder, defined by the *Diagnostic and Statistical Manual of Mental Disorders* (DSM) as "a pervasive pattern of grandiosity." The disorder includes fantasies of unlimited success and power and the need for self-gratification, even if that involves exploiting and hurting others. It can start small, with verbal sleights and bullying, but the "malignant narcissist" needs increasing power and control over others to serve his ego—and the only way to exercise that power and control can be through escalating terror and violence.

6 Recent limitations in socioeconomic mobility combined with increasing racial diversity might be threatening narcissistic personalities and provoking ever more violence in the U.S. The old-school 20th-century American Dream rewarded the *Mad Men*-type of society where the white men comfortably ran the workplace, the women stayed at home or did clerical work, and the minorities were invisible servants holed up in their own enclaves. This structure no longer works. On one side, consolidated money and power has led to an oligarchy driven by tech and finance, which in turn financially froze out the lower and middle classes via inflation, job dissolution and outsourcing. On the other side, social-media democracy has empowered many diverse groups to fight for change. Given these upheavals, the future is uncertain and we are all in flux.

7 Tragically, violence might seem like the easiest way to restore the old order, especially for past beneficiaries—white men who can catch quick fame through ready access to guns. Statistically, mass shooters are mainly white men, but, notoriously, several minorities have joined in as well. In one way or another, they may all feel threatened, destabilized and betrayed, unable to find solid ground. It could be that violence in America will subside when its narcissists accept that the old order and the old dreams are gone. To heal the injured narcissist to a state of self-worth, we need new dreams along with plenty of training and the right kind of jobs so the dreams can be fulfilled.

Write an essay in which you explain how Jean Kim builds an argument to persuade her audience that violence in America is exacerbated by self-centered mythologies that conflict with reality. In your essay, analyze how she uses one or more of the features listed in the box above (or features of your own choice) to strengthen the logic and persuasiveness of her argument. Be sure that your analysis focuses on the most relevant features of the passage.

Your essay should NOT explain whether you agree with Kim's claims, but rather explain how she builds an argument to persuade her audience.

SAT PRACTICE TEST 6 ANSWER KEY

Section 1: Reading	Section 2: Writing and Language	Section 3: Math (No Calculator)	Section 4: Math (Calculator)
1. A	1. C	1. B	1. A
2. D	2. A	2. A	2. C
3. B	3. D	3. C	3. C
4. B	4. C	4. B	4. A
5. B	5. A	5. D	5. B
6. D	6. B	6. B	6. B
7. A	7. C	7. D	7. B
8. C	8. A	8. C	8. D
9. D	9. B	9. A	9. A
10. D	10. D	10. A	10. C
11. C	11. C	11. A	11. C
12. D	12. A	12. D	12. A
13. A	13. B	13. C	13. A
14. A	14. D	14. B	14. C
15. B	15. C	15. D	15. C
16. C	16. B	16. 6	16. B
17. B	17. A	17. 9	17. B
18. D	18. B	18. $2 \leq x \leq 2.33$ or	18. C
19. C	19. D	$3.67 \leq x \leq 4$	19. C
20. A	20. B	19. 7/5 or 1.4	20. A
21. B	21. C	20. 5/12 or .417	21. A
22. D	22. D		22. D
23. C	23. A		23. C
24. D	24. C		24. A
25. A	25. D		25. B
26. C	26. C		26. C
27. B	27. A		27. B
28. C	28. B		28. A
29. D	29. A		29. A
30. A	30. D		30. C
31. C	31. A		31. 11
32. C	32. C		32. 1/5 or .2
33. C	33. C		33. 5/2 or 2.5
34. D	34. C		34. 200
35. C	35. C		35. 945
36. B	36. A		36. 11
37. C	37. C		37. 21.1
38. A	38. A		38. 14
39. B	39. D		
40. C	40. C		
41. A	41. A		
42. D	42. D		
43. C	43. A		
44. A	44. B		
45. C			
46. D			
47. D			
48. A			
49. B			
50. A			
51. D			
52. C			

Total Reading Points (Section 1)

Total Writing and Language Points (Section 2)

Total Math Points (Section 3 + Section 4)

Scoring Your Test

1. Use the answer key to mark your responses on each section.

2. Total the number of correct responses for each section:

    1. Reading Test   Number correct: _____ **(Reading Raw Score)**

    2. Writing and Language Test   Number correct: _____ **(Writing and Language Raw Score)**

    3. Mathematics Test—No Calculator   Number correct: _____

    4. Mathematics Test—Calculator   Number correct: _____

3. Add the raw scores for sections 3 and 4. This is your **Math Raw Score**: _____

4. Use the table on page 460 to calculate your **Scaled Test and Section Scores (10–40)**.

    Math Section Scaled Score (200–800):   _____

    Reading Test Scaled Score (10–40):   _____

    Writing and Language Test Scaled Score (10–40):   _____

5. Add the **Reading Test Scaled Score** and the **Writing and Language Test Scaled Score (sum will be 20–80)**, and multiply this sum by 10 to get your **Reading and Writing Test Section Score (200–800)**.

    Sum of Reading + Writing and Language Scores: _____ × 10 =

    Reading and Writing Section Score: _____

Scaled Section and Test Scores

Raw Score	Math Section Score	Reading Test Score	Writing/ Language Test Score	Raw Score	Math Section Score	Reading Test Score	Writing/ Language Test Score
58	800			29	540	27	29
57	790			28	530	26	29
56	780			27	520	26	28
55	760			26	510	25	27
54	750			25	510	25	27
53	740			24	500	24	26
52	730	40		23	490	24	26
51	730	40		22	480	23	25
50	720	39		21	470	23	24
49	710	38		20	460	23	24
48	700	37		19	460	22	23
47	690	36		18	450	21	22
46	680	35		17	440	21	21
45	670	35		16	430	20	20
44	660	34	40	15	420	20	19
43	660	33	39	14	410	20	19
42	650	33	38	13	390	19	18
41	650	32	37	12	370	18	17
40	640	32	37	11	360	18	16
39	630	31	36	10	350	17	16
38	620	31	35	9	340	16	15
37	610	30	34	8	320	15	14
36	600	30	33	7	300	15	13
35	590	29	33	6	280	14	13
34	580	29	32	5	270	13	12
33	570	28	31	4	250	12	11
32	570	28	31	3	230	11	10
31	560	28	31	2	210	10	10
30	550	27	30	1	200	10	10

PRACTICE SAT 6 ANSWER EXPLANATIONS

Section 1: Reading

1. **A**   **Inference**

Although Fanny expresses hope that Sir Thomas Bertram *may continue to like Mr. Rushworth* (lines 2–3), Edmund expresses *dread* (line 7) about *the impression [that five hours in Mr. Rushworth's company] must leave on Sir Thomas* (lines 7–8). In other words, Edmund *believes that his father will grow to dislike Mr. Rushworth.* Choice B is incorrect because Edmund expresses no regrets for his own actions. Choice C is incorrect because Fanny is certainly not trying to sabotage the engagement. Choice D is incorrect because Edmund is predicting exactly what his father will do, and indeed he turns out to be correct.

2. **D**   **Interpretation**

In lines 28–30, in describing Sir Thomas' thoughts the passage states, *Advantageous as would be the alliance, and long standing and public as was the engagement, her happiness must not be sacrificed to it.* This reveals the fact that the engagement *has been well-known for a long time.*

3. **B**   **Textual Evidence**

As indicated in the explanation to the previous question, the best evidence is found in lines 28–30.

4. **B**   **Word in Context**

In saying that *Sir Thomas resolved to speak seriously to her,* the passage is saying that he *decided* that he must have a serious discussion with her. Choice D is incorrect because agreement requires more than one person.

5. **B**   **Inference**

The final three paragraphs of the passage explain the relationship between Maria and Henry Crawford. Here, the narrator indicates that *Crawford had destroyed [Maria's] happiness* (line 83) by *leaving* (line 75) and devastating Maria emotionally, to the point that her feelings needed to be *tranquilized* (lines 75–76). In other words, Henry Crawford is *a former love interest of Maria who has spurned her.*

6. **D**   **Interpretation**

The paragraph in lines 63–73 indicates that, after her conversation with her father, Maria *was in a state of mind to be glad that she had secured her fate beyond recall; that she had pledged herself anew to Sotherton* (Rushworth's estate). In other words, she was happy that she had assuaged her father's fears that she was entering a marriage she did not want. Therefore, she resolves *to*

behave more cautiously to Mr. Rushworth, that her father might not again be suspecting (lines 70–72) that she did not want to marry Mr. Rushworth.

7. **A**   **Interpretation**

The sentence in lines 73–82 indicates that, after Henry Crawford left, Maria had feelings that needed to be *tranquilized* (line 75) but as time passed, *her mind became cool enough to seek all the comfort that pride and self revenge could give* (lines 81–82). In other words, her *feelings had transformed from desperation to vengeance.*

8. **C**   **Interpretation**

In lines 54–57, the narrator indicates that Sir Thomas believes that a *well-disposed young woman, who did not marry for love, was in general but the more attached to her own family.* In other words, a loveless marriage tends to bring *solidarity with the rest of the family.*

9. **D**   **Textual Evidence**

As indicated in the explanation to the previous question, the best evidence is found in lines 54–57.

10. **D**   **Word in Context**

The statement that Maria *was in a state of mind to be glad that she had secured her fate beyond recall* (lines 64–65) means that she was happy that she had made a decision that could not be *retracted* (taken back).

11. **C**   **Tone**

The statement that Maria *must escape from [her father] and Mansfield as soon as possible, and find consolation in fortune* (lines 93–95) indicates the *desperation* that Maria feels to move on to Sotherton estate. The statement that *Her mind was determined, and varied not* (lines 96–97) indicates clear *defiance* in the face of that desperation.

12. **D**   **Purpose**

The first paragraph begins with the statement that *for hundreds of years, humans have worried about rats as agents of disease.* This sentence alone indicates the *extent of an attitude.* The rest of the paragraph gives examples of this attitude in 11th-century Persia and in modern-day New York. Although the rest of the passage goes on to dispute some common ideas about how diseases are linked to human and rat activity, this paragraph does not *dispute* this *widespread belief.*

13. **A**   **Word in Context**

The phrase *how pathogens carried by rats corresponded with Katrina's flooding* (lines 23–24) refers to the degree that these germs *coincided with* flooding due to natural disasters.

---

14. A   **Graphical Inference**

The graph indicates that there were 80 reported cases of the plague in the United States from 2000–2014, and that 8 of these, or 10%, resulted in death.

---

15. B   **Inference**

Lines 35–43 describe the nature of Blum's work and the reasoning behind it. In particular, Blum says that his work is *laying the groundwork for a potentially powerful tool in disaster relief: a mathematical model that . . . can be used to guide smarter policies.* The next paragraph goes on to explain that, until now, policymakers have been misguided by erroneous assumptions about how diseases are spread.

---

16. C   **Textual Evidence**

As indicated in the explanation to the previous question, the best evidence is found in lines 40–43.

---

17. B   **Purpose**

When the author says that *on a "good" day, [researchers] handle up to a dozen disease-carrying rats* (lines 33–34), he uses quotation marks around *good* to make the point that most readers would not agree that handling disease-carrying rats would be "good." In other words, he is indicating that *the goals of scientists do not always correspond to the goals of non-scientists.*

---

18. D   **Interpretation**

When the author states that *it doesn't matter where the rats are, but where people think they are* (lines 46–47), the author is making the point that both individuals and *policymakers* (those who drive government action) *are guided more by perception than by fact.*

---

19. C   **Word in Context**

The phrase *they will concentrate countermeasures in those places* (lines 49–50) means that policymakers will *focus* their efforts in the places where they think they are most needed.

---

20. A   **Interpretation**

In lines 57–60, we get a summary of one of Blum's findings: *a greater human population density doesn't necessarily mean more rats. In fact, Blum found that rats moved in when humans abandoned spaces.* Choice B is incorrect because the passage indicates that the plague virus is transmitted by fleas, not rats. Choice C is incorrect because the opposite correlation was found. Choice D is incorrect because the passage

mentions nothing about how rats are affected by *hantavirus.*

---

21. B   **Interpretation**

In lines 68–71, the passage states that *the much-feared plague is not a concern at all because the plague bacteria does not naturally exist in the U.S. except in scattered rural areas.* In lines 14–15, the author states that *as a bacterial disease, plague can be treated with antibiotics.* In other words, the author believes that the plague is an *isolated and manageable health risk.*

---

22. D   **Textual Evidence**

As indicated in the explanation to the previous question, the best evidence is found in lines 68–71.

---

23. C   **Cross-Textual Inference**

The authors of the two passages disagree about the significance of *Common Sense* in inspiring the American Revolution: Adams doubts *that this pamphlet was of great importance in the Revolution* (lines 38–39), but Powell claims that, with its appearance, *suddenly, increasing numbers spoke openly for independence* (lines 85–86). They disagree also about the soundness of its arguments: Adams says that Paine's *"Arguments" from the Old Testament on the unlawfulness of the monarchy were ridiculous, either from foolish superstition or willful sophistry* (lines 14–17), but Powell stands with Washington's claim that *Common Sense* offered *"sound doctrine and unanswerable reasoning"* (lines 75–76). They also disagree about the genius of its author: Adams called his plan for democracy *foolish* (line 22) and said that his best arguments were ones *which [Adams] had been repeating for nine months* (lines 31–32), but Powell agrees with Bailyn's quote in lines 91–103 that claims that the pamphlet was brilliant.

They agree, however, that *Common Sense* had extensive popular appeal. Adams expresses dread about *the effect so popular a pamphlet might have among the people* (lines 25–26), and Powell states that the pamphlet was so popular that its ideas *leaped across borders* (lines 77–78) and was well received across the globe.

---

24. D   **Purpose**

Adams uses the word *delicacy* sarcastically to describe Paine's use of such hyperbolic phrases as *"The Royal Brute of England,"* and *"The Blood upon his Soul."* Therefore, Adams is making the point that Paine was not *particularly subtle in his characterizations.*

---

25. A   **Interpretation**

In lines 16–21, Adams criticizes Paine's *plan to a form of government* as being *so democratical, without any restraint or attempt at any equilibrium or counterpoise, that it must produce confusion and every evil work.* In other words, Adams believes that Paine's proposal for the American government relies far too much on democracy, which is the rule of the people. Choice B is incorrect because Adams is not criticizing Paine's style of rhetoric in this sentence. Choice C is incorrect because Adams is not suggesting that Paine is not adamant about independence, and indeed he praises Paine's arguments for independence. Choice D is incorrect because this sentence is discussing Paine's proposed *form of government*, and not a system of economics.

---

26. C   **Cross-Textual Inference**

Adams criticizes Paine's attack on the monarchy as being *not argumentatively sound.* In lines 14–17, he states that *the "Arguments" from the Old Testament on the unlawfulness of monarchy were ridiculous, either from foolish superstition or willful sophistry* (specious reasoning).

---

27. B   **Textual Evidence**

As indicated in the explanation to the previous question, the best evidence is found in lines 14–17.

---

28. C   **Inference**

Passage 2 quotes George Washington's praise for Paine's *sound doctrine and unanswerable reasoning* (lines 75–76) in *Common Sense.* Adam disagrees about the *cogency of Paine's writing,* and states that *Common Sense* contains elements that *produce confusion* (lines 20–21) and that are *foolish* (line 22).

---

29. D   **Purpose**

The last line of the quotation expresses wonder at the fact that a man with a *relatively humble background* could have written something as profound as *Common Sense.* Choice A is incorrect because, although some of these positions are public service positions, the point that Bailyn is making is not that Paine had extensive experience in public service, but rather that he did *not* have the experience one would expect of a great pamphleteer. Choice B is incorrect because Bailyn says nothing about ethical standards. Choice D is incorrect because Bailyn is not remarking about Paine's education, but rather his relatively simple background.

---

30. A   **Cross-Textual Inference**

The doubts that Adams expresses in lines 39–41 are doubts that *Common Sense was of great importance in the Revolution.* The author of Passage 2 disagrees, and indeed states that, after *Common Sense* appeared, *suddenly, increasing numbers spoke openly for independence* (lines 86–87). In other words, the pamphlet *converted many colonists to the cause of independence.*

---

31. C   **Textual Evidence**

As indicated in the explanation to the previous question, the best evidence is found in lines 86–87.

---

32. C   **Tone**

Passage 1 is clearly *critical* of Thomas Paine and *Common Sense,* calling Paine a *Disastrous Meteor* (line 2) and his plan *foolish* (line 22), whereas Passage 2 is *laudatory* (complimentary), calling Paine a *genius* (line 103) and his pamphlet *brilliant* (line 93).

---

33. C   **Thesis**

The *timely lesson* is that the dramatic changes in metabolic energy, as revealed by the owls in Homestead Cave, are due *not [to] climate change, but [to] human activity* (line 26) that changes the ecology of millions of species. In other words, *human activity can have a more significant impact on global ecology than global warming does.*

---

34. D   **Word in Context**

The author says that *despite all these [dramatic climatological] changes, life was pretty stable* in the Homestead Cave, in other words, *the total amount of biological energy . . . remained steady* (lines 16–19). Even though the climate had changed from *rainfall-rich coolness to its present hot, dry state* (lines 13–14), life had remained *consistently vigorous.*

---

35. C   **Purpose**

The first four paragraphs describe the *lesson* (line 8) of Homestead Cave, which is the lesson that humans can cause more dramatic ecological changes than even climate change can. Homestead Cave is particularly useful for demonstrating this fact because the 13,000 years in which it has been the home to owls have *spanned some profound environmental upheavals* (lines 9–10). That is, it is useful because of its *longevity as a habitat.*

---

36. B   **Inference**

After describing the human activity that caused the degradation of the habitat of the Atlantic cod, the author says that *that nuance was lost in the public narrative, which was exclusively about climate: "Climate Change Fuels Cod Collapse," said the headlines* (lines 54–57). The media *focused excessively on climate issues to the exclusion of ecological issues.*

---

37. C   **Textual Evidence**

As indicated in the explanation to the previous question, the best evidence is found in lines 54–59.

38. A   **Word in Context**

In line 88, the author uses the phrase *climate frame* to refer to the limited scope that the media impose on discussions about the environment. Therefore, *frame* refers to *the scope of a discussion*. Choice B is incorrect because, although ecological degradation is certainly a *problem*, the phrase *climate frame* is referring to the nature of the discussion of the problem, not the *proportions of the problem* itself. Choice C is incorrect because the author is not referring to any particular *setting of a phenomenon*. Choice D is incorrect because this paragraph is about the nature of the public discussion of a problem, not the scientific *study* of the problem.

39. B   **Graphical Analysis**

The two graphs indicate the total "ecological footprint" of humanity in 1961 and 2005. Each rectangle shows the total human impact, in hectares, for a particular geographical region. This is what the author is referring to when he refers to *human activity* (line 26) that has an impact on the global ecology.

40. C   **Purpose**

The eighth paragraph describes the *human activities that have altered the ecosystem of the Atlantic cod*, specifically overfishing, bottom-trawling, and dam-building.

41. A   **Inference**

In lines 80–85, the author states that the *Laudato Si* was *a full-throated denunciation of the ideology of unlimited economic growth, a lamentation of environmental degradation, a call for people to respect both ecosystems and individual animals: a radical, existentially challenging work, of which climate was just one facet*. In other words, it does not merely focus on the issue of climate change, but rather *articulates a well-balanced position with regard to the human impact on the global environment*.

42. D   **Textual Evidence**

As indicated in the explanation to the previous question, the best evidence is found in lines 80–85.

43. C   **Purpose**

The first paragraph of the passage mentions Einstein's General Theory of Relativity in order to *illustrate the effects of competition in scientific discovery*. Myhrvold's point in the first paragraph is that this *act of genius* (line 4) was *not born, fully formed, in some eureka moment* (lines 5–6), but rather that Einstein was *driven to complete it by a fierce (though collegial) rivalry with mathematician David Hilbert*. Choice A is incorrect because Myhrvold does not discuss the phenomenon described by the General Theory of Relativity at all. Choice B is incorrect because Myhrvold is not discussing the difference

between theoretical and applied science. Choice D is incorrect because, although Myhrvold goes on to argue for government investment in scientific research and innovation, he is not doing so in this first paragraph.

44. A   **Interpretation**

In this paragraph, Myrhvold's main point is that *without government support, most basic scientific research will never happen* (lines 28–29). He then goes on to describe the bygone days when *company research laboratories used to do this kind of work: experimental evidence for the big bang was discovered at AT&T's Bell Labs, resulting in a Nobel Prize. Those days are gone* (lines 36–40). Myhrvold then goes on to explain that *companies now understand that basic research is a form of charity—so they avoid it* (lines 42–44).

45. C   **Textual Evidence**

As indicated in the explanation to the previous question, the best evidence is found in lines 42–44.

46. D   **Purpose**

This paragraph as a whole discusses Myhrvold's claim that companies avoid the *charity* (line 44) of doing basic research. The three examples cited—the transistor, the graphical user interface, and giant magnetoresistance to boost hard-disk capacity —are all examples of inventions that did not earn their inventors any profit.

47. D   **Word in Context**

Throughout the passage, Myhrvold uses the term *basic research* (lines 43, 56, and 67) to describe the *kind of pure research that has delivered enormous prestige and great intellectual benefits but no profits* (lines 30–32), that is, *essential* research that earns researchers scientific prestige but not money.

48. A   **Word in Context**

In lines 66–72, Myhrvold is describing the situation in which research would be left to the private sector. But since private companies would be afraid to lose profit to their competitors, they would have to do this research *largely in secret* (line 69), thereby suppressing the innovation that thrives on the open sharing of ideas. Myhrvold believes that this suppression of innovation is due to *corporations competing with each other for economic advantage*.

49. B   **Interpretation**

In lines 20–26, Myhrvold describes the opinion that Matt Ridley espouses in his new book, namely that *government should leave it to companies to finance the research that they need* (lines 25–26). Myhrvold then goes on to describe how *dangerously wrong* (line 27) such arguments are. Therefore, he believes that Ridley's book is a *poor guide to public policy*.

---

50. A   **Interpretation**

In lines 75–78, Myhrvold describes how to motivate great scientific minds: we must *stoke the competitive instincts of the smartest people around and persuade them to share their discoveries, in exchange for a shot at glory and riches.* In other words, great minds are motivated by *prestige and money.*

---

51. D   **Textual Evidence**

As indicated in the explanation to the previous question, the best evidence is found in lines 75–78.

---

52. C   **Inference**

The *wide-ranging benefits* described in line 63 must not include *immediate corporate advantage*, because the basic scientific research that brings such benefits is shunned by *profit-driven companies* (lines 61–62).

Section 2: Writing and Language

1. C   **Transitions/Coordination**

The two clauses within this sentence show a stark contrast. Therefore, a contrasting conjunction like *although* is most appropriate.

---

2. A   **Transitions/Cohesiveness**

The sentence as a whole describes an important lesson that the writer learned when he worked in his father's office in the 1980s. Since this lesson was about professional boundaries and the etiquette for greeting one's boss, choices A, B, and C may all seem to be acceptable introductions to this discussion. However, notice that the question asks us to consider how to *set up the sentence* that follows. The sentence that follows uses the past tense to refer to a period of time when *working in an office meant dressing the part.* Without the reference to *1989* in the original phrasing, the sentence that follows does not make sense. Choices B and C are incorrect because they use the present tense and so do not provide a logical context for the sentence that follows. Choice D is incorrect because the paragraph is not about different standards for men and women.

---

3. D   **Development**

Although this sentence does not have a sharply different tone from the rest of the paragraph, it is inappropriate to a discussion of workplace professionalism. Neither the musical fads nor the political climate are relevant to this discussion about behavior in the workplace.

4. C   **Verb Tense/Verb Aspect/Verb Mood**

The original phrasing is incorrect because the writer is clearly talking about an actual event, which requires the indicative mood rather than the subjunctive mood. The other verbs in this sentence clearly indicate that this story is being told in the past tense, so choice C is correct. Although choice D is in the past tense, it is incorrect because it applies the consequential (or "perfect") aspect, which illogically implies a status-as-consequence.

---

5. A   **Diction/Clear Expression of Ideas**

The original word, *scourge* (a cause of trouble) is the best choice for this context, since *nepotism* (the practice of giving unfair advantage to family members) is rightly seen as a type of corruption and potential trouble in the workplace. Choice B is incorrect because *mishap* implies an accident beyond one's control, rather than a deliberate decision. Choice C is incorrect because a *setback* is something that hinders one's progress toward a goal, which is not relevant to this context. Choice D is incorrect because *tragedy* is far too strong a word for this context and also implies a situation that is out of one's control.

---

6. B   **Modifier Form**

The original phrasing is incorrect because it is awkward and forms a comma splice. Choice C is incorrect for the same reasons. Choice D is incorrect because deleting the underlined phrase also forms a comma splice. Only choice B avoids the comma splice and idiomatically coordinates the modifying phrase and the main clause.

---

7. C   **Cohesiveness**

The thesis of the passage is that *Thriving in different work environments means being a chameleon* and adapting oneself to the standards and expectations of each individual workplace. The only choice that provides an effective connection to this thesis is C, because it indicates that what is "professional" depends on the *specific time and place.*

---

8. A   **Verb Mood**

The original phrasing is best because it is in the subjunctive mood, which is necessary when describing an indirect command: *we were told that . . . we were to ask for the caller's name.* Choice B is incorrect because it is not idiomatic: we may say *we were told to ask*, but not *were told that to ask*. Choice C is incorrect because it is in the indicative mood rather than the subjunctive mood. Choice D is incorrect because the auxiliary *could* implies permission or ability, rather than an indirect command.

9. B — Coordination

This phrase contains four elements that are related to the verb *give*: a direct object (*the message*), an indirect object (*the CEO*), and two adverbial modifiers (*when he was available* and *in his office*). To properly coordinate these ideas, the objects to the verb take priority, and the modifiers must then be coordinated with their referents by the Law of Proximity. The original phrasing is incorrect because it subordinates the direct object. Choice C violates the Law of Proximity, because the modifier *when he was available* must immediately follow its referent, *the CEO*. Choice D is incorrect because it subordinates the direct object. Only choice B correctly coordinates these four elements.

10. D — Redundancy

The underlined word should be deleted because it is redundant: the phrase *followed the same protocol* implies that the writer was repeating a procedure he had used before.

11. C — Coordination/Development

The reference to *this skill* in the inserted sentence only makes sense if the sentence that precedes it clarifies that skill. Sentence 2 is the only choice that provides a clear referent: *being a chameleon*. Therefore, this sentence belongs immediately after sentence 2.

12. A — Diction/Clear Expression of Ideas

The first paragraph makes it clear that the National Gallery of Art has a long and respectable history, so the best word in this context should indicate this prestige. The original word, *foremost*, is best because it suggests prestige without implying any particular criterion or task. Choice B is incorrect because *unbeaten* suggests a competition, which is not relevant to this context. Choice C is incorrect because *ultimate* means the best or most extreme with regard to a particular criterion, but no such criterion is indicated here. Choice D is incorrect because *optimal* means superior at performing a particular task or serving a particular function, which is also not appropriate in this context.

13. B — Dangling Participles

The original phrasing creates a dangling participle: the subject of the participle *conceived* must also be the subject of the main clause. Since *the museum* is the only logical subject for this participle, the only acceptable choice is B.

14. D — Logical Comparisons

To be logical, the sentence must compare items that belong to the same category. It is not logical to compare a museum to *other great nations*, but it is logical to compare a museum to *those [museums] of other great nations*.

15. C — Parallelism

The sentence indicates a list of three things that Mellon *offered*, so the list must follow the Law of Parallelism. The three items must have the same grammatical form, in this case the infinitive form: *to donate . . . to use . . . and to include*.

16. B — Dangling Participles/Sentence Fragments

The original phrasing is incorrect because it produces a dangling participle: the subject of the participle *located* must be the subject of the main clause. Since the only logical subject of this participle is *the National Gallery of Art*, choices A and D are incorrect. Choice C is incorrect because it creates a sentence fragment.

17. A — Development

This sentence should be deleted because it essentially paraphrases the ideas in the previous sentence without providing any development.

18. B — Redundancy

The term *irrevocable* implies that the damage is *permanent*, and hence *enduring*. Every choice except B is redundant.

19. D — Diction/Clear Expression of Ideas

This paragraph is clearly discussing the long-term damage that light exposure can do to paintings. Only choice D, *degradation*, captures this idea.

20. B — Redundancy

The original phrasing is incorrect because the verb *comes* does not agree with the subject *sources* and because this verb conveys a redundancy. Only choice B avoids the redundancy and agrees with the verb.

21. C — Pronoun Antecedent Agreement/Logic

The use of the pronoun *which* is illogical. As an interrogative pronoun, its antecedent is the immediately preceding noun, which (depending on how the sentence is parsed) could be *paints* or *components*. However, neither word represents things that *are harder to reverse*. Only choice C corrects this semantic problem, by clarifying the point that ultraviolet rays *create a problem* that is hard to reverse.

22. D — Idiom

The correct idiomatic phrasing here is *works . . . to find*. No other choice is idiomatic.

23. A — Comma Splices/Modifier Form

The original phrasing is best, since it forms an adjectival phrase that modifies the noun *bat*. Choices B and C are incorrect because they both produce comma splices.

Choice D is incorrect because it misuses the progressive form of the participle and thereby indicates a current action rather than a current state of being.

---

24. C   **Punctuation/Comma Splices**

This sentence contains three independent clauses, and these clauses must be coordinated logically. Because the second and third clauses both explain the first clause, it is best to follow the first clause with a colon, which implies explanation. Choice A is incorrect because it forms a comma splice. Choice B is incorrect because the conjunction *so* is illogical in this context. Choice D is incorrect because the pronoun *where* requires a place to serve as its antecedent.

---

25. D   **Pronoun Antecedent Agreement/**
Possessive Form

Choice A is incorrect because the pronoun *its* disagrees in number with its antecedent *bats*. Choice B is incorrect because *they're* is the contraction of *they are*. Choice C is incorrect because *there* is not a possessive pronoun. The correct possessive form is *their*.

---

26. C   **Logical Comparisons**

The phrase *unlike other nocturnal animals* begins a comparison that must be completed logically. The only choice that provides a logical comparison is choice C: *bats*. The subjects of the other choices are not in the same category as *nocturnal animals*.

---

27. A   **Logical Comparisons/Pronoun**
Antecedent Agreement

The original phrasing provides the most logical comparison. Logic requires that we compare the *navigational and hunting skills* of one type of animal to the *navigational and hunting skills* of another type of animal. Choice B creates an illogical comparison. Choice C creates a fragment. Choice D is incorrect because the pronoun *that* does not agree with the antecedent *navigational and hunting skills*.

---

28. B   **Development/Cohesiveness**

The sentence that follows refers to the bats' remarkable *aerial maneuvers*, which is most directly associated with *flying acrobatically at full speed*. The other choices indicate true facts about bat navigation, but they each create a *non sequitur* with the sentence that follows.

---

29. A   **Development/Cohesiveness**

This sentence is most appropriate as an introduction to the paragraph as a whole, which is about the bat's ability to find its way deftly around its environment. This sentence makes a very general claim, which is then supported by the details that are provided in the paragraph.

---

30. D   **Clear Expression of Ideas/Diction**

Choice A is incorrect because applications cannot be *resourceful* (able to overcome difficulties), because applications are not willful agents. Choice B is incorrect because the application that is described in the sentences to follow is real and not *theoretical* (existing only in theory). Choice C is incorrect because *no-nonsense* (simple and straightforward) has too informal a tone for this context, and furthermore does not aptly describe the mobility aid, which is fact quite sophisticated. Choice D, *viable* (capable of working), is appropriate for describing application that could feasibly help millions of blind people.

---

31. A   **Idiom/Logical Comparisons**

The original phrasing most logically and idiomatically describes the comparison between the processing done by the mobility aid and the processing done by bat brains. Choice B is incorrect because it erroneously implies that bats use microprocessors. Choice C is incorrect because it illogically compares a *way* to *echoes*. Choice D is incorrect because it creates an ungrammatical and illogical comparison.

---

32. C   **Possessive Form/Pronouns**

Choice A is incorrect because *their* disagrees in number with the antecedent *bat*. Choice B is incorrect because *it's* is a contraction, not a possessive pronoun. Choice C is the correct possessive form of the pronoun, and it agrees with its antecedent.

---

33. C   **Logical/Idiom**

Since the sentence refers to *several obstacles*, the blind person must discriminate *among* them. The phrase *discriminate between* would be appropriate for exactly two things. The other choices are not idiomatic.

---

34. C   **Pronoun-Antecedent Agreement/**
Modifier Form

Choice A is incorrect because the use of the pronoun *which* implies that the year 1863 declared slaves free. Choice B is incorrect because a colon should not separate a modifying phrase from the clause that it modifies. Choice D is incorrect because the present perfect participle *having declared* is illogical, since the Proclamation does not have a status-as-consequence. Choice C correctly coordinates the modifier with the main clause.

---

35. C   **Diction/Clear Expression of Ideas**

Choice C is best because *advocating the passage of the Thirteenth Amendment* is a clear example of *work[ing] to expand anti-slavery policies nationwide*. Choice A is incorrect because *propositioning* means "making a request of." Choice B is incorrect because the passage of an amendment cannot be *designed*. Choice D is incorrect because the amendment was passed, and not merely *intended*.

---

36. A   **Parallelism**

The original phrasing best maintains the parallel structure established in the preceding sentence: *Gone are the open slave markets . . . Gone also are the days when . . . .* The other choices disrupt this parallel structure.

---

37. C   **Coordination/Comma Splices**

The original phrasing is incorrect because it forms a comma splice. Choice B is incorrect because a colon should never separate a modifier from the clause that it modifies. Choice D is incorrect because the phrase that follows the semicolon is not an independent clause. Choice C logically coordinates the main clause and the participial phrase.

---

38. A   **Graphical Analysis**

The original phrasing provides the most accurate information from the graph. The six bars representing 2012 add up to approximately 6,000 cases. The other three statements are inaccurate, based on the graph.

---

39. D   **Development**

This sentence *expands on the point made in the previous sentence* (specifically that the 6,000 cases processed by the IOM are a small fraction of the problem) by *providing specific details* (specifically about the number of victims both worldwide and in the United States).

---

40. C   **Idiom**

The correct idiomatic phrasing here is to say that *human trafficking [has a status] **as** the [second] most profitable form of international crime.*

---

41. A   **Cohesiveness/Redundancy**

Choice A provides the most concise and effective way to combine the sentences. Choices B and C are redundant, since being *afraid* is the same as having *fear*. Choice D is incorrect because the pronoun *it* has no clear and logical antecedent.

---

42. D   **Idiom/Parallelism**

Choice D best maintains the parallelism in the list *to marshal . . . and to bring.*

---

43. A   **Diction/Clear Expression of Ideas**

Choice A, *initiative*, best describes the effort of the Blue Campaign to raise public awareness about human trafficking. Choice B is incorrect because *achievement* focuses on giving credit for the program rather than on the program itself. Choice C is incorrect because *scheme*

has too negative a connotation for this context. Choice D is incorrect because *enterprise* suggests a business venture rather than a social program.

---

44. B   **Conclusion/Cohesiveness**

Choice B best links to the previous sentence, which describes the great *cost* of our previous efforts to end slavery. It also effectively concludes the passage by expressing a positive hope. Choices A, C, and D are incorrect because they do not link to the previous sentence.

Section 3: Math (No Calculator)

---

1. B   **Algebra**
                                       (linear equations) EASY

Original equation: $3b = 2$

Divide both sides by 3: $b = \dfrac{2}{3}$

Divide both sides by 2: $\dfrac{b}{2} = \dfrac{1}{3}$

---

2. A   **Algebra (simplifying expressions) EASY**

Given expression: $\dfrac{x^3}{x} + \dfrac{x^5}{x^3}$

Simplify using the identity $\dfrac{x^m}{x^n} = x^{m-n}$: $x^2 + x^2$

Combine like terms: $2x^2$

---

3. C   **Algebra (inequalities) EASY**

Original inequality: $m < -3$
Multiply both sides by −3 and "flip" inequality:
                                                        $-3m > 9$
Combine the two given inequalities into
one statement: $9 < -3m \le 2n$
By the Transitive Law of Inequality: $9 < 2n$
Divide by 2: $4.5 < n$
Since n must be greater than 4.5, the least integer value it can take is 5.

---

4. B Algebra (expressing algebraic quantities) EASY

When Janie sits 3 dogs, she charges $12 per hour for the first dog and $5 per hour each for the other two, for a total of $22 per hour for all three dogs. Therefore, if she sits them for n hours her charge is $22n$. If she also takes all three dogs to the dog park, she charges an additional $10 (remember, she charges a flat fee for a trip to the dog park with up to three dogs), and so she charges a total of $(22n + 10)$.

5. D   **Algebra (linear relationships) EASY**

If Oprey Reef has an area of 400 square meters and is growing at a rate of 2.5 square meters per month, then it will have an area of $400 + 2.5m$ square meters after m months have passed. Similarly, if Pelican Reef has an area of 360 square meters and is growing at a rate of 3 square meters per month, it will have an area of $360 + 3m$ square meters after m months have passed. Their areas will be equal when $400 + 2.5m = 360 + 3m$

Subtract 360 and 2.5m from both sides: $40 = 0.5m$

Multiply both sides by 2: $80 = m$

---

6. B   **Problem Solving (numerical reasoning) MEDIUM**

Since the only fact we are given is that x is less than −10, let's choose a convenient value for x, like −100. Now we can simply plug this value into the choices and choose the one with the least value:

A) $\dfrac{1}{x^2} = \dfrac{1}{(-100)^2} = \dfrac{1}{10,000} = 0.0001$

B) $\dfrac{1}{x^3} = \dfrac{1}{(-100)^3} = \dfrac{1}{-1,000,000} = -0.000001$

C) $\dfrac{1}{x^4} = \dfrac{1}{(-100)^4} = \dfrac{1}{100,000,000} = 0.00000001$

B) $\dfrac{1}{x^5} = \dfrac{1}{(-100)^5} = \dfrac{1}{-10,000,000,000} = -0.0000000001$

Remember that numerically "least" doesn't mean "closest to zero;" it means "farthest to the left on the number line." Among these four numbers, choice B, −0.000001, is farthest to the left.

---

7. D   **Advanced Mathematics (complex numbers and radicals) MEDIUM**

Original expression: $\sqrt{-27} + \sqrt{-48}$

Factor out $\sqrt{-1}$ from both terms: $\sqrt{-1}\sqrt{27} + \sqrt{-1}\sqrt{48}$

Substitute $i = \sqrt{-1}$: $i\sqrt{27} + i\sqrt{48}$

Factor the perfect square from each radicand:
$$i\sqrt{9}\sqrt{3} + i\sqrt{16}\sqrt{3}$$

Simplify square roots of perfect squares: $3i\sqrt{3} + 4i\sqrt{3}$

Combine like terms: $7i\sqrt{3}$

---

8. C   **Algebra (interpreting expressions) MEDIUM**

The equation $n = 416 - 4T$ or, equivalently, $n = -4T + 416$, is a linear equation in "slope-intercept" form. The "slope" of this linear relationship is −4, which represents the "change in n per unit change in T." Since n represents the number of cars requesting full service and T represents the temperature in degrees Fahrenheit, this slope represents the fact that 4 *fewer* (this is the meaning of the minus sign) cars request full service for every 1-degree increase in temperature.

---

9. A   **Additional Topics (circles and arcs) MEDIUM**

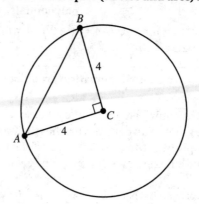

When solving a geometry problem, it is usually very helpful to mark up the diagram, and even occasionally to re-draw it. In this case, the diagram is drawn to scale, so we can just mark it up. When we are asked to find an arc length, we should remember that an arc is just a part of the circumference, and we can always find the circumference of a circle with the formula $C = 2\pi r$. Therefore, our strategy should be to find the value of r, then use this to find the circumference, then use this to find the arc length. To find the value of r, we must use the fact that the right triangle has an area of 8 square units. Therefore: $\dfrac{1}{2}(r)(r) = 8$

Multiply both sides by 2: $r^2 = 16$

Take the square root of both sides: $r = 4$

This means that the circumference of the circle is $2\pi(4) = 8\pi$. Since the central angle of arc AB is 90°, it represents 1/4 of the circumference, or $(1/4)(8\pi) = 2\pi$.

---

10. A   **Algebra (simplifying expressions) MEDIUM**

Original expression: $\dfrac{a}{b}(a-b)(a+b)$

FOIL the product of binomials: $\dfrac{a}{b}(a^2 - b^2)$

Distribute: $\dfrac{a^3}{b} - \dfrac{ab^2}{b}$

Simplify: $\dfrac{a^3}{b} - ab$

---

11. A   **Advanced Mathematics (composition of functions) MEDIUM**

We simply need to find the equation that is equivalent to $y = g(f(x))$.

Substitute $f(x) = -\dfrac{1}{2}x + 1$: $y = g\left(-\dfrac{1}{2}x + 1\right)$

Substitute $-\dfrac{1}{2}x + 1$ as the input to $g(x)$: $y = -4\left(-\dfrac{1}{2}x + 1\right) - 1$

Distribute and simplify: $y = 2x - 4 - 1 = 2x - 5$

Since this equation is now in slope-intercept form, we can see that its y-intercept is −5.

12. D Advanced Mathematics (factoring polynomials) MEDIUM

If $p(x) = 6x^2 + 2x$, then $p(x) - 4 = 6x^2 + 2x - 4$, which can be factored as $2(3x - 2)(x + 1)$.

13. C Advanced Mathematics (graphical analysis) MEDIUM

The x-axis is equivalent to the line $y = 0$, so the points at which the graph of an equation touches the x-axis can be found simply by setting y equal to 0 and solving for x. If we take the equation $6x - xy = x^2 + 9$ and set y equal to 0, we get:

$$6x = x^2 + 9$$

Subtract $6x$ from both sides: $0 = x^2 - 6x + 9$

Factor: $0 = (x - 3)^2$

Therefore, by the Zero Product Property, the x-intercept is $(3, 0)$.

14. B Advanced Mathematics (quadratic equations) MEDIUM-HARD

First we should recognize that the solution is presented as a nonsimplified solution from the quadratic formula: if $ax^2 + bx + c = 0$, then $x = \dfrac{-b \pm \sqrt{b^2 - 4ac}}{2a}$. However, the equations are not exactly in standard quadratic form, so we must first subtract the constant term from both sides so that each equation has 0 on the right side:

A) $2x^2 + 3x + 5 = 0$

B) $2x^2 + 3x - 5 = 0$

C) $2x^2 - 3x + 5 = 0$

D) $2x^2 - 3x - 5 = 0$

Now notice that the solution "fits" the quadratic formula only if $a = 2$, $b = 3$, and $c = -5$. This corresponds to the equation in choice B.

15. D Advanced Mathematics (rational functions) MEDIUM-HARD

If this equation is true for all values of x (except $x = 2$), as we are told, then we can just choose a value of x that lets us solve easily for b. A good option is $x = 0$:

$$\frac{x^3}{x - 2} = x^2 + 2x + 4 + \frac{b}{x - 2}$$

Substitute $x = 0$: $\dfrac{(0)^3}{(0) - 2} = (0)^2 + 2(0) + 4 + \dfrac{b}{(0) - 2}$

Simplify: $0 = 4 - \dfrac{b}{2}$

Multiply by 2 on both sides: $0 = 8 - b$

Add b to both sides: $b = 8$

Equivalently, we could have simply used long division (or synthetic division) to divide x^3 by $x - 2$ to show that the remainder is 8. Or, if you are *exceptionally* clever and recall the Remainder Theorem, which says that whenever the polynomial $P(x)$ is divided by $x - k$ the remainder is $P(k)$, you can see that b must be equal to $(2)^3 = 8$.

16. 6 Algebra (linear equations) EASY

If the point $(a, 1)$ is a solution, we can solve this equation by simply substituting $x = a$ and $y = 1$. When we substitute these values into $y = \dfrac{1}{3}x - 1$ we get $1 = \dfrac{1}{3}a - 1$

Add 1 to both sides: $2 = \dfrac{1}{3}a$

Multiply by 3: $6 = a$

17. 9 Advanced Mathematics (solving quadratics) EASY

Substituting $x = 3$ into the equation gives us: $2(3)^2 - b(3) + b = 0$

Simplify: $18 - 2b = 0$

Add $2b$ to both sides: $18 = 2b$

Divide by 2: $9 = b$

18. $2 \leq x \leq 2.33$ or $3.67 \leq x \leq 4$ Advanced Mathematics (inequalities) MEDIUM

Original inequalities: $2 \leq 3|3 - x| \leq 3$

Since the problem asks us to find *one possible* value of x, we don't have to worry about finding the general solution. Therefore, we can find a particular solution by assuming that $3 - x$ (the expression inside the absolute value) is non-negative. This means that $3 - x \geq 0$ and therefore $x \leq 3$. Now, recall that if a number is non-negative, then it is equal to its absolute value. Therefore, if $x \leq 3$, we can rewrite the inequality and just ignore the absolute value signs: $2 \leq 3(3 - x) \leq 3$

Distribute: $2 \leq 9 - 3x \leq 3$

Subtract 9 from all three sides: $-7 \leq -3x \leq -6$

Divide by -3 and "flip" the inequalities: $\dfrac{7}{3} \geq x \geq 2$

Since 7/3 is 2.333 . . . , you may enter any value between 2 and 2.33.

To get the *complete* solution set, you must consider the possibility that $3 - x$ could be negative, and so $x > 3$. Remember that *if a quantity is negative, then its absolute value is its opposite.* Therefore, if $x > 3$, then the inequality can be rewritten as: $2 \leq 3(x - 3) \leq 3$

Distribute: $2 \leq 3x - 9 \leq 3$

Add 9 to all three sides: $11 \leq 3x \leq 12$

Divide by 3 on all three sides: $\dfrac{11}{3} \leq x \leq 4$

Since 11/3 = 3.666 . . . , you may enter any value between 3.67 and 4.

19. **7/5 or 1.4** — Additional Topics (complex numbers) MEDIUM-HARD

Original expression: $\dfrac{2+i}{2-i}$

To simplify the quotient of complex numbers, multiply numerator and denominator by the *complex conjugate of the denominator*: $\left(\dfrac{2+i}{2-i}\right)\left(\dfrac{2+i}{2+i}\right)$

Multiply: $\dfrac{4+4i+i^2}{4-i^2}$

Substitute $i^2 = -1$ and simplify: $\dfrac{4+4i+(-1)}{4-(-1)} = \dfrac{3+4i}{5} = \dfrac{3}{5} + \dfrac{4}{5}i$

Therefore, $a = \dfrac{3}{5}$ and $b = \dfrac{4}{5}$, so $a + b = \dfrac{7}{5} = 1.4$

20. **5/12 or .417** — Additional Topics (areas) HARD

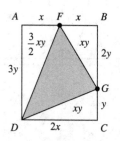

As with every SAT geometry question, it's best to mark up the diagram. Since F is a midpoint of its side, AF and FB must have the same measure, so let's call them both x. Since BG is twice as long as GC, let's say that GC is y units long and BG is $2y$ units long. This means that the rectangle has a height of $3y$ and a width of $2x$, so its area is $(3y)(2x) = 6xy$. Now we can find the area of the three nonshaded triangles fairly easily, because their bases and heights are all labeled. Using the triangle area formula $A = (1/2)(b)(h)$, we can calculate the areas of the three nonshaded triangles: xy, xy, and $\dfrac{3}{2}xy$. The sum of these three areas is $\dfrac{7}{2}xy$, which is $\dfrac{\frac{7}{2}xy}{6xy} = \dfrac{7}{12}$ of the total area. Therefore, the *shaded* triangle is $1 - \dfrac{7}{12} = \dfrac{5}{12}$ of the total area.

Section 4: Math (Calculator)

1. **A** — Problem Solving and Data Analysis (proportions) EASY

The phrase *at this rate* tells us that we can set up a proportion based on equal rates: $\dfrac{12 \text{ gallons}}{\$24.36} = \dfrac{16 \text{ gallons}}{\$x}$

Cross-multiply: $12x = 389.76$

Divide by 12: $x = \$32.48$

2. **C** — Problem Solving and Data Analysis (averages) EASY

Recall that the sum of any set of numbers is equal to their average times the number of numbers in the set. Therefore, if the average of a and b is 6, then

$$a + b = (6)(2) = 12$$

If the average of a, b, and c is 8, then:

$$a + b + c = (8)(3) = 24$$

Subtract the first equation from the second equation:

$$c = 12$$

3. **C** — Algebra (multiplying binomials) EASY

We can find the value of xy in terms of a and b by simply using the given equations to substitute:

$$xy = (3a + b)(a - b) = 3a^2 - 3ab + ab - b^2 = 3a^2 - 2ab - b^2$$

4. **A** — Algebra (linear systems) EASY

A system of two linear equations will have no solution if and only if the graphs of those two equations are parallel lines, which means they have the same slope but different y-intercepts. (If they have the same slope <u>and</u> the same y-intercept, then their graphs are identical and therefore the system has infinitely many solutions.) Remember that in standard $ax + by = c$ form, the slope of a line is always $-a/b$. Notice that choice A is the only system in which the lines are parallel. They both have a slope of -2, and the first line has a y intercept of 0, but the second line has a y-intercept of 1.

5. **B** — Problem Solving and Data Analysis (tables) EASY

The table shows that the tem has a total of 13 attackers and 14 midfielders. There are 6 attackers who are in the 12th grade and 5 midfielders who are in the 12th grade, so $(6 + 5)/(13 + 14) = 11/27$ of this group are 12th graders.

6. **B** — Algebra (linear inequalities) EASY

If he Arkady needs \$5,000 for the down payment, but already has \$300 saved, he only needs to save \$4,700 more. If he saves \$40 each week, he will have saved \$40w after w weeks. Since this amount must be at least 4,700 dollars, $4{,}700 \leq 40w$.

7. **B** — Advanced Mathematics (geometric sequences) EASY

After the first bounce, the ball rises to 80% of its previous height, or $(0.8)(10) = 8$ meters. After the second bounce, it rises to $(0.8)(8) = 6.4$ meters. After the third bounce, it rises to $(0.8)(6.4) = 5.12$ meters.

8. **D** — Additional Topics (geometric sequences) EASY-MEDIUM

When the ball hits the ground for the first time, it has traveled 10 meters. It then goes up and down 8 meters before it strikes the ground for the second time, then up and down 6.4 meters before striking the ground for the third time, then up and down 5.12 meters before striking the ground for the fourth time. Therefore, the total distance it travels is $10 + 2(8) + 2(6.4) + 2(5.12) = 49.04$ meters.

---

9. A   Algebra (equivalent expressions) MEDIUM

If $u = x + 2$, then $x = u - 2$. We can use this equation to substitute into $(x-1)^2 \sqrt{x+2}$ to get $(u-2-1)^2 \sqrt{u-2+2} = (u-3)^2 \sqrt{u}$.

---

10. C   Advanced Mathematics (functional analysis) MEDIUM

Use the definition of $g(x)$ to translate $g(a) = 8$:
$$g(a) = 5a - 2 = 8$$
Add 2 to both sides: $5a = 10$
Divide both sides by 5: $a = 2$
Evaluate $g(a+2)$: $g(a+2) = g(2+2) = g(4) = $
$$5(4) - 2 = 20 - 2 = 18$$

---

11. C   Advanced Mathematics (graphical analysis) MEDIUM

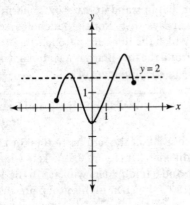

The equation $f(x) = 2$ has real-valued solutions wherever the graphs of $y = f(x)$ and $y = 2$ intersect. Therefore, we should draw the line $y = 2$ on all of the graphs and choose the one that gives four distinct intersection points. As the figure above shows, the only choice that works is C.

---

12. A   Algebra (interpretation of expressions) MEDIUM

The number 25 is the "slope" of the supply function $S(p) = 25p + 100$, where S represents the number of units supplied to the market and p is the price, in dollars. Like every "slope," it represents the change in the function value (usually y, but in this case S) for every unit increase in the input (usually x, but in this case p). Therefore, 25 represents the change in the number of units supplied for every dollar increase in price.

---

13. A   Advanced Mathematics (functional analysis) MEDIUM

The equilibrium price, as the question explains, is the price at which the supply and the demand are equal. Therefore, we simply set the supply and demand expressions equal and solve for p:
$$25p + 100 = -35p + 1,300$$
Add $35p$ to both sides and subtract 100 from both sides:
$$60p = 1,200$$
Divide by 60: $p = 20$

---

14. C   Advanced Mathematics (nonlinear systems) MEDIUM-HARD

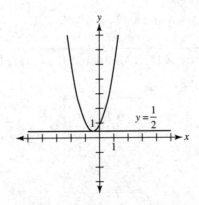

The graph of the equation $y = 2x^2 + 2x + 1$ is an "open-up" parabola, and the graph of the equation $y = b$ is a horizontal line. The only way that a horizontal line can intersect an "open-up" parabola in exactly one point is if it passes through the vertex of the parabola. Therefore, to solve this problem we must find the coordinates of the vertex of the parabola. The line of symmetry of the parabola described by $y = ax^2 + bx + c$ is the vertical line $x = -\frac{b}{2a}$. This line of symmetry must pass through the vertex, so the vertex must have an x-coordinate of $-\frac{b}{2a} = -\frac{2}{2(2)} = -\frac{1}{2}$. We can now find the y-coordinate by plugging $x = -\frac{1}{2}$ into the quadratic equation: $y = 2\left(-\frac{1}{2}\right)^2 + 2\left(-\frac{1}{2}\right) + 1 = 2\left(\frac{1}{4}\right) - 1 + 1 = \frac{1}{2}$. Therefore, the vertex of the parabola is $\left(-\frac{1}{2}, \frac{1}{2}\right)$, and so the horizontal line that passes through this vertex is the line $y = \frac{1}{2}$.

---

15. C   Algebra (word problems) MEDIUM

Let's let $a = $ the number of easy puzzles that Joaquin solves, and $b = $ the number of hard puzzles that he solves. If he solved 30 puzzles, then $a + b = 30$. If he earned a total of 375 points, then $10a + 25b = 375$. Now let's solve the system:
$$a + b = 30$$
$$10a + 25b = 375$$

Multiply both sides of the first equation by 10:

$$10a + 10b = 300$$

Subtract this from the second equation: $15b = 75$

Divide by 15: $b = 5$

Substitute $b = 5$ into the first equation: $a + 5 = 30$

Subtract 5 from both sides: $a = 25$

Therefore, Joaquin solved $25 - 5 = 20$ more easy puzzles than hard puzzles.

---

16. B   **Problem Solving and Data Analysis (medians) MEDIUM**

The median of 200 numbers is the average of the 100th and 101st of these numbers when listed in order. The sum of the two bars on the left is just under 100, and the sum of the first three bars is clearly greater than 130. Therefore, the 100th and 101st numbers are in the third bar, which represents a Richter scale number of 1.5.

---

17. B   **Advanced Mathematics (solving quadratics) MEDIUM**

Although this question can be answered by finding the two solutions and then taking their sum, it turns out that these solutions aren't very pretty: $-2 + \sqrt{14}$ and $-2 - \sqrt{14}$. So it is helpful to remember that, for any quadratic equation of the form $ax^2 + bx + c = 0$, the sum of the two (perhaps identical) solutions will always be $-b/a$, and the product of those solutions will always be c/a. Therefore, we simply need to put the equation into standard quadratic form and find $-b/a$. The equation $2(x^2 + 4x) = 20$ can be rewritten as $2x^2 + 8x - 20 = 0$, and so $-b/a = -8/2 = -4$, which is obviously the sum of $-2 + \sqrt{14}$ and $-2 - \sqrt{14}$.

---

18. C   **Problem Solving and Data Analysis (study design) MEDIUM-HARD**

A proper study requires a *control group*, which is a group that is identical in every relevant way to the experimental group *except* for the treatment variable. Without a control group, it can be difficult if not impossible to tell if any effect is due to the treatment or to some other variable. The treatment variable in this case is the taking of the zinc supplements. Therefore, the best comparison group is one that is identical to the treatment group (100 adults with cold symptoms who are taking some kind of pill), but differs in the treatment: the subjects take a harmless sugar pill (a "placebo") instead of the actual zinc supplement.

---

19. C   **Problem Solving and Data Analysis (percent change) MEDIUM-HARD**

Let's define x as the minimum cost, in dollars, of purchases that Philip must make to save enough on shipping and handling costs to cover his annual fee of $80. First, we must calculate the amount he would spend in total on those purchases if he did *not* have the annual membership. With the 3.6% tax and 2% shipping and

handling on every purchase, the total would be $(1.036)(1.02)(x) = 1.05672x$. If, however, he did not have to pay shipping and handling, the total would be only $1.036x$. The difference between these two is $1.05672x - 1.036x = 0.02072x$.

This difference must be at least $80 in order for Philip to cover his annual fee, so $0.02072x \geq 80$. Dividing both sides by 0.02072 gives $x \geq 3,861$.

---

20. A   **Advanced Mathematics (rational expressions) HARD**

Notice that this question is not asking us to "simplify" the expression. In fact, each answer choice is written as a sum, which is an "expanded" version of the original. Fortunately, the answer choices have some elements in common that help us simplify this problem. Notice that each sum contains fractions with the same denominators: $(x + 1)$ and $(x - 1)$. The common denominator, then, is their product: $(x + 1)(x - 1) = x^2 - 1$, which is the denominator in the original expression. This shows us that one way we can solve this problem is by simplifying each choice until we find one that is equivalent to the original expression:

A) $\dfrac{2}{x+1} - \dfrac{1}{x-1} = \dfrac{2(x-1)}{(x+1)(x-1)} - \dfrac{1(x+1)}{(x+1)(x-1)} = \dfrac{2x-2}{x^2-1} - \dfrac{x+1}{x^2-1}$

$= \dfrac{x-3}{x^2-1}$

B) $\dfrac{1}{x+1} - \dfrac{2}{x-1} = \dfrac{1(x-1)}{(x+1)(x-1)} - \dfrac{2(x+1)}{(x+1)(x-1)} = \dfrac{x-1}{x^2-1} - \dfrac{2x+2}{x^2-1}$

$= \dfrac{-x-3}{x^2-1}$

C) $\dfrac{2}{x+1} + \dfrac{1}{x-1} = \dfrac{2(x-1)}{(x+1)(x-1)} + \dfrac{1(x+1)}{(x+1)(x-1)} = \dfrac{2x-2}{x^2-1} + \dfrac{x+1}{x^2-1}$

$= \dfrac{3x-1}{x^2-1}$

D) $\dfrac{1}{x+1} + \dfrac{2}{x-1} = \dfrac{1(x-1)}{(x+1)(x-1)} + \dfrac{2(x+1)}{(x+1)(x-1)} = \dfrac{x-1}{x^2-1} + \dfrac{2x+2}{x^2-1}$

$= \dfrac{3x+1}{x^2-1}$

---

21. A   **Advanced Mathematics (exponentials) MEDIUM-HARD**

We can use the given equations to substitute into the expression $\dfrac{b}{a}$: $\dfrac{b}{a} = \dfrac{4^{-3k}}{2^{3k}}$

One way to simplify this expression is to express both exponentials in terms of the same base. Since $4 = 2^2$, we can rewrite the expression as

$$\dfrac{b}{a} = \dfrac{4^{-3k}}{2^{3k}} = \dfrac{(2^2)^{-3k}}{2^{3k}} = \dfrac{2^{-6k}}{2^{3k}} = 2^{-6k-3k} = 2^{-9k}$$

22. D   **Problem Solving and Data Analysis (scatter plots) MEDIUM-HARD**

The point corresponding to the year 2004 has coordinates of approximately (4.8, 3), which means that in 2004, the population density of leopards was 4.8 individuals per square kilometer and the population density of baboons was 3 individuals per square kilometer. The point corresponding to 2006 has coordinates of about (4.5, 5.6). This means that the population density of baboons went from 3 to 5.6, which is a change of approximately (5.6 − 3)/3 = 2.6/3 = 0.87 or about 87%, which is closest to choice D.

23. C   **Data Analysis and Problem Solving (scatter plots) MEDIUM**

Choice A is incorrect because the population density of baboons *increased* between 2000 and 2010, from about 1.2 to about 8 individuals per square kilometer. Choice B is incorrect because the population density of leopards *decreased* between 2000 and 2010, from about 5.8 to about 3.5 individuals per square kilometer. Choice D is incorrect because if two variables vary inversely, then their products are (approximately) constant. However, if we take the product of each pair of coordinates, we get (5.8)(1.2) = **6.96** for 2000, (5.1)(2.9) = **14.79** for 2002, (4.8)(3) = **14.4** for 2004, (4.5)(5.6) = **25.2** for 2006, (4)(7.9) = **31.6** for 2008, and (3.5)(8) = **28** for 2010. Since these products are not even approximately equal, we cannot say that the two variables vary inversely with one another. Choice C, however, is correct, because the 6 points fall very close to a "line of best fit" relating the two population densities.

Population Density of Baboons and Leopards in Western Cape of South Africa, 2000–2010

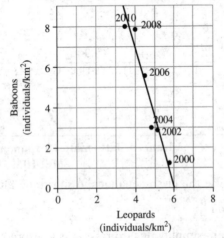

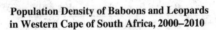

24. A   **Advanced Mathematics (exponentials) MEDIUM-HARD**

The correct answer is A, because in order to increase a number by x%, we must multiply it by $(1 + x/100)$.

Therefore, increasing a number by 1% is equivalent to multiplying it by 1.01. So if an initial population P_0 grows at a rate of 1% *every* year, the population after t years is $P = P_0 (1.01)^t$, which is an exponential function. Choice C looks very similar to choice A, but it is *not* an exponential relationship, but rather a *linear* relationship, because each year the population is growing by a *constant* amount, which is 2% of the *original* population. For instance, in choice C, if the initial population were 100, then each year the population would grow by (0.02)(100) = 2, so after t years the population would be $P = 100 + 2t$, which is a linear relationship, not an exponential one. Choices B and D also indicate linear relationships.

25. B   **Problem Solving (numerical reasoning) MEDIUM-HARD**

It's very important to remember the difference between proving that something *can be true* and proving that something *must be true*. When solving *must be true* questions like this, it's often best to try first to find counterexamples for the statements, that is, examples that satisfy the conditions of the problem but do *not* satisfy the statements. A statement with a counterexample obviously does *not* have to be true.

Let's start by choosing values for a and b. Since a must be between 0 and 1, let's choose $a = 0.5$. Since b must be between −1 and 0, let's choose $b = -0.5$. Now we can check statement I. Since $(0.5)^2 = 0.25$ and $(-0.5)^2 = 0.25$, it is *not* necessarily true that $a^2 > b^2$. Since statement I is not necessarily true, we can eliminate choices A and D. When we plug these values in for statement II, we get $(0.5)^2 > (0.25)^2$, which is true. However, one successful example does not prove that statement II *must* be true, so let's check statement III. Since $(-0.5)^3 < \left(\dfrac{0.5}{-0.5}\right)^3$ simplifies to $-0.125 < -1$, which is *not* true, we can eliminate choice C, and so the correct answer must be choice B.

26. C   **Algebra (inequalities) MEDIUM**

Recall the formula that *average speed = total distance traveled ÷ total time*. The total time of the trip is 1 hour and 18 minutes, which is 1.3 hours. We can find the total distance traveled by using the formula *distance = average speed × time*. If he drove for 30 minutes (or 0.5 hour) at 64 mph, he traveled (64)(0.5) = 32 miles. If he then drove for 48 minutes (or 0.8 hour) at 50 mph, he traveled (50)(0.8) = 40 miles. Therefore, he traveled a total of 32 + 40 = 72 miles in 1.3 hours, which means his average speed was 72 ÷ 1.3 = 55.38 mph, which is closest to choice C.

27. B   **Advanced Mathematics (graphing parabolas) MEDIUM-HARD**

Let's start by assuming that the smaller banners have a height of h and a length of l, and therefore have an area of hl. The larger banners have a height of $(1 + k/100)h$ and a length of (1.40)*l*. Since the larger banner has an area that is 75% larger than the smaller banner:

$$(1 + k/100)h(1.40)l = 1.75hl$$

Divide both sides by *hl*: $(1 + k/100)(1.40) = 1.75$
Divide both sides by 1.40: $1 + k/100 = 1.25$
Subtract 1 from both sides: $k/100 = 0.25$
Multiply by 100: $k = 25$

---

28. **A**   Algebra (interpreting systems) MEDIUM-HARD

First, let's simplify our given equations to make them easier to work with.

First equation: $x + a = 4x - 8$
Subtract *x* from both sides: $a = 3x - 8$
Second equation: $y + b = 4y - 8$
Subtract *y* from both sides: $b = 3y - 8$
Since $a - b$ is equal to 1: $a - b = (3x - 8) - (3y - 8) = 1$
Simplify: $3x - 3y = 1$

Divide both sides by 3: $x - y = \dfrac{1}{3}$

Add *y* to both sides: $x = y + \dfrac{1}{3}$
Which means "*x* is 1/3 greater than *y*."

---

29. **A**   Problem Solving and Data Analysis (percentages) MEDIUM-HARD

One way to approach this question is to pick values for *x* and *y*. Since *y* must be 150% greater than *x*, let's choose $x = 100$ and so $y = 250$. (Be careful here—notice that *y* is not 150! If it is 150% *greater* than 100, then it is $(1 + 150/100)(100) = (1 + 1.5)(100) = (2.5)(100) = 250$.) Therefore, $x + y = 100 + 250 = 350$. To see what percentage 350 is greater than 250, we use the formula $(350 - 250)/250 = 100/250 = 0.4$ or 40%.

---

30. **C**   Additional Topics (volumes) MEDIUM-HARD

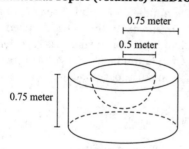

To find the volume of the fire pit, we must subtract the volume of the hemisphere from the volume of the cylinder. Recall (from the reference information at the beginning of the test) that the volume of a cylinder is $\pi r^2 h$ and the volume of a sphere is $\dfrac{4}{3}\pi r^3$. Since the diameter of the cylinder is 1.5 meters, its radius is 0.75 meter, and its height is also 0.75 meter. Therefore, its volume is $\pi(0.75)^2(0.75) = 0.421875\pi$. The hemisphere has a radius of $0.75 - 0.25 = 0.5$ meter, so it has a volume of

$\dfrac{2}{3}\pi(0.5)^3 = .083333\pi$. Therefore, the fire pit has a volume of $0.421875\pi - 0.083333\pi = 0.338542\pi = 1.063561$ cubic meters, which is closest to choice C.

---

31. **11**   Problem Solving and Data Analysis (averages) EASY

Recall the formula $average = sum \div n$: $32 = \dfrac{352}{n}$
Multiply both sides by *n*: $32n = 352$
Divide both sides by 32: $n = 11$

---

32. **1/5 or .2**   Problem Solving and Data Analysis (rates) EASY-MEDIUM

Since the auditorium began to fill 20 minutes prior to the lecture, by the time it was 12 minutes prior to the lecture the auditorium had been filling up for 8 minutes at a rate of 12 students per minute. This means that $(8)(12) = 96$ seats were filled, which is $96/120 = 4/5$ of the seats, and so $1 - 4/5 = 1/5$ of the seats are empty.

---

33. **5/2 or 2.5**   Algebra (equivalent expressions) MEDIUM

Original expression: $\dfrac{(x+1)(x-2)}{2} + 3x$

Distribute the 0multiplication in the numerator:

$$\dfrac{x^2 - x - 2}{2} + 3x$$

Distribute the division: $\dfrac{1}{2}x^2 - \dfrac{1}{2}x - 1 + 3x$

Combine line terms: $\dfrac{1}{2}x^2 + \dfrac{5}{2}x - 1$

---

34. **200**   Algebra (systems of inequalities) MEDIUM

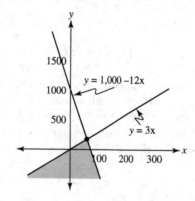

The graph above shows the solution set to the given system of inequalities. The solution set to $y \le 1,000 - 12x$ is the set of all points *on or under* the line $y = 1,000 - 12x$, and the solution set to $y \le 3x$ is the set of all points *on or under* the line $y = 3x$. The solution to the system, then, is the region where these two sets overlap. The point in this region with the maximum *y* value is the intersection point of the two lines. We can find the *x*-value of this point by substituting $y = 3x$ into $y = 1,000 - 12x$:

$$3x = 1,000 - 12x$$

Add $12x$ to both sides:

$$15x = 1,000$$

Divide by 15:

$$x = \frac{1,000}{15} = \frac{200}{3}$$

Now plug in to $y = 3x$ to find the y-coordinate:

$$y = 3\left(\frac{200}{3}\right) = 200$$

---

35. **945**   **Additional Topics (trigonometry) HARD**

When you see an expression like $\sin\left(\frac{5\pi}{4}\right)$, it's important to remember that the "input" to any trigonometric function is always an angle measure, and if that angle measure does not have a degree symbol next to it, it is a *radian measure*. For instance, $\sin(1°)$ means the sine of a 1° angle, but $\sin(1)$ means the sine of a 1 *radian* (or approximately 57.3°) angle. An angle measure of $\frac{5\pi}{4}$ radians is equivalent to a measure of $\frac{5\pi}{4}\left(\frac{180°}{\pi}\right) = 225°$. If the sine of $x°$ is equal to the sine of 225° and the tangent of $x°$ is equal to the tangent of 225°, then the two angles are "co-terminal," which means that their terminal rays coincide when they are graphed in standard position on the xy-plane. This means that $x = 225 + 360n$, where n is any integer. If x must be between 720 and 1,080, then the only possibility is $n = 2$, which yields $x = 225 + 360(2) = 945$.

---

36. **11**   **Advanced Mathematics (quadratics) MEDIUM-HARD**

Original equation:

$$\frac{4}{1-x} = \frac{2}{x+2} - \frac{1}{2}$$

Multiply by the common denominator:

$$(2)(1-x)(x+2)\left(\frac{4}{1-x}\right) = \left(\frac{2}{x+2} - \frac{1}{2}\right)(2)(1-x)(x+2)$$

Simplify: $(8)(x+2) = (2)(2)(1-x) - (1-x)(x+2)$

Distribute: $8x + 16 = 4 - 4x - (x + 2 - x^2 - 2x)$

Distribute and combine like terms: $8x - 16 = x^2 - 3x + 2$

Subtract $8x$ and add 16 to both sides: $x^2 - 11x + 18 = 0$

Any quadratic of the form $ax^2 + bx + c = 0$ has two solutions that have a sum of $-b/a$; therefore, the two solutions of this quadratic are $-(-11)/1 = 11$.

---

37. **21.1**   **Problem Solving (nonlinear systems) HARD**

If $h_1 = h_2$, then: $-4.9t^2 + 28t + 10 = -4.9t^2 + 7t + 19$

Add $4.9t^2$, subtract $7t$, and subtract 10: $21t = 9$

Divide by 21: $t = \frac{9}{21} = \frac{3}{7}$

Substitute $t = \frac{3}{7}$ into either equation to get the height:

$$-4.9\left(\frac{3}{7}\right)^2 + 28\left(\frac{3}{7}\right) + 10 = 21.1$$

---

38. **14**   **Advanced Mathematics (interpreting quadratic models) HARD**

Average speed is can be found with the formula *average speed = total distance ÷ total time*. We are interested in the time between launch and when Projectile 1 reaches its maximum height. At the launch, $t = 0$ seconds, and so the height is $-4.9(0)^2 + 28(0) + 10 = 10$ meters. We can find the time at which it reaches its maximum height by noticing that the height function is quadratic in t, and so its graph is a parabola that reaches its greatest height at its vertex. Recall that the axis of symmetry of any quadratic function in the form $y = ax^2 + bx + c$ is is $x = -\frac{b}{2a}$. Therefore, the value of t when Projectile 1 reaches its maximum height is $t = -\frac{b}{2a} = -\frac{28}{2(-4.9)} = \frac{20}{7}$. The height at that time is therefore $-4.9\left(\frac{20}{7}\right)^2 + 28\left(\frac{20}{7}\right) + 10 = 50$. So the total distance it traveled is $50 - 10 = 40$ meters in $\frac{20}{7}$ seconds; therefore, its average speed is 40 meters ÷ $\frac{20}{7}$ seconds = 14 meters per second.

(It's not a coincidence that this number is half of 28, which is the middle coefficient in the quadratic. In this function, 28 represents the vertical speed, in meters per second, of Projectile 1 when it is launched. When it reaches its maximum height, its vertical speed is 0. The average of 28 and 0 is, of course, 14.)